AN HISTORICAL GEOGRAPHY OF EUROPE
1500–1840

An historical geography of Europe

1500–1840

N. J. G. POUNDS

CAMBRIDGE UNIVERSITY PRESS

CAMBRIDGE

LONDON · NEW YORK

NEW ROCHELLE

MELBOURNE · SYDNEY

Published by the Press Syndicate of the University of Cambridge
The Pitt Building, Trumpington Street, Cambridge CB2 1RP
32 East 57th Street, New York, NY 10022, USA
296 Beaconsfield Parade, Middle Park, Melbourne 3206, Australia

First published 1979

Text set in 10/12 pt VIP Times, printed and bound
in Great Britain at The Pitman Press, Bath

Library of Congress Cataloguing in Publication Data

Pounds, Norman John Greville.
An historical geography of Europe 1500–1840.

Includes bibliographical references and index.
1. Europe – Historical geography.   I. Title.
D21.5.P634   940.2   79–11528

ISBN 0 521 22379 2

Contents

Maps and diagrams

Maps and diagrams

Abbreviations

A.A.A.G.	*Annals of the Association of American Geographers* (Washington, D.C.)
A.A.G. Bij.	*Afdeling Agrarische Geschiedenis Bijdragen* (Wageningen)
Acad. Besanç.	*Académie des Sciences, Belles-Lettres et Arts de Besançon* (Besançon)
Acad. Roy. Arch. Belge	*Académie Royale Archéologique de Belge* (Brussels)
Acta Bor.	Acta Borussica (Berlin)
Acta Hist. Neer.	*Acta Historiae Neerlandica* (The Hague)
Acta ˙Pol. Hist.	*Acta Poloniae Historica* (Warsaw)
Actes Coll. Int. Dém. Hist.	*Actes de la Colloque Internationale de Démographie Historique, Liège, 1965*, Liège, n.d.
Agr. Hist.	*Agricultural History* (Berkeley, Calif.)
Am. Hist. Assn Ann. Rept	*American Historical Association, Annual Report* (Washington, D.C.)
Am. Hist. Rev.	*American Historical Review* (Lancaster, Pa.)
Ann. Bourg.	*Annales de Bourgogne* (Dijon)
Ann. Bret.	*Annales de Bretagne* (Rennes)
Ann. Dém. Hist.	*Annales de Démographie Historique* (Paris)
Ann. ESC	*Annales: Economies–Sociétés–Civilisations* (Paris)
Ann. Fac. Nice	Annales de la Faculté des Lettres et Sciences Humaines de l'Université de Nice (Nice)
Ann. Géog.	*Annales de Géographie* (Paris)
Ann. Hist. Ec. Soc.	*Annales d'Histoire Economique et Sociale* (Paris)
Ann. Hist. Rév. Fr.	*Annales Historiques de la Révolution Française* (Paris)
Ann. Hist. Soc.	*Annales d'Histoire Sociale* (Paris)
A. Litt. Nantes	Annales Littéraires de l'Université de Nantes (Paris)
Ann. Midi	*Annales du Midi* (Toulouse)
Ann. Mines	*Annales des Mines* (Paris)
Ann. Norm.	*Annales de Normandie* (Rouen)
Ann. Siles.	*Annales Silesiae* (Wrocław)
Ann. Soc. Arch. Brux.	*Annales de la Société d'Archéologie de Bruxelles* (Brussels)
Antem.	*Antemurale* (Rome)
Arch. Frank. Gesch. Kunst	*Archiv für Frankfurts Geschichte und Kunst* (Frankfurt-on-Main)
Balt. Scand.	*Baltic and Scandinavian Countries* (Toruń)
Basl. Zt.	*Basler Zeitschrift* (Basel)
Beitr. Öst. Eis.	Beiträge zur Geschichte des Österreichischen Eisenwesens (Berlin)

Beitr. Wtgesch. Nürn.	*Beiträge zur Wirtschaftsgeschichte Nürnbergs* (Nuremberg)
Bg. Hüt. Zt.	*Berg- und Hüttenmannische Zeitung* (Freiberg, Saxony)
Bibl. Arch. Hist. Inst. Fr. Arch.	*Bibliothèque Archéologique et Historique de l'Institut Français d'Archéologie d'Istanbul* (Paris)
Bibl. Ec. Fr. Ath. Rome	*Bibliothèque de l'Ecole-Française d'Athènes et de Rome* (Paris)
Bibl. Ec. Htes Et.	Bibliothèque de l'Ecole des Hautes Etudes (Paris)
Bibl. Fac. Liège	Bibliothèque de la Faculté de Philosophie et Lettres de l'Université de Liège (Paris)
Bibl. Soc. Hist. Dr. Flam.	Bibliotheque de la Société de l'Histoire du Droit des Pays Flamands, Picards et Wallons (Lille)
Boh.	*Bohemia: Jahrbuch des Collegium Carolinum* (Munich)
Bull. Comm. Hist. Ec. Soc. Rév. Fr.	*Bulletin de la Comm. Hist. Ec. Soc. Rév. Fr. (Paris)*
Bull. Comm. Roy. Hist.	*Bulletin de la Commission Royale d'Histoire* (Brussels)
Bull. Inst. Arch. Liège	*Bulletin de l'Institut Archéologique de Liège* (Liège)
Bull. Inst. Hist. Belge Rome	*Bulletin de l'Institut Historique Belge de Rome* (Brussels)
Bull. Phil. Hist.	*Bulletin Philologique et Historique de la Comité des Travaux Historiques et Scientifiques* (Paris)
Bull. Soc. Ant. Pic.	*Bulletin de la Société des Antiquaires de Picardie* (Amiens)
Bull. Soc. Belge Géog.	*Bulletin de la Société Belge de Géographie* (Brussels)
Bull. Soc. Sci. Dauph.	*Bulletin de la Société Scientifique de Dauphiné* (Grenoble)
Bull. Stat.	*Bulletin Statistique* (Brussels)
Cah. Ann.	*Cahiers des Annales* (Toulouse)
Cah. Ann. Norm.	*Cahiers des Annales Normandes* (Caen)
Cah. Brux.	*Cahiers Bruxellois* (Brussels)
Cah. Hist.	*Cahiers d'Histoire* (Grenoble)
Cah. Hist. Mond.	*Cahiers d'Histoire Mondiale* (Paris)
Camb. Ec. Hist.	*Cambridge Economic History of Europe*, vols. I– , Cambridge, 1941–
Casa Veláz.	*Casa de Velázquez* (Madrid)
Ciba Rev.	*Ciba Review* (Basel)
Civ. Venez.	*Civiltà Veneziana* (Venice)
Coll. Ec. Réf. Soc.	Collection des Economistes et des Réformateurs Sociaux de la France (Paris)
Comm. Hist. Ec. Soc. Rév. Fr.	Commission d'Histoire Economique et Sociale de la Révolution Française (Paris)
Comm. Roy. Hist.	Commission Royale d'Histoire (Brussels)
Con. Hist. Dém. Rév. Fr.	*Contributions á l'Histoire Démographique de la Révolution Française, Comm. Hist. Ec. Soc. Rév. Fr., Mém. et Doc.*, 18 (1965)
Deutsch. Akad. Wiss.	Deutsche Akademie der Wissenschaften zu Berlin, Schriften des Instituts für Geschichte, 1st ser.: Allgemeine und deutsche Geschichte (Berlin)
XVIIᵉ S.	*XVIIᵉ Siècle* (Paris)

Ec. Hist. Rev.	*Economic History Review* (London)
Eng. Hist. Rev.	*English Historical Review* (London)
E.P.H.E.	Ecole Pratique des Hautes Etudes (Paris)
Et. Hist. (B)	*Etudes Historiques* (Budapest)
Expl. Entr. Hist.	*Explorations in Entrepreneurial History* (Cambridge, Mass.)
Forsch. D. Landesk.	*Forschungen zur Deutschen Landeskunde* (Stuttgart)
Forsch. Soz. Wtg.	Forschungen zur Sozial- und Wirtschaftsgeschichte (Stuttgart)
Hans. Gbl.	*Hansische Geschichtsblätter* (Lübeck)
Hist.	*History* (London)
Hist. (P)	*Historia* (Prague)
Hist. Quant. Ec. Fr.	*Histoire Quantitative de l'Economie Française* (Paris)
Hist. Stud.	Historische Studien (Berlin)
Hommage Labrousse	*Conjoncture économique: structures sociales – hommage à Ernest Labrousse,* Paris, 1974
Htes Et. Méd. Mod.	*Hautes Etudes Médiévales et Modernes* (Geneva)
Int. Conf. Ec. Hist.	*International Conference of Economic History*
Inst. Nat. Et. Dém.	Institut National des Etudes Démographiques (Paris)
Jb. Gesch. Mitt. Ostd.	*Jahrbuch für die Geschichte Mittel- und Ostdeutschlands* (Tübingen)
Jb. Ges. Loth. Gesch.	*Jahrbuch der Gesellschaft für Lothringische Geschichte und Altertumskunde* (Nancy)
Jb. Nat. Stat.	*Jahrbücher für Nationalökonomie und Statistik* (Jena; Stuttgart)
Jb. Schw. Gesch.	*Jahrbücher für Schweizerische Geschichte* (Zurich)
Jb. Ver. Meck. Gesch.	*Jahrbücher des Vereins für Mechlenbürgische Geschichte*
Jn. Ec. Hist.	*Journal of Economic History* (New York)
Jn. Ec. Soc. Hist. Orient	*Journal of Economic and Social History of the Orient* (Leiden)
Jn. Eur. Ec. Hist.	*Journal of European Economic History* (Rome)
Jn. Mines	*Journal des Mines* (Paris)
Jn. Pol. Ec.	*Journal of Political Economy* (Chicago)
Jn. Roy. Stat. Soc.	*Journal of the Royal Statistical Society* (London)
Kw. Hist. Kult. Mat.	*Kwartalnik Historii Kultury Materialny* (Warsaw)
Loc. Pop. Stud.	*Local Population Studies* (Nottingham)
Med. Hum.	*Medievalia et Humanistica* (Boulder, Colo.)
Mélanges F. Braudel	*Histoire économique du monde méditerranéen, 1450–1650: mélanges en l'honneur de Fernand Braudel,* 2 vols., Toulouse, 1973
Mém. Acad. Roy. Sci.	*Mémoires de l'Académie Royale de Science* (Paris)
Moy. Age	*Le Moyen Age* (Paris)
Nass. Ann.	*Nassauische Annalen* (Wiesbaden)
New Camb. Mod. Hist.	*New Cambridge Modern History,* 12 vols. and vol. XIV (atlas), Cambridge, 1957–70

Nouv. Et. Hist.	*Nouvelles Etudes Historiques* (Budapest)
P & P	*Past and Present* (London)
Paris–Ile	*Paris et l'Ile de France* (Paris)
Pet. Mitt.	*Petermanns Mitteilungen* (Jena)
Pop.	*Population* (Paris)
Pop. Stud.	*Population Studies* (London)
Proc. Roy. Soc. Med.	*Proceedings of the Royal Society of Medicine* (London)
Pub. Fac. Lett. Clermont-Ferrand	Publications de la Faculté des Lettres et Sciences Humaines de l'Université de Clermont-Ferrand (Paris)
Pub. Fac. Strasbourg	Publications de la Faculté des Lettres de l'Université de Strasbourg (Paris)
Pub. Univ. Dijon	Publications de l'Université de Dijon (Paris)
Quell. Forsch. Aggesch.	*Quellen und Forschungen zur Agrargeschichte* (Stuttgart)
Rec. Trav. Hist. Phil.	*Recueil de Travaux d'Histoire et de Philologie* (Louvain)
Rev. Belge Phil. Hist.	*Revue Belge de Philologie et d'Histoire* (Brussels)
Rev. Géog. Alp.	*Revue de Géographie Alpine* (Grenoble)
Rev. Hist.	*Revue Historique* (Paris)
Rev. Hist. Ec. Soc.	*Revue d'Histoire Economique et Sociale* (Paris)
Rev. Hist. Mod. Cont.	*Revue d'Histoire Moderne et Contemporaine* (Paris)
Rev. Hist. Sid.	*Revue d'Histoire de Sidérurgie* (Nancy)
Rev. Nord	*Revue du Nord* (Paris)
Rhein. Vbl.	*Rheinische Vierteljahrsblätter* (Bonn)
Rocz. Dz. Spol. Gosp.	*Roczniki Dziejów Spolecznych i Gospodarczych* Poznań)
Sc. Ec. Hist. Rev.	*Scandinavian Economic History Review* (Stockholm)
Schm. Jb.	*Schmollers Jahrbuch für Gesetzgebung, Verwaltung und Volkswirtschaft im Deutschen Reich* (Munich)
Schr. Rhein.–Westf. Wtgesch.	*Schriften zur Rheinish–Westfälischen Wirtschaftsgeschichte* (Cologne)
Schw. Zt. Gesch.	*Schweizerische Zeitschrift für Geschichte* (Zurich)
Soc. Hist. Suisse Rom.	Société d'Histoire de la Suisse Romande (Lausanne)
Stud. Dz. Gór. Hutn.	*Studia z Dziejów Górnictwa i Hutnictwa* (Wrocław)
Stud. Gen.	*Studium Generale*
Stud. Hist. (B)	*Studia Historica* (Budapest)
Studi Fanfani	*Studi in onore di Amintore Fanfani*, 6 vols., Milan, 1962
Stud. Stor.	*Studi Storici* (Rome)
Taschb. Aargau	*Taschenbuch der Historischen Gesellschaft des Kantons Aargau* (Aarau)
T. Ec. S.G.	*Tijdschrift voor Economische en Sociale Geografie* (Rotterdam)
T.K.N.A.G.	*Tijdschrift van het Koninklijk Nederlandsch Aardrijkskundig Genootschap* (Amsterdam)

Tr. Am. Phil. Soc.	*Transactions of the American Philosophical Society* (Philadelphia)
Veröff. Planck	*Veröffentlichungen des Max-Planck-Instituts für Geschichte* (Göttingen)
V.S.W.G.	*Vierteljahrschrift für Sozial- und Wirtschaftsgeschichte* (Leipzig)
Westf. Geog. Stud.	*Westfälische Geographische Studien* (Münster)
Zt. Aggesch.	*Zeitschrift für Agrargeschichte und Agrarsoziologie* (Frankfurt-on-Main)
Zt. Berg. Hüt. Sal.	*Zeitschrift für Berg-, Hütten- und Salinenwesen im Preussischen Staat* (Berlin)
Zt. Ges. Staatsw.	*Zeitschrift für die Gesamte Staatswissenschaft* (Tübingen)
Zt. Harz Gesch.	*Zeitschrift des Harz-Vereins für Geschichte und Altertumskunde* (Wernigerode)

Preface

In 1973 the first volume of *An Historical Geography of Europe* was published. It presented a survey of the geography of the continent at five widely separated periods of time, from the fifth century B.C. to the fourteenth century A.D. It stressed what has come to be called the 'horizontal' approach, and gave little space to the evolutionary processes which occurred between the periods chosen. Such a method is open to criticism. The choice of the periods for intensive study is not automatic, and several periods of great interest and historical significance received no consideration. The choice must be arbitrary, unless regularly recurring periods are chosen – every five hundred years, for example. Such a method would have been very difficult to use, because some periods, the fifth and sixth centuries A.D., for example, would be quite impossible to document on the scale contemplated.

The author tried to use what might be called 'peak' periods in European history, the culminations of long historical processes. At one time he considered using those examined by the art critic Clive Bell in his study of *Civilisation*. The fifth century B.C. was an inevitable choice; perhaps also the Carolingian period in the late eighth and early ninth centuries, but the age of the Flavian emperors hardly marks the climax of the Roman empire. Most would regard the thirteenth rather than the fourteenth century as the culmination of medieval civilisation, and the period around 1100 was chosen because a survey seemed to be needed between the ninth century and the fourteenth.

This volume departs from the format of its predecessor. In the first place it covers a span of only three hundred years rather than the eighteen hundred of the earlier volume. Documentation is incomparably more abundant than for the period before 1500 and spatial distributions can be studied with greater precision and in greater detail. Post-Napoleonic Europe differed greatly from Reformation Europe, but change from the one to the other was very far from revolutionary. It was therefore difficult to adopt a 'horizontal' approach in this volume. Periods do not distinguish themselves with sufficient clarity, and, indeed, it is difficult to discover significant change during the period in certain areas and in some fields of human activity, such as agriculture and urban development. The method adopted has therefore been to present a 'horizontal' picture both for the years about 1530, when the book begins, and for the 1840s, when the impact of the Industrial Revolution was beginning to be felt in much of continental Europe. For the centuries between these terminal dates change and development in the spatial pattern has been traced topic by topic, chapter by chapter, thus combining the 'vertical' with the 'horizontal' methods. This technique was first used successfully by Professor J. O. M. Broek in his study of the Santa Clara Valley of California, and was followed by Professor H. C. Darby in *A New Historical Geography of England*.

The chief problem in studying a region as large and as complex as Europe has proved to be one of organisation. A topical treatment in the 'vertical' chapters seemed to be the most practicable and convenient. Information has therefore been organised under the heads of population, urban development, agriculture, manufacturing and trade and transport. A chapter has not been given to the history of the physical environment, as could well have been the case. Instead, in the interests of keeping the length of the book within reasonable bounds, this topic has by and large been incorporated into the chapter on agriculture.

The five chapters which emerge must look remarkably like economic history. Indeed, the author claims to write as an historian who has also studied and worked in the field of geography. The spatial distribution of economic activity in the past is itself an important fact in historical explanation. In example after example its distribution is found to be the consequence of the physical opportunities offered by the environment, or at least of man's perception of them. The writer's primary purpose has been to introduce into history the spatial dimension which has all too often been lacking from historical writing. In both this volume and its predecessor he has emphasised the distribution of population and economic activity and their relationship to the physical environment, rather than technology and economic organisation, though the latter are in fact inseparable from the former.

As in the previous volume, both Russia and the British Isles have been omitted, except for incidental references where relevant. Constraints of space would have prevented their adequate treatment, and, in any case, both have been very fully treated in other books.

Department of History,   N. J. G. Pounds
Indiana University,
Bloomington, Indiana.

1

Europe in the early sixteenth century

The face of Europe in the early years of the sixteenth century was still in most respects medieval. The horizon of the human mind had expanded; a new world had been brought into existence beyond the Atlantic; authority had been questioned as never before; the printing-press was disseminating knowledge more widely, but the material things of life had changed little since the fourteenth century. The population was still rural and agricultural to the extent of at least 80 per cent, and almost every village settlement existing at this date had been known two centuries earlier. Nor had there been any significant change in the pattern of cities and towns. A few had declined in importance; others had grown in size, but the great majority were still as they had been in the fourteenth century, small and cut off from their fields by defensive walls, but nonetheless closely bound up with the life of the countryside.

Despite the genius of Leonardo da Vinci and the speculations of Copernicus, this was not an age of invention. Ships were increasing in size, and navigational aids were more widely used, but none of these involved any new discovery. Mechanical devices in use at this time had been known for centuries. No advances were made in the use of power beyond the further development and diffusion of the windmill. No new crops were to be introduced until late in the century, and, though the practice of fallowing had been abandoned in a few small areas, as, for example, in the Low Countries, the three-course system of agriculture prevailed almost everywhere, except where a two-field system was still in use. There may have been some small increase in agricultural productivity, but the practice of agriculture remained basically medieval. Perhaps the invention and spread of the blast-furnace in the closing decades of the fifteenth and early years of the sixteenth century constituted the most important technical advance of the age.

If there had been little change during the previous century in the structures of the rural and urban scene – field systems, crop-rotations, settlements – their organisation had undergone profound alteration. Demesne farming in western Europe had long been declining in importance. Land was being leased increasingly to prosperous peasants, while their lords lived more and more on rents in cash and in kind. In eastern Europe, on the other hand, the reverse was happening, as market conditions made demesne farming and the sale of grain increasingly profitable. Here the status of the peasant was being depressed as the lords laid acre to acre and exacted increasingly heavy labour dues on their estates.

The sixteenth century was nevertheless an age of lavish and ostentatious expenditure on the construction of palaces and chateaux and on extravagant ceremonies. These, however, were for the few; the mass of the people lived in poverty as abject as that of the thirteenth or fourteenth century. Indeed, their plight might even have been worse, for their labours had now to support a vaster superstructure. Government was more wasteful, armies were larger[1] and warfare more costly, and it was the peasant who bore most of their cost. The sixteenth century was marked by violent movements of social protest, prompted by religious abuses, by excessive taxation and tithe and by low living standards and the prospect of imminent starvation.[2] Most savage of all these risings was the German Peasants' War (1524–5). Their objectives, expressed in the Memmingen Articles, included the prevention of arbitrary taxation and tithing and the exaction of excessive labour dues. They demanded the right to take wood, fish and game, but, above all, they complained of 'the labour services which are daily increased and daily grow'.[3]

The scale of economic activity was increasing. Larger ships were being built; mining enterprises were more ambitious and were organised on a capitalist basis. The volume of trade was increasing, as most of Europe was very slowly drawn into a single economic system, in which estate farming in Poland was adjusted to the demand for bread crops in western cities, and bullion, imported through Spanish ports, was used by merchants on Europe's steppe frontier. The economic crises of the fifteenth century had been spasmodic and local, influencing one branch of production and one region and not another. The price rise of the sixteenth century, on the other hand, was general. It spread from west and south across the continent; no part was spared. To this extent an economic unity had been achieved within the limits of traditional Europe.

There was change also in the pattern of trade. The great discoveries brought Atlantic ports and sea routes to the fore. The internal routes of Europe, however, were very far from being neglected; indeed, the volume of goods transported over them increased, but with changing emphasis on commodities and places of trade. Lyons became the leading commercial centre in the west. Italian manufacturing and commercial centres had lost some of their earlier importance, and the Flanders cities paled before Antwerp, as Antwerp was to do within the century with the rise of Amsterdam. New commodity fairs sprang up, like the wool fair of

Medina del Campo, in Old Castile. New ports like Livorno (Leghorn) and Le Havre responded to new commercial needs. Some amongst the older ports decayed, while others – Riga, Danzig, Saint-Malo, Lisbon and Cadiz – reached a new peak of prosperity. In eastern Europe new towns sprang up, and a few grew rich on the profits of trade in grain, metals and forest products. Even today, some retain the faded evidence of their Renaissance splendour.

The physical scene

Superficially regarded, the Europe of the early sixteenth century differed little from that of the nineteenth or twentieth. There was the same pattern of mountains, hills and plains as we see now. The same rivers flowed seawards, subject to the same rhythm of flood and low water. A closer inspection, however, reveals thousands of ways in which Renaissance Europe differed from that of today. Valleys were wetter and rivers flooded more readily. The water table generally stood higher in the rocks, and some areas which are today under the plough were then undrained fenland. The forest cover was more extensive, and its fauna more varied, and in certain minor respects man's experience even of the weather was different.

The physical regions of Europe

Over most of Scandinavia there stretched a worn-down plateau, made up of old, hard rocks, metamorphosed by geological processes and intruded by metalliferous veins. Its higher surfaces had been scraped bare of soil by the movement of ice during the Ice Age, and over the lower ground the detritus carried from the uplands formed an uneven cover of clay, sand and gravel. Quite apart from the harshness of its climate, this was an uninviting land with a thin, poor and unrewarding soil.

The second region was the great plain which extended from the Pyrenees northwards and eastwards until it merged into the vastness of Russia. It was built of younger and softer rocks than the highlands of Scandinavia. East of the river Rhine this plain was partially covered with clay and sand transported by the ice and deposited when it had reached its maximum extent. Around the outer margin of the area of glaciation outblowing winds had distributed a fine, dust-like deposit, known as *loess* or *limon*. In some areas this was only a thin veneer, since removed by erosion or incorporated into the soil by ploughing. In others it accumulated to a depth of several metres. Its importance lay in the ease with which it could be cleared and cultivated and in the abundant crops which it yielded. The great European plain was in consequence a region of greatly varying fertility, ranging from the fertile *limon* of the Beauce, the 'granary of Paris', to the sterile heaths of Brandenburg which Frederick the Great attempted with so little success to tame and cultivate.

To the south of the plain lay a belt of hills, from Spain to Poland and the Balkan peninsula. It consisted of a number of separate plateaux or massifs, cut off from one another by wide valleys and extensions of the northern plain. This region was built of hard rocks, older than those which composed the plain, younger than Scandinavia. Like the latter they had been intruded locally by mineral-bearing lodes. These hills rarely rise to more than 500 to 1000 metres. Their climate is a degree or two cooler than in the nearby lowlands; the rainfall is many millimetres greater, and snow commonly lies for much of the winter. This region was never covered by the Quaternary ice-sheets, but its soil, leached by percolating water, is nonetheless poor and infertile.

These massifs are part of the basement or foundation on which Europe is built. They were thrust up like islands through the younger rocks of the plain, or were caught up in the earth-movements which folded the Alpine system. Much of this region has always been forested, and its population relatively sparse. Agricultural land was largely under grass, and such crop-farming as was carried on emphasised the hardy cereals like oats and rye, and fodder crops.

The Alpine system makes up the last of the major landform regions of Europe. It extends from the extremity of the Spanish peninsula to the Black Sea coast and the southern headlands of Greece, from which it is continued through the Greek islands to Asia Minor and beyond. A branch from the French Alps runs the length of Italy as the Apennines, and is continued in Sicily and in the Atlas mountains of North Africa. Crossing points were relatively few, especially in the Pyrenees and the Alps of France, Switzerland and Austria, and the Alpine system has always provided the most significant barrier in Europe to transport and communication.

The Alpine system brings together a great range of physical conditions, not only of terrain but also of climate and soil. The sequence of the seasons is even more significant here than elsewhere, because some parts of the region – the grassy slopes of the higher mountains, for example – can be used economically for only part of the year. The practice of transhumance (the seasonal movement of part of a community together with its animals between two or even three differing environments in order to make use of marginal resources) is met with throughout the region. A consequence of the marginal character of much of the Alpine region has been the predominance of pastoralism. Crop-farming was restricted to the valleys and lower slopes, where alone the growing season is long enough. Even so, crops were in most parts of the region restricted to quick-growing and hardy cereals and fodder crops.

The Alpine system has always been characterised by the relative isolation and independence of its constituent parts. The valleys, cut off by mountains and often approached only by a difficult mountain road, had always supported a self-sufficing and inbred community. Life was hard in this environment; 'plein de difficultés', as Montaigne wrote, 'les meurs des hommes éstranges, chemins inaccessibles, logis sauvages, l'air insupportable'.[4] Famine crises were intensified by the isolation. There were, however, exceptions. Traffic was funnelled through a few passes and along a small number of routes where, as Bishop Burnet pointed out in the seventeenth century, 'the inhabitants seem to live at their éase', though they did so only at the expense of the travelling public.[5]

The last of the distinctive regions of Europe is the smallest, the coastlands of the Mediterranean Sea. The European shore of the inland sea is bordered by the mountains of the Alpine system, but sedimentation by the Alpine rivers has created a succession of alluvial lowlands and coastal plains. These occur from southern Spain to the Aegean. They range from a few square kilometres to lowlands as extensive as the plain of Lombardy or of Andalusia, and in quality from coarse sand and gravel to the richest alluvium. They supported the classical civilisations of the Mediterranean and have continued, despite problems of water management, to feed an appreciable part of the population of the region.

The Alpine system forms a climatic divide. The contrast between the cloudy skies to the north and the brilliance of the Mediterranean has become a commonplace of travel literature from the Renaissance travellers to Goethe, who described with wonder the transformation in crops and climate as he progressed from the Tyrol down the Adige valley to Verona.[6] 'North of the Alps', wrote D. H. Lawrence, 'the everlasting winter is interrupted by summers that struggle and soon yield; south of the Alps, the everlasting summer is interrupted by spasmodic and spiteful winters that never get a real hold . . . North of the Alps, you may have a pure winter's day in June. South of the Alps, you may have a midsummer day in December or January or even February.'[7] Climates north of the Alps have mild or warm summers, cool or cold winters, and rainfall at all seasons of the year. There are nonetheless important variations between west and east as well as between south and north. In western Europe, where the oceanic influence is most strongly felt, mild winters are associated with cool summers and rainfall comes most heavily in the winter months. As one progresses eastwards winters become cooler and summers warmer, while a maximum rainfall in summer gradually replaces that of winter. There is no arbitrary division between the 'continental' climate of central and eastern Europe and the 'maritime' climate of western. The one merges into the other, with occasional periods of continental severity in the oceanic west and, on the other hand, the penetration of maritime conditions into eastern Europe. Rainfall, in addition to moving from a winter to a summer maximum, becomes smaller in amount towards the east, though the volume of precipitation also varies with altitude.

These physical conditions are of profound human importance. They influence every facet of life from styles of clothing and of architecture to the practice of agriculture. In the wetter lands of the west and the cooler lands of the mountains and of the north the climate favours grass and fodder crops rather than cereals. The latter become relatively more important away from the western margins of the continent, though everywhere the quality of the soil is no less important a determinant than the characteristics of the climate.

Northern Europe, comprising broadly Scandinavia and the Baltic region, has a climate of cool summers and cold winters which become progressively more extreme as one moves northwards and eastwards. Over a large part of the region, summers are too cool and too short for cultivated crops. The agricultural frontier extends across Norway, Sweden and Finland and into Russia. It is a zone within which the probability of crop failure increases. The farmer advances into it, driven by population pressure or tempted by a succession of good harvest years, but always he is repelled by the ultimate failure of his crops.

Climate is merely a statement of probabilities. The weather which is experienced from day to day and influences the growth of the crops and the success of the harvest often departs widely from the pattern of climate. In the sixteenth century such departures were probably no greater than in other ages, but man was ill equipped to face them. The later Middle Ages appear to have been characterised by increased storminess. Sailings between Scandinavia and Iceland diminished in number, and after about 1410 the route to Greenland was abandoned and its small colony perished in the worsening climate.[8] There were storm-surges at many points on the European coast, and large areas were inundated. It is difficult to write in general terms of the climatic fluctuations of the early sixteenth century. Northern Europe became colder, and the pack-ice spread more widely and lasted longer in the year. Within Europe there was a sequence of severe winters. 'There were years of distress in all northern countries; farms or farmland had to be abandoned to the ice in Iceland, Norway and the Alps. Growing of cereals completely ended in Iceland.'[9] The twenties and thirties of the sixteenth century, however, were marked by a temporary improvement. The vast body of climatic evidence assembled by Weikinn[10] shows that these were, in general, years of mild but very wet winters, with severe floods on all the rivers from France to Poland. The winter of 1513–14 was an exception; it was very cold and led to great suffering and misery. The journal of a Paris burgess described an acute frost in the closing weeks of 1522, so severe, indeed, that newly sown grain was killed and 'il convient de nouveau ressemer les dictz bledz'.[11] Problems during these years, however, lay rather in the flooded fields, bridges swept away, roads made impassable and houses in Paris collapsing as their foundations were sapped by the rising waters of the Seine.[12]

During the middle years of the sixteenth century winters became more severe, frost more frequent and snow more abundant. Contemporaries more often recorded hard frosts and frozen rivers than disastrous floods, and many climatic historians have since taken these years to mark the beginning of what they term the 'little Ice Age'. In Provence wine yields were reduced by the cooler and more cloudy summers.[13] In northern Europe cultivation contracted on the hillsides, and the treeline sank lower in the mountains. The glaciers of the Alps crept farther down their valleys; the snow cover on the passes became deeper and travel more difficult and hazardous. Vineyards and olive groves were killed by the frost, and ports on the shores of the Baltic were closed by ice for a longer period in winter. Everywhere the intensity of insolation was lowered by perhaps several per cent.[14]

The slight change in climate was reflected in the rivers. The snow melt was less vigorous in summer, and the Rhine – and doubtless other rivers – carried less water so that some of their channels in the Low Countries became too shallow for navigation. This in turn facilitated the drainage and reclamation projects undertaken at this time.[15] Rivers silted more readily. The Zwin, the river of Bruges, ceased to be navigable above Sluys for sea-going ships. The coastline advanced along the Scheldt estuary, and near the mouths of other rivers in western Europe natural silting went hand in hand with endyking and reclamation.

Forest

The area under forest was beginning to contract and was indeed to continue to do so until the present century. In the sixteenth century most of Europe's forests, except in Scandinavia, were of broad-leaved trees. Beech and oak were most widespread, but alder, willow and ash were common on damp and low-lying ground. Conifers, now so widespread in all parts of Europe, were found in few places outside Scandinavia and the Baltic region. Even the Black Forest was clothed

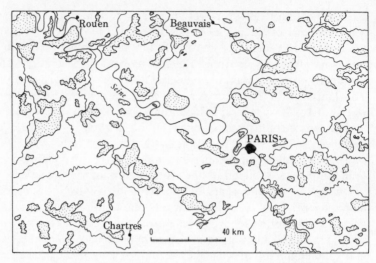

Fig. 1.1 Distribution of forest in the Paris region in the sixteenth century

with deciduous woodland, and over the German and Polish plains broad-leaved trees predominated. In Germany conifers were abundant only in Pomerania and Prussia, but east of the Baltic and over much of Scandinavia they predominated and from their vast resources were to supply the navies of western Europe with masts and spars.[16]

Everything points to a change in the character of Europe's forests, beginning in the fifteenth and sixteenth centuries. Conifers were spreading at the expense of deciduous trees. They had been introduced into the hilly areas of central Germany by 1500, and were established on the plain of the Rhine, where the lower water table dried out the sandy soils and made them less suitable for broad-leaved trees.

The earlier Middle Ages had seen severe inroads into the forests of Europe. They recovered somewhat in the fourteenth and fifteenth centuries; demand for timber was reduced and depopulation in the course of war allowed the woods to recover. In France, it was said, the forests came back with the English. In the sixteenth and following centuries there were renewed attacks on the woodlands, until, over much of Europe, the timber shortage reached crisis proportions in the eighteenth. The reasons did not lie altogether in the growth of population and the expansion of the area under cultivation. Technological developments made increasing demands on the supply of wood. Domestic building, much of it in wood, became more elaborate, and where brick and tile were used, these had to be baked in wood-fired kilns. Ships were increasing in size, and Venice, having exhausted the sources

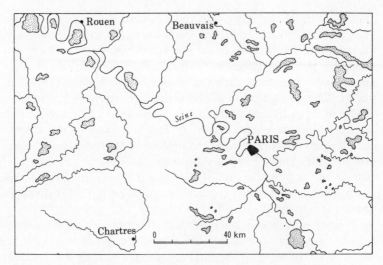

Fig. 1.2 Distribution of forest in the Paris region in the eighteenth century

of ships' timber which formerly grew along the Adriatic coast, was obliged to turn to the Alpine foothills in search of suitable trees.[17] At the same time the demand for timber for industrial purposes had increased sharply. Wood fuel had long been used to evaporate brine at the salt-springs and to refine iron on the hearth. To these were added the manufacture of glass, the burning of bricks and the production of wood-ash for soap-making. But the most extravagant consumer of wood was the iron industry. The newly introduced blast-furnace used immense quantities of charcoal (see p. 51), and the subsequent refining yet more.

In central and eastern Europe there was, however, no scarcity. Forests were more extensive and local demands on them were smaller. Mager has estimated that in Prussia at least 40 per cent of the land was still under forest as late as the eighteenth century.[18] Nonetheless, the destructive exploitation of the eastern forests had already begun, and those close to navigable waterways were being cleared to provide timber and potash for western Europe. From the fourteenth century there had been a growing shortage of good-quality timber for shipbuilding, and in the sixteenth, the merchants of Danzig, Elbląg and other ports were pressing their search for merchantable timber deep into Lithuania.[19] Everywhere the extent of the Baltic forests was contracting, not so much before the peasant's plough as from the insatiable demand for timber for naval and industrial use.

The forests of Mediterranean Europe had never been as extensive as those north of the Alps, and their destruction had begun in classical times, if not earlier. Except in the mountains, they provided little good timber, and for this the naval powers of the Mediterranean competed fiercely. By the sixteenth century only a few areas of high forest remained along the European shores of the Mediterranean, amongst them Albania and parts of the Dalmatian coast and, on the opposite shore of the Adriatic Sea, Monte Gargano and Calabria. By the sixteenth century even these were becoming depleted, and with the disappearance of the southern forests went the decline of Mediterranean fleets. In this respect the Turks had an advantage denied to their rivals, the oak forests of the Pontic region of Asia Minor. The Venetians and Spaniards were obliged to turn to northern Europe for their naval supplies, and even for fully built ships.[20]

Timber was as necessary as food to a pre-industrial society. It was needed *à chaufer et à bastir*. Much food was inedible until it had been cooked and in winter some form of domestic heating was necessary even to preserve life. Vauban's elaborate calculations showed that 700 arpents of woodland (about 425 hectares), allowing twenty years' growth – which was probably the minimum necessary – could be made to yield annually 350 cordes of *gros bois*, 49,000 bundles of firewood and 12,250 faggots.[21] This, he estimated, would have supplied about 110 households with wood for heating, cooking and constructional needs, especially if it could have been supplemented with the trimmings from hedges, fruit trees and vines.

If Vauban was correct – and he was in general a careful witness – the wood supply of most communities in western Europe fell desperately short of what was deemed necessary for domestic use. It was very scarce in Mediterranean Europe, and adequate only in central and eastern. At the fairs of Medina del Campo, it was said, food cost less than the fuel needed to cook it, and the Swiss traveller Felix Platter said of Montpellier that it was fortunate that winter was short, since the fuel supply would not last longer.[22] The forests also supplied pannage for pigs which over the northern half of Europe supplied much of the peasants' small intake of meat.

The area under forest was growing smaller in most parts of France and had almost disappeared from much of the Low Countries. Extensive woodlands were preserved by the king and nobility for hunting, but peasant clearings were nonetheless authorised, and large areas were sometimes conceded to charcoal burners and iron-masters. The vast forests of the Saulx-Tavanes in Burgundy were thus leased for fuel.[23] Elsewhere the competition between the iron-master and the peasant for timber led to violence as early as the sixteenth century[24] as well as to a gradual destruction of this essential resource.[25] Devèze's generalised map of the forested areas of northern France in the early sixteenth century[26] can be compared with that prepared by the Cassinis (figs. 1.1 and 1.2). While no precision can be claimed for the former, the contraction is nonetheless apparent. Devèze claims that in the thirty-one departments for which data are available, 16.3 per cent of the land was forested about 1550. By the twentieth century this had fallen to about 9 per cent.[27] The scarcity of timber, apparent in the sixteenth century, gradually became more acute. Attempts to conserve the woodlands were ineffective. Too many individuals and institutions had prescriptive rights in them, and the destructive exploitation by charcoal burners, glass-makers and others seemed impossible to prevent or even restrain. The long-distance transport of timber was practicable only by water, and the larger cities were supplied by *flottage*. Paris, for example, drew from Burgundy and the Morvan, and timber from the Black Forest was floated down the Rhine. In such agricultural regions as Beauce, Picardy, Flanders and Brabant the situation had become desperate by the eighteenth century, and one wonders how the rural population survived such cold winters as that of 1709–10.

Nationalism and the political map

The impact of central government on human activities had been slight during the Middle Ages, and even in modern times there were areas of political obligation which in 1789 were not sure whether they belonged to France or Germany and suggested that they might have been independent of both.[28] Such uncertainty was more common in the sixteenth century, but already that sense of belonging to a larger group, which we call nationalism, was beginning to pervade the more articulate classes of Europe. A feudal organisation of society was giving place to a more modern concept, that of the state, enclosed by precise boundaries and endowed with rights over all who lived within them. This twofold process, the creation of the state and the diffusion of a sense of unity within it, was only in its infancy in the early sixteenth century. The state was still not fully aware of its territorial limits and resources, and many of its subjects continued to think more in terms of feudal obligations and local loyalties than of national aspirations, as, indeed, some continued to do into the nineteenth century.

In 1546 Charles V was passing along the eastern or imperial bank of the Meuse in what is today Lorraine, when he noticed the newly founded French town of Villefranche on the opposite bank. He complained that it had been built on imperial territory, but, in the words of the chronicle, 'the records of the district, covering two centuries, were brought and examined, and it was shown that the inhabitants of the new

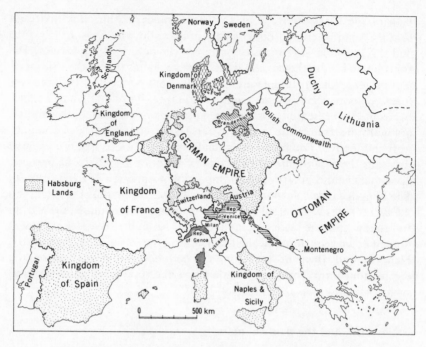

Fig. 1.3 Europe: political map, about 1530

town were subjects of the French king'.[29] The question asked by the
emperor of the citizens was the medieval one: Whose are you? To whom
do you owe loyalty and allegiance? even though in this instance the
mutual boundary of France and the empire had long been established
along the river, where it was to remain until the eighteenth century.

Boundaries gained precision in a piecemeal fashion, usually when a
lawsuit required definition in a particular area. Such a case was that of
Claude de la Vallée, *prévôt* of Clermont-en-Argonne, who had been
fined for some misdemeanour while in office by the courts of the Duke
of Lorraine. He escaped to France where he claimed that only the courts
of the King of France had jurisdiction over Clermont.[30] On this occasion
the French kings did not press their claims, and it was left for Richelieu
to annex the Clermontois to France. The solution in such cases was
usually to adopt a conspicuous physical feature, most often a river, as
the line of the boundary.

In the Low Countries the conversion of barriers between personal
obligations into boundaries between political units presented even
greater difficulties. It gave rise to territorial enclaves and exclaves and to
countless places in which sovereignty was actually divided. The Tournaisis, for example, was made up of about eighty named settlements;

over a half of them were politically divided between Tournai and neighbouring states.[31]

These incidents occurred along boundaries that had become relatively well established. In some parts of western and more widely in eastern Europe boundaries were still ill-defined zones – frontiers in the strict sense. The limits of Bohemia and Poland, of some German states and Swiss cantons, ran through forest and waste in which men from both sides cut timber, grazed their animals and pursued quarrels which no courts existed to resolve. The Swiss boundary in the Jura and the division of grazing rights were not effectively settled until the nineteenth century.[32] The task of 'clearing up all this feudal debris'[33] was to last, at least in central Europe, into the twentieth century.

Despite the many instances of vagueness and uncertainty, sixteenth-century rulers could be expected to have a very considerable knowledge of the lands which they ruled. They were helped by the newly invented printing-press, which disseminated the facts of history and geography. Maps began to be printed with some pretension to accuracy in the location of towns and villages, rivers and hills. Above all, more people were travelling, not only along the familiar routes of trade and pilgrimage, but also to areas which had no commercial or spiritual attraction. There was an intense desire to know what the inhabited world was like. A. L. Rowse has written of the 'Elizabethan discovery of England', and commended the achievement of John Leland who, well before the middle of the century, 'was totally inflamed with a love to see thoroughly all those parts of [this] opulent and ample realm'. Topographical writings became increasingly common in many parts of Europe, presenting their peculiar blend of popular history, geography and folklore.

This genre had developed in the fifteenth century. In 1457 Aeneas Sylvius (Pope Pius II) wrote his descriptive letter on Germany,[34] and at about the same time Gilles le Bouvier produced his *Livre de la description des pays*, a simple narrative account of regions, rivers and resources.[35] *Le débat des hérauts* was written soon after 1460; in it two protagonists extolled the wealth and resources of their respective countries.[36] The Heralds' Debate is a dry academic exercise, but at about the same time a *Ballade contre les Anglais*[37] had appeared. The latter was profoundly different; it belonged 'to another world of thought ... it has in it the venom of a life-and-death struggle between two peoples'. The English are seen 'not only [as] enemies; they are foreigners, men of another "sort" '.[38] The sixteenth-century topographical writings were born of a marriage of such deeply felt emotions with a detailed knowledge of the land and its history. Such a product was Leland's *Itinerary*, as were also, despite their wide differences in style and character, the Swiss history of Johann Stumpf, the *Germania* of

Jakob Wimpfeling, the *Bischreibung etlicher Gelegenheit Teutschen Lands* of Sebastian Brant, the *Cosmographia* of Sebastian Münster, and the Polish history of Jan Długosz.

In 1492 Conrad Celtis, in a public oration at the University of Ingolstadt, called upon his audience to 'consider it . . . the height of shame to know nothing about the topography, the climate, the rivers, the mountains, the antiquities and the peoples of our region and our own country'.[39] Most of the topographical writers echoed this sentiment, though their emphasis varied. The Germans tended to emphasise the German-language area. Johann Stumpf sought to define the limits of Germany 'by examining customs, character and language';[40] to Ulrich Mutius, Germany was the area 'in which the German language or any of its dialects was spoken',[41] while Johann Rauw towards the end of the century sought to define the boundaries of German speech. From this emphasis on the language-area there grew a sense of a *Germania irredenta*: 'our famous harbour [Danzig]', wrote Celtis, 'is held by the Pole, and the gateway to our ocean [the Sound] by the Dane'.[42] To the east, he added, lived communities 'separated from the body of our Germany . . . [such as] the Transylvanian Saxons who also use our racial culture and speak our native language'. Wimfeling sought to embrace Alsace within Germany, despite its location to the west of the Rhine, by appealing to place-names and the language used in monuments and inscriptions.[43] In these writings there is a curious anticipation of the ideas of J. G. Herder, if not also of some Germans in the present century.

In these writings we find the German humanists striving for a definition of Germany with which they could become emotionally involved. They had tried the classical model of Tacitus' *Germania* and it had failed; they had looked to the German empire, and found it too diffused and abstract. So they settled for the German folk-area. Indeed they had no alternative, however disastrous for the future of Europe their choice may have been.

Italy, like Germany, had a common language, but was divided between many states. Northern peoples, both French and German, had at intervals broken across the Alpine barrier to devastate the plains of Italy. At least as early as the time of Petrarch some Italians had conceived of Italy as a land distinct from all others and in fact cut off from them by the barrier of the Alps. It was with considerable satisfaction that they echoed Cicero's words to the effect that God had erected the Alps as a protection for their country. Indeed, they had constantly before them the classical model of a united Italy.

Machiavelli exhorted his fellow countrymen to deliver Italy 'from the Barbarians',[44] but, like his contemporaries, nonetheless approved the fragmentation of the country into city-republics. They found no inconsistency between their intense loyalty to their own state and hostility to others on the one hand, and their belief in the unity of Italy. Francesco Guicciardini could write a Florentine history filled with local pride and fierce condemnation of other city-republics and also a history of Italy, in which he lamented the inability of Italians to combine against a common enemy. 'I want to see three things before I die', he wrote; 'a well ordered republic in our city, Italy liberated from all the barbarians, the world delivered from the tyranny . . . of priests.'[45]

French nationalism was at this time less vociferous, perhaps because it had less to protest against than German and Italian. It had been tempered in the wars with England, and France had achieved a degree of political unity which Germany and Italy were not to attain until the nineteenth century. There was a concept of community within France, even though its boundaries might long continue to be debated. French topographical writings plead less and describe more fully. They are filled with praise of *la douce France*, the fertility of its soil and the abundance of its vegetable and mineral production. 'This best garden of the world, our fertile France', wrote Shakespeare, showing how he had succumbed to French writings about their own country.

French nationalism in the early sixteenth century, like both German and Italian, was firmly based upon language. In Germany it was Luther's *Mittelhochdeutsch*; in Italy, the Tuscan dialect. In France, no less, there were local dialects and even, in peripheral regions, distinct languages. France differed, however, in having a central government able to impose one particular dialect, make it the official language and encourage its use in a national literature. By the Ordinance of Villers-Cotterets (1539) Francis I initiated certain judicial reforms and at the same time required that official acts be recorded and published in the *langue d'oïl*, the dialect of northern France and the Paris basin. At the same time a conscious attempt was made to use this chosen language as a medium for a literary development. Claude de Seyssel urged his contemporaries to use French rather than the classical languages in their writings, and thus initiated a literary trend which complemented the political movement towards unity.

The Spanish peninsula had never, not even during the period of Roman domination, formed a political, certainly not a cultural, unit. Its internal divisions were intensified during the Middle Ages. While Catalans to the east and Portuguese to the west were pursuing their commercial and maritime schemes, the Castilians – by far the most numerous of the peoples of the peninsula – were locked in a deadly struggle with the Moors. To the barrier of language was added a difference in outlook between the medieval, crusading Castilian and the more forward-looking, commercial and industrialised peoples of the west, the north and the east of the peninsula. Under Charles V Spain became the focus of a world empire, a role for which Castile was well cast, but not one calculated to unify the peninsula. Spain was perhaps the only European state in which local feeling was intensified during the sixteenth century, so that national unity seemed farther away at its end than when the century began.

One may question how deeply this sense of nationhood was experienced by the majority of the people in the nation-states of Europe. For most their mental horizon was a narrow one, and their longest journey no greater than that to the nearest market town. The inhabitants of the next valley or of an adjoining town were different, untrustworthy, even hostile. Such primitive, almost tribal, emotions were gradually sublimated, but there was no sudden change from local to national feeling. This transition was made first by the literate classes, the officials, scholars and merchants, who were the public for whom the topographers wrote, but even they cherished their ancient and local laws and customs. Any attempt to abridge them might lead to protest and even rebellion. Philip II's crime in the Low Countries was not his support of the Counter-Reformation, but his violation of the rights and privileges of the individual provinces. Europe was still a mosaic of communities, cut off one from the other by barriers of prejudice and custom, upon which governments were trying to impose administrative unity.

A common language was probably the most powerful force in creating a nation, but only a degree less important was the existence of a common foe or the experience of a deep emotional crisis. The French had endured such an experience in the Hundred Years' War; the Czechs in the Hussite wars; the Dutch in the war against Spain. Such an ordeal brought home to each of these people the truth that the differences within each of them were slight compared with the barriers between themselves and other nations. The struggle against the outsider was an emotional experience in which most of the people participated, and often enough their achievements were exaggerated to heroic proportions after the event. It became the role of the topographical writers to elaborate this body of heroic legend, and nowhere was this done more skilfully than in Switzerland, so that it is difficult today to distinguish between fact and fiction in the history of the Swiss revolt. Amongst the Dutch the experience of revolt was no less profound and far-reaching. In the early sixteenth century the Low Countries were made up of small, separate and quarrelsome states. Yet, in Renier's words, 'the Dutch nation was born, coherent, and distinct from other national units. It was born because, during the second half of the sixteenth century, a state came into existence, within whose territory men lived and strove together, and shared experiences so crowded and so intense that they found themselves overnight where it had taken the people of other national states centuries to arrive.'[46]

The dominant powers in Europe were France and Spain. Both were populous and powerful, able to maintain large armies and to carry on their mutual conflicts from one end of Europe to the other. Around these two were grouped most other political divisions of Europe. Italy and Germany, despite the wealth and culture of the one and the size and resources of the other, were only pawns in the struggle of France and Spain, of Valois and Habsburg.

Italy was divided at this time into more than a dozen principalities. Their number had diminished as Milan, Venice and Florence, to mention only three, extended their territory by conquest and the absorption of smaller city-republics. Their mutual quarrels, endemic since the earlier Middle Ages, exposed Italy to invasion, and from the French incursion of 1494 to that of the imperialists in 1526 the whole country was repeatedly fought over and ravaged, and in 1527 the city of Rome was sacked as never before.

Germany in the narrow sense was, for the greater part, embraced within the German empire, which gave it the illusion of unity and a certain aura within the European states system. In reality, however, it presented a picture of even greater disunity than Italy. Territorial states and imperial cities, each of them independent and sovereign in all but name, reached a total of some three hundred. A few, like Bavaria, Brandenburg and Electoral Saxony, were extensive and powerful enough to demand a price for their friendship. Most were too small to play any independent role, and some cities could survive only by forming urban leagues. An attempt to introduce some order and stability into this changing scene by organising the states into a number of *Kreise* had failed, and now, in the third decade of the century, a new factor of discord was introduced, the Protestant Reformation. Its effect was to polarise the German states, to increase the authority of the princes within their territories, and, in the following century, to precipitate the most damaging war so far even in Germany's long history of conflict.

The western border of Germany was in theory clear and unambiguous, running from the Scheldt to the Meuse and from the Meuse to the Saône and Rhône. In practice it was blurred in many areas by conflicting feudal loyalties and obscured by the creation of the Burgundian state. By a combination of marriage, inheritance and conquest, the Burgundian dukes, scions of the French Valois, had in the fourteenth and fifteenth centuries got possession of the French Duchy of Burgundy, of the Free County of the same name, which lay within the theoretical boundary of the empire, and of the greater part of the Low Countries. This ill-assorted bundle of territories was held by a variety of legal titles. All retained their 'customs', and the dukes had little success in creating political unity within them or establishing a centralised administration. Marriage, which had done much to bring these territories together, took them, after the death of the last duke in 1477, to the emperor Maximilian and joined them with the Habsburg lands in southern Germany and Austria. Philip of Habsburg in the next generation married Johanna, heiress of Castile and Aragon as well as of the Spanish empire in the New World. Their son, the emperor Charles V, was ruler of all the lands which had thus been brought together. To these he added Bohemia and those parts of Hungary which escaped the Turkish conquest when their last king, Lewis, perished as he fled from the battlefield of Mohács (1526).

The emperor thus came to rule almost a quarter of the land area of Europe, if we exclude Russia, Scandinavia and the British Isles, with perhaps a similar proportion of its population. To this he added the economic power which he derived from the Spanish empire. Superficially regarded, the power of the Habsburgs was overwhelming. They could control at some point most of the routes from the Mediterranean to northern Europe, and they were in a position to dominate most of the sea routes which followed Europe's coastline. They controlled much of Europe's metal production, as well as the sources of most of the gold and silver which passed into circulation. Never, it might have seemed, had so many of the determinants of power been united in the hands of a single ruler since the end of the Roman empire.

Yet the power of the Habsburgs fell short of what one might have expected. Their lands were scattered; movement between them was far from easy, and much depended on the willingness of the Swiss to open their passes to the movement of imperial troops and the freedom of Spanish ships to sail up the English Channel to the Low Countries. Other problems also faced the Habsburgs: social unrest in Spain, particularism in the Low Countries and hostility to Habsburg rule in the Czech and Hungarian lands. Above all, the empire over which Charles V ruled was split by the religious upheaval of the Reformation. Charles V devoted his energies to preserving the spiritual unity of his inheritance. He failed, but long before the settlement of Augsburg (1555) it was apparent that north Germany had espoused the Protestant cause and that much of the south had remained loyal to the emperor and faithful to the church. The religious wars were interrupted during the latter half of the sixteenth century, but revived with greater fury in the seventeenth. Warfare then ceased to be an instrument of religious policy. It became more controlled and humane, until the new religion of nationalism restored to it something of its old ruthlessness and savagery.[47] The religious wars saw the eclipse of the power of the German emperors and the reduction of their authority in central Europe to the ancestral Habsburg lands.

The Habsburg empire was threatened no less from without. The battle of Mohács (1526) marked the end of the Hungarian kingdom, which had long served as a buffer protecting Austria and the empire from the Ottoman Turks. In 1529 the Turks for the first time attacked Vienna. They were repulsed, but for a century and a half Europe's eastern frontier lay only a few miles down the Danube from the city, and the energies of the Austrian Habsburgs were largely consumed in protecting Europe's eastern flank.

Along the steppe road which leads from southern Poland towards the Black Sea and in the Mediterranean basin Europe was also threatened by the forces of Islam. Rhodes fell to the Turks in 1522 and the Greek islands not long after. The Moslems were a constant threat to Europe's seaborne commerce, and not until they were defeated at Lepanto (1571) by a combined Spanish and Venetian fleet was the danger reduced. At the same time the corsairs of the Barbary coast carried on a less organised but more persistent campaign against Europe's ships and coastline.

Spain became the focus of Habsburg power, especially after the abdication of Charles V (1556) when the Austrian lands passed to his younger brother, Ferdinand. It provided a more secure base than either Austria or the Low Countries. Through the port of Seville was channelled the bullion of the New World, without which the emperor could not have retained the loyalty of his armies. The Spanish empire in the New World was, nevertheless, a constant drain on Spanish man-power and resources. No less than 200,000 migrated from Spain, most of them from Castile, and this was unquestionably a factor in the economic decline of Spain.[48] In the long run it is doubtful whether the benefits which Spain derived from her empire outweighed the obligations it imposed.

Scandinavia had, since the Viking age, played only a passive role in the history of Europe. It was, with the exception of Denmark, a sparsely populated frontier region, whose leading products – fish, timber and iron – were largely handled by German merchants. The kingdom of Denmark, most developed of the Scandinavian states, embraced southern Sweden and profited from the tolls levied on the traffic which passed through the Sound. Norway, chiefly important for its fisheries, had been linked with the Danish crown since 1397, but Sweden had been restless under Danish rule, and in 1523 a movement with overtones of Swedish nationalism placed Gustavus Vasa on the throne and initiated a period of expansion.

The eastern tier of states, from the Baltic to the Adriatic, underwent profound changes as the Middle Ages ended. Their traditional role had been in some sense to provide a frontier, or buffer, between Europe and the east. By the mid-fifteenth century the Turks had conquered the Balkan peninsula south of the Danube and, in the early sixteenth, followed this with the occupation of Hungary and the Romanian Provinces. The mountainous province of Transylvania remained under the rule of its native princes, though nominally a vassal state of the Turks. The Polish and Czech states had been built around tribal nuclei, but in the fourteenth century their traditional dynasties, the Piasts and Přemyslids respectively, had come to an end. The Polish throne had been inherited by the Lithuanian Jagiełłos, whose combined state, the largest by far in Europe, reached from the Baltic Sea to the Russian steppe. The extinction of the native Czech dynasty, however, led to a succession of foreign and predominantly German rulers, whose presence served chiefly to fan the flames of Czech nationalism. In 1526, following the death of Lewis who had united the thrones of Hungary and Bohemia, Ferdinand of Habsburg, brother of Charles V, was elected King of Bohemia, thus commencing that association of Bohemia with Austria which lasted until 1918.

The events of the fifteenth and sixteenth centuries drew the countries of eastern Europe into ever closer relationship with those of central and western. Not only were the art styles of the Italian Renaissance diffused as far as Poland and Slovakia; the Reformation itself, both Lutheran and Calvinist, was widely accepted in Hungary, Transylvania and Poland. Commercial links between central and eastern Europe were strengthened, and before the end of the century the western states of Europe were to rely heavily on the eastern for the supply of corn and timber, as well as flax and hemp, resin and animal products.

Population

In the early decades of the sixteenth century the population of most of Europe was again expanding after its contraction during the closing centuries of the Middle Ages. The evidence is fragmentary, but all of it points in the same direction. Some time in the fifteenth century the number of births in the aggregate began to exceed that of deaths. The reasons are obscure. Perhaps epidemic diseases were less virulent; perhaps the availability of agricultural land led to a lower average age at marriage.

Russell has estimated that the population of continental Europe, excluding Russia, amounted to about 42 million at the beginning of the

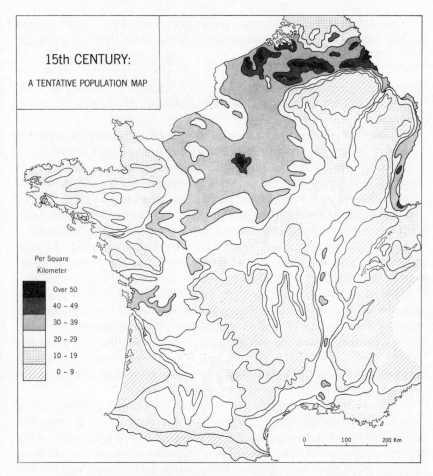

15th CENTURY:

A TENTATIVE POPULATION MAP

Per Square
Kilometer

Over 50

40 – 49

30 – 39

20 – 29

10 – 19

0 – 9

0   100   200 Km

Fig. 1.4 Population density in western Europe at the end of the Middle Ages

sixteenth century.[49] He may be right, but the evidence on which he bases his judgement is scanty and far from unambiguous. It consists essentially of tax records, and, since taxes were as a general rule levied on the heads of families, what we have is usually the number of 'hearths' or households. A prolonged and inconclusive controversy has centred on the size of the multiplier to be used for converting hearths to aggregate population. There was, in fact, no 'normal' size for the household. A further difficulty lies in the fact that the hearth tended to become a notional unit of taxation, and the number of hearths at which a community was assessed ceased gradually to bear any close relationship to that of real households.

Urban population is in general better documented than rural, though it did not make up more than a fifth of the total. Not only did the authorities keep records of the numbers of householders for purposes of taxation, but many of them also counted people, or 'mouths', in order to ensure an adequate food supply. This was especially the case in Italy, which became, in terms of its demographic history, the best-documented country in Europe.[50]

During the fifteenth century the Dukes of Burgundy instituted a series of hearth-counts within their domains in the Low Countries and Burgundy, a practice which was also adopted by some of their neighbours. They suggest that the population began to rise during the second half of the fifteenth century and by the 1540s had reached a density of 40–50 to the square kilometre in Brabant[51] and Hainault.[52] There was a belt of relatively dense population – over 40 to the square kilometre – extending across the Low Countries from the neighbourhood of Calais to that of Liège. To north and south densities diminished sharply in the sandy heathlands of the Campine and the forests of the Ardennes.

The population of the northern Low Countries was very unevenly distributed. The province of Holland, with perhaps 275,000 inhabitants, was the most densely inhabited with almost 50 to the square kilometre. This high density was supported in part by the fisheries. The predominantly agricultural provinces were much less densely settled. Friesland probably had little more than 30 to the square kilometre, and the sandy regions of Veluwe and Overijssel much less than 20.[53]

Evidence for France at this date is scanty, but nevertheless points to a relatively sparse population which had not yet recovered from the depredations of the Hundred Years' War and of the epidemics of the fourteenth century. The latter were especially severe in southern France, and hearth-lists for ducal Burgundy reveal a countryside which had been devastated and almost depopulated. The densities which existed before the great catastrophes of the fourteenth century were probably not regained until late in the sixteenth and in some areas probably not before the eighteenth. Over most of France, the density of population did not rise above 30 to the square kilometre, and the few large towns lay like oases amid a thinly peopled, indeed in places almost deserted, countryside.

The demographic history of central Europe is no better documented, and estimates of the population of Germany in the early sixteenth century range from seven million to almost twice this total.[54] Amongst the few areas which have been intensively studied is the Münsterland. Here Ditt found that densities were less than 15 over much of the area, and that population was more dense only along the Rhine.[55] Population was even sparser in Mecklenburg, where it fell to less than 5 in parts of this forested region.[56] Another region which has been intensively investigated is Saxony. Blaschke found an average density of about 32, which is low in view of its mining activity and its rich loess soils.[57] Germany is likely in the early sixteenth century to have had a population of some 12 million.[58]

The population of Poland may have been somewhat denser than that of northern Germany because the late medieval decline was felt less severely, if indeed it was experienced at all. There is a broad measure of agreement amongst Polish scholars that the population, within contemporary boundaries, was of the order of three million in the mid-sixteenth century, an average of about 20 to the square kilometre.[59] The density declined towards the east and was unquestionably very much lower in the forested kingdom of Lithuania.

The Alpine region, from France to Austria, was sparsely peopled. There was little cropland and agriculture was greatly restricted by the rigours of the mountain climate. Baratier has shown how abruptly densities fell off as one passed from the hills of Provence into the Alpes-Maritimes.[60] Large villages were to be found along many alpine valleys, especially those which opened southwards to the Italian plain, but within the mountains population had declined sharply. Its closely knit communities had suffered disastrously from epidemic disease, and vacant lands in the nearby plains were a constant invitation to the mountain peoples to migrate from this region of hardship. Indeed, there were communities which were no larger at the end of the eighteenth century than they had been at the beginning of the sixteenth.[61] Birth-rates were generally high in the mountains, but were compensated by a vigorous out-migration.

Fifteenth-century tax records for the cantons of Zurich[62] and Basel[63] and an episcopal visitation of the diocese of Lausanne,[64] which were used in compiling fig. 1.4, all suggest a sparsely settled countryside, even in the central plain of Switzerland, dotted with small and mainly agricultural towns. Densities rose to 30 and more near towns like Zurich and Geneva, but sank to less than 10 in the Jura and the Alps.[65] The Danube valley and Austria were even more sparsely settled than Switzerland, and large areas were visited only in summer by transhumant flocks and herds.

The mountains of Bohemia and the Carpathians of Slovakia and Romania supported a small but fertile population and fed a stream of migrants to the plains.[66] Little is known precisely of the density of population in these regions.[67] Hungary was probably populous before the Turkish invasions, which reduced the plains almost to a desert.[68] There is no acceptable evidence for the population of the Balkans at this time. A late-medieval source has been taken to suggest a total of

700,000 for Transylvania[69] – about seven to the square kilometre – and a hearth-count made under Sultan Suleiman I in the European provinces of the Ottoman empire suggests a total of 5,700,000.[70] But no one familiar with south-eastern Europe could ever place any reliance on such a total, which would in any case have excluded Albania, Croatia and perhaps also Montenegro. The overall density of population may have been as low as ten, though a much denser population would have been met with in such areas as the Skopje, Bitola and Sofia basins and near Edirne, Sarajevo and Beograd.

With Mediterranean Europe we enter a realm at once more populous and better documented. Italy not only had a large and literate middle class to which the size of the population was of interest, but also experienced difficulty in its urban food supply and thus felt a need to have a record of numbers. These urban records were studied by Beloch at the beginning of this century,[71] and Cipolla has observed[72] that more recent research has left his figures 'substantially unaltered'. Density varied greatly, but in no major province, except Sardinia, did it on average fall below 30. Most populous were the highly urbanised regions of Tuscany, Umbria, the Ligurian coast and the Lombardy plain. Piedmont was less populous and less urbanised than the territories of Milan and Venice,[73] and was one of the least densely populated of the Italian states. Northern Italy suffered severely in the course of the wars of the early sixteenth century, and an English ambassador reported that 'we found neither men nor women working in the fields nor any living soul except three poor women working in one place who were gleaning the few grapes that remained'.[74] Nevertheless, the fiscal documents for the district of Monza, lying to the north-east of Milan, for the year 1541 suggest an average density of about 32 to the square kilometre.[75] The abundant archives of the city of Venice contain a survey of population in 1548.[76] Most of the territory lay within the fertile plain of the Po, and was intensively cultivated to satisfy the needs of the city. Densities were amongst the highest in Europe, rising to more than 50 in the territories of Verona and Vicenza, to over 60 in the Padovana and 80 in the delta region (fig. 1.5). A decade later Carlo Borromeo, Bishop of Bergamo, conducted a visitation of his diocese which extended from the plain north of Milan into the Alps and spanned an area of some 2500 square kilometres.[77] If allowance is made for those villages for which no data are given, the rural population must have been about 111,500 'souls'. To this must be added that of the twelve urban parishes of Bergamo, which had, according to Beloch, a population of about 19,500.[78] The diocese thus contained some 130,000, a density of 52.

The Spanish peninsula is much less adequately documented than the Italian, though reliable aggregate totals can be established. The popula-

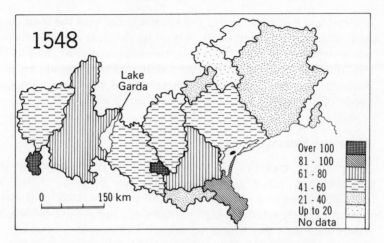

Fig. 1.5 Population density in Venezia, mid-sixteenth century

tion of Spain has been put at about 7.4 million in 1541 and that of Portugal at 1,124,000 in 1527.[79] It was increasing rapidly in both, but overall densities remained low in comparison with those of Italy. The highest average densities were in Castile, but these disguised the contrast between the densely peopled Basque province and Old Castile and the thinly settled regions of Estremadura and La Mancha. There was a vigorous migration from north to south, due in part to the fact that Andalusia was the gateway to the New World. Seville itself had a boom-town atmosphere,[80] and became in Cervantes' words 'the asylum of the poor and the refuge of the outcasts' of northern Spain.[81]

Table 1.1 *Approximate population of Europe, c. 1530*

France	13,000,000
Low Countries	1,500,000
Germany (incl. Austria)	12,000,000
Swiss Confederation	800,000
Poland	2,500,000
Czech lands	2,000,000
Hungary	2,000,000
Balkan peninsula	1,200,000
Spain and Portugal	8,524,000
Italy	11,000,000
Scandinavia	1,600,000
Total	56,124,000

Catalonia had been during the later Middle Ages the most populous and developed region of Spain, but in the sixteenth century its economy was irreparably damaged by the commercial revolution, and its leading city and port, Barcelona, increased only slowly.[82] Lisbon, by contrast, profited from the change to become one of the largest cities of the peninsula.

The urban pattern

The previous discussion has by and large ignored the important distinction between urban and rural population. In general, the densely peopled regions of Europe, such as northern Italy and the Low Countries, were relatively highly urbanised, and in thinly peopled areas towns were few and widely separated. Urbanisation, however, is difficult to measure because the majority of Europe's towns were in terms of function no more than large villages. By the early sixteenth century an urban map had been established which was to remain virtually unchanged until the nineteenth century. There had, in fact, been little change since the mid-fourteenth. Only in eastern Europe had the wave of new towns continued through the fifteenth century. Elsewhere, with a declining population and economic recession, a few small towns even disappeared, or, like Therouanne, were razed in war and never rebuilt.

It was always difficult to define a town. Legally it was a community separate and distinct from those of the surrounding countryside. It was endowed with limited though variable rights of self-government, and its inhabitants were exempt from the arbitrary impositions of a lord, free to move, to acquire property and to engage in whatever economic activities they chose. This, however, did not prevent most small towns from being predominantly agricultural, distinguishable only with difficulty from large villages. Indeed, many an unincorporated village in Flanders was far less agricultural and more industrial than half the formal towns of Europe.[83] The range of activities carried on by townspeople increased with the size of the town, but the functions of small towns – and most were small – were highly restricted.

Lenzburg, in the Swiss canton of Aargau, was such a small town.[84] It embraced a walled area of only 2.4 hectares. Its population never exceeded 500. They owned the surrounding fields, in which most were employed. The few crafts were of a kind usually met with in villages. Lenzburg had a weekly market, which served mainly for the exchange of local products and had little contact with more distant centres. There were thousands of towns in the Rhineland and in central and eastern Europe like Lenzburg. In England they would in all probability have reverted to the status of villages, like the decayed boroughs in Devon and Cornwall. In continental Europe they were saved from this fate by their defences. Every incorporated town had walls and gates to emphasise its separateness from the villages. Without fortifications it was not a town, and its population not readily distinguishable from those who lived in the surrounding countryside and worked in the fields.[85]

Little attempt had been made during the Middle Ages to portray towns pictorially. They had sometimes formed part of the background of Italian paintings, but were usually highly stylised. By the early sixteenth century it had become common to draw and engrave a faithful representation of a particular town. Dürer's Nuremberg, Leonardo da Vinci's Imola, Bufalini's Rome, Truschet and Hoyau's Paris, and *some* of the illustrations in Schedel's *Liber chronicarum* and Sebastian Münster's *Cosmographia* have pretensions to accuracy in their portrayal of both the plans and buildings of towns.

The earliest urban pictures were simple horizontal views, which presented the town's walls and skyline. These were followed by oblique representations, which showed both the plan of the streets and the elevation of at least the more important buildings. These engravings found a market amongst urban patricians and also, in this age of sieges, with the artillery-masters.[86] The genre culminated in the *Civitates orbis terrarum* of Braun and Hogenberg but was continued during the following century in the yet more ambitious series of engravings of Matthäus Merian and his sons.

These engravings invariably represented a town as walled with fortified gates and numerous towers. Within lay closely spaced houses dominated by the spires of churches and by other public buildings. Streets were narrow, except the principal axes of the town, which were usually wide enough for the erection of wooden stalls. In most there was a central open space which served as market-place. It was commonly overlooked by the church of the principal or oldest urban parish, and sometimes also by a gild – or market – house in which the urban patricians conducted private as well as municipal business. Within the walls, especially of the larger towns, were extensive areas which had not been built up. When the defences were rebuilt or extended in the thirteenth or fourteenth century, the city fathers sometimes built too generously, anticipating an urban expansion which never took place. Braun and Hogenberg show wide areas of orchards and crops within the outermost line of walls of numerous cities, including Basel, Brussels, Cologne, Milan and Zurich. The idea that such areas were deliberately contrived in order to provide the city with a food supply in time of siege does not bear serious consideration. Urban sieges – not infrequent in the wars of the sixteenth and seventeenth centuries – were always too short for such autarkic production to have been an object of policy.

On the other hand, all towns controlled an area extending for a limited distance beyond their walls. This was the *Bannmeile*, within which the town exercised jurisdiction. In most instances it extended only for a mile or two. Nuremberg was exceptional in having a *Bannmeile* of 65 square kilometres.[87] Within this area, and even beyond it, citizens had from the earliest stages of urban growth owned land and produced crops. During the later Middle Ages an increasing number of them had invested in rural land on a scale which had dangerously reduced their operating capital. Citizens, especially in the smaller towns, cultivated the surrounding fields themselves or with the help of hired labour. More distant possessions were often farmed at a rack-rent or – a growing practice – were leased *en métayage*. Suburban lands were often culti-vated intensively; some were planted with vines – a consequence of relatively high land values close to the city.

There must have been some five to six thousand cities and towns in Europe in the sixteenth century, ranging from the few giant cities of over 100,000 inhabitants to several thousand small places like Lenz-burg, each with less than a thousand. They were spread thickly in the Low Countries, the Rhineland, central Germany and northern Italy, but there were few in Europe's frontier regions to the north and east. This pattern of cities and towns exercised one of the best minds of the age, Giovanni Botero. In a very perceptive work[88] he defined the causes 'of the greatness of a city' as 'the commodity of the site and the fruitfulness of the country'. He realised that the pattern of towns, and their density or frequency, was dependent on the richness of the soil and the wealth of the countryside which supported them. But large cities, he knew, required a more substantial basis than a prosperous agriculture; 'for many provinces there are, and they very rich, that have never a good city in them, as, for example Piedmont . . . and there is not a country throughout all Italy that hath more plenty of corn, cattle, wine, and of excellent fruits of all sorts'. Nor was Paris, the largest city in western Europe, 'situated in the most fertile part of France'.

Botero had thus established his model: urbanism was a function of the fertility of the land and of its capacity to support people, and he was looking for an explanation of those cities and regions which did not fit his scheme. He looked beyond the market needs of the surrounding countryside. Large cities might serve regional or even continental needs. 'It will also greatly help to draw people to our city if she have some good store of vendible merchandise . . . [such as] tapestry in Arras, rash [satins] in Florence, velvets in Genoa, cloth of gold and silver in Milan, and scarlet in Venice' (see p. 241). Convenience of trade was seen as a factor in the growth of cities; a 'store of navigable rivers . . . [and] good havens of the sea' might give rise to commercial towns, but Botero was quick to note that a good harbour alone did not make a centre of trade. 'What port is more safe or more spacious than the channel of Cattaro' (Gulf of Kotor, on the Dalmatian coast), he wrote. 'And yet is there not any memorable city in that place.' Botero was no determinist, and emphasised repeatedly that man's use of his environment was conditioned by his perception of what it had to offer him. The sites of religious cults, he noted, sometimes grew to great size, and Rome – a city of some 55,000[89] – was indebted 'to the blood of the martyrs, to the relics of the saints, to the holy consecrated places, and to the supreme authority in beneficial and spiritual causes'. Universities also contributed to the size of cities; 'the commodity of learned schools is of no small moment to draw people'. In Paris, faculty and students of the Sorbonne made up a total of at least two or three thousand. At Louvain, a student body of over 1300 made up about 12 per cent of the population of the city,[90] and to the total of students and masters must be added the perhaps large body of people for whom, directly or indirectly, they provided employment. Above all, large cities owed their size to their selection as seats of 'supreme authority and power', for government 'draweth dependency with it, and dependency concourse and concourse greatness'. Botero was right; the 'primate' cities in Europe were the political capitals, though he went a little farther than the evidence warranted when he claimed that the size of the capital was directly related to the extent of the country which it administered.

Fig. 1.6 shows the distribution of the larger cities of Europe in the first half of the sixteenth century. Evidence for the size of towns is scanty, and in many instances consists of nothing better than a subjective judgement based on the area within the walls or the number of houses in a sixteenth-century plan. Even where hearth-lists or head-counts exist it is not always certain to what they relate. Did they include the population of suburbs without the walls or even the inhabitants of the *Bannmeile*? The map was conceived as representing large and medium-sized towns about 1530. The data used were derived from sources ranging from the late fifteenth to the late sixteenth century. In some instances it was practicable to interpolate a likely total. One was nevertheless left with such insoluble problems as the size of Rome after its sack by the soldiers of Charles V or of the Budapest cluster of settlements after their capture by the Turks.

It proved impossible on a continental map to represent towns of less than about 5000 inhabitants, partly because of their great number, partly because of the problem of distinguishing between them and large villages from which they scarcely differed in function. The frequency of small towns varied greatly. It was greatest in Germany and least in France and Spain. Walker has estimated that in Württemberg there was

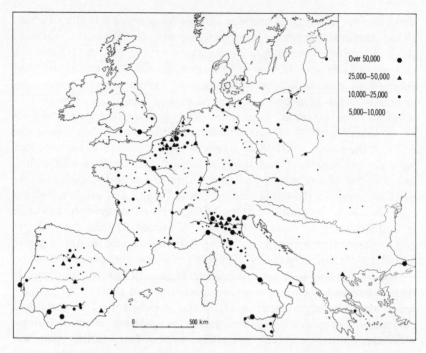

Fig. 1.6 The chief cities of Europe in the first half of the sixteenth century

on average one town for approximately every 55 square kilometres, and that in Prussia and Hanover, amongst the least urbanised of German provinces, there was a town for every 200 square kilometres.[91] 'A stroller through Württemberg', he wrote, 'could expect to strike a recognizable and incorporated town every seven kilometres.' In Alsace there were thirty-five towns, all of them very small except Strasbourg, Colmar and Sélestat – on average one for every 75 square kilometres.[92] Fig. 1.7 shows the distribution of *all* towns in one restricted area: Switzerland. An urban hierarchy is apparent with large and medium-sized cities rearing their walls and steeples above a multitude of small and humble towns and *bourgades*.

The distribution of towns, irrespective of their size, was very irregular. It depended in part on terrain and soil, as Botero had noted, and towns were especially numerous along the loess belt which extends (see above, p. 3) from the Low Countries to Silesia, and correspondingly few in the Alpine region and in areas of infertile sands and gravel. France paradoxically had fewer towns for its area than Italy or Germany. The reason probably lay in the fact that the primary urban network derived

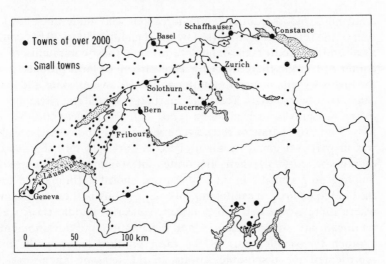

Fig. 1.7 The towns of Switzerland

from the *civitas*-capitals of the Roman empire. Most of the latter became the seats of bishops and thus pre-empted as it were the urban functions of their dioceses. Outside the boundaries of the Roman empire there were no towns in the early Middle Ages, and the political fragmentation later led to a spate of competitive town-building. The immense number of towns which emerged in central Europe was offset by their small average size. The few which in the early sixteenth century exceeded 5000 population could not in the aggregate have contained more than 400,000, or 5 per cent of the population.[93] Agriculture was of increasing relative importance with the diminishing size of towns and the German *Zwergstadt* of 500 to 1000 inhabitants was functionally little different from a village.

The degree of urbanisation can be measured for only restricted areas. In Brabant in 1526, about 35 per cent of the population lived in towns, and in Hainault about 29. It has been claimed that in 1514 some 46 per cent of the inhabitants of the county of Holland were urban, though this is likely to have included a large fishing and maritime sector. About half the population of the city-state of Geneva lived in its central place, and about a quarter of the canton of Zurich were in its chief town. Bergamo contained about 18 per cent of the population of its diocese, and over the whole north Italian plain some 20 per cent of the population lived in cities of over 10,000.

Agriculture and rural conditions

Over Europe as a whole the urban sector of the population, the craftsmen, traders, rentiers and churchmen who made up some 15 per cent of the total, were supported by the remaining 80 to 90 per cent who lived and worked on the land. From every rural community in every corner of Europe there flowed a small stream of farm produce towards the towns – grain, live cattle, butter and cheese, wool, skins and hides. It came from two sources. The larger part represented the payments made by the peasants to their masters: rents, *taille, champart* and tithe. These passed into the hands of the seigneurs, both lay and ecclesiastical, and was in part consumed by themselves, in part sold into the market to defray the costs of their elaborate entertainment and extravagant building programmes. In most of Europe almost nothing came back to the land to be used in capital improvements. Only in the Low Countries, where there was a rich and politically powerful middle class, was any significant investment made in land reclamation and development.

Much the smaller part of the farm produce entering the market represented the disposable surplus of the peasants themselves. The money received for it was used to purchase salt, clothing, seed, tools and whatever else the otherwise autarkic rural community could not supply from its own resources. A model devised by Wilhelm Abel,[94] admittedly for the eighteenth century, represents about 40 per cent of the gross output of the peasant farm as disposed of in services, taxes and other seigneurial obligations, and 20 per cent as sold off the land, leaving about a third as the net income of the farm family. The exactions of the seigneur were heavy everywhere,[95] and fully explain why agriculture was unprogressive, with no surplus for investment in agricultural improvements. The social literature of the time is filled with protest against the exactions of the lords which reduced the peasantry to misery.[96] The Memmingen Articles of the revolting German peasants of 1524 shows that the gravity of their lords' exactions was uppermost in their minds. In parts of central and eastern Europe, where peasant obligations had been relatively light, they were being increased as the lords, in that movement which is sometimes known as the 'second serfdom', increased their control over the peasants and their land.

An unprogressive agriculture was practised in most of Europe, little changed from that which had inadequately fed the overgreat population of the fourteenth century. Everywhere, except in the mountainous areas, cropland was largely under cereals, and bread grains provided the staple diet of all except the rich. Wheat was the bread crop *par excellence*, but only a minority of the population even tasted bread made from it. It was the most important crop on the 'strong heartie and fat Soyle' of the Paris basin and northern France.[97] It was grown on the better soils of the Limagne and the Rhineland,[98] on the loess of central Europe, and in parts of Poland, from which it was exported to the west.

But the only areas where wheat was widely cultivated were in southern Europe: Provence, Languedoc, the Spanish Meseta and Italy. In the Low Countries and parts of Germany and Switzerland a form of wheat known as spelt or dinkel was grown. It had the advantage of milling easily but did not crop as heavily as the standard variety.[99] Nevertheless, it entirely displaced wheat in parts of the Low Countries.[100]

While wheat was everywhere the preferred bread grain, rye supplied the basic food of the majority. Contemporary writers made much of the fact that rye would grow well on light, sandy and infertile soils. It could resist the hazards of the weather and, if it did not yield more heavily, it was at least more reliable than wheat. Sometimes, especially in north-western Europe, a mixture of wheat and rye, known as *méteil*, or maslin, was grown, probably as a kind of insurance. Rye was the most widely cultivated cereal in much of western Europe and throughout central and eastern. In Poland the typical estate in the sixteenth century produced four times as much rye as wheat.[101]

Both wheat and rye were autumn-sown. They grew through the winter and spring, and were harvested in July or early August. They were less hardy than the strains which are cultivated today, and the young plants were sometimes destroyed in winter by excessive rain or severe frost. On such occasions the land had to be ploughed afresh and sown with a spring crop (see p. 175). The cropping system which had developed in much of Europe during the Middle Ages called for the alternation of autumn- and spring-sown grains with fallow. Wheat or rye was thus followed by oats or barley. The two groups of cereals were thus in joint production, with the autumn-sown grains cropping as a general rule rather more heavily than the spring-sown. The volume of production of these cereals on a Polish estate described by Wychański[102] as:

Autumn-sown			Spring-sown		
	Production	Yield-ratio		Production	Yield-ratio
Rye	174 hl	5.0	Oats	204 hl	4.2
Wheat	44 hl	5.2	Barley	43 hl	6.8
	218			247	

The spring-sown grains were not held in high regard. The *Maison Rustique* regarded oats as 'un vice et chose inutile', but admitted that they were valuable as a fodder, and, cooked as a gruel or porridge, served as human food. Barley, like oats, lacks gluten, and cannot make a light bread, as wheat and rye are able to do. It was used for malting; it was fed to animals, and, cooked in a kind of soup, entered into the human diet.

Oats are particularly tolerant of poor soil and harsh climate, thus compensating for the disadvantages of their low yield and weak straw which could not be used for thatching. Rye and oats formed the typical crop association over much of Europe, but at greater altitudes and higher latitudes oats alone were grown. Oats were the principal – even the only – cereal crop in the Alpine regions and in such areas as the Auvergne and Eifel.

In northern Europe wheat disappeared from the farm system. The cultivation of rye extended into Denmark and southern Sweden, while oats constituted the only cereal crop in most of Norway, Sweden and Finland.[103] This was reflected in the diet. Bread was virtually unknown in these areas. Instead, flat oaten cakes and a gruel made from oats, together with milk products, made up the greater part of the human food supply. Fortunately, those areas where oats were the principal cereal crop were usually able to produce a compensatory supply of protein in the form of butter and cheese.

Although cereals provided the basic human food supply, they were unreliable crops and their yields were low. They were the pillars of an agricultural system which was to prove tragically durable. They were, however, supplemented by 'garden' crops, without which it would have been difficult to sustain life. Almost every rural household had its garden, in which were grown beans and peas, source of much of the peasants' intake of protein, as well as green vegetables, roots and herbs, not to mention industrial crops such as flax, hemp and dyestuffs. Around the houses of the rich were large·gardens which contributed an important part of the food supply. All treatises on agronomy which were written for a well-to-do clientèle contained long chapters on the management of gardens. Their soil, Olivier de Serres explained, should be well dressed, but in return produced every year without any need for fallowing. The garden was a private preserve. It was, as a general rule, neither tithed nor subjected to the *Feldzwang* of the village community. New crops could be tried out in the garden – not that the peasant was much given to experiment and innovation. It is probable that the potato was first grown in the garden, as also were maize, sunflower, tobacco and many vegetables and roots, such as chicory and mangold. Only after the success of such crops had been demonstrated beyond cavil in the private garden were they allowed to share in the communally controlled fields. Few records were ever kept of garden crops, so that this highly important branch of agriculture forms one of the darkest corners in the history of early agriculture.

A three-field system prevailed over much of Europe, except the Mediterranean region. The use of a fallow year was a concession to the fact that manure was available only in very small quantities, and was in shortest supply in those areas – the 'champagne' regions of north-western Europe – where it was needed most. A disadvantage of the system was that it produced the less desirable spring-sown grains in quantities which were approximately equal to the bread grains. For this reason a two-field system was retained (or reverted to) in the middle Rhineland, where cities created a large demand for the winter cereals.[104] The aggregate amount of grain produced was smaller, but it consisted wholly of bread crops. In eastern Europe, especially in Poland, a two-field system was also practised in some areas, but here the reason is more likely to have been the abundance of land which made a more intensive use unnecessary. In areas of Mediterranean climate, including the Dalmatian coast,[105] autumn-sown grains alternated with fallow, since here there was little possibility, except in the mountains, that spring-sown grains would grow and mature during the hot, dry summer.

While the two- and three-field systems prevailed over much of Europe, they were by no means the only systems in use, and were, in fact, in slow retreat before a variety of cropping methods which made a more intensive use of the soil. A powerful factor was the growth of population, especially of urban population, and the increasing demands which it made upon the food supply. Long before the end of the Middle Ages, the practice of fallowing had been abandoned, temporarily at least, in parts of the Low Countries, and peas and beans were being grown as field crops in its place. By 1500, turnips, green vegetables and fodder crops, the so-called artificial grasses, were beginning to be used in rotation with cereals. At the same time, a convertible husbandry, in which a period of cultivation alternated with long leys of several years,[106] began to be practised. In the Low Countries this more intensive cultivation was made possible by the gradual relaxation of medieval tenurial restrictions, and made necessary by the growing population. A system of ley-farming was also carried on in hilly areas, where the high rainfall, and consequent poverty of the soil, made continuous cultivation impracticable.

The sixteenth century was a period of rising grain prices, and efforts were made both to increase the area under cultivation and to improve the yield. Manure was more widely and more carefully used, but the extension of cereal farming was unfortunately incompatible with a more generous supply of farmyard manure. The *Maison Rustique* – always rather exacting in its requirements – claimed that for a good crop on 'raw, rough and tough [that is, acidic] Soyle you must labour [plough] it most exquisitely, harrow it and manure it very oft with great store of dung'. Such quantities of manure were not available, and crops on such soils were generally poor. Olivier de Serres recommended the use of pigeon and poultry manure, as well as of marl and lime. Beans and lupins, he found, would enrich the soil. The productivity of sixteenth-century agriculture was, however, always restricted by the small animal population and hence the feeble supply of manure.

The writings of the sixteenth-century agronomists showed a keen appreciation of the differing qualities of soils and of the uses to which they could be profitably put. Olivier de Serres, for example, prefaced his book with a discussion of the soil. Its quality, he wrote, depended on the balance between the elements of clay and sand within it. The best soil, according to the *Maison Rustique*, 'is that which is blacke, crumbling and easily turned over ... [and] falleth into small pieces in ones hand'.[107] The presence of ruined farm buildings indicating a settlement long since abandoned was a favourable sign, for the soils, 'cuits et recuits à la longue, avec le meslinge des sables et chaux des batimens desmolis, par feu ou vieillesse, se sont rendus plus friables, et en suite aisez à cultiver'.[108]

The texture of the soil seems to have been the only criterion of its quality. The use of lime and manure and the ploughing in of nitrogenous plants were considered beneficial because they helped to produce a crumbly texture. Deep ploughing of 'strong' or heavy soil was recommended, because it improved the drainage, and the frequent use of harrows, and especially of a roller fitted with spikes, was encouraged because it broke up the lumps and produced a fine tilth. Limited though their knowledge of soil was, sixteenth-century writers were nevertheless thinking in terms of adjusting crops and cropping systems to fit the qualities of soil that were available.

Agricultural tools and equipment had changed little in western and southern Europe for several centuries. The plough, the basic tool of the farmer, was in general a heavy instrument – built of massive beams, usually of oak, carefully jointed together. It was commonly supported on wheels in the front, and was equipped with an iron coulter and a ploughshare which was at least tipped with iron. There were many local variations in the design of the plough. It had to be lighter in design in areas – those, for example, of scattered settlement – where a large team was not available. The light classical plough, *aratrum* or *araire*, had survived in southern Europe and, in one form or another, in the Balkans.[109] In east-central Europe, however, the use of the heavy wheeled plough was spreading.[110] It may have been diffused by the German immigrants and settlers, but its adoption was certainly encouraged by the growing demand in western Europe for Polish grain.

In other respects there were small improvements in farm equipment. The scythe began to replace the sickle. It allowed the harvester to cut close to the ground, to make the most of the hay harvest, and, when he wished, to obtain a long wheat straw for thatching. The harrows shown in sixteenth-century paintings and drawings were massive wooden frames fitted with large iron spikes. One cannot be sure how widely such improved tools were used. The bourgeois who invested in a rural estate may have used them – hence the frequency with which they appeared in the pictorial art of the Low Countries – but it is unlikely that the peasant had the opportunity to use such sophisticated tools before the nineteenth-century.[111] In eastern Europe also, where labour was abundant and the seigneur's control over it increasing, there was little inducement to improve its efficiency by equipping it with better tools.

Yet capital was invested in land reclamation reflecting the growing population and the rising price of grain. In the Low Countries and elsewhere in north-western Europe marshland was reclaimed. Spectacular though some of these undertakings were for their age, they added little to the area of agricultural land. Elsewhere cropland was extended marginally in most communities. In many parts of France land was· cleared to make way for peasant farms in much the same way that it had been in the twelfth and thirteenth centuries.[112] In some areas vineyards of questionable value gave place to cropland, and in the south the *garrigue* was cleared to make way for the vine.

Despite the rising population and a strong market demand for bread grains, little was done to improve either yields per hectare or yield-ratios. Indeed, it is likely that on average they declined somewhat as marginal land was brought under cultivation.[113] Yield-ratios varied not only with the weather but also from one cereal crop to another and from one region to another. But even on the good soils of northern France they exceeded 8:1 only on rare occasions,[114] and on soils of medium quality the return was at best fivefold. In Provence wheat generally gave less than a fourfold return,[115] and the return was often less than threefold on the poor, sandy soils of Berry[116] or the stiff glacial clays of Dombes.[117] A similar range in yield-ratios was to be found in central and eastern Europe. In Poland yields were occasionally as high as sixfold on the best soils, but were more often fourfold or less, with a tendency to decline during succeeding centuries.[118]

The basic reason for both low yields and yield-ratios was the lack of manure. Even the best soils cropped poorly because they were given over almost exclusively to arable husbandry, and few animals were kept beyond those necessary for draught purposes. The soil, furthermore, was poorly ploughed, and weeds were not destroyed. The number of those who followed the advice of the agronomists and ploughed both frequently and deep must have been very small, and Goubert found that in parts of northern France four-fifths of the peasants, in fact, had no plough.[119] Seed was poorly selected, despite the oft-repeated advice to keep the best for sowing, and there must have been many occasions when peasants had their store of seed corn looted or stolen, and were obliged to buy and sow whatever was available in the market.

In mountainous and hilly areas the balance between arable and pastoral agriculture was better. Much of the land, especially the higher plateau surfaces, could only be used for grazing. Flocks and herds were brought up from the valleys for the summer months, but spent the winter stabled on the lower ground, where their manure was available for the fields. This helps to explain why yield-ratios in these infertile regions were often but little less than on the plains of Picardy and Artois.[120]

In the Alps, as also in the Pyrenees and the higher mountains of eastern Europe, the balance was tipped even more strongly towards pastoralism. The *Urbäre* of Austrian monasteries[121] show how, in the later Middle Ages, peasant tribute in grain was gradually replaced by payment in cheeses. The same was happening in Switzerland, where the victory 'du bétail sur le blé'[122] was assured by 1500. Burgesses from the cities began to buy up alpine pastures just as elsewhere they acquired suburban vineyards and market-gardens. Urban population provided a large market for the dairy produce and live cattle of the mountains, and not even the high price of grain seems to have brought about a revival of corn-growing in the mountain valleys.

Not only was Europe dotted with islands of pastoralism which broke the vast sea of grain; it was also surrounded by a *Weidezone*, in which animal-rearing was the primary, if not the only, objective of agriculture.[123] Scandinavia, the plains of eastern Europe beyond the belt of commercial corn-growing, the grasslands of Hungary, Moldavia and Wallachia, and the steppe of central Spain all supported vast numbers of animals. In Scandinavia the emphasis was on dairy cattle. Writers, from the author of the *Heimskringla* to Malthus, have described how the cattle passed the short summer on the saetars, returning to the valleys in autumn. Only as many cattle could be kept as there was fodder to support during the winter. The human diet was made up mainly of oaten cake and gruel, butter and cheese, and there was an export of dairy produce to the towns. Denmark, more accessible to the markets of western and central Europe, exported live cattle by way of the cattle fairs of Schleswig[124] to the pastures of north-western Germany, where they were fattened for the market. The movement occurred principally in early spring and in the autumn, in herds of up to 1000 head. During the sixteenth century this cattle trade was increasing with the growth in population and the improvement in living standards of the more prosperous sections of the community.

The movement of cattle from Europe's eastern frontier was on an even larger scale. The cattle were bred on the grasslands which,

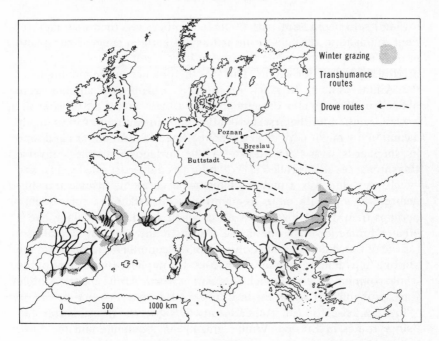

Fig. 1.8 Transhumance and drove routes in Europe in the sixteenth century

interrupted by mountains and forest, stretched from the Ukraine to the plain of Hungary. They were driven in vast herds across Poland to the markets of Poznań, Frankfurt-on-Oder and, above all, the small town of Buttstadt, near Weimar. At Buttstadt, it was said, as many as 16,000 or 20,000 animals changed hands in a single day during the fairs. A more southerly stream came from Moldavia, Wallachia and Hungary towards Vienna and the cities of southern Germany.[125]

Quite distinct from these mass migrations of animals to the markets of western and central Europe were the seasonal movements between plateau and valley, mountain and plain. These sometimes extended over great distances, as between northern and southern Spain or from the Carpathian mountains to the Black Sea coastlands. Their purpose was to gain a profit from marginal lands capable of economic use for only a part of the year, such as mountain pastures buried under snow in winter and lowlands burned dry by the summer heat. Reference has already been made to such transhumant movements in Scandinavia, but they belong pre-eminently to the Mediterranean region.[126] Two types of transhumance have been distinguished, both of which were practised in the sixteenth century. In normal transhumance the inhabitants of a valley or lowland settlement sent part of their number, together with most of their animals, to the hills or mountains in early summer. The upland grazing was thus used while the lowlands were left free for making hay or growing fodder for winter. This was the practice in the mountains of the Alpine system. In much of southern Europe the animals were obliged by the summer drought to vacate their winter pastures in the lowlands until after the first rains of the following autumn. Alternatively a community might have its permanent home in the mountains and send its shepherds with flocks down to the lowlands in winter – inverse transhumance, as it is called. The two forms could exist side by side, and which prevailed was a matter of historical accident. Inverse transhumance was met with more frequently in the Balkans, a consequence perhaps of war and invasion against which a mountain village had a greater protection than one in the plains. In any event, it was characteristic of transhumance that only part of the community took part in the seasonal movement. Nomadism, by contrast, implied a movement of the whole community, and, though common in North Africa and the Middle East, probably did not occur in Europe at this date.

Fig. 1.8, based on Elli Müller's study,[127] shows the principal transhumance routes in Europe. Winter grazing, in Aquitaine and the Ebro valley, bordered the Pyrenees. There was a large-scale movement of sheep and goats – almost 66,000 animals passed through Castellane, in the Alpes-Maritimes, in six weeks in 1516[128] – between the plains of Provence and the French Alps. There were similar movements in Italy between the Maremma, the Campagna and the Tavoliere of Apulia on the one hand and the Abruzzi mountains on the other.[129] In the Balkans the mountaineers descended to the Sava and Danube valleys and to the coastal plains of Albania, Greece and Macedonia with their flocks.

The transhumant movements of flocks and herds were highly organised. Pastures, either upland or lowland, were rented; the migration paths were kept open and were reserved for the transhumant animals at certain times of the year, and there were toll-stations at which payment was made for their rights of passage. Nowhere, however, was the seasonal migration of stock more highly organised than in Spain. After the *reconquista* much of the grassland of Castile became a vast sheep run, within which the flocks migrated along their *cañadas* between winter grazing in the south and their summer homes on the plateaux of Old Castile. The sheep were shorn in the course of their spring migration, and the wool sold at the fairs, especially that of Medina del Campo, which had grown up along their route. Estimates of the number of animals which took part in these migrations varied, but throughout the first half of the sixteenth century it ranged from 2 to 3.5 million.[130]

During the Middle Ages local specialisation in agricultural production had, with the exception of that in wine, been of only minor importance. By the sixteenth century this was no longer so. A growing appreciation of the qualities of the soil and the constraints of climate, coupled with improvements in the methods and organisation of transport, had led to the development of monocultures, dependent on sale and export. The rye production of eastern Europe, butter and cheese in the Alps, livestock on Europe's northern and eastern frontiers, and increasingly intensive wine production in certain favoured areas, all illustrate how the farmer, even the peasant farmer, was generating a marketable surplus of increasing size. It is impossible to measure this change with any precision. Of course, there remained many areas which were relatively self-sufficient, but elsewhere, notably in the Low Countries and northern France, the Lombardy plain and Tuscany – areas where the urban population was increasing most rapidly – there was a growing reliance on distant sources for some essential commodities: 'in the western parts of the Low Countries the farmers began to grow all sorts of commercial crops . . . instead of corn . . . Only a regular supply of corn made it possible for the farmers thus to specialise in the cultivation of commercial crops or on cattle breeding.'[131] In the Netherlands in the narrower sense, the reclaimed polders tended to be used mainly for dairy farming; the heathlands of the east for beef cattle, and the croplands near the cities for vegetables and industrial crops, while the basic bread crops were imported on an increasing scale from Germany and the east.[132]

Foremost amongst the specialised crops was wine. It had formerly been produced very widely, even in areas as unsuited climatically as the English Midlands, Flanders and Brandenburg. It was the growing ease with which a better wine could be imported from southern France or the Mediterranean, rather than any change in climate, which led to the abandonment of the more northerly vineyards. By the sixteenth century very little wine was being produced along the Seine valley below Paris. Viticulture had disappeared from the Low Countries,[133] and the more northerly vineyards had ceased production along the Rhine, but in central Europe, less accessible to imports from France, the vine was still grown in Saxony, Mecklenburg, Pomerania and Prussia.[134] It was, nevertheless, in retreat, as the economics of growing grain for export and of importing wine gradually asserted themselves. By contrast, in areas favoured by both climate and transport, the vine 'swept aside all other kinds of vegetation and forms of cultivation'.[135] Thus in one area of Europe after another, the law of comparative advantage was inexorably forcing the restriction or abandonment of some subsistence crops, and, in their place, the cultivation of others for export. The largest commercial wine production was in south-western France, the valleys of the Rhône and Rhine, and on certain coasts and islands of the Mediterranean. The last was becoming, with the conquests of the Turks, an uncertain source of supply, and malmsey wine – the rich Greek wine shipped from Monemvasia – disappeared from the tables of the rich. It was many decades before southern Spain and Portugal filled its place with their heavy and fortified vintages.

The trend towards commercial production and trade in farm products was restricted by two factors. Foremost was the increase in rural population, which began again to press against resources as it had done in the thirteenth century. The effect of the fragmentation of farm holdings was to emphasise yet again the self-sufficient character of peasant agriculture. At the same time, tenurial conditions all too often checked experiment and the conversion of land to those crops which under the prevailing economic conditions seemed the most profitable. It was no accident that innovation in farming was most noteworthy amongst the bourgeois landowners of north-western Europe.

The bipartite manor, with its demesne cultivated by the labour of its dependent villeins, was over most of Europe a thing of the past. In most cases, labour dues had been commuted for a rent in money or in kind, and the demesne was broken up and leased in small tenancies. At the same time, the status, if not always the personal fortunes, of the peasant had tended to rise. For this the scarcity of labour in the years following the Black Death was in part responsible. Price movements in the fifteenth century also tended to help the peasant. On the other hand, a century of almost incessant warfare, with its attendant loss of life and destruction of crops, farmstock, tools and homes, dealt a severe blow to the well-being of the peasantry. Under such conditions the type of tenure known as *métayage* spread widely in the fifteenth and sixteenth centuries.[136] The lord provided the land and a minimum of stock, seed and equipment, and took a fraction – sometimes as much as two-thirds – of the crop. Tenures of this kind became the most widespread in France and Italy. Elsewhere farm-holdings were leased, commonly for a term of a few years, at a fixed annual rent, coupled in many instances with certain servile obligations.

The lords suffered no less than the peasantry in the disturbed conditions of the later Middle Ages.[137] Their participation both in warfare and in the expensive forms of entertainment which character-ised the later phases of feudalism, cost them heavily, so that many were obliged to alienate at least part of their lands. Some were bought by aspiring members of the peasant class, who thus came to form a class of rich peasants, or yeomen. Others were purchased by the rising urban middle class, which thus entered the ranks of the rural landowners and hoped thereby to achieve the status of landed gentry. Conditions of land tenure were changing rapidly in the early sixteenth century, but, whoever held legal title to the land, the continent was, at least from the Duero to the Oder, one of peasant farms. In general, they were small and with the growth in population they were becoming smaller. Each was made up of a large number of scattered parcels, a result in part of division between heirs. A community in Poitou in the sixteenth century possessed eighty separate tenures, divided into no less than 1298 parcels of land:[138]

Under 3 hectares	20
3–5 hectares	11
5–10	23
10–15	10
15–20	6
20–25	4
25–30	3
Over 30	3
Total	80

At Sardon (Gard) in 1590 more than half of the total of fifty-four peasant holdings were of less than one hectare, and only eight had more than five.[139]

It is probable that holdings were on average larger in northern France and in central Europe. Nevertheless, even in eastern Germany, traditionally regarded as the home of the great estate, less than a fifth of the land was held in units of over 100 hectares,[140] and in Mecklenburg almost a half were of under 20 hectares. Even the estates, or *Rittergüter*, to which these holdings belonged, were very much smaller than has commonly been supposed, and the great majority were of less than 250 hectares.

In eastern Germany and Poland the trend in the development of landholding was opposite to that in the rest of Europe. There had, in the later Middle Ages, been a movement towards greater freedom for the peasant. This was then checked and ultimately reversed. The Elbe became 'the boundary between freedom and serfdom'[141] as estates, cultivated directly by their lords with servile labour, were created in the east. By the end of the fifteenth century 'most of the peasantry were well on their way to becoming serfs', and 'by the end of the sixteenth century the process of enserfment was just about completed'.[142] This movement is generally attributed to the growing demand for bread grains in the west European markets, a demand which the new estates of the east were well suited to satisfy. It must, however, be noted that the movement to create or extend estates and to depress the status of the peasantry was also felt in areas, such as Bohemia and Hungary, which were not important sources of grain for the west, and that it could not have taken place if the central government had not been heavily dependent on the political support of the nobles. The conversion of *Grundwirtschaft* into *Gutswirtschaft*, of lordship over land into direct exploitation of the land, was pursued in most of eastern Europe throughout the century. Peasants were dispossessed and villages destroyed to make way for vast demesne farms. In Poland the peasants were often relocated in long 'street' villages in order to leave the fields unencumbered, and were also called on to perform excessive corvées. In Hungary, a system of hereditary serfdom was imposed in 1514, after the peasant revolt led by Dózsa.[143] In 1557, King Zygmunt August of Poland, under pressure from his own nobility, instituted wide-ranging 'reforms', whose purpose was to reorganise the system of landholding and to increase agricultural production.[144] At the same time, the peasants' labour dues, or corvée, were regularised and made more oppressive, and peasant land, whenever the opportunity arose, was absorbed into the demesne.

In Italy the break-up of the demesne proceeded on lines similar to those in France, only at a faster pace. In Tuscany, the *mezzadri* were 'poverty-stricken and in debt . . . [they] were more and more becoming members of the proletariat and assumed the character of underpaid workers . . . almost entirely without capital'.[145] The average size of the peasant holding was becoming smaller.[146] In the village of Montaldeo, in Piedmont, for example, the size-structure of peasant holdings in 1548 was as shown in table 1.2.[147]

Table 1.2

	Number	Percentage of area
Under 0.5 hectares	40	2.5
0.5–1	33	6.3
1–3	49	22.9
3–5	14	13.9
5–10	14	25.0
10–20	4	14.0
Over 20	1	15.4

In those areas of the Balkan peninsula which were effectively occupied by the Ottoman Turks a species of feudalism was introduced. Much of the land was divided into small fiefs or timars which were allocated each to a Turkish official or spahi. The latter had no more than a life interest in the timars and were called upon for military service in proportion to their holding. The peasants, who had continued to cultivate the soil since the pre-Turkish period, had security of tenure. They could pass on their holdings to their children, and their obligations in the form of rent and corvée were not excessive.[148] Their status, was, however, to change radically as gradually timars became hereditary; their obligations became more onerous and their status was depressed to that of serfs.

Settlement

The pattern of human settlement had not changed greatly since the early fourteenth century. Some small settlements had disappeared during the period of declining population in the late fourteenth and fifteenth centuries, never to reappear. No new settlements were established, except in areas such as the Balkans which had been devastated by war. Although the geographical pattern of settlements changed little, they underwent profound change in detail. The houses and farm buildings of which they were made were built of wood and clay. They decayed and were vulnerable to fire. There was a continual process of renovation and rebuilding, and the actual site of cottage or farm was likely to change with each rebuilding. In some parts of Europe, notably the estate villages of eastern Europe, it became the policy of the lord to reduce the formless jumble of houses to some more regular pattern. In this way originated many of the interminable street villages of Poland.

It is difficult to determine the actual size of villages at this time. Even in northern France and the southern Low Countries, for which hearth-lists survive, it is not always possible to say whether all the households allocated to a named place were in one nucleated settlement or scattered over the area of a parish. Only by projecting back from eighteenth-century cadastral maps and using whatever archaeological data there may be, can the pattern of human settlement be established. Such evidence, however, suggests that the morphology of settlements had not greatly changed between the later Middle Ages and the early nineteenth century. Nucleated villages with their surrounding open fields predominated in the rich agricultural belt of northern France, the southern Low Countries and parts of Germany and elsewhere where physical conditions encouraged the traditional three-course system of cultivation. In areas of poorer soil hamlets and isolated farmsteads were more common. In the east European areas of late medieval settlement the 'forest' and 'street' villages prevailed, with the farmsteads aligned on each side of a single road.

Each of these very broad types of human settlement can be further subdivided. Many village forms can be understood in terms of the social and economic needs of the community. Others have no such rationale. A fuller discussion of types of rural settlement is given in the first volume of *An Historical Geography of Europe* and for reasons of space is not repeated here.[149]

Manufacturing and mining

The Renaissance was not characterised by any significant developments in manufacturing technology, except in the fields of mining and metallurgy. Change occurred rather in the structure and organisation of industry. The towns had never possessed a monopoly of manufacturing, and throughout the Middle Ages a residual industry had survived in rural areas, concentrating on the lowest qualities of production. In the later Middle Ages urban crafts began to decline in importance, and those of the countryside to increase. The reasons are not far to seek: the rigid organisation of the urban gilds and their inelasticity in the face of changing demand, the unruliness of the urban craftsman, and the relative cheapness of unorganised rural labour. But the condition which, more than any other, made possible this revival of rural industry was the emergence of a class of merchant capitalists. They provided the capital which the peasant–craftsman lacked. They supplied him with raw materials and marketed his products, whether these were textiles or light metal goods.

Textile industries

The textile industry was without question the most widespread branch of manufacture, and the one employing the greatest number of workers. It made use of wool, flax and hemp, cotton and silk. Cloth for local use was produced within the self-sufficing local community, and was also the largest single category of goods entering into long-distance trade. Apart from foodstuffs, it was the only commodity in mass demand, the only one which in due course could provide the basis for an industrial revolution.

Woollen cloth in all probability clothed more people than all other fabrics together, though in some areas linen ran a close second. There was no part of Europe where sheep were not raised, and from certain areas – England, Spain and southern Italy amongst them – wool of high quality was exported to regions of more concentrated cloth production. Foremost amongst the latter were, apart from England whose cloth was entering continental Europe in increasing quantity, the southern Low Countries, northern France and the north Italian plain. The reputation of the Low Countries had, until the fourteenth century, been based upon the manufacture and export of a heavy, well-fulled cloth, woven from the best English wool. It was the élite fabric of the Middle Ages, but production declined during the fourteenth century and almost disappeared in the fifteenth. The reasons were complex: the decline in the supply of English wool; changes in fashion and in the channels of trade; civil disturbance in the cloth-making cities of Flanders and Brabant; and the unwillingness of the master craftsmen to modify their methods or their type of product in the face of changing demand.

By the early sixteenth century, the broadcloth industry was almost extinct in the *villes drapantes* of Bruges and Ghent, Ypres and Courtrai, but it had left a formidable legacy of clothworking in the Low Countries. The decline of the urban industry was paralleled by the rise of the rural craft. A coarser and thinner cloth was produced in the villages; it was less expertly woven and was only lightly fulled. It was cheap but serviceable, and far better suited to mass demand than the heavy broadcloth which could command only a luxury market. The weaving of the 'new draperies' took place mainly in the villages of Flanders and northern France. The region was, in Coornaert's words, 'saturé de draperie'. The chief centre of the new industry was Hondschoote. It had been a village, unincorporated and without gilds, and even in the early sixteenth century when it had grown to be a place of 15,000 people, it remained straggling and unwalled. Other rural places were following the example of Hondschoote: Bergues-Saint-Winnoc, Armentières, Neuve-Eglise. In these overgrown villages an industrial proletariat was emerging, dependent on those who supplied them with thread, who finished and marketed their cloth, and even owned the looms they used.

Cloth-making had spread from its focus in Flanders eastwards into Brabant and southwards into Artois and Picardy. The towns had here adapted themselves more successfully to the new trends, largely because their fortunes had not previously been bound up so closely with a single type of cloth. But here too the cities – Arras, Cambrai, Amiens, Abbeville, Beauvais – were each as much the commercial foci of small manufacturing regions as industrial centres in their own right.

The only other part of continental Europe which could rival the southern Low Countries and northern France was northern Italy and Tuscany. The local wool was not of high quality, and for the better kinds of cloth Italy had been dependent upon an unreliable supply of imported wool. The Italian craftsmen remained more flexible than those of the Low Countries, and were not above using flax and cotton in their fabrics (see p. 240). They also remained more narrowly urban, and only the spinning branch was at all widely diffused through the countryside. Most of the cities of northern and central Italy had large but relatively unspecialised cloth industries, and exported their products to much of the Mediterranean region. The huge cloth production of the Low Countries and northern Italy tends to obscure the fact that in every town there were weavers engaged in making an indifferent local wool into a mediocre cloth to satisfy an undiscriminating local demand.

In parts of northern Europe flax was scarcely less important than wool. It differed from the latter, however, in being grown very largely by the peasants who prepared and wove it. It was a simpler material to use, and did not require to be finished, beyond bleaching, with which the peasant was commonly prepared to dispense. Flax was climatically suited to northern Europe, and linen was an important rural product in a broad belt extending from Brittany to Poland. In a few places, northern France, Switzerland and Flanders amongst them, the flax was carefully prepared and woven, and good-quality linen produced, but in general the fabric was coarse and its use largely restricted to the peasantry. The quality can, however, be greatly improved by using woollen or cotton thread along with the linen, the latter serving as the warp and the admixture as the weft. The result was a light fabric, softer than pure linen and more durable than poor quality woollens or cottons. Such mixed fabrics were produced under the name of fustian and barchent in Swabia and northern Switzerland and in the later Middle Ages and early sixteenth century they commanded a wide market in the Mediterranean world.

Other fabrics were of only minor importance. Cotton was grown on a very small scale in Sicily and was also imported from the Levant and North Africa. It was woven, generally with the admixture of flax or wool, in the cities of northern Italy and, to a smaller extent, of southern Germany. Silk was of greater importance, though the volume of production was probably less than that of cotton fabrics. Its manufacture had been introduced into southern Italy from the Byzantine empire, and had spread northwards through the peninsula during the later Middle Ages. Silks in part displaced broadcloth as a luxury fabric. Their manufacture was stimulated by kings and aristocracy, and remained essentially an urban occupation. By the early sixteenth century it was of slight importance in southern Italy, but its more northerly centres of production, Lucca, Genoa and Venice, retained their importance, and the craft of silk-weaving had spread to other towns in northern Italy. Indeed, its great mobility was its characteristic feature. Louis XI, in 1466, encouraged Italian silk-weavers to settle in Lyons, where they founded the industry which still survives. Weavers from Lyons took the industry to Tours, Blois, Montpellier, Paris, but always with the patronage and encouragement of king or nobility.

The leather industries

The leather industry in some ways resembled the manufacture of cloth. Both provided essential articles of clothing; both used materials mostly of animal origin to produce commodities of widely differing quality and usefulness, and both were carried on in almost every community in Europe. The leather industries consisted essentially of treating skin or hides in such a way that they would not putrefy or decay. This was a relatively simple process, accomplished most often by the use of tannin derived from the bark and galls of oak trees. The stench of the tanyard pervaded the village community in many parts of Europe, as coarse leather was made from the hides of local oxen. The tanning industry was in most places restricted by the slender supply of hides. Only where cattle were very numerous, as, for example, near the Alps and at the points where the vast herds from the eastern and northern frontiers reached the European heartland, could the leather industry be of more than local importance. In many of the larger cities, however, the immense consumption of meat resulted in a large supply of hides and thus in a large tanning industry. Efforts were made to exclude the tanyards from the perimeter of the city, but their heavy demand for water usually took them to the river-bank, where they polluted the city's water supply as surely as they did the atmosphere. Softer and more delicate forms of leather were prepared by scraping and thinning skins and hides in the course of tanning. Sometimes leather was brightly coloured by introducing dyestuffs into the tanning process. This was the art of the cordwainer. It was as a general rule an urban craft, serving the needs of the wealthier classes which alone could afford such luxuries.

The consumer good industries, which today account for a high proportion of all manufacturing activities, were relatively unimportant in the sixteenth century. Few such goods were in demand, and most were made within household or community. Soap was known but used only by a very small minority. It was made from tallow and lye derived from wood-ash. The most important sources of soap were the north Italian cities, notably Venice and Genoa. Potting was carried on where a suitable clay was available, but the product was in most instances only a coarse earthenware. The poor most often used wooden vessels and platters, and the well-to-do ate off pewter. Glass-making was more developed. Glass was used increasingly in windows and for decorative vessels. The Italians, particularly the Venetians, had already established a high reputation for their wares, and the craft was in the sixteenth century spreading in France and Germany (see p. 244). By the end of the Middle Ages paper was widely used as an alternative to parchment. Most was made from rags and cloth waste. The chief centres of production were the north Italian cities, but the craft was spreading to France and the Rhineland. Printing was established mainly in the larger commercial cities of Italy and western Europe.

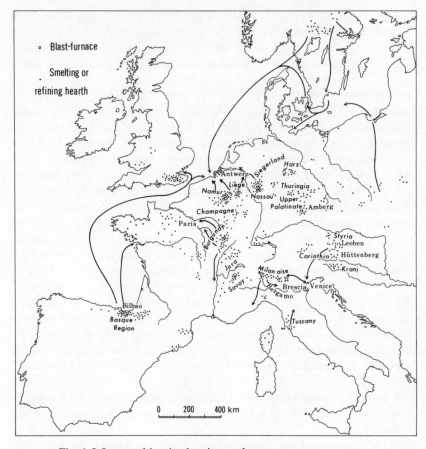

Fig. 1.9 Ironworking in the sixteenth century

Metal industries

These formed a group second in importance only to clothworking. Iron was used in small amounts almost everywhere, for nails, plough-coulters, weapons and tools, armour, chains and, more recently, ord-nance. In addition widespread use was made of the non-ferrous metals, copper, lead, tin and, though indirectly, zinc. Pewter, an alloy of lead and tin, was used for plates and drinking vessels, and latten, a copper alloy, for bowls. But metals were expensive and their use was sparing. Wills sometimes bequeathed small quantities of 'old iron', which were given what might seem to have been exaggerated values in inventories of personal property.

Iron was the least valuable of the metals. Its ores were amongst the commonest minerals in the earth's crust, and could be obtained from

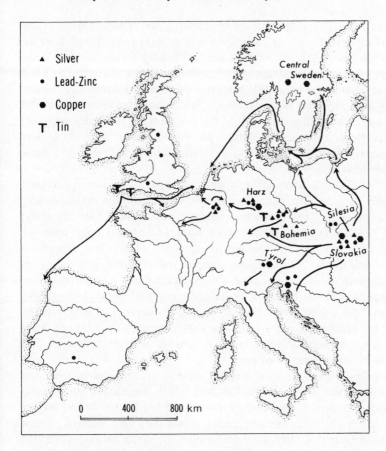

Fig. 1.10 Non-ferrous metals in sixteenth-century Europe

shallow pits in many areas without the use of costly equipment or the employment of skilled miners. It mattered little that most were inferior both in quality and metal content. Nevertheless, they could be made, in the hands of skilful ironworkers, to yield a serviceable metal. On the other hand, some ores acquired a high reputation and yielded an iron which was in demand throughout Europe. Those of northern Spain and the Italian Alps, of Dauphiné and Franche-Comté, Lorraine and Liège, the Rhineland and central Sweden were well known, and gave rise to important smelting and refining industries.[150] But to these must be added the countless centres of less importance, which were to be found from southern Spain to Poland (fig. 1.9).

The iron industry also called for an inordinate amount of fuel which increased greatly wherever the blast-furnace replaced the so-called 'direct' process. In consequence iron-smelting and -refining were of the greatest importance where large reserves of ore were found close to extensive forests. Scarcity of fuel was a limiting factor in the Italian industry, and the great advantage of the Rhineland and central Sweden was their almost inexhaustible supplies of timber for charcoal. Iron-working also required power to work the bellows which provided the blast. Though a small stream would do, problems arose in dry weather, when its flow diminished. Water power was also used to power trip-hammers which beat refined iron into bars and sheets and drew malleable iron into wire.[151]

These marketable forms of iron were the raw material of specialised and highly skilled craftsmen. 'One smith', wrote Biringuccio, 'is master only of massive iron things, such as anchors, anvils, well chains, or guns; another of ploughshares, spades, axes, hoes, and other similar tools for working the earth and for reaping the harvests. Others are masters of more genteel irons such as knives, daggers, swords, and other arms for wounding with the point and edge. Others again make scythes and saws, others gauges, chisels, hatchets, drills, and similar things, including locks and keys. Still others make crossbows and muskets, and others make armour for protecting and arming the various parts of the human body . . . there are as many kinds of special masters as there are things that are made or can be made of iron.'[152]

Two other forms of iron deserve mention. The newly invented blast-furnace (see p. 251) yielded an iron which would flow and assume the shape of a mould. This cast-iron was hard but brittle. It was useless for making tools, weapons and armour, but men had learned to cast guns and slabs with it. The second was steel. By contrast, this was tough as well as hard, ideally suited for tools and weaponry. It was usually the product of elaborate processes, some of whose stages belonged rather to magic than to science. Most, however, involved some form of case-hardening, by which the soft or bar-iron of commerce was transformed into steel by the absorption of carbon.

If smelting and refining were rural occupations, the fabrication of ironware was more often urban. Few towns were without a gild of smiths, and in some they were divided into gilds of armourers, cutlers and other specialised branches. The locus of the industry was determined in large measure by the nature of the product and the volume and weight of raw materials used. Some were consumer-oriented. The locksmith, cutler and armourer were to be met with in towns and some towns acquired a high reputation for the quality of their wares. The north Italian cities of Bergamo, Brescia and Milan, close to the iron-smelting region of the Alps, were renowned for the quality of their armour and plate steel. Liège and Cologne, both near areas producing soft or bar-iron, made light iron goods.

There is no means of knowing how large was the European iron industry in the early sixteenth century. While the number of craftsmen who worked in iron in the towns can sometimes be estimated from gild records, the number of those who worked in the countryside is quite unknown, and many were undoubtedly employed only seasonally. For only a few areas can one estimate reliably the number of furnaces and hearths, but by extrapolating from these examples Sprandel has estimated the total European production of iron of all varieties at about 40,000 tonnes a year early in the sixteenth century.[153]

Trade

The sixteenth century differed from those which had preceded it in the pattern of trade more than in any other respect. Late-medieval trade, apart from that between village and market, had been predominantly one between the Mediterranean and north-western Europe. The Mediterranean Sea was in the broadest sense the focus of European trade. Commodities from the Middle East and southern Asia – raw and fabricated cotton, silks and dyestuffs; wine, alum and spices – were conveyed from the Middle Eastern ports to those of the north-western Mediterranean and from here were distributed to western and central Europe. These were requited by the export of woollens, fustians and linen, armour and weapons, pewter and other metals. All parts of Europe contributed to the flow of goods towards Africa and the Middle East.

This system lasted well into the sixteenth century, but two years before that century began, Vasco da Gama and his fleet of Portuguese ships had reached the Indian port of Calicut. He returned with a cargo of spices which would otherwise have found their way to Europe by way of Alexandria and Venice. For a time the volume of pepper reaching European markets by the traditional routes declined, but within a few years had recovered. 'The Portuguese did not reduce the Levantine spice trade to permanent insignificance';[154] and in the mid-century only about 6 per cent of the spices handled in the Antwerp market had been brought to Europe by the Portuguese.[155] The threat of oceanic trade to the commerce of the Mediterranean may have been no more than a cloud on the distant horizon, but there were many Italian merchants who viewed it with as much alarm as they did the conquests by the Ottoman Turks.

In the early sixteenth century the latter constituted the more immediate threat. The Turks had conquered much of the Balkan peninsula and were spreading through the Greek islands. They ended the alum export of Phocaea and that of wine from Greece and Crete. The butt of malmsey wine in which the Duke of Clarence was drowned may well have been one of the last to be shipped from the Peloponnesian port of Monemvasia. It was not oriental spices which were disappearing from the Mediterranean markets but a host of less esoteric and more bulky goods which had sustained the greater part of Mediterranean commerce.

Just as there was no sudden extinction of Mediterranean shipping and decline of Mediterranean ports so there was no eruption of oceanic commerce. There had been an Atlantic trade since prehistoric times. In the later Middle Ages, apart from the infrequent and irregular sailing of Italian and Majorcan galleys to England and the Low Countries, there was an intensive movement of small craft along the Atlantic shores of Europe. The Italians, 'especially the Genoese, were . . . numerous and influential both in Seville and Lisbon',[156] and, before they reached India, the Portuguese had established sugar-growing and viticulture in the Azores, Madeira and the Canaries. Long before 1500 Bretons, Normans and Flemings were loading sugar in the Atlantic islands and selling it in Antwerp.[157] Trade with Iceland, Ireland and Norway was active, and a round ship had been developed suited to these stormy northern seas, which the long Mediterranean craft navigated with such difficulty.

It is impossible to exaggerate the volume of trade carried on in little ships from countless ports along the Atlantic coasts of Europe. Most had a capacity of from ten to thirty tonneaux, no more than about 45 cubic metres, but what they lacked in size they made up by their numbers. In the mid-sixteenth century there were up to two thousand arrivals and clearances by such vessels at Nantes, in addition to the large Flemish 'hulks' of over 200 tonneaux which occasionally made their appearance.[158] La Rochelle carried on a similar trade in which the Breton, 'le transporteur universel',[159] played a leading role. They shipped the salt and wine of western France to the Channel ports and the Low Countries, returning with metal goods and salt fish. They picked up Basque iron and Spanish wool, coarse linen and canvas from Brittany and cloth from south-western England, and on occasion they made the longer voyage to the Atlantic islands for sugar or Madeira wine. In this way the seamen of Atlantic Europe were preparing for their future in the American and colonial trades.

A similarly intense local coasting traffic was to be found along both shores of the English Channel, with frequent commercial intercourse between them, and up the rivers of the Netherlands and in the dozens of small ports which encircled the Zuider Zee.[160] Those of the northern Netherlands were part of the trading system of northern Europe, and their merchants helped to relay westwards the products of the Baltic. The small ports both in Mediterranean and in Atlantic Europe formed groups each of which was tributary to a large port, which supplied it with exotic and luxury goods and received from it grain and whatever its catchment area produced. The Adriatic was thus tributary to Venice; the Ligurian and Provençal coasts to Genoa; north-western France to Rouen, and the southern North Sea to Antwerp.

The Baltic also formed such a trading sphere in which dozens of small ports were subordinated to Lübeck or Danzig. Superficially it resembled the Mediterranean. But in the latter Europe traded with the developed area of the Middle East, in some respects more developed than itself, while the Baltic trade was essentially an exchange of goods between a developed western Europe and an underdeveloped or pioneer fringe to the north and east. This was reflected in both the character and the organisation of Baltic trade. The Baltic region supplied primary materials: timber and wood-ash, furs and skins, grain and salt fish. Its imports, apart from the salt which it could not produce, were made up of wine and the products of west European industry.

Baltic trade had formerly been largely in the hands of the merchants of the Baltic ports, which, under the informal leadership of Lübeck, formed the loose association known as the Hanseatic League. Both the political and the economic importance of the Hanse had been declining; outsiders, notably the Dutch, were intruding into their commercial space, and they were in the early sixteenth century increasingly at the mercy of the territorial states which encircled their sea.[161] At the same time the volume and importance of Baltic trade with western Europe were increasing. Demand for Baltic timber, especially for shipbuilding, was growing and, if furs had been in some measure replaced by silks as a mark of wealth and status, the demand for wood-ash (for glass and soap manufacture) and corn was tending to grow. At the same time the territorial lords of the lands around the eastern Baltic were finding profit in this trade. They were in the early sixteenth century beginning to organise their estates to produce larger export surpluses. Since river transport from their estates to the Baltic coast was of vital importance, those ports which lay close to the great Baltic rivers, the Oder, Vistula, Niemen and Dvina, had an advantage. The small and less-well-sited ports were declining in importance, and ceased to send representatives to the periodical *Hansetäge*, while Stettin, Danzig, Elbląg, Königsberg and Riga gradually increased in importance at their expense.

There is little evidence for the actual volume of merchandise leaving and entering the Baltic during the early sixteenth century. Grain, predominantly rye, appears to have been the most bulky and the most valuable export commodity.[162] It came mainly from the south Baltic ports, especially Danzig. Timber must have been a close second in the total Baltic trade, and by far the most important export of the east Baltic ports, Königsberg and Riga.[163] Flax and hemp were, however, increasingly important amongst the exports of Lithuania and White Russia. To these commodities, which made up the bulk of the export trade of the Baltic, must be added Swedish copper and iron; copper from the Fugger mines of Slovakia which was shipped down the Vistula to Danzig,[164] and salt fish from the fairs at Skåne in southern Sweden. It is evident that the decline of the Hanse as a political and economic force was not reflected in any falling-off in Baltic trade. The latter was, in fact, tending to grow, as timber for the navies, flax for the linen industries and grain for the swelling population in western Europe inflated demand.

It is a commonplace of pre-industrial economic history that water transport was preferred for the movement of all except the lightest and most valuable goods. It was cheaper and, despite the dangers of shipwreck and piracy, was often safer than overland transport. That is why the coasts of Europe, from the Baltic to the Adriatic, were alive with small craft, which sailed up tidal rivers far beyond the reach of craft today and were pulled up on a beach for unloading and loading, just as they had been in the Mediterranean since Homeric times. Inland transport made use of rivers which would now be judged unnavigable.[165] Rivers too shallow and swift for upstream travel could nonetheless be used to float timber downstream. Logs were even made up into rafts which could carry other commodities. Rivers could only transport goods between places which lay along their courses. There was talk of *improving* rivers, but no one seriously contemplated changing their course or of supplementing them with canals except on a small and local scale. Opportunities for inland navigation were thus limited, and, except in a few instances, the volume of traffic carried was small. There are instances of the development of 'feeder' roads to carry merchandise to the river-banks,[166] and in Poland an elaborate transhipment point emerged on the Vistula, where the great road from the steppe reached it near Kazimierz Dolny. But river transport was slow. Though sails and oars were used, boats had for much of the time to be pulled by men or animals, and this in turn necessitated the maintenance of a towpath. Even on the Rhine, the inadequacies of the *Leinpfad* along the river's upper course were a major factor in the small use that was made of it. Boats were commonly ill made and far from watertight. Many a cargo must have been lost in this way, and the salt taken up the Loire was always diminished by solution in the river water.

Any well-used river was certain to become encumbered with toll-stations which each charged what the traffic would bear and provided no form of service in return. The Rhine was at this time the most notorious example, with, at most, over thirty toll-stations.[167] But navigation of the Seine system essential for the supply of Paris was equally impeded. There were no less than eighteen toll-stations in 100 kilometres of river below Paris.[168] Some obstacles were even more burdensome than tolls. A few towns, notably the larger Rhineland cities, exercised a *Stapelrecht*, by which they were able to pre-empt any goods which passed along their sections of the river. A few were even able to insist on an *Umschlagsrecht*, by which all goods had to be transferred from one boat to another at the city before continuing their journey. Frankfurt-on-Oder prohibited boats from sailing past the town, and thus severely restricted shipping on the river and the trade of the port of Stettin.[169]

The superiority of rivers to roads was indeed restricted to a few rivers and a narrow range of commodities. Travellers, as Boyer has shown, manifested 'a decided preference . . . for land routes'.[170] One trusted to the river, wrote Bautier and Mollat, only goods that were 'too bulky to be carried overland'.[171] Thus in the sixteenth century maritime and river traffic had detracted very little from the volume of trade that went by road. To this generalisation there were, however, exceptions. Great use was made of water transport in the Low Countries, and here navigation began to be improved by the construction of sluices as early as the twelfth century. At first they were simple stanch- or flash-locks, through which a boat was carried by a sudden rush of water. In the later Middle Ages these began to be replaced by chamber-locks with a gate above and below. Such devices were of great importance in the sixteenth century, and many inland cities, such as Lille, would communicate with the maritime ports only by their use.[172] By the sixteenth century a few artificially created waterways were in use in the Low Countries and northern Italy, where Leonardo da Vinci devised the mitre-gate to replace the awkward portcullis type of lock-gate.[173]

Europe was criss-crossed by a complex network of routes. These were rarely defined clearly, except where they crossed bridges or mountains, and they often diverged into competing tracks, between which the traveller chose according to the weather or the season.[174] Most routes had been established during the Middle Ages; very few outside Italy derived from the road system left by the Romans.[175] None were properly built or adequately maintained, and the quality of the surface usually varied with the character of the rock that was being traversed. Roads that had been traced over clay rock or alluvium might be impassable for much of the winter, and travellers sometimes took a hilly route rather than one through gentler terrain because its surface was drier. In the sixteenth century an increasing interest was being taken in itineraries because more people were travelling. In 1553 Charles Estienne published his guide to the routes of France, which served as a model for later road-books.[176] A few years later the first road-map appeared.[177] Countless travellers recorded both the routes they took and their impressions of the quality of both road and overnight accommodation. It was possible to travel by a fairly direct route between all towns of large and medium size. Rauers has constructed a road-map for central Europe on the basis of early itineraries.[178] The net of roads, clearly recognisable as such, was dense in the Rhineland and western Germany, though much thinner to the east. The road pattern was in process of continual change. The building of a new bridge or the collapse of an old one could make a important difference to the flow of traffic. The rise of new commercial centres: Medina del Campo or Seville, Antwerp or Amsterdam was necessarily accompanied by the development of new routes.

Bridges, ferries, even toll-stations served as fixed points through which the routes had to pass; so also did inns and hospices. The traveller looked for shelter and security at night, and this he could not usually find on the open road. Nowhere did accommodation serve to fix the route more strongly than in mountains. There was, for example, an infinity of routes across the Alps, but only a small number were used. Some, like the Brenner, were relatively low and easy, but the others, like the difficult Great St Bernard, had hospices which gave the traveller shelter as well as protection during the most arduous part of his journey. The most-used passes were, in fact, the Mont Genis, on the route from Lyons to northern Italy; the Great St Bernard, the St Gotthard, Reschen-Scheideck and Brenner.[179] There was no close season for the Alpine roads as there was at sea. 'The fittest times to passe the Alpes', wrote Fynes Moryson, 'are the winter moneths, when no snow is newly fallen, and the old snow is hard congealed, or else the moneths of June, July and August, when the snow neere the high wayes is altogether melted.'[180]

Unless heavy rains had made the roads difficult the traveller could often cover 50 or even 70 kilometres a day, but this was arduous and he sometimes interrupted his journey, if it was a long one, for a day or two. Charles de Bernenicourt, for example, left Béthune in Flanders on 20 September 1532 and reached Naples on 22 November. He had spent forty-four days on the road, travelling by way of Lyons, the Mont Cenis Pass, Bologna, Florence and Rome.[181] His average day's journey was about 35 kilometres. Important news could be carried as much as 100 kilometres in a day.[182] Merchandise, however, travelled very much more slowly than the ordinary traveller. By the sixteenth century a four-wheeled waggon, illustrated in many contemporary manuscripts, was in widespread use, but pack-animals – chiefly mules – were impor-tant in the Alpine region and southern Europe,[183] and human porterage was used especially by the chapmen who travelled from village to village with their wares.

Amongst the more important commodities were spices. They came from south-eastern Asia either by the overland or the oceanic route to respectively Venice or Lisbon. Venetian spices were distributed mainly by the Alpine routes to central and western Europe, and only occasionally by galley to western ports. The Portuguese spices were distributed by sea, most going to Antwerp for redistribution in northern Europe.[184] Throughout the first half of the sixteenth century the Lyons fairs handled spices brought across the Alps from Italy or up the Rhône valley from Marseilles; in either case, it was overland spices.[185] The volume of spices in European trade was small. The twice-yearly Portuguese fleets brought some 40–45,000 quintals a year to Antwerp – about 4500 tonnes, though units of measurement are uncertain.[186] A similar, though more variable, amount passed through the Middle East and Europe's Mediterranean ports. Pepper made up, as a general rule, some 90 per cent of the cargoes, with ginger, cloves and cinnamon accounting for most of the remainder.

Textiles composed the largest category of goods in European trade, but they defy evaluation. The market was dominated by light fabrics. Foremost amongst them were the 'new draperies' of the Low Countries and northern France and the mixed fabrics of southern Germany and north Italy.[187]

The loosely woven and lightly fulled cloth of Hondschoote, Lille and of other centres in north-western Europe found a market in much of France and Spain, and were sold in the Rhineland and Germany. Here they met the competition of mixed fabrics, woven from a combination of wool, flax and cotton (see p. 237). Swabia and the Lake Constance region were a major source of these cloths, whose export was largely handled by the company of merchants trading from the small town of Ravensburg.[188] Cloth, chiefly fustian, barchent and linen, was distributed over much of west Germany, but the largest market lay in the Mediterranean basin, and the biggest traffic was across the passes of the Engadine to northern Italy and the ports of Venice and the Ligurian coast. Raw cotton for the barchent manufacture moved in the opposite direction. But the Ravensburg merchants were no specialists. They dealt in leather and skins; dyestuffs, alum and all materials of the cloth-maker's art, as well as in metals and spices. They had in 1507 switched their purchases of pepper from Venice to Antwerp, a significant straw in the wind of European commerce.

Most of Europe's demand for cloth was satisfied by local weavers, but many areas, in addition to those mentioned, produced an exportable surplus. In general it was light fabrics of medium quality, and much of it was linen. Many towns of northern France sold 'new draperies', and *toiles* of linen or hemp were made in much of north-western France for sale in central and eastern Europe.[189] In the early sixteenth century the largest market for light and cheap cloth was in the colonial trade of Spain and Portugal,[190] already demonstrating its importance for the manufacturing industries of Europe.

Countless other consumer goods entered into the trading pattern of Europe in the early sixteenth century: leather and skins, dyestuffs and alum, pewter, brass and other metal goods, but in most instances one knows too little about the provenance and the volume of the goods traded to be able to present a picture of their role in European trade. Three groups of commodities provide, however, an exception: the metals, salt and grain. The grain trade is well documented because it was a matter of life or death to so many communities, and trade in minerals is relatively easy to study because its distribution was narrowly circumscribed and was subject to a degree of governmental or monopolistic control.

Iron was exported mainly from northern Spain, the Italian Alps and the metal-bearing regions of the Ardennes, Eifel and Siegerland (fig. 1.9). The non-ferrous metals were more narrowly localised than iron, and their movement easier to trace. Copper, in demand for both bronze and brass and for use as coinage, was produced mainly in Slovakia and at Mansfeld in the Harz. From these sources it was distributed to Italy and north-western Europe (fig. 1.10). Lead and calamine (metallic zinc was not known) were distributed from the Ardennes–Eifel, the Harz and the Ore mountains of Bohemia. Closely associated with lead was silver, much of which was circulated in the form of coinage. The minting of silver 'dollars' at Jáchymov (*Joachimsthäler*) was begun in 1519.[191] Most of the tin in the European market, used for both bronze- and pewter-making, came from south-western England,[192] but in the early sixteenth century it was also mined in the Bohemian Ore mountains.[193]

Salt, like food and clothing, was needed everywhere. It was obtained from a few inland salt-springs, particularly those of the Jura, Lorraine, Lüneburg and Salzburg, and from coastal saltpans. The latter were the more important and were to be found chiefly along flat coasts where the summer sun was hot enough to evaporate sea water. This, in effect, restricted them to coastal regions lying south of the Loire. A few were, however to be found on the Breton and Normandy coasts.[194] From the saltpans of the Biscay coast there was an export of salt not only up the Loire but also by coastwise shipping to the British Isles, northern France and the Low Countries.[195] From here some of it made its way in Dutch or Hanseatic ships to the Baltic, where it met the competition of Lüneburg salt and ultimately that of the Polish salt-*mines* of Wieliczka and Bochnia.[196] Competition was intense between rival salt-springs, and also between them and the salt brought inland from the coast. Transport costs were the chief factor, but governments sometimes intervened to assist or restrict the movement of salt.[197]

Most of the trade of early-sixteenth-century Europe was conducted on a local scale. It consisted of the supply of bread grains, live animals and other products of agriculture to the towns, and was carried on mainly through the mechanism of the local market. Quantities were small, and the peasant and even his lord often made the market journey to sell only a bushel or two of corn or a few chickens. Under such conditions there was a strong tendency for 'local market areas' to emerge, that is, 'districts having a strong tendency towards a differential price level'.[198] Such areas must have been nearly self-sufficing, and the flow of commodities between one such area and another was too small to smooth out the price differentials between them.

There was, nevertheless, a long-distance movement of foodstuffs; the larger cities could not otherwise have been supplied. The larger the city, the greater was the tendency for the production of perishable food-stuffs – vegetables especially – to predominate in its immediate vicinity, thus forcing the city merchants to draw their grain supply from ever greater distances. The maintenance of a supply of bread grains was an essential function of city government. In many cities, notably those of northern Italy, a department of the urban administration – the *casa d' abondanza* – was charged with purchasing and maintaining a store of grain in the city for use in emergency. In France, grain jobbers or *blatiers* bought in one market and sold in another according to their knowledge of prices. Since prices were higher in the larger towns than in the small-town markets, there was a movement of corn to the former. All large towns had their areas of regular supply, together with a very much broader but less definite area which was drawn upon in time of crisis (fig. 1.12). On such occasions, however, one city could secure its grain supply only by cutting into the normal supply area of another.

The increase in population during the sixteenth century, in particular the growth of the larger towns, placed a burden on traditional modes of food supply. The availability of more distant sources of bread grains was a condition of their continued expansion. Corn was a bulky commodity to transport, especially by land. As Braudel has shown,[199] a journey of only 200 kilometres could very nearly double its price. Corn was therefore almost invariably carried by water, except for the short market journey. Inland centres of population were dependent on river boats. Small craft brought the grain from Artois down the Scheldt, Lys and other Flemish rivers to the towns of Douai, Bruges, Ghent, Ypres, and throughout the century there was a running feud between upstream and

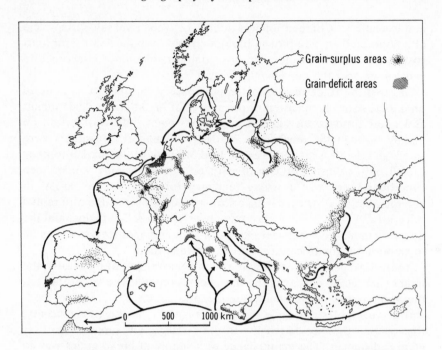

Fig. 1.11 Grain-surplus and -deficit areas and the grain trade in the sixteenth century

downstream towns for control of the grain boats.[200] The northern Netherlands was supplied from the lower Rhineland, with some grain brought by coastal shipping from Picardy.[201] Paris and Rouen were both supplied mainly from within the basin of the river Seine. Each had 'a fairly well defined sphere of influence',[202] with Rouen dominating the lower Seine. Geneva, which was growing in size and importance, experienced greater difficulty in ensuring its grain supply. Its immediate region provided little, and it relied on grain from Vaud, transported by boat down the lake. This had to be supplemented by supplies brought overland from as far away as Aargau and Thurgau.[203] In the early sixteenth century the plains of eastern Germany and Poland were still of only minor importance in the grain trade, but small amounts were shipped down the Vistula, Bug and San from Ruthenia and Volhynia to Danzig.[204] Estates which produced the grain for export were in most instances distant from a navigable river, and trade was possible only because the cost of overland transport to the shipping point was borne by the unpaid labour of the peasantry (see p. 43).[205]

The countries of northern and western Europe were still on balance self-sufficing in their supply of bread grains except in time of crisis; only the Low Countries were normally dependent on imports.[206] Not so the

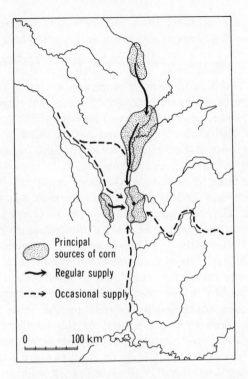

Fig. 1.12 The grain supply of the city of Lyons

Mediterranean countries, where concentrations of population had long outgrown the local food supply. Tuscany could grow less than half its requirements. Venice and Genoa were major importers. At Venice imports continued to grow throughout the first half of the century, and by 1550 had risen to about 170,000 quintals annually.[207] Even the Papal States, one of the less-urbanised parts of Italy, required a regular import. Indeed, one of the factors in the persistent warfare between the city-republics of Italy was the urge to command the grain supply of neighbouring territories. The Mediterranean basin, on the other hand, had been blessed since classical times with a number of grain-surplus areas. Foremost amongst them were southern Italy – especially Apulia – and Sicily. These continued to form the granary of Italy, and were supplemented by the plain of Albania.[208] Other deficit areas were Portugal and the region of Constantinople. The former drew from Spain, in which serious shortages had not yet become apparent, and from North Africa. Constantinople continued to be supplied from the Aegean and Black Sea coasts.[209] Egypt and the Levant contributed at first to the grain supply of Italy, until the increasing demands of Constantinople and the exigences of war brought this trade to a close.

The only other foodstuff to enter into long-distance trade was wine. The areas of production were more circumscribed than those of the bread grains, and the resulting movement more concentrated. On the other hand, the quality of wines differed greatly from one region to another, so that some producing areas were also importers. The popes at Avignon, for example, had shown a preference for the wine of Saint-Pourçain, produced far away in the northern Auvergne, and transported with great difficulty by road and river to Provence.[210] In the sixteenth century, as during the later Middle Ages, the chief exporters of wine were Gascony, Burgundy and the Rhineland. The movement was almost exclusively northwards. Gascon wine travelled by sea to Great Britain and the Low Countries, from which some was distributed, again by sea, to north German and Baltic ports.[211] Burgundian wines had necessarily to travel overland for at least part of their journey to the market. Large quantities were transported northwards until they reached the navigable tributaries of the Seine, by which they were carried to Paris and Normandy.[212] Some even continued its journey up the Oise to the Compiègne wine fairs, and thence overland to the southern Low Countries. The quantities of wine consumed in the cities were immense; at Antwerp in the 1540s about twenty litres on average were drunk by each inhabitant in a year. Almost half of this was French wine; the rest, Rhenish. [213] Rhineland wines, from Alsace to the outskirts of Cologne, were carried down the Rhine to the Low Countries, from which some, in competition with French wines, made their way to Great Britain and the Baltic.

Economic growth

The following chapters will examine the development of population, of the urban pattern, of agriculture and manufacturing and trade between the early sixteenth century and the beginning of the Industrial Revolution in continental Europe. Progress was uneven and significant economic growth occurred only in western Europe before the middle years of the nineteenth century. There was growth wherever and whenever the gross national product increased more sharply than the population. Such increase was due to innovation – in agriculture, in manufacturing or in transport and the transactions which constituted the linkages between these activities.

No people has a monopoly on innovation. The inventions which prepared the way for the Industrial Revolution were in the main pioneered in Great Britain, and in continental Europe were first adopted in Belgium and France. They could have been made almost anywhere in Europe. That they were not must be attributed in the main to social and economic conditions. Innovation is made – or at least accepted – only if the inventor has freedom to use and profit from his invention. For this reason the abolition of restrictive gilds and patents of monopoly, such as occurred in the more advanced countries, was a precondition of their success. Similarly, innovation in agriculture was conditional on ownership or at least control over the land, so that the innovator could be sure of reaping the benefits of his innovation. Communal rights over land, short-term tenancies and share-cropping leases were all inimical to agricultural progress.

These conditions of economic progress taken together amount to an assurance in law and custom of property rights in land and in ideas and innovations. This, as North has argued,[214] is a precondition of economic progress, but one which was achieved only in very restricted areas of Europe, notably Great Britain and the Low Countries. It was conspicuously absent from Spain and Portugal, from Italy and from eastern and south-eastern Europe, and was not strongly felt in France and central Europe.

A second factor in economic progress during these centuries was the increasing scale of economic activity and its growing concentration at a few centres. This was the case, not only with manufacturing, but also with commercial and financial activities. The prosperity of the Low Countries owed much to the predominance of Antwerp and later of Amsterdam in these latter fields. The continued growth of a few large cities and the relative if not absolute decline of the many small is a further illustration of this trend. Not only were the economies of scale achieved, but the speed and efficiency of all forms of business and commercial transactions were achieved. At the same time managerial skills were developed. The entrepreneur had improved access to the market and greater knowledge of market conditions. At the same time commercial institutions evolved to concentrate capital at points where it could be used.

But such progress was very far from general. It, like innovation in agriculture and manufacturing, was dependent on a system of law and custom which encouraged and rewarded the entrepreneur, in this case the financier and business manager. Progress had been made in Italy in the later Middle Ages, but the advantages enjoyed by the Italian cities were lost in the sixteenth century as the focus of commercial activity shifted from the Mediterranean to the Atlantic. Spain and Portugal were well placed geographically to benefit from this development, but in the long run failed to do so. They never evolved the legal–social conditions which would encourage and reward the entrepreneur and the innovator.

These were really achieved only in Great Britain and the Low Countries, especially the Netherlands. Some progress was made in this direction in France and in some of the German states, notably Brandenburg–Prussia, but here it sprang more from governmental policy than from a favourable social attitude to manufacturing and commerce. In much of Europe there was no progress before the second half of the eighteenth century. Indeed, in the Balkan peninsula and much of eastern Europe there was retrogression, as invasion, war and the revival of neo-feudalism destroyed what little scope there had been for the entrepreneur and the innovator. These regional variations in opportunity and achievement will be examined in the next six chapters.

2
The population of Europe from the sixteenth to the early nineteenth centuries

Population was growing rapidly throughout most of the sixteenth century. This expansion had begun in most areas before the end of the previous century and in some was continued into the seventeenth. Then the rate of growth slackened and late in the century it appears to have ceased. The total may even have declined locally, so that the nadir of European population in modern times was reached in the early 1700s. Then slowly it began to expand. The rate of growth accelerated in the second half of the eighteenth century and continued through the nineteenth. Such in broad outline was the course of population change in modern Europe. Not every part of the continent conformed with this model. There were some where the seventeenth-century decline was scarcely experienced and others where it had begun well before 1600. The eighteenth-century recovery began earlier in England than in continental Europe, and earlier in western than in eastern. Nevertheless, there is sufficient unanimity to suggest that there were common features to the demographic history of all parts of Europe.

For most of these centuries the population of Europe displayed characteristics similar to those of the Middle Ages. Both birth-rates and death-rates were high, and the expectation of life short. Population was always pressing against available resources, and any reduction in the accustomed supply of food, even on a small and local scale, was likely to be followed by hardship, even by famine. Disease was endemic, erupting periodically to epidemic proportions, and causing heavy mortality in a population already weakened by malnutrition. It was for good reason that the Tudor litany of the English church prayed: 'From plague, pestilence and famine / Good Lord deliver us.' These were ever present in the sixteenth century, as they had been throughout the Middle Ages.

In the late eighteenth century, when population was again beginning to increase, Thomas Malthus demonstrated how a population, obeying its natural instinct to grow, was always pushing against a resource base which could be expanded only a great deal more slowly. 'It may be safely asserted', he wrote, 'that population when unchecked, increases in a geometrical progression of such a nature as to double itself every twenty-five years ... The yearly increment of food would ... have a constant tendency to diminish, and the amount of the increase of each successive ten years would probably be less than that of the preceding.' From this constraint man succeeded in freeing himself – if only temporarily – during the age of Malthus himself.

Birth-rates and mortality rates were influenced by food supply, by the spread of epidemic diseases, by the incidence of war and by social attitudes to marriage and the family. It is to the interplay of these factors that one must look for an understanding of the changes in the size, distribution and structure of the population of Europe during modern times.

Population and food supply

Every four or five years there was a harvest failure. In Langland's words in the *Vision of Piers the Ploughman:*

> ere five years be fulfilled such famine shall arise
> Through floods and through foul weather fruits shall fail.

Conditions had not greatly changed by the sixteenth and seventeenth centuries, though crop failures were somewhat less frequent than Langland had suggested. The greater part of the population lived so close to the margin of subsistence that any harvest which fell significantly below the average bore with it the threat of famine. Most of the famine crises during the pre-industrial period were due to the weather. It is unlikely that any season of bad weather spanned the whole continent. Severe conditions in the west or north might be compensated for by favourable conditions for agriculture in the east or south. Conditions which might in a particular area be detrimental to the dominant crop could in fact be favourable to others. It was the poorly developed means of transport and lack of flexibility in the cropping systems which made famine so much more disastrous than it might otherwise have been.

Harvest failure could usually be anticipated weeks or even months ahead, leading dealers to buy up supplies of grain and others to hoard. Under normal conditions the price of bread crops tended to rise in spring and early summer, as the stocks on hand began to diminish. The expectation of scarcity led to a much sharper rise than usual, removing the bread grains from the reach of the mass of the population. The poor were driven to mix their scanty supply with inferior and decayed grain, and ergotism, caused by eating diseased rye, was not uncommon.[1] They had resort to other plants, including chestnuts – a regular item of food in central France – and the bark of trees, which the human stomach was unable to digest. Undernourishment and malnourishment left the mass of the population vulnerable to every disease, hastened the spread of

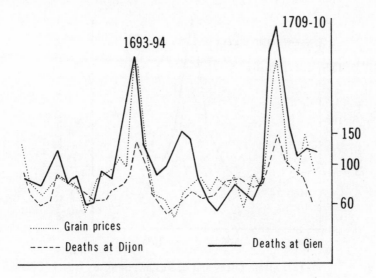

Fig. 2.1 Grain prices and deaths at Dijon and Gien

epidemics and often made common pulmonary complaints fatal.

Even in years of abundant harvests excessive reliance on farinaceous foods brought its problems. The diet was deficient in anti-scorbutic elements; the lack during winter of vitamin A, derived mainly from green vegetables and dairy produce, exposed people more readily to infection, and at all times there was a shortage of protein. In almost every case of which we have record, high grain prices were accompanied or closely followed by high mortality. Meuvret has commented that every sharp rise in grain prices brought with it 'a brutal increase in mortality and a fall no less brutal in the number of conceptions'.[2] In Brittany, wrote Goubert, 'three out of four mortality crises occurred immediately after sharp rises in [grain] prices': in 1773, 1782 and 1786. Only that of 1779 was due to an epidemic unrelated to a price rise.[3] Meuvret collated mortality at Dijon and at Gien (dép. Loiret) with the nearest available grain prices, those for Rozoy-en-Brie (fig. 2.1). Despite the fact that these places are from 120 to 200 kilometres apart, the correlation between the two sets of statistics was high, and the disastrous crop years of 1693–4 and 1709–10 – probably the worst that modern Europe has known – were marked by excessively high mortalities. Similarly high correlations between grain prices and mortality have been demonstrated for the crises of 1811–12[4] in France and for 1816–17 in much of Europe.[5]

The correspondence of the intendants,[6] that mine of information on local conditions in France in the later seventeenth and early eighteenth

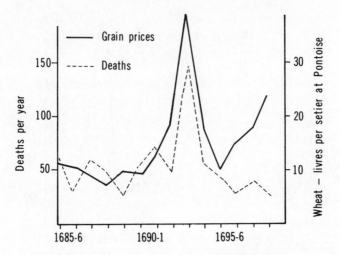

Fig. 2.2 Grain prices and deaths at Pontoise

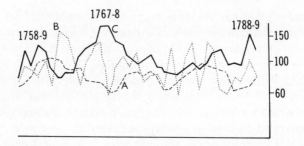

Fig. 2.3 Grain prices and mortality. The dotted lines show deaths as a percentage of conceptions for (A) Dijon and (B) Gien. The heavy line (C) shows wheat prices as a percentage of those of the previous five years

centuries, supplies colourful detail on the severity of these *crises de subsistance*. The intendant of Limoges declared that 70,000 people were reduced to begging their bread even before March, and had since lived on rotted chestnuts; even these would soon be exhausted. From Hainault to Bordeaux and from Normandy to Dauphiné there were reports of the complete failure of crops, and along the Loire valley the hay harvest was destroyed by floods. Coastal regions were able to import grain and even Scotland and Ireland were called upon to relieve the scarcity in Gascony, but the inland provinces would have found it

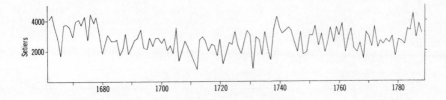

Fig. 2.4 Fluctuations in the grain harvest, based on tithe payments to Saint-Trophime, Arles

impossible to transport grain even if the intendants had been able to secure any. In Champagne the peasants ate bran and roots and the well-to-do were reduced to a diet of buckwheat. Everywhere there was appalling mortality, and the intendant of Montauban declared that in the parishes of his province from a half to two-thirds had succumbed.

The *crise de subsistance* of 1693–4 was due primarily to an excessively wet winter, spring and summer. There is no significant evidence of severe cold. The next crisis, however, arose from *le grand hiver* of 1708–9, probably the hardest winter of modern times. Autumn-sown crops were in many areas frozen in the soil and killed. There was a desperate and generally unsuccessful attempt to plough and sow the ground with spring corn, but this sent up the price of barley and oats and put them beyond the reach of the peasants. Land was abandoned for lack of seed, and by the summer of 1709 there was acute starvation in all parts of France until the better harvest of 1710 restored the country's food supply.

The year 1740 was also one of severe weather, high grain prices and acute mortality, especially in north-western Europe. The winter of 1739–40 had been long and hard, and spring delayed. A 'glacial' cold persisted throughout Europe. Harvests were late and yields low. Merchants hoarded grain and forced prices so high that the poor could not afford to buy. The government of the Austrian Low Countries intervened to secure a more equitable distribution of foodstuffs, and undoubtedly prevented mortality from becoming more severe. The number of marriages was greatly reduced and the level of conceptions was low during the crisis period. 'It is quite certain', wrote Gisèle Van Houtte, 'that there exists a correlation between want of bread and irregularities in population growth.'[7]

After the middle years of the eighteenth century conditions began to change. There continued to be food crises, especially in France in 1758–9, 1767–8, 1788–9, 1811–12 and 1816–17. But none appear to have been of the magnitude of those of the previous century. Fluctuations in the price of grain were much reduced – probably by government

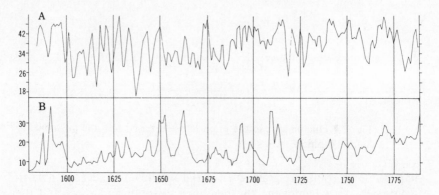

Fig. 2.5 Wheat prices (B) in livres per setier, and date of the wine harvest (A) in days after 1 September. A late wine harvest denotes a cool, cloudy and generally wet summer, and commonly coincides with a poor grain harvest and high prices

action – and there is no reason to suppose that mortality was greatly influenced by them.

It would be extravagant to attribute the stagnation in population growth, which occurred in the seventeenth century, only to these recurring *crises de subsistance*. There were also medical and social factors, but the fluctuations in the level of food supply were of great importance. There was a connection between undernourishment on the one hand and the spread of epidemic disease on the other, but this is difficult to demonstrate. Nor is it possible to trace in detail the volume of food production during these centuries, for the price series reflect only the scarcity-value of corn in the urban markets, not the amount that was available in the countryside.

There appear to have been few food crises during the sixteenth century, when population in general was increasing steadily, but this may in part be due to the fact that sources are fewer and less detailed. The frequency of famine crises diminished in the second half of the eighteenth century. At the same time population increase became measurable in many parts of Europe, and one is tempted to relate these two phenomena. The minor crises of the later eighteenth century gained much publicity and led to well-documented food riots.[8] The bad harvests which preceded the French Revolution were politically significant in part because such disasters had ceased to be expected.

Crises of disease

It is impossible to dissociate the population increase of the later eighteenth century from the fact that food supply was probably more abundant and certainly more regular. But the fall in the mortality rate, which was the principal factor in the expansion of population, was also due in part to the fact that certain epidemic diseases were less virulent. Starvation and even malnutrition exposed people to disease and increased the probability that they would succumb to such ever-present complaints as influenza and bronchitis. It may also have made them more vulnerable to epidemic diseases, such as smallpox, typhus and plague. But it was not primarily for this reason that epidemics spread.

During the sixteenth and early seventeenth centuries the most severe epidemic disease was the plague, but during the later seventeenth its outbreaks became less serious, and the last of significance occurred in Provence in 1720. Outbreaks had been locally severe, but none were widespread, and extensive areas had no recorded outbreak. The hallmarks of the plague differed from those of most other diseases. Mortality usually increased sharply during the heat of summer and commonly remained high into September. It then declined during the autumn months, but the disease sometimes lingered through the winter and erupted again, though less virulently, during the following summer. The evidence for the severity of a plague outbreak lies mainly in burial records, but it is always difficult to distinguish between deaths due to the plague and those which arose from fevers and other diseases of the warmer months. It does appear, however, that the young were more susceptible than other age-groups.

The Great Plague of London of 1665 was the last major British outbreak. Infection was carried to the Low Countries, leading to a series of outbreaks in Flanders.[9] Mortality, however, does not appear to have been particularly severe, but it then spread to Brussels where it was a great deal more virulent.[10] Fig. 2.6 demonstrates the seasonal pattern of plague deaths. During this period the recorded deaths reached over 4000, almost 10 per cent of the total population. More significant from the demographic point of view was the fact that some 35 per cent of the dead were children, and that this must have been reflected in a diminished birth-rate some twenty years later. This, however, was not the end of the plague in the Low Countries. There were renewed epidemics in 1667–8 and in 1693–5. The latter coincided with a period of bad harvests, but one cannot say to what extent malnutrition contributed to the spread of the plague; it is unlikely that they were wholly independent of one another.

In the city of Amiens there were outbreaks in 1582–4; in 1596–8, a time when many parts of western Europe suffered severely; in 1619 and 1627; and there were recurrent outbreaks between 1631 and 1638, and again at the same time as the Brussels epidemic of 1668–9.[11] In Burgundy the plague broke out sporadically from 1628 to 1631, but a

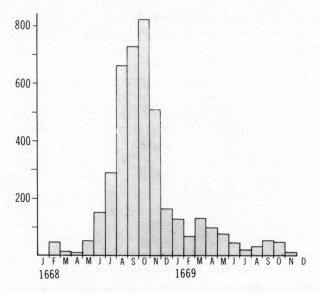

Fig. 2.6 Plague deaths at Brussels, by month

severe epidemic of 1636 was the last in this region.[12]

In Germany the plague was widespread during the first half of the seventeenth century, in part at least because it was disseminated by armies during the Thirty Years' War.[13] In Catalonia it was severe in 1589–92, 1629–31, 1650–4 and, as in many other parts of Europe, in 1683–95.[14] The city of Valladolid, together with much of Old Castile, experienced an outbreak in 1599 and again in 1647–53 and 1677–85.[15] Italy was ravaged by plague in the late sixteenth and early seventeenth centuries and the northern cities were decimated.

In the later years of the seventeenth century the plague disappeared from western Europe. The outbreak in Marseilles of 1720 appears to have been due to an infected ship from the Levant, and it did not spread beyond Provence.[16] There were sporadic outbreaks in Poland in 1708–10, and heavy mortality in Danzig as well as in several other Baltic ports. There were minor occurrences in Germany, Bohemia and Austria during the following years, but thereafter the record is silent. The plague had disappeared from Europe.

Smallpox became important only in the seventeenth century, when it gave rise to localised epidemics. The medical diary kept by a Plymouth doctor, John Huxham, from 1728 to 1752, clearly associated the heaviest mortality during this period with epidemic smallpox.[17] Inoculation against smallpox had long been known, and was described in 1718 in one of the letters of Lady Mary Wortley Montagu.[18] It does not

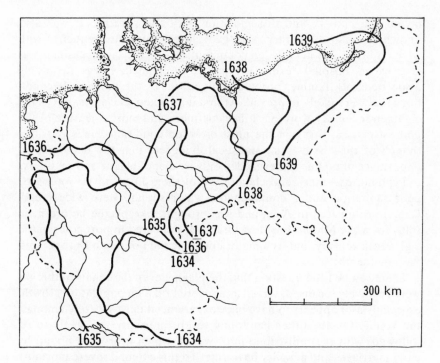

Fig. 2.7 Diffusion of the plague in Germany during the Thirty Years' War

appear to have been particularly effective, and near the end of the century began to be replaced by the newly discovered method of vaccination.[19] It was not, however, until the nineteenth century that any significant reduction was made in mortality from smallpox.

Syphilis, which had come to the fore in the early sixteenth century, had ceased to be epidemic by the seventeenth. Leprosy was dying out at this time, and Louis XIV closed the leper houses of France in 1662.[20] Diphtheria was not important outside southern Europe before the eighteenth century, but malaria, influenza and measles – particularly severe amongst children – were common, and occasionally reached epidemic proportions. Contemporaries described and named a number of forms of fever, not all of which can be related with certainty to modern febrile diseases. It is clear, however, that 'putrid' and 'nervous' fevers – to be identified with respectively typhus and typhoid – as well as 'scarlatina' or scarlet fever were all dangerous and of considerable importance to demographic history. The greatest importance probably attached to typhus. It was transmitted by body lice, and spread most rapidly 'when cold produces the uncleanliness and overcrowding that favour the activity and dissemination'[21] of the parasite. It was also known as 'camp', 'military' and 'gaol' fever, from the frequency with which it broke out in crowded communities. For the same reason it was also called hospital fever. Typhus, it is claimed,[22] was invariably associated with famine, probably on account of the unhygienic conditions that were likely to prevail. At first it attacked all classes, but as the eighteenth century wore on, it became more and more a feature of the poorest classes, living in the most crowded conditions. It is possible, though of this there is no statistical evidence, that the demographic importance of typhus was exceeded only by that of plague and smallpox.

Typhoid, dysentery and cholera, all of them likely to be spread by poor sanitation and a contaminated water supply, were widespread. Cholera originated in Asia, and was brought, like plague before it, in ships from the Middle East and Orient. It appeared in port cities in the eighteenth century, but as a major epidemic did not reach Europe until the nineteenth.

There can be little question that the plague, even though its outbreaks were relatively localised, served as a severe brake on population growth, especially as it appears to have been experienced most severely amongst the young. On the other hand, any severe mortality was likely to be followed, with the redistribution of wealth which it brought about, by early marriages and a higher birth-rate. To this extent a severe mortality was to some extent self-correcting. Smallpox, typhus and the fevers never assumed the 'killer' role in the eighteenth century that had been played by the plague in the sixteenth century, and this change in the character of the dominant diseases must have contributed in some degree to the 'vital revolution'.

War and mortality

The third check on population growth was war. From its very nature warfare was destructive of life, not only of the soldiery who participated directly, but also of the civil population caught up in the movement of armies. At the beginning of the modern period armies were poorly organised, inadequately controlled and highly destructive. They lived off the land, and the passage of an army led at least to food shortage and malnutrition. The movement of large bodies of soldiers also spread epidemic diseases, and refugees all too often infected those who gave them shelter. Geneva in 1686 suffered a high mortality from diseases brought to the city by the Huguenot refugees from France. Nor were those who went down to the sea in ships immune. Crews, confined in a small space for long periods of time, were particularly susceptible to diseases like typhus and cholera, which they communicated to those

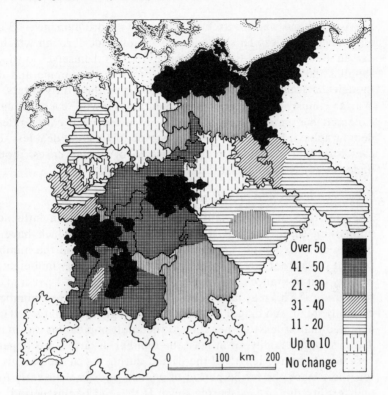

Fig. 2.8 Percentage loss of population in Germany during the Thirty
Years' War

ashore at ports where they called.

Warfare was highly destructive in the sixteenth and at least the first
half of the seventeenth centuries when religion imported an added
degree of savagery. The Thirty Years' War (1618–48) caused appalling
losses in central Europe. Franz has estimated[23] that in extensive areas
more than half the land was wasted, and that mortality was more than
40 per cent over at least a quarter of Germany (fig. 2.8). Grimmelshausen[24] and Callot, in their different ways, depicted the horrors of
this, the most destructive of European wars before the twentieth
century. The wasting of the Rhenish Palatinate by the French army
under Turenne (1674) has been described as 'the most thorough
application within the limits of the historical consciousness of western
Europe of what we now call a "scorched-earth" policy'.[25] The devastation of Burgundy in 1636 was only a degree less severe.

In the later seventeenth century and during the eighteenth warfare
lost its religious component. Armies became better organised and

provisioned and warfare itself 'in some ways more humane'.[26] Soldiers may have dealt less harshly with the countryside through which they passed, but they nevertheless continued to help themselves to whatever supplies they needed. Warfare still led to scarcity, famine and death, though the scale was less extreme than during the Thirty Years' War. Warfare must have restricted population growth, even though, as Coleman has emphasised,[27] its role has often been exaggerated. Its demographic influence, however, was probably a great deal less significant than that of either epidemic disease or famine crises, though it undoubtedly contributed to the severity of both.

Social conditions and population growth

The structure of society and of the family exerted an influence on population trends no less marked than the crises which have been discussed. Most people married and had families, and the number of celibates was not great. Moheau estimated in the mid-eighteenth century that in France ecclesiastics made up only about 1 per cent of the population.[28] This may have been on the low side, but their number was certainly small, and that of lay celebates not a great deal larger. It can be assumed that at least 90 per cent of the adult population was married. The size of the family, or at least the number of births, was dependent very largely on the length of the period during which the parents lived together. Since the fertile period of women ends in their early forties, and fertility diminishes sharply towards the end of this period, much depends on the age at marriage. Any factor which favours early marriages is likely to contribute to a higher birth-rate, and postponement of marriage, which could readily happen in time of war or epidemic or following a poor harvest, would have had a negative effect on the birth-rate and thus on the size of the next generation.

It is possible to derive the average age at marriage and the size of the family within any community from parish registers, but these are far from numerous for the earlier part of the modern period. Those which have been analysed are mainly from France and the southern Low Countries. They suggest that age at marriage was relatively high during the seventeenth and early eighteenth centuries, but tended to become lower towards the end of the eighteenth. At Carentan, in Normandy, fifty-seven out of seventy-five women were aged 25 or more at marriage, and only three were below 20.[29] At nearby Port-en-Bessin the age at marriage was most often 26 or 27 for women, and 62 per cent were over 25.[30] In the city of Amiens the bourgeoisie married at a significantly greater age than the plebeian classes. Amongst the latter men tended to marry at about 26 in 1674–8 and at 27 half a century later, while for women the average age was only a little younger, from

24 to 25 years.[31] The average age at marriage for those moderately well off was for men generally from 28 to 30, and for women from 25 to 27. This contrasted with the general tendency for the wealthier classes to marry at a younger age, as Henry has demonstrated for Geneva.[32]

The period between successive births within a particular family ranged in general from two to three years, but tended to shorten in the eighteenth century. At Duravel, in Quercy, for example, the average intergenesic period was 32 months in the period 1693–1720, but only 23 months in 1770–1800.[33] At Saint-Malo the average lapse of time between successive births was one of the shortest found hitherto – 21.4 months in the later seventeenth century and 22.4 in the early eighteenth.[34] With marriage generally at an age of not less than 25, the fertile period for women could not have lasted much more than fifteen years. This would suggest that the size of the completed family could not greatly exceed six children. The influence of age at marriage on the number of births is well shown in the justly famous study of the population of Crulai (table 2.1).[35] If it can be assumed that average age at marriage for women fell by two years or more in the course of the eighteenth century – and for some communities there is good evidence that it did – one might expect the number of births to have been increased by one. Similarly, a reduction of the intergenesic period by some four months could have had a similar result.

Table 2.1 *Size of family according to age at marriage*

	Woman's age at marriage		
Number of children	20–4	25–9	30 and over
0	2	5	10
1–3	6	12	27
4–6	17	39	57
7–9	43	40	6
10 and over	32	4	0
	100	100	100

This discussion presumes the absence of any prudential check on the size of the family, other than the postponement of marriage. It is evident from the study of registers that in some communities greater restraint was practised than Malthus had believed possible, and it is probable that a rudimentary birth-control was widely used in the eighteenth and possibly also the seventeenth centuries.

'Marriage . . . was contingent', wrote Ohlin,[36] 'upon access to a livelihood: in rural society it was postponed until a homestead was available as married couples were expected to live *hors de pot et feu* and not with their parents; in the cities the ban on marriage during apprenticeship ensured similar prudence.' Age at marriage was thus heavily dependent on the economic situation; employment opportunity led to earlier marriages. A severe mortality might liberate peasant holdings for the young to inherit; the spread of domestic crafts permitted the peasant family to supplement an income from a small-holding and thus encouraged early marriages. In Brittany, in West-phalia, Bohemia and Silesia, the adoption of the domestic manufacture of canvas and coarse linen in the seventeenth century was followed by a period of earlier marriages and greater fertility. A system of partible inheritance also encouraged early marriage, especially if the peasant was able to pursue a domestic craft.

A combination of late marriages and long intergenesic periods led to a smaller family size than is sometimes supposed to have been the case. Very large families have been well publicised, but were in fact rare, and completed families of not over five or six were the norm. Indeed, Moheau claimed that only one family in 27,000 had more than twelve children.[37]

The birth-rate, despite the rarity of really large families, was high throughout this period. In general, it amounted to 35 to 40 per thousand in rural areas, though it was appreciably lower in towns.[38] Deprez obtained crude birth-rates of 38 to 43 per thousand in Flanders at the beginning of the eighteenth century.[39] These tended to fall during the century and were from 33 to 37 in 1792. In some areas a very much lower birth-rate has been postulated, less than 25 per thousand, for example, in a community in Quercy in 1780–1800.[40] One suspects, however, in cases such as this that still-births and children who died in their earliest months of life were not recorded. On the other hand, it is suggested that as this was a region of small, fragmented peasant holdings where the pressure of population was felt acutely, there was in some degree a voluntary restriction of births. In this particular community the number of baptisms per thousand of population declined steadily for much of the eighteenth century (table 2.2). In any case, it does appear that the birth-rate, at least in France, was tending to fall in the late eighteenth century. One must assume that the lower age at marriage was in some degree offset by the voluntary restriction of conceptions.

Birth-rates even as low as those recorded for Quercy would under current conditions have sufficed to maintain a steadily rising population. That it did not do so during much of the period under discussion was due to the very high level of mortality. The overall death-rate was between 30 and 40 per thousand, but this hides the fact that it was in fact subject to extreme fluctuations. Mortality crises gave rise at intervals to very greatly inflated totals. Children always formed a high proportion of

Table 2.2 *Baptismal rate per thousand at Duravel, Quercy*

1700–9	32.6
1710–19	29.2
1720–9	31.3
1730–9	32.1
1740–9	30.8
1750–9	29.1
1760–9	25.3
1770–9	26.3
1780–9	23.8
1790–9	24.4

Source: Denise Leymond, 'La communauté de Duravel au XVIIIᵉ siècle', *Ann. Midi*, 79 (1967), 363–85.

burials, in general 40 per cent and more during crises. Even so, it is questionable whether children who died before baptism were regularly recorded. It was this high mortality amongst children and adolescents which brought the net reproduction rate close to unity, and prevented any great increase in total population.

There appears to have been a decline in child mortality during the century, but the evidence is scanty. Leymond has compared the rates for the Beauvaisis in the period 1656–1735 with this for Duravel (Quercy) in 1770–80, and demonstrated a very considerable improvement by the later eighteenth century (table 2.3). On the other hand, age-specific death-rates derived from the unusually good registers of Auriol, near Marseilles, show very little change between 1676 and the French Revolution.[41]

Table 2.3 *Percentage of children surviving to the ages indicated*

Age at death	Beauvaisis 1656–1735	Duravel (Quercy) 1770–80
Up to 1 year	28.8	19.9
1 to 4	14.5	15.4
5 to 9	3.8	3.6
10 to 15	4.0	2.7
Surviving first year	71.2	80.1
Reaching 21	48.9	58.4

Source: see table 2.2.

Nevertheless it becomes increasingly apparent that in France generally mortality fell more rapidly than the birth-rate, especially after about 1750.[42] The last really severe famine crisis was in 1740; the last outbreak of plague, in 1720. It is true that other epidemic diseases may have become more virulent, but the chief causes of *crises de mortalité* had disappeared from the scene. It seems probable, furthermore, that the younger age-group benefited more than the old, and that a larger percentage of those born grew up to become parents in their turn. [43] 'It seems', wrote Louis Henry, 'that the first drop in mortality was due to the absence of those major catastrophes which, until the beginning, or even the middle, of the eighteenth century, destroyed in a few years, if not months, the surplus [of population] accumulated during a few decades free from such calamities.'[44] It is the simple fact that, despite a diminished birth-rate, more children were surviving into adulthood in the later eighteenth century than ever before that goes farthest to explain the increase in population which occurred in those years (tables 2.4 and 2.5).

Table 2.4 *Infant mortality in the seventeenth and eighteenth centuries*

	1676–1700	1771–90
Auneuil	15.7%	14.4%
Clermont	17.1	14.2
Moux	19.3	14.5
Beauvais	27.1	20.9

Source: P. Goubert, *Beauvais et le Beauvaisis de 1600 à 1730* (Paris, 1960), 61.

Table 2.5 *Infant mortality in the Auvergne*

	1740–60	1770–90
Parish A	31.8 per 1000	29.3 per 1000
Parish B	25.0	24.7
Parich C	23.7	21.9
Parish D	28.0	25.0

Source: A. Poitrineau, *La vie rural en Basse-Auvergne au XVIIIe siècle (1726–1789)*, Pub. Fac. Lett. Clermont-Ferrand, 2nd ser., 23 (1965), 61.

The household and family

For the period before regular censuses began to be taken, estimates of total population must be based in large measure on the number of hearths or households. The hearth had been used since the later Middle Ages as a unit of taxation, and most eighteenth-century estimates of French population were based on households rather than on the absolute number of persons. The use of hearth-lists raises two problems. In the first place, the hearth tended to become for purposes of taxation merely a unit of assessment, and increasing prosperity might lead only to an arbitrary increase in the number of hearths assessed. Secondly, even if the number of hearths was recorded with reasonable accuracy, this took no account of the very great variations through both space and time in the size of the hearth. It differed between town and country; between different rural areas, and between the seventeenth and eighteenth centuries. The houses of Paris in 1770 had, according to Moheau,[45] almost 25 inhabitants; those of Lyons only a little less; but in Rouen, only 6. In Provence the average urban 'houseful' was almost 6, while 4⅓ was reckoned a high estimate for rural areas. Even within the latter there were great variations. Tomas found[46] that in the Forez the household commonly consisted of 4 or 5 persons in the Loire valley, while in the surrounding mountains it often rose to 10. Urban households were commonly larger than rural, but Hélin found the reverse to be the case in the province of Liège at the end of the eighteenth century.[47] On the other hand one finds in some rural areas evidence for a large, patriarchal family consisting of more than two generations, together with collateral members of the family. The extended family was likely to occur in any part of peasant Europe, and was not entirely unknown in the city. It was relatively common in mountainous areas, notably the Auvergne, and received its fullest development in the *zadruga* of the Balkans, where, as Mosely has shown,[48] it was admirably adapted to pioneering in this insecure and thinly peopled region. Berkner has demonstrated from a small area in Austria how the extended family alternated with the nuclear family of parents and children, according to whether grandparents and other elderly relatives had to be supported.[49]

The size of the household was clearly subject to very great variations in most parts of Europe, and probably tended to become larger with increasing size of the population after about 1750. The graph (fig. 2.9) was based on a very large sample of English households, but it is unlikely that it is wholly inapplicable to much of western Europe. Laslett found 4.75 a convenient multiplier in his study of a large sample of English households, and if one has to choose for continental Europe, it must be between 4.5 and 5.0, remembering that this can be gravely distorted in large cities and in areas where the extended family was frequently to be found.

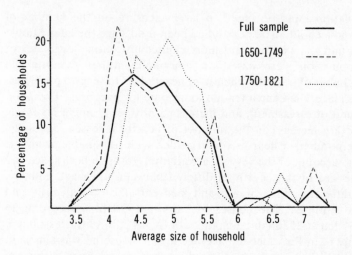

Fig. 2.9 Household size in England, seventeenth and eighteenth centuries

Population structure and migration

It was, by and large, a young population. Expectation of life at birth was probably no more than about 30 years and in many areas little more than 25. Mortality among the young, especially those in the first two or three years of life, was particularly heavy. In addition to epidemic diseases which afflicted all age-groups, they were especially vulnerable to measles, which occasionally assumed epidemic proportions, and, during hot summers, to a fatal form of diarrhoea. Parish registers for the seventeenth and eighteenth centuries demonstrate the high mortality amongst children and minors, who in some areas and for prolonged periods may make up almost half the total of those buried. Those who lived through the teens had a moderately good chance of reaching old age. Evidence for age at death of a narrow and admittedly atypical group of adults – members of a religious order in Liège – shows a gradual increase in longevity.[50] But this was a sheltered and, in all probability, a better-nourished group than the majority, which probably on average reached ages considerably less ripe (table 2.6).

Age structure throughout this pre-industrial period resembled that of some underdeveloped countries today. Whenever the data allow a population pyramid to be constructed it is found to be concave, with a very broad base (figs. 2.10 and 2.11). The population pyramids for small communities commonly show the distortions from migration, mortality crises and war. Fig. 2.11 shows the age and sex structure of a parish near Rodez in 1690.[51] Almost a third of the population was aged less than 10

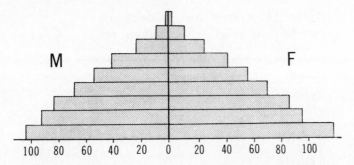

Fig. 2.10 Structure of population in France in the eighteenth century (ten-year age-groups)

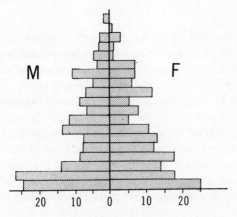

Fig. 2.11 Structure of population at Inières (five-year age-groups)

years, and there was a marked overplus of females aged from 15 to 29, due, it is claimed, to the fact that many of the young males had gone to seek employment in nearby towns.

Not all this out-migration was permanent. In many areas the poverty of the peasantry forced them to seek work away from home whenever their own lands did not call for their labours. They moved into the forests in winter to cut timber and make charcoal. The peasants of Burgundy shared in the grain harvest in northern France before returning for their own grape harvest. The Central Massif, like many such areas of poor soil and harsh climate, provided a ready source of labour for surrounding lands. The intendant of Limoges reported in 1695 that 'almost all who are able to work leave their homes in March

Table 2.6 *Average age at death of members of religious institutions in Liège*

Period	Average age at death
1520–49	45.77
1550–99	47
1600–49	50.2
1650–99	53.7
1700–49	52.8
1750–89	55.6

Source: J. Ruwet, 'Les inégalités devant la mort: les Pays-Bas et la principauté de Liège du XVIᵉ au XVIIᵉ siècle', *Actes Coll. Int. Dém. Hist.*, 441–55.

and go to work in Spain and in every province of this kingdom',[52] leaving their wives to look after their own harvests before their return in the following November. The Limousin was a source of itinerant masons, of whom some 6000 worked out of this area in 1695. By 1768, their number was put at 15,000. The intendant of Dauphiné noted that 'all the inhabitants of the mountains leave every *winter* in search of a livelihood in regions less harsh'.[53] A traveller in the Tarentaise (Savoy) early in the seventeenth century 'found not a single man in the villages of the Haute-Tarentaise, which had been emptied by the winter emigration'.[54] In the high Auvergne, poverty was such that 'the subsistence of half the population was dependent on the seasonal migration of the other half'.[55]

The annual exodus from the French Alps and Central Massif was paralleled by that from the mountains of Switzerland and Austria. Thomas Platter, who died in 1582, wrote that the men departed before winter, leaving the women at home to spin.[56] To many it was for a season's work in the cities; for some, a lifetime in the service of the French king; or of the pope, for the migrants came chiefly from the Catholic cantons. The plain of Lombardy and the Italian peninsula as far south as Naples used labour from the Alps in a variety of crafts, of which masonry was perhaps the most important. A report of 1647 described the mountaineers from the Lake Maggiore region as 'passing most of their time far from their hearths in distant lands', and in 1656 a third of the men of Val Travaglia were absent, one of them observing that 'we only spend the winters beside our hearths, and the rest of the year we wander through the world, practising our craft of masons'.[57]

These quotations raise an important question; what was the general

Fig. 2.12 The major movements of peoples in the seventeenth and eighteenth centuries

season of migration? From the Central Massif it appears to have been a summer movement; in Dauphiné, the peasants were away from home in winter; in the Italian Alps, in summer. These movements bore no clear relationship to the labour needs of the mountain economy, where the women continued to manage the farms during the absence of the men.[58] The latter left home at whatever time of the year there was a demand for their labour, for the mountains were, in Braudel's words, a 'fabrique d'hommes au service d'autrui'.

If differential birth-rates between one area and another gave rise to movements of migration, this was conspicuously the case between the countryside and the town. One finds in city after city that in the aggregate the number of deaths greatly exceeded that of births. In Orléans, for example, 4240 deaths were recorded in the first third of the

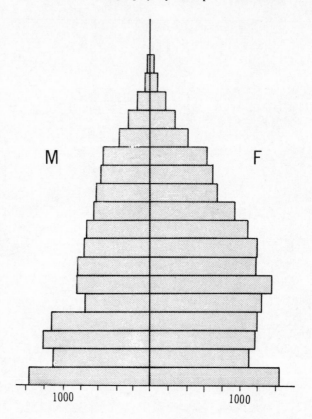

Fig. 2.13 Population structure of Nancy, 1815 (five-year age-groups)

eighteenth century as against only 1870 births, and in the middle third, 3563 deaths and 1566 births.[59] It is doubtful whether any of the larger European cities could have maintained themselves – certainly they could not have grown – without a continual influx of people from the countryside. This is reflected in the structure of urban populations. The lower age-groups were small in the cities as they were large in the countryside. There was also in all probability an overplus of young unmarried males, thus complementing the deficiency in this group in many rural areas. Fig. 2.13 illustrates the age structure of the population of Nancy in 1815.[60] It is, of course, distorted by a long period of warfare, the deficit of males above the age of 20 being accounted for in part by casualties. The feature which distinguishes this graph from figs. 2.10 and 2.11, however, is the small size of the youngest age-groups. Other evidence suggests that age at marriage was higher in towns than in rural areas, not only because of the institution of apprenticeship, but also because immigrant countryfolk had to establish themselves in work before setting up a home. It appears also that the number of celibates – many of them household servants – remained relatively high. The result was a low birth-rate, with a net reproductive rate of less than unity.

It is not easy to determine the place of origin of these immigrants to the city. During the Middle Ages, the adoption of toponymic surnames provided a rough guide to the source of a sample of the urban population. By the sixteenth century inheritable surnames were already well established, and it was not until the French Revolution that any attempt was made to record the place of birth of the urban population. Paris increased greatly in size after the outbreak of the Revolution, and fortunately the sources of this influx is roughly known. Out of 4031 listed inhabitants of the Popincourt quarter, only 1190 had been born in Paris; 2736 had migrated from the provinces.[61] Most came from northern and north-eastern France, but every part of the country was represented in the population of the city in 1793. The migrants were mostly young, between 15 and 30; many of them succeeded in gaining employment only as servants – a quarter of the adult males were 'domestiques', and few of these were ever able to marry.[62]

Refugee movements

In contrast both with the regular movements of seasonal workers and transhumant shepherds and with the considered migrations from the countryside to the towns was the flight of refugees from war and persecution. There were countless movements of people of this kind, many of them involving only small communities. The largest without question was the forced migration of the Moriscoes from Spain in 1609–10. Lapeyre has estimated that their numbers amounted almost to 300,000, of whom nearly a half lived in the province of Valencia.[63] Most migrated directly to North Africa, but some from Aragon and Castile made their way into southern France and thence by way of the Provençal ports to Tunis. Next in number were the Huguenots who left France after the revocation of the Edict of Nantes in 1685. Only a small fraction – perhaps not much over 10 per cent – of the Protestant population actually migrated. Scoville has put their number at about 200,000, spread over a period of several years.[64] The largest group went to the United Netherlands, in which the dominant religion, like their own, was Calvinist. Smaller groups went to Brandenburg and the Protestant states of the north. Another such migration was the 'long march' of the Serbs from Raška to Hungary in 1690 in the face of the Turkish attack. They probably numbered no more than 30,000, but the territory which they abandoned was then partially occupied by Albanians, and has since been in dispute between Albania and Yugoslavia. It is less easy to give a total for those who fled from the southern Low Countries to the United Provinces during the Dutch wars of the later sixteenth century, though they must have numbered tens of thousands.

These movements were large and sudden enough to have had important economic consequences, but more important in the long run were the slow, sustained movements of migration, *migrations de glissement*. The migrant was impelled, not by war or persecution, but by the attraction of a better land beyond the horizon. Modern history does not provide examples from within Europe on the scale of the eastward movement of the German peoples during the Middle Ages, but on a smaller and more local scale instances are numerous and, taken together, of great importance. Amongst these drifts of population was that of the Swiss into Germany after the Thirty Years' War[65] and into eastern France later in the same century; of Savoyards into the Rhône valley, of the French into Catalonia in the sixteenth and seventeenth centuries, of Castilians into Andalusia, and the numerous migrations of eastern Europe. The Swedes settled the eastern shore of the Baltic Sea, and their descendants today still inhabit the coastal regions of Finland. There was a movement of Poles from the Vistula basin into Lithuania and the Ukraine, to settle and develop the vast estates which the Polish aristocracy had carved for themselves from the ruins of the Tatar empire.

In the plains of Hungary the defeat and withdrawal of the Turks had left an empty land in the early eighteenth century, 'for the most part desert and uncultivated', wrote Lady Mary Wortley Montagu. Into it there migrated, with the active encouragement of its Austrian rulers, settlers from lands to the west. Communities of Czechs, Slovaks, Germans, Croats and Serbs were established especially in the south-eastern sector of the plain, the Banat, where wartime destruction had been most severe. There they formed a mosaic of ethnic communities, many of which have survived into the twentieth century.[66]

The Balkan peninsula had always been characterised by the intense mobility of its peoples. In addition to long-distance transhumance practised in much of the region, there was also a continuous shifting of settlements, so that the migration of Serbs from the Kosovo area, noted above, was not altogether unusual. These movements, largely from the Dinaric mountains into the gentler region of hills and forests bordering the Sava and Danube, have been preserved in the folk-memory of the southern Slavs, so that Cvijič was enabled to map them.[67] In the seventeenth and eighteenth centuries the Šumadija and northern Bosnia became a pioneer fringe, in which the Serb and Croat peasants cleared the forest and created new agricultural land, as German settlers had done during the Middle Ages.

To these movements within Europe and the Mediterranean must be added the migration from Europe to the European empires beyond the seas. Some 200,000 must have left Spain for the New World in the course of the sixteenth century. Portuguese migration may have been even larger, amounting according to Magalhães-Godinho[68] to 600,000 by the mid-seventeenth century. Over 50,000 Frenchmen, mainly from Normandy and Brittany, went to Canada. Add to this the British migration to North America and, at a later date, to South Africa and Australasia; the Dutch who settled in North America, South Africa and Indonesia; the Swedes, Germans and Italians – and one has a total migration *from* Europe of at least a million long before the great migratory movements of the nineteenth century began.[69]

Migrants who took part in such *glissements* had usually some idea of the conditions which awaited them. Friends had been there before, and most could usually settle amongst people of the same stock with whom they had a common language. Furthermore it was rarely the poor and distressed who took part in such movements; they lacked the means to make the journey and to establish themselves in their new homes, unless they were assisted in the operation, as were the German peasants planted in the Banat of Hungary. It was rather people of some substance who, as a general rule, could perceive the opportunities which lay beyond the horizon and marshal the resources to achieve them.

The growth of the population

Any discussion of the history of European population must draw heavily on the example of France, for it is only in France that the evidence is at once abundant and readily available. Indeed the French were pioneers in the eighteenth century in creating the science of demography and more recently in analysing the structure of the population.

France

The population of France, within its present limits, may have risen to 14 million before the Black Death. It unquestionably fell catastrophically in the later fourteenth and fifteenth centuries, the result of war and of repeated outbreaks of plague. There is no evidence for the extent of this contraction, though the *cerche de feux* of Burgundy, compiled in 1431, represents a countryside which had been almost depopulated.[70] French scholars have made great use of parish registers in tracing the history of the population. In 1539 Francis I by the Edict of Villers-Cotterets required the parish clergy to keep such records. (Thomas Cromwell had issued a similar directive in England in the previous year.) Although it

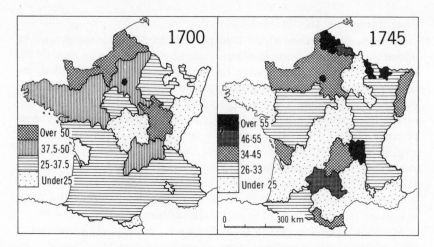

Fig. 2.14 The population of France (inhabitants per km²) in 1700 and 1745

was imperfectly obeyed, enough evidence survives to show that population was increasing through the sixteenth century.[71] The religious wars later in the century do not appear to have stemmed the growth, which was checked only by the famine crises of the 1590s.[72] Growth was, however, resumed after 1600 and continued until the thirties or forties of the seventeenth century. The sources do not allow one to estimate the total population of France with any pretension to accuracy, though Mandrou suggested that France had a population of about 14 million in 1600.[73] If this was the case the losses of the later Middle Ages had been made good, perhaps by 1560 in some areas.

The reign of Louis XIV was marked by renewed recession. Parish registers indicate a declining birth-rate, and from Amiens comes evidence of a higher age at marriage.[74] A series of mortality crises struck France, and for long periods and over large areas deaths exceeded births.[75] Over the period as a whole, wrote Goubert, 'the rate of replacement of the generations oscillated around unity'.[76] The French began to concern themselves with the size of their population, and even before the famine of 1692–3 rudimentary censuses were carried out in some areas. In 1686 Vauban published anonymously a short memoir on how a census should be conducted. The distress of 1693 gave a new urgency to the problem.[77] An attempt made at that time to enumerate the population has left few records, but four years later the intendants were called upon to supply data on towns, villages and hamlets and the number of persons in each. The report for the *généralité* of Paris was published in 1881[78] and was seen as the first of a series to be made public. Few others, unfortunately, are available.[79] The manuscript reports of the intendants were however the basis of the *Etat de France* which the comte de Boulainvilliers published in London in 1728.[80] The most competent of the regional surveys of this period was written not by an intendant but by Vauban himself, his 'Description géographique de l'élection de Vézelay'.[81] Early in the eighteenth century the government again contemplated a census. At this time, however, Saugrain produced the first edition of his *Dénombrement du royaume de France,* followed in 1720 by a second, revised and more complete, edition.[82] In it he listed the number of households in almost every town and commune of France. His sources were the intendants' reports, supplemented by tax. records and perhaps some data from the recent abortive census. This vast body of statistical material, despite its lacunae, its use of hearths and the uncertainty regarding Saugrain's manipulation of the intendants' data, nevertheless allows one to estimate with only a small margin of error the population of France and its distribution at the end of the reign of Louis XIV. All the evidence points to a total of about 19,000,000.[83] Apart from the Paris region, the densest population was to be found in northern France, from Normandy to the Low Countries, and in Burgundy. The most sparsely inhabited areas were Alsace and Franche-Comté, which had suffered harshly during the wars of the seventeenth century; Berry; the Auvergne; and the mountainous regions of the Alps and Pyrenees.

Demographic studies made much progress during the eighteenth century, without, however, inducing the government to hold a general census.[84] Instead the intendants were again called upon to supply figures, which they did with varying degrees of care and skill. The total obtained by Contrôleur-General Orry in 1745 was too low – only a little over 17 million.[85] A comparison of Orry's figures with those compiled at the beginning of the century was probably the source of the widely held opinion that the population of France was actually declining. Mirabeau in 1754 wrote with some alarm of the fall in the population. This pessimistic view was however refuted by the abbé Expilly, who included short demographic studies in his *Dictionnaire géographique,* and later summarised his totals in a *Mémoire au roi.*[86] His work was ambitious in concept, but carelessly executed, and some of his figures were copied inaccurately from Saugrain. He did, however, use parish registers to obtain baptismal and burial series and from these computed population totals. His estimate of about 24,125,000 in 1778 is acceptable.[87]

While Expilly was publishing his elaborate Dictionary, Messance (a pseudonym; the author's real name is unknown) published a statistical study of the *généralités* of Auvergne, Lyons and Rouen in which he used baptismal and burial records from a sample group of parishes to

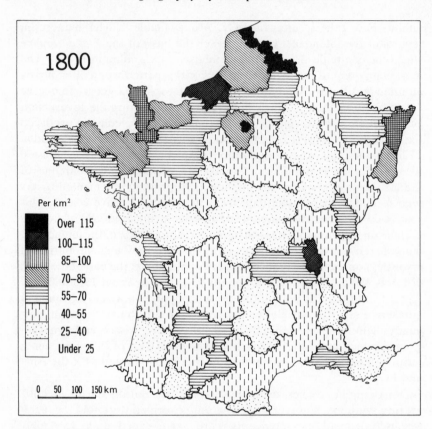

Fig. 2.15 The population of France in about 1800

estimate the total population. This method was, however, used more skilfully by Moheau, the pen-name of Montyon, who in 1778 published a study of the population of the whole of France.[88] He first attempted to devise a multiplier which would enable him to convert the number of households into a population total, but found their variation in size to be too great and too irregular for this method to yield more than a very approximate total. He then used baptismal, marriage and burial rates, obtaining ratios from sample parishes and applying his findings to the whole country. Lastly, though with scant success, he tried to evaluate population on the basis of food and salt consumption. Moheau's several lines of enquiry suggested to him that the total population of France was between 23.5 and 24 million. Necker in 1784 estimated it to be about 24,802,000,[89] and at the outbreak of the Revolution it fell little short of 27 million. A number of attempts were made during the Revolutionary and Napoleonic period to estimate the population of France. None was based on any kind of census, and the results are not wholly reliable. In 1801 the total population was put at 27,350,000. The first formal census, held in 1831, revealed a population of 32,569,223.[90]

The latter half of the seventeenth century was a period of stationary and locally of declining population; the later eighteenth was characterised by steady increase. When did the change occur from the one phase to the other? The period before 1740 was marked by a series of crises. The years from 1690 to 1715 were 'one of the worst [periods] known to the French; continual warfare, conscription of men, seizure of horses, taxation, famine and epidemics combined their efforts'[91] to reduce the population. A few good years followed. Births began to exceed deaths and, despite local reverses, including the last *mauvaise année*, that of 1740–1, the population began imperceptibly to increase.

The middle years of the century were climatically more favourable and grain prices were generally low. The total number of births was, however, restricted by the fact that the parents of these years belonged to the generation which had been decimated by the crises of the first part of the century. It was probably not until after 1750 that the upward trend became pronounced. Births became more numerous as the larger generation born between 1720 and 1740 reached child-bearing age. The good years in the mid-eighteenth century were followed in the 1770s and 1780s by another spell of lean years which culminated in the bad harvest of 1788. The resulting hardships must again have cut back on the number of births and increased the level of child mortality.

There had always been regional variations in fertility and in the rate of population growth, accompanied by migration from areas of high fertility to those of low. Such regional variations became more pronounced during the eighteenth century. Fertility was high in Brittany and in such mountainous regions as Dauphiné[92] and Forez,[93] and was compensated for in part by a steady out-migration. The rate of growth remained lowest in the cereal-growing plains of the Paris basin and Picardy. Here a quasi-monoculture combined with a traditional mode of land tenure to produce mortality crises of more than usual severity.[94] Gradually during the eighteenth and early nineteenth centuries the present population map began to take shape, with its high densities in the peripheral areas, especially the north of France, and relatively low densities over much of the interior.

A paradoxical feature of the distribution of population in France was the contrast between the region of *bocage* and the reputedly more fertile *champagne*. Densities were greater 'on the cold, impermeable soils of the Breton massif than on the limestone soils which bordered the Paris basin: denser on the "black" lands where buckwheat and rye prevailed, than on the "white" lands with their abundant crops of cereals'.[95] The reasons are not hard to find. Settlements in the *bocage* were small, even isolated, protected by the badness of their roads from intrusion. Land was not scarce even though its quality was poor, and holdings could grow by subdivision and enclosure from the waste. In many such areas, furthermore, domestic crafts, especially the manufacture of textiles, provided yet another support for a growing population. By contrast, the nucleated village of the plains of the Paris basin felt the full rigour of every crisis. It was dependent to an excessive degree on cereal crops, and only the introduction of new crops and farming methods (see pp. 172–84) saved these regions from an even greater relative decline.

The Low Countries

During the later Middle Ages the southern Low Countries were one of the most densely peopled areas of Europe, while the northern – approximately the Netherlands of today – remained a thinly populated and relatively undeveloped region. These roles were to be reversed in the course of the sixteenth and seventeenth centuries. The barrier between the two was a belt of damp, alluvial valleys and dry, sandy heathland, which had proved resistant to medieval peasant settlement. To the south, population declined during the later Middle Ages,[96] increased in the early sixteenth century, and again declined in the seventeenth. The sixteenth-century revival was chiefly in the clothing centres of west Flanders (see p. 227) and in the city of Antwerp which had inherited the roles of the Flemish ports and increased its population more than tenfold in the course of the century. In 1576 it was sacked by Spanish soldiers, and its population fell abruptly.[97] Six years later Hondschoote and its neighbouring villages in west Flanders were ravaged. The provincial council of Namur reported that 'the open country remained empty and uncultivated, without people or inhabitants . . . on account of the excursions, extortions and pillaging perpetrated daily by the garrisons [Spanish] at Namur, Gembloux [and other fortresses] so that no one dared to live in the open country'.[98]

Towards the end of the century the fighting ebbed away to the north. Antwerp was recovered by the Spanish forces in 1585, its commerce destroyed and its population reduced by a half. The southern Low Countries revived, but their recovery was short-lived. The numbers of baptisms recorded in the registers began to decline, and the region shared in the general depression of the seventeenth century. In the parish of Theux near Liège the numbers of births, after fluctuating during the early decades of the century, reached their peak in the 1640s, and then fell steadily until the end of the century. It was not until about 1760 that an increase again became apparent.[99] A group of villages near Brussels showed a similar trend, with population at its lowest in the

1680s.[100] Brabant, which had a population of more than 450,000 at the beginning of the sixteenth century, recorded no more than 373,000 in 1700.[101] In a group of parishes to the west of Brussels, a region which suffered greatly during the wars, the population had fallen catastrophically even before 1600:[102]

1557	4104 households
1600	2380
1698	4301
1766	5721

The population of the *châtellenie* of Ypres showed a similar trend,[103] and the study of parish registers from other parts of the Spanish Low Countries provides confirmatory evidence.[104]

The Low Countries suffered like France from famine crises and epidemics. In Brussels alone more than 4000 deaths were ascribed to the plague of 1668–9,[105] and the years 1693–4, 1709–10 and 1740–1 were marked by crop failures, starvation and heavy mortality.[106] The Ardennes region provided a partial exception to the prevailing picture of stagnating or declining population. The hills of Liège, Namur and Luxembourg, with their cloth manufacture and iron-smelting and refining industries, were in a position to profit from the wars which ravaged the rest of the Low Countries. They provided, furthermore, a refuge for those who fled from campaigns fought in the plains.[107]

The population of the southern Low Countries is estimated by Mols[108] to have been about 1,750,000 when the War of the Spanish Succession ended (1713) and the region passed from Spanish to Austrian rule. There followed a period of steady growth. A total, including the bishopric of Liège, of about 2,800,000 was reached before the French Revolution. Growth continued during the period of the Revolutionary and Napoleonic wars and, yet more sharply, during the period of industrial expansion which followed. It had reached 4 million by the time of the Belgian revolt from the United Netherlands, and 4,337,196 by 1846.[109]

Demographic history in the northern Low Countries differs sharply from that of southern, and, indeed, exhibits features which conflict with that of much of the rest of Europe. The rapid growth of the sixteenth century was continued through much of the seventeenth, and did not show signs of declining until the eighteenth. Growth was most vigorous in the western Netherlands, the provinces of Zeeland, Holland and Friesland. In Holland alone the population is estimated to have increased from about 275,000 in 1514 to 672,000 a century later,[110] leading to a rapid urban growth and spilling over into commercial ventures overseas. 'The Dutch Commonwealth', wrote Sir William

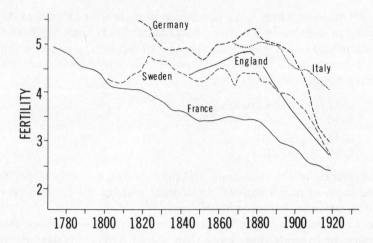

Fig. 2.16 Decline in fertility rates in the late eighteenth and nineteenth centuries

Temple in 1673, 'was born out of the sea . . . And after the Union, a greater confluence of People falling down into the United Provinces than could manage their Stock, or find employment at Land, Great multitudes turn'd their endeavours to the Sea.'[111] Rural population grew by about 110 per cent, but urban almost trebled within this period. By 1622, the population was 54 per cent urban, and Holland was the first major European province to become predominantly urban. Amsterdam itself grew from about 30,000 to 200,000 within a century.[112] The rate of population growth was smaller in other provinces. In Friesland it grew from 72–80,000 in the early sixteenth century to more than 129,000 in 1714.[113] Away from the stimulus of maritime trade, however, the population grew very much less rapidly. In the eastern and southern Netherlands, where much of the soil was poor and unrewarding, growth was slow. That of Overijssel grew from about 52,000 at the end of the fifteenth century only to some 70,000 by 1675, and the Veluwe, also a region of sandy heathland, increased only from 36,000 to 40,700 in a similar period.[114]

The rate of population growth declined everywhere in the Netherlands during the last quarter of the seventeenth century, with the decay of Dutch commercial activity which had supported it. This decline was most marked in the western Netherlands, where almost every town with the exception of Amsterdam was smaller in the eighteenth century than it had been in the seventeenth. The province of Holland, focus of Dutch commercial activity, declined by 11 per cent between the late seventeenth century and the mid-eighteenth, and then its population remained virtually static until the end of the century. Eastern and southern Netherlands, which did not experience the sharp increase of the sixteenth and seventeenth centuries, also escaped the decline of the early eighteenth. The demand for foodstuffs in the urbanised western Netherlands led to an increase in agricultural production on the poor soils of the east and south. The mainstay of continued population growth in such areas as Twente and Veluwe was, however, the domestic cloth industry, supplemented by the paper industry. By the second half of the eighteenth century the rate of population growth began to slacken here too. The market for the homespun textiles weakened in the face of foreign competition and there was acute distress with, it is said, half of the population or more impoverished. Renewed economic growth in the early nineteenth century, coupled with the rising price of foodstuffs and the introduction of new crops (see p. 210), gradually overcame the grievous overpopulation of these regions, and prepared the way for further expansion.

Dutch scholars, equipped with population series for sample areas from both the 'maritime' Netherlands and the heathland regions, have projected backwards the curve of population growth for the whole country. It is assumed that the Netherlands, within its present territorial limits, had a population of 0.9 to 1.0 million at the beginning of the sixteenth century. This rose almost to 2 million before the end of the seventeenth. Thereafter it stagnated, decline in 'maritime' Netherlands being partially compensated for by continued increase in the east and south. The total barely exceeded 2 million by 1795. Thereafter with the solution of certain of its economic problems the earlier growth was resumed, and a total of 3 million was reached by 1850.[115]

Germany

The Germans have sadly neglected their own demographic history. Their sources are, however, scanty, and they lack the parish registers which throw so much light on development in western Europe. The population of Germany increased during the sixteenth century and the first decades of the seventeenth. Land which had passed out of cultivation in the later Middle Ages was again brought under the plough. Contemporaries were unanimous that, in the words of Sebastian Franck, Germany was 'teeming with children', that the land was crowded and food scarce. Population may have doubled or even tripled in Westphalia.[116] In Saxony the pre-Black Death population had been greatly exceeded by 1550,[117] and the population of Germany as a whole may have risen from about 12 million in 1500 to 15 million a century later.[118]

The rate of growth began to slacken late in the sixteenth century, and ceased during the Thirty Years' War. Franz has estimated[119] that when the war ended in 1648 Germany had lost 40 per cent of its rural population and a third of the urban. Comparatively few of the losses resulted directly from the fighting; most were due to famine and disease induced by the war. The scale of destruction varied from one part of Germany to another. It was greatest in the south-west, which had suffered acutely in the peasant risings of the previous century, and also in Franconia, Thuringia and north-eastern Germany. Here the destruction was catastrophic. In 1637 General von Werth described the Rhineland as 'a country where many thousands of men have died of hunger and not a living soul can be seen for many miles along the way'.[120] There was great mobility after the war, as peasants moved into and recolonised the wasted lands. The birth-rate was high, as was commonly the case when land was abundant and the peasant could receive a tenement for the asking. In some areas the population loss was made good in a generation or two. Elsewhere the process took longer. Large areas of Prussia were still depopulated in 1718,[121] and parts of Mecklenburg remained deserted even longer. Population growth nevertheless continued through the eighteenth century. That of Brandenburg–Prussia more than doubled between 1740 and 1805 and increase in the lower Rhineland was probably even more rapid. By 1800 the population of Germany, excluding Switzerland and the Habsburg lands, was close to 20 million.

Growth was most rapid in those areas where manufacturing was developing, as in Brandenburg and the Prussian Rhineland provinces. The county of Mark, the small and hilly territory which contained much of the Westphalian iron-working industry (see p. 256) grew by a third in a period of seventy years. The wholly agricultural state of Cleve, lying along the lower Rhine, grew by only 10 per cent in the same period (table 2.7). Prussia was the fastest-growing German state. Its population was about 4 million in the mid-eighteenth century. Mirabeau recorded a total of almost 5.5 million, and by 1800 this had risen to 9,300,000. More than 10 million were recorded in 1816; and in 1843, 15,471,765.[122]

Table 2.7 *Population of Mark and Cleve*[123]

	Mark	Cleve
1722	99,704	85,988
1740–2	104,422	81,146
c. 1770	117,882*	
c. 1780	124,188*	92,000*
1792–3	132,113	94,880

This growth was assisted by a substantial immigration; large numbers of Swiss moved to Germany; the Low Countries, notably the bishopric of Liège, supplied settlers to the devasted areas of Hesse and Thuringia, and many Huguenots settled in Brandenburg. Germans themselves, however, moved into the wasted north-east of their own country, where they were joined by immigrants from Scandinavia, Poland and the Habsburg lands. This movement of peoples – possibly larger in the aggregate than the eastward movement of the Germans during the Middle Ages, brought about a significant shift in the French–German language boundary in the west[124] and lasting changes in the ethnic composition of the German people.

Demography attracted little attention in Germany before the nineteenth century. Busching was assiduous in collecting and publishing totals for towns and provinces, but was quite uncritical in his acceptance of them. The only writer who can stand comparison with the French demographic writers of the eighteenth century was Johann Peter Süssmilch, whose treatise anticipated in some respects the studies of Messance and Moheau.[125] He collected statistics of births, marriages and deaths in both urban and rural environments, and attempted to derive total populations from them. He was the first German scholar to give serious attention to such matters as the sex ratio, age structure and expectation of life of the population as a whole.

Only the Prussian government attempted before the Revolutionary Wars to hold any kind of census. After 1815, however, the situation, from the demographic point of view, was greatly eased. The number of political units was reduced and in many of them attempts were made to count the population. The population of Germany within the boundaries established at Vienna was of the order of 23.4 million in 1815. By the mid-century this had increased to 33.5 million, a growth of 45 per cent. Rates of growth varied greatly. It continued to be most rapid in Prussia – a growth of 65 per cent, followed by Hesse-Cassel and Saxony. It was fastest in areas where manufacturing industry was expanding; slowest in such predominantly agricultural states at Württemberg and Bavaria.

Switzerland and Austria

The Alpine region provided a partial exception to the generalised picture which has been built up of population growth, stagnation or decline, and renewed growth. It differed from areas already discussed in being protected in some measure both from war and epidemic disease. On the other hand, most people lived close to the margin of subsistence and had little opportunity to import food in time of emergency. The towns of the Swiss plateau were ravaged by epidemics in the seventeenth century, and in 1610–11 Basel lost more than a quarter of its population,[126] but Switzerland was spared the horrors of the Thirty Years' War. Grimmelshausen in the mid-seventeenth century noted, with apparent surprise, that in Switzerland people 'went about their business in peace; the stables were filled with livestock ... Nobody stood in fear of the foe, nobody dreaded pillage, nobody was afraid of losing his property, his limbs or his life.' Armies sometimes crossed the Alps, using the more accessible passes; Lower Austria and the eastern Alps were exposed to raids by the Turks until late in the seventeenth century, but after the end of the religious wars in 1531 there was little fighting in Switzerland.

Scarcity of food was thus the most effective check on the growth of population in much of the Alpine region. In the sixteenth and above all the seventeenth centuries population was continuously pressing against the limited food resources. Wheat almost ceased to be eaten in Geneva, and was replaced by rye, spelt and mixed grains. Famine crises were common, and remote valleys must have been particularly vulnerable.

There was necessarily a large-scale migration from the Alpine region, but one of the most important outlets for surplus population was in the service of other countries. The Swiss cantons had adopted a system of compulsory service, which made them a formidable military force, but their defeat at Marignano (1515) led them to withdraw from active participation in international affairs and their redoubtable fighting force became available for recruitment by the French and Italians.[127] Bickel has estimated that 900,000 to 1,000,000 Swiss were killed in other peoples' wars between the fifteenth and the eighteenth centuries, and that at any one time 50,000 to 60,000 were serving in foreign armies. Migration and foreign military service drained away fully half the natural increase in the population of Switzerland during a period of three centuries.[128]

The population of Switzerland at the beginning of the sixteenth century was probably of the order of 800,000.[129] It had risen to 1,000,000 by 1600 and to 1,200,000 by 1700. Of this total some 150–180,000 lived within the mountains, a total which remained very stable until the nineteenth century. The increase in population took place on the Swiss plateau, and above all in the towns, where the development of the Swiss textile industries provided supplementary employment. By 1800, the population of Switzerland, within its present boundaries, was about 1,680,000; by 1820 it had risen to 1,956,000, and at the mid-century, to 2,393,000.[130]

Scandinavia

As the Great Northern War was ending in 1660 the Danish government levied a poll-tax. It showed that the Danish population had been reduced by war and disease from about 600,000 to no more than 480,000. The following century was, however, one of steady growth, and a partial census of 1769 suggests a total of about 810,000. By 1801 this had risen to 926,000, and by the mid-nineteenth century to 1,414,600.[131]

Norway, Sweden and Finland had always been very much more sparsely populated than Denmark. Much of their territory lay too far north for agriculture and Scandinavia suffered more than the rest of Europe from the severe winters in the seventeenth and eighteenth centuries.[132] Crop failures were followed by heavy mortality, especially in 1696–8, 1708–10, 1738–42 and 1772–3. Even the birth-rate has been said to vary 'in accordance with the harvest results'.[133] The years 1696–8 were amongst the most severe known in northern Europe, and in Finland, it is said, 28 per cent of the population died of famine.[134]

In none of these countries is there evidence for the size of the population before the mid-seventeenth century. A poll-tax of the time of Gustavus Adolphus suggests a population of about 900,000 in Sweden. By 1720 this had increased to 1,440,000, and by 1815, to 2,452,000.[135] The impetus for this growth was, according to Utterström, a period of low mortality, especially infant mortality, during the first half of the eighteenth century, and this he attributed to 'a period of unusually mild, and probably dry, winters'.[136] Growth continued through the nineteenth century, and by 1850 the population had reached 3,483,000.

Growth was somewhat slower in Norway, where the hazards of climate were even greater. From about 444,000 in 1665, the population rose to 616,000 in 1735, to 748,000 in 1769 and to 883,000 in 1801. Thereafter growth was more rapid. Drake has suggested that in these years the adoption of vaccination and the spread of an additional source of food, the potato, drastically reduced the death-rate.[137] By 1845 the population had reached 1,328,000.

Eastern Europe

The growth of population in eastern Europe was assisted by the high ratio of land to people and perhaps also by the relative weakness of epidemics, itself a consequence of its sparsity in much of the area. In Poland there was little to interrupt its growth from the early Middle Ages to the mid-seventeenth century. The population of the historic provinces – Mazowsze and Great and Little Poland – cannot have been much more than 2,500,000 in 1500. By 1650 it had increased to 3,830,000.[138] That of the lands of the Jagiellonian crown, which included Lithuania and much of the Ukraine, is a great deal less certain. These eastern lands were very sparsely inhabited, so that the population of the Polish–Lithuanian Commonwealth, the largest territorial state in Europe, was no more than 7,500,000 in 1500 and 11,000,000 by 1650.[139]

In 1655 there began that series of invasions and wars which Polish historians call the 'Deluge'. The whole country was fought over by Swedes, Brandenburgers and Tartars. The war lasted only five years, but it was as if the destruction of the Thirty Years' War had been concentrated into this short period. When it was over, Poland had lost a third of its population[140] and the country had not recovered from these losses when the wars of Charles XII of Sweden made further inroads early in the next century. The period which followed was one of relative peace and prosperity. The level of population of 1650 was probably regained a century later. According to Korzon's estimates Poland (with Lithuania) had a population of 11,420,000 on the eve of the First Partition (1772).[141] The latter deprived Poland of 35 per cent of her population and 29 per cent of her territory. The twenty years before the Second Partition were marked by a high birth-rate. A census was held in 1790 but omitted the clergy and the numerous gentry class. Corrected for this, the population must have been about 8,800,000.[142] In 1796 the Polish state was extinguished. It was revived in 1807 as the Grand Duchy of Warsaw, and this, with extensive boundary changes, became in 1815 the 'Congress' Kingdom of Poland. A Napoleonic census showed a population of 4,335,000 in the Grand Duchy, but the first – and only – census ever taken in Tsarist Russia was not held until 1897. It recorded a population of 9,400,000 in 'Congress' Poland.[143]

The study of population in the Habsburg lands is complicated by internal migration and shifting boundaries. Even the nuclear Austrian lands were interpenetrated by the episcopal lands of Salzburg, Brixen and Freising. Growth was slow in most of Austria before the nineteenth century. In 1754 the population was about 2,750,000, a third of it concentrated in the present province of Lower Austria. By 1816 Austria, which now embraced the church lands, had a population of about 3,350,000. Thereafter growth was more rapid, and the total reached 4,560,000 by 1850.[144]

Outside the ducal lands of Austria the Habsburgs held three extensive blocks of territory: the Czech and Polish lands, Hungary, and the Dalmatian and Balkan lands. The first consisted of Bohemia, Moravia and, until its conquest by Frederick the Great in 1741, Silesia, together with Galicia, acquired in the Partitions of Poland, and Bukovina, gained in 1775. The second was made up of the historic kingdom of Hungary, including Slovakia and Transylvania, and the last of Krain, Croatia, the Dalmatian coast, the Military Frontier district, and Austrian possessions in northern Italy.

The Czech lands, with Silesia, were the most densely peopled, and during the eighteenth and nineteenth centuries their population grew most rapidly, much of it finding employment in the textile and metallurgical industries.[145] The birth-rate was high in the mountainous fringe of Bohemia where domestic crafts, especially weaving, were important.[146] There is, nevertheless, no satisfactory measure of population before the mid-eighteenth century. In 1754 the population of Bohemia was about 1,972,000, and that of Moravia and Czech Silesia 1,048,000, densities respectively of 38 and 39 to the square kilometre. The second half of the eighteenth century was a period of growth. By 1785 the population of the Czech lands had risen to about 4,250,000, and by 1815 to more than 4,800,000. The nineteenth century was a period of uninterrupted growth, and by 1850 the population had risen to almost 7 million.[147]

Galicia was Austria's share in the Partitions of Poland. It was relatively thinly peopled when Austria received it, but under Habsburg rule the population increased rapidly. The average density is supposed to have reached 40 to the square kilometre by 1800, and 60 by the mid-century. This was a very high density for a population almost exclusively rural and practising a primitive form of agriculture. Galicia became in the nineteenth century one of the most overpopulated and depressed rural areas in Europe.

The population of Hungary, including Slovakia and Transylvania, may have reached from 3.5 to 4 million before the Turkish invasion of the sixteenth century.[148] It then fell sharply, and in the early eighteenth century the plains were 'desert and uncultivated, laid waste by the long war between the Turk and the emperor'.[149] They were resettled in the course of the eighteenth century (see p. 90) and the population recovered. Joseph II's census of 1787 showed about 7,117,000, with some 1,400,000 in Transylvania.[150] Population continued to increase during the Napoleonic period, reaching 10 million for Hungary and Transylvania in 1800 and 13.3 by 1850.

The southern provinces of the Habsburg empire present a more confusing picture, and Istria and the Dalmatian lands did not pass into Austrian possession until 1815. The population of Krain, Istria and Dalamatia was then about 500,000. By 1850 it had increased to 800,000. The Habsburg empire as a whole had a population of about 23.3 million at the beginning of the nineteenth century. By 1850 and with the inclusion of the Dalmatian and north Italian territories, this had risen to 35,768,000.

Balkan peninsula

Romania and the Balkans are demographically the least known of the major divisions of Europe. The sparse population had been further reduced by the Turkish invasions. It is known to have increased rapidly during the eighteenth and nineteenth centuries, and densities increased from an average of about 3 to the square kilometre in 1718 to 10 by 1800 and 18 by 1834.[151] In the middle years of the nineteenth century, the population of the Romanian provinces had reached about 4.2 million, and that of the Balkan peninsula south of the Danube probably not more than 6 million.[152]

Italy

A highly urbanised society is likely to be a well-documented one, and Italy is no exception. The Italian city-republics taxed and also fed their citizens, and for both purposes frequent head-counts were necessary. Venice established a precedent with its census, now lost, of 1338. The Florentine *catasto* of 1427 derived from the Venetian example. Later censuses of the fifteenth and sixteenth centuries contain a vast store of information on population and social structure which is now being analysed.[153] No other cities conducted surveys on quite so elaborate a scale, but there are few which have not preserved some record of their population in early modern times. On the basis of such data Beloch estimated that at the beginning of the sixteenth century the population of Italy was about 10 million and that it increased to about 11 million by 1559. Growth was restricted by both warfare and epidemic disease. There were numerous outbreaks of the plague, and in 1630–1 Italy was struck by its worst outbreak in modern times. Milan is said to have lost 86,000 people; Venice, 60,000, and Mantua, 50,000. The death-toll in only nineteen cities in northern Italy was put at 393,000.[154] Italy's population was reduced to its lowest level since the later Middle Ages. But after 1657 the plague left Italy, and the population began slowly to recover. By 1700 it had reached about 13.5 million, and fifty years later 15.5. Growth was more rapid in the later eighteenth century, and a total, excluding Corsica which was annexed to France in 1770, of 17.8 million was reached in 1800, and of 22.6 million in 1845.

Throughout this period of over three centuries the rate of growth was higher in peninsular than in northern Italy, and highest in Sicily.[155] Age at marriage was low and birth-rates high. The land, some of it passing out of cultivation because of soil erosion in the mountains and lack of drainage in the plains, could not support the growing rural population, and there was a flight of young people from the countryside to the towns. The city of Naples doubled in size within the century, without ever developing the basic activities to support so large (426,600 in 1796) a concentration of people. Catania increased almost threefold, and Palermo by almost 40 per cent (see p. 145). It is a curious fact that

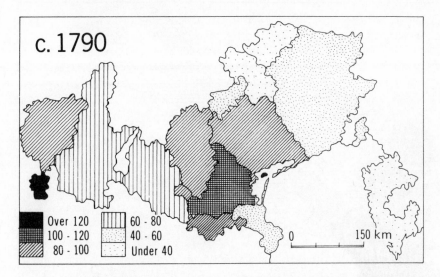

Fig. 2.17 Population density in Venezia (inhabitants per km²), late
eighteenth century. Compare with fig. 1.5

urban growth during the eighteenth century was almost restricted to
southern Italy, where the economy was least able to support it. Most
northern cities grew little if at all. Verona, for example, reached a
population of over 56,000 in 1593. It had already declined somewhat
before it was struck by the plague epidemic of 1630–1 which killed 60

Table 2.8 *The population of Italy (in thousands)*

	Northern Italy	Peninsular Italy	Sicily	Sardinia	Corsica	Total
1500	(9000)		695	250	(100)	10,000
1550	4745.9	5020.5	884	300	120	11,070
1600	5412	6239.4	1130	330	120	13,231
1650	4254.9	5592.7	1147	375	120	11,489.6
1700	5659.9	6177.4	1126	330	120	13,413.3
1750	6510.6	7000.2	1346	430	132	15,420.8
1800	7206.3	8452.7	1638.5	497	177.6ᵃ	17,794.5ᵇ
1845	9438.8	10,594.5	2040.6	546	–	22,598.5ᵇ

[a] Estimated; Corsica was then part of France.
[b] Excludes Corsica, which was then part of France. Totals include Nice, but
exclude South Tyrol, Gorizia (Görz) and Savoy.
Sources: J. Beloch, *Bevölkerungsgeschichte Italiens* (3 vols., Berlin, 1937–61);
Raum und Bevölkerung in der Weltgeschichte, ed. E. Kirstein, E. W. Buchholz
and W. Kollmann, II (Würzburg, 1956); C. Cipolla, in *Population in History*, ed.
D. V. Glass and D. E. C. Eversley (London, 1965), 570–87.

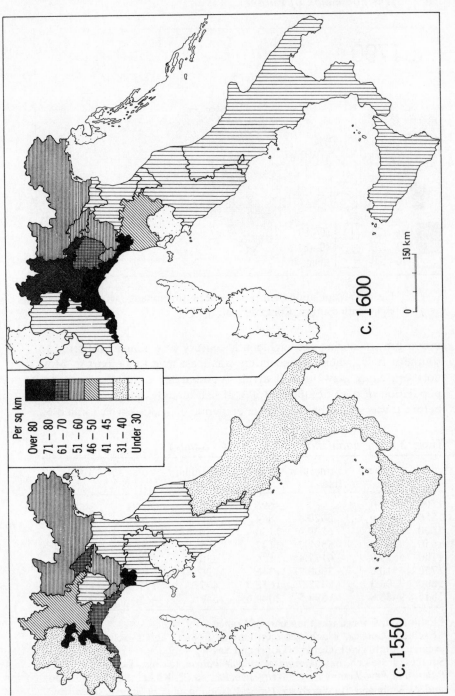

Fig. 2.18 Population distribution in Italy, c. 1550 and c. 1600

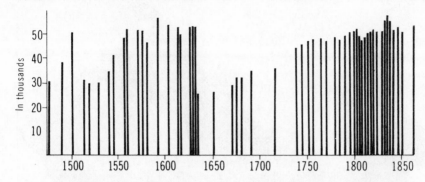

Fig. 2.19 The population of Verona. Note the very slow recovery from the plague outbreak of 1632

per cent of its population. It never quite regained its earlier population before the mid-nineteenth century (fig. 2.19). Growth in the north could be largely absorbed by the countryside. Rural population doubled in some areas. Figs. 1.5 and 2.17 show the distribution of population in Venice's *terra firma* in 1548 and 1790. The increase during the intervening years was particularly great in the fertile lands along the Adige, Brenta and Po.[156] Such rural densities could not be supported on the thin mountainous soils of the south, where poverty intensified as the population grew.

Table 2.9 *Percentage growth in the population*

	Northern Italy	Peninsular Italy	Sicily
1550 to 1750	37	39	52
1750 to 1845	44	51	58

Iberian peninsula

Population was increasing steadily through much of the sixteenth century. Areas newly conquered from the Moors were thinly peopled, and there was a drift of people southwards from Old Castile. The population of Spain in 1541 was about 7,414,000; half a century later it had risen to 8,485,000 despite the migration to the New World.[157] Growth was most rapid in Castile. Madrid grew to be a large city, and there was a steady expansion in Valladolid, Toledo and other towns.

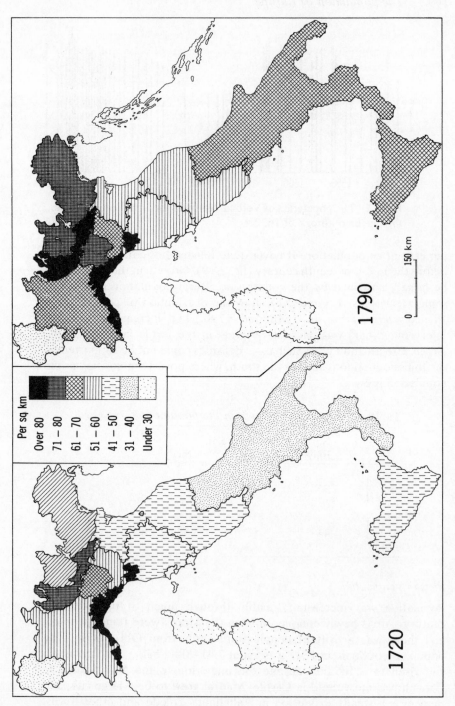

Fig. 2.20 Population distribution in Italy, 1720 and 1790

Then, late in the sixteenth century, this period of growth ended. Towns in Old Castile began to decline. The birth-rate dropped, and the drift of people towards the coast ceased to be compensated for by a high birth-rate in the interior provinces.[158] The decline of the population in coastal regions, particularly the kingdom of Aragon, which included Catalonia, was postponed for a decade or two, [159] but eventually the whole peninsula, including Portugal, experienced the recession. Contemporaries recognised the seriousness of the decline. 'This general evil', the Council of Castile called it, and de Moncada wrote that 'it is notorious that Spain has too few inhabitants'. The immediate cause is clear. Registers show a decline in the number of baptisms beginning in rural parishes in the 1570s and spreading to the towns before the end of the century. The marriage rate also fell, and it is likely that average age at marriage increased.[160]

This sudden change is not easy to explain. Migration, especially of younger men, to the New World was a factor; so also was the celibacy of the excessive number of clergy and other religious. Social and tenurial conditions on the land, including the grazing rights of the Mesta (see p. 40) sometimes made it difficult for a peasant to acquire a holding. There was furthermore a growing unwillingness, especially on the part of the Castilian, to undertake the rigours of agricultural work. Spain became 'a nation . . . dependent on foreigners not only for its manufactures but also for its food supply, while its own population goes idle, or is absorbed into economically unproductive occupations . . . one became a student or a monk, a beggar or a bureaucrat. There was nothing else to be.'[161]

Social attitudes and institutions provide, however, only part of the answer. The Iberian peninsula was afflicted no less than the rest of Europe by the scourges of famine and epidemic disease. Indeed, there is reason to believe that the plague occurred more frequently and with greater virulence here than elsewhere. There were numerous outbreaks during the sixteenth century, but none was as devastating as that which began to spread in 1589 and in the course of the next decade covered much of Spain. It began in the ports of the north coast, where Santander is said to have lost 70 per cent of its population. It spread southwards through Castile and, as Bennassar has shown,[162] only the utmost vigilance by the city authorities in maintaining a quarantine prevented mortality from being a great deal more severe. In Valladolid and Segovia 18 per cent of the population is said to have died of the plague at this time. Catalonia suffered no less than Castile. A sequence of plague epidemics – in 1589–92, 1629–31, 1647–52, 1683–95 – repeatedly cut back on the population of the towns, and that of 1647–52 moved along the whole Mediterranean coast and entered Castile by way

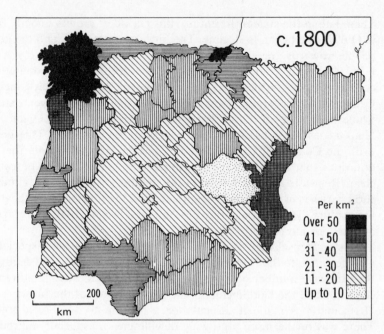

Fig. 2.21 Distribution of population in Spain and Portugal, *c.* 1800

of Cadiz and Seville. The Barcelona 'bills of mortality' show severe losses throughout the century. In 1558 the number rose to 4088, and in 1589–90 to 11,792, about 30 per cent of the population of the city.[163] It is hard, wrote Elliott, to avoid the conclusion 'that the plague of 1599–1600 marks the turning-point in the demographic history of Castile'.[164] Subsequent outbreaks prevented recovery and helped to turn the Meseta into an empty steppe in which the migrant sheep found few to dispute their passage.

There is little evidence for the size of the population of Castile between the sixteenth century and the eighteenth. It probably stood at about 6 million in 1594; by 1650 it had fallen to at most 4,500,000, but had recovered perhaps to 5 million by the end of the century.[165] By this date *la mortalidad catastrófica* had come to an end, and the population of Spain as a whole began to grow: 7,500,000 in 1717 and 9,308,000 a half century later. By this time the present population pattern had been achieved, with a relatively dense settlement near the coast and a vast empty interior, of which George Borrow and Richard Ford have left unforgettable descriptions (fig. 2.21).

Growth continued during the nineteenth century in both Spain and Portugal despite the Carlist wars in Spain and the Peninsular War in both.

Table 2.10

	Spain			Portugal	
	Thousands	Per km²		Thousands	Per km²
1787	10,409	20.7	1750	2,800	31.6
1797	10,541	20.9	1800	2,900	32.8
			1820	3,000	33.9
1857	15,455	30.7	1841	3,412	38.6

Conclusion

The model of population growth, decline and renewed growth, described at the beginning of this chapter, is, as has been seen, applicable to all parts of Europe. Only its timing and the intensity of its fluctuations varied. The sixteenth-century period of growth began early in Spain and in much of eastern Europe but was delayed in Italy and the Netherlands. In the Iberian peninsula this period of growth ended perhaps as early as the 1580s, but continued into the seventeenth century in France and Italy and until late in the century in the Netherlands. The population decline of the late seventeenth and early eighteenth centuries was relatively slight in France and Switzerland, but extreme in Germany and Poland. Renewed growth in the eighteenth century, called by Helleiner the 'vital revolution', began slowly, almost imperceptibly, everywhere. It was well under way in many areas – especially Germany and eastern Europe – by the 1730s, but in the Low Countries was delayed until late in the century. All Europe saw continued growth from the mid-eighteenth century into and through the nineteenth. It was slowed by warfare, but never interrupted.

Each country, each region of Europe provided a variation on this theme of growth, decline and renewed growth. The factors which shaped both theme and variations were of two kinds. First there were those which lay beyond the ability of man to control: the weather and harvests and the spread of epidemic disease, and, secondly those which derived from political action, from social customs and institutions and from human innovation and discovery. To some extent the latter factors were dependent on the former; age at marriage for example, was influenced by grain prices, and thus by the weather.

The first group of factors is the easier to evaluate. The influence of harvest failure on *crises de mortalité* is too obvious to require comment; so also are the consequences of epidemic disease, even though its nature, apart from plague and smallpox, is not always easy to diagnose. The plague itself ceased gradually to be significant in the later years of the seventeenth century, and effectively disappeared from Europe after the Provençal outbreak of 1720. Vives is emphatic that repeated outbreaks of plague were a major factor in the decline of population in the Iberian peninsula. It must be remembered, however, that typhus, sometimes mistaken for plague, did not disappear in the eighteenth century, and that smallpox became more virulent. It was not until the early nineteenth century that vaccination against smallpox made much progress. Nor has it been demonstrated conclusively that improvements in sanitation, quarantine and medical and hospital care had any great effect in reducing mortality until well into the nineteenth century.

One is obliged to conclude that the most important single factor in the growth of population in the eighteenth century, and perhaps also in the sixteenth, was the more abundant supply of foodstuffs, made possible by a sequence of good harvest years. There were, however, developments in agricultural technology; new crops were introduced, and some – maize and the potato, for example – had an important influence on the food-producing capacity of the land. The last widespread subsistence crisis was in 1740. Thereafter, there were, of course, many poor harvests, and consequent distress, but none which led to widespread famine. Furthermore, developments in transport and in the organisation of trade were making it easier for one region to supply the deficiencies of another.

The socio-economic factors in demographic history included warfare with its attendant destruction of crops and farm equipment, and also the number of celebates, the age at marriage and the size of the completed family. Marriage presupposed the means to support a wife and family, and could be and often was postponed when food was scarce and grain prices high. On the other hand, the practice of partible inheritance, which had the effect of increasing the number of farm-holdings – albeit at the expense of making them smaller – might result in earlier marriages. A domestic craft, coupled perhaps with a smallholding, could provide a livelihood and contribute to early marriage. On the other hand, the large, nucleated village and open-field system, with a rigorous social and seigneurial control, exercised through the manorial court, were usually incompatible with a divided inheritance. Here the peasant had commonly to await his father's death or retirement before entering into his inheritance and marrying. For this reason the fertile *limon* soils of the Paris basin and northern France were relatively sparsely settled, and their population showed little tendency to increase. By contrast, early marriage was more likely in areas, such as Brittany, the *Geest* of the Netherlands and north-western Germany, and the mountains of Bohemia, where settlement was more scattered and constraints on land clearance and the division of holdings less rigorous. In such areas the fluidity of social and economic relationships made it practicable, and even desirable, to supplement the farm income by developing domestic crafts. These in turn further encouraged early marriage and large families by providing a means of subsistence. This appears to be the reason for that inversion of the traditional relationship of dense rural population to good soil, which in the eighteenth century produced a greater density of population in the Sudeten mountains and the hills of Normandy than in the plains of Beauce.

3
The pattern of cities

There have been three periods in the history of Europe when the foundation and building of cities was a major preoccupation of western man. The first was in the classical period, when the Greeks and Romans developed their *poleis* and *civitas* capitals. The second occurred during the Middle Ages, roughly from the eleventh to the fourteenth centuries, and the third was associated with the industrial and commercial developments of the late eighteenth and nineteenth centuries. Each built on the settlement pattern which had preceded it. Medieval urbanism derived in part from classical. Most ancient cities in western and southern Europe survived the Dark Ages, and were supplemented by the new towns of the Middle Ages. Only in central and eastern Europe was there no tradition of classical urbanism on which to build. The urban development associated with the Industrial Revolution was similarly established on a foundation of medieval urbanism. It assumed two directions, first a selective growth amongst the older towns, some of which found themselves well placed for a new role in industry. Many small and obscure medieval towns, such as Essen and Dortmund; Berlin, Chemnitz and Plzeň, came into prominence during the period of industrial growth and grew in the nineteenth century to be giants amongst the cities of Europe. Other cities grew during this period from village origins; such were the coal-mining towns of northern France and central Belgium; ironworking centres such as Oberhausen, Charleroi and Zabrze, and mill-towns like Elbeuf and Verviers.

Urban development in the sixteenth century

The pattern of towns in Renaissance Europe was essentially that of the later Middle Ages. No new towns were founded in the sixteenth century, except fortresses, a few of which developed some urban functions. Many towns were extended and in part rebuilt, but in ground plan and style most remained medieval. More than three-quarters of the population of Europe lived in rural areas, yet it was the towns which represented Europe's cultural and artistic traditions. They were the repositories of much of the accumulated wealth of the continent. They were the seats of bishops and the centres of learning and public administration. They were poles of attraction for every traveller who could expect to find there both accommodation and sights to entertain him. It was in the towns that country people sold their agricultural surplus and bought goods which they could not produce in their villages. Rural settlements were linked by paths and trackways with their urban 'central place'. Roads, familiar from itineraries and road-books, joined towns with one another, linking them into a system within which there was a continual circulation of people, goods and ideas.

Though the overall urban pattern underwent no significant change, the size of some cities and towns altered greatly during the century. The great majority were no larger in the sixteenth than they had been in the fourteenth, and their functions had undergone no significant change. Amongst the larger cities, however, there was a selective growth. Whereas in the fourteenth century there had been very few of 50,000 and probably no more than four with a population of 100,000, there was by 1600 a very significant growth in both the size and the number of giant cities.

Capital cities. Growth occurred mainly in two types of city: the political capitals and the ports. Giovanni Botero, writing late in the sixteenth century, expressed succinctly the chief reason for their expansion: 'the greatest means to make a city populous and great is to have supreme authority and power; for that draweth dependency with it, and dependency concourse, and concourse greatness'.[1] The peripatetic courts of medieval kings had become gradually less mobile. In the course of their migrations they had tended to delimit a focal or nuclear area within their states, where their landed possessions were most extensive and food production most abundant. There, at last, they anchored themselves, and began to pass an increasing portion of their time in their capital cities. This fixing of the seat of government was in part necessitated by the growing business of government itself. The transition from the medieval to the modern period was characterised by the assumption by government of a greater range of functions. A rudimentary civil service evolved under the control of the chancery; more elaborate records were kept, preserved and consulted. These developments brought an influx to the capital of royal servants, petty officials and hangers-on of government. At the same time the royal court attracted those seeking profit or employment or merely wishing to bask in the light of royal pleasure. These in turn gave employment to robe-makers and perruquiers; goldsmiths and jewellers; swordsmiths and armourers, and architects and builders of all kinds, all of whom attracted swarms of humbler servants. As if by a kind of multiplier effect, the addition of a seigneurial household brought more business to the markets and to those who unloaded wine and fuel from river barges and performed other menial tasks.

The landed aristocracy played an important but variable role in the development of cities. Fra Salimbene once commented that when Louis IX visited Sens the women who welcomed him seemed like hand-maidens, whereas in Pisa or Bologna the noblest ladies would have been present. Then he recollected that in France, unlike Italy, 'it is the burgesses only who dwell in cities'.[2] In like vein, Botero commented that 'it is not of small importance . . . that the gentlemen in Italy do dwell in cities, and in France in their castles. . . For the Italian divideth his expense and endeavours part in the city, part in the country, but the greater part he bestows in the city. But the Frenchman employs all that he may wholly in the country, regarding the city little or nothing at all.'[3] The 'noble' families had lived in Italian cities from early times, building castle-like palaces, and carrying on feuds between their tall *turri* and through the streets of the town. They brought income to the city and stimulated employment, but the reverse of the coin shows brawling and civil disorders such as Shakespeare represented in the streets of Verona. Outside Italy, only the capitals, the seats of royal power, attracted the nobles of the land, and there they built palaces rather than castles and, as a general rule (the Fronde constitutes a conspicuous exception) conducted themselves with more decorum than the Montagues and the Capulets.

Paris became the archetype of the capital city. It had been a royal residence since the beginning of the Capetian dynasty, for the Capets had first been Counts of Paris. A royal residence at the north-western end of the Ile de la Cité was replaced by the Louvre on the right bank of the river. The building occupied much of the sixteenth century and was continued through the seventeenth. Later in the sixteenth century the Tuileries gardens were laid out; the Pont-Neuf was built linking the Ile de la Cité with both banks of the river; the Place des Vosges (Place Royale) and Place Dauphiné were constructed, and early in the seventeenth century the Luxembourg palace was built near the edge of the city on the south bank. The façades of new buildings were ordered to be of stone with which the city was well supplied. Paris began to take on the aspect of a city of art and culture. It was, however, still contained within the walls built by Charles V in 1370. These embraced about 450 hectares on both banks of the river, and within this area lived some 200,000 people,[4] the largest urban agglomeration in Europe with the possible exception of Constantinople. Except where the French kings had cleared land for their own building projects, there was extreme congestion.[5] Houses were of up to six storeys, some of them occupied by as many as half a dozen families; all except the newer buildings were of wood and plaster.[6] Streets were narrow and dirty, though some were paved with stone slabs during the eighteenth century.[7] A fifteenth-century tax assessment shows the distribution of wealth within the city.[8] The richest quarters were on the right bank, in a broad belt reaching from the Louvre towards Saint-Denis. The left bank, including the Sorbonne and the Latin Quarter, appears to have been one of the poorest and most congested, even though sufficient open space remained for the building of the Luxembourg palace early in the seventeenth century and the laying out of its gardens.

Enclosing the right bank was an old meander of the Seine, a tract of damp land which, fertilised by the sweepings of countless stables, provided fresh vegetables for the city and obstructed its growth in this direction. The local region, however, was very far from satisfying the city's needs. Food and fuel, the most significant of its imports, were brought from as far away as Picardy, the Central Massif and Brittany. Meat travelled on the hoof from Normandy, some of it pausing to fatten in the meadows and grazing lands along the lower Seine.[9] Most other commodities came by river boat. Paris would have been inconceivable without the Seine and its system of tributaries and canals. Fuel and timber for construction was rafted down the river, some of it coming by way of the Canal de Briare from the Forez and the upper valley of the Loire. Wine came mainly from Burgundy by the Seine and Yonne, but some was brought upstream from Rouen; grain came from Picardy, by the Oise, from Brie and Champagne by the Marne, or from Beauce and the Vexin. Fish – most of it salted – came up the Seine, together with salt from the Bay of Bourgneuf. All were unloaded at quays which lined the Seine, and were carried by an army of porters to the city markets.[10] These to the number of almost thirty, in addition to the great market of Les Halles, were to an eighteenth-century observer a scene of utmost confusion, and it was recommended that the visitor keep away from them.[11] The only fair of significance was that of Saint-Germain, held late in the winter, near the abbey church, in a 'Barn of Frame or Wood, tiled over; consisting of many long Allies, crossing one another, the Floor of the Allies unpaved, and of Earth'.[12]

Paris received vast quantities of foodstuffs, fuel and raw materials for its crafts, but little ever left the city. It was a consumer rather than a producer. Its income derived from the tax revenue of the kings and the rents paid to the nobles who gathered to his court. Paris, like classical Rome, had little basic industry before the nineteenth century, and for much of its livelihood it was parasitical on the French nation. Nonetheless it continued to grow. There is little precise evidence for its size before the early eighteenth century when Saugrain reported a total of 166,665 hearths. There was a continual inflow of people from rural

France.[13] Paris, in Mercier's words, was 'un gouffre où se fond l'espèce humaine', and Messance estimated, doubtless with some exaggeration, that on an average every household contained more than twenty-four persons.[14]

The characteristics of Paris – a vast, underemployed population, without basic industries to employ and support it – belonged in some degree to most capital cities. The capital of Habsburg Spain was, until 1561, Valladolid. It lay in the midst of the plains of Old Castile. It was a route centre for the region, though its small river, the Pisuerga, was not navigable. The surrounding plains were noted for their grain production, but the city itself had little commercial importance; Medina de Campo, forty kilometres to the south, was far more important for finance and trade. Nor was it important for its manufactures; a far smaller proportion of its population was engaged in crafts than in any other city of Old Castile. Nevertheless, its population grew to 6750 *vecinos*, or households, in 1530 – a population of perhaps 35,000. It was a large, crowded and dirty city[15] when, in 1559, the court of Philip II left it. The population fell at once, but revived again late in the century before its long decline throughout the seventeenth century.

In 1561 Madrid was chosen as the chief residence of the king and the capital of Spain. It was at the time a very small town, of Moorish origin, lying close to the southern flanks of the Sierra de Guadarrama, the range which separates New Castile from Old. The site had little to recommend it. It was central to the peninsula and reputedly healthy. It had at the time no developed road system, and its local river, far from being navigable, could not even yield an adequate water supply. The surrounding land, much of it scrub-covered steppe, was far indeed from the Tierra del Pan, the 'land of bread', which surrounded Valladolid.

The old town was razed, and a new city laid out. For a time it was doubted whether the site was suited to be the capital of Spain, and Philip II in fact spent much of his time at the palace–monastery El Escorial, which he built 40 kilometres to the north-west, at the foot of the Sierra. But by the early seventeenth century, the decision had become irrevocable, and Madrid enjoyed a period of rapid growth, when it became the cultural as well as the political centre of Spain. The central square, the Plaza Mayor, was built to the east of the palace, in 1619, and in 1625 Philip IV ordered walls to be built to enclose the new city. It covered about 75 square kilometres, within which the original medieval town remains distinguishable by its less-regular street pattern.[16] There is no way to trace the growth of population in detail, but by the second half of the eighteenth century this had reached 150,000, and the built-up area had spread well beyond the wall of Philip IV. A new line of walls was begun in 1782, but its purpose, like that of the Farmers-General Wall

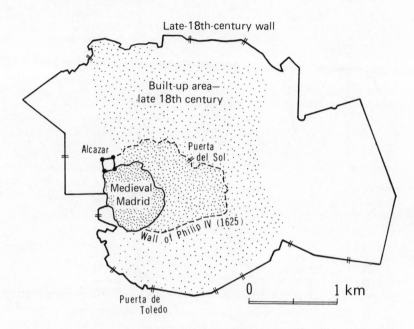

Fig. 3.1 The growth of the city of Madrid

around Paris, was rather to delimit the city's jurisdiction and to check smuggling than to provide an effective military defence.

In Italy and Germany political fragmentation prevented the emergence of large capital cities. In northern Italy, the clearest example of growth was Turin, which became the capital of the Counts of Savoy and Piedmont. In the mid-sixteenth century it was still a town of less than 15,000, but the territory subject to the house of Savoy increased in extent and the city of Turin grew with it. Growth was maintained through the seventeenth century, despite the ravages of the plague of 1630–1. The population reached about 24,500 in 1600, 42,500 by 1700, and 56,750 by the mid-eighteenth century.[17] By contrast, Milan, as capital of the Visconti and later Sforza Dukes of Milan, had reached the peak of its pre-industrial development before 1500. The wealth of the Milanais could not support further growth. There was little further building, and the population was probably smaller in 1600 than it had been by 1500.[18] A similar cessation of growth characterised Venice, Florence and Naples from the later sixteenth at least until the early eighteenth century.

The only exception in Italy to this generalisation was Rome. The classical city whose walls, built under the emperor Aurelian, had enclosed an urban area of 1372 hectares was partially abandoned during

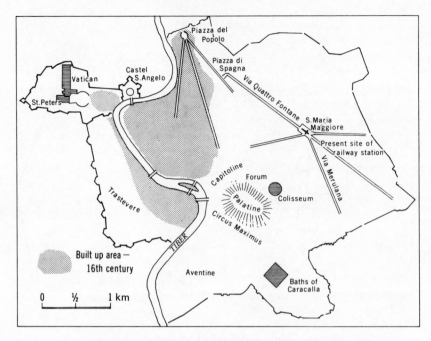

Fig. 3.2 Rome after the planned rebuilding of the sixteenth century

the centuries which followed. The medieval city occupied only the north-western sector of the ancient city, the area of flat land, liable to flooding by the Tiber, which extended northwards from the Capitoline hill, together with the suburb of Trastevere. There were few settlements on the hills of the eastern half of the city, and only religious foundations had intruded amongst the ruins of the Palatine and the Forum.[19] The life of the city had been disrupted by the feuds of the patrician families and its economy ruined by the flight of the papacy to Avignon. In 1417 the popes returned its ancient dignity. St Peter's was begun in 1506 and the Vatican palace enlarged. Palaces were built for the leading families who attended the 'court' of the pope. This restoration and extension of the ancient city was interrupted by its sack by the soldiers of the emperor in 1527.[20] Its population, at this time about 55,000, was reduced by some 20 per cent, but quickly grew again and reached 100,000 by 1600. Somewhat slower growth continued through the seventeenth and eighteenth centuries. It was a cosmopolitan population, as much as a quarter of it having come from outside Italy. One of the largest Jewish ghettoes in Europe was to be found near Sant'Angelo, under close papal supervision. Rome was more visited than any other city, and the guidebooks and itineraries for travellers of this period are too numerous to count. The census of 1526–7 listed no less than 236 'inns, hosteleries and taverns'.[21]

A building programme, largely inspired by the popes themselves, continued through the sixteenth century. Sixtus V (1585–90) continued the work of Julius II in replanning the city, cutting broad, straight streets through the maze of classical and medieval buildings and alleys, to link the key points of the city. The building of churches and palaces continued throughout these centuries, and Rome became, not the largest, but incomparably the best-built and most beautiful city of Europe. This building programme was made possible because the popes ruled the richest and most extensive empire Europe had known. It mattered little that it had been diminished by the Reformation; the New World had, in Acton's words, been called into being to redress the balance of the Old.

The provisioning of Rome presented in all probability a greater problem than that of Paris, because the surrounding region, the Campagna, was depopulated and largely abandoned by agriculture. The attempts of the popes to stimulate farming had little success, and the city's grain supply came largely by sea from Romagna and Ancona, from Sicily, Spain, Provence and even, after 1591, from the Baltic.[22] Animals were driven in from the Apennines, and wine and fish were brought by sea to Civita Vecchia and carried overland. Some foodstuffs, but above all timber, were brought down the Tiber from Umbria.

The Low Countries had no central administration, but the Burgundian dukes in the fifteenth century and the Habsburgs after them made Brussels the chief centre of their authority. The peak of its prosperity was reached by 1500. In 1526 it had 22,036 households, representing a population of at least 90,000. After the mid-sixteenth century the Habsburg rulers deserted Brussels; the Low Countries became a battleground, and the city's brief age of splendour was over. By 1709, its population had fallen to about 50,000, and not until the end of the century did it regain its earlier size.[23]

In none of the petty German capitals was there any significant growth in the sixteenth and seventeenth centuries. Prague, the capital of the Bohemian state, ceased to be a royal residence with the death of King Lewis at Mohács, and Vienna, seat of the Austrian Habsburgs, remained a small frontier town, girt by its walls and ever watchful against the Turks, throughout the sixteenth and seventeenth centuries. Nowhere in central Europe had centralised political authority developed a capital city comparable with those of France, Spain and the Catholic Church, before the end of the seventeenth century.

To this, however, Poland offered a partial exception. Authority had been exercised in turn from Gniezno, Poznań and Kraków. The state had, however, been expanding towards the east, and the union with Lithuania (1569) created a politically united territory which reached from the Baltic almost to the Black Sea. Kraków was too eccentric to serve as an administrative centre for the combined Polish–Lithuanian Commonwealth. It was decided that the joint diet, or *sejm*, should meet alternatively at Piotrków and the small Vistula town of Warsaw which had been the capital of the duchy of Mazowsze. The diet which chose a successor to the last of the Jagiellonian kings (1573) met here, and during the last years of the sixteenth century its political importance began to increase. Lastly, in 1596, King Zygmunt III moved his residence from the Wawel in Kraków to the castle in Warsaw.[24]

This transference of the seat of authority, similar in some ways to that of the Spanish court from Valladolid to Madrid, was followed by the rapid growth of Warsaw. From about 10,000 its population grew to 20,000 by the mid-seventeenth century. The old city was largely rebuilt. The castle, lying on its southern edge, was reconstructed in baroque style, and numerous churches and the palaces of the Polish magnates were built especially to the west and south. Building continued through the seventeenth and eighteenth centuries, interrupted only by the Swedish war of 1655–60. When Bernardo 'Canaletto' Belotto came to Warsaw in 1767 and was given the task of recording the sights of the city, his paintings portrayed what was probably the most courtly and beautiful city in Europe.

At the same time the two Scandinavian cities, Copenhagen and Stockholm, began to grow in size and to take on the air of capitals. Both had been built largely of wood, the houses of Stockholm having been prefabricated in Finland, it was said, and shipped to the city and assembled there.[25] Fires were unusually frequent and destructive, but after each a little more of the city was rebuilt in masonry. Copenhagen owed its first significant rebuilding, and also many of the architectural monuments which survive today, to Christian IV (1588–1648). Both Stockholm and Copenhagen grew during the sixteenth and seventeenth centuries with the increasing power, prestige and commerce of their respective countries. The growth of Stockholm received the deliberate encouragement of the Swedish government, and, in addition to its role as capital of a Baltic empire, it served as the chief port of Sweden. Its population is said to have grown to at least 42–43,000 by 1676.

Only one other capital city underwent any significant transformation during these years: Constantinople. During much of the Middle Ages it had been by far the largest city in Europe. It was reduced to a population of perhaps 80,000 at the time of the Ottoman conquest (1453),[26] but it quickly grew, however, as the capital of the Ottoman empire, and may have reached 500,000 in the mid-sixteenth century and

600–750,000 towards the end of the seventeenth.[27] By this time the city had filled out most of the space enclosed by the Theodosian walls and had spilled over to the Galata and Pera suburbs beyond the Golden Horn. The former imperial palace at the eastern extremity of the triangular peninsula of Constantinople became the Topkapi, the residence of the sultans. The Church of Hagia Sophia was converted to a mosque, and other mosques – some of them, like the mosque of Sulaiman, of great size – were built in immense numbers, and, in fact, represented most of the investment in public buildings under the Turks.

Travellers were unanimous that Constantinople was a crowded, dirty and ill-planned city. Buildings were mainly of wood, and fires were frequent. There was only one practicable road, that running from the Topkapi to the principal city gate on the west. All others were narrow, darkened by the jutting upper storeys, and almost impassable.[28] It was also a cosmopolitan city. Turks made up little more than half the population. The rest were mainly Greeks, Armenians and Jews, the last mainly Sephardic from Spain. The non-Turkish inhabitants lived mostly in closed communities, or ghettoes, chiefly along the shores of the Golden Horn. The city carried on an important trade, but it was primarily 'an administrative and military city'.[29] Its crafts catered only for the needs of the urban population.

The food supply of so large a city presented serious problems which the Turks seem never to have solved satisfactorily. Constantinople did, however, have one particular advantage. It lay on the coast, equally accessible from Black Sea and Aegean ports. Most of the food came in by ship; only animals appear to have been driven across the steppe which lay to the west. Grain supply, as in the Italian city-republics, was entrusted to an official, but was, in the opinion of Baron de Tott, so badly administered that food riots, famine and epidemics were the inevitable consequences.[30]

Port cities. After capital cities, ports were the chief growth points in the sixteenth and seventeenth centuries. During the later Middle Ages the leading centres of maritime trade had been the Mediterranean ports, especially the Italian. Venice and Genoa were intermediaries in a trading network which reached from the Middle East to the Baltic. Goods, imported from North Africa and the eastern Mediterranean, were redistributed either overland by way of the Alpine passes, or by sea to the ports of western Mediterranean and Atlantic Europe. The northern ports, especially those of the Baltic, exported only a narrow range of commodities (see pp. 277–82), while the Atlantic ports generated relatively little trade, except in wine and salt. One of the obstacles to a more vigorous development of trade between the

Mediterranean and western Europe during the later Middle Ages was its unbalanced nature; there was little for Italian ships to bring back to the Mediterranean.

The great discoveries and the commercial revolution which followed changed this, and revolutionised the pattern of seaborne trade. The trade between Europe and the lands newly opened up in Asia and the New World dwarfed all that had passed through Venice and Genoa. 'Compared with all other traffic flows of the period', wrote Chaunu, 'the Spanish–American trade was enormous',[31] and only the Portuguese trade by way of the Cape of Good Hope could compare with it. And this trade passed through only two groups of European ports, those which lay respectively at the mouths of the Guadalquivir and the Tagus. It is not surprising that their growth was rapid during the century of Spanish predominance.

Seville was the chief port of southern Spain. It had long carried on a fairly small traffic with the Italian ports, and a colony of Genoese merchants was settled here.[32] It lay 84 kilometres from the sea, on the Guadalquivir, which was navigable by all except the largest ships. At the mouth of the river was San Lucar de Barramedo, a small and unsatisfactory port, and 30 kilometres to the south, the excellent natural harbour of Cadiz. North-west of the Guadalquivir mouth stretched the straight, sandy coast of Las Marismas, the marshy lower valley of the river. Beyond was the mouth of the small Tinto river, and on it the port of Palos, from which Columbus set sail in 1492.

Seville was already a city of at least 25,000. It quickly became the Spanish focus of the growing traffic with the New World, and the Casa de Contratación, or government department charged with administering this trade as a state monopoly, was established here in 1503; and after a short period when the government tried to extend the New World trade to other ports, Seville acquired a commercial monopoly. It was through Seville that most of the bullion from the Spanish empire entered Europe. As time passed, however, fewer of the galleons made the difficult voyage up the river, and instead docked at Cadiz which in time took over the role of principal port of the Indies.

This, however, did nothing to hinder the growth of Seville. Its population in 1530 was about 45,000 – the largest city of Spain – and reached 90,000 by 1594.[33] It was, like any rapidly growing port city, crowded and cosmopolitan. It attracted the best and the worst elements in contemporary Spain, many of whom crowded on to the ships for the New World, and few of whom returned. Seville had, in consequence, a highly unbalanced sex-ratio, with an excessive number of widows. Only a steady migration from the rest of Castile could have allowed it to grow. The population probably reached its peak in the 1580s. In 1599–1601,

Fig. 3.3 The ports of Portugal and south-western Spain

the city was hit severely by the plague. Immigrants were no longer coming down from the Meseta in as great a number, and much of the port business of Seville was passing to Cadiz.[34] The seventeenth century was a period of slow decline. In the eighteenth century, the population stood at about 80,000, and was exceeded by that of Cadiz.[35] Not until well into the nineteenth century did Seville regain the size it had known during its age of greatness.[36] The food supply of Seville had always been a problem. Wine and olive oil were produced locally, grains were supplied mainly from the plain of Andalusia, now being restored to cultivation after the wars with the Moors.

The mouth of the Tagus lay 330 kilometres to the north-west of that of the Guadalquivir. It was the finest natural harbour on the coast of the Iberian peninsula, and had replaced Oporto as the chief port of Portugal during the Middle Ages. In the fifteenth century the seaborne trade of Portugal began to increase, as Portuguese navigators opened up the west coast of Africa and advanced into the Indian Ocean. It was canalised through the port of Lisbon, which became the emporium for the New World of Asia as Seville was for America. That the population of Lisbon grew is self-evident, but there is little statistical measure of its growth. It was larger than Seville in the fifteenth century; Boxer suggests some 40,000.[37] It may have risen to 80,000 in the sixteenth and to 100,000 in the seventeenth,[38] and when Lisbon was struck by the earthquake of 1755 it may have had a quarter of a million inhabitants.

The Atlantic ports of France, from Bordeaux to Saint-Malo, Le Havre and Rouen, all experienced growth during the sixteenth century. In part this was a reflection of the development of transatlantic and colonial trade; in part, also, of the growth of internal trade in France itself. France was late in developing a colonial trade, and when she did so, in the later seventeenth and eighteenth centuries, a great deal of it passed through Bordeaux. La Rochelle and Nantes were more important for the local trade in wine, salt and the coarse fabrics made in the cottages of the interior, and Saint-Malo added to these the pursuit of the Newfoundland fisheries. Rouen had long been the port for the Paris basin. In 1516 Francis I founded Le Havre de Grace to replace the port of Harfleur which had silted and become difficult to use. It grew very slowly before the late eighteenth century, and was more important for the Grand Banks fisheries than for France's external trade.[39] Rouen remained the chief port for Paris. But the Seine was a difficult river to navigate, and the construction of docks at Le Havre towards the end of the *ancien régime* tipped the balance in favour of Le Havre, which slowly replaced Rouen in seaborne trade.

Only in the Low Countries was the growth of port cities more rapid than in south-western Spain, and only Antwerp and Amsterdam could rival the more southerly cities of Seville and Lisbon. During the later Middle Ages the chief emporium for trade with the Mediterranean had been Bruges and its outports along the river Zwin. Merchandise, in the words of the *Libel of English Policie*, was

> into Flanders shipped full craftily,
> Unto Bruges as to her staple fayre:
> The Haven of Scluse hir Haven for her repayre.
> Which is cleped Swyn tho shippes giding:
> Where many vessels and fayre are abiding.

In the fourteenth century the trade of Bruges began to decline. The reason most often given is the supposed silting of the port. The waterways which led up to the city had always been shallow and difficult to navigate, and most ships had unloaded at Sluys or Damme, and their cargoes had been brought upriver by lighters. These physical conditions did not change materially during the later Middle Ages. It was the volume of traffic which contracted. By the fifteenth century Flanders no longer supplied the greater part of the cloth export. It came increasingly from Brabant and the region to the east of Flanders. The ports of the Zwin were less well suited than those of the Scheldt for this developing trade. The Scheldt, furthermore, was more easily navigated, and allowed the largest ships from the Mediterranean or the Baltic to tie up at the quays in Antwerp. Antwerp also had links both by road and river with the Rhineland, and cloth from Brabant was sold in Cologne and throughout Germany. It was, in short, better placed to profit from the expanding market in central Europe than the older commercial centres of Flanders.[40]

Flanders sought to extinguish the competition of its upstart rival on the Scheldt by annexing it (1356), but, restored to Brabant in 1406, Antwerp enjoyed almost a century of unhindered growth. Its fairs, together with those Bergen op Zoom, to the north, were amongst the most important in north-western Europe, and the city increased steadily in population through the fifteenth century. By 1500 it contained almost 7000 hearths, and by 1526 this had increased almost to 9000, suggesting a total population of 40–50,000.[41] In 1543, the third and last line of walls was built to include the growing population. A new bourse was erected in 1531; new, wide streets were planned, and private houses were rebuilt with stone in an attempt to reduce the danger of fire. Ludovico Guicciardini, writing in the mid-century, described the wide, straight streets and the handsome buildings as well as the immense range and variety of the goods which were unloaded or loaded at its quays along the Scheldt.[42]

Growth continued until the outbreak of war in the Low Countries (1568). The population of the city may by this date have reached 90–100,000.[43] It had become the largest city in north-western Europe, Paris excepted. The war, however, shattered its prospects, and the population and trade of the city both declined in the following years. The catastrophic decline of Antwerp was, however, precipitated by the events of 1576, when the Spanish soldiers of Don John of Austria mutinied, plundered and burned the city, and murdered thousands of its inhabitants. Already, however, the revolting Dutch had seized Flushing and interrupted its shipping, and after the early 1580s the convoys from Spain ceased to come to the Scheldt. The population of Antwerp fell to less than half its total before the war began, and, though it recovered somewhat in the seventeenth century, it did not regain its earlier prosperity until after its conquest by the French at the end of the eighteenth.

The commercial mantle of Antwerp fell upon Amsterdam which had grown up as one of many small fishing and trading towns around the Zuider Zee. It lay on the small river Amstel, where it discharges into the IJ, itself a branch of the Zuider Zee. The site, built mainly of alluvial clay and peat, was ringed by polders and unreclaimed meers, of which one of the largest, the Haarlemmer Meer, to the south-west of the city, remained undrained until the mid-nineteenth century.

Amsterdam grew more slowly than Antwerp. In the mid-sixteenth century, when it was described by Guicciardini,[44] it had a population of less than 30,000, and its trade was little more than a coastwise traffic carried on mainly in hulks, belonging to its own citizens. The very factors which brought about the collapse of Antwerp contributed to its rise: the wars, the flight of merchants – many of them Jewish – from the southern Netherlands, and the closure of the Scheldt, the true beneficiary of which was not the Zeeland towns which had brought it about, but Amsterdam. At the time of the truce of 1609 the population of Amsterdam was still no more than 50,000 but already the first ships of the Netherlands East Indies Company had sailed to Asia and back, and their cargoes, made up mainly of pepper and spices,[45] were being marketed in the city. In 1609 the Bourse, or exchange bank, was opened, and Amsterdam began to take over the financial as well as the commercial functions of Antwerp.

Growth was extremely rapid during most of the seventeenth century. The population had reached 100,000 by about 1620, and 200,000 by 1645. The city itself was largely rebuilt during these years. Brick replaced wood, and the tall houses with ornamented gables began to rise in concentric rows above the canals. The city developed no important manufacturing industries, and its prosperity was built primarily on its trade. Yet its harbour, along the river IJ, was one of the least satisfactory. To reach it ships had to sail around the peninsula of north Holland and, as they approached the harbour, to negotiate a shallow which no amount of dredging seemed able to clear. The draught of ships was restricted, and it proved necessary in the end to give them a greater buoyancy by attaching to them air-filled drums.[46]

The food supply of Amsterdam was easier to manage than that of other cities of comparable size. Holland itself was a considerable producer of animals and animal products; the fishing industry was pursued from every port around the Zuider Zee, and any local deficiency in cereals was readily made good by imports, since Amsterdam was the western emporium of the Baltic grain trade. Furthermore, there was a heavy investment by the city's merchants in land reclamation.[47] Many of the polders to the north-west of Amsterdam were reclaimed early in the seventeenth century, including the Beemster Polder, which in the opinion of Sir William Temple, provided 'the richest Soil of the Province'.[48]

In the nineteenth century the foremost rival of Amsterdam was Rotterdam, situated on a branch of the Rhine, about 35 kilometres from the sea. During the period of Dutch ascendancy, however, it remained relatively small, in part because the lower Rhine had not been straightened and its navigation improved. By 1600 it still had a population of less than 15,000. It grew through the seventeenth century but by 1690 had barely exceeded 50,000,[49] and even this level was not maintained during the eighteenth century.

Another legatee of the decline of Antwerp was Hamburg. In the later Middle Ages it had been a relatively unimportant Hanseatic town, over-shadowed by Lübeck and Stettin, whose access to the central European hinterland was superior. During the sixteenth and seventeenth centuries, however, Hamburg enjoyed a comparative immunity from the religious wars which decimated the population and destroyed the trade of her rivals. Some of the refugees from the southern Netherlands settled in Hamburg, bringing with them more advanced business methods than those known to the rather backward Hansards. Jews from the Iberian peninsula came here, and the Merchant Adventurers of London transferred their staple for English cloth from Antwerp to Hamburg.[50]

The city lay on the north-eastern shore of the Elbe, 125 kilometres from the sea. The navigation of the estuary was not easy, and the larger vessels could reach its quays only on the tide. Access to the city was improved only by dredging during the nineteenth century. On the other hand, Hamburg's hinterland was broadened by the construction of canals, beginning in the sixteenth century, across Brandenburg from the Elbe to the Oder (see p. 298).[51] With the support of the commercial nations of north-western Europe, the merchants of Hamburg set about controlling the maritime trade of central Europe. In the eighteenth century Justus Möser described the activities of 'the grasping, monopolising merchants of Hamburg and Bremen', and looked back nostalgically to the time when all Hanseatic towns had equal opportunities.[52] Hamburg was thus the only north German port, indeed the only German city, to grow continuously through the pre-industrial period. Its population early in the sixteenth century was some 16,000. This grew to over 22,000 by 1600; to about 45,000 at the outbreak of the Thirty Years' War, and to 60,000 at its conclusion. By the mid-eighteenth century the population of Hamburg had reached 80,000, and had turned 100,000 at the end of the century.[53]

By contrast, other port cities of north Germany experienced a short period of growth in the sixteenth century, followed by a long period of decline which lasted through the seventeenth and, in some instances, the eighteenth century as well. Danzig, replacing Lübeck, became the foremost Baltic port in the sixteenth century (see p. 55).[54] Its population grew from some 30,000 to about 65,000; immense profits were made by its merchants in the main from the grain trade, and much of the city was rebuilt. It became the finest Renaissance and baroque city in northern

Europe. Quays were developed along the Motława, a branch of the Vistula, and opposite the city was built a range of granaries and warehouses, made necessary by the interruption of navigation during the winter half year. This period of prosperity lasted into the second half of the seventeenth century, when warfare destroyed the trade on which its prosperity had been founded. It never regained what it lost during these years. By 1750, its population had fallen to 46,000 and by the end of the century the city was smaller than it had been in 1500.[55]

Early modern urbanism

The European town was, at least until the eighteenth century, still medieval in appearance, in plan and even in function. It continued to be walled, even though its walls served no other function than to separate it from the countryside and to emphasise its differing status. Not a single town portrayed by the cartographers and engravers of the sixteenth and seventeenth centuries was without its defences, though many a small German town, illustrated by the Merians, was protected by nothing more than a ditch, a bank and a wooden palisade, with a small, stone-built gateway. Those cities which had grown most rapidly during the later Middle Ages extended their walls to enclose an even larger area. Antwerp was one of the last to do so; its final enceinte was built in 1543. Many had built too generously, and their walls continued until the eighteenth century to enclose large open spaces and gardens. Cologne, for example, had almost as much open space within its walls in 1815 as it had about 1600.

Medieval urban defences, consisting of curtain walls, set with towers and gates, had been built by the citizens themselves, and their cost had often stretched the municipal finances to their limit and even run the city deep into debt. They continued into the seventeenth century to have their uses. They could not stand up to a siege train, but still protected the citizens from marauding bands such as disturbed much of Germany during the Thirty Years' War. The newer defences were lower but very much thicker, fitted with gun platforms and embrasures designed to provide cross-fire *along* the walls. The construction called for skilled military engineers, and their cost was beyond the reach of most towns. They could in effect only be built by governments. Amongst the earliest examples of the new style of urban defences were those built to protect the Trastevere, or right-bank suburb of Rome, from attack from the north. The latest walls of Milan were designed to support guns and resist artillery, and the defences of some other towns were in some measure adapted to the new military technology, with bastions at particularly exposed points; but most towns felt no need to turn themselves into fortresses, and the new mode of defence became significant only in those of strategic importance.

Within the circuit of its walls, the street plan of the sixteenth-century city differed little from that of two centuries earlier. Most streets were narrow; few were paved, and all became the repositories of domestic waste which was at infrequent intervals collected by the employees of the town. The urban plan had, in most instances, developed gradually without any guiding ideas to determine the location of streets and open spaces. But urban law in Europe, unlike that in Moslem lands, protected streets from encroachment by the houses along each side of it, and, though generally very narrow, they never ceased to be passable, even by wheeled vehicles.

Two groups of towns provided exceptions to this generalisation: those which derived their lay-out directly from the planned construction of the Romans, and those – most of them very small – which were similarly laid out during the Middle Ages. Most of the former were in Italy. Turin – or at least the oldest parts of the city – preserved its classical ground plan to perfection, and the early modern development of the city merely extended its pattern of straight streets and square city blocks. In most other cities, the regular plan had been somewhat distorted during the early medieval period when urban life was at its lowest ebb, though it remains recognisable even today. Medieval planned towns were numerous in most parts of Europe. In some instances they consisted of a planned suburb grafted on to an older, unplanned nucleus, as at Poznań, Breslau, Kraków, Plzeň and Prague. Much social and legal history is implicit in the contrasting ways in which the streets of a town developed. But the medieval planners were never rigid in the interpretation of their ideas. They were prepared to distort their town blocks and to bend their streets, though they seem never to have resolved the problems of fitting a gridiron pattern of streets within the curving line of a town wall nor that of locating churches, public buildings and open spaces in relation to a regular system of streets. This was left to the more sophisticated and erudite planners of the Renaissance.

Urban building was more often of wood and clay than of stone and brick. Wood was, except in southern Europe, more readily available to urban builders than stone. Few large cities – Paris and Rome were significant exceptions – had abundant sources of good building stone within easy reach, and in most the use of masonry was reserved for churches, public buildings and sometimes the basements or ground floors of houses, as well, of course, as for town walls. Brick construction had been much used by Romans, but during the earlier Middle Ages the only bricks and tiles used were those retrieved from Roman sites. The use of bricks was revived in northern Europe during the later Middle Ages. The reason lay in the absence of building stone in the glaciated north German plain and southern Scandinavia and in the compensating abundance of clay suitable for brick-making. Throughout the later Middle Ages brick was used from the Low Countries to Poland for the building of churches and town halls, and during the Renaissance began to appear in the houses of prosperous burgesses from Amsterdam to Danzig.

Most urban houses did not rise more than two or three storeys. Only where pressure on space was severe, as in the congested city of Genoa, did they rise to five, six or even seven.[56] Houses were larger, taller, more pretentious around and close to the town square, for it was here that the local patricians chose to live, and there they built tall façades with stepped and decorated gables, which still form a notable feature of many north European towns from Brussels to Warsaw.

The spread of masonry construction offered many advantages. It was less likely to harbour rats than houses built of wooden framing infilled with wattle and plaster, and, in consequence, its inhabitants were less vulnerable to disease. It was warmer in winter and cooler in summer, and above all, it burned less readily. Fire was a perennial threat to the pre-industrial city. Fireplaces, hearths and ovens were made of stone, brick or clay, even in houses which were otherwise of wood, but the amount of masonry was often far too small; the mortar was readily burned out, and joists were even notched into chimney stacks in such a way that they could be ignited. Fires could thus spread with the greatest ease, and could quickly engulf much of a town. The journal of a Mons burgess recorded a fire at Armentières in 1518 which destroyed 1300 houses, leaving only 3 standing.[57] Four years later 1200 houses were burned in Valenciennes, and in the following year the greater part of the small town of Reulx was destroyed. Almost every city and town in Europe had its catalogue of fires; Constantinople recorded no less than twenty-two major fires between 1633 and 1701.[58]

Water supply and the disposal of sewage and waste were always major problems. In no instance did the aqueducts of the Romans continue in use. Their giant arches and tunnels were conspicuous features of the landscape, but they failed to inspire Renaissance man to comparable building activity. Towns relied on springs rising either within their walls or only a short distance from them. Pipes, usually of lead, carried the water to public fountains. These became during the Renaissance more and more colourful and decorative, often belying the quality of the water which they dispensed. Most large towns drew water from their rivers, with little reference to its quality. At most they held it in cisterns to allow sediment to settle and occasionally they restricted the discharge of waste into the stream.[59] This remained substantially the situation until the development of the science of hydraulic engineering in the eighteenth century. Cities, especially large cities, were always chronically short of water, a fact which helps to explain the frequency of serious fires.

There were no sewers in medieval and Renaissance towns. In monasteries toilets were often built *over* a stream; in castles, they projected from the walls and discharged into the moat or ditch below. This convenient if insanitary way of disposing of excreta was rarely possible in towns – though the town ditch was not infrequently used in this way. The sweepings of stables were usually carted to the surrounding fields, but domestic waste was more often thrown into the streets, from which cleaners removed it at intervals to the river. The earliest sewers were in fact small rivers, such as the Fleet in London, which had been walled in and covered over. Rivers were so polluted by human as well as industrial waste, such as the drainings from tanyards, that they could not provide a safe drinking water. Yet there were few which were not used as a source of supply. Disease spread in such conditions, and the increasing incidence of fevers in the late eighteenth and early nineteenth centuries is to be related directly to the growth of larger urban centres without sufficient care to prevent the contamination of the water supply.

Most towns could not have maintained themselves without a steady influx of peasants from the countryside. Except in the small *Agrarstädte*, the death-rate in towns seems always to have been higher than in rural areas, and the birth-rate lower.[60] Many – perhaps most – of the immigrants were those who stood no chance of inheriting land in their native villages. In the towns they became craftsmen, or servants, or joined the mass of unskilled and destitute who were recorded in the tax-books quite simply as *pauvres* or *non taillables*. Many did not marry because they never possessed the means to set up house. At Lyons, in 1529–31, over 60 per cent of the adults for whom there is evidence of place of birth had been born outside the city.[61] Immigration was heavily male – another reason for celibacy. The immigrants were drawn from a very wide area, almost a quarter of them from other towns. The city attracted people, but often could not hold them. If they failed to obtain employment in one, they moved on to another. Only about a twentieth of the immigrants to Lyons came from beyond the French-speaking area;[62] language was evidently a factor in determining the direction of migration. Large towns attracted immigrants from a very much wider area than small. Strasbourg drew settlers from much of western Europe, though a majority came from Germany. Paris in the eighteenth century was found to have citizens from all parts of northern France, as well as many from southern.

Small towns, however, continued throughout the pre-industrial period to be fed with immigrants from their surrounding countryside. Haguenau in northern Alsace derived all of its citizenry from distances of less than 30 kilometres, and similar instances of predominantly short-distance migration could be found in many parts of western Europe.[63] The direction of migration was determined in part by religious conviction. A Catholic would have been unlikely to settle in Strasbourg, and a Protestant would not have been well received in Haguenau. In part, also, the decision to migrate must have been influenced by news of economic opportunity. Areas of expanding industrial activity in the late seventeenth and eighteenth centuries, such as northern France and the lower Seine valley, received a stream of rural immigrants. It seems that in many instances migration was in the first instance to nearby small towns, and only then, after the migrant's break with his home village was complete, did he move on to a more distant and larger town.

This overwhelming dependence on immigration explains, of course, the fluctuations, often extreme, in the size of towns. The supply of immigrants might be interrupted, or a significant part of the footloose and perhaps unwelcome population of one town might move on to others where, it was hoped, its presence might be more highly rewarded. The high urban death-rate was due in part to the fact that many immigrants were already in middle life; in part to the fact that the incidence of disease was greater than in rural areas. The disastrous outbreaks of plague during early modern times were mostly urban; so also were the worst outbreaks of typhus, also a disease carried by human parasites. Cholera, increasingly important in the eighteenth and early nineteenth centuries, derived from the infected water supply of cities, and all communicable diseases were transmitted more readily in crowded urban conditions than in rural.

Urban planning

Few new towns were founded in the sixteenth and seventeenth centuries, and the urban net bequeathed by the Middle Ages was adequate for most modern needs. Yet there was an immense interest in urban planning, stemming in large part from the rediscovery of the classical writers on the subject. Opportunities to employ this new-found knowledge were, perhaps unfortunately, few.

The works of Vitruvius, rediscovered in the fifteenth century, were the most important formative influence on the town-planners of the Renaissance. He had advocated a planned lay-out for a town, preferably circular, with radiating streets, and open spaces judiciously sited for the health and amenity of the citizens. His ideas were adopted in somewhat theoretical fashion by Alberti and Leonardo da Vinci, whose notebooks contain many suggestions for the improvement of towns. Leonardo conceived a plan to sweep away the city of Milan, at the time in all probability the largest in southern Europe, and to replace it with ten 'new towns'. In this way he hoped to break up 'the great congregation of people who herd together like goats one on top of another, filling every place with foul odour and sowing seeds of pestilence and death',[64] but such a project was far beyond the political and economic realities of his age.

Italian architects and planners went on to produce a series of models for the ideal city, each of them a variation on the theme of Vitruvius, but in practice all that they were called upon to do was to modify existing cities and to replan odd corners of them. The most significant of such opportunities was in Rome. When, in 1417, the popes returned to the city they found it half in ruins. The work of rebuilding began at once. Churches were restored, and on the right bank of the Tiber Pope Nicholas V (1447–55) began work on a new papal palace, the Vatican, and sketched the general plan of St Peter's and its approaches. Early in the next century Julius II, the most ambitious and visionary of the builder–popes, planned to cut broad thoroughfares through the maze of streets and alleys which had spread over the Campus Martius and composed the medieval city. On the northern edge of the city he created the large square known today as the Piazza del Popolo, from which, he planned, broad avenues should radiate across the Campus. One of these, the Via del Corso, constitutes the central axis of modern Rome. To the east of the medieval city lay the region of the 'hills' abandoned since the later years of the empire, though enclosed within the Aurelian wall. In the fifteenth century, settlement began again to spread into this area, and in the later sixteenth century a building-plan was imposed on it.[65] Sixtus V (1585–90) encouraged his architect, Fontana, to plan a series of avenues to converge on the church of Santa Maria Maggiore. At the same time Fontana constructed a water-supply system for the area and designed impressive buildings to accord with his plan. This was urban planning on a more ambitious scale than had been known hitherto, and, since Rome was the most-visited city in Europe, its fame spread, and it became an inspiration to town-planners throughout the continent.

In no other Italian, or even European, city were there changes as drastic as those imposed on Rome. No other institution had wealth comparable with that of the papacy. Nevertheless the central piazza of Venice was replanned and rebuilt to produce a central area 'unequalled among the great cities of the world'.[66] The centre of Vicenza was partially rebuilt by Palladio, and there was also extensive new building, according to the principles of Vitruvius, in Milan and Bologna. Parts of other Italian cities, including Genoa, Naples and Palermo, were rebuilt, and in some of them new boulevards were cut through the maze of medieval streets. In Turin the classical ground plan was extended without modification along the lines prescribed by the Roman planners.

The opportunities to plan a city *ab initio*, on a virgin site, and to apply more fully the principles of Vitruvius, were few indeed. Most of the new towns of the sixteenth and seventeenth centuries owed their origin to military necessity. They were fortresses, and the lay-out of streets and squares had to be subordinated to the overriding requirements of defence. The most familiar and best presented of such towns is Palma Nova, built close to the eastern frontier of the Venetian republic in 1593 by the architect Scamozzi. It was nine-sided, with a radial pattern of streets emanating from a central piazza. Around it was cast a star-shaped pattern of walls, moats, hornworks and bastions which occupied altogether a far greater space than the town itself. A not-dissimilar plan was adopted at Livorno (Leghorn), which had been developed as a port early in the sixteenth century to replace Pisa and Porto Pisano.[67] It consisted of rectangular blocks contained within a polygonal perimeter and centring in an arcaded piazza. The plan, however, was abandoned before it had been completed.

The ideas of Vitruvius spread to France, and the first opportunity to apply them arose in 1545 when the king ordered a new town – Vitry le François – to be built to replace Vitry-en-Perthois, recently destroyed by the army of Charles V. It was planned by an Italian engineer as a series of rectangular blocks of unequal size, enclosing a central square. Around the whole was built a line of defences, also roughly square in plan. Later in the century similar fortress towns were founded at Hesdin, in Artois; at Marienbourg and Philippeville in the Ardennes; at Rocroi and Villefranche in the Meuse valley, and at Brouage on the Atlantic coast of France. In the following century the 'upper town' of Longwy in Lorraine, Neuf Brisach in Alsace, and Montlouis in the eastern Pyrenees were built. All were variations on the Vitruvian theme of a small town, square or polygonal in plan, with a radial or rectangular street plan. All were conceived as fortresses and were located close to the boundary between France and the Habsburg empire. They served no important economic purpose and are today little larger than when they were founded. To this short list of fortress towns might be added Henrichement, in the province of Berry, which was founded by the Duc de Sully in 1608 as a refuge for the Protestants of the region.

Commercial development called for the creation of a number of ports during the sixteenth and seventeenth centuries. Le Havre (see p. 128) was planned as a small square town, made up of sub-rectangular blocks. Francis I was dissatisfied with it, and in 1541 commissioned an Italian architect to lay out another town nearby, which proved to be little different. Brest was founded by Richelieu on a site which had long been occupied by a small town, and was built on as regular a gridiron pattern as the hilly terrain permitted. Naval and commercial requirements called for another Atlantic port, and in 1665 Colbert established the planned town of Rochefort on the Charente. At about the same time a small port was developed on the Breton coast by merchants trading with the east, and soon acquired the name of Lorient. Its early development was haphazard, but in the eighteenth century a planned town was grafted on to the earlier settlement.

In contrast with the fortress towns, which had little prospect of growth once their military functions had been fulfilled, the Atlantic ports were founded to meet the needs of an expanding trade. When Saugrain compiled his *Dictionnaire géographique*, Le Havre had a population of about 8000, but by 1801 had reached 16,000. Brest had reached 14,000 by the end of the seventeenth century, and 27,000 in 1801.

To this period of planned urban development also belongs the category of *Residenzstädte*. They were built to provide a semi-urban setting for princely palaces and the homes of the wealthier members of the landed aristocracy. The earliest was Charleville, established in 1608 on the river Meuse. Its founder, Charles of Gonzaga, Duke of Nevers and Rethel, laid out the town as a series of rectangular blocks enclosing a large and impressive central square, with an arcaded and covered sidewalk – rather Italianate in style.

A few years later Richelieu built a château at Richelieu, in Touraine, and planned the town of the same name. The latter was sited at a discreet distance from the château, and departed from the established plan for new towns in being aligned along a single axial street. It clearly had no military pretensions, and owed little to Vitruvius. The most grandiose attempt made in France to organise town, palace and park into a whole was, however, Louis XIV's creation of Versailles. The design was traced in 1661–5. The three elements were disposed symmetrically on each side of a central axis. The town was made up of regular blocks through which cut three wide, tree-lined boulevards, to converge at the principal entrance to the palace. For this the model was clearly Julius II's plan for Rome, with its avenues diverging from the Piazza del Popolo. The immense palace was spread symmetrically across the axis, with its principal façade facing into the garden and park, whose main lines were also made to converge on it.

The Vitruvian inspiration had run its course at Versailles. The scale of the palace dwarfed all other attempts to weld the elements of a *Residenzstadt* into a coherent whole. But it was backward-looking, providing only for courtly elegance, and consuming, it is said, 60 per cent of the tax income of France during its period of construction. Lauguier, within a century of its construction, condemned 'the hollowness and artificiality of Versailles, which had sacrificed content to form'. Versailles was, in his opinion, 'the most overestimated work of art that has ever been created'.[68]

The only other attempt at large-scale planning in pre-Revolutionary France was at Nancy. The duchy of Lorraine, of which Nancy had long been the capital, was granted in 1738 to Stanislas Leszcziński, who for a short time had been King of Poland and had been given Lorraine as consolation for his loss of Warsaw. The city consisted of a small medieval nucleus, to which had been added in the later Middle Ages a suburb made up of rectangular blocks. Between the two there remained in the seventeenth century an extensive open space, and it was here that Stanislas laid out the square which bears his name, with, to the north of it, the Place de la Carrière, one of the most elegant examples of eighteenth-century civic planning.

At Nancy the planned development of the eighteenth century was made possible in part by the demolition of the medieval walls of the city. In Paris, also, the destruction of the wall of Charles V allowed the extension of the Louvre towards the north-west and the creation of the Tuileries gardens. In city after city, urban architects found scope for their activities in developing wide boulevards where previously there had been only wall and ditch and the open space which, for reasons of security, had been left on each side of them.

In France the piecemeal rebuilding of older cities continued through the eighteenth century. Property was cleared; townhouses were built for members of the aristocracy; squares and piazzas were laid out, and wide streets driven through the built-up areas, leaving untouched on each side the narrow streets, squalid alleys and ill-built and insanitary housing which made up the greater part of every European town in this age. The high cost and sometimes even the sheer impossibility of acquiring property rights over enough urban land made extensive rebuilding impossible.

The Low Countries, in which occurred the most vigorous urban growth in the early modern period, presented unique opportunities for urban planning, though little use was ever made of them. Antwerp, the fastest-growing European city in the first half of the sixteenth century, developed without plan, and the area within the newly rebuilt fortifications was at the mercy of private speculators. Brussels provides another example of lost opportunities. In 1695 much of it was destroyed by the French army of Villeroi, and a disastrous fire in 1731 completed the destruction. But in the course of rebuilding the only planning occurred around the royal palace, on the eastern edge of the city.

The Netherlands present a rather different picture. Amsterdam grew as rapidly in the seventeenth century as Antwerp had done a century earlier, but here urban growth was closely supervised and controlled. The late-medieval city had consisted of some half a dozen rows of houses lying parallel to the river Amstel (see p. 285). A further series of parallel streets was added in the seventeenth century, separated by canals, so that the city came to be made up of alternating streets, rows of houses and waterways. Although the houses were built by the burgesses, their design was controlled by the urban authorities, which also dug and maintained the canals. The Hague, seat first of the Counts of Holland and then of princes of the Netherlands, was in effect a *Residenzstadt*, though the urban development of the seventeenth century around the Binnenhof was elegant, if somewhat uncontrolled.

Italian concepts of urban planning did not reach Germany in any significant fashion until after the Thirty Years' War, and did not really influence urban development until the eighteenth century. Germany became after the Reformation a refuge for Protestant refugees from France and Austria, and at least three small towns were founded in order to provide them with homes: Freudenstadt, in Württemberg (1599), Lixheim, in the Rhenish Palatinate (1608), and Erlangen, near Nuremberg, established in 1686 to house French Huguenots. All were small rectangular towns, laid out in a gridiron pattern. A few German towns, notably Hamburg and Emden, added suburbs during this period, but there were few other instances of planned urban growth other than the creation of *Residenzstädte* by the German princes.

The most ambitious *Residenzstädte* were Mannheim and Karlsruhe, founded respectively by the Elector Palatine and the Margrave of Baden. Both were established on or close to the Rhine, a fact which was to stand them in good stead during the nineteenth century. Mannheim was twice destroyed in war during the seventeenth century. In the early eighteenth century the site was cleared and a new city built, and in 1720 the Elector Palatine moved his capital there from Heidelberg. The city consisted of a rectangular pattern of 136 blocks, with the electoral palace bordering the Rhine to the west, the whole enclosed within a complex system of fortifications. There was nothing original in the plan of Mannheim, but Karlsruhe, founded a few years later and 60 kilometres to the south, broke new ground. It attempted, like Versailles, to weld together the three elements palace, park and town. The plan was a variant of Vitruvius' radial concept; the *Residenz* lay at the centre of a circle, with the town occupying one sector of the enclosing circle, and the park the remainder.

Ludwigsburg, near Stuttgart (1709), Neustrelitz (1726) and Ludwigslust (1765), the last two in Mecklenburg, are examples of small

Residenzstädte dependent on the palaces of German princes. In several instances, however, the palace with its ornamental gardens was added to an older city, often replacing part of its defensive walls, sometimes occupying the site of housing destroyed to make way for it, frequently incorporating into its design a new and elegant suburb laid out on a geometrical plan. Würzburg, Munich, Dresden, Potsdam, Rastatt, Darmstadt, Kassel, Stuttgart, Weimar and Berlin all exemplify in their different ways the imposition of a *Residenzstadt* on a medieval nucleus.

Scandinavia had, by and large, escaped the wave of urbanisation which had spread across most of Europe during the Middle Ages, and it was not until the sixteenth and seventeenth centuries that the need was felt for urban centres. The seventeenth was the century of Scandinavia, when economic growth combined with determined leadership to allow Denmark and Sweden to play a significant role in the politics of Europe.

Christian IV (1588–1648) of Denmark was the foremost founder of cities of his age. He more than doubled the urban area of Copenhagen, building a planned suburb to the north of the old town. He also founded, within the space of some thirty years, at least half a dozen towns, comparable, as Lavedan has pointed out,[69] to many of the medieval *bastides* of southern France, though his architects and planners seem mostly to have been Dutch. Norway belonged at this time to the Danish crown, and here too Christian IV established towns. The ancient settlement of Oslo had been destroyed by fire in 1624; it was refounded on a nearby site and continued to bear its founder's name, Christiania, until 1925, when its original name was revived. It was rather unimaginatively planned as a series of rectangular blocks, but royal ordinances controlled closely the character of the building and required – a very unusual step for Norway – that all should be in masonry.

Sweden was not behind Denmark in the foundation of towns. Gustavus Adolphus is himself credited with establishing sixteen. These include the port of Göteborg (1620) and the inland town of Jonköping (1627), as well as many small towns as far north as Luleå. The economic justification for their foundation was, in many instances, a great deal less powerful than the king had supposed. He had difficulty in peopling them, and Umeå, also in northern Sweden, was occupied only by a handful of peasants who were located there against their wills. Most of these new towns grew very slowly, and remained into the nineteenth century merely 'rural settlements equipped with town charters'.[70]

Stockholm, however, was different. Its medieval nucleus was two small islands situated where the narrow Lake Mälaren began to open towards the Baltic Sea. In the seventeenth century the city began to spread to the mainland both to north and south as a series of parallel streets intersecting at right angles.

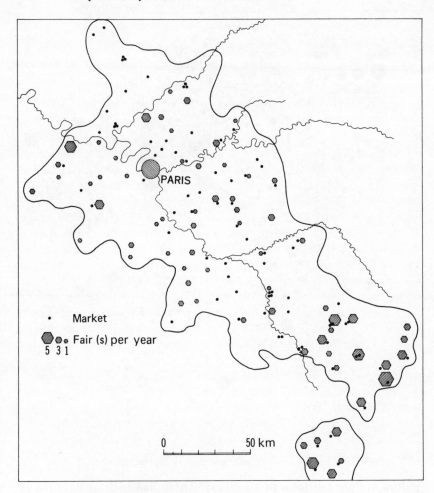

Market

Fair (s) per year
5 3 1

0   50 km

Fig. 3.4 Markets and fairs in the *généralité* of Paris

The function and size of towns

The pre-industrial town was essentially a place of exchange, where the peasant and the grain-jobber could dispose of their rural surplus; where the craftsmen, whether rural or urban, could sell their products, and where goods of distant origin could reach the rural consumer. Of course, towns performed other functions; they were centres of manufacture and of administration; they provided homes for a rentier class; they contained a community of lawyers, churchmen and other professional people, but underlying all these was their role as market-places.

It is for this reason that the number of small towns exceeded by so

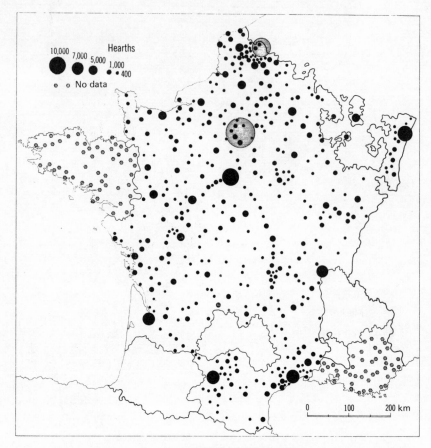

Fig. 3.5 Cities and towns in France, early eighteenth century

wide a margin the total of all others. There had to be a network of
market centres if local communities were to rise above the level of
subsistence. There was no town that was not also a place of exchange.
Most had weekly or twice-weekly markets, and it was generally assumed
that a peasant would be able to get to market, do his business and return
home within a day. This ideal was not always realised. There were many
areas of scanty population, where market towns were few and a market
journey a rare event. Vauban compiled a list of markets and fairs within
the *généralité* of Paris (fig. 3.4). In this moderately populous region few
places lay more than 12 kilometres from a market. There were even
areas where markets were so closely spaced that a peasant might be able
to choose between several. Such was the case in parts of the Rhineland
and western Germany; only in Bavaria and eastern Germany did their
spacing exceed the normal day's journey of a peasant and his cart.[71]

The services of a town to its surrounding area were not limited to buying and selling on market day. A tanner in the Alsatian town of Wissembourg had customers in twenty-five villages within a radius of 15 kilometres, and a map showing the distribution of debtors to a wealthy citizen of the town was broadly similar.[72] Within this area, also, members of the local bourgeoisie were investing their savings in land, so that the peasants themselves did not control more than 50 per cent of it.

The largest towns, no less than the smallest, had market functions, but in the former they were overlaid and obscured by others: government and administration, manufacturing, retailing. In small towns the markets were conspicuous because they were the dominant function. The classification of towns into large, medium-sized and small is difficult because the data are both incomplete and unreliable. Saugrain in 1720 produced a revised hearth-list, though his estimates, especially for the larger towns, must be treated only as rough estimates. Using the size classification suggested by Mols,[73] we have in France about 1720:

Very large towns (over 40,000 population)	5
Large towns (20–40,000)	11
Medium-sized towns (5–20,000)	100
Small towns (2–5000)	385

Evidence is less complete and less reliable for Germany and central Europe. On the evidence of Büsching[74] there were only 6 very large and 20 large towns amid a vast number – up to 3000 – of small and very small towns. More reliable data from Prussia in the early nineteenth century also shows how few were the large towns or even towns of medium size:[75]

Size of town	Number	Total population
Over 10,000	26	836,079
3500–10,000	136	765,936
2000–3500	194	508,933
1000–2000	407	597,947
Less than 1000	258	186,937

In Italy data are available only for the larger cities. The number of very large towns remained considerable. In 1600 at least 11 exceeded 40,000, and Naples had more than 250,000; a further 20 could be regarded as large. Altogether 10 per cent of the population of Italy lived in its 30 largest cities. Most declined in size during the seventeenth century, but by the middle years of the eighteenth were again increasing. By 1800 no less than 35 belonged to the categories of 'large' and 'very large'.

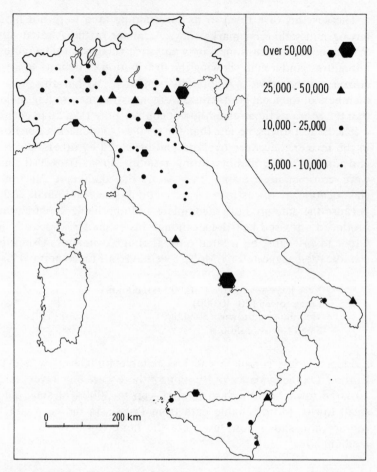

Fig. 3.6 Cities and towns in Italy in the sixteenth century

In Poland, by contrast, only a handful of towns could even be described as 'medium-sized', and four-fifths of the legal towns could not even qualify as 'small':[76]

Medium-sized towns (over 10,000)	8
Small towns (2–10,000)	100
Very small towns (1–2000)	over 400
Dwarf towns (under 1000)	about 100

The numerical preponderance of the small town throughout the pre-industrial period is apparent, and even in terms of aggregate population they probably exceeded the collective size of the large. The small town was relatively uncomplicated in its function and social structure. It was a community of up to about 5000 inhabitants in which every face was familiar, and everyone's business a matter of common knowledge. It was, as a general rule, dominated by a few settled and established families, which ran the small businesses and owned much of the urban property. The small town would have consisted of one, or at most of two or three parishes, and its ecclesiastical population would have amounted to no more than a handful of priests or ministers. There would have been a few rentiers, living on income from rural property, but the *noblesse*, even the *petite noblesse*, were of little importance in the small town.

All small towns contained craftsmen, though in most they were too few to support any kind of gild organisation. At Weissenburg, in Bavaria, twenty-two separate crafts were practised,[77] but the élite amongst them were the butchers, bakers and tanners, showing both the closeness of their ties with the surrounding countryside and also their overwhelming dependence on local consumption. Most small-town craftsmen were organised into gilds, but these were necessarily few in number, each corresponding with a group of related trades. They were conservative and exclusive, more intent on preserving status than on supervising workmanship. Mack Walker has commented upon their 'social prudery and political stubbornness'.[78] They were immune to innovation in technology and business organisation. Immigrants were generally unwelcome and were made to feel unwanted. Only as servants had they much chance of employment, and their numbers help to explain the abundance of the domestic staff in many citizens' households. The small town was clearly not in the forefront of economic progress. The majority were poor, even depressed. They had failed to maintain their growth of the sixteenth century, and in the seventeenth suffered from both warfare and the general recession. During the eighteenth century it was, as a general rule, the larger towns which grew, attracting the manpower and the business which had hitherto sustained the smaller. The letters of the intendants present a picture of utter depression:[79] Montreuil, filled only with 'petit peuple', and carrying on no trade; Montdidier, 'extremely poor'; Montargis, in the *généralité* of Orléans, 'drowned in its debts', and Gien, ruined by the departure of the *réligionnaires* (Huguenots); Beaugency, by the collapse of its bridge and the vileness of its wine, and Vendôme and Châteaudun, by the decline of their trade. Dourdan was 'la plus gueuse ville de la généralité', and only for Clamecy had the intendant a good word.

Such towns drifted into the nineteenth century, their quaintness unimpaired because there was no rebuilding, no economic growth. Guérande, in Brittany, was one of them. It lay, in the words of Balzac, 'entirely outside the social stream which gave character to the nineteenth century. It had no regular and active links with Paris, and was barely joined by a bad road with the *sous-préfecture* and regional capital . . . this and others like it watched the progress of civilisation as if it were a spectacle . . . The aspect of the feudal age could be recaptured here. One could not walk without sensing at each step the ways and customs of the past, every stone spoke of it; the attitudes of the middle ages survived there as superstition.'[80] There were thousands of Guérandes in eighteenth-century Europe, though few found a pen as eloquent as that of Balzac to describe them.

Urban decay was not restricted to western and central Europe. In eastern also the local and the distant markets of the small and medium-sized towns were declining. At least from the sixteenth century the peasantry was increasingly subject to the 'new feudalism' (see p. 43), and the product of their labour was sold more and more by their lords direct to merchants, without passing through the local market. At the same time their own spending power was reduced. In Poland and the Czech lands[81] the business of the small towns decayed, though the large – notably Breslau, Toruń, Warsaw, Kraków and Prague – maintained their commercial ascendancy, because they were the business centres for the magnates and the merchants, as the small town had formerly been for the peasant.

Medium-sized and large towns had a more complex social structure and fulfilled more varied functions than the small. Such urban growth as there was before the industrial age was almost wholly in the larger towns. They concentrated more and more the wealth and the talents of the population; they were the seats of governmental authority and the centres of education and culture. Every town of medium or large size served the immediate needs of its local region; it was its market centre, but to this it added other functions. Its crafts extended far beyond the needs of the local peasantry. It contained jewellers, goldsmiths and silversmiths. There were tailors and wig-makers and others who satisfied fashionable needs rarely met within the small towns.

To some extent these necessities arose from the presence in the larger towns of classes of people who were not to be found elsewhere: members of the nobility and of the ecclesiastical hierarchy, together with a large body of lawyers and officials, known collectively in France as the *noblesse de robe*. The town of Vannes, in Brittany, with a population of about 14,000 in 1700, had 486 members of the clergy and of the religious orders.[82] Dijon, a town of much greater size – about 25,000 – had perhaps as many as 1500, inclusive of the inmates of religious foundations.[83] In Bayeux, a smaller town than Vannes, the clerical population amounted to 5–600, about 6 per cent of the total.[84] At Louvain, the religious together with the members of the university made up almost 17 per cent of the population at the end of the sixteenth century.[85] In all Roman Catholic countries the episcopal cities tended to have a large clerical population. In Germany, where many of the larger cities had become Protestant, it was very much smaller, and was least in the Netherlands and Scandinavia.

In most of the larger towns a group of the landed nobility preferred life in the city to virtual isolation on their estates. Not all were rich, and many had incomes smaller than those of the wealthier merchants. At Bayeux most 'lived simply in a house of moderate size, simply furnished, with two or three servants'.[86] The situation must have been broadly similar in other towns. At Vannes the *noblesse* and their retinues amounted almost to 500, but there was a tendency for the landed wealth of the nobility to pass gradually into the hands of the merchant class which alone seemed able to increase its possessions.[87] The *noblesse* stood apart from other classes within the city. Their younger sons may have entered the higher levels of the ecclesiastical hierarchy, but they disdained commerce and the crafts and lived as a general rule on the income from their often poorly administered estates. Yet their daughters were sought by – and often given in marriage to – the wealthier burgesses and members of the *noblesse de robe*. It was to these latter that they turned when in financial difficulties, which was not infrequently, and to them they pledged, and sometimes lost, their lands.

In most medium-sized and all the larger towns there was a large body of professional people: doctors, lawyers, officials of the courts of law and of the government's local administration. In France they outnumbered the churchmen and the nobility together. There was a complicated hierarchy of officials, serving overlapping administrations; 'un luxe parasite d'inutiles fonctionnaires', Roupnel called it.[88] In Dijon there were more than 1200 such officials, ranging from the judges of the *parlement* to the junior servants of the courts. With their families and dependants, some 6–8000 persons lived from public office in a city whose total population could not have much exceeded 25,000. In short, less than half the adult male population of Dijon at the end of the seventeenth century can be considered productive.

This may have been an extreme case, but in every seat of a *généralité* or of an *élection* there were courts, lawyers and officials, collectors of the *taille* and administrators of the *gabelle*. The peasant and craftsman had an immense body of officialdom, ecclesiastical as well as lay, to support by their labours, larger indeed than that borne on the shoulders of the medieval peasant.

All cities and towns had a wide range of crafts, but very few had any dominant specialisation or any product which they exported for sale in distant markets. In Dijon, from 1600 to 1800 'masters' were grouped into no less than 130 different crafts or occupations, of which only the tanners, *vinaigriers* and jewellers seem to have been particularly numerous or important. 'There was none', wrote Roupnel, 'that was not strictly proportionate in size to local needs . . . none that would be of interest to a more general and more distant market.'[89] Dijon was, according to the categories adopted above, a large town, yet its industrial structure was little different from that of the smallest; its market was essentially local. Bayeux, a town which in the later eighteenth century bordered on the large, 'was composed of shopkeepers and petty tradesmen and those involved in the administration of the town and surrounding area'.[90]

The German town of Fulda, comparable in size with Bordeaux, had in the late eighteenth century some 270 gild members. Of these the butchers, bakers and shoemakers, whose clientele can only have been local, made up 120. In the largest German towns the food industries and the crafts which served local needs were always amongst the most numerous. The only craft whose products could have been distributed widely was the weaving of linen, fustian and woollens, and even these were probably sold mostly to a local public.

Most of the larger towns of the pre-industrial period thus appear to have owed their size more to the services which they performed than to the number of their artisans, the range of their industrial production, or the volume of trade which they carried on. Many of the citizens lived on the rent from rural property, on the taxes and tithes on rural production, or by exploiting one another. 'The town was in fact parasitic on the countryside.'

Examples have been drawn mainly from France, but the situation differed only in degree in the towns of the southern Low Countries, of Germany, Spain and Italy. At Valladolid, even after the Spanish court had abandoned the city for Madrid, primary and secondary activities supported only 19 per cent of the *vecinos*, or households.[91]

A consequence of the distorted occupational structure of the towns, especially of the larger, was the immense number of poor and destitute. They were attracted to the city, but few occupations were open to them beyond those of servant and retainer. A thousand of the population of Vannes was classed as *mendiants* and *indigents*.[92] According to Hufton, over half of those rated in the tax lists of Bayeux 'hovered dangerously on the fringe of destitution'.[93] This situation was common to much of Europe throughout the pre-industrial period. Rome was filled with beggars, and Montaigne declared that scarcely anyone lived by the work of his hands.[94] English travellers on the Grand Tour were continuously struck by the poverty of continental peoples and by the fact that so many were reduced to beggary. Joseph Addison found the population of the

Papal States 'wretchedly poor and idle'.[95] Bishop Burnet, in travelling from Paris to Lyons, discovered 'all the marks of an extreme Poverty . . . in the buildings, the Cloaths, and almost in the Looks of the Inhabitants'.[96] Such observations were made by every traveller who troubled to record his impressions. Somewhat more objectively, tax records show how large was the proportion of the population which a grasping city government was obliged to treat as exempt from taxation. The problem basically was the continued migration to the towns of a surplus population from rural areas, without any commensurate development of unskilled and semi-skilled employment. The situation was exacerbated by war and harvest failure, which drove even greater numbers to the supposed security of the towns, and was not moderated until the development of factory industry in the late eighteenth and nineteenth centuries.

Urban food supply

Only the smallest towns could hope, within the limitations imposed by weather and harvest, to have an assured food supply from their local region. All others had to draw upon the resources of a very much larger area, and were thus always at the mercy, not only of the elements, but also of the manipulations of corn-dealers, of warfare and of the difficulties of transport. Access to a source of food was a precondition of the growth of a large city. Seville derived much of its supply from the plain of Andalusia; Valladolid and other cities of Old Castile lay in the grain-growing plains of the northern Meseta. Coastal cities of southern Europe derived their bread grains, generally by sea, from areas which traditionally had a surplus: southern Italy, Sicily and North Africa.[97]

Urban food supply was dependent in part on the degree of control which the city could exercise over the surrounding countryside. This might amount to an absolute control, such as was exercised by the Italian city-republics over their *contadi* and by the Swiss urban cantons and the free imperial cities of Germany over their surrounding territories. In such instances the food supply was in large measure assured. There were, however, exceptions. Geneva was one of the worst placed, lying as it did within a kilometre or two of both the French and Savoyard boundaries, across which it was difficult or impossible to move food supplies. Its lack of hinterland, in the opinion of Bergier, 'posed the most severe problem in the economic history of the city',[98] Augsburg, free imperial city though it was, also had almost no territory of its own.[99] On the other hand, the lack of political control over the surrounding territory mattered little in a centralised state such as France, though even here the competition between neighbouring cities could occasionally become fierce and bitter. Those Flanders towns which never made good their claims to control the surrounding rural areas engaged in a cut-throat competition for the limited supply of grain, resorting at times to a species of piracy as they strove to get possession of bargeloads of grain making their way along the waterways of the Low Countries.[100] Another highly urbanised area was Venezia. Venice was itself one of the largest cities in southern Europe, and its immediate hinterland included Padua, Verona, Vicenza and other large cities. The local region, fertile though it was, was quite inadequate to supply the urban demand. There was in the sixteenth century a heavy investment in land reclamation, but all the larger cities, especially Venice itself, were heavily dependent on imports.[101]

The continued growth of large cities in north-western Europe during the sixteenth century necessitated an ever broadening search for a regular source of food.[102] The cities of the Low Countries as well as port cities, such as Hamburg and Lübeck, became overwhelmingly dependent on grain imports from the Baltic, and before the end of the century the largest cities in the western Mediterranean, notably Venice, were buying rye from Danzig. Paris, as the largest city in western Europe, presented the acutest problem and its food supply had been a major preoccupation of French kings. The problem grew in magnitude with its expansion. Writers continually stress the immense food consumption of the city.[103] The memoir on the *généralité* of Paris, prepared in the 1690s by the intendant, gives particular attention to the ability of the region to supply food and of the rivers to transport it,[104] and a separate report on the Paris markets listed both the quantities of goods handled and the sources from which they principally came.[105] The grain supply became critical in the seventeenth century, with the continued growth of the city. Merchants buying for Paris dominated the small town markets of the Paris basin, where their activities forced up prices for the local people.[106]

In many cities a local official was charged with responsibility for maintaining the supply of essential foodstuffs. He usually bought up grain when it was cheap after the harvest and released it during the year to local retailers. Nevertheless, crises were not infrequent in the larger towns in the seventeenth and eighteenth centuries. At Lyons, for example, 40,000 people were reported by the intendant to have died of starvation during the crisis of 1693–4. This was unquestionably an exaggeration, but at Beauvais the population whose wealth was assessed fell from 3019 in 1691 to 2252 five years later.[107] Even Danzig, the foremost grain-exporting port of the age, suffered from local scarcity, largely because merchants engaged in the export trade had engrossed most of the corn, and a department of the city government (Urząd Zapasów) was constituted in the sixteenth century to handle the city's

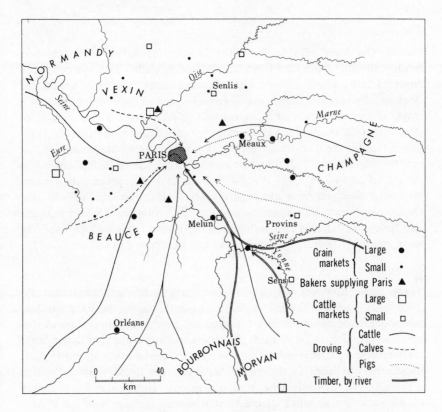

Fig. 3.7 Food supply of Paris, late seventeenth century

food supply.[108]

Urban food supply was greatly influenced by tenurial conditions in the surrounding countryside. In France especially the local patricians and *nobless de robe* were busy buying up parcels of rural land. If they managed these lands themselves or leased them *en metayage*, they could contribute very materially to the urban food supply (see p. 61). If they leased them to 'farmers' or – an increasing practice in the eighteenth century – grassed them down and reared animals, they not only contributed to the numbers of the unemployed but also reduced the urban food supply. In the later eighteenth century there were bread riots in many French cities, notably the industrial centres along the lower Seine valley. In central and eastern Europe the problem was less because the towns were themselves smaller, but here the urban supply of bread grains was frequently at the mercy of the landed aristocracy which controlled the marketable grain surplus[109] (see p. 44).

The industrial city

During the later Middle Ages the centres of industrial production tended to shift from the town to the countryside. The reasons were complex and varied, and amongst them were the rigidity of urban gild systems, the relative cheapness of rural labour, and the emergence of a class of entrepreneurs able to organise and market the products of domestic craftsmen. Manufacturing remained a predominantly rural pursuit until the factory system returned it to the town during the nineteenth century. This does not mean that the pre-industrial town was devoid of craftsmen; only that, with significant exceptions, their numbers were few and their clientele entirely within the local urban area. One is continually being surprised at the small number of weavers, dyers and fullers, of tanners and metalworkers in most cities and towns. They were regularly fewer in number than the butchers and bakers.

Urban crafts

There were, however, important exceptions to this generalisation. At Lyons, for example, the silk industry was dominant in the sixteenth and seventeenth centuries, and continued to prosper during a period of acute depression. About 1690 the intendant reported that some 8000 craftsmen were employed within the city, most of them working in their own homes in front of the broad 'weavers' windows', many of which survive in the Croix-Rousse area of the city. But demand was highly elastic, and the number of craftsmen is said to have fallen within a decade to 2500.[110] There is no doubt, however, that Lyons was one of the few cities in the pre-industrial age that had a basic industry which supported directly a large part – perhaps a third – of the total population.

Liège was also primarily an industrial city. Its basic industry was metalworking with glass and textiles of lesser importance.[111] This was due in part to the fact that gild organisation within the city was weak and its jurisdiction ineffective. Licences to work within the city could be easily obtained by non-gild-members, and gild regulations were habitually ignored.[112]

Leyden, particularly after its siege by the Spanish forces in 1573, grew to be 'the foremost textile centre in Europe'.[113] About 1660 its 35,000 inhabitants were overwhelmingly dependent on the manufacture of woollen textiles. Several of the older textile centres of Flanders tried to revive their fortunes by introducing the manufacture of the 'new draperies'. In general, however, the traditions of the older industries, strongly supported by the gilds, were too strong, and in very few did the newer branches of weaving establish themselves.[114] The clothing industry of the southern Low Countries spread into northern France as an urban craft, particularly where the local gilds were weak and the urban authorities lax in their supervision. The manufacture of says was thus established in Amiens late in the fifteenth century by a group of refugees from the north. In the sixteenth, two-thirds of the population is said to have lived from the cloth industry.[115] The industry grew in importance; 'no town in France', it was said, 'had gathered within its walls as many weavers'.[116] Beauvais and Reims were second only to Amiens as weaving towns.[117]

In Spain craft industries, never of great consequence, tended nonetheless to be concentrated in the towns. Almost three-quarters of the population of Segovia was supported by manufactures in the late sixteenth century,[118] and the town of Medina del Campo was also primarily a craft town, when it was not preoccupied with its wool fairs.[119] In Italy, also, craft industries tended to be concentrated in the towns, because the latter exercised a firm control over their *contadi* and could, whenever they wished, check any rural development which conflicted with their interests. At Venice there was a short period of quite intensive industrial activity in the later sixteenth and seventeenth centuries, based on the production of woollen cloth.[120] Genoa pursued a number of export industries, prominent amongst them the weaving of textiles. The Genoese silk industry remained pre-eminent until the seventeenth century, when it was overtaken by that of Lyons.[121] At Florence also there was a large urban cloth industry, and it is claimed that some 20,000 out of a total population of 70,000 were in one way or another supported by it.[122]

In western and north-western Europe towns could exercise no effective control more than a mile or two beyond their walls, and thus had no direct means of restraining rural industries. The urban textile industries of the towns of the Low Countries suffered severely from rural competition, and in some instances were virtually extinguished. The result, however, was eventually to create a new kind of industrial town. Weaving and cloth-finishing tended to become full-time occupations, rather than adjuncts to agriculture, and the villages in which they were carried on grew into small, sprawling settlements, without the constraints imposed by urban government or city walls.

The earliest of these industrial villages emerged in west Flanders. Hondschoote, Bergues-Saint-Winnoc, Armentières, Tourcoing, Neuve-Eglise, Bailleul became during the later Middle Ages and sixteenth century centres for the manufacture of the 'new draperies'.[123] Some suffered in the wars of the sixteenth century; others from changes in taste and popular demand, but the industry and the towns in which it was carried on survived the crises and expanded again in the later seventeenth and in the eighteenth centuries. Such an industry was 'domestic' and scattered. It was controlled from a centrally placed town from which merchant capitalists supplied and controlled the domestic workers of the surrounding small towns and villages. Such a town was Lille, which had grown rapidly in the sixteenth century and in 1698 had a population of some 55,000.[124] The oldest amongst its 6000 houses were of wood and plaster, but the newer buildings, reflecting the growing wealth of its 4000 merchant capitalists, were in 'white stone and brick, whose red colouring, mingled with the white of masonry, produced a pleasing sight'.[125]

Another region in which villages had grown into industrial towns was the northern fringe of that belt of hills and plateaux which extends from the Ardennes in northern France to the Harz mountains in Germany. Dinant, once famous for its copper- and brassworking – 'dinanderie' it was called – declined in importance after it had been ravaged by the armies of Charles of Burgundy. By the early seventeenth century its metal industry had been reduced to a single bell foundry. Verviers, in the parallel valley of the Vesdre, was only a village with fulling mills along its river at the beginning of the sixteenth century. Weavers then moved into the valley, some of them refugees from the destroyed weaving centres of west Flanders.[126] Verviers grew rapidly. No attempt was ever made to organise a system of gilds, and labour remained mobile and relatively cheap. Instead, the town was controlled by an oligarchy of rich merchant capitalists, who would certainly have done nothing to encourage any organisation of craftsmen. In 1674 the town was enclosed by a defensive wall on the orders of the Bishop of Liège, but already its built-up area extended for several kilometres along the Vesdre. By the end of the eighteenth century its population had reached 10,000.[127] Beyond the hills which enclosed Verviers other weaving towns grew up in the neighbouring valleys: Eupen, Monschau, Burtscheid, Vaals. To the east of the Rhine, similar small industrial towns were growing in the valleys of the Sauerland. Prominent amongst them were Elberfeld and Barmen, stretched out along the valley of the Wupper, a tributary of the Rhine, and, like Verviers, without gilds or other institutions to restrict the exploitation of weavers by the merchant capitalists.

Many of the small industrial towns of the Eifel and Sauerland were based on the metal industries. The smelting of iron and refining of bar-iron were of necessity rural occupations, but the small towns, such as Altena, Iserlohn and Siegen, carried on certain fabricating industries, such as making screws and wire goods, and served, above all, as marketing centres for the products of rural craftsmen.

Rural crafts were giving rise to urban industry also along the lower

Seine valley. Rouen had been during the later Middle Ages the chief industrial centre of Normandy, but in the course of the sixteenth and seventeenth centuries a narrow gild structure had prevented its adaptation to changing market demands. Protestant craftsmen established the manufacture of Holland-style woollens at Elbeuf, 25 kilometres upstream from Rouen. The textile industry of Rouen declined as that of Elbeuf, Darnetal, Louviers and neighbouring villages grew. By the time of the revocation of the Edict of Nantes (1685), which led to the migration of many of them, there were 3000 textile workers in Elbeuf. A century later this had increased to 5000, with twice as many more living in the rural areas and supplying the weavers with thread.[128] The textile industry was distributed through the small towns of 'Upper' Normandy: Bolbec, Montivilliers, Lillebonne, Yvetot – the last described as nothing more than 'a main street, a half a league in length, with low, wood-built and slated houses'.[129]

4
Agriculture from the sixteenth to the nineteenth centuries

The sixteenth century was a period of expansion in agriculture, when fresh land was brought under the plough to support a growing population. The following century was marked by stagnation and even contraction, while the eighteenth witnessed renewed growth which continued into the nineteenth. This periodisation is far from precise; it is a rough framework within which to fit the fluctuations in population and in agriculture and production. The growth, contraction and renewed growth in agriculture was in part a response to changes in population, but it can be argued no less that fluctuations in agricultural production were an important factor in demographic change.

The nineteenth-century view that the cause of the trade cycle lay in the weather and cyclical changes in crop yields has long since been discarded as too simplistic. It is, however, less easy to dismiss the weather as a significant factor during the pre-industrial period. People then lived close to the margin of subsistence, and as late as 1820 William Jacob could write of Westphalia that 'the surplus of the production of the soil in the best years so little exceeds the consumption, that there is no store on hand to meet such years of scarcity as will sometimes occur'.[1] In earlier centuries it could have been said that the yield in the best years barely sufficed for current needs. Famine crises at irregular but not infrequent intervals cut back on the population, and it is not difficult to relate the demographic history of these centuries to the sequence of bad harvests which occurred at intervals during the seventeenth and in the early years of the eighteenth century (see pp. 6–7).

There was little or no measurable change in climate during the three centuries covered in this book. But climate is only an expression of the probability that a certain type of weather will occur, and fluctuations in weather were sometimes extreme. The later Middle Ages appear to have been characterised by increased storminess, the later sixteenth century by more severe winters. It is difficult to discern a pattern in the climatic fluctuations of the sixteenth and succeeding centuries, and impossible to generalise. Severe winter cold or summer drought in one area might be accompanied by very different conditions at no great distance. Crop failures never occurred over the whole continent at the same time, though before the railway age there were rarely adequate transport facilities to bring relief to areas affected. Nevertheless, certain years stand out as particularly disastrous over large areas of western Europe, leading to a rise in grain prices and widespread starvation. Such were the periods 1587–98, 1649–53, 1662–3, 1693–4, 1709–13, 1724–5, 1769–70, 1789–90 and 1816. It would appear that crises were less severe, less widespread and less prolonged after *le grand hiver* of 1708–9. Nevertheless, even minor fluctuations could affect adversely the simple style of husbandry practised in pre-industrial Europe.[2]

This is demonstrated by a weather diary, kept on an estate near Pithiviers, in the Gâtinais of Poitou, for the years 1755 and 1756.[3] It contains a month-by-month description of the weather and of its influence on crops. These years do not appear to have departed much from the average and the vintage was only a day or two late in 1755 and a little early in 1756 – evidence that the summer weather was in no way unusual. The winter of 1754–5 was cold and rather wet, which hindered spring ploughing. A very warm April was followed by a sharp frost in early May, which severely damaged the grape vines on the lower ground. The summer was too dry, though the drought was interrupted by heavy storms. A wet period in August ruined much of the wheat crop, but spared the oats which were harvested later because sowing had been delayed by the late winter. A cool, dry autumn favoured plough-ing, and winter corn was sown by 10 October. The hay harvest was poor; vegetables and roots did well, but a 'prodigious quantity' of all sorts of insects 'did immense damage to most fruits'.

The following winter was mild and very rainy. 'The earth was so wet, that no ground could be tilled, nor could any carriage go to the fields'. The wheat 'came up very thin', and the spring grains were sown late. Spring and summer were cooler than usual and very wet, and 'weeds . . . got the better of the wheat', though insect pests had been killed off by the cold weather. The oats harvest was good, but so many weeds were harvested with the wheat that, since they were not given time to dry out, 'corn piled up in the barns heated to that degree that part of the grain was injured' and provided a poor seed for the next year. The roads were so wet that summer that wood could not be carried from the forest and this essential task had to be postponed until late in the autumn. Grass grew well, but the weather was too wet for haymaking. Autumn was cool and dry, thus helping the ploughing. The winter grains were sown in good time and the lord of Denainvilliers must have asked himself what combination of ills would disturb his routine and threaten his harvest during the coming year. Unfortunately the diary breaks off and we do not know.

The Denainvilliers diary and other comparable records suggest that the farmer suffered more from excessive rain than from drought or severe winter cold. Rain hindered haymaking and harvest, but, above all, it kept the husbandman off the land and made it impossible for him to plough and sow. One of his most serious difficulties on all except the lightest soils was drainage, but it was not until well into the nineteenth century that adequate means of soil drainage began to be introduced into continental Europe.

There were evidently severe losses even in relatively good years like 1755 and 1756. Bad crops were disastrous. The summer of 1788 was one of unparalleled drought. Harvests failed in much of north-western Europe, and in Spain there was a famine crisis.[4] The following winter was extremely cold, 'the coldest of the century', according to an English observer. The harvest of 1789 was again a poor one, and grain prices rose. There were food riots in parts of France, thus helping to create the atmosphere of revolt which precipitated the Revolution. During the next twenty years summers tended to be wet, and there were a number of severe winters, notably those of 1794–5 and 1813–14. Harvests were poor in France in 1802 and 1803; in 1811 they were ruined in many areas by severe summer storms.[5] The end of the Napoleonic Wars was followed in 1816 and 1817 by wet summers and poor harvests.[6] Thereafter severely abnormal weather became less frequent. Poor harvests alternated with good, but there were no further *crises de subsistance*, except in 1846–7, when widespread crop failure in western Europe followed a severe winter.[7] Departures from the average may have been smaller during the middle years of the century, but the chief reasons for the general absence of famine crises were improved means of transport, the ever widening market for corn, and governments' willingness and ability to bring relief.

Weather, however, was not the only factor influencing the quality and amount of agricultural production. The husbandman was restricted by the conditions of his tenure, by the custom of his village community, by the scarcity of land available to him, and, above all, by lack of capital. The institutional framework within which he worked was of human origin, and could be modified by human action. But interlocking vested interests made such change difficult to achieve, and even the political and social revolution of the end of the eighteenth century, though it brought about a fundamental change in the ownership of land in France, made little difference anywhere to the practice of agriculture.

Nevertheless agricultural production did increase between the sixteenth and the nineteenth century, but this was achieved without any profound changes in the practice of farming. Such as occurred were small-scale and local before the nineteenth century: marginal improvements in the tools and equipment of farming; the diffusion of better types of plough; an increased attention to manure and a wider use of lime; the introduction of a few new crops and, here and there, a modification of the pattern of crop-rotation and the elimination of fallow. Many areas of Europe were quite unaffected by such changes, and the practice of agriculture in 1800 was not recognisably different from that of three centuries earlier. The overall growth, however, was sufficient to support a population which had more than doubled and an industrial population which had greatly increased in the period.

Land tenure

At the beginning of the sixteenth century most of the land belonged either to the lay aristocracy or to the church. In some areas, notably Scandinavia, there were extensive royal estates, but these derived in part from the confiscation of monastic land, and around the larger cities the bourgeois class had acquired extensive possessions. Comparatively little land was cultivated directly by those who owned it, except in eastern Europe, and most was leased in small peasant tenancies or was 'farmed' in larger units by the more prosperous peasants.[8] In Scandinavia and the Protestant states of Germany and cantons of Switzerland, the lands of the church largely passed into lay hands in the course of the Reformation. Elsewhere they generally remained in ecclesiastical hands. In France church lands are said to have made up 10 per cent of the whole and were locally far more extensive. In the Beauvaisis they made up more than 18 per cent,[9] and over a quarter in Picardy and the Laonnais.[10] Around Toulouse, on the other hand, they amounted only to 6.5 per cent.[11] In the principality of Liège, ruled by its prince–bishop, the lands of the church made up about 17 per cent.[12] In some of the Catholic states of Germany a very large proportion of the land was held by the church. Ecclesiastical land made up 56 per cent of the area of Bavaria, noted for the number and the rich endowments of its monasteries. In Italy, the monasteries had lost much of their landed wealth during the Middle Ages, but here no less than 15 per cent of the country continued to be ruled (as distinct from owned) by the papacy, whose actual possessions were relatively small. In Spain vast areas, especially in the southern Meseta, had passed into the possession of the religious orders in the course of the Reconquista.[13]

It is important to know how much land was held by the church, because ecclesiastical landlords were in general amongst the least progressive. Much of the remainder of the land was held by lay lords. It had formerly been organised in manors, but by the sixteenth century the system had broken down over much of Europe, and the labour obligations of the peasants had, as a general rule, been largely commuted, and the demesne itself leased or farmed. Much of the land thus released from direct manorial control passed into the hands of the peasants in some form of perpetual tenancy. They owed *cens* or conventionary rent, and usually other relics of their former feudal dependence, but as a general rule inflation had reduced the burdensome nature of their obligations, and the peasant in much of western and central Europe had relative security of tenure at a fairly small price, even if his tenement was on average uneconomically small.[14]

Estates varied greatly in size. The poorest members of the nobility held little more than a good-sized peasant holding with a mere handful of dependants. At the opposite extreme was the small number of really large estates. That of the Saulx-Tavanes in Burgundy consisted in the eighteenth century of some 3280 hectares – 2225 of it in woodland – all under the direct control of the lord, together with a further 8100 hectares over which the Saulx-Tavanes exercised seigneurial rights, receiving quitrents and mill, oven and other dues. The lands were mainly in three groups, spread over twenty parishes, but were within these areas highly fragmented, consisting in some places of small parcels interspersed with those of the peasants.

Most estates were, however, very much smaller than that of Saulx-Tavanes. The average size of a 'grande domaine' near Montpellier was only 66 hectares in 1547, and 84 in 1677.[15] Here too their number and size were tending to increase, and this could only have been at the expense of peasant holdings. It does not follow that the latter had been suppressed; it is possible that the decline in population had left some of them unoccupied. Everywhere the size of estates ranged downwards until they were indistinguishable from the farms of the well-to-do peasants, and their owners, like the 'barefoot *szlachta*' in Poland, distinguishable only by their status from the peasantry whom they despised.

The situation was, however, changing during the three centuries covered by this book. There was always a market for land. Members of the aristocracy on occasion borrowed heavily on the security of their estates, or sold parcels of land to meet current obligations. Nowhere did this happen on a larger scale than in France, where the attractions and extravagances of the royal court were a constant drain on landed revenue. Whole estates were thus dissipated, but always a new aristocracy was being fed into the system from below. Urban merchants and manufacturers, lawyers and other functionaries bought rural land or foreclosed on the mortgages they had given. By the seventeenth century, land in the close proximity of Dijon had, with the exception of that which continued to belong to the church, been snapped up by prosperous members of the bourgeoisie.[16] It was the wisest form of investment, and it yielded a further dividend to the class-conscious citizen; it brought him closer to the noble status to which he aspired. The land which he acquired came from the communal possessions of the village, from impoverished nobles, and from a peasantry ruined by warfare. It was held by a variety of titles, ranging from allodial tenure to perpetual tenancy, by payment of a *cens* and the discharge of other obligations to a lord. It commonly consisted of small, fragmented parcels, many of which were in turn leased to the local peasantry.

The area held by the bourgeoisie tended to increase until the Revolution of 1789, and in the later eighteenth century may have amounted to 30 per cent of the land of France.[17] The greater prosperity of the burgesses of the Netherlands allowed them, especially during the first half of the seventeenth century, to buy up much of the real estate around their cities and to drain and reclaim part of it. In Italy the *contadi* of the cities had largely passed into the possession of the urban patricians, and there were few merchant families which did not end as members of the landed aristocracy. Indeed, the urge to invest in land intensified in the sixteenth and later centuries as a hedge against the weakening position of Italian trade.[18] Only in Spain was there little attempt by the urban patricians to move into the ranks of the landed classes.

In western, central and southern Europe, with the exception of Spain, the tendency was for estates to be broken up into tenancies and for labour services to be commuted for a money payment. In east-central and eastern Europe an opposite trend manifested itself. Peasants who had owed only minor services found their obligations increased; independent tenancies were absorbed into estates and cultivated as part of the demesne, and a more or less free peasantry was reduced to serfdom and used to cultivate the enlarged demesnes of their lords. This development, known as the 'second serfdom' (*zweiter Leibeigenschaft*) has in recent years received a great deal of publicity from scholars in the east European countries, because – so it would appear – it provided a classic example of the application of marxist theory. One of the earliest significant publications on this subject, that of Jerome Blum,[19] placed the beginnings of this depression of a free peasantry in the early Middle Ages. It was interrupted by the immigration of free Germanic settlers, but revived again in the later Middle Ages. Blum related these developments primarily to political and social conditions, in particular to the weakness of the central governments which permitted the nobles to concentrate greater power in their own hands. Since the publication of Blum's article, a spate of studies from the Communist countries – in particular, those of Marian Małowist – have linked the development of the second serfdom with the demands of the west European markets for bread grains. Various refinements on this view have been elaborated: the low yield-ratios in eastern Europe and the need to cultivate large areas in order to secure an exportable surplus; the movement of prices against the corn-grower, which necessitated the export of larger quantities to cover the import of the same volume of western luxury goods; the demand for corn to feed the armies fighting the Turks. What all these explanations have in common is their insistence on the profit motive for the creation and assertion of seigneurial rights over the peasantry.

It is nonetheless clear that the landed aristocracy could never have had their way if there had been a strong central government, such as existed in some western countries. By the end of the fifteenth century, in each of the east European countries, wrote Blum, 'the noble had become the government so far as the peasants who lived on his manor were concerned'. It remained to give legislative expression to the claims newly advanced by the nobles. In Poland, Bohemia and Hungary, the labour dues owed by the peasants were increased in the course of the sixteenth century and restrictions were placed on the movement of the latter.[20] Every pretext was used for appropriating peasant land and adding it to the demesne, and the suppression of independent holdings (*Bauernlegung*) has since been seen as the characteristic sin of the landowners. In the absence of adequate statistics there has probably been a tendency to exaggerate the severity and extent of the second serfdom. In Poland it was clearly related to the market. It was of minor importance in the mountainous regions of southern Poland and in areas of White Russia remote from the rivers which flowed to the Baltic. It was pursued most vigorously in the hinterlands of the Baltic ports. It was of much smaller importance in Bohemia and in Hungary, which lacked a means of water transport to western markets.

Even in areas which had the advantages of cheap and easy movement to European markets, great estates never covered all the land, and some free and independent peasants were able to survive until the emancipation movements of the eighteenth and nineteenth century. Żytkowicz has studied the villages belonging to the Polish crown in the Kraków principality, and has calculated the percentage of free and independent peasants (table 4.1).[21] It is noteworthy that the proportion of free peasants was always greater in the hilly and mountainous region to the south of Kraków, but that even along the fertile Vistula valley, they continued to make up at least a third of the peasantry. They formed an even larger proportion on the lands of the Bishop and cathedral chapter of Chełm, lying on the rich grain land of Ruthenia, between Lublin and L'vov.

The demesne farm (*folwark*) was not usually of great size; on average

Table 4.1 *Percentage of free peasants*

	1564	Early 17th century	1660
North Kraków	68.6	55.8	40.9
Central Kraków	67.5	50.3	33.0
South Kraków	74.7	65.9	56.6

Table 4.2 *Percentage of land held by peasants*

	Lands of the Bishop of Chełm	Lands of the chapter of Chełm
1605	85.7	–
1614	–	79.6
1646	–	58.5
1651	70.4	–
1666	69.3	–
1676	–	50.4

it did not exceed some six *włoki* or a hundred hectares,[22] and many were a great deal smaller. The great landowners, of course, held many such *folwarki*, but the majority of the *szlachta* cannot have held more than one or two. The average *folwark* would have produced from 4.0 to 10.5 tonnes of grain, about half of which would have been spring grains for which there was no export market.[23] The marketable surplus from any single *folwark* must thus have been quite small, and it is doubtful whether, without some contribution from the free peasantry, the sales of the estates could have made up the quantities passing through the Baltic ports, small as these in fact were.

The revival of demesne farming, with labour supplied by unfree serfs, was most marked in the lands of the Polish crown; less so in Bohemia and Hungary. It was also apparent in Germany to the east of the Elbe, but attempts thus to reverse the course of history were rare and in general unsuccessful in western Europe. Abel has measured the creation of estates in the Mittelmark of Brandenburg.[25] At the end of the Middle Ages 1265 Hufen (about 8000 ha) were in estates. By the end of the eighteenth century this had increased to 4820. More than a quarter of the latter derived from lands that had been abandoned (*Wüstungen*) during the later Middle Ages, and almost a fifth came from land laid waste during the Thirty Years' War. Less than a quarter came from the suppression of peasant tenancies (*Bauernlegung*), and only about 2 per cent from the reclamation of waste land. In Mecklenburg there was also a steady decline in the number of peasant holdings (*Bauernwirtschaften*) as land was absorbed into estates and the peasants themselves reduced to servile status:[26]

1729	6235
1755	4900–5000
1776	2631
1794	2440

The estates of eastern Germany varied greatly in size, and, as a general rule, embraced large areas of forest and of other land of little agricultural value. As a general rule they each contained over 100 hectares of cropland, and some had 400 or more.[27] The latter was worked by the part-time labour of dependent peasants. Bread grains formed the predominant crop, but the *Gutsbetrieb*, unlike the Polish *folwark*, also produced flax, hops, vegetables and fodder crops, some of which were sold for export. Occasionally a *Gutsbetrieb* was broken up into small units which were leased to 'farmers', and the *Gutsherrschaft* tended to merge into a *Grundherrschaft*, or lordship over territory, that confusing association of rights, some of them of little pecuniary value.

Estates (*Gutsbetriebe*) covered a relatively large proportion of the agricultural land to the east of the Elbe: over 50 per cent in Mecklenburg and parts of East Prussia, and over a third in most of eastern Germany. In western Germany, on the other hand, it is doubtful whether such estates embraced more than 5 per cent of the agricultural land.

The peasantry

No less than 75 to 80 per cent of the population of Europe belonged to the peasant class. This was not, however, a homogeneous group, and it displayed a distinct social stratification. The gulf between the rich peasant and the poor was almost as great as that which separated the peasantry itself from the gentry. Serfdom had largely disappeared from western Europe by the sixteenth century. Peasants were free to leave their holdings, but as long as they held them they were bound by certain contractual obligations to their lords. Some were onerous: the corvée, the duty to use the lord's mill and baking oven, and to pay heriot and merchet; but the peasant was not, except in a few backward areas, bound to the soil and the property of his lord.

East of the Rhine, burdensome medieval restrictions lasted longer, and serfdom (*Leibeigenschaft*) survived into the nineteenth century (see p. 324). But protest against it had come at an early date. The Memmingen Articles, drawn up by the revolting German peasants in

1525, declared that 'it has been the custom to hold us for bondmen . . . we assert that we are free and will be free'. Serfdom was abolished in Switzerland by the Protestant reformer Ulrich Zwingli, in 1525. Elsewhere it was eroded slowly, but had largely disappeared from western Germany by the time of the Napoleonic Wars.[28] Within the Habsburg lands the peasant was freed of most of his servile obligations by the reforms carried out by Joseph II in the 1780s, though vestigial traces of his servile status survived until 1848. In Prussia serfdom disappeared with the reforms of Stein and Hardenburg. Serfdom, which had come late to eastern Europe (see p. 324), was not finally ended in Hungary, Galicia and Bohemia until 1848. It lasted in Romania until 1864, and in Russian-held Poland until 1863–4, though its more restrictive aspects had disappeared well before these dates.

Elsewhere the status of the peasant depended mainly upon the extent of the land which he held. This might range from a substantial, well-stocked and well-equipped farm of, perhaps, 50 hectares down to a small parcel of less than a hectare in extent. Below the smallest tenant farmer was the mass of landless rural labourers. This spectrum can be divided into at least four distinct classes. At their head was the small group of well-to-do farmers, able to lease extensive holdings and to undertake to farm the local tithes or the manorial rights of their lords. They were close to the lower fringe of the gentry, a barrier which many of them were able to overstep. They formed everywhere a very small minority, and were rare outside northern France and the Paris basin. It was the absence of this imaginative tenant class which in part explains the stagnation of agriculture in much of continental Europe.[29]

Next came the *laboureur* class, which, by a combination of allodial holdings and leaseholds, had put together an adequate farm, and with their families could live on it comfortably if not well.[30] In parts of northern Germany the *laboureurs* reared large herds of cattle, which they drove to the markets of the Low Countries. They employed domestic and field labour, and their homes were well furnished by the standards of the age. Their holdings, called *métairies* in France, had from 10 to 30 hectares. In the community of Duravel in Quercy the *laboureurs* made up from a quarter to a third of the whole community, and over France as a whole they may have amounted to 20 per cent of the rural population. They were not rich and independent enough to become enterprising and progressive farmers, but they were the backbone of the western European farming community.

Below them were the *brassiers* or *manouvriers*. They possessed at most 3 or 4 hectares and many had little more than a garden, and were obliged to sell the labour of their arms – hence their name – to better-off members of the community. Such employment was usually only seasonal, and they always lived close to starvation. Many migrated for part of the year in search of work, providing temporary labour for the grain or wine harvest, in the forest or at construction sites.[31] It was probably the *brassiers* whom La Bruyère had in mind when he wrote his famous *caractère* of the peasant, comparing him to

> certain wild animals . . . dark, livid and quite tanned by the sun . . . chained, as it were, to the land, always digging and turning up and down with an unwearied stubbornness . . . At night they retire to their burrows, where they live on black bread, water and roots; they spare other men the trouble of sowing, tilling the ground, and reaping for their sustenance, and, therefore, deserve not to be in want of that bread they sow themselves.[32]

The peasant, wrote Darlington, 'fareth very hardly and feedeth most upon bread and fruit'.[33]

The *brassier* merged into the landless labourer class, whose lot was even more unenviable. These two classes formed together the rural proletariat. They were most numerous in north-western Europe, where there was least scope for the creation and extension of farm holdings; least so in eastern Europe, where land was relatively abundant. Their number was almost certainly much greater in the eighteenth than it had been in the seventeenth century. During the latter, many would have died in the course of the *crises de subsistance*; in the following century such crises were less severe, and, as Hufton has pointed out, a higher proportion of the indigent were able to survive.

All the evidence points to the small average size of the peasants' arable holding in western, central and southern Europe. The *brassiers* greatly outnumbered the *laboureurs*. The Poitevin abbey of Sainte-Croix, for example, had eighty tenures made up predominantly of small holdings (table 4.3).[34] In a valley in Savoy holdings were even smaller (table 4.4).[35] Subdivision could scarcely go farther. The alternative was,

Table 4.3

Hectares	Held by	
Under 5	31	*Brassiers* (67.5%)
5–10	23	
10–15	10	*Laboureurs* (25%)
15–20	6	
20–5	4	
25–30	3	*Fermiers* (7.5%)
30–5	2	
Over 35	1	

Table 4.4

Hectares	Holdings	Percentage
Under 1	187	52.4
1–5	124	34.7
5–10	26	7.3
10–25	14	3.9
Over 25	6	1.7
	357	100.0

of course, migration, and Savoy became an area which in the eighteenth and nineteenth centuries lost population on a greater scale than almost any other region of western Europe. Another region in which the vast majority of tenancies were far too small to support a peasant family was the Central Massif of France. Here, at Duravel,[36] three-quarters were of less than 5 hectares (table 4.5).

Table 4.5

Hectares	Number	Percentage	Area	Percentage
Under 5	316	74.9	598	27.0
5–10	64	15.0	442	19.9
10–15	16	3.9	204	9.2
15–20	13	3.1	221	10.0
20–30	5	1.2	136	6.1
30–40	3	0.7	121	5.5
Over 40	5	1.2	494	22.3
	422	100.0	2216	100.0

In the principality of Liège three-quarters of the holdings were said in the eighteenth century to have been of less than 3 hectares,[37] and in the hilly region of Hervé, to the south-east, the great majority contained less than 2 *bonniers* (about 1.75 hectares).[38] Even in Saxony, where population densities were in general much lower than in western Europe, holdings were still uneconomically small (table 4.6).[39]

Table 4.6

Hectares	Percentage
Under 5	32.1
5–20	51.8
20–100	14.3
Over 100	1.8

Table 4.7

Hectares	Number	Percentage	Percentage of area
Under 0.5	18	13.6	1.0
0.5–1	24	18.2	3.7
1–3	51	38.6	19.3
3–5	18	13.6	14.7
5–10	14	10.6	21.8
10–20	5	3.8	14.3
20–30	1	0.8	4.3
Over 30	1	0.8	20.9
	132	100.0	100.0

This minute division of farm-holdings was not restricted to western and central Europe. At Montaldeo, in the northern Apennines near Alessandria, 84 per cent of their total number were of less than 5 hectares (table 4.7).[40] Two centuries later 93.5 per cent of the peasant holdings were of less than 5 hectares. Not surprisingly, Doria wrote of the 'meseria cronica e fame' of the village community.

Holdings of less than about 5 hectares – the critical size would vary with soil and terrain – clearly could neither support nor employ a peasant family, the members of which must have turned elsewhere for a supplementary income. This would have consisted chiefly of employment on peasant holdings of larger than family size, that is of more than 15 or 20 hectares. The latter were comparatively few, and could have given employment to only a minority of the *brassiers*, who would in any case have been in competition with the landless labourers. It seems certain that in most communities throughout the greater part of Europe the amount of peasant labour available was greater than that required to cultivate the land. The alternatives were migration, seasonal or permanent, and complete destitution. The seasonal migrant hoped to return to his village with a small sum of money or a store of food. If he did not, he had at least been able to *manger hors de la région* and at no cost to his family. The towns provided shelter for large numbers of migrants from the countryside, but, until the industrial age, could employ most only as servants.

The average peasant was both over-taxed and underemployed. Even when no corvée was exacted – and this was the case in much of western Europe – *cens*, tithe, *champart* and the commuted value of other obligations were a very heavy, though uneven, burden on the peasantry. In two communities in the Brunswick region of Lower Saxony, dues and taxes amounted respectively to about 35 and over 50 per cent of the gross yield of cereals, or 20 and 32 per cent of the gross agricultural production.[41] Such obligations left little even for the better endowed amongst the peasants to live on.

Peasant holdings were not only small but also much fragmented. This was due in part to the distribution of the tenement through the fields of the community, but also to the tendency to divide each parcel between heirs in those regions where inheritance was customarily partible. It was not uncommon for a holding of only 10 hectares to be divided into forty or even fifty separate and widely scattered pieces of land.[42] Some attempt was made in the sixteenth and seventeenth centuries to consolidate scattered lands as small parcels came into the market or were mortgaged and seized for non-payment of debts. Urban investors in particular thus put together sizeable blocks of land. This process of *remembrement* continued in western Europe into the seventeenth century, bringing about, in some areas, a complete change in the aspect of the countryside. Then, with the renewed growth of population, the trend was reversed, and over much of central and western Europe holdings began again to be divided as population pressed more strongly against resources.

Most peasant land was held by payment of a conventionary rent or quitrent (*cens*), but in many areas, notably Italy and southern France, *métayage* or share-cropping was the most widespread condition of tenure. Rents had always been paid at least partly in kind, and it was not a big step to relate the payment to the size of the crop. The chief reason for the development of *métayage*, however, was that demesne and other lands were leased to penniless peasants, unable to raise the capital necessary to stock and equip their holdings. This was provided by the lord, commonly for a term of years, and the tenant undertook to pay him a fraction, usually a half, of the yield of nature. Commonly the lands acquired by the bourgeoisie were leased *en métayage*, and the *demifruits* (half the crop) which they yielded went to supply the urban markets. Ninety per cent of the landlords of the Toulouse region are said to have leased their lands 'on shares'.[43] In Burgundy much of the land was held in this way.[44] The system was general in Italy, where urban capitalists had gained possession of much of the land (see p. 42), but was much less common in northern France and the Low Countries and rare in central and northern Europe.

Métayage has been condemned as a wasteful and inequitable mode of land tenure. The landlord rarely, if ever, took any interest in the management of his lands, and the tenant paid so large a share of his crop in rent that he had little inducement, even if he had the knowledge and capital, to make improvements. Tenancies held *en métayage* were invariably small and inadequately equipped. The share-cropper was

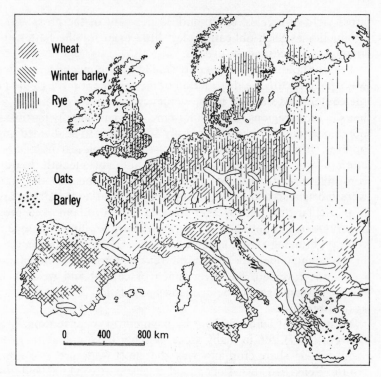

Fig. 4.1 Cereal crop associations in Europe, seventeenth and
eighteenth centuries

only 'a semiliterate dirt farmer whose half-produce was a euphemism for
bare subsistence'.[45]

The crops

No fundamental change occurred either in the crops grown or in the
cropping systems used between the Middle Ages and the late eighteenth
century. Indeed, it was not until the nineteenth century that a medieval
system of agriculture gave place generally to one which can be called
modern. Throughout these centuries agriculture was characterised by its
self-sufficiency and lack of specialisation, by its low yields and inadequate
provision of capital. It was called upon everywhere to supply first the
needs of its local region. Only a very small proportion of the total
production passed into the market; even the cornlands of the Vistula
basin could not have exported more than 2 or 3 per cent of their gross
output. Conversely, local scarcity could not easily be relieved from
distant sources. Transport and marketing institutions had not been
developed to make this possible except on a very small scale, a fact

which is made abundantly clear by the correspondence of the French
intendants during the crisis of 1693–4.

Almost every part of Europe produced cereals, however unsuited the
soil might have been for bread grains. This contributed to the low
yield-ratios, which, over most of Europe, were only marginally better on
the eve of the Industrial Revolution than they had been during the
Middle Ages. Low yields meant that vast areas had to be sown with
grain crops, and this in turn reduced the area available for livestock
farming and kept the supply of manure small. It was a vicious circle out
of which it needed both capital and initiative to break. The landlords, in
general, lacked the latter, and the peasants, both. The economic
exclusiveness of the local community greatly increased its vulnerability
to bad weather and harvest failure, which were not infrequent from the
late sixteenth century to the early eighteenth.

Lack of capital, lastly, was a condition of life in pre-industrial Europe.
The peasant lived too close to the margin of subsistence to be able to
invest in his land. Many of the aristocracy had the means to do so, but
lacked the will. On the Tavanes estates in Burgundy in the 1780s, 4.3
per cent of gross revenues is said to have been reinvested, but, 'if
repairing stone walls and roofs of farm buildings are excluded, the rate
falls to zero'. In other words, there was no net investment in agriculture,
and the land was milked by the nobility 'in order to live *noblement* on
the banks of the Seine'.[46]

The bread crops. The bread grains provided the basic food supply. Only
wheat and rye could be used in making true bread. Barley, oats,
buckwheat and maize, which were widely grown in pre-industrial
Europe, lacked gluten and could not be made to rise when baked. They
yielded at best a rather solid and indigestible oaten or barley cake, but
were more often cooked and eaten as a porridge or soup. The peasant
diet, wrote Vauban with the *élection* of Vezelay in mind,[47] was mainly
oats and barley, with a few wild fruits and garden vegetables. Only the
best off amongst them could eat bread made from rye with perhaps a
little wheat and barley added.

Wheaten bread was eaten by the burgesses of the towns, but the high
price of wheat – commonly 40 per cent above that of rye and double
that of oats – removed it from the peasants' table except in areas, such
as Picardy and Artois, particularly well suited to wheat-growing. Rye
was eaten far more often than wheat, even in countries such as France
and England, which prided themselves on their fine white bread.[48] John
Locke found that in Aquitaine the ordinary food of the poor was 'rie
bread & water. Flesh is a thing [which] seldome seasons their pots', and,
he added somewhat gratuitously, 'they make noe distinction between

flesh & fasting days'.[49] In areas where the autumn-sown grains did not yield well, or had been killed by the severity of winter, the coarser, spring-sown grains – oats and barley – had to suffice, and frequently the coarse grains were mixed with rye in bread-making. Thomas Malthus compared the diet of black rye bread which he encountered amongst the peasants of Denmark with 'the flad brod made of oatmeal' which was general in the mountains of Norway.[50] And if the coarse grains should fail, as they sometimes did, the peasant was reduced to chestnuts, where they were available, and then to grass, hay and the bark of trees. In the years 1628–30, which were marked by disastrous crop failures, the peasants near Geneva were reduced to a diet of 'bran, cabbage and acorns'.[51] During the crises of the 1690s and 1709–10 peasants were forced to eat grass, roots of wild plants, bran and even partially rotted chestnuts.

Under normal conditions towns fared better than the countryside, because they usually had the wealth to purchase the more desirable bread grains and, in many cases, to hold a store of them for times of crisis. Hémardinquer has compared the consumption of the different bread grains in town and country.[52] In Venice, in 1764, the bread was 84.5 per cent wheat and the rest maize. In other Italian cities, the average was only two-thirds wheat, and in rural areas one-third, the rest being made of rye and maize. Evidence from the Netherlands is not dissimilar. In the cities of Amsterdam and Rotterdam bread was to the extent of 70 to 75 per cent of wheat, with the rest made of rye and buckwheat. In the provincial towns the proportion of wheat was very much lower, especially in the less wealthy region of the northern Netherlands (table 4.8).

Table 4.8 *Percentage of grains in bread*

	Wheat	Rye	Buckwheat
Southern Netherlands: Towns	54.7	17.3	28.0
Countryside	53.3	30.2	16.5
Northern Netherlands: Towns	33.0	38.0	29.0
Countryside	30.0	58.0	12.0

The predominantly starch diet of both the urban and the rural population was supplemented with milk, most often taken sour, and with vegetables. Meat was mostly eaten by townspeople. Peas and beans as well as green vegetables and roots were grown in the garden plots. There were few cottages without a small garden, where, cut off from neighbours and exempt from the *Feldzwang* of communal cultivation, the peasant could grow whatever he wished. Without the produce of his garden the peasant's diet would have been totally inadequate. Meat was rarely eaten by the richer peasants, and not at all by the rest. There is good reason to suppose that the peasant's diet was better in central and eastern Europe than in western, because the pressure of population was substantially less. In Poland in the sixteenth century it consisted of rye bread and barley and millet gruel, supplemented by eggs, cheese, legumes and a small amount of meat.[53] The diet of the French peasant in the eighteenth would have been considerably less varied and nourishing.

Throughout Europe, except in the hills and mountains and on the northern frontier of cultivation, the bread grains were linked, together with fallow, in a cropping system. In most of southern Europe, as well as in parts of central and eastern, a two-field system prevailed, with an autumn-sown grain – either wheat, spelt or winter barley – alternating with fallow. Elsewhere, a three-field system was used in which autumn- and spring-sown grain and fallow succeeded one another. In Mediterranean Europe a spring-sown corn was in general precluded by the fact that its growing period would be too short before the beginning of the hot, dry summer. A two-field system survived in parts of eastern Europe where there was little pressure on the land, and also in parts of the urbanised Rhineland, where there was a heavy demand in the urban markets for wheat, and little for the coarse grains.[54]

In the areas of three-field cultivation the two sets of grains – panifiable and coarse – were in joint production. If wheat and rye were the primary object of the cultivator, oats were a by-product and their price correspondingly low. If, however, the winter grain should fail – a not improbable contingency – the fields might be resown with barley or oats in the spring, and the coarse grains would for the coming year assume the role of the principal bread grain and command a correspondingly inflated price. In any case, barley and oats tended more and more to form the bread grain of the poorer peasantry, who used their wheat and rye to sell or to discharge their obligations to their lord.

In marginal regions, however, they had little choice; wheat was not grown and rye was scarce. In mountainous areas and in hilly areas with a poor, acid soil, oats alone were grown. Malthus found only oaten cakes along his route from Oslo to Trondheim, and oats were important in such areas as the Ardennes–Eifel plateau and the valleys of the Alps, where a winter-sown crop was precluded by the severity of the frost. It is difficult to speak of a field system in such conditions. Corn was, as a general rule, grown in closes, and the peasant determined his own cropping system. Sometimes he alternated between crop and fallow; at others, two or more years under corn were followed by a period under grass.

Buckwheat, another crop of marginal soils, could not be grown where there was great risk of late spring frosts. Its cultivation spread through much of northern and north-western Europe in the fifteenth and sixteenth centuries,[55] but it became a really important article of diet only in Brittany[56] and on the light and sandy soils of the Netherlands, north Germany and Poland. Its seed was bitter to the taste and of low food value, but was used as an alternative to the coarse grains.

Other grains of local importance were spelt and dinkel. Both were variants of wheat. Spelt had been of great local importance in the southern Low Countries since the early Middle Ages.[57] It cropped well and yielded a good bread wheat, but the glumes which clung to the grain made it difficult to mill. This was probably the chief factor in preventing its spread. Dinkel was a poorer and more primitive grain. Its habitat was very largely the province of Württemberg, where it was grown to the exclusion of the standard wheats.[58]

One might expect, in a three-field system, that the volume of winter and of spring corn would approximately balance. After allowing for differences in yield-ratios this is indeed what one finds in a great many instances. An example of a very close balance between the areas under winter and spring grain is quoted by Berthold for Altenburg in Thuringia (table 4.9).[59] The value of cereal production within the

Table 4.9 *Areas under grain (in hectares)*

Wheat	4.33	Barley	9.62	Peas	4.33
Rye	13.47	Oats	8.18	Vetch	0.35
				Fallow	13.12
Winter corn	17.80	Spring corn	17.80		17.80

Prussian state about 1800 amounted, according to Krug, to the totals shown in table 4.10.[60] If allowance is made for the greater unit value of

Table 4.10 *Value of cereal production (in million Täler)*

Winter corn:	Wheat	11.2
	Rye	42.0
		53.2
Spring corn:	Oats	19.2
	Barley	14.0
		43.2

the winter grains, there was probably little difference in volume between autumn- and spring-sown corn.

Sometimes considerable discrepancies arise between the two sets of figures which can be accounted for only by departures from the rigid three-course system. In the Low Countries, for example, it became increasingly the practice to replace fallow with a crop, if only fodder or artificial grasses. Indeed, the beginning of this process is seen in the example already cited from Altenburg. It was but a short step from varying the sequence of grain crops to taking two similar crops in successive years and to adopting a sequence of crops spread over more than three years. It was not altogether conservatism or ignorance which deterred the peasant from taking such steps, but the constraints imposed by communal organisation, conditions embodied in leases, and lack of capital. Such changes interfered with communal ploughing and harvesting, and, above all, with the traditional rights to *vaine pâture*, the privilege of turning stock out to graze the cornfields after harvest. A typical French lease required that the land be ploughed and sown 'selon la coustume du pays scavoyr un tiers en bons bleds, un tiers en gros bleds, un tiers en guéret'.[61] A more intensive cultivation, furthermore, would have necessitated a larger supply of manure than the community could supply and an expenditure on seed which it could not afford.

Changes in the traditional routine of cropping were therefore made most readily in areas where these constraints were least in evidence, such as the Low Countries, and other areas where enclosed fields held in undivided ownership prevailed. Progress was least evident in the large, open-field communities of northern France and on the autocratically ruled estates of the east. In time the cropping systems would become so individual and varied that it would be difficult to produce a generalised map of them. This had not yet happened in the eighteenth century, and for the period up to the Revolutionary Wars one can map their regional variations.

The southern region of Mediterranean climate was characterised by the cultivation of wheat and barley. These were autumn-sown, and were reaped usually in early summer. Rye was almost unknown, and oats cultivated mainly in the mountains. The rotation used was, as a general rule, a simple alternation of crop and fallow, such as had been practised since classical times. The general lack of summer rain made it difficult to grow grass and fodder crops; hence there was a shortage of animals, other than sheep and goats, which could use the abundant rough, coarse grazing. In particular draught animals were few, and, partly for this reason, a light plough was used which only stirred the surface of the ground.

France was traditionally a wheat-growing country, yet it was rye which fed the majority of the people. Wheat was dominant only in the extreme south and in parts of the Paris basin and northern France.[62] Rye prevailed elsewhere with oats in hilly areas.[63] In Brittany rye and buckwheat provided the basic diet; in the Central Massif, rye and oats,[64] and in Gévaudan of south-eastern France, rye and barley.[65] The heavy clays of the Pays de Dombes, in the Saône valley, yielded five times as much rye as wheat, and on the dry Causses to the south-west, it was again rye and barley which prevailed.[66] On the borders of the Mediterranean, where the long hot summer began to preclude spring-sown grain, strange compromises between the northern and the southern systems were to be found. At Lourmarin, to the north of Aix-en-Provence, a lease prescribed a system consisting of 'one-third in wheat, one-third in rye and . . . one-third fallow'.[67] The Beauce, to the west of Paris, was wheat-growing country, as it has remained,[68] but to the north, over much of lower Normandy, rye was the prevailing bread crop. The boundary was in the main a matter of soil. The fertile plain of Alençon was a region of white, wheaten bread, set amid the rye-growing *bocage* of western Normandy.[69] The spring-sown crops were oats and barley, with a tendency for the former to be more important in the north and on acid soils, and the latter in the south and on more fertile ground. On sandy soils, especially in the Sologne and in Brittany, buckwheat tended to be the spring crop.[70]

The Rhineland and Germany were in the eighteenth century, as they had been during the earlier Middle Ages, rye and oats country. Wheat, however, acquired some importance on the better soils and near the towns, and barley in dry areas, such as the plain of Alsace.[71] In Holstein

Table 4.11 *Areas cropped (in hectares)*

Grain crops		
Wheat	825,000	7.5%
Rye	4,510,000	41.0
Barley	2,000,000	19.0
Oats	2,805,000	25.5
Spelt	440,000	4.0
Buckwheat	330,000	3.0
	10,910,000	100.0
Other crops		
Legumes	708,000	
Industrial crops	685,000	
Roots (incl. potatoes)	415,000	
	1,808,000	
Fallow and long ley	5,200,000	

and Denmark, according to Malthus, bread was made entirely of rye.[72] All the evidence of cropping suggests the predominance of rye amongst the autumn-sown grains and of oats, with barley a close second amongst those sown in spring.[73] Berthold has estimated on the basis of a very far from random group of holdings the areas cropped in Germany at the end of the eighteenth century (table 4.11).[74] Wheat was of far greater importance in some areas than his figures suggest. The lands of the abbey of Berge, near Magdeburg, lying, it should be noted, in the fertile Börde of Saxony, produced almost as much wheat as rye.[75] In Württemberg, dinkel was grown as a winter crop on about 40 per cent of the cropland, and spelt was cultivated in north-western Germany.

In Poland and Lithuania the cropping pattern was broadly similar to that in Germany, with a marked predominance of rye and oats. Wyczański has estimated the production of the grain crops in the four historic provinces of Poland in 1560–70 (table 4.12).[76] On the lands of

Table 4.12 *Production of grain crops (in tonnes)*

Rye	602,393	43.9%
Wheat	172,577	12.6
Oats	457,885	33.3
Barley	140,595	10.2
	1,373,450	100.0

the Archbishop of Gniezno, the area under rye was tending to increase relative to that under other crops;[77] presumably the rotation was modified to yield more of the exportable grain. Grain production reached its peak in the last decades of the sixteenth century, and had declined somewhat when the disastrous series of wars began in 1654. Thereafter production collapsed to only about a third of its previous level and export ceased for a time. Even at the end of the eighteenth century production is estimated to have remained at only two-thirds of its level about 1600. Closely similar crop associations were to be met within East Prussia, where the percentage break-down of cereal crops at the end of the eighteenth century was:[78]

Winter	Wheat	5.5%
	Rye	45.0
Spring	Barley	19.5
	Oats	30.0

In Bohemia wheat predominated on the good soils. In about 1600 the area under cereals is thought to have been divided:[79]

Winter { Wheat   32%
         Rye   23

Spring { Barley   7
         Oats   38

The tendency was, however, for rye to gain at the expense of wheat until, in the early nineteenth century, it covered three times the area of the latter.

Little is known of the cropping patterns in the Hungarian plain and the Balkans. The former attempted to profit from the market in western Europe, but lacked the means to transport bulk cargoes to the west. There was, however, a demand for bread grains in the mining areas and to supply the Habsburg armies facing the Turks. Rye was the chief cereal, with barley, oats and spelt as spring-sown crops.[80] In the mountains of Upper Hungary (Slovakia), the crop association was broadly similar; on the Šintava estates the total production of the bread grains in 1761 was that shown in table 4.13.[81] In the Balkan peninsula an association of winter and spring crops – in general rye and oats – passed southwards into a cropping system better adjusted to the Mediterranean climatic régime.

Table 4.13 *Production of bread grains (in local units)*

Wheat	2,693	9.1%
Rye	14,967	50.8
Barley	4,287	14.6
Oats	7,522	25.5
	29,469	100.0

Crop yields and yield-ratios. Agriculture throughout the centuries covered by these chapters used much land for only a small return. Even the population pressure in the later sixteenth century and again at the end of the eighteenth made little difference to the intensity with which the land was cropped because the controlling factor was the poverty of the soil and the scarcity of manure. The productivity of the land is measured by the yield of crops from each acre or hectare and by the yield-ratio, or relationship of the crop harvested to the amount of seed used. Contemporary farm accounts commonly record the volume of

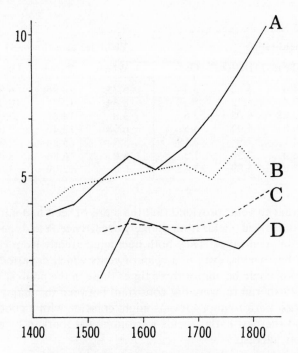

Fig. 4.2 Yield-ratios. A = Great Britain and the Low Countries;
B = France, Spain and Italy; C = central Europe and Scandinavia;
D = eastern Europe

seed and the amount of harvest so that the yield-ratio is, as a general rule, determinable. They rarely record the area used, so that the yield per unit area is much more difficult to discover. Even the calculation of the yield-ratio has its pitfalls. It is not always clear whether tithe had been subtracted before the harvest was measured; it was, it must be remembered, the usual practice for the local priest – or in Great Britain the lay impropriator – to go about amongst the shocks and pick out every tenth or eleventh sheaf, taking good care that it did not fall below the average size. Nor is it always clear whether the harvest can be regarded as net or gross; whether seed for the next year's crop had or had not been subtracted. Lastly, harvesting was a wasteful process, and enough grain was left in the field for gleaners and for animals exercising the right of *vaine pâture*.

Table 4.14, compiled from a series of hind's accounts of the middle years of the eighteenth century for a barton in Cornwall,[82] illustrates the order of magnitude of both yields and yield-ratios. In this instance the accounts are so detailed that the qualifications mentioned above do not apply. It is unlikely that the amount of seed used to the hectare varied

Table 4.14

	Yield-ratio			Yield per acre (bushels)		
	Wheat	Barley	Oats	Wheat	Barley	Oats
1756–7	4.6	5.53	3.74	5.75	10.96	6.91
1757–8	7.4	5.32	5.23	8.34	10.7	10.47
1758–9	2.98	6.88	3.5	3.8	14.2	7.0
1759–60	c.6.0	6.04	4.5	6.58	12.46	9.0
1760–1	4.1	7.5	3.19	5.34	5.28	5.86
1761–2	n.d.	3.36	1.5	8.0	6.86	3.0
1762–3	5.89	5.89	1.83	6.9	12.09	3.67

greatly from year to year, provided that the store of seed had not been consumed or destroyed – a far from unlikely occurrence. Yields per acre thus varied with yield-ratios. They both fluctuated greatly from year to year, and the best yields, even in a span of years which departed little from the normal, could be almost three times those in the poorest years. Fluctuations, furthermore, were not consistent between the major grain crops. The worst performance for oats might coincide with a good year for wheat, and the best barley yields were in a year marked by a very indifferent oats harvest.

A series has been compiled for the lands of the abbey of Fontmorigny, in Berry.[83] The fluctuations in the amounts harvested were so great that the house made it a practice never to sell grain off its estates unless it had a store of at least 2000 bushels in its barns. Despite the extreme fluctuations in yields and yield-ratios from year to year, certain generalisations can be made. The first is the obvious conclusion that cereals cropped more heavily on good soil than on poor, but the differential was a great deal less than might have been supposed. Seed was commonly sown more thinly on poor soil, so that the comparison of yields per hectare can be quite misleading. A lower ratio of seed to land may in fact have increased the yield-ratios. In the Auvergne the yield-ratios of wheat and rye were on average about four to one, whereas they were rarely more than five or six to one on the best *limon* soils in the north of France.

Yield-ratios, secondly, improved somewhat towards the end of the Middle Ages, a fact which is probably to be related to the contraction in the area of arable and the abandonment of marginal land. They appear to have maintained this upward trend during the sixteenth century,[84] probably as a result of marginal improvements in the use of manure, in selecting seed, and in the techniques of husbandry. There *may* have been an effort to adapt the crop to the soil, though there can have been no conscious movement towards regional specialisation. Yield-ratios either ceased to increase or actually fell during the seventeenth century, before increasing again in the eighteenth.

Thirdly, there was a marked contrast in the trends in yield-ratios between the major provinces of Europe. The upward trend was very strongly marked in Great Britain and the Low Countries. There was a slight upward trend in western and southern Europe, but central and' eastern experienced a long period of declining yield-ratios, which, in the case of the latter, lasted until late in the eighteenth century. In Poland, which is well documented in this respect, there was a progressive decline in yield-ratios from the highest levels, which were achieved in the sixteenth century.[85] This was probably due to the rapid expansion of cultivation to meet a growing market demand and to the consequent cultivation of inferior soil. It is certain that the sharp contraction in the cultivated area during and after the wars of the 1650s was followed by an increase in yield-ratios.[86]

Slicher van Bath regarded a yield-ratio of 10 for bread grains as the highest that could be achieved in pre-industrial Europe. Such a ratio was indeed a rare phenomenon, and it implied not only a good soil but also a generous use of manure. An estate in the Po valley, near Rovigo, which represented the investment of a Venetian merchant family, is said to have yielded from elevenfold to thirteenfold, but the land in this instance was a rich alluvium and it supported also a large number of animals.[87] Slicher van Bath has quoted even higher ratios from the Netherlands, but these seem to have been achieved under quite exceptional conditions. As a general rule, yields were very rarely more than sixfold in continental Europe, though somewhat higher in England. This must have had considerable significance in the differential economic growth of the two regions. As a general rule, wheat and barley cropped more heavily than rye, and oats commonly produced the lowest ratios. Since oats were often grown on the poorest soils, this is not remarkable.

Low yield-ratios were due in part to poorly selected seed and in some instances to poor soil, but primarily to lack of manure.[88] The irony of the situation was that regions where the largest proportions of the land were cropped were those where animals were fewest and the supply of manure least adequate. In Picardy there was on average a good deal less than one cow to each peasant household. An eighteenth-century source reported that in Beauce the peasant did not even have the space to keep a cow, and that he lived 'misérablement au milieu d'un pays fertile'.[89] In Flanders, where large numbers of cattle were stall-fed and their manure was readily available, as much as 150 loads might be spread in the course of a year on a farm of 22 hectares.[90] Barnaby Googe, whose treatise on agriculture of 1577 was heavily dependent on farming practice in the Low Countries, stressed the importance of manure for a good cereal crop.[91]

Marl was used in those parts of Europe where it could be found, and near the coast, especially in Normandy and Brittany, it was the practice to spread sea-sand, which contained a proportion of lime in the form of finely divided shells.[92] In parts of northern France, burned lime was used in the eighteenth century, but its high cost and the difficulties in transporting it in effect restricted its use to limestone regions which had little need of it. These additives, however, were not manure. Their only functions were to correct the acidity of the soil and to lighten its texture. Seaweed, which was added to the soil in coastal regions of Brittany, did, however, contribute certain nutrients to the soil.

Other food crops

The bread grains were supplemented by legumes, roots and green vegetables, grown as a general rule in the small garden plots by which almost every cottage was surrounded. Occasionally peas and beans were grown in a corner of a fallow field.[93] The use of turnips was spreading, but the only new food crops of revolutionary importance were maize and the potato. Both were brought to Europe from the New World during the sixteenth century and were first introduced into Spain, to which neither was particularly suited. Their spread was slowed both by their climatic requirements and by the resistance of the peasantry to crops so radically different from those to which they had become accustomed.

The earliest varieties of maize were introduced from the West Indies, and required a hot and humid climate. They were followed by those from Mexico and Peru, more suitable for the climates of Europe.[94] Maize was being grown in Castile in 1530, and at Tarragona in 1573 a provincial church council decided that maize should be tithed. By 1554 it had spread to northern Italy, where it was of some importance in the diet of Venetians during the famine of 1590–1.[95] By the end of the sixteenth century maize had been established on peasant holdings in northern Portugal and north-western Spain.[96] From here the crop spread to southern France. It was cultivated in the Lauragais at the beginning of the seventeenth century.[97] Duhamel de Monceau found maize to be widely cultivated in Guyenne, but clearly did not altogether approve of it. Bread made from it, he wrote, was 'heavy and hard to be digested', and the crop was, furthermore, 'a great impoverisher of land'.[98] It was recorded in the Saône valley in 1630–40, where it was known as 'blé de Turquie', suggesting that it had come by way of south-eastern Europe or the Mediterranean.[99] Nevertheless, maize was slow in penetrating the Balkan peninsula. It does not appear to have been widely grown in Greece before the middle years of the eighteenth century, and the earliest known mention of it in Bulgaria – as 'türckisches Korn' – was not until 1786.[100] The name by which maize is most often known in eastern Europe – *kukurydza* (Polish), *kukuřice* (Czech), *kukuruz* (Serbo-Croat), *kukoticza* (Hungarian) – is in fact Turkish. The spread of maize in the Balkans, together with the terminology used for it, is consistent with its introduction through the Dalmatian ports by the Venetians, who may have obtained it from Spain.

Maize had the great advantage of a very high yield-ratio. At a time when the bread grains were yielding little more than five to one, maize could offer from twenty to thirty. There was resistance to its use as human food, perhaps because satisfactory means of cooking it had not been devised. It did not fit readily into the rotations in general use, and, when first adopted, was commonly sown on a small part of the fallow. It was used as a fodder, and was consumed by human beings only in time of direst need. In 1675–9 John Locke observed, near Saintes, in western France, 'plots of Maiz in several parts, which the country people call bled d'Espagne, &, as they told me, serves poore people for bred. That which makes them sow it, is not only the great increase, but the convenience also which the blade & green about the stalke yeilds them, it being good nourishment for their cattle.'[101] It was in Italy, the Balkans and the Hungarian plain[102] that maize cultivation became most widespread, and here in the nineteenth century the crop became the 'bread of the poor'.

The history of the potato has been called the 'success story' of modern agriculture, but it was a success long delayed. The root had reached Spain from the New World by 1570, and was used as human food at Seville in 1573. It was treated as a luxury in France in 1616, and was grown in Italy at about the same time and in Germany shortly afterwards.[103] By 1712, it was known in Bohemia. Yet it was a rare crop before the second half of the eighteenth century. Like maize, it could not easily be fitted into any cropping system in current use, and the peasant developed a prejudice against it as food. Not until the prices of bread grains rose sharply in the mid-eighteenth century did the peasant begin to accept the potato as a regular part of his diet.[104] It was introduced to Ireland about 1750, and quickly spread, with consequences which are now familiar. Frederick the Great ordered it to be grown in Brandenburg–Prussia. The famine of 1771–2 led to a healthy respect for the heavy-cropping potato, and the amount grown rose sharply. In the Kurmark the potato crop increased:[105]

1765	5,200 tonnes
1773	19,000 tonnes
1801	103,000 tonnes

At the same time the cultivation of potatoes made progress in northern France, despite the resistance of the peasantry. It was, however, the French Revolution which did most to encourage its cultivation.[106] By disturbing tenurial systems and cropping routines, it provided the opportunity for a change. The acreage under potatoes began to increase sharply, and the potato became in parts of northern France and Germany, as it had already done in Ireland, 'le pain des pauvres',[107] cultivated as much by the peasant in his garden as by his lord on the demesne farm. In 1819 the Comte de Chaptal could report that the potato had at last come to be accepted as a valuable food crop.[108] It had been known in Sweden from the mid-seventeenth century, but was not widely cultivated until late in the eighteenth, and then, so it would appear, largely because it could be used for the distillation of liquor. It was not generally adopted for human food before the nineteenth.[109]

The third new crop to gain importance during these centuries was the sugar-beet. Unlike maize and the potato, it was native to Europe, but its virtues were long neglected, and might have remained so but for the Napoleonic Wars and the cessation of sugar imports from the West Indies. The presence of sugar in a number of temperate plants was recognised before 1750, but it was not until 1786 that Franz Carl Achard began the systematic examination of the beetroot grown on his estate at Caulsdorf in Brandenburg.[110] In 1799 he secured a patent from the Prussian government for the manufacture of sugar and was urged to press ahead with his research. He built a beet-sugar factory at Cunern, in Silesia, and at about the same time Count Vrbna put up another at Horowitz in Bohemia. In 1804 a factory was built in Russia, and by 1812 there are said to have been a dozen in central and eastern Germany. The first was not built in France until 1811 but before the wars ended a large number of small sugar-making establishments were operating.

This rapid spread of sugar-beet cultivation and the proliferation of factories was due solely to the almost complete cessation of the import of cane-sugar. The defeat of Napoleon and the termination of the continental blockade at once altered the picture. Imports of cane-sugar were resumed and sugar-beet growing was almost completely abandoned. A few factories remained active near Arras, however, and within a year or two the cultivation of sugar-beet again began to spread.[111] In 1819 the Comte de Chaptal reported that it was becoming customary in northern France to take a crop of beet between the ploughing up of artificial grasses and the sowing of the first wheat crop. The beet prepared the ground for cereals and its waste provided fodder. Furthermore, work on the beet took place mainly in winter, when farm labour was underemployed.[112]

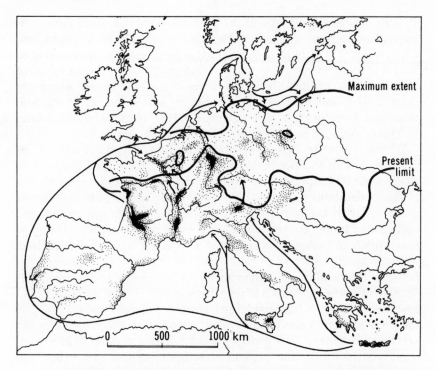

Fig. 4.3 Viticulture and the wine trade. The maximum extent of
vine-growing was probably reached in the thirteenth and fourteenth
centuries

In Germany the practice of growing and processing the beet did not
revive until 1827, after which it expanded rapidly. In the Netherlands,
the industry, established by the French, was abandoned in 1815 and not
revived until 1860. The Belgian industry had its origins in 1833, and the
Italian in 1840. The industry, however, remained small until late in the
nineteenth century. In 1839, less than 5 per cent of the sugar consumed
derived from beet.

Viticulture

The cultivation of the vine was in retreat across Europe from Normandy
to Poland.[113] One by one, vineyards were abandoned along the lower
Seine, in northern France and in Flanders. Guicciardini found extensive
vineyards around the towns of the southern Low Countries, and noted
that they cropped 'reasonably', adding, however, that the grapes were
small.[114] The vine disappeared from the environs of Cologne, and by the
late eighteenth century there were few vineyards left in the north
European plain. The vine disappeared also from the interior of the

Balkan peninsula, but around the margins of the Ottoman empire its cultivation became well established. In the regions of Hungary and Croatia under Austrian rule one peasant household in three is said to have had a small vineyard in the sixteenth century. Wine was sold in the local markets of the plain, but there was little export except to Austria.[115] Count Bethlem described in his autobiography of the later seventeenth century how he supplemented the vintage of his own estates in Transylvania by purchases from the local peasantry.[116]

Within the broad belt of general viticulture, which extended from southern France to Transylvania, were areas of specialised production, where wine was produced for export. Such areas required not only the physical conditions necessary for a good grape harvest, but also means of transport to the centres of consumption. Water transport was the cheapest and most convenient, since good wine did not take kindly to rough roads and unsprung waggons. Amongst the regions of specialised viticulture in the sixteenth century was the region of Old Castile lying between Valladolid and Salamanca. At its centre lay Medina del Campo, at whose fairs much of the wine was sold.[117] The presence of the royal court at Valladolid until 1561 created a market and encouraged the production of a good-quality wine. Production declined later in the seventeenth century. Vineyards were consolidated in order to give them some protection in the prolonged struggle against shepherds and migrant flocks, and the quality of wine inevitably suffered.[118]

The Bordeaux region had formerly been the most important source of commercial wine in western Europe. Its vineyards had, however, suffered severely during the Hundred Years' War,[119] and did not regain their earlier pre-eminence for several centuries. In the sixteenth century the export of wine from the ports of the Gironde began to revive. At the same time the northern consumer, especially the Dutch, developed a taste for distilled liquor, especially that of the Charente valley (Cognac) and of southern Gascony (Armagnac). Brandy was a desirable product in areas which lacked cheap means of transport, since its greater value allowed it to support higher freight charges to the coast. It was exported from southern France in the sixteenth century, but its production and export did not become really important until the late seventeenth and eighteenth, when the art of distilling wine was perfected.

Paris was probably the largest market for wine in the whole of Europe. Ordinary wine for the city's use had come mainly from the nearby valleys of the lower Seine and of its tributaries. Summers in Normandy were, however, too cool for effective viticulture, and vineyards were gradually abandoned in the course of the seventeenth century. Those which lay close to towns were replaced by gardens. They continued to be cultivated close to Paris up to the Revolution, and those

of Argenteuil, 15 kilometres to the north-west, were especially important.[120] The chief source of quality wine for the Paris market and indeed
for the whole of northern France was Burgundy, that vast area which
extended from the headwaters of the Seine to the Jura and the
Lyonnais. Its incomparable advantage was its possession of a network of
rivers which provided an effective system of transport both to Paris and
also the lower Rhône valley. It was, indeed, the ease of transport which
had, since classical times, contributed most to the creation of the great
vineyards which survive today in the region of Chablis and along the
sunny limestone slopes of the Côte d'Or and the Maconnais. Roger
Dion has argued[121] that the great export vineyards developed close to
the climatic limit of effective viticulture, whence the wine could be
shipped to markets in north-western and northern Europe. Burgundy,
like the middle Rhineland, had these advantages to perfection.

An exception to the generalisation that viticulture was in retreat along
its northern margin from the sixteenth to the eighteenth century is the
rise of the vineyards of Champagne. The vine had grown here since the
early Middle Ages, and even in the ninth century the Reims area was
supplying monasteries in the Low Countries. In the later Middle Ages
and sixteenth century the wines of Beaune, in Burgundy, were in
greatest demand in the towns of Flanders and Brabant, whither they
were transported by way of the towns of Champagne. Inevitably,
attempts were made to improve the wines of the latter region and to
profit from this lucrative trade. By the late seventeenth century the
wines produced around the city of Reims were beginning to acquire
both the qualities and the reputation which they have since retained,
and during the following century they quite displaced Beaune in public
esteem in north-western Europe. It is noteworthy that the use of glass
bottles, sealed with corks, for wine was introduced in the late seventeenth century. Without this innovation the development of Champagne
wines would have taken a very different course.[122]

Despite the retreat of wine-growing in the vicinity of Cologne and
Bonn, the middle Rhineland and Moselle valley remained an important
region of specialised viticulture. Its most important centres lay in the
vicinity of Mainz, whence the wine was shipped by river boat to the
ports of the Low Countries for export. In the eighteenth century this
became one of the major sources of supply to the English market, where
hock, from Hochheim on the Main, provided a generic name for
Rhenish wine. Elsewhere in Germany, vine-growing received a setback
during the Thirty Years' War from which it never fully recovered. It
disappeared in the course of the sixteenth and seventeenth centuries
from most of north Germany, as well as from much of central and
southern. It survived and regained its former importance in Hesse and

Württemberg, and also in Bohemia and northern Silesia, where the vineyards at Zielona Góra are today the most northerly example of commercial viticulture in Europe.

The olive

Bread, wine and olive oil formed traditionally the basic human diet in the Mediterranean region. Bread and wine remained important into modern times, but the olive gradually became less significant. It has a more restricted habitat than almost every other commercial plant regularly grown in Europe and is highly sensitive to frost. The young tree may take as many as twenty years to come to fruition and thus represented a capital investment beyond the reach of most peasants. If it was destroyed in the course of war it might not be replaced, and if killed by frost its owner might consider olive-growing too hazardous to be pursued. Olive groves were most extensive in the south of Spain, and in Andalusia they covered a vast area and provided an important export. In the south of France, another important source of olive oil, cold winters did great damage to the groves. Fifteen 'disastrous winters' have been listed between 1570 and 1789,[123] each of which did irreparable damage. A report on agriculture in the community of Vinsobres (Drôme) in 1789 recorded that the olive trees were in poor condition and likely to die. At two communities in Gard the area under olives steadily declined from the sixteenth until the end of the eighteenth century.[124] That no greater effort was made to preserve the groves was probably due to the increasing availability of animal fats, coupled perhaps with the fact that, with an increasing population, it was necessary to use the land for field crops.

Industrial crops

The number and importance of crops which were grown for other purposes than direct consumption by man or beast was increasing. The oldest, and still the most important, were flax and hemp.[125] Flax was grown throughout northern Europe from Brittany to the Baltic. The retting and scutching, spinning and weaving of flax were peasant occupations throughout northern Europe (see p. 237). Hemp, usually grown as a garden crop, was also woven into coarse fabrics and twisted into ropes. The mulberry tree was grown to satisfy the voracious appetite of the silkworm. Sericulture had spread from Italy to France in the later Middle Ages, and in the sixteenth century the mulberry was widely grown in Provence and the Rhône valley, as well as in Italy.[126] Olivier de Serres devoted a section of his treatise to the cultivation of mulberries and the rearing of silkworms,[127] but then he came from the

Vivarais, near Lyons, important for the domestic production and reeling of silk, and would naturally have been familiar with the processes. At Sardan (dép. Gard) the area under mulberry trees grew from none in the seventeenth century to more than 20 per cent in 1791.[128]

The cultivation of oil-seeds of various kinds spread through western Europe, especially rape- and cole-seed, oil-bearing varieties of Brassica. They were particularly important in northern France and the Low Countries, and Young commented on the number of windmills to be found around Lille for crushing the seed and extracting the oil.[129] The latter was used in part for cooking and currying of leather; in part in lamps which were the only alternative to candles before the nineteenth century.

Vegetable dyes were the only source of colouring matter, except for a few simple chemicals used in pigments, before the nineteenth century. Although imported indigo was increasingly used for blues, woad, madder and other traditional vegetable dyes continued to be grown.

Beer was brewed in most areas where wine was not made, and was the chief drink throughout northern Europe from Brittany to Poland. It competed, though without great success, with wine in the Paris market, but had greater success in such regions as Champagne and Lorraine, where local wines were poor and good wine expensive.[130] Brewing was more important in the Low Countries and Germany than in France, and a few centres, amongst them Hamburg, Brunswick, Einbeck and Leipzig, gained a reputation for the quality of their brew, which was widely exported. Most beer was, however, a weak home-brew, 'a harmless and healthy drink in an age when water was commonly impure'.[131]

It was brewed from any grain, though oats were the commonest and malted barley the preferred cereal. Wheat was too expensive to be used in this way. Brewing was clearly related to the adequacy of the local grain supply. It was curtailed during the recurring crises and occasionally it was enacted that only the inferior grains might be used for this purpose. The use of hops for flavouring became common in the sixteenth century. They were widely grown in Germany, the Low Countries and northern France.[132]

In Normandy the decline of viticulture left the field clear for the planting of apple trees and the making of cider.[133] Cider began to be widely consumed in the mid-sixteenth century, but was regarded generally as a plebeian drink, inferior to both beer and wine. Nevertheless, the *Maison Rustique* described the process of cider-making,[134] and in the course of the seventeenth century cider became more socially acceptable, an indication, Braudel has suggested, of the depression of the times.[135] It never made much headway in Paris and never achieved any importance in central Europe. Cider and the distilled liquor, calvados, made from it, remained a near-monopoly of north-western France.

Tools and equipment

At the beginning of the nineteenth century the tools of the European peasant remained essentially those of the later Middle Ages. All were clumsy, heavy and made almost exclusively of wood.[136] They broke readily and were quickly worn out, and their manufacture and repair called for a heavy investment of time in every rural community. The plough, the basic tool of agriculture, had not changed significantly in design since the early Middle Ages or even in some areas late classical times. Throughout most of western and central Europe the type of plough in general use was the heavy, four-square instrument, commonly, though not always, mounted on wheels to insure that it cut to an even depth, and fitted with coulter and mouldboard, which respectively cut and overturned the turf, thus burying the weeds. Not until late in the eighteenth century did a lighter and more efficient instrument, made largely of iron or steel, begin to replace the medieval plough in the west, and its use did not spread widely until the nineteenth. In Hungary east of the Danube, not even a metal coulter and metal-tipped ploughshare had appeared by the early nineteenth century. In Poland, on the estates of the Archbishop of Gniezno,[137] a heavy wooden plough was in general use on the demesne, but a lighter, Mediterranean-type plough, without mouldboard and drawn by a horse, was also employed, probably by the peasants who lacked the animal-power to draw a heavy plough.[138]

In southern Europe the light plough was used everywhere. It merely stirred the soil without turning it over, but it had the merit of needing only a single draught animal and of being light and portable, an important consideration in this hilly region of small fields. Scarcity of fodder would have precluded the use of a heavy plough, with its large team, in most of the Mediterranean region, and the general absence of clay soils would have made it less desirable. The northern plough appeared in Languedoc and perhaps also in northern Italy, but it gained no real importance, and the classical plough continued to scratch the stony soils.[139]

Seed was sown broadcast and covered at once by a harrow which followed the sower. A seed drill was invented in Italy, but did not gain acceptance, perhaps because there was no need to economise in labour. The harrow consisted of a simple wooden frame with crossbars, from which spikes of iron or wood projected downwards into the soil, breaking up the clods by their passage and burying the seed. Olivier de Serres recommended the use of a roller fitted with spikes to compact the earth around the seed.[140] He also urged that seed grain should be carefully selected, a practice which, if it had been widely adopted – as it certainly was not – would have led to the emergence of better strains. He also recommended to his readers that they always sow seed grown on another site: 'prendre du bled de vostre voisin pour semer'[141] – a time-honoured practice but one without any scientific basis. It is doubtful whether any such advice ever reached the peasant and unlikely that he would have heeded it had it done so.

Harvesting was traditionally by means of the sickle, which left much of the stalk to be ploughed back into the ground. Occasionally the scythe, the usual instrument of haymaking, was used if a long straw was needed for thatching.

Corn as a general rule was not threshed until it was needed for milling, or until the dark days of autumn and winter when there was less to be done in the fields. The grain was separated from the husks, sometimes by treading it with the bare feet,[142] more often with a jointed flail. Threshing was one of the most arduous tasks in the peasant's year, but was not mechanised until well into the nineteenth century. It is not surprising that the peasant did not favour species, such as spelt, in which the grain did not separate easily. Finally, the grain was winnowed, a task which was performed out of doors on a dry day with a light breeze to blow away the chaff. In most communities a small area was reserved as a threshing floor. Cereals intended for breadmaking were usually milled only a short time before use, owing to the difficulty in keeping flour in good condition. The hand quern continued to be used, especially in homesteads remote from a mill, but the watermill and, less frequently, the windmill were of growing importance. Such mills represented a large capital investment, and were usually built by the lord of the manor, who then compelled dependent members of the community to use them, paying in return for the service a fraction of the corn brought to be milled. Insistence on 'suit of mill' lasted until the end of the eighteenth century in many parts of Europe, and into the nineteenth century in some.

Transport on the farm and within the village was by four-wheeled waggon or two-wheeled cart, which scarcely changed in their basic design throughout the period under discussion. They were heavy and clumsy vehicles, commonly drawn by the same beasts that pulled the plough. Those seen on the roads and at the markets of Poland today are clearly mirrored in the drawings of 'Canaletto' Belotto, Callot, Brueghel and others.[143]

The efficiency of labour was greatly reduced by the poor quality of tools and equipment. A ploughman could cultivate only from 0.3 to 0.4 hectares a day, and less if the soil was heavy or his team small. He could sow rather more, but harvesting was an even slower process than ploughing. Only about 0.2 hectares of corn could be cut in a day with a sickle.[144] On the assumption that a rye crop called for two ploughings, the labour required for 1000 kilograms of rye – enough to support four people for a year – in ploughing, sowing, harrowing and reaping must have demanded at least a hundred man-days in western and central Europe, in addition to the time required for threshing, winnowing and milling. The time requirements would have been greatest in eastern Europe, where tools and equipment were even less adequate. Add to this the labour – much of it female – required for putting the corn into shocks, for transporting it, for feeding and maintaining draught animals, and in performing such necessary tasks as cutting ditches and maintaining hedges, and it is clear why the food production of any agricultural community was very little more than that necessary for its own support. The margin for distribution to the nobility, church and bourgeoisie was small, and must on many occasions have been achieved by depressing yet lower the living standards of the peasantry.

Land-use

The sixteenth century and the early years of the seventeenth were a period of rising grain prices, and this was reflected in all parts of Europe in an increase in the area of cultivated land. Everywhere one finds evidence of the ploughing-up of the waste, of the reoccupation of the *Wüstungen* of the previous century, of the replacement of meadow and vineyard by cropland,[145] and the reclamation of marsh and fen. This activity, which bears some resemblance to the land clearance and settlement of the twelfth and thirteenth centuries, came to an end during the middle decades of the seventeenth. Grain prices fell; some cropland passed out of cultivation, and the area under grass and rough grazing increased. In the Hervé (Belgium), arable fell from two-thirds of the total area to less than a fifth, and over much of western Europe, 'the transition from arable farming to animal husbandry reached a peak in the seventeenth and first half of the eighteenth century, above all between 1719 and 1725, a time of especially low cereal prices'.[146]

In the Netherlands the reclamation of coastal marshes and inland meers provided something of a barometer of land values and economic conditions. It assumed two forms. Along the coast and the estuaries of the large rivers it consisted in enclosing a tract of alluvium with a wall to protect it from the sea and in slowly drying it out and ridding its soil of salt. The coast of Zeeland, Holland and Friesland slowly advanced at the expense of the sea, and the waterways of the combined delta of the Rhine and Maas were narrowed and in some instances completely closed. Coastal reclamation must be distinguished from the contemporary drainage of the lakes and meers, especially of Holland.[147] The

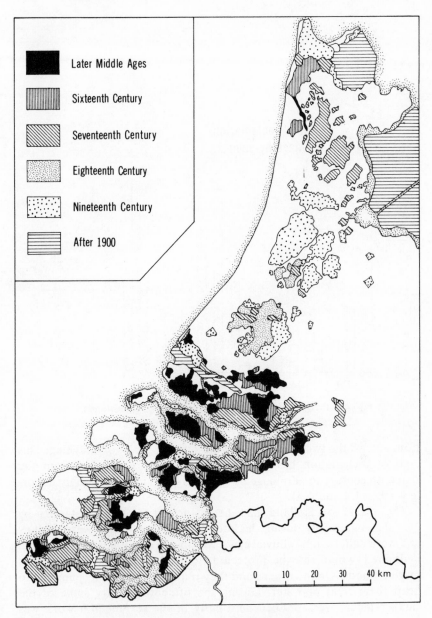

Later Middle Ages

Sixteenth Century

Seventeenth Century

Eighteenth Century

Nineteenth Century

After 1900

0   10   20   30   40 km

Fig. 4.4 Land reclamation in the Netherlands

former called for no mechanical aids; the latter required pumps, and could be carried on effectively only after the introduction of windmill drainage in the later Middle Ages.[148] Coastal land was being reclaimed

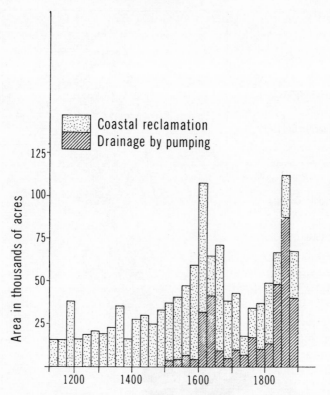

Fig. 4.5 Progress of land reclamation in the Netherlands

from at least the twelfth century by the simple process of endyking. This type of reclamation has continued until the present, but from the sixteenth century the drainage of the meers became increasingly important (figs. 4.4 and 4.5).

The meers of Holland had been formed in most instances by peat-digging, mainly during the later Middle Ages. They were shallow and were underlain by alluvial clays. Most were surrounded by land and, if drained, would thus be protected from all except the most violent marine floods. On the other hand they required continuous pumping to keep them clear of water. During the fifteenth century some of the smaller meers were drained, and early in the seventeenth work was begun on the larger Beemster Polder. The very active drainage and land-reclamation programme of the seventeenth century was facilitated by the growing volume of investment capital in the hands of the Dutch merchants, and necessitated by the rising population and increasing demand for foodstuffs. There was much less activity during the later seventeenth and eighteenth centuries when population had ceased to grow; the demand for new land was less pressing and the easier projects had all been accomplished. In the first half of the nineteenth century the pressure of population was again increasing (see p. 99); and at the same time the remaining meers were found to pose a serious risk of flooding to neighbouring settlements. Furthermore, the steam-engine was now available to pump water from the meers into canals which led it directly to the sea. In 1840 work was begun on the Haarlem Polder, the largest of the meers, and was completed in 1852. Other meers were drained at the same time, the deepest of them – i.e. those requiring the most powerful pumps – being left until last. In all, some 6000 square kilometres of land were added to the area of the Netherlands between the early sixteenth and the mid-nineteenth century. Until about 1715, coastal reclamation accounted for about 80 per cent of this increase. Thereafter the drainage of meers became increasingly important, and during the nineteenth century was the source of most of the new land.

The Dutch acquired the reputation of being the most expert in Europe at draining and reclaiming land, and their services were in demand from the Baltic to Italy. This does not mean that the projects would not have been undertaken without them, only that they might have been executed more slowly and certainly less expertly. Abel has claimed that altogether about 40,000 hectares were reclaimed on the German North Sea coast.[149] Dutch settlers were established along the lower marshy valley of the Vistula; they helped in the reclamation of the coastal marshes of Schleswig, where their work was in part undone by the storm surge of 1634. On the coast of Flanders, the damage wrought by the great flood of 1404 was largely repaired by the late sixteenth century. But the dykes were poorly maintained by the Spanish authorities, and were neglected during the war with the Dutch. There were repeated incursions of the sea, and the land was less extensive towards the end of the seventeenth century than it had been early in the sixteenth.[150] The coast of west Flanders was bordered by sand dunes, upon which Dunkirk and Gravelines had been built. Behind were marshes and tidal flats. These were partially drained in 1617–24, but again inundated in the mid-century, when the sluices at Dunkirk were opened to give protection to the town. The resulting marshes were not finally drained until the early nineteenth century.[151]

Alluvium brought down by the rivers of northern France and redistributed by the waves had built up a narrow coastal plain between the chalk hills of Artois and Picardy and the coast. Here, as in the Low Countries, the sand-flats, exposed at low tide, were partially protected from the sea by sandy and usually dune-crowned spits and bars. They were little by little enclosed and reclaimed from the sixteenth century to

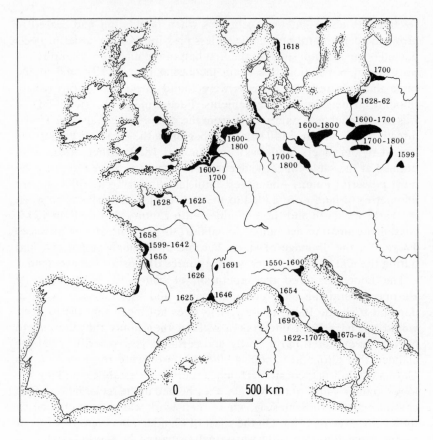

Fig. 4.6 Coastal reclamation in Europe

the eighteenth. Other coastal areas which were reclaimed at this time were the marshes along the Seine estuary and the Gulf of Saint-Malo. But the most ambitious of French projects was the drainage of the marshes of Bas Poitou, between Niort and the sea.[152]

Inland marshes were drained and brought under cultivation in countless areas of Europe. Most lay in the broad marshy valleys which had formerly carried away the meltwater from the continental ice-sheet. Drainage was undertaken especially in the valleys of the Elbe and its tributaries, and of the Oder, Warthe and Vistula.

Reclamation of the Padovan marshes, to the west of Venice, was, like that of the Holland meers, prompted both by the food needs of the city and by the need to regulate the floods on the Adige which had become more serious with the deforestation of the Alps.[153] In all, it is claimed, 100,000 hectares were drained in Venezia and brought under cultiva-

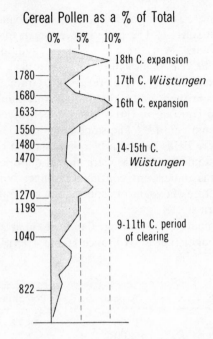

Cereal Pollen as a % of Total

Fig. 4.7 Cereal pollen in the peat of Rote Moor in West Germany

tion in the sixteenth century. Small areas of the Tuscan Maremma, the Pontine Marshes and Campania were also drained in the early seventeenth.

An independent line of enquiry, the measurement of cereal pollen in peat bogs in Germany, confirms the evidence for the expansion of arable farming from its low level in the later fifteenth century to a peak about 1640 (fig. 4.7). This was followed by a sharp decline to the lowest level, about 1730, that had been experienced since the mid-fifteenth century.[154] Thereafter the percentage of pollen from cereals continued to increase until the end of the century, after which the precise dating of the evidence becomes unreliable.

The area under cultivation began to increase again during the middle years of the eighteenth century. Population grew and grain prices rose. In France land-clearance was stimulated by the promise of reduced taxation. Locally, as in Brittany[155] and Burgundy,[156] there was a considerable increase in the area of arable, but over France as a whole the expansion was of the order of only 2.5 per cent.[157] The greater landowners were apathetic and the peasants powerless to extend the area of cultivated land. The result was increasing pressure on agricultural resources and growing poverty and destitution. In Germany the agricultural recession was more severe, and cropland was abandoned more widely than in western Europe. The price of rye began to fall in the 1640s as the Thirty Years' War drew to a close, and, despite fluctuations, did not begin to rise significantly for a century. In the mid-eighteenth century these trends were reversed. Grain prices increased and fresh land was brought under the plough. In Poland also the cultivated area began to contract in the mid-seventeenth century, and increased again in the eighteenth.[158] The same course of development was seen in Spain, where fields began to be abandoned in Castile by 1600, and in Italy where some rural areas were almost depopulated. The pattern of land-use thus underwent continual change, but it is impossible to present this picture of expansion, contraction and renewed expansion in quantitative terms.

About 1700 Vauban estimated the average land-use in a square league of land which he thought typical of France (table 4.15).[159] He

Table 4.15

	Arpents	Percentage
Cropland	1500	38.72
Vineyard	300	7.74
Garden	100	2.58
Meadow	400	10.32
Woodland	700	18.06
Waste, roads, built-up	875	22.58
	3875	100.00

may have based his calculations on the *élection* of Vezelay, which he knew so well. He would have found, had he pressed his enquiries farther, that the proportion of the land under field crops would have been very much greater in northern France, and lower in southern; that 10 per cent was well above the average for meadow, and that in many parts of France a great deal more than a fifth of the land was waste. In some parts of the south vineyards may have covered as much as 20 per cent of the land. In northern France as much as four-fifths might have been under cereals or fallow, while in Normandy and the north-west the practice was spreading of ploughing up grassland and cultivating it for a year or two before allowing it to revert to grass. Meadow and woodland were essential to the rural community. Without the former there could be no hay, and without hay the ploughing oxen could not be fed through the winter. But meadow was almost everywhere the scarcest form of land, and the shortage of fodder, at least before the adoption of artificial grasses, was one of the severest constraints on agriculture.

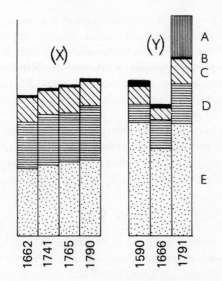

Fig. 4.8 Changes in land use in Aspères (X) and Sardan (Y). A = mulberries; B = meadow; C = olives; D = vines; E = field crops

Evidence from two communities in Languedoc (fig. 4.8) illustrates not only the contraction of agriculture in the seventeenth century and its expansion in the eighteenth, but also the changing relationship between crops.[160] The graphs show, apart from the predictable changes in the area under cereals, the increase in viticulture and the expansion of mulberry cultivation at one of them.

The area of woodland, rough grazing and meadow was greater in Germany than in France. The proportion of the land under field crops diminished from west to east and also from the south towards the Baltic coast, but was always higher on loess soil than elsewhere. About 57 per cent of Thuringia is said to have been under cultivation late in the eighteenth century.[161] In Congress Poland cropland formed an even smaller proportion of the whole than in much of Germany (see table 4.16).[162]

Table 4.16

	Thousand hectares	Percentage
Cropland	4196	33.68
Meadow	748	6.00
Woodland	3745	30.06
Waste	3770	30.26
	12,459	100.00

The area under crops was small within the Alpine region, and was tending to diminish as pastoral activities increased. The harsher climate of the late sixteenth and of the seventeenth centuries may have led to a reduction in the area under coarse grains. Certainly the Alps became increasingly a specialised producer of dairy foodstuffs, and Switzerland in particular began to acquire its reputation for cheese which was exported to Italy and south Germany.

Cropland in Scandinavia occupied only a very small proportion of the land. The Danish islands were well cultivated, as was Skåne and the plains of central Sweden, but forest prevailed in the hills, though 'the bottoms consisted chiefly of rich grass fields, & only here & there a spot of corn'.[163]

Forests

The disappearance of the forests from western and southern Europe created a problem of growing magnitude, and even in Sweden, where the softwood forests were almost limitless, there was concern over the inroads made by the charcoal-burner. In 1721 Réaumur expressed the general concern. Everywhere, he wrote, the woodland was less extensive than it had been fifty years earlier;[164] the iron-masters continued to make inroads on the surviving forests, and population – and in consequence demand – was increasing. A few years later Buffon was even more forthright; there was scarcely enough timber to satisfy basic needs, and it was essential to replant trees after they had been cut. Oak was the most desirable species, but conifers would do well on light and sandy soil. No land, he conjectured, however poor, could fail to yield some profit if it were afforested.[165]

Nothing came of these proposals, and in 1796 the official *Journal des Mines* presented an even more gloomy picture.[166] Forges had been forced to close in the Pyrenees, and the furnace at Allevard (dép. Haute-Savoie) could get fuel for only five months of the year. The forests were being destroyed indiscriminately, and in southern France – and doubtless in Italy and the Balkans as well – the efforts of man were ably seconded by those of the goat. In many areas, the woodlands had disappeared, and the rural population was dependent on the *bois de haies* and *bois de fosses*, the trimmings of the hedges and ditches.[167] In Germany the forests were generally thought to be better managed, but this was only because they were more extensive and their destructive exploitation less apparent. Only in eastern Europe and the Baltic region were forest resources truly abundant. Prussia was said to have been one-quarter forested in 1830, and the deforestation was restricted to the vicinity of the rivers which transported the timber to the coast. In Sweden and Finland forests covered an even larger proportion of the land. They were largely of softwood, which commanded a lower price than the hardwoods of the German forests. The threat to them came chiefly from the peasant. From the sixteenth century settlement was penetrating the northern forests, which were cleared by felling and burning the trees. After a few years' cultivation the land was allowed to revert to forest before again being cleared for the plough.[168] This practice of burn-beating was very destructive of forest resources in Finland. In Sweden the government was more protective, and limited the output of the iron industry, which was the chief consumer of timber.

The clearing of the forests led in some areas where the soil was too poor for regular cultivation to the formation of heathland. The Lüneburg Heath and the heaths of the Low Countries developed in this way.[169] Attempts were made during periods of rising population to reclaim heathland, but with very little success. The acid soils severely restricted the range of crops that could be grown, and without a heavy use of manure gave only a very poor return on seed.

Pastoralism

There was no part of Europe where farm animals were not reared, and in some pastoralism was carried on to the total exclusion of arable farming. In most parts of the continent, however, their numbers were few and their quality poor. There were two reasons for this. In the first place, stock had not been bred for either milk or meat production, and the yield of these was low. The only animals which were subject before the eighteenth century to any careful process of selection were sheep, and this was for the purpose of obtaining a good-quality wool. Animal-rearing, secondly, was an inefficient way of using the land. When it was a question of obtaining a maximum supply of food, as it was in the thirteenth century, the sixteenth and again in the later eighteenth, the land would be sown with bread grains rather than used to rear fatstock and dairy animals. Only when the pressure of population was relaxed, as it was in the late fourteenth and fifteenth centuries and again in the seventeenth and early eighteenth, was land available on a significant scale for rearing stock, and it was during these periods that the consumption of meat and other animal products increased most significantly.

During the earlier part of the period arable and animal husbandry were seen as alternative ways of using the land. If the land was cultivated under a three-course system, it could not at the same time be grazed, and if market conditions led to an expansion of cereal-growing there was likely to be a corresponding decline in the number of animals kept, with the exception, of course, of ploughing oxen. This simple picture began, however, to be blurred by the introduction in the fallow year of crops which could not in any way serve directly as human food. Arable and pastoral husbandry gradually became complementary instead of mutually exclusive. The reasons for the change were twofold. In the first place farm animals provided the manure whose absence had been a major cause of low yields. In the second, fodder crops, in particular the so-called artificial grasses – lucerne, vetch, sainfoin, alfalfa – began to be grown on part, then on most, of the fallow. This is the chief reason why the renewed population growth in the eighteenth century, with its increased demand for bread grains, was not accompanied by a renewed cycle of contracting production of meat and dairy goods. At the same time the break-down in primitive self-sufficiency, which had once characterised most rural communities, contributed to the meat supply. In the Pays de Bray, in Upper Normandy, a reporter noted in 1727 that 'dans une ferme où il se recolte six acres de mauvais bled, il s'i fauche douze acres de bon foin'.[170]

The selective breeding of farm animals achieved few significant successes before the nineteenth century. In some areas, Spain and England for example, sheep were well bred, but at the end of the eighteenth century cattle developed little meat and their milk yield was low. There were, furthermore, very heavy losses through epidemic cattle diseases which at intervals in the eighteenth century spread through much of Europe.[171] Pigs remained the chief source of meat only because they made no demands on cropland, and could be left to fend for themselves in the woods, where they bred indiscriminately. Horses, of course, contributed nothing to the food supply, as in much of Europe there was a deeply rooted antipathy to eating horsemeat or using mare's milk. Care was, however, taken in breeding horses. The noble, who showed no interest whatever in the quality of his cattle, was nonetheless keenly interested in the finer points of his horses.

Draught animals were required everywhere – to convey farm produce to the market, to carry crops from the fields and, above all, for drawing the plough. The light, southern plough needed one or at most two oxen. The heavy northern plough required a team. The ox was the traditional draft animal in most parts of Europe, though there was no uniformity in the size of the ox-team, which depended on the type of plough, the quality of the soil and, above all, the resources of the community. In some areas the horse was preferred, as in Picardy and the northern Beauvaisis and in much of Poland. The horse was faster, but the ploughman often preferred the steadier movement of the ox. It is likely that the horse was used mainly on light or *limon* soil, such as covered much of northern France. Occasionally a horse was used to lead a team of slower oxen, as if inspiring them to more vigorous movement.

In much of northern France, the animal equipment of farms and rural communities amounted to little more than that necessary to maintain the plough-teams, and it was often difficult to feed even this. Meadow, suitable for the production of hay, was naturally scarce, and there was an inadequate supply of winter feed. A reason for the use of horses was that they could be fed on oats which were, in a sense, a by-product of the cropping system. But even within the grain-growing, open-field regions of northern France there were areas where animal-rearing had, at least since the later Middle Ages, been of some importance. In the northern Beauvaisis meadowland was of slight extent – Goubert cites a series of plans showing that it amounted to less than 1 per cent of the area – and animals were few.[172] In the southern Beauvaisis, by contrast, both meadow and woodland were more extensive, together making up about 30 per cent of the area, and in the Pays de Bray in 1727 more than two-thirds of its area was said to have been under grass.[173] A survey of land-use in the *généralité* of Paris, made on the eve of the Revolution, shows how variable was the extent of meadowland, ranging from under 4 to over 20 per cent of the agricultural land.[174] Its extent was a very rough measure of the importance of cattle.

In the lower Seine valley and western Normandy pastoralism formed an important and in some areas the dominant agricultural activity. The large open fields of eastern Normandy gave place in western to smaller enclosed fields, and cropland to meadow and pasture. In the peninsula of Cotentin and the coastal region of Auge cattle-rearing was the chief farming activity. Butter and cheese were produced for the Paris market, and cattle, fattened on the grazing of the coastal 'marais' of Auge, passed through the markets of Sceaux and Porissy to Paris at the rate of 2600 to 2800 a week in the later eighteenth century.[175] A memoir of the intendant of 1698[176] commented on the expanding area of grazing, adding that cattle, bred in Poitou or Brittany, were brought here to be fattened before being sent on to Paris.

Brittany was even more suited than Cotentin or Auge for cattle-rearing and dairying, but here grain crops were dominant. It lay too far from the only significant market, Paris, for specialised animal-rearing to have been practicable, and Brittany continued, in its obstinate self-sufficiency, to concentrate on the cereal crops which it grew so badly.[177] The peasant commonly kept a cow, which even shared the cottage with him, but this was subsistence, not commercial, pastoralism, intended to supplement the inadequate diet of oats and *blé noir* (buckwheat).[178]

The developing cattle industry of Bray, western Normandy, Anjou and Maine was as much a response to the urban markets of Rouen and Paris as it was a concession to the heavy soil and damp climate. It was made possible only by an import of bread grains.[179] In the Central Massif a development similar to that of Normandy was taking place.

A rather primitive grain-growing economy with subsidiary animal-farming was giving place to a greater concentration on the cattle and dairy industry. It lacked the stimulus of a large urban market, such as Paris provided for Normandy, but found a substantial outlet for its cheese and fatstock in Rouergue, Quercy and Toulouse, where for climatic reasons cattle-rearing was of slight importance.[180]

In the Low Countries a high level of urban demand sustained an important cattle-raising industry. Guicciardini found that in the province of Holland the basis of agriculture was grazing and fattening cattle.[181] One village near Haarlem, so he claimed, had 2000 head. The land reclamation of the sixteenth and early seventeenth centuries, which yielded much damp land,[182] had the effect of increasing the relative importance of cattle-rearing. Cattle were driven into Flanders from Lorraine and Franche-Comté for fattening;[183] most peasants were able to maintain a cow, and the relative abundance of butter and cheese added immeasurably to the quality of the diet. Only in areas with a light dry soil, such as Overijssel and the plateaux of Brabant and Hainault was grain cultivation much practised.

In the hilly country which borders this belt of open country, crop-farming was in rapid retreat before the advance of pastoral farming. This movement was particularly rapid in the seventeenth century. There was a market in the more urbanised regions of the Low Countries for cattle; the soil in the hills was poor and unrewarding, and – a factor of considerable importance with the peasantry – grain paid tithe, whereas animal products, as a general rule, did not. By the beginning of the eighteenth century, almost 80 per cent of the agricultural land was grazing, and cropland had been reduced to about a fifth in the district of Hervé, to the south-east of Liège. There was during this period 'une harmonisation incontestable entre l'utilisation du sol et ses qualités naturelles'.[184]

In the Ardennes, Jura, Alps and all such areas of poor and acid soil and cool, moist climate, crop-farming was in retreat, most rapidly in areas where animal products could find a market and the bread grains be imported; least so where the poverty of communications and lack of market imposed a higher degree of local self-sufficiency. In Switzerland the movement from self-sufficiency to specialisation and trade was accomplished during the years of peace which followed the settlement of the religious question in 1532. The mountain cantons gradually abandoned crop-farming except on a very small scale in some of the better-favoured valleys, and those cantons which lay wholly within the Swiss plateau, such as Aargau and Solothurn, gave themselves to grain production. By the sixteenth century in the central Alps, 'la victoire du bétail sur le blé' was complete.[185] Switzerland found a market for its butter, cheese and livestock in the towns of the Rhineland and of northern Italy. There were cattle markets along the foothills of the Alps, notably at Aosta, and these in turn fed the demand of cities such as Milan. In the eighteenth century cattle-rearing and dairy-farming even spread from the mountains where hitherto it had been chiefly practised, towards the lowlands.

The Austrian Alps showed a similar development. The amount paid as seigneurial dues in the form of cheese increased steadily, and from Styria there was an export of cattle to the town markets of both Bavaria and Venezia. At the same time the expansion of mining within the Alps, especially in Tyrol, created an internal demand for most varieties of foodstuffs, and helped to maintain crop husbandry in this unpropitious environment.[186] In other regions of the eastern Alps, distance from markets and the difficulties of transport postponed the contraction of arable and its replacement by grazing. In the Pitztal cropland reached its greatest extent about 1775, and it was not until the nineteenth century that it yielded place to pastoral farming.[187]

Sheep and pigs were less closely related to the cropping system than cattle. Apart from being pastured on the stubble after harvest, sheep were in the main grazed over the unimproved grassland which covered the hills. The downs of Artois and the Central Massif, and above all the dry scrub of southern Europe all suited sheep-rearing, and the flocks often formed the only means of using such marginal land. But land which is marginal at one season of the year may be incapable of any economic use at another. Only by the practice of transhumance could such lands be used (see p. 40). In the Balkan peninsula there were vast areas of such land, within which enormous flocks of sheep and goats migrated between plateau and plain, and produced the skins which were amongst the more important of the exports of this region.

In central Europe the pressure of population was very much less acute than in western, and the compulsion – so strong in northern France – to use for bread grains every hectare that could be made to bear a crop was less keenly felt. There was everywhere a better balance between pastoral and arable farming. The monastery of Berge, lying close to Magdeburg in the fertile Börde region, had in the sixteenth century two demesne farms with the livestock shown in table 4.17.[188] A valuation of 1696 of an east German estate – Wustrau in Brandenburg – showed a not dissimilar proportion: 60 hectares of cropland, with 30 head of cattle and 300 sheep, as well as a small vineyard and fishing and hunting rights.[189]

The situation was broadly similar in Poland and Bohemia. The estates were well stocked, and the gentry increasingly active in the cattle trade. On the lands of the Archbishop of Gniezno, the size of flocks and herds

Table 4.17

	Berge	Presten
Cropland	24 *Hufen* (=*c.* 170 ha.)	16 *Hufen* (=13 ha.)
Cattle	101 head	82 head
Sheep	214 head	842 head
Horses	19 head	29 head
Pigs	94 head	64 head

increased during the sixteenth century, declined in the seventeenth under the impact both of prolonged and destructive wars and of a decline in western markets, but rose again in the eighteenth.[190] The peasantry, however, found its status depressed and almost certainly disposed of fewer animals towards the end of this period than at its beginning.

Western and central Europe were enclosed on east and north by a pastoral zone which embraced much of Scandinavia and the northern coastlands of Germany, eastern Poland, Hungary, Wallachia and Moldavia. From many parts of this *Weidezone* cattle were driven to market centres in central Europe. This traffic developed strongly in the sixteenth century and probably reached its greatest intensity towards 1600. It then fell off, was interrupted by wars and did not again revive until late in the eighteenth century (fig. 1.8). It was a long journey from the grazing lands on Europe's eastern frontier to the markets in central Europe, and many animals were driven as store cattle to be fattened off in the meadows of the North Sea marshes and the river valleys of north-west Germany and the Low Countries.[191] The herds, numbering as a general rule from 250 to 400, were driven to markets on the fringes of central Europe. Those from Denmark were commonly sold at cattle markets held in western Schleswig, but the greatest numbers were driven from Europe's steppe frontier.[192] They came from as far away as Moldavia and the Ukraine. Those which kept to the north of the Carpathian mountains made for markets at Poznań, Frankfurt-on-Oder and, above all, Buttstadt in Thuringia. Here in the sixteenth century was the largest cattle market in Europe where as many as 1600 to 2000 head of cattle changed hands in a day. The movement out of Wallachia and the Hungarian plain impinged on Budapest and Vienna, but was greatly impeded by the Turkish wars in the sixteenth and seventeenth centuries. After the expulsion of the Turks early in the eighteenth the Great Alföld became one vast cattle range within which grazing was the only profitable form of land-use and live cattle the only practicable export. Only very slowly and as population increased did an inefficient arable farming begin to displace the herds from the more fertile areas of the plain.[193]

Animals were driven to the towns of western Germany, the Rhine-land and the Low Countries. Here the meat consumption was immense. Early in the eighteenth century, Hamburg is estimated to have received some 4 million kilogrammes of meat, including pork and mutton, a year, and this, in a city of 70–75,000, represented some 50 kilogrammes of meat per head.[194] Consumption was no less heavy in Cologne, Lübeck and Amsterdam, and in Frankfurt-on-Main the demand was satisfied by cattle driven from as far away as Scandinavia and Transylvania.

The new agriculture

There was little evidence in continental Europe, at least before the Napoleonic Wars, of that revolution which was transforming agricultural production in England. For this there were a number of reasons, of which absenteeism, inefficient farm management and lack of capital investment in the land were foremost. Then the tyranny of village custom, which had been breached in England, made change, such as the cultivation of the fallow or the more careful breeding of stock, difficult, if not impossible. Warfare and banditry, from which every part of Europe suffered at some time, resulted in the destruction of stock, buildings, seed and the tools of farming so that no capital accumulation was possible. Lastly, the prolonged depression which marked the second of the three centuries covered by this chapter and which extended into the third, with its tendency for agricultural prices to remain stable or even to fall, did nothing to encourage experiment or innovation.

The agricultural revolution in continental Europe during these centuries consisted essentially in (1) the very gradual abandonment of fallow and adoption of new and more varied systems of crop-rotation, (2) the introduction of new field crops, made possible by the cultivation of the fallow, (3) a small increase in many areas in the number of farm animals and some improvement in their quality, leading to an increase in the supply of manure, and, lastly, (4) a tendency towards local specialisation in agricultural products and a resulting increase in the volume of trade. None of these developments involved a technological revolution, such as had been achieved by the diffusion of the heavy plough during the early Middle Ages. Indeed, the only truly novel feature was the appearance of a number of new crops, several of them leguminous, whose beneficial effects on the soil encouraged their use on fallow. For the rest, the improvement was strictly one in management, in the better organisation of the land and the more successful marketing of its surplus products.

It is not surprising, therefore, that progress was most marked in areas, such as Flanders and northern Italy, where a more modern attitude to commerce and investment was present. Indeed, it might be said that farming was marginally more efficient in those areas where urban patricians had invested in land. Government, outside England, played no significant role in the improvement of agriculture. Indeed, as a general rule it did the reverse, because, obsessed with the need for cheap bread, it did its best to maintain an agricultural system which had been developed around the grain crops. In very few states – notable amongst them the Prussia of Frederick the Great – did public authorities encourage the introduction of new crops and rotations.[195]

A breach with traditional methods of farming was made first in Flanders and the southern Low Countries. From early in the Middle Ages, the growth of towns and commerce had created a market for farm produce, and provided both the incentive and the capital for a more intensive cultivation. Thierry d'Hireçon's lands in thirteenth-century Artois achieved yield-ratios which would have been high even by early-nineteenth-century standards. This was done by means of a heavy use of manure, which itself necessitated a larger number of animals than was usually to be found. In Flanders itself large areas were more suited to rearing cattle and sheep than to crops. Animals were often stall-fed, and a large supply of manure became available for use in the fields. Thus Flanders and neighbouring areas moved at an early date towards a more intensive use of the land. The diversification of agriculture was followed by the introduction of industrial, fodder and root crops and the complete elimination of fallow. The result was a large increase in the total production of foodstuffs at the expense of some reduction in that of bread grains. The Low Countries were, however, well placed to import corn, and did not lack the means to pay for it.

The spread of Flemish methods of farming was very slow,[196] by and large because the peasant *dared* not depart from his traditional corn-based agriculture. Nevertheless the practice of cultivating the fallow with roots or leguminous crops was diffused from Flanders into other parts of the Low Countries and into northern France.[197] Elsewhere change came through the initiative of a landowner who had read Olivier de Serres – whose following appears to have been very small – or Duhamel de Monceau. Arthur Young could find very few estates or farms deserving his praise, and by the time of the French Revolution it was still only a minute minority of landowners who had progressed beyond traditional methods. Yield-ratios were increased in some areas, such as Artois, during the eighteenth century; the cultivation of artificial grasses was widely adopted in the stock-rearing areas of Normandy, but there was no agricultural revolution anywhere in continental Europe before the nineteenth century.[198]

One of the obstacles to improved husbandry was the extreme fragmentation of holdings. The consolidation of these strips and fragments of land had been encouraged by legislation in England, and, in the eighteenth century, the open-field village was in rapid retreat. In continental Europe strips were sometimes consolidated by purchase or inheritance, but, except in Sweden, there was no coherent policy of bringing order out of the confusion to which the structure of agriculture had been reduced. In 1749 Swedish legislation provided the mechanism for the voluntary consolidation of the scattered parcels of farm-holdings. It had little success, and was followed eight years later by another act which permitted any peasant to demand that his land be reduced to a single compact tenement.[199] There was nevertheless strong resistence from the peasantry, and the movement had probably made little progress by the end of the century.

The enclosure movement in Sweden may have derived from the English example, but in France and Germany only a minority of landowners were aware of contemporary developments on the other side of the Channel. Jethro Tull's *Horse-Hoeing Husbandry* (1731) was translated into French and, misguided though it was in certain respects, provided the basis of Duhamel de Monceau's treatise on agriculture of 1753–61.[200] This latter work, abbreviated and edited, was translated back into English and published in London in 1759.[201] Despite his wrong-headed ideas on the nature and value of manure, which he derived from Tull, Duhamel de Monceau was a true pioneer in French agriculture, and his writings 'ushered in the movement of agricultural improvements that was to take place in the nineteenth century'.[202] He emphasised the value of careful ploughing and clean tillage, the cultivation of artificial grasses and other fodder crops on the fallow, the selection of good seed, the construction of sound farm buildings and the use of the best tools available. On the vital issue of the greater provision and better use of manure, Duhamel de Monceau was silent, as was Tull before him.

The intensive methods used by the Dutch spread eastwards into Ostfriesland and Schleswig, and were supplemented and reinforced by those introduced through Hanover, which remained until 1837 part of the British crown. George III interested himself in farming in his German principality, and even founded at Celle a society to encourage improvements. Frederick the Great sent young farmers to England to study farming methods that might be used with profit on the sandy wastes of his own country, and a number of other German rulers tried to introduce English techniques.[203] Many books were published to describe and illustrate them, but it is doubtful whether these were read by the practising farmer. Clover was widely adopted as a fallow crop; the cultivation of roots, especially the turnip, spread on light soils, and the number and quality of the animals must have improved in consequence; potatoes were very widely cultivated by the end of the eighteenth century, and were tending in some areas to rival the bread grains as the basic human food because of their heavy yield. But there was no great improvement in yield-ratios; no enclosure of the commons, and but little attempt to improve the quality of farm-stock by selective breeding. Progress, even in the first quarter of the nineteenth century, was still far from uniform, and depended primarily on the vision and energy of the local aristocracy. Jacob in the Münsterland saw 'numerous marks of recent improvement', but a short distance away near Minden he found only 'poverty and negligence', the consequence of the feudal tenures under which the land was held. Almost all farm equipment was primitive and inefficient: harrows with tines of wood and ploughs 'stirring but scarcely turning the soil'.[204] The agricultural revolution in most of western and central Europe had to await the mid-nineteenth century. If the influence of the agronomes had been slight in France and Germany, it was negligible in Spain and Italy and non-existent elsewhere.

Agricultural regions

It is difficult, in a Europe in which local communities were basically self-sufficing and agricultural specialisations few, to delineate farming regions such as those which can be defined today. One can nevertheless group the agricultural practices of the eighteenth century into a small number of broad types, and, within limits, map the distribution of each. Readily distinguishable are the following five types of farming.

(1) *Extensive crop-farming*, in which a small part of the land – less than, let us say, a fifth – was cultivated, commonly on a shifting basis and almost always in a climatically marginal area.[205] Animals were usually kept, some of them transhumant, but were generally subordinate to crop-farming. Such was the farming practice in much of Scandinavia. Here soils were poor, and animals ranged too widely for their manure to be collected and used, except perhaps in winter. It was usual to clear a patch of land by burning the trees and other growth, to plough or dig in the ashes, and to take as many crops as possible before abandoning the land and making another clearing.[206] Variations in this pattern of alternate husbandry were to be met with in some of the hilly areas of central Europe, in the Alps, the forested Baltic region, Brittany and the Central Massif.

(2) *Animal-rearing*, with subordinate arable farming. This included not only the transhumant sheep-rearing of southern France and the Spanish and Italian peninsulas, but also the cattle-rearing of parts of the

Hungarian plain and of eastern Poland. It included those Alpine and Pyrenean areas where transhumant pastoralism was the chief occupation, and fodder to tide the animals over winter almost the only crop. The fattening of store cattle in the marshy lowlands of Friesland, north-western Germany and Holstein, as well as in parts of Normandy and the Central Massif, are other examples of dominantly pastoral farming.

Such animal-rearing was extensive; the density of stock was very low, and it was, as a general rule, a way of using land that would have been regarded as submarginal to the peasant farmer. In most instances it was in some degree transhumant, insofar as the animals were obliged to alternate with the seasons between different grazing grounds. In the case of cattle-rearing on the grasslands of eastern Europe it was necessary to drive the animals to richer pastures in central Europe for fattening. Extensive animal-rearing was based upon a long-distance trade to a far greater extent than extensive crop-farming, which was by and large self-sufficing. It could be practised only where there were convenient outlets for the products. The wool from the flocks of the Spanish peninsula moved to the ports of northern Spain; the butter and cheese of the Alps, to the plains of northern Italy and the Danube valley, while the cattle from the frontier regions of the east were driven to the pastures and markets of central Europe. There was, of necessity, some movement of bread grains into these pastoral regions, but most were so interrupted and broken up by areas of arable husbandry that this raised no serious difficulty.

(3) *Mixed farming*, in which arable husbandry and animal-rearing were combined and mutually dependent. Such farming could assume many shapes. In France and parts of Germany it took the form to an increasing degree in the eighteenth century of growing fodder crops on land which would previously have been fallow and of increasing the number of cattle and using their manure on the arable. It would have included the extension and improvement of meadow and the introduction of artificial grasses in order to provide a larger supply of winter feed.

(4) *Arable-farming*, which concentrated on the production of bread grains. This is sometimes regarded as the typical agriculture of pre-industrial Europe. It was, however, normal only on a belt of light, fertile soil which extended from the Beauce, to the west of Paris, north-eastwards across France, the southern Low Countries and northern Germany to Poland. An analogous agriculture was practised in parts of the Spanish Meseta and of the Lombardy plain. A three-course rotation, with fallow, was most often used, with a two-course system of alternating cropland and fallow in southern Europe and in some parts of central

and eastern. Only the best soils could have supported continuous cereal cultivation, interrupted only by fallow, without a generous supply of manure.

Such an agriculture tended to support nucleated villages, unenclosed fields, the practice of *vaine pâture* and an unchanging routine amongst the peasant farmers. Arthur Young found the Beauce, a classic example of this type of farming, to be 'one universal flat, uninclosed, uninteresting and even tedious'. He described the soil as excellent, but condemned its management. In Picardy, he found 'no scattered farm-houses . . . all being collected in villages which is as unfortunate for the beauty of a country, as it is inconvenient to its cultivation'.[207] Travellers and commentators on the agricultural scene without exception noted the poverty and misery of the population in such areas. Basically this was due to the contemporary obsession with grain production and to the reluctance to make any change in farming routine which might be thought to lower the output of bread crops, even if aggregate production would thereby have been increased. This resulted, as has been already emphasised, in a very small supply of manure and hence in feeble yield-ratios. In this lies the explanation of the paradoxical situation that the greatest poverty and the least productive agriculture were often to be found in areas of the highest natural fertility.

(5) *Intensive agriculture*, in which the maximum use was made of the land under given technological conditions. Fallow was not used; as much manure was applied as possible, and labour was used intensively. This category of agriculture included the cultivation of the gardens which surrounded most cottages; the areas of commercial vegetable production found near most towns; vineyards and olive groves, and the highly intensive corn-, fodder- and vegetable-farming met with in parts of Flanders, Holland and the Lombardy plain. In such areas the peasant was usually free to experiment with new crops and new methods. Potatoes, maize and oleaginous crops were largely grown under such conditions. Cattle were sometimes stall-fed, and their droppings used on the land. Sometimes the urban sewage was carried to the surrounding fields, as is done in China today. The yield-ratios of the cereals were in consequence high, and the level of welfare of the cultivators in general considerably above that of the rural classes.

It is not easy to map these major types of farming. The evidence consists of a large number of studies of the economy of local areas, supplemented by the subjective judgements of travellers and administrators. There are few acceptable statistical series which can be used for the period before the nineteenth century, and the number of observers with the acumen of Vauban or Arthur Young was small. The problem lies in the richness and variety of Europe, in the frequent changes in terrain, soil and economy, in the influence of social institutions and organisations, which make generalisation difficult even for small areas. The five categories of farming enumerated above are arbitrarily defined segments of a spectrum, which ranges from the primitive slash-and-burn at one extreme to garden cultivation at the other. There are no boundaries, no thresholds within this gradation, and the placement of each category on the map must to a high degree be one of personal judgement, inadequately buttressed by the sources.

5
Manufacturing and mining

The system of manufacturing which the sixteenth century had inherited from the Middle Ages remained almost unchanged in technology, and but little modified in structure and organisation until the latter half of the eighteenth century. From the middle years of the latter, however, there was an accelerating development in both, as markets broadened, technological innovations were adopted, and new forms of organisation were devised to cope with new conditions. In the early nineteenth century the rate of change was intensified as Europe was engulfed in that wave of innovation known as the Industrial Revolution. The three centuries or more spanned by this book can be divided into periods, or, since they were not strictly contemporary in all parts of the continent, stages of development.

The first stage, a continuation with modifications of the industrial structure and pattern of the Middle Ages, was characterised by traditional technology and organisation. Units of production were small and, except in mining and some branches of metallurgy, consisted of nothing more than a workshop giving employment to a handful of operatives. Indeed, it is even possible that, as an increasing proportion of industrial production came to be carried on in rural cottages rather than in urban workshops, the average size of the manufacturing unit actually declined. The ratio of capital to labour remained very small, except in mining and some branches of metalworking. Many textile workers did not even own the tools and working capital which they used; these were supplied by merchant capitalists. In some branches of production, notably the urban textile industries, there were instances of workshops with a dozen or twenty operatives. Nevertheless, attempts to create even larger units of production – factories, in fact, if only they had used mechanical power – achieved no lasting success. Manufacturing remained small-scale and predominantly domestic almost everywhere at least into the eighteenth century, and in many areas even longer. The failure to develop a system of large-scale or factory production was due, in large measure, to the lack of mass demand for most manufactured goods, to the shortage of investment capital, and to an imperfect concept of management which could derive no significant economies from production on a larger scale.

The second stage in the development of European manufacturing industries began when these shortcomings and inadequacies began to be overcome. In the most advanced areas this was in the first half of the eighteenth century, but it was a very gradual process. It was marked by the appearance of specialised producers of goods which had been in wide demand: bar-iron and coarse, durable fabrics whether of the traditional wool or linen or of cotton. The scale of production began to increase locally and in certain branches of manufacture, and attempts were made to adopt some form of mechanical power. But growth was restricted both by prevailing attitudes to the use of labour-saving devices and by restrictions imposed by the gilds on the size of units of production. Only when the innovator could be assured of a just reward for his effort and risk-taking could any significant progress be made in both industrial technology and marketing practice.

The third stage began after the conclusion of the Revolutionary and Napoleonic Wars. These had demonstrated the economic backwardness of continental Europe when compared with Great Britain, and at the same time had removed many of the institutionalised obstacles to growth. Sustained growth in the economies of European countries began in the 1830s and 1840s.[1] At this time the first railways were built, thus providing a stimulus both through the investment demands which they made and also the opportunities which they provided for the speedy transport of bulky goods and raw materials.

The events of the first third of the nineteenth century initiated a period of continuous growth which lasted through the rest of the century and into the twentieth. It was characterised by the completion of the present railway net; the emergence of a factory system with a narrow specialisation of labour, and the creation of a mass demand, both within Europe and beyond, for the products of manufacturing.

The sixteenth and seventeenth centuries

The immediate effect of population growth was an increase in the demand for basic commodities, but at the same time the increased availability of labour depressed the labour market. Wages failed to keep pace with rising prices in much of Europe, and the real income of the artisan classes was lowered more than at any time since the thirteenth century. An abundant, and therefore cheap, supply of labour had the effect of discouraging innovation and the introduction of labour-saving devices.

Except for a few goods of high price, in demand only amongst a very limited segment of society, there was no European market. The price of pepper, or of copper, might not vary except within narrow limits between Spain and Poland, Italy and England. But for most other commodities there was a series of local markets, and 'such price variation as existed within the area was of less importance than that between areas'.[2] For most producers of manufactured goods the only market which mattered was the local market. Purchasing power was low; 'the poor of the eighteenth century entered the market as little as possible',[3] and there was in consequence no scope for the emergence of mass demand or for the development of large-scale production. Local production was to meet local demand, and for most varieties of goods there was no other kind of market. 'Thus', wrote Landes,[4] 'provincial patterns of dress lingered much longer on the Continent than in Britain and longest in those semi-isolated rural areas where status and home were most firmly fixed.'

One must not, however, underrate the scale and importance of those industries which had developed to supply distant markets. They were concerned with the preparation and fabrication of metals and minerals which from their nature were highly localised. They embraced the production of quality cloth, bar-iron, printed books and works of art. But none of the products of highly localised origin, with the exception of salt, entered into the budget of the mass of the people. Arthur Young, commenting on the ill-clad and under-equipped peasantry of France, remarked that 'the wealth of a nation lies in its circulation and consumption; and the case of poor people abstaining from the use of manufacturers of leather and wool ought to be considered as an evil of the first magnitude . . . a large consumption among the poor being of more consequence than among the rich'.[5] Mass demand in the sixteenth century was probably even less developed than in the eighteenth.

Nevertheless, industrial production was expanding during the six-teenth century. Nef had referred to an 'industrial revolution' during these years. A revolution implies a fundamental change in the organisa-tion and processes by which manufacturing is carried on. There was growth – for a period in the mid-sixteenth a vigorous growth – in the production of metals and minerals. Iron production was greatly expanded by the introduction of the blast-furnace, the only significant technological innovation of the Renaissance. Industries based on miner-als and metals – the manufacture of weapons, of brass and copper ware, and of glass – grew. The production of cloth almost certainly increased, and with it that of alum and dyestuffs. Nef wrote of a 'remarkable industrial development at the end of the fifteenth and beginning of the sixteenth century . . . most striking in Italy, in South and East Germany and the adjacent countries to south and east, in the Rhineland, Lorraine, Franche-Comté', as well as the Low Countries.[6] But there was no 'revolution'.

In most of these areas growth began to flatten out in the late sixteenth century and ended during the first half of the seventeenth. The upward surge in population came to an end, and governments began to adopt increasingly restrictive and mercantilist policies. In France edicts of 1581 and 1597 laid down the rules for a uniform organisation and conduct of craft gilds. Merchants were forbidden to accumulate larger stores of raw materials than they needed, and patents of monopoly were granted for the manufacture of various goods of a broadly luxury nature. The state intervened repeatedly in the conduct of business, and 'little room was left in French industry for private initiative, except within the framework of the royal enactments and under the supervision of the royal officials'.[7] Government regulation interfered most with those industries which produced on the largest scale. It inhibited growth, and had the effect of perpetuating the late-medieval system of small units of production.

In the Low Countries, economic growth in the early sixteenth century was followed by decline, intensified in the south by war, the closure of the Scheldt (pp. 128–30) and the decline of Antwerp. Only in the north, the United Provinces, was growth continued until late in the seventeenth century, a remarkable instance of economic movement against the prevailing trend, explicable in terms of a legal and institutional system which encouraged the entrepreneur. In Spain, with which Portugal was linked from 1580 to 1640, economic recession set in earlier and more abruptly. Here, by contrast with the Netherlands, the downturn can be related to the government's failure to encourage private enterprise and to the priority which it gave to short-term measures to raise money over long-term plans to create opportunity. In Italy a relatively high level of prosperity was maintained until late in the sixteenth century. Then, in the course of the seventeenth, Italy declined from 'one of the most advanced of the industrial areas of western Europe [to] an economically backward and depressed area'.[8] The cloth industries of Milan and Venice; the silk manufacture of Como and Genoa, the building industry throughout Italy all declined catastrophically.

In Germany the economic decline of the seventeenth century was less marked because the previous advance had been less rapid. It probably antedated the Thirty Years' War, but was felt unevenly.[9] There was an expanding market for cloth in eastern Europe, but evidence suggests that the overall production of consumer goods had failed to keep pace with increasing population long before 1618, and that real incomes were falling.[10] In Poland urban life was in decay, as the gentry turned increasingly for their purchases to the merchants who exported their grain. On the other hand, there was a movement of craftsmen out of

Germany during the Thirty Years' War into the relative peace of
Poland, and Polish manufacturing, especially of cloth, benefited accord-
ingly.[11]

Scandinavia was Europe's pioneer fringe during the sixteenth and
seventeenth centuries, an area in which local communities were very
nearly self-sufficing and exports were restricted to primary products like
metals and forest products. Sweden, the most developed of the Scandinavian countries, apart from Denmark, did not experience a recession
as did central and western Europe;[12] self-sufficiency can be a protection
against the cycle of boom and depression, and the only significant
exports, iron and copper, continued to be in demand in the west, which
was torn by recurring wars.

The prelude to industrialisation

Europe began to recover from the depression of the seventeenth
century at some time during the early eighteenth. It is difficult to assign
a date even for a single country because the long-term trends are
obscured by short-term fluctuations in the economy due to military
campaigns, the weather and crop failure. Provence, it has been claimed,
never experienced the depression of the seventeenth century.[13] The
Netherlands did not experience the recession until after about 1660, and
never fully recovered from it before the nineteenth century. In Poland,
the recession turned to a depression during the period of invasion and
war known as the 'Deluge' (*Potop*), and the country, economically
weakened and politically divided, succumbed to its neighbours during
the following century.

In France 'a wave of prosperity' followed a succession of bad harvests
and epidemic diseases about 1740, and from this date the evidence
suggests an almost continuous increase in production.[14] In Germany the
latter half of the seventeenth century was marked by a slow recovery
from the devastation of the Thirty Years' War, leading about 1700 to a
period of industrial growth, which intensified after the mid-eighteenth
century. Mandrou has emphasised that, as a result of forty years of good
harvests, the peasant's purchasing power was greatly increased, to the
benefit, in particular, of the textile and small hardware industries.[15]

The pre-industrial stage was thus characterised by the very slow
emergence of a mass demand for simple consumer goods. It saw also the
evolution of the institutional framework necessary if rapid industrial
growth was ever to be achieved: banks to mobilise short-term capital,
commercial houses, and the infrastructure for the bulk transport of
commodities. Governments, especially in France, Prussia and the Habsburg empire, encouraged the foundation of new industries, and in some
instances provided capital for them. Larger numbers of workers were

gathered under one roof, not to benefit from the provision of mechanical power, but rather to secure closer supervision of work and a better integration of processes. Some of the earliest factories were attached to gaols and poorhouses in order to give profitable and disciplined employment to their inmates. Colbert established such a factory at Sedan to manufacture cloth (see p. 232), and a generation later factories capable of employing hundreds were built in England. In Bohemia and Moravia and to a lesser extent in Poland, the landed aristocracy themselves established factories to employ the half-free labour which they controlled and to use the raw materials generated on their own estates. Workshops were appended to the big house in much the same way as stables.

It has often been assumed that the use of mechanical power, generated by either water or steam, was an essential feature of the factory. Max Weber, however, defined in the factory as 'a capitalistically organised production process employing specialised and co-ordinated working methods within a workshop and utilising invested capital'.[16] The factory was thus seen as a function of management, not of technology. In this sense these large productive institutions of the pre-industrial era were unquestionably factories.

These developments anticipated the Industrial Revolution. They made it relatively easy to introduce mechanical power because they had succeeded in organising labour. But in the type of manufacture which they pursued they looked back to an earlier age. Most were concerned with producing either the munitions of war or consumer goods for the rich. They were established to make 'fine' cloth or glass ornaments. At least a dozen factories were founded in the eighteenth century to produce Chinese-style porcelain. Nowhere does one find, in the pre-Revolutionary era, any encouragement for the mass production of coarse, cheap wares suited to the needs and the pockets of the majority of the population.

The Industrial Revolution

The opening phase of the Industrial Revolution forms the last stage in the history of manufacturing to be discussed in this book. The revolution itself consisted essentially in the application of power – specifically steam power – to manufacturing processes. It was made necessary, like all technical innovations, by scarcities existing in certain sectors of production: in cotton thread, in fuel for smelting, in coal. An innovation, such as machine-spinning, coke smelting or pumping and winding machinery for deep mines, increased production in one branch and thereby created scarcities in other and complementary branches. The result inevitably was to create larger units of production. The factory system spread very rapidly between the end of the Napoleonic Wars and the year of revolutions, 1848, and became the dominant mode of industrial production. It represented a large capital investment – far larger than had previously been customary except in mining undertakings – and this in turn brought institutions into play whose purpose it was to mobilise investment capital: banks, partnerships, joint-stock companies. The owners of industry tended to become faceless men, far removed from the actual operations which earned them their incomes. There were exceptions; Krupp of Essen and De Wendel of Hayange were family undertakings, but most of the mushrooming factories of northern France, Belgium and western Germany were capitalised by share-capital and bank loans.

The factory, secondly, imposed a discipline on the worker. The hand-loom weaver under the domestic system had no life of leisure, but he could, and commonly did, interrupt his work to help for example with the local harvest. The factory system permitted no such liberties. It was continuous, unremitting work from the time when the worker was summoned by the factory bell until, twelve or even fourteen hours later, the bell was again struck to signify the end of the working day.

The factory system, lastly, was ill-suited to produce quality goods. What it produced was uniform in texture and generally coarse in quality. It held no appeal to sophisticated taste, and its sales were dependent on an ever broadening market. There was little expansion, and more often contraction, in the output of quality goods from the older centres of production. Sir John Clapham, commenting on the decay of the woollen industry of East Anglia and the rise of the West Riding cloth industry, noted that it was 'the ordinary case of a pushing, hardworking locality with certain slight advantages, attacking the lower grades of an expanding industry'.[17] This is what the Industrial Revolution was about, for the same could have been said of the weavers at Roubaix and Tourcoing, Rouen and Elberfeld, Chemnitz and Łódź.

It would be a mistake to assume that the mass market for certain manufactured goods, notably textiles, which developed in the latter eighteenth and early nineteenth centuries was entirely a domestic or local one; that those who wove the cloth provided the market for it. To some extent, of course, they did, but no entrepreneur ever set up a cotton mill merely to clothe his operatives and their rural contemporaries. He sought to satisfy an existing market, not a hypothetical one, and the market which he envisaged was that provided by the hundreds of millions of consumers in the underdeveloped world. Behind the Industrial Revolution, wrote Hobsbawm, 'lies this concentration on the colonial and "underdeveloped" markets overseas'.[18] He was writing of the British Industrial Revolution; 'our industrial economy grew out of our commerce, and especially our commerce with the underdeveloped world'. But what he wrote was applicable, though to a lesser degree, to the Industrial Revolution in continental Europe. The cheap French textiles from Languedoc (see p. 233), the Spanish cottons from Catalonia and the cloth of northern France were in part destined for an overseas – much of it Middle Eastern – market. The German textiles of the Wupper valley and of Chemnitz found a market in eastern Europe, and the Łódź industry was established by entrepreneurs from Saxony in order to satisfy the Russian demand.

Mechanical power and the factory system lie at the heart of the Industrial Revolution, but the realisation of their full potential was dependent on improvements in transport. In continental Europe the improvement of river navigation and the creation of a network of canals had begun long before the revolution in industrial techniques, and played a vital role in transporting coal and marketing the products of industry. It was the railway, however, which was the essential precondition of the full development of the factory system and the effective use of steam power. The first railway in continental Europe was built in 1835, ten years after the first public railway in England, but the subsequent growth of a European system was rapid, and by the mid-century the main outlines of the rail network had been completed.

The factory, the railway, the Industrial Revolution itself are inconceivable without the steam-engine. Its development in the eighteenth century was in response to the needs of mining. Larger units of power than could be provided by the water-wheel were needed to keep the mines dry and to haul coal and ore to the surface. In the pre-industrial age the steam-engine was used almost wholly for raising water. Vertical motion was then converted to rotary motion, and from this it was but a short step to harnessing the power of steam to the mechanism of the textile or rolling mill, and from this to mounting the engine on wheels and allowing it to run on a track. Yet it took considerably more than a century for Newcomen's atmospheric engine to develop into Locomotion I. This development was pioneered in England, and it was from English workshops that continental Europe derived both its first steam-engines and the men who drove them. Newcomen engines were erected in the mines of Belgium and Upper Hungary in the 1720s. One was even installed in Paris to raise the water of the Seine to supply the city. They were in use in Spain, Germany and even Russia before the atmospheric principle was superseded late in the century by that of Watt's expansion engine. The adoption of the latter on the continent was hindered by the Revolutionary and Napoleonic Wars, but when they were over Europe was ripe for the rapid diffusion of mechanical power in factory and mine.[19]

Rural and urban industry

During the later Middle Ages there had been a shift of emphasis from urban manufacturing to rural. The latter had, of course, always existed. Mining and smelting of metalliferous ores were necessarily carried on in the countryside. The rural community had never ceased to produce much of its rough cloth and leather goods, its tools and equipment of wood and iron; and the peasant was also in some measure both carpenter and mason. Fluctuations in the agricultural calendar, with periods when the farm-worker was underemployed, offered scope for domestic crafts, practised in the living-room of the cottage.

The expansion of rural crafts beyond the needs of the village community occurred as soon as control of manufacturing passed from the hands of urban 'masters' and craft gilds into those of merchant capitalists. The stultifying effects of gild regulations on the one hand and the underemployment of rural labour on the other provided the opportunity for the 'putting out' of work on a commission basis to rural workers. This change was most important in the textile industries, in part because these together formed the largest sector of medieval and early-modern industry; in part because they were not particularly capital-intensive and the textile processes were broadly familiar to all countryfolk. Spinning, in particular, had never ceased to be a predominantly rural occupation, even when most of the weaving was concentrated in the towns.

By the sixteenth century a significant fraction of total manufacturing had deserted the towns for the rural areas. All branches of the textile industry, except dyeing and the finishing of the better-quality fabrics, as well as the leather, glass, paper, woodworking and metal-goods industries, decayed in many of their urban centres and expanded in rural areas. Rural crafts grew in importance everywhere, but most rapidly, as Kellenbenz has demonstrated, in areas least favourable to agriculture, where a subsidiary occupation, either part-time or seasonal, was made necessary by the rising population.[20] Domestic crafts flourished in areas of poor soil, like the *Geest* of the Low Countries and north Germany, and in mountainous regions where there was a close season on outdoor work.

The use of water power was undoubtedly a factor in tipping the balance against urban crafts. Fulling mills had been worked by water from the thirteenth century, though as a force attracting industry from the town to the countryside their significance has perhaps been exaggerated. More important, because the industry would have been inconceivable without it, was the use of streams to power hammer, rolling and slitting mills, used in the production of wire, nails and other forms of iron ware, as well as to produce the blast in furnaces.

A more sophisticated style of craftsmanship had in the meanwhile evolved in the towns, catering for the more extravagant demands of the land-owning nobility and of the rising bourgeoisie. It was dominated and controlled by gilds or corporations of masters, whose rules insured the maintenance of small-scale units of production, conservative in both their techniques and the style and quality of their products. A few towns were able to break with the traditions of the gilds and to make a cheaper and coarser product – amongst them Lille, Amiens and Beauvais. At Beauvais the traditional cloth industry recoiled before the manufacture of coarse serges,[21] much of it carried on in large workshops which in scale approximated factories. At Amiens, also, there was a large manufacture of coarse cloth, which employed over half the active population.[22] But the urban industry was under constant pressure from the countryside. The city craftsmen continuously complained of the poor quality of rural fabrics, an excuse for refusing to allow them to be finished by urban fullers and dyers.

In most small towns in France and throughout central Europe the gilds retained control of urban manufacturing, maintained some sort of standards and kept the scale of production small. Indeed, the trend during the sixteenth and seventeenth centuries was towards strengthening 'corporations', and not until the eighteenth was any significant breach made in their privileges. In 1731 an Imperial Letter Patent attempted to give the public authorities in German towns some degree of control over local gilds.[23] In particular, gilds lost their power to restrict the mobility of labour and to exclude certain categories, illegitimates for example, from profitable employment. In France, where towns were less able than in Germany to control economic activity in their surrounding regions, the powers of the gilds began to be eroded even earlier. Louis XVI's minister Turgot then addressed a memorandum to his master in which he declared that he regarded 'the destruction of the guilds and complete abolition of the hindrances imposed by these establishments upon industry and the poor but hard-working class . . . as one of the most beneficial deeds Your Majesty could perform for his people'.[24] In 1791 craft gilds were finally abolished in France, and they disappeared in the course of the Revolutionary and Napoleonic Wars from the rest of Europe.

Gilds were in general highly restrictive, but one must beware of generalising. There were towns in which the gilds were weak and ineffective, and industry was able to develop on a quasi-factory basis. Among these were Lille and Sedan and such settlements as Hondschoote, Armentières and Verviers, which remained unincorporated during their period of industrial growth.

The destruction of the privileged position of gilds at the end of the eighteenth century was part of the general process of industrialisation, along with the introduction of the factory system and the adoption of steam power. The change, however, did not in general bring industry back to the towns which it had deserted three or more centuries earlier. The new magnet was the coalfields, and from the latter years of the eighteenth century the larger coalfields began to attract a miscellaneous range of manufacturing industries. First to feel the pull of the coalfields was the iron industry, followed by the smelting of non-ferrous metals. In Great Britain the movement of industry to the coalfields had been pioneered by the textile industries because these were among the first to adopt the steam-engine as a motive force. In continental Europe, the mechanisation of the spinning and more especially the weaving sectors came relatively late, and in most industrial centres was in fact preceded by the creation of at least a rudimentary railway net. This allowed fuel to be brought to existing centres of manufacture, and removed the necessity for the textile industry to shift to the coalfield. By the time that mills in Chemnitz, Elberfeld or Verviers were ready to adopt steam power, the railway was there to bring them the fuel they needed. Nevertheless, all the larger and some of the smaller coalfields attracted manufacturing industries, became populous and urbanised, and developed in the course of the nineteenth century into scarred and smoke-blackened industrial areas.

Three major regions were emerging during the early decades of the nineteenth century. The largest and most complex spanned northern France and the southern Low Countries and reached into north-western Germany. The second centred in the Ruhr coalfield, but included also the textile industries of Krefeld, Mönchen-Gladbach and the Wupper valley, as well as the light metal industries which were carried on around Iserlohn, Altena and Remscheid, in the hills to the south. The last industrial region to emerge in these years was that which spread over the coalfield of Upper Silesia and northern Moravia. Industrial centres – as distinct from regions – grew up on the smaller coalfields of western and central Europe: Alès, Saint-Etienne and Le Creusot, the Saar valley, Saxony and the Plzeň–Kladno area of Bohemia. In all these regions and centres small towns mushroomed into large industrial cities and villages quickly took on the size and function, if not always the status, of towns.

Textile industries

Throughout this period the textile industries employed more people and produced goods of greater total value than any other sector of industry with the exception only of agriculture. Clothing was a universal need.

The potential market was immense, and it might be expected that mechanisation would be applied first to this branch of manufacture. Throughout this period the industry had a two-fold organisation. It was in part an urban craft, carried on by artisans in their own homes or workshops, subject to the obsolete regulations of their gilds. It was also a part-time rural occupation, which supplemented work on the land and provided a small income for an economically depressed peasantry. The Comte de Mirabeau remarked – and there have been many who have echoed his words – that the more crowded the population and the more sterile the soil, the more readily did the peasant take to domestic crafts.[25] It is probable that the greater part of the textile production came from the cottages of the rural areas. Spinning was almost wholly a rural occupation, even for the supply of urban weavers. There were periods of the year, harvest-time for example, when the supply of yarn was gravely reduced by the calls of agricultural work, and it was the shortage of thread which provided the inducement in England to experiment with spinning machines.

In the following pages the textile industries of continental Europe will be discussed in all their variety: woollens, linen, cotton, mixed materials and luxury fabrics. This discussion will for convenience be organised in four separate regions: the Low Countries, France, central Europe and southern Europe, each of which has certain distinctive characteristics. A general picture will then be presented of the European industry on the eve of the French Revolution, to be followed by a discussion of the slow encroachment of the factory and the machine on the traditional hand industry of the continent.

The Low Countries

The traditional broadcloth industry of Flanders continued to decline through the sixteenth century. This was at first compensated for by the rise of the 'new draperies' (p. 47), but their prosperity was short-lived. Bergues-Saint-Winnoc began to decline as a weaving centre early in the century, and Armentières ceased to grow about 1540. Only at Hondschoote did the cloth industry continue to prosper. From about 11,000 pieces of cloth in 1495 its production rose to 40,000 pieces by 1531, and to 82,000 by 1561. A level of about 90,000 pieces a year was then maintained until the industry was ruined by warfare in the Low Countries, and the town of Hondschoote was itself destroyed in 1582.[26] Both the town and its dominant industry revived in the seventeenth century, but suffered again in the course of the wars of that century, and was finally abandoned in the eighteenth.

The 'new draperies' had been based upon imported Spanish and English wool, and were dependent on a system of marketing carried on through the larger cities and ports of Flanders. A contracting market and the disturbed political situation in the later sixteenth century brought about the collapse of the industry. It never disappeared completely from the villages of Flanders, but over most of the former cloth-making region of the southern Low Countries its place was taken by the production of linen, which called for a smaller capital investment and made no demands on imported raw materials.[27]

The decline of the Flemish cloth industry, both that of the traditional fabrics and of the 'new draperies', was accompanied by an expansion of clothworking both in Brabant to the east and in Holland to the north. To a limited extent there was actually a migration of weavers from the older centres of production to the newer. The outbreak of the war against Spain (1568) and the subsequent division of the Low Countries into the independent United Provinces in the north and the Spanish Low Countries in the south not only reduced the market for the products of Flanders but greatly encouraged production in the northern provinces.[28]

The heirs of the clothing industries of the southern Low Countries were the provinces of Holland and North Brabant, the heathlands of the eastern Netherlands and the Pays de Liège. Of these the province of Holland, and in particular the city of Leyden, was the first to develop a significant cloth industry. Holland's cloth industry during the Middle Ages had been small and had done little more than satisfy local demand. Its period of prosperity dated from the Dutch revolt and from the migration to the town of Leyden of clothworkers from the south, some of them in fact from the Hondschoote region. The population of Leyden grew from about 12,000 in 1581 to over 44,500 in 1644 and to 70,000 by 1670. For much of the seventeenth century Leyden was one of the foremost centres of cloth production in Europe – if not the largest. By 1660 no less than 40 – 45,000 persons in and around the town lived by the industry, and total production during the first half of the century, according to Posthumus, may have been 130–200,000 pieces of cloth a year.[29] The wool – most of it imported from Spain – was spun mainly in the villages, while weaving was carried on in the town, mainly by full-time craftsmen, in workshops of up to twenty craftsmen. The cloth was mostly light serges or says, not unlike that of Hondschoote. The Leyden industry was dependent on an export market, and the ships which brought its wool from Bilbao to Amsterdam carried back Leyden *laken* to southern Europe. It always suffered, however, from a shortage of wool. The English prohibition of wool export robbed it of the long-combing wool which it had used in its serges and worsteds, and forced it to concentrate on woollens, which had a less ready market in southern Europe.[30] Late in the seventeenth century the Leyden industry began to decline in the face of English competition and by the end of the eighteenth it was of negligible importance. The cloth industry of Holland, however, was not restricted to Leyden. It was also carried on in Amsterdam, Delft, Gouda, Haarlem and Utrecht where the scale was smaller, but a superior-quality cloth was made to meet the needs of the burgesses of these cities.

The heathlands of the southern and eastern United Provinces – very roughly the provinces of North Brabant, Overijssel and Gelderland – proved very receptive to the textile industries because there was little scope for the expansion of agriculture on their sterile soils. There had long been a small, domestic linen industry. The woollen industry was established near Tilburg in North Brabant before the end of the sixteenth century, and in the Twente district (prov. Overijssel) in the course of the seventeenth.[31] In the eighteenth century weavers were amongst the most numerous craftsmen in the Veluwe, but there was already a tendency for the industry to concentrate in the few towns of these regions: Tilburg, Eindhoven, Enschede, Almelo, where it still remains.[32]

Another beneficiary of the destruction of the clothing industry of Hondschoote and Armentières was the Vesdre valley, in the Ardennes to the south of Liège. Immigrants from Flanders settled in the Pays de Liège in the latter years of the sixteenth century. The region had certain advantages for the textile industry: cheap labour, abundant water power and a freedom from restrictive corporations.[33] The woollen industry which grew up in and near Verviers was based, like much of the Low Countries industry, on imported Spanish wool and produced mainly light fabrics such as serges and worsteds. Its development was rapid. It imported wool by way of the Dutch ports and sold its cloth by way of the Rhineland fairs to central and eastern Europe. Its market, it was said, extended from the Rhine to the Volga.[34] By the eighteenth century it was dominated by a narrow group of merchant clothiers. Spinning was carried on in the cottages of the Ardennes countryside, but weaving became to an increasing degree an urban pursuit, and Verviers itself, no more than a village in the sixteenth century, grew, as Hondschoote and Armentières had done, to be a specialised, industrial town. In 1674 the Bishop of Liège, within whose principality it lay, had it enclosed by walls and attempted – unsuccessfully – to impose a gild structure on it.

In the second half of the eighteenth century the Vesdre valley became one of the foremost centres of the woollen textile industry in Europe, and manufacturing spread across the hills to Eupen, Burtscheid, Monschau and Malmédy in Germany.[35] A major factor in its industrial growth, apart from the expansion of demand, was the cheapness and abundance of labour in an area of very restricted agricultural potential. The conversion of much of the Hervé region, lying to the east of Liège, from crop-farming to pastoral agriculture in the eighteenth century freed labour for the textile industry. The French conquest of the region and its absorption into France in 1794 further broadened its market. The labour supply was less than adequate for the increased demand for cloth, and in 1799 the Cockerills introduced machine spinning to the area (p. 345). Indeed, the Verviers district was the first in the whole region of the Low Countries and lower Rhineland to adopt both the factory system and the mechanisation of the spinning processes. In 1815 the boundaries in western Europe were again redrawn and Verviers found itself outside the customs barrier of France. It lost the large market which it had enjoyed for twenty years, but the creation of the United Netherlands opened up another, at least until 1831, and encouraged the further mechanisation of the Verviers woollen industry.

The growth of the woollen industry in the Low Countries had been preceded by that of linen and hempen cloth. The peasantry had never ceased to grow flax and hemp, to scutch and prepare it, and to weave linen for their own use. In the sixteenth century a demand began to emerge in the New World for linen, and large quantities were shipped to Spain for export to America. In traditional centres of the woollen industry, such as Ghent and Courtrai, merchants were handling far larger quantities of linen than of woollens in the seventeenth century.[36] The linen industry continued to prosper through the eighteenth century in both the Netherlands and Flanders, and the bleaching of the cloth produced by the peasants became an important specialised occupation in some towns, including Turnhout, Termonde and Dordrecht. It was, however, beyond the southern boundary of the Low Countries, in west Flanders and Artois, that the linen industry was developed on the largest scale.

The cotton industry came late to the Low Countries, and it was not until the closing years of the eighteenth century that cotton began to displace linen in the cloth industry of Ghent and the Flanders towns.[37] It remained small until after the Napoleonic Wars, when it began to grow in response to the demands of the colonial market.

France

The manufacture of textiles weas practised everywhere in late-medieval France. The cloth of Reims, Provins and Troyes was sold over much of western Europe, and poorer cloth, woven in rural areas like Périgord, commanded a local market.[38] When the industry began to recover from the depredations of the Hundred Years' War it tended to follow the example of the Low Countries and to concentrate on light fabrics. Lille was authorised by the emperor to weave says, and its rural *châtellenie* was restricted to the spinning of thread for the urban weavers.[39] In the

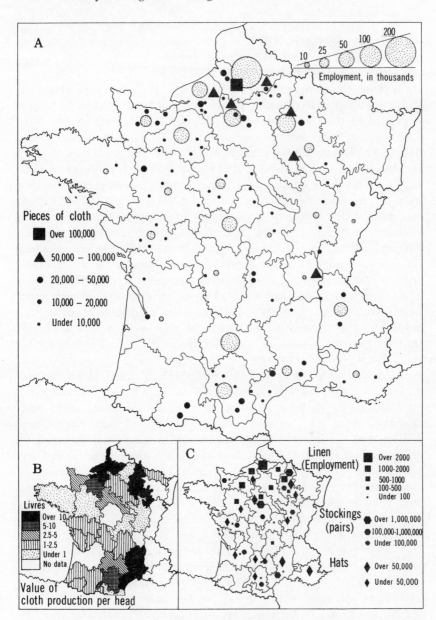

Fig. 5.1 Clothworking in France in the early eighteenth century

early sixteenth century the craft of *sayeterie* was introduced at Amiens,[40] and spread to Beauvais, Reims and other cities of northern France. The clothing industry expanded during the sixteenth century, but production began to stagnate almost everywhere before its end. It was depressed throughout the seventeenth century. Sully, Richelieu and above all Colbert attempted to stimulate production, but their efforts were largely restricted to the luxury branches. The Gobelins tapestry works were founded near Paris and the weaving of fine cloth established at Sedan, Troyes and Rouen but the efforts of the government were frustrated by the lack of a mass demand and the smallness of the luxury market. Colbert himself favoured small production units closely supervised by a corps of inspectors and dependent on a domestic market.[41] This basis was inadequate unless supplemented by an export trade, which did not become significant until the eighteenth century. The efforts of the French government in the end achieved little. They were concentrated on a narrow range of luxury goods and were subjected to an excessive degree of control by a paternalistic government. A side-effect of this close supervision, however, was that manufacturing became very much better documented. Reports and letters of the intendants, returns of the inspectors and surveys by the Contrôlleur-General yield a wealth of information, some of which is used in fig. 5.1.[42]

In about 1700 more than 80 per cent of the French cloth industry was concentrated within three regions:[43] northern France, Champagne and Languedoc. The first was the most important and, even without Lille, for which no figures have survived, produced almost a third of the cloth made in France. Amiens, which concentrated on light and rather coarse fabrics, was the largest manufacturing centre,[44] and was followed by Beauvais and Rouen.[45] The wool came mostly from Picardy, and was spun in the villages. Much of the weaving, however, was carried on in the towns. Over half the population of Amiens was said to have been supported by the cloth industry, but there were many villages which also depended on weaving.[46] Another important centre of the cloth industry of northern France lay along the lower valley of the Seine. The over-regulated industry of Rouen had declined, but weaving had greatly expanded in the small towns of the Seine valley, the Pays de Caux and the *généralités* of Caen and Alençon.[47] This industry, the intendant claimed,[48] was one of the largest in the country. Rouen, Darnetal, Elbeuf and Louviers, he wrote, produced 'draps très fins', but outlying towns like Bolbec, Lisieux, Caen, Falaise, only 'draps communs et serges'. Another official claimed that in 1709 40,000 were employed in the cloth industry in the Rouen *généralité*, and that Elbeuf alone had over 8000 craftsmen.[49]

The Champagne region resembled that of northern France. Its chief

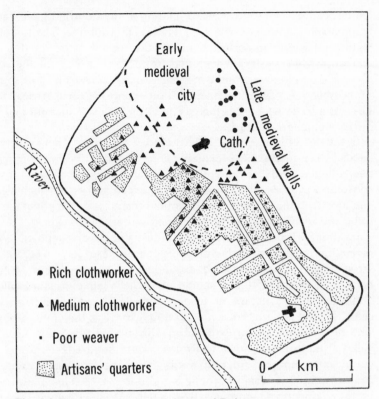

Fig. 5.2 The domestic cloth industry of Reims

centres were Reims, Provins, Meaux, Sens, Joigny, but cloth-making was carried on in almost every small town.[50] At Sedan was Colbert's 'factory' for fine cloth. Local wool was used for ordinary cloth but imported Spanish wool for that of Sedan, though this seems sometimes to have been adulterated with the inferior local product.

The third cloth-making region of France was Languedoc, consisting of the *généralités* of Montpellier, Toulouse and Montauban. The intendant of Montpellier reported that most of the cloth made within his province was woven by peasants in the villages, hamlets and scattered farmsteads of the Cevennes, 'quan il ne sont pas occupé au travailles de la terre'.[51] He added that the cloth was sold to merchants of Nîmes, Montpellier and Saint-Hippolite, who finished and marketed it. These peasant–craftsmen were illiterate, he wrote, and kept no records, and he distrusted the information which they provided. The actual production may have been considerably above the level indicated by the reports of the inspectors. The south-western margin of the Central Massif had also an important cloth industry, with its focus in Toulouse. The Languedoc cloth region used imported Spanish wool for the better-quality cloth, and wool from the local sheep and from North Africa for the coarser types.[52] The industry could command a market over much of southern France but was primarily dependent on export to North Africa and the Levant, a trade which was increasing in the late seventeenth and much of the eighteenth centuries.

In the rest of France poor-quality cloth was woven to help satisfy local needs.[53] The intendants repeatedly complained of its shortcomings: 'of poor quality, badly woven and inadequately fulled';[54] 'fit only for local consumption'.[55] It was almost without exception woven in the home, and mostly in the countryside. It clothed the mass of the population and some was even exported to the French settlers in Canada.[56]

In about 1700 the French cloth industry was very depressed, but it revived in the course of the following century, especially where it could serve an export market.[57] It expanded in Alsace, where Mulhouse became the focus of 40,000 people who 's'occupent dans leurs vallons et domiciles de la filature et lissage dans les saisons où l'agriculture cesse'.[58] Everywhere, however, rural industry was the child of poverty. The most significant growth during this period was along the Seine valley from Louviers down to Rouen, where hundreds of *métiers* wove cloth from imported Spanish wool. 'Nowhere else was there such a concentration of quality woollens production.'[59] This industry was better equipped and more heavily capitalised than elsewhere, and it was here that the most successful attempt before the Revolution was made to introduce English mechanical techniques.

Although woollens were by far the most important textiles in France, flax and hemp were nonetheless widely used. Flax was much grown in northern France, and when the manufacture of 'new draperies' collapsed in Flanders and Hainault its place was largely taken by that of linen *toiles*. The manufacture was encouraged by Colbert, and in the late seventeenth century 100,000 pieces a year were being produced in the region of Cambrai, Valenciennes, Saint-Quentin and Peronne. In Valenciennes alone there were in 1670 700 masters and 2000 artisans. During the eighteenth century the industry became increasingly rural – 'la seule occupation des familles pauvres'.[60] The industry was concentrated in the low-lying region of the Scarpe and Lys valleys which produced the best flax. Here the women spun the flax and the men wove it during the winter months when the land ceased to call them.[61] The linen industry was, however, spread through the whole of northern France, but was in most areas only a poor cousin of the woollen. It was everywhere closely bound up with agriculture.[62] Linen-weaving was a

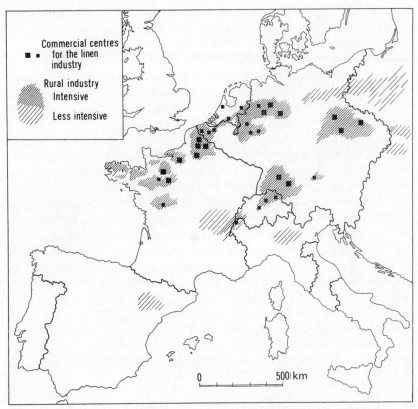

Fig. 5.3 The European linen industry in the eighteenth century

mark of rural poverty, and the deeper the poverty the greater was the reliance on domestic weaving. West of the Seine *toiles* increased in importance at the expense of woollens,[63] which they largely displaced in western Normandy and Brittany.[64] Linen was not only the chief clothing material; it was used as sail-cloth, and was exported in quantity to Spain and southern Europe. The industry grew steadily in the seventeenth century and production at Léon, a major centre in northern Brittany, rose from 20,000 pieces to more than 80,000.[65]

The chief threat to the linen industry came from cotton. The latter was of only slight importance at the beginning of the eighteenth century, but in 1740 an attempt was made to establish cotton-weaving at Rouen.[66] It was however, unsuccessful until John Holker, an English émigré, familiar with the textile processes developed in Lancashire, introduced English equipment. The manufacture secured royal patronage and was at once successful. It was from the start a factory industry, producing first cotton velvets – a luxury fabric, it should be noted – but then cheaper cotton prints. Holker was later appointed Inspector-General of Manufactories, and devoted himself to updating and re-equipping the textile industry throughout France.[67] The cotton industry grew rapidly in the Seine valley, and cotton-spinning replaced woollen in the cottages.[68] It was adopted in Languedoc and Alsace; a cotton mill was established at Toulouse in 1791,[69] and in town after town the destruction of restrictive corporations allowed cotton-weaving to replace woollen. In the Lille area cottons began to displace both woollens and linen, and quickly became the dominant branch of industry in the developing towns of Tourcoing and Roubaix.

Lace-making (*passementerie*) and stocking-knitting (*bonneterie*) also supplemented the income from agriculture and were in fact even more widely distributed than linen-weaving. They used only small quantities of thread and their product was relatively valuable in proportion to its bulk and weight. For this reason they were important in such areas as Brittany and the Central Massif. They only provided work for women, and fitted best into the economy where the men were otherwise fully employed or absent from home as migrant workers. Hosiery manufacture was heavily concentrated in Champagne,[70] where almost half the French production is reported to have come from the districts of Reims and Soissons, closely followed by Châlons and Orléans.

Central Europe

Woollens had predominated in the textile industries of France and the Low Countries since the Middle Ages. In central Europe, by contrast, linen provided much of the clothing of the masses. The small woollen industry was largely urban.[71] Its chief centre was Aachen and the nearby towns of Düren, Burtscheid, Eupen and Montschau.[72] It was given impetus in the sixteenth century by immigrant weavers from the Low Countries, who also carried their craft as far as Saxony and Pomerania. Frederick the Great tried to foster the cloth industry in Prussia, but late in the century Mirabeau could find only a handful of weavers in most towns.[73] The market for all except the coarsest cloth was dominated by the products of Leyden, Verviers and Aachen.

The woollen industry developed more vigorously in lands to the east of Germany. Employment more than doubled in Bohemia between 1766 and 1797,[74] and in Moravia growth was even faster.[75] The reason lay in the huge market for coarse cloth offered by the Habsburg empire. Production was stimulated by the immigration of weavers from western Europe.[76] At the same time members of the landed aristocracy invested in manufacturing, and some, notably the Lichtenstein, Kiński, Harrach,

Chamaré and Salm families, built factories in which weaving was carried on under supervision by their servile dependants,[77] while *Fachleute* toured rural areas, instructing the peasantry in better methods of spinning.

The woollen industry was widely developed in the towns of northern Bohemia, especially Litoměřice, Liberec and Hradec Králové, where much of it was concentrated in small, factory-like buildings.[78] Its growth in the later eighteenth century was, however, most rapid in Moravia. Craftsmen from the Low Countries established themselves in Jihlava (Iglau) and in 1763 built the first factory in Brno. Jihlava was a small, gild-ridden town in the uplands of western Moravia, and was quickly outpaced by Brno which had no such restrictions and established itself as the chief woollen centre in central Europe.[79]

The linen industry was more important than the woollen almost everywhere in central Europe. Its chief centres were Swabia, where it had been a manufacture of major importance during the Middle Ages, Westphalia and Bohemia.[80] In the sixteenth century south German linen and fustian were sent to Italy, but the decline of the Mediterranean market allowed north-western Germany to come to the fore.[81] The Münsterland became the leading linen-producer, with Minden, Bielefeld and Ravensburg the chief centres of 'cette immense manufacture', as Mirabeau called it,[82] but it was, he added, only 'une ressource contre la misère'. Jacob early in the nineteenth century noted that in this region flax was grown 'in small patches on each farm' and that the spinning-wheel was active in every cottage.[83] Linen, unlike woollens, did not require to be finished, but it had to be bleached if it was to be marketed. This was usually done by specialised urban craftsmen. Linen from Westphalia was commonly sent to bleacheries in the Netherlands. The urban engravings of towns, made by the Merians in the seventeenth century, often showed the pieces of linen laid out to whiten in the open spaces beyond their walls. In the eighteenth century the Wupper valley, in the hills of Berg, developed as a leading bleaching centre, and its chief towns, Elberfeld and Barmen, handled immense quantities of flax and linen for the Westphalian industry.[84]

Northern Switzerland formed part of the south German linen-working region, and, like the latter, developed on the export of good-quality linen cloth to Italy. The industry fell off during the Thirty Years' War, but later revived and prospered until, in the later eighteenth century, cottons cut into its market.[85] At St Gallen an attempt was even made to produce linen 'prints' – unsuccessful as it proved – to meet the competition of cottons.

Linen manufacture was also a traditional craft in Bohemia and Silesia. In the sixteenth century it was exported to Mediterranean markets.

Production was expanded after the Thirty Years' War largely in rural areas by part-time craftsmen.[86] It was organised by merchant–capitalists, many of them German, who in effect competed with the magnates for the labour of the latter's serfs.[87] Eventually the aristocracy entered the linen industry as they had done the woollen by erecting small factories on their estates.

By the end of the eighteenth century the central European linen industry was being threatened by the manufacture of cottons. Cotton had been much used in south Germany during the later Middle Ages, and it was cotton-weavers from Augsburg who carried the craft to Chemnitz in Saxony in the sixteenth century; from there it spread to Plauen, the small weaving centres of the Ore mountains and thence to Bohemia and Silesia.[88] A cotton factory was established at Schwechat in Lower Austria, and Mirabeau found cotton-weavers in Pomerania and East Prussia. The most vigorous expansion of the cotton industry took place, however, in the Rhineland, where it cut into the hitherto predominant role of linen.[89] There was a gradual shift from linen to cottons, made all the easier by the general similarity in the techniques employed. The rising demand was principally for 'prints', and in all the cotton-weaving centres a calico-printing factory was as necessary as bleaching works had been to the linen industry. Augsburg became an important centre for calico-printing, and from here the craft spread to Saxony, Bohemia and other centres of cotton-weaving, and even to Hamburg through which some of the cottons were exported to overseas markets.

The central European textile industry had developed during the eighteenth century within boundaries which were relatively stable. But during the Revolutionary and Napoleonic Wars these were changed radically, and the boundary of France was advanced to the Rhine while puppet states were established beyond it. The textile industries of the left bank of the Rhine, including those of Aachen and Verviers, found the whole French market opened to them.[90] They were quick to take advantage of the change and enjoyed a short-lived period of unparalleled prosperity. Even the Napoleonic Confederation of the Rhine, which lay to the east of the river, found the new boundary far from impenetrable, and the textiles of Berg were able to enter the French market. The Cockerills, who had established themselves as makers of textile machinery in Verviers, found no lack of customers. English-style spinning-machines and looms were introduced into the Aachen region soon after 1800, and by 1812 the first power loom was at work. One of the more conspicuous results of the boundary change was the rapid growth of the towns of Mönchen-Gladbach and Rheydt. These had previously been linen-weaving centres of minor importance. Late in the eighteenth century cotton-spinning and -weaving were introduced by craftsmen from Berg. After 1794, when they found themselves within the French customs area, there was a rapid expansion of the cotton industry, restricted only by the continental blockade and the difficulty of importing raw cotton.

After 1814 this changed. The boundary of France was restored approximately to the line of 1789. The Verviers region was included with the United Netherlands, but Berg, Aachen and the whole left bank, with the exception of Alsace, were reabsorbed into a German Confederation, less complex than it had been previously, but nonetheless still made up of over thirty territorial units, each with its own tariff system and commercial regulations. The inevitable loss of markets was accompanied by renewed competition from an English textile industry which was larger and more efficient than before the Revolutionary Wars. The textile industries which had developed over the previous twenty years in western Germany required for their prosperity an all-German market, and, until this was established with the creation of the Zollverein, they experienced a prolonged depression.

Southern Europe

The chief centres of the medieval cloth industry in southern Europe were Catalonia, Tuscany and northern Italy. All declined in the fifteenth century, recovered in the sixteenth, but declined again almost to extinction in the seventeenth and eighteenth. Spain, with an abundant supply of the best wool, had a unique advantage from which it failed to profit. The gild-ridden industry of the Meseta towns disappeared, and survived in the towns of Catalonia only on a reduced scale.[91] In the eighteenth century an attempt was made to revive the woollen cloth industry by establishing a number of 'royal' textile factories – woollens at Guadalajara and Segovia; tapestries at Madrid; silks at Talavera. Foreign craftsmen were brought in, and the factories were technically successful, but were burdened, like all state-run enterprises, by an overgreat and inefficient bureaucracy. They were located in the empty heart of Spain rather than near the coast, and were financially a failure. In the end all were closed or were sold to private individuals.[92]

Far greater success attended the eighteenth-century attempts to introduce a cotton textile industry. It owed its origin to the initiative of the merchant class of Barcelona and the patronage of Charles III. There had previously been a small cotton industry in Barcelona, as there was in many Mediterranean towns. In the 1760s it grew rapidly. In 1760, it is said, there were 353 looms in Barcelona. By 1784 this had risen to 2102, together with 948 tables for making cotton prints.[93] The cotton industry replaced the woollen and spread to other towns of the region, notably Manresa and Malaro. The industry scarcely spread beyond the Catalan littoral, but here for a few years it was a major export industry. It was carried on in factories or mills – there were 60 in 1784. This made it particularly vulnerable, and most of the cotton mills, as well as the surviving woollen mills, were destroyed by the French. Recovery after 1815 was slow until the 1830s, when mechanised spinning and weaving were introduced, and the industry grew rapidly in Barcelona and its satellite towns.[94]

The Italian cloth industry had formerly been second only to that of the Low Countries. It was carried on mainly in the towns of northern Italy, and Italian cloth formed a return cargo for the ships which brought spices, silks and wines from the Levant.[95] The industry stagnated in the later Middle Ages; it recovered in the sixteenth century – Mantua reached the peak of its production in 1558[96] – but then entered on its long decline from which it was not rescued until the nineteenth century. The wars, coupled with the shift in the focus of trade from the Mediterranean to the Atlantic, were fatal to the cloth industry, but one city was in some measure protected from these influences. Venice had only a negligible cloth industry until about 1510. This then began to grow rapidly, profiting from the destruction of rival crafts in its Italian hinterland and from its freedom to import wool and to control what remained of Mediterranean trade.[97] By 1600 the Venetian cloth industry was twice the size of that of Milan or Florence. Thereafter it too declined, as its products were driven from the Mediterranean by the competition of the Dutch and British and later the French. In 1700 Italy 'had sunk to the undistinguished position of a basically agrarian country cut off from the mainstream of economic life'.[98] The Italian cloth industry was restricted to the production of coarse, cheap fabrics for a predominantly peasant society.

The Balkan peninsula, today a not unimportant source of textiles, had only a primitive domestic craft industry before the mid-nineteenth century. The spinning-wheel was only beginning in the late eighteenth century to displace the distaff and spindle, and weaving was practised on the simplest of looms.[99] There were no full-time professional weavers; clothworking was an occupation of everyone, and nearly every house had its loom.

Luxury fabrics

By the end of the Middle Ages silk had become the élite fabric in most of Europe. It clothed the cardinals at Rome and courtiers throughout western Europe, and to the bourgeoisie a piece of silk was a treasured possession. In the later Middle Ages silk-weaving had become established in many parts of Italy, and Italian craftsmen took their skills to Lyons, Tours and Amboise, to Zurich and Cologne. Yet silk-weaving was the most difficult branch of the textile industry to establish. Silk was very expensive; its market was narrow and demand highly elastic and subject to changes in fashion and purchasing power.[100] The silkworm, secondly, was a delicate creature, and rearing it an arduous and highly seasonal occupation. It was dependent furthermore on the cultivation of the mulberry, climatically a rather demanding tree. It could be grown anywhere in Italy and southern France, but Buffon failed to establish it on his estate in Burgundy, and Frederick the Great's mulberry groves in Brandenburg almost succumbed to the hard frosts of 1785–7.[101] Such extravagances did not survive the Napoleonic Wars, and the silk industry in northern Europe was thereafter restricted to places which could import raw silk from southern Europe. Reeling and throwing silk were aided from the sixteenth century by the use of water power, and in Italy tended to concentrate along the streams which flowed from the Alps to the plain of Lombardy. Weaving remained the prerogative of highly specialised and full-time craftsmen. They usually worked in the towns, often in small factories or workshops.

Venice was noted in the sixteenth century for the extreme elaboration of its products. The industry declined generally in the late sixteenth and seventeenth centuries, but some branches of production, Genoese damask and the best-quality Venetian, maintained their commercial position.[102] The first important silk industry to be established outside Italy was that of Lyons, followed in the later sixteenth century by the Zurich manufacture, established 'after the Italian manner'. The Swiss industry was further reinforced by the arrival of French Huguenots and later by refugees from the Revolution. Italians established silk-weaving in Geneva and Basel, which became notable for its production of ribbons.[103] From Lyons the industry was carried to Tours, Amboise and Paris, and late in the sixteenth century it reached northern France. Demand continued to increase, and in the eighteenth century silk-weaving was established in Saint-Etienne, the lower Rhineland, Saxony, Brandenburg, Bohemia and London. In these latitudes there was no real possibility of rearing silkworms, and the industry had to be based on imported silk. Few of these undertakings survived long, but that of Krefeld was an exception. It was created by the von der Leyen family which in 1721 established a small factory to make ribbon and velvet. They were helped by the absence of a gild organisation and by the King of Prussia, who granted extensive privileges to Krefeld, including exemption from military conscription for its workmen. The industry grew rapidly during the eighteenth century, and by 1786 the von der Leyens are said to have employed 3400 weavers and to have owned 815 looms. The majority probably worked in mills, but there was some domestic employment in the surrounding countryside. 'An impression is gained', wrote C. F. Meyer, an official of the Prussian government, 'of visiting one of the most flourishing industrial towns of England.'[104]

The French conquest brought an end to the special privileges of the von der Leyen firm; competition from Lyons and other French producers was intensified, and the supply of raw materials from southern Europe became difficult. The von der Leyens succumbed, but other firms were established. The market revived after 1815 as demand broadened for silk. By 1835 there were 28 silk mills in Krefeld, and by 1848 this had increased to 98.

Towards the end of the Middle Ages it became customary to hide the rough surfaces of walls with woven fabrics. Both damask – most often at this date a mixed fabric of silk and linen – and tapestry were used. Silk damasks became a product of the French and Italian silk-weavers.[105] Tapestry-weaving was more closely associated with the southern Low Countries, where Arras, Brussels, Tournai and Bruges had acquired a high reputation for their work by 1500. Flemish craftsmen later in the century carried the art of tapestry-weaving to many parts of Europe, but nowhere were their efforts crowned with greater success than in Paris. There, in 1601, Flemish tapestry-weavers were established in an old dyeworks, which had belonged to the Gobelins, in the Faubourg Saint-Marcel.[106] In 1664 the works became a royal factory, producing for the use of the king and of those whom he wished to favour. This famous mill continued in operation, with only a slight interruption, until the Revolution, and was reopened in the nineteenth century. The Gobelins provided a model for other tapestry-weavers, and some of its craftsmen were enticed to St Petersburg, Brussels and elsewhere, until fashions changed and other methods of covering the walls of chambers – notably the use of wallpaper – were devised.

Consumer good industries

Between 1761 and 1774 Duhamel de Monceau published under the title *Descriptions des arts et métiers* a series of monographs or studies by different writers of the crafts which were considered the most important at this time.[107] Over a hundred were gathered into twenty-seven volumes. Some are brief and uninformative; others detailed, even prolix, and illustrated by engravings of tools, machines and processes. Between them they surveyed the current state of industrial technology; they examined the state of mining, quarrying and metalworking; of fishing, the carbonising of wood and the forging of anchors; of burning of lime and the baking of bricks. But in reading these monographs one feels that this is a very skewed list. The manufacture of surgical and astronomical instruments or the craft of cabinet-making or of inlay work rate more space than weaving, and the simple carpenter is ignored. A keynote is struck by the Comte de Milly; the useful arts, he wrote, have always been the foundation of national prosperity, and his desire to further the latter leads him to contribute an essay on the manufacture of Chinese porcelain.

Duhamel de Monceau viewed the crafts through the eyes of the French aristocracy, and gave the greatest space to those which contributed to their comfort and pleasure. He tells us not a word on how a plough was made, or on how the coarse woollen and linen fabrics which clothed the masses were woven and finished. Yet, as his contemporary Arthur Young was quick to note, the future of French industry rested with the mass demand of the latter (p. 218), rather than with the esoteric crafts which delighted the rich.

It was a narrow range of industries which supplied the daily wants of most people. Apart from agriculture and the textile industries, the most important was probably tanning and leather-working. These were almost as universal as weaving, and scarcely less necessary. They provided footwear – which was not regularly worn by the peasantry – saddlery harness and upholstery. The transport industry was dependent on leather. The tanyard was a feature of every village, and the larger towns, where animals were slaughtered in greater numbers, had a regular tanning industry. Tanning was most strongly developed in areas where animal husbandry was relatively important. In Brittany the intendant declared it to be second only to textiles,[108] and the industry was concentrated in southern Poland, where the drove routes entered central Europe from the steppe. Tanning was an antisocial industry, creating an offensive smell and polluting the streams. Perhaps for this reason it was unimportant at Paris; instead 'the butchers sell their skins and hides at Rouen, where these industries are on a large scale'.[109] Such concentrations were not unusual. Nantes, Poitiers, Dunkirk and Lille were regional centres of the tanning industry. Much of the leather was shaved to make it thin and pliable, treated with chemicals and dyestuffs, and used for making light shoes and purses, book-bindings and upholstery.[110]

There were few food industries more sophisticated than those of the baker, butcher and brewer. Among them, however, was that of the sugar-refiner. Until early in the nineteenth century sugar was obtained almost exclusively from the cane. It was imported into Europe in the form of molasses, and was refined principally at the ports. In the sixteenth century Antwerp came to the fore, and was followed by Cologne[111] and port cities trading with the West Indies, such as Nantes, Hamburg and Bordeaux.

Other industries which used raw materials of colonial origin also grew up in the port cities. They included the preparation of tobacco, the roasting of coffee and the making of soap and candles. The principal ingredients of soap were vegetable oils and wood-ash. The import of ashes from the Baltic region contributed to the growth of the soap industry in the northern ports, as the availability of olive oil did to that in the southern. The intendant of Provence complained that oil was so scarce that the industry had to rely on imports from the Mediterranean littoral;[112] ashes were also imported from the Levant.[113] Marseilles was probably the foremost European soap-making centre; about 1760 there were no less than '38 soap factories with 170 boilers and a thousand workmen'.[114] No other port could rival this concentration, but soap-boilers were nonetheless prominent at Nantes, Rouen, Amsterdam and Hamburg.

The manufacture of paper increased steadily from the sixteenth to the eighteenth centuries in pace with the expansion of book-printing and the spread of literacy. Parchment gradually ceased to be used, except for legal documents, and its place was taken by paper made, as a general rule, from rags. At first, paper mills tended to cluster in the textile-producing areas. Ravensburg in Swabia had in the early sixteenth century fifty paper mills. They then developed in most large cities, where there was both a demand for paper and a supply of rags to serve as raw material. The expansion of paper-making is inseparable from that of printing, for most of the paper made went through the press. As early as 1500, it is said, no less than 236 European towns had their printing-presses.[115] By the eighteenth century there were presses in every large and medium-sized town, and many, notably Paris, Lyons, Amsterdam, Cologne, Basel, Vienna, Venice, were outstanding centres for the publication of books.

The ceramic and glass industries, like the textile and leather, satisfied a very wide range of demand. At one extreme were the glass of Venice and the porcelain of Meissen; at the other the coarsest of earthenware. They were alike in requiring mineral raw materials and an abundance of fuel. The principal determinants of the pottery industry were the presence of beds of clay together with a nearby market. Wherever there was clay there were potters, and little of what they made ever travelled more than a few miles. There was no really élite pottery before the seventeenth century; the rich used metal plates and dishes – most of them of pewter – and the poor ate off wooden trenchers. The first pottery to gain a reputation far beyond its place of manufacture was Italian majolica, a coarse ware covered with enamel and decorated. It was made in many towns, but some of the finest came from Urbino, Faenza, Siena and other places in central and northern Italy. The manufacture prospered through the sixteenth century, and large quantities of majolica ware were exported. Late in the century Italian craftsmen, traditionally from Faenza – hence faience – carried the manufacture to France. Potteries were established at Nevers, Rouen, Moustiers (Provence), Marseilles, Strasbourg, Niderviller (Lorraine).

The industry also spread to the Low Countries, again borne by Italian emigrants, first to Antwerp, then to Haarlem and Rotterdam. In the mid-seventeenth century the manufacture of majolica-type pottery was begun at Delft, where, with its distinctive design and colour, it became the dominant pottery in north-western Europe for over a century. Majolica potters also migrated to Spain, where they worked at Seville and Talavera; to Switzerland – Winterthur; to Germany – Frankfurt-on-Main, Hanau, Kreussen (Bavaria), Dresden, Potsdam and several other towns; to Copenhagen in Denmark; to Sweden, Austria, Hungary and England. During this period earthenware or stoneware continued to be made in many parts of Europe, and in some, notably the Netherlands, the lower Rhineland, Bavaria and Saxony, it began to take on some of the mannerisms of Renaissance Italian pottery, and to use mineral dyes and lead or salt glaze.

Throughout these years the model to which potters aspired was the Chinese porcelain, now being imported into Europe first by the Portuguese and later by the Dutch and English. They admired its smoothness of texture, its translucent quality and its colour and decoration. Several attempts were made in France to imitate it, but none of them was successful until in the early eighteenth century the ingredients of the Chinese product were made known in the west.[116] These were not the clays of the potter, but a granite-like substance known as petuntse or china stone, and china clay, derived from the disintegrated felspar of granite. The restricted occurrence of these materials, together with the high cost of manufacture and the limited demand, greatly restricted the manufacture of true porcelain. Bottger early in the century discovered china stone and china clay in the Erzgebirge of Bohemia, and established a successful pottery at Meissen, in Saxony, which still operates today. The manufacture was established in Vienna, Bayreuth, Plaue (Brandenburg), Höchst (Franconia), Nymphenburg (Bavaria), Frankenthal and several other places, most of them fairly close to the Erzgebirge, which supplied much of the raw materials. Most of these porcelain works acquired their skills from runaway craftsmen from the ducal works at Meissen.

The chief centre of porcelain manufacture in western Europe was Sèvres, 10 kilometres to the south-west of Paris. After many years of effort the Sèvres factory produced a true porcelain, but it was generally content to make 'soft-paste' porcelain, which did not call for scarce raw materials. Limoges, which had deposits of the latter nearby, also produced true porcelain for a time, but most of the French porcelain factories produced an imitation from crushed glass, clay and bone-ash. No less than about seventy works attempted with varying degrees of success to make porcelain in continental Europe in the course of the eighteenth century. Few achieved any lasting success, and those which did owed it to royal or princely patronage.[117] All the larger porcelain factories, such as Meissen – the premier works during most of the eighteenth century – Sèvres, Nymphenburg, were either owned by or received considerable help from royal patrons. Very large sums were invested in the industry, and it seemed, long before the end of the century, that porcelain was overproduced. By the time of the Revolution the small demand for luxury china was being overshadowed by a growing demand for cheaper, mass-produced ware. It was the Staffordshire Potteries which set the model in the nineteenth century, with their use of cheap materials, standardised designs, and printed and 'transferred' patterns. The continental market was dominated by the products of Staffordshire kilns, but some of the older centres of quality wares – Paris, Berlin, Copenhagen, Munich amongst them – adapted to the new market, and produced competent china of standardised designs.

Glass-making was more restricted. It was dependent on quartz-sand and used large quantities of fuel in order to fuse its raw materials. It catered, furthermore, for a narrower market. The demand for window glass grew during the sixteenth century, followed by that for domestic and ornamental glassware. Italian glass-makers, notably those of Venice, set a standard to which the rest of Europe aspired; licences granted to glass-workers in seventeenth-century Liège called for the production of glasses 'à la vénitienne'.[118] Italian craftsmen were established near Paris in the sixteenth century to produce glass for the royal court.[119] This particular enterprise failed, but others were abundantly successful – so much so that they placed a severe strain on the supply of fuel, despite the fact that most were located in forested regions of Normandy, the Orléanais, the Morvan and the Argonne. After its earlier period of growth the industry stagnated during the reign of Louis XIV, but expanded again in the eighteenth century when there were, it is said, no less than three hundred 'glass houses' in France.

In the sixteenth and early seventeenth centuries Hesse and the Thuringian Forest in central Germany developed an important glassmaking industry, organised on a capitalist basis.[120] It succumbed to the Thirty Years' War and, though it was revived on a craft basis, redevelopment was largely in Bohemia. There had been a glass industry here during the Middle Ages. This grew during the sixteenth century until it was considered a threat to the timber resources. The solution was to move deeper into the forests which border Bohemia, and here the glass-workers played an important part in settling those empty regions which separated German from Czech. The magnates, on whose lands the glass works were established, encouraged the industry, and the Bohemian glass trade, centred mainly in the mountains of northern Bohemia, grew through the eighteenth century, supplying quality glassware to much of Europe.[121]

Great progress was made during the eighteenth century both in the manufacture and decoration of glass. The demand for window glass, especially for sheets of increasing size and strength, led to the production first of crown- or bull's-eye-glass, and then of plate-glass. The production of table-glass was a craft industry, calling for no large investment. The manufacture of sheet-glass was a more complex process, requiring large furnaces for both melting the glass and annealing it, and also mills to polish the sheets. It was a factory–rather than a craft–industry, and was carried on in few places before the nineteenth century. Amongst them, however, were Saint-Gobain in Picardy which became the chief centre in France, and Charleroi, in the Austrian Low Countries, which became the largest source of window glass.

The manufacture of clocks and watches was, by and large, a development of the later seventeenth and the eighteenth centuries. It was in part an urban craft, carried on by skilled craftsmen who were often proud to engrave their names on the faces of the timepieces which they made. But it was also a rural craft, practised especially in areas where the length and severity of winter precluded outdoor work. The Black Forest developed clockmaking in the early eighteenth century.[122] At the same time watchmaking developed in Switzerland. It began in the Jura mountains of Neuchâtel in the late seventeenth century and spread through this region and across the plateau to the Alps of Vaud. The number of watchmakers is said[123] to have increased more than sevenfold during the last half of the eighteenth century. The industry was at this time exclusively a domestic craft. Demand, however, was restricted to the wealthier classes, and small groups of clock- and watchmakers appeared in some of the larger cities. Augsburg and Nuremberg became centres of the craft in the sixteenth century, and Fynes Moryson, early in the seventeenth century, wrote of the men of Nuremberg that they 'are esteemed the best workmen for clockes and some like thinges'.[124] Paris, Lyons, Geneva and other cities developed the craft in the course of the seventeenth century, and in some the number of craftsmen was enough to form an independent gild of clockmakers.[125]

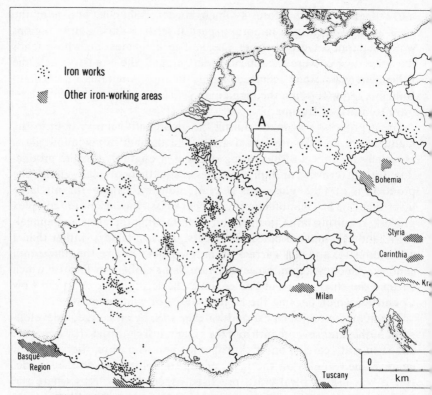

Fig. 5.4 The European iron industry in the later eighteenth century. For inset A, see fig. 5.5; for B, see fig. 5.8

The metal industries

The early sixteenth century was a period of rapid expansion in the metal industries. The output of copper, silver, mercury and lead, as well as of iron, increased rapidly.[126] This was due in part to the greater volume of coinage in circulation; in part to the increased demand for tools and for weapons and ornamental and decorative metalwork. It was made possible by improvements in mining technique – notably in the cutting of adits for drainage – and by developments in smelting and refining. Indeed, the most significant technological innovations before the Industrial Revolution were in the field of metallurgy.

Ironworking

The smelting process had traditionally been carried out on a hearth with a charcoal fire and bellows powered by a water-wheel. The heat was sufficient to bring the metal to a soft, spongy mass, through which were distributed particles of slag and charcoal. The skill of the ironworker lay in manipulating the ore, exposing it to an oxidising blast from the bellows, and alternately heating and hammering it until he had reduced it to a bloom of impure iron. This was, finally, passed between rolls both to squeeze out the remaining slag and also to bring it to a manageable shape, the bar-iron of commerce.

There were few parts of Europe where it could not be made, but the quality of the iron depended in large measure on that of the ore. Ores varied greatly in chemical composition, size of the reserves, and grade or ratio of metal to ore. Above all, they differed in the presence or absence of beneficial elements like manganese, or of deleterious, such as sulphur and phosphorus. Some, like the ores worked at Allevard in Savoy, at Müsen in the Siegerland, or in the Alps of Milan, yielded an iron of high quality for steel-making, largely because of their manganese content. Others produced a metal which defied the efforts of the iron-masters to refine it into a serviceable metal. Amongst these were the low-grade, phosphoric ores of Lorraine and Luxembourg, known contemptuously as *minette*, which, until the introduction of the basic process in 1879, were suited only for making iron castings. The limestone beds of eastern France which contained the *minette* were overlain by a discontinuous, superficial deposit of clay, in which were found nodules and masses of a brown ore of superior quality. Reserves were very small and have long since been worked out. But it was these ores, rather than the *minette*, which yielded the iron for which eastern France was noted in the seventeenth and eighteenth centuries.

Most ore deposits were small and were quickly exhausted. Few could support a smelting works for more than a decade or two, and the ironworker was traditionally mobile as he exploited one ore-body after another. The history of iron production became one of gradual concentration on a few larger reserves. The presence or absence of traces of phosphorus, sulphur or manganese could greatly influence the metal. The ironworker learned empirically which ores to use and which to avoid. The phosphoric ores of eastern France and Lower Saxony were little used before the mid-nineteenth century. The high-grade spathic ores of the Siegerland, of Styria and of central Sweden were amongst the most favoured.

The quality of the ore was, however, not the only factor influencing the location of iron works. No less important was the supply of fuel. Smelting and refining were inordinately extravagant of charcoal, and the more complex technically the industry became the greater was its need for fuel. A single iron works was capable within a few years of exhausting the timber supply for miles around, and this in turn imposed a degree of mobility on the industry.

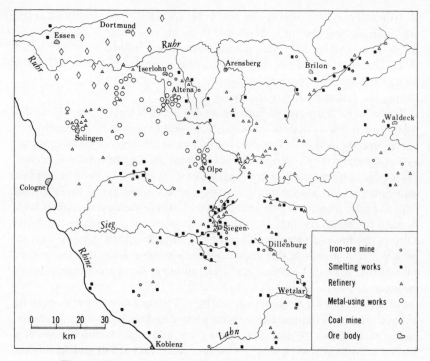

Fig. 5.5 Ironworking in the Siegerland and neighbouring areas about 1800

The earliest iron works had relied upon the wind to provide a draught. The hearth and above all the blast-furnace used bellows, commonly mounted in pairs and usually worked by a water-wheel. In any iron-producing region the availability of water power set a limit to the industry no less certainly than did the supply of charcoal. In some such regions – the Sauerland, lying to the south of the river Ruhr, for example – almost every metre of fall in some of the streams was used. Attempts were made to obtain a blast by other means, notably by a suction device known as a *trempe*,[127] which was used in the Alps of Dauphiné, but there was no effective alternative until the steam-engine began to be used for this purpose in the nineteenth century.

Iron, lastly, was heavy and difficult to transport, and a navigable waterway was a very important asset. The Siegerland and Sauerland had the Rhine; the manufacturing regions of northern Spain and central Sweden were close to the sea; the Urals industry used the network of Russian rivers. Where there was no such convenience, the type of ironware produced had of necessity to be small goods, easily packaged and transported; in short, what has often been called 'Birmingham wares'.

Diffusion of technology

Between the fifteenth and the nineteenth century the technology of ironworking underwent more profound changes than that of any other branch of manufacturing. The blast-furnace increased the volume of metal available; puddling speeded up the parallel refining process; coal and coke were introduced as fuel in order to relieve the growing pressure on the forests, and the cementation and crucible processes aimed to satisfy the demand for steel, which was growing at the expense of that for soft iron. In the course of the nineteenth century the discovery of the open-hearth and then the Bessemer processes allowed the volume of steel-making to keep in line with that of smelting.

The development of the blast-furnace during the fifteenth century was fundamental to all later inventions. Where it was achieved, and by whom, is unknown. It probably occurred in eastern France or the Rhineland. In all probability the sides of the hearth were raised and a strong blast developed. Temperatures ran higher and, instead of a soft bloom of iron, a pool of metal formed on the floor of the hearth. This was, in effect, the *Stücköfen,* whose sides had to be broken down in order to extract the 'pig' of iron which had formed. The next stage was simple. Vents were constructed at the level of the floor of the hearth and were alternately closed with fire-clay and opened to allow the hot metal to flow out into moulds. The essential features of the modern blast-furnace – with the exception only of the hot blast, which was not introduced until 1828 – were present before 1500.

The iron which flowed from the blast-furnace when its vents were tapped differed fundamentally from that which had been made on the hearth by the skill of the ironmaster. The latter was soft and malleable; the former hard and brittle, capable of being poured into a mould and of forming castings, but useless for welding or forging. It was high-carbon or cast-iron, and in itself it had no uses except to make castings.

Iron castings first appeared on a large scale during the sixteenth century. The fluid iron was run into moulds to give decorative firebacks; it was used to cast pots and other vessels of increasingly complex design, and, above all, it was used in cannon-founding. It is doubtful whether those who developed the blast-furnace regarded castings as their principal end-product. What they wanted was more bar-iron which could be made into nails, tools and other forms of ironmongery. This, however, could only be achieved by a further process which reduced the level of carbon in the iron from perhaps 5 per cent to 0.5 per cent or less. Smelting had therefore to be followed by refining, a process in which the carbon was literally burned away on a hearth, under the oxidising stream of air from the bellows, until the desired level was attained.

This was the *indirect* process. It yielded a bar-iron purer than that obtained by the older *direct* process, but incomparably more costly in terms of fuel consumption. The advantages offered by the indirect process in the production of bar-iron were only marginally greater than those of the traditional method, and the superiority of the blast-furnace really lay in its ability to produce high-carbon iron and thus castings. The spread of the blast-furnace was slow. It reached south-eastern England early in the sixteenth century, central Germany by the middle years and the borders of Bohemia before its end. A blast-furnace represented a larger capital investment than any industrial equipment known hitherto, and with its adoption control of the industry passed from the craftsman to the merchant–capitalist. In central and eastern Europe it was more often managed by the landed aristocracy, and in the Urals in the eighteenth century it was thoroughly feudalised, and labour was provided by serfs.

There were three important constraints on the use of the blast-furnace: its inordinate consumption of fuel, the often poor quality of the metal it yielded and the inability of refineries to cope with the increased flow of iron. The charcoal shortage became acute. In France there were widespread complaints of the iron-masters who bought up the available timber.[128] Even in Sweden there were fears – almost certainly exaggerated – for the continued supply, and the output of iron was in fact restricted by the government. In 1709 Darby succeeded in smelting iron with coke at his Shropshire furnace. Although he made no effort to hide the secret of his success, over half a century was to pass before he found imitators. Coke smelting became general in Great Britain before the end of the century, but it was not until after the Napoleonic Wars that it made much progress in continental Europe.

In the meantime a solution had been found to another aspect of the problem, a more rapid and efficient means of refining pig-iron. In 1784 Henry Cort took out a patent for a method of converting high-carbon iron to soft or wrought iron, using coal fuel in a reverberatory furnace. This was the puddling process which, in association with a rolling mill, was quickly diffused across Europe. Its technology was easy to grasp; it filled an obvious need, and, above all, it could use any form of solid fuel.

None of these developments had made it easier to produce steel, the most prized and the most expensive form of iron. Chemically it consisted of iron with a small admixture of carbon; physically it had a distinct crystal structure imparted to it by tempering. The traditional way of producing steel was by a kind of case-hardening, but the quality of the resulting metal varied because absorption of carbon was always uneven. The problem was to produce steel of uniform quality in large enough masses to make the moving parts of machines. The solution was found by a watchmaker, Benjamin Huntsman, looking for a metal from which to make springs of even tension. It might have seemed obvious that the answer was to melt down the steel and thus to achieve an even distribution of carbon. In doing so, however, it seemed impossible not to change the carbon content by oxidising and removing it. Huntsman used crucibles made of a refractory clay, in which he placed bars of cement-steel. He then fused lids on to the crucibles with molten glass, so that nothing could enter or leave. The crucibles were heated until the metal inside them had melted. They were then broken open and the steel poured into moulds. The process yielded only small pieces of steel at a time when there was a growing demand for large masses to be forged or worked into flywheels, cylinders and shafts. This necessitated the pouring simultaneously of the contents of a great many crucibles, a task of immense difficulty. It was the solution of this problem which, early in the nineteenth century, established the reputation and founded the fortunes of the German firm of Krupp, although Krupp's method of making *Gussstahl* was subsequently superseded by the open-hearth and converter processes and, most recently, by the electric furnace (p. 342).

Ironworking was an industry strongly oriented towards the sources of its fuel and energy. A tendency nevertheless developed for the three stages – smelting, refining and fabricating – to become spatially distinct. This was in part due to their dependence on water power which was often inadequate to support more than one branch of the industry at any one place. It was also due to some extent to the fact that smelting was organised on a capitalist basis whereas refining and fabricating remained in some degree in the hands of craftsmen. There was thus a movement of pig-iron from furnace to refinery, and of bar-iron from the latter to the workshops of the nailers and other craftsmen. The fabricating industry in general remained rural because of its dependence on water power, but tended to be oriented to the market. This is well illustrated in the map (fig. 5.5) of the distribution of ironworking in the Sauerland and Siegerland.

Sixteenth to eighteenth centuries

By the sixteenth century a number of ironworking regions had emerged (see p. 50). Foremost amongst them were the Basque province Navarre and the western Pyrenees. The local ores were of a high quality and their coastal location gave them a unique advantage. Spanish iron was shipped to much of western Europe, but production began to decline in the seventeenth century, and by the eighteenth Spain had almost ceased to be a major source of iron.

Spain's principal competitor in the European market was Sweden. The Swedish industry had developed in the latter Middle Ages, and ingots, known as *osmund* iron, were exported by the ships of the Hanse to western Europe.[129] In the sixteenth century the Swedish iron-masters, perhaps in consequence of their adoption of better, water-powered hammers, began to export bar-iron. In the second half of the sixteenth century this grew to be Sweden's most valuable export, and in the seventeenth accounted for up to three-quarters of the total. Sweden had the inestimable advantages of ores of high quality and almost unlimited forest resources. In the sixteenth century production was concentrated in the province of Uppland, where the ores of Dannemora were amongst the best available. Mining and ironworking later spread westwards into Vastmanland, Orebro and Varmland, and north-westwards into the mountains of Dalarna. The volume of iron produced is said to have increased fivefold between 1600 and 1750.[130] This rapid expansion owed much to the introduction of the masonry-built blast-furnace and the Walloon process of refining bar-iron.

Swedish authorities displayed an unusual concern at a very early date for conserving their resources. They attempted to spread the industry over as wide an area as possible by separating refining from the smelting of the ore and pushing the former out into the forests of Varmland and Dalarna. In the eighteenth century this anxiety extended also to ore reserves. From 1720 a quota was allocated to each mill and in 1747 excess capacity was ordered to be destroyed.[131] The advantages of curtailing production were not restricted to the conservation of resources. Swedish iron was in great demand, especially in England, and the limitation of output had the effect of forcing up the price. The total iron production has been put at 40,000 tonnes about 1600.[132] In 1788 it was still only about 68,000. Internal demand was small, for Sweden never developed iron-using industries before the later nineteenth century, and most of the output was exported. Exports, however, never rose much above 45,000 tonnes a year owing in large measure to restrictions on production. The only iron manufacture which figured significantly amongst Sweden's exports was ships' anchors. The industry continued to be dominated by peasant proprietors, who, Jars noted, were often themselves the workers, and, though the manufacture of tinplate was introduced in the later eighteenth century, Swedish iron production was remarkably unprogressive. Gabriel Jars claimed that even the cementation process for steel-making was little used.[133] The industry ceased to expand after about 1770. This was due at first to the rapid growth of the Russian iron industry, which flooded western Europe with a cheaper iron than the Swedes could produce. Then technical advances in Great Britain, Sweden's largest market, led to a drastic reduction in imports of iron. It was not until the mid-nineteenth century that the Swedish iron industry again began to grow.

In western and central Europe the cycle of growth in the sixteenth century, followed by decline and renewed growth in the eighteenth, brought about considerable changes in the location of the iron industry. During the eighteenth-century period of expansion those regions which were best endowed with resources and water power gradually asserted their superiority. Those whose only advantage was their isolation from competition – Brittany and the north German plain – for example, continued to smelt and refine iron for local use, until improved transport in the nineteenth century deprived them of the protection which their remoteness had conferred.

By the later eighteenth century most of the iron production – that of Sweden excepted – was from about a dozen regions, whose importance, both relative and absolute, had been increasing throughout the previous hundred years. These regions can be divided on the basis of terrain and type of ore into three groups.

The first, and in terms of the volume of production the least important, was made up of those iron works which were located within the Alpine system. They included the mines and iron works of the Basque region, the Pyrenees, Savoy and Dauphiné. In each the output was small and technology in general old-fashioned, but the metal produced was often of a high quality, and for this reason production continued, often under difficult physical conditions.[134] In northern Italy there was a small but important production in the Alps of Bergamo and Brescia[135] and in the Ligurian Apennines near Genoa.[136] Iron ores from the island of Elba were also smelted on the Tuscan mainland, where fuel resources were greater.

The iron ores of the Austrian Alps were abundant, easy to extract and of high quality, and were accompanied by abundant fuel resources. The local market, however, was small, and transport difficult and costly. The industry of Styria, Carinthia and latterly of Krain, which lay beyond the Karawanken Alps to the south, remained small. It was largely controlled by merchants from the towns of Leoben, Steyr and St Veit, who sold the metal in Poland, Hungary and the Balkans.[137] The industry expanded in the eighteenth century, but was, like ironworking elsewhere within the Alpine region, slow to adopt western technological innovations and methods of business organisation. Output in Styria was estimated at 20,000 tonnes in 1777, and that of Carinthia at 4000. Production was even smaller in Krain,[138] but the trend was upwards in all provinces. There was also a very small output in Tyrol and Slovakia.

A second group of iron works was based on the ores contained in the primary massifs (see p. 4) of central Europe. Ore bodies were often small and difficult to mine, but their quality was usually high and they yielded an iron suitable for steel-making.[139] Iron had long been worked in Brittany, Maine and Anjou and was used mainly for agricultural tools. There, however, the growing fuel crisis of the eighteenth century compelled many forges to close, and yet others were destroyed during the Revolution. The Armorican industry was extinguished early in the nineteenth century.[140]

The iron industry which developed in the Ardennes and Eifel had larger reserves of ore at its disposal and more extensive forests, and it possessed furthermore the immense advantage of proximity to the markets of the Low Countries and the Rhineland. The early adoption of the blast-furnace led to the separation of the smelting and refining processes. The former continued in the interior of the region, where charcoal was most abundant, while refining and with it the rolling of sheets, the drawing of wire and the fabrication of ironwares were attracted to the tributary valleys of the Meuse, Moselle and Rhine where both water power and water transport to the market were available.[141] The Meuse valley and the Pays de Liège became in the eighteenth century a highly important source of nails and of all iron goods made from drawn wire.

East of the Rhine resources for the iron industry were even greater. The ores of the Siegerland were 'probably the most valuable . . . in Germany',[142] and those of the Lahn–Dill region, the Westerwald and the Taunus were little inferior. The spread of the blast-furnace, with its immense appetite for fuel, had the effect of driving the refineries and fabricating works into areas where the competition for charcoal was less intense.[143] In fact, they concentrated during the eighteenth century in the deep valleys which drain to the Ruhr, Rhine and Fulda, where there was water power to turn their rolls and lift their heavy hammers. Here wire, sheet and strips were produced, to be dispatched by pack animal across the hills of the Sauerland to the workshops around Altena, Iserlohn and Solingen.[144] The flow of materials was approximately from south-east to north-west, from the ore and charcoal of Siegen to the nailers' and cutlers' workshops of the Sauerland and the markets of Cologne, Düsseldorf and Aachen.

To the east of the Siegerland and deriving its skilled labour and entrepreneurs in part from it, lay the iron-producing districts of the Harz (fig. 5.6), Thuringian Forest and Upper Palatinate. The industry in the Harz mountains expanded greatly in the sixteenth century; its capacity was doubled, and by 1600 several blast-furnaces were active. The region suffered disastrously from Tilly's army during the Thirty Years' War,

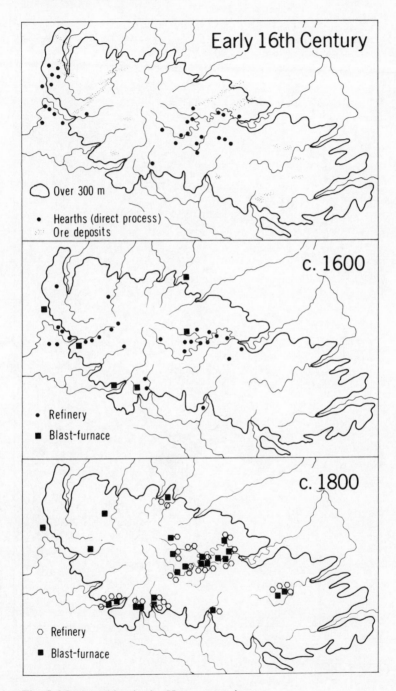

Fig. 5.6 Ironworking in the Harz mountains

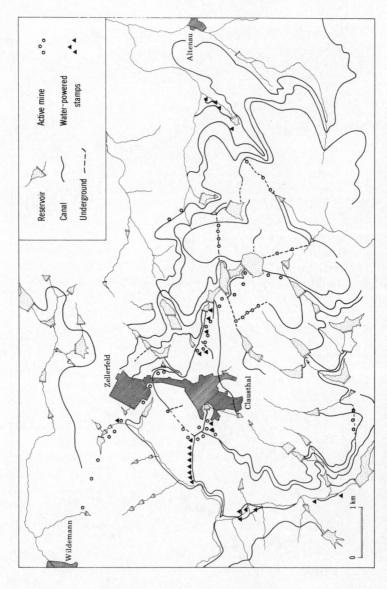

Fig. 5.7 The Clausthal–Zellerfeld mining region in the high Harz. Note the overwhelming dependence of mining and ore-dressing on water power

but had more than recovered by 1700 and continued to increase its production during the following century.[145] The history of ironworking in the Thuringian and Palatinate forests followed a broadly similar course. The former was noteworthy for its arms manufacture, especially around Suhl. In all these areas the industry survived the Napoleonic Wars, but slowly succumbed during the nineteenth century to industries equipped with the new technology and located close to the coalfields.

Ironworking developed later in Bohemia and its surrounding mountains than in western Germany. The region, however, was rich in small ore deposits and its forests were extensive. Water-powered smelting hearths were established in the later Middle Ages, and in the mid-sixteenth century the *Stücköfen* made its appearance, to be overtaken a century later by the blast-furnace. During the eighteenth century the direct process was largely abandoned, and by 1800 there were nearly fifty active furnaces, producing over 10,000 tonnes of iron, more than two-thirds of them in the Plzeň basin and neighbouring Brdy Forest.[146] Output declined during the Napoleonic Wars, but expanded rapidly, with the introduction of new technology, in the 1830s and 40s.

The iron industry of the Bohemian massif spread northwards into Saxony and eastwards into Silesia and Poland, where ores may have been more restricted but the forests were unlimited. Technological innovation was diffused eastwards. The blast-furnace did not begin to replace the hearth until early in the eighteenth century, and not until late in that century did it appear in Poland. Silesia, which passed under Prussian rule in 1741, became an oasis of advanced technology, thanks in large measure to the encouragement given by Frederick the Great. It was here in 1789 that iron was first smelted successfully with coke fuel in continental Europe.[147]

Ironworking had long been carried on in the Holy Cross mountains, near Kielce in central Poland, but methods continued to be simple and output small until the last decades of the eighteenth century. In the 1780s a number of blast-furnaces were built, some of which, ruinous and overgrown, still remain. They were feudally owned, and were operated by the unfree labour of the great estates.[148] Development was interrupted by the last partitions of Poland and the Napoleonic Wars which followed. After 1815, when the so-called Congress Kingdom of Poland became an autonomous territory within the Tsarist empire, the development of industry in this region was again pursued by Stanislas Staszic, as director of industry and trade. The older iron works were revived and new ones established in the forests of central Poland. An elaborate use was made of water power, calling for sophisticated hydraulic engineering. The Polish Rising of 1830 was followed by the suppression of the Congress Kingdom and the abandonment of these

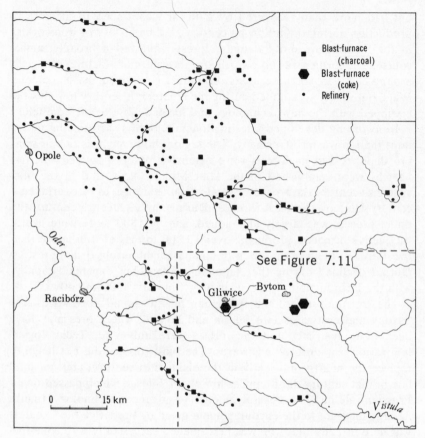

Fig. 5.8 Ironworking in Upper Silesia in the late eighteenth century

plans. The development of the Congress Kingdom was a curious by-product of industrial history, an attempt to create, using only traditional means, a western-style industrial complex (fig. 5.9).

The third group of iron works was dependent on ores of Secondary geological age. These occurred in beds of varying thickness over broad areas of western and central Europe from Périgord to Poland. The beds were shallow and easily worked, but their metal content was low, and most contained a high level of the deleterious element phosphorus. In France these deposits made up over three-quarters of known ore reserves, and over half of those in Germany. The bedded ores of Perigord and Limousin began to be worked on an important scale in the sixteenth century.[149] The blast-furnace was introduced about 1800 and there were soon no less than twenty-eight works in the department of

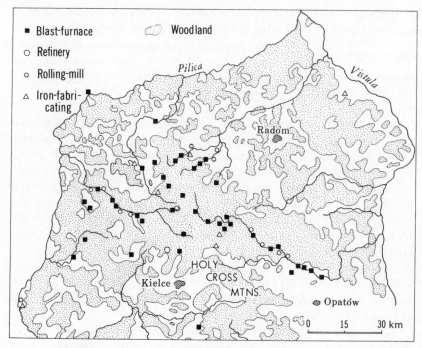

Fig. 5.9 Ironworking in the Kielce–Holy Cross mountains region of central Poland in the early nineteenth century

Dordogne alone.[150] Most French iron works before the mid-nineteenth century lay in a half circle, enclosing the Paris basin on the west, south and east, and following the outcrop of the ore-bearing Jurassic beds. Works were clustered most thickly around Nevers, in Burgundy and in Champagne. Smaller numbers were to be found in Berry, Lorraine and Normandy. From the limestone plateaux of Burgundy, iron works were spread eastwards, across the Saône valley and through the Jura (Franche-Comté) as far as the Swiss border.[151] At the heart of this region lay the region around Chaumont, the present département of Haute-Marne. Its industry had developed during the Middle Ages and sixteenth century, received a set-back in the seventeenth, but expanded again in the eighteenth and reached the peak of its prosperity in 1830s and 40s.[152] Its advantages were considerable. Superficial ores – the *fer fort* – were extensive and very easily worked. The fields, it was said, were 'criblés de petites excavations faites au hasard', and the Napoleonic *Journal des Mines* called for a more systematic exploitation of this valued resource.[153] Forests were abundant, and not until the nineteenth century was there any real shortage of charcoal. The region to the south-east of Paris produced bar-iron, which was mostly marketed at Saint-Dizier on the Marne or Gray on the Saône. Eastern Champagne and northern Burgundy became the chief source of iron in France.[154] The importance of this region grew during the Napoleonic Wars, and was finally extinguished, very abruptly as it happened, by the competition of the coal-based industry of Le Creusot, Lorraine and northern France (see p. 340).

Lorraine, which today is known to have the largest reserve of iron ore in Europe and has, after the Ruhr, the most important smelting industry, does not figure conspicuously in the map of iron works in the late eighteenth century. The reason lay, as a memoir of the Revolutionary government pointed out,[155] in the unsuitability of its *minette* which yielded only a 'cold-short' iron – *cassant à froid*. Nevertheless the *minette* yielded an iron highly suited for castings, and was occasionally blended with better ores. Some of the later centres of the Lorraine steel industry – Hayange, Moyeuvre, Herserange, Villerupt – had already in the eighteenth century developed a smelting and refining industry. Indeed, the de Wendel family was active at Hayange as early as 1704. But the industry grew less rapidly here than elsewhere in France, and even declined during the Revolutionary period.

The bedded ores of Lorraine extend into Luxembourg and southern Belgium where, however, they were not worked on a significant scale until the middle years of the nineteenth century.[156] Comparable ores near Salzgitter in Lower Saxony did not begin to be exploited until the latter half of the century.

The new technology

By the end of the eighteenth century, ironworking was carried on by the indirect process almost everywhere. The demand for fuel, as has been noted (p. 252) was greatly increased and there was an acute scarcity in some areas. At the same time demand for iron was increasing sharply. Inevitably increasing attention was given to the use of mineral fuel in ironworking. There were serious objections to using coal in the furnace, since its sulphur imparted dangerous qualities to the smelted metal. The solution, adopted successfully by Abraham Darby in 1709, was to use coke. But this normally required a larger furnace, higher smelting temperatures and a stronger blast. Nor was any coal suited for making furnace coke, and only by trial and error was the proper combination of furnace and fuel discovered.

Nevertheless, the use of coke in the blast-furnace spread rapidly in Great Britain after about 1750. By 1788, more than three-quarters of the pig-iron had been smelted with coke, and most of the remaining charcoal furnaces disappeared a few years later. No such progress was seen in continental Europe. In the 1760s Gabriel Jars was sent by the French government to examine the progress made in coke smelting in Great Britain. This report, published as *Voyages métallurgiques*, was widely studied for the light it threw on the English process. His descriptions of the processes which he witnessed were far from clear, owing in part to the lack of a scientific terminology, and his reports on the iron made from coke-smelted pig were not encouraging.[157] Coke-smelted iron could not, he reported, be made to yield a serviceable bar-iron. Nevertheless, attempts were made to follow Jars's somewhat confusing recipe. The first was probably at Sulzbach, on lands of the Count of Nassau-Saarbrücken, and was described by de Genssane. An account of the experiment was published by Duhamel de Monceau, and Goethe roundly condemned it as trying to do too many things at once.[158]

The failure of the Sulzbach experiments did not discourage others. Attempts were made to smelt with coke at Juslenville, near Liège; at de Wendel's works at Hayange; at Dijon, using coal from Montcenis, near Le Creusot, and in Languedoc with coal from Alès. All were uniformly unsuccessful. Another visit was made to England, this time by la Houlière who returned to France accompanied by an experienced iron-master, William Wilkinson. This led to a large-scale smelting operation at Le Creusot. But the government's support was wavering and ineffectual; the works were closed and were ultimately converted to a factory for glass-crystal.[159]

Thus, almost a century after Darby's innovation, coke smelting had still not been adopted successfully in western Europe despite the pressing need for iron and the growing shortage of timber. The first effective use of coke took place, not in the west where there had been so many experiments, but in Upper Silesia where the Prussian government was in need of iron for military purposes. The Prussian government, unlike the French, acted vigorously. The advice of William Wilkinson was sought, and it is commonly held that he visited Silesia. Coke was first used at Małapanew. It was a failure, but the furnace was rebuilt and its blast increased. The next experiment was successful, and this was followed by the construction at Gliwice in 1794 of a furnace specifically designed for the use of coke fuel. So far the purpose was to produce iron for castings, especially cannon. In 1802 a coke-fired works was established at Chorzów (Königshütte) for the purpose of making iron for the refinery. It also was successful, and additional furnaces were built three years later.

So matters rested until after the Napoleonic Wars, during which Great Britain made further advances, while continental Europe – Silesia excepted – stagnated technologically. A significant change did however take place in the field of communications. Eighteenth-century advances had, more often than not, been shrouded in secrecy or described in terms which were very nearly incomprehensible. This gradually ended. A scientific vocabulary began to be used, and a periodical literature – the French *Journal des Mines* was the first – began to disseminate technical information to all who would read it.

Coke smelting was reintroduced to western Europe through Belgium. A furnace was built at Couvin, in Namur province in 1823, to smelt with coke and was operated successfully. Two years later John Cockerill built his furnace at Seraing, near Liège. In France the use of coke was introduced in Berry in the 1820s; at Saint-Etienne in 1822; at Maubeuge in 1830; at Denain, in the département of Nord, in 1837, and in the Boulonnais in 1838–9. It was reintroduced at Le Creusot after the works had been bought by Schneider Frères in 1836, and was first used successfully in the Saar at Dillingen in 1838. Coke-smelting came last to Germany, the country which, as events were to show, had the largest reserves of coking coal. Not until 1849 was iron first smelted with coke in the Ruhr, but thereafter progress was very rapid.

In contrast with the slow diffusion of coke smelting was the rapid spread of Cort's puddling process (see p. 252). The latter, though extremely arduous, was technologically simple, and its adoption solved two problems – the scarcity of charcoal fuel and slowness of the traditional refining hearth. Lastly, pig-iron, which was already being transported considerable distances to the refineries, could as easily be moved to the coalfields. Puddling was adopted in central Belgium in 1820 and at Saint-Etienne and on the coalfield of northern France soon afterwards, and it spread from there to Aachen and the Rhineland where coal could be obtained by water transport from the Ruhr. In the 1830s it was adopted on the Saar and Ruhr coalfields. In 1835, with the advent of railways in central Europe, the demand for puddled iron for rolling rails increased sharply. Puddling and rolling mills – the two were always associated – sprang up on all the major coalfields. Many – those, for example, at Aachen and Düsseldorf – were geographically divorced from the smelting process and were dependent on pig-iron from in some instances distant sources. It was through the puddling process, with its extravagant demand for coal, that the coalfields exercised their magnetic attraction for heavy industry.

Shipbuilding

The growing significance of waterborne commerce gave great importance to the ship- and boat-building industry. The number of sea-going vessels must have increased at least twenty-five-fold between the sixteenth and the early nineteenth century. With the growth in numbers went some increase in size and considerable modification in design. Nonetheless the average size of ships about 1800 was little more than a hundred tons. Every effort was made to crowd on as much canvas as possible, and by the late eighteenth century it seemed impossible to add to the sails of a fully rigged ship. Its size was limited by the extent of the sails which it could carry, so that there was little further increase in ship size until the coming of steam.[160]

Until the 1840s sea-going ships were built exclusively of wood. The largest shipbuilding industries were to be found in the chief maritime countries, particularly England and the Netherlands. In north-western Europe, however, ships' timbers were a scarce commodity, and the yards around the Zuider Zee were heavily dependent upon imports. Though some oak was available in parts of north-western Europe for the primary structure of a ship, deals for planking and spars for masts had to be imported. These were supplied mainly by Scandinavia and the eastern Baltic until imports from North America began late in the eighteenth century.[161]

Though shipbuilding was concentrated in areas generally lacking in suitable timber, construction was also to be found on coasts where there were forests. The Spanish and Portuguese fleet were largely built along the coast of Galicia and the Asturias, and the Baltic region was not unimportant, though its many small ports faced strong Dutch competition in this respect. The little port of Elbląg, situated on one of the branches of the Vistula, retained for example a small shipbuilding industry from the Middle Ages until the early nineteenth century.[162] It declined in importance with the ascendancy of Dutch shipbuilders, and concentrated on small river and coastal craft, but demand continued for its relatively simple products as long as wooden sailing ships were used commercially. Elbląg was but one of many similar Baltic ports which profited from the relative cheapness of materials to exploit the lower fringe of this expanding market.

The introduction of steam power and the construction of iron ships brought about a fundamental change in the distribution of the shipbuilding industry. Iron plates were first used in river barges in the late eighteenth century, but in sea-going ships not until the 1840s. The use of steam power to propel a ship crept in very slowly in the 1830s and 40s, and was used only as a supplement to sail. The relocation of the shipbuilding industry did not come until the latter part of the nineteenth century.

The mining industries

The expansion of metalworking was made possible only by the contemporaneous developments in mining technology. Improvements in pumping were a precondition of deep mining. If most iron-mines before the nineteenth century were little more than shallow pits, coal-mines were becoming deeper, and the increased coal production of the late eighteenth and nineteenth centuries was made possible only by the introduction of the steam-driven pump.

Coal-mining

Coal had long been mined in small quantities, but medical opinion held that its use was unhealthy, and its combustion in stoves and furnaces unsuited to the purpose was unpleasant. On the other hand it was a readily accessible fuel in many parts of Europe. There were an immense number of coalfields, most of them very small in their total reserves and today no longer used. In most instances the coal seams came to the surface and were easily recognised. In some cases these outcrops lay on the flanks of hillsides, so that drifts could be driven into them without problems of drainage. This happened along the Meuse valley upstream from Liège, and in that of the Ruhr, and these two areas were the first European coalfields to achieve more than local importance.

Early coal-mining was carried on as small partnerships and sometimes even as a part-time activity on small plots of land leased for the purpose. Unlike the metalliferous-miner, the coal-miner had no right to enter land and search for coal without the consent of the owner, and his market was restricted by the cost and difficulty of transport and the prevailing prejudice against it. It is impossible to know with any degree of certainty how many of the coalfields were being exploited in the sixteenth century. There is evidence for mining in the Burgundian fields of Autun, Le Creusot and Champagnac by the middle of the century.[163] That of Saint-Etienne in the Lyonnais was being worked and coal was exported by river from the Liège and Ruhr fields.

The earliest uses of coal were for burning bricks and lime, but its sulphurous fumes detracted from its usefulness in preparing food and heating the home. The shortage and high price of wood were in its favour. 'Sea-coal' was used in London, but was strongly condemned by writers such as John Evelyn, and in Paris its use was prohibited by the doctors.[164] Despite these fears coal became increasingly widely used. By 1670 the Rive-de-Gier mines, near Saint-Etienne, were supplying some 20,000 tonnes a year to the Lyons region. The Canal de Briare, opened in 1664 (see p. 300), linked the Loire system with the Seine and allowed coal from Burgundy and the Bourbonnais to reach Paris, while Rouen had since the sixteenth century imported English coal. Stoves and chimneys were adapted to the new fuel. Jars reported that in the Saint-Etienne region people used it for every domestic purpose without harm to themselves and with great benefit to the country. Morand wrote in the *Description des arts* that the high cost of wood was no longer a hardship, since a cheaper fuel was now available, adding that it would keep the masses from idleness and allow the forests to regenerate.[165]

By the second half of the eighteenth century the prejudice against the use of coal was being overcome; it remained only to make its use technically more efficient. By about 1750 the output of coal in France had climbed to about 450,000 tonnes a year, and was increasing sharply in the Austrian Netherlands. The greatest potential appeared at this time to lie in the coalfield which extended from near Valenciennes in northern France across the southern Low Countries and into Germany at Aachen. Erosion had removed the coal measures between Namur and Huy, and to the west of Mons the seams dipped from view beneath a cover of Secondary and later deposits. This coalfield was the best known in Europe. Buffon regarded the Liège region as 'perhaps in all Europe the area most richly endowed with coal',[166] and both Morand and Jars gave it pride of place amongst European coalfields. The reason was that the river Meuse had cut its valley lengthways across the coalfield revealing the seams along the valley sides for almost 30 kilometres and facilitating both mining and transport. The *exposed* coalfield also extended westwards from Namur for about 80 kilometres, though beyond Charleroi it was partially hidden. It had long been mined around Mons and Saint-Ghislain, where the coal was considered to be of a very high quality, and very small concessions, some of them relating to a single seam, were granted by the landowners. But to the west, where it was entirely covered by later deposits, attempts to trace its course had been unsuccessful.[167]

In 1713 France relinquished her control of the Mons area and with it the not inconsiderable coal production of this region. This led to a search on the French side of the new boundary for the continuation of the Charleroi-Mons field. The alignment of the coalfield, however, changes direction, and exploratory pits were sunk too far to the south. The brothers Jacques and Pierre Desandrouin then secured a concession to search to the north of Valenciennes. In 1720 they struck a poor seam near Fresnes, but reached a workable coal at Anzin in 1734. Many pits were sunk during the following years, and in 1757 the Anzin company was formed, absorbing the smaller undertakings and exercising for a time a virtual monopoly of coal production in French Hainault. By the time of the Revolution, the Anzin company was producing about 37,500 tonnes a year, and a number of mines had already been opened on the Aniche Concession to the west. But still the greater part of the coal basin of northern France remained undiscovered beneath the thickening chalk of Artois (p. 335).[168]

Although coal production increased on the French sector of the northern basin, the Belgian fields of Liège and Mons (the Borinage) remained the most highly regarded and the most productive. They were in the view of a contemporary 'le plus vaste et le plus richement doué de notre continent'.[169] Next in importance, but a very long way behind, came the Saint-Etienne coalfield. Most other coalfields in western Europe were of little more than local importance. Statistics of production are, however, inadequate and unreliable, despite the efforts of the Napoleonic government to publish them in the *Annales des Mines*. Total production west of the Rhine was probably of the order of 2.3 million tonnes in 1814, of which more than three-quarters came from the coal basin of Belgium and northern France.[170] By 1825 this had increased to 3.3 and by the late 1830s to 6 million. Thereafter growth was more rapid, as the western extension of the northern coal basin was explored and brought into production, and French production drew level with Belgian.[171]

The largest reserves of coal in Europe lay, not, as had been supposed, in Belgium and northern France, but in the Ruhr basin and Upper Silesia, the one largely hidden by a thick cover of later rocks, the other on the eastern frontier of pre-industrial Europe where demand was small. Coal had been extracted since the Middle Ages from shallow pits sunk into the exposed sector of the Ruhr field, and shipped down the river Ruhr to the Rhine. The political fragmentation of the region hindered exploitation. The Prussian government did much to stimulate mining in its sector of the coalfield in the County of Mark and to increase its efficiency, and production was increased from about 61,000 tonnes a year in the 1760s to about 189,000 in the 1790s and to 210,000 at the beginning of the next century.[172] In the following years coal-mining advanced northwards into the hidden field, and total output increased to about 1,666,000 tonnes in 1850, still less than half that of the Borinage. On the other hand, the minute fields in northern Westphalia, Hanover and Saxony, like the small French basins, retained an importance out of all proportion to their resources.[173]

The Upper Silesian coalfield was in its extent and resources as large as that of the Ruhr, and its seams furthermore were visible at the surface over an extensive area. Coal had been worked by the peasantry from shallow pits long before the Prince of Pless in the eighteenth century granted the first concession. There was however little demand for coal and it would have been many years before a mining industry could develop were it not for the nearby deposits of lead- and zinc-ores. There was no lack of demand for these metals, and in 1786 the Prussian government bought an English-made steam-engine to work the pumps at the Tarnowskie Góry lead-mines. The first large demand for coal was to satisfy the needs of this machine. Other steam-engines followed, and these, together with the smelting furnaces for lead and zinc and the newly built blast-furnaces (p. 259) constituted for many years the only significant market for Upper Silesian coal. Coal production remained small and did not exceed 100,000 tonnes a year by 1820. The coming of the railway in 1845 brought about a more rapid expansion of mining, and output reached a million tonnes by the mid-century.

The Upper Silesian coalfield extended into both Habsburg Moravia and Russian-held Poland. Attempts were made at Dąbrowa in the latter to open up mines in the 1840s but met with little success. A few small mines were developed in the Austrian sector, but in neither was coal-mining of importance before the late nineteenth century.

Nowhere else in Europe, except Bohemia, was coal-mining of any importance. There were several small basins within the Bohemian massif, as well as extensive deposits of brown coal. The latter were worked intermittently in the eighteenth century, but there was no serious exploitation of them until late in the nineteenth. Bituminous-coal production reached only about 15,000 tonnes by 1810, but increased rapidly during the following years, reaching about 150,000 tonnes in 1825 and 625,000 twenty years later.[174]

It is not easy to estimate the total European production of coal before the mid-nineteenth century.[175] It is nevertheless very doubtful whether total output could have exceeded 1,000,000 tonnes in 1700 or 1,500,000 in 1750. By the end of the century it must have been (excluding Great Britain) between 3.0 and 5.0 million, of which at least a third came from the present territory of Belgium. By 1825 production had risen to at least 6 million tonnes and by 1850 to 24 million.

The non-ferrous metals

These played a relatively more important role in pre-industrial Europe than at any time since. Lead was used for cisterns, pipes and roofing; copper, pewter, brass and bronze, for making vessels and utensils of all kinds, and the precious metals for decoration, ornament and currency. Europe is noteworthy more for the variety of its metalliferous ores than for their abundance. With very few exceptions they are associated with the Hercynian rocks, and were located in a very few mineralised areas. The most important were the highlands – the Eifel and Sauerland – on either side of the Rhine, the Harz mountains and the mountains of Saxony and Bohemia. Within the Alpine system, the southern Meseta and the rocks of similar geological age found in the Balkan peninsula were highly mineralised. The highly important lead–zinc deposits of

Upper Silesia occurred as replacement deposits in limestone. Lastly, the Scandinavian massif – older geologically than the Hercynian system – was also intruded by mineral-bearing lodes. Production was mainly from a small number of mineralised regions. Most lay within the belt of hills which extends from the Ardennes, through the Western wald, Harz and Thuringian Forest to Bohemia and the mountains of Upper Hungary and Transylvania. To the north lay the mineralised regions of Sweden, Norway and the western fringe of the British Isles; to the south, the extensive resources of the Spanish tableland, and of the Austrian and Dinaric mountains.

Emphasis was at first on silver. The Harz mines continued to produce until the Thirty Years' War, but were greatly exceeded in importance by the newly opened mines of Saxony, Bohemia and Slovakia. Silver production reached its peak in the Ore mountains about 1530. The focus of mining activity then moved across the mountains into the Bohemian basin, where the Fugger were active at Jáchymov by 1529.[176] Mining at Pr̆ibram and Kutna Hora revived after the destruction of the Hussite wars. The most vigorous developments, however, took place in the Carpathian mountains, where the Fugger family of Augsburg, in collaboration with local entrepreneurs, the Thurzo family, introduced German capital and mining techniques. There was a short period of intense activity based on the towns of Banská Bystrica, Kremnica and Banská Stiavnica. In 1541 the Fugger withdrew from their Slovak ventures; the volume of ore production contracted, but mining continued at a lower level into the eighteenth century.[177]

Silver-mining was associated with that of copper, and in several areas the two were produced jointly. The chief sources of copper were Sweden, the Harz, Vosges[178] and Slovakia. Sweden had been the major source in the later Middle Ages, but was in the course of the sixteenth century overtaken by Slovakia. Copper production rose sharply from the Fugger mines and continued at a high level long after they had abandoned their enterprises in Slovakia.[179] These were taken over by other mining capitalists like the Manlicks, Paumgärtners and Welsers, and production continued though with interruptions through the seventeenth and eighteenth centuries on a scale sufficient to warrant a visit by Gabriel Jars to Banská Bystrica.[180] Slovak copper was largely sold in the markets of western and southern Europe. Smelted near the mines, it was sent across Poland to the Baltic ports, westwards to south Germany, or to Venice. The largest copper market was Antwerp – until the destruction of the latter by the Spaniards in 1576. Thereafter Amsterdam became the leading copper market.[181]

Production in Slovakia began to decline in the late sixteenth century because the market was oversupplied, and when it revived after the

Thirty Years' War, Europe was 'flooded with Swedish copper'.[182] The large Swedish copper deposit at Falun – Stora Kopparberg – was opened up during the later Middle Ages, but production did not become significant internationally until late in the sixteenth century.[183] Mining was carried on by a large number of small enterprises, but they were concentrated in the Falun district, and were rigidly controlled by the Swedish crown which took a royalty on copper produced. During the seventeenth century, copper, 'the noblest commodity which the Swedish crown produces or can boast of', as Oxenstierna described it, was the chief export and the principal means of Swedish war finance. Production was encouraged by the government, and Swedish agents abroad manipulated the market in order to secure the highest price. Maximum production was achieved about 1650 when Sweden produced more than half the copper entering into European trade. The mines were, however, nearing exhaustion, and copper production declined through the seventeenth century and almost entirely ceased in the eighteenth.

Much of the copper was alloyed with tin or zinc to make bronze or brass. There was thus a demand for these metals, as there was also for lead, the basis of pewter. Lead and zinc were commonly associated. It was an easy matter to smelt lead, but zinc was to pre-industrial technology one of the most intractable of metals. Its smelting temperature is above its boiling point, so that it separated off as a vapour and thus was lost. Eventually a condenser, known as a muffle furnace, came to be used to trap the zinc vapour, but this was not used until about 1800. Metallic zinc was unknown until the later eighteenth century, and brass was usually made by adding calamine, the commonest zinc-ore, to molten copper.[184] The mines of Vieille Montagne, in the Ardennes near Liège, together with those of the Harz mountains were able to satisfy most of Europe's demand for zinc, but towards the end of the eighteenth century Upper Silesia became an important – ultimately the dominant – source of supply.

There is little evidence before the nineteenth century of the volume of production of the non-ferrous metals. In general it was very small. Sweden's copper production at the peak of its prosperity was no more than about 3000 tonnes.[185] The Upper Silesian zinc output in 1809 was only about 100 tonnes a year.[186]

6
The pattern of trade

During the three centuries from the sixteenth to the early nineteenth the prevailing economic principles were those commonly known as mercantilism or cameralism. This body of doctrine took shape gradually, but its end was abrupt as the ideas of free trade and international competition spread to continental Europe from Great Britain. Two aspects of mercantilist doctrine are particularly significant in the context of this chapter. The first was the view that the precious metals were the ultimate repository of wealth. A country should aim to accumulate bullion; its export trade should exceed its imports in value, with the excess paid for with precious metals. In Mun's words, written in the early seventeenth century, 'wee must ever observe this rule: to sell more to strangers yearly than we consume of theirs in value . . . because that part of our stock which is not returned to us in wares must necessarily be brought home in treasure'.[1]

The second aspect of mercantilism derived from the first. One country should be dependent upon another only to the smallest degree possible; it should grow or manufacture as much as it could of what it needed. To do otherwise would be to give hostages to its neighbours and rivals, and to risk an outflow of bullion. Mercantilist policies were applied with varying degrees of completeness and understanding. In Great Britain and the Netherlands they were tempered by the high degree of freedom and initiative allowed to the individual merchant. In France and Prussia the state assumed a vigorous and authoritarian role in dictating economic policy. Everywhere, however, freedom of trade was restricted in the supposed interests of well-being and security, of opulence and power, as Mun expressed these objectives of mercantilist policy. Everything was done to prevent the export of raw materials and the migration of skilled craftsmen. The import of manufactured goods was discouraged and domestic crafts and industries were promoted.

Despite these restrictive policies the amount of trade increased throughout the period. Its volume is difficult to measure, and for many branches of trade there are no statistics. Series are lacking for all continental countries before the nineteenth century. A measure of the scale of the growth of trade is the increase in the imports of England and

Wales by about 430 per cent between 1697 and 1791, and of exports (not counting re-exports) of 690 per cent.[2] The commerce of France is said to have grown by over 300 per cent between 1716–20 and 1772–6.[3] The expansion of Dutch trade in the previous century was probably even more rapid, though there are no adequate statistics to show it.[4] The general course of European trade was marked by growth in the sixteenth century, recession in the middle and later years of the seventeenth, and renewed growth in the eighteenth. This became very rapid in the nineteenth as factory industries developed and many of the restraints on trade were abandoned.

Much of Europe's external trade was with colonial dependencies. Not only Spain and Portugal, but also Great Britain, France and the Netherlands acquired overseas possessions, whose purpose was in the main commercial. Colonial trade involved no concessions to rivals and enemies, and those colonies were most valued which contributed most to the economic needs of the home country. But the growing volume of imports of colonial origin – there was a more than threefold increase in the value of Asiatic goods auctioned in Amsterdam between 1648 and 1780[5] – had to be requited by exports, even if they had been obtained at concessionary prices. The colonial trade thus encouraged export industries, particularly the manufacture of light textiles and ironware, and prepared the way for the technological innovations of the later eighteenth century.

Europe's internal trade was hindered throughout the period by embargoes, tariffs and tolls. All countries protected their own agriculture and crafts by prohibiting or restricting imports, and, furthermore, did their utmost to injure those of their neighbours by restricting the export of raw materials and part-finished goods. Such restraints were even imposed on movements *within* a single country. France abandoned its internal tariffs only with the Revolution; and the reduction of such obstacles to trade between the German states did not even begin until 1819, and it was not until 1841 that most members of the German Confederation had been brought within a customs union.

To these obstacles to internal trade were added the physical difficulties which arose from the poor condition of the roads and navigable rivers. The letters of the French intendants are filled with complaints: in Poitou the roads were so bad that people could not get to the fairs and markets;[6] in Alsace there was not a single paved road;[7] in the Auvergne roads were unsuited to wheeled traffic.[8] Such conditions tended to drive traffic back to the rivers, but these – shallow, silted, encumbered with obstacles – were of little use. Throughout Europe, from Spain to Poland, attempts were made to improve them for navigation and to construct linking canals (see p. 298), but such projects met with only limited success. Technical difficulties were in many instances too great, and some areas which called loudly for improved means of transport had no rivers to improve. The Limousin, for example, exported no wine because it had no navigation.[9] Such conditions occurred widely. Some improvements were effected in the eighteenth century, especially in France. Internal navigation was made easier in the early nineteenth, but there was no revolution in transport until the coming of the railways. It is not surprising that the volume of Europe's internal trade grew a great deal more slowly than that of external trade, and that those industries were most favoured which had convenient links with the coast and ports.

This chapter will examine the changing pattern of Europe's trade over the period of three centuries, first the external or seaborne trade of the continent; then its internal trade, carried on by road, river and canal. The former was made up not only of commerce with the Americas, the Middle East and Asia, but it also embraced a very important coastwise trade. The Baltic trade in iron and ships' timbers was intra-European, but it also formed part of Europe's maritime trade, scarcely distinguishable from that with Canada or Africa. The maritime trade of Europe is conveniently divisible, according to the three spheres in which it was carried on, into Mediterranean, oceanic and northern. These overlapped and reacted on one another. Antwerp and Amsterdam were as much ports engaged in the northern trade as in the oceanic, and Seville was a meeting place of Mediterranean and Atlantic. Nevertheless, the fortunes of the three and the types of goods in which they dealt were sufficiently distinct to warrant separate treatment.

External trade

The Mediterranean

Mediterranean trade recovered from the impact of the Portuguese voyages, but its renewed prosperity was short-lived. Genoa and Venice had been the foremost amongst the many Mediterranean ports of Europe. Genoa had never played an important role in the spice trade; her merchants had tended to use 'round' ships rather than galleys for the transport of bulk cargoes: grain, cotton, alum, timber.[10] This trade was not tied to particular ports, and the Genoese were able to cut their losses in the eastern Mediterranean and concentrated on their trade with Spain and north-west Africa and on the processing of imported raw materials. Genoese trade declined, but Genoa as an economic force remained potent into the seventeenth century. Venice, on the other hand, strove to make its traditional system work in changing circumstances. By the mid-sixteenth century Venetian ships were as numerous in Alexandria and Tripoli as they had been a century earlier, and 'in the late sixteenth century the Mediterranean and oceanic routes competed on fairly even terms'.[11] But Venice was faced not only with the rivalry of the Portuguese, which had indeed lost its edge, but also with the competition of other Mediterranean ports. Of these Livorno (Leghorn), founded early in the century by the Duke of Tuscany to replace the silting port of Pisa, grew slowly at first, but late in the century broadened its trade and became a major port for grain and mixed cargoes.[12] In the mid-sixteenth century the port of Ancona developed an important Mediterranean trade when Florentine merchants began to ship their cloth by this route.[13] Dubrovnik (Ragusa) had long traded in the shadow and under the protection of Venice, but in the early sixteenth century expanded its activities and, with the help of a large fleet – some 180 ships – and a more cordial relationship with the Turks, became a major port in its own right. Other ports, amongst them Split (Spalato) and Senj (Segna) also came to the fore;[14] 'Italian [i.e. Venetian and Genoese] domination of the Balkan and eastern Mediterranean trade was being undermined by the rise of local merchants and local shipping.'[15] There were, however, other factors in the eclipse of the two giants of Mediterranean commerce: the failure of Italy's export industries; the renewed danger of piracy in the Mediterranean,[16] and the increasing importance of the land route across the Balkan peninsula, which favoured Dalmatian ports rather than Venice.

Venice, the symbol of Mediterranean trade, served primarily as the link between central Europe and the commercial system of the inland sea. In 1508 the Fondaco of the German merchants beside the Grand Canal, which had served their needs since the thirteenth century, was rebuilt.[17] The trade which flowed through the Fondaco fluctuated, but showed no marked downward trend before the late sixteenth century. The cargoes which entered and cleared the port of Venice were, however, increasingly carried in other than Venetian ships.[18] Venetian merchants, discouraged by competition and the growing risks of navigation, were, like successful merchants everywhere, putting their money into farms on the *terra firma*. In 1602 the Venetian senate ruled that goods brought to the port should be carried either in Venetian ships or in vessels of their country of origin. This was aimed at the carrying trade of ports like Split and Dubrovnik, but it led in fact to an abrupt decline in the trade of Venice itself, which became a port of local significance, serving the needs of its own inflated population and immediate hinterland.

The final blow to the trade of the Italian cities came from the merchants of north-western and northern Europe. The English were the first in the field. Their cloth trade with the Mediterranean had formerly gone by way of the Antwerp emporium.[19] The collapse of the latter encouraged them to deal directly with their customers in the eastern Mediterranean. In 1581 a company, the predecessor of the Levant Company, was formed to trade with the Ottoman empire. Exports to the Mediterranean were primarily of cloth, followed in importance by pewter and other metal goods. Return cargoes were made up of cotton, silks, dried fruits, wine and oil. The company continued to carry on trade with the Levant until 1825.[20] It was, however, faced with very strong competition – from the Dutch, the Hansards and the French.[21]

The Dutch were the true heirs of the Portuguese, and it was in Dutch hands that the oceanic spice trade ultimately triumphed over the land trade across the Middle East. They were, however, preceded by the Flemings, who for a short period before the eclipse of Antwerp did business directly with Naples and Venice,[22] though most of their Italian trade went overland.[23] About 1590 there was a sudden change in the commercial situation. There had been imports of grain from Atlantic Europe to meet local shortages at intervals through the century. From 1586 there was a series of bad harvests, and by 1590 there were famine conditions in many of the larger Italian cities. The Duke of Tuscany sent agents to Danzig to make purchases, and these were quickly followed by Venetian emissaries. Grain shipments from the Baltic began to arrive in the winter of 1590–1 and increased in volume during the following years.[24] The crisis did not last, though there continued to be a small import of Baltic grain into Italy. The northerners had forced themselves into Mediterranean trade and were not easily dispensed with. Some of the grain ships were Hanseatic, sailing direct from the Baltic;[25] a few were Italian which had sailed north in search of grain, but an increasing proportion were Dutch, bringing grain transhipped in the ports of the Netherlands.[26] The grain ships returned with cargoes of Mediterranean products: wine and dried fruit, rice and cotton. The range of imports brought into the Mediterranean by the Dutch increased as Amsterdam became the focus of north-west European trade, and it was not many years before they were selling in Venice the spices which they had themselves brought from the East Indies by way of the Cape. Not only was Mediterranean trade depressed in the seventeenth and eighteenth centuries, but only a diminishing proportion of it was left in the hands of the Italians themselves. Venice and Genoa, Marseilles and Barcelona were henceforward concerned mainly with local trade, while the Dutch, English and French sold the products of western Europe in the markets of the Levant.

The Baltic

Trade between the Baltic region and north-western Europe grew significantly during the sixteenth century, but it ceased to be dominated by the merchants of the Hanse. There was little opportunity, in a Europe dominated increasingly by powerful governments, for the autonomous cities which made up the League to carry on an independent policy. Attendance at the periodic Hansetäge, its only central organ, declined; its sea was invaded increasingly by Dutch and British ships, and, if the fortunes of the Hansards revived later in the century, this was only because the energies of the Dutch were absorbed in their struggle against Spain. Lübeck continued to be important for Sweden's trade,[27] but for the rest the trade of the Hanse was virtually destroyed by the Thirty Years' War and the Swedish invasion. The last meeting of the Hansetag took place in 1669.

The heirs of the Hansards were the British and the Dutch. English ships were in the Baltic in the mid-sixteenth century, importing cloth and returning laden with corn and naval supplies.[28] The Eastland Company was formed in 1579, with its principal Baltic trading centre at Elbląg. The Muscovy Company had been formed a few years earlier to trade with Russia by way of Archangel, but soon diverted its activities to the Baltic port of Narva, from which its members reached Novgorod and Moscow.[29] During the later decades of the sixteenth century English merchants did well in the Baltic. Their trade was predominantly in cloth, and towards the end of the century they were supplying some 90 per cent of the Baltic import.[30] After 1600, however, they began to encounter increasing difficulties. Dutch competition became more vigorous and successful; the feud between the Eastland merchants and the Merchant Adventurers grew in intensity, the latter claiming a monopoly on the export of unfinished cloth to the Dutch, who finished and sold it to the Baltic. They complained of the high Sound dues levied by the Danes, of the hostility of the Danzigers and of the unreliability of the Russians.[31] Their trade declined, and by the mid-seventeenth century two-thirds of the cloth trade was in the hands of the Dutch. Thereafter British trade with the Baltic held steady through much of the eighteenth century, but this was only because its emphasis had changed. Grain disappeared from Britain's Baltic imports, and was replaced by Swedish iron, flax and hemp from Livonia, and Norwegian timber. British ships now sailed to Stockholm, Riga and Narva rather than to Danzig and Elbląg.[32]

Great Britain's need for iron and naval supplies from the more northerly Baltic lands increased, and her continuing problem was to find some means of paying for them in this predominantly bilateral trade.

The Dutch could, at least in the earlier period, offer a far greater range of goods in return. In the course of the eighteenth century, however, bills of exchange began to be used, thus removing one important constraint on trade.

Throughout the seventeenth century the Dutch dominated the trade of northern Europe. Here, as in the Mediterranean, they had been preceded by the Flemings. Antwerp had for a time been the terminus of Baltic trade,[33] but in the later years of the sixteenth century it was gradually replaced by Amsterdam. Indeed, many of the Dutch merchants who engaged in the Baltic trade were themselves refugees from Antwerp. Amsterdam's trade had begun to grow long before the war with Spain came to a temporary halt in 1609. It was in fact the Baltic trade which provided the sinews of war. By 1600, wrote Christensen, 'the Dutch were unquestionably the world's leading seafaring nation'.[34] Dutch trade with the Baltic continued to increase, despite wide year-to-year fluctuations, until the 1620s. There was then a sharp drop, brought about by the Swedish invasion of north Germany. A new peak was reached about 1650, after which the volume of trade stabilised at a lower level. There was a further decline in Dutch Baltic trade in the eighteenth century.

In the eyes of contemporaries the explosion of Dutch trade in northern Europe was little short of miraculous. 'By extraordinary enterprise and efficiency, they had managed to capture something like three-quarters of the traffic in Baltic grain, between half and three-quarters of the traffic in timber, and between a third and a half of that in Swedish metals. Three-quarters of the salt from France and Portugal that went to the Baltic was carried in Dutch bottoms. More than half the cloth imported to the Baltic area was made or finished in Holland.'[35] By 1650, as Wilson has shown, 'the Dutch economy had expanded to a point where further growth was difficult and gains already made were but precariously held'.

The Dutch were fortunate in having a wide range of goods with which to pay for their imports. In terms of volume, and generally also in value, salt made up more than a half of the eastbound cargoes of the Dutch. This was followed by salted herring, which tended to increase in volume as the Dutch developed their 'great fishery', the summer and autumn herring catch off the Scottish coast.[36] Wines, spices and textiles were of smaller importance. Of these exports to the Baltic, only the herring and a fraction of the textiles were products of the Dutch themselves; the rest had been brought into the Netherlands in the course of Dutch Atlantic and oceanic trade.

The Baltic trade is the earliest for which comprehensive statistics are available. This is due entirely to the fact that most of the shipping

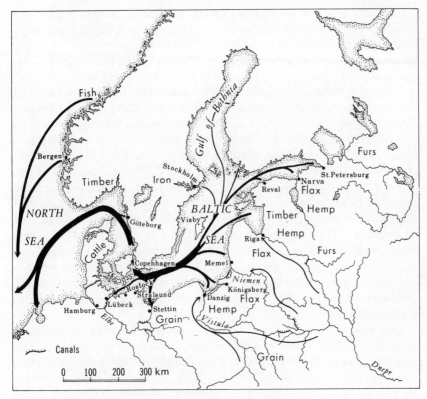

Fig. 6.1 The trade of the Baltic about 1800

entering and leaving the Baltic Sea sailed through the Danish Sound, the Öresund, and was there called upon to pay a toll to the Danish government. A record of some kind of the passage of ships was kept from the late fifteenth century. By the middle years of the sixteenth the reporting became sufficiently detailed and careful to permit a picture to be built up of both the cargoes carried and the origin and destination of the ships.[37] The Sound Registers have, however, to be handled with circumspection. They relate only to traffic through the Sound; they omit all shipping which passed through the Great Belt (the Little Belt seems not to have been used), which *may* have amounted to 15 per cent of the whole, and also that – probably only a very small percentage – which took the overland route from Lübeck to Hamburg. It is evident from a comparison between the cargoes known to have left Baltic ports, especially Danzig, and those declared to the Danish authorities in the Sound that there was under-reporting.[38] There were furthermore omissions and errors in recording, and a frustrating tendency to lump together goods of very diverse character and origin. Light goods were sometimes smuggled; grain tended to be under-reported, and the only commodity to be fully recorded – because it could not easily be hidden – was timber.

The grain trade was crucial to Baltic commerce in the sixteenth and seventeenth centuries. Its source was mainly the plains of Great Poland, Ruthenia and Livonia. The exportable surplus fluctuated greatly. The annual average during the first half of the seventeenth century was about 68,500 lasts (about 175,000 tonnes). This fell to about 56,000 lasts during the second half and to less than 32,000 between 1700 and 1749. This decline in exports is not easy to explain. It does not appear to have been due to any shortage at the producing end: this is implicit in the price movements, and in western Europe population was beginning to increase at the time when exports declined most sharply. Exports were largest during the period when famine crises were most frequent in western Europe, but it seems likely, as Faber has argued, that western and southern Europe were in fact able to increase their per capita food production (see pp. 209–10) and needed less from the Baltic in the eighteenth than in the seventeenth century.[39]

The record of the timber trade by contrast was one of continual growth. The Dutch at first dominated it, as they did that in grain. The logs were rafted down the Baltic rivers, some of them even supporting loads of corn, and were shipped from the same ports as the grain.[40] But the timber trade began to contract during the seventeenth century in the southern Baltic, probably because of the exhaustion of forests close to the navigable rivers, and merchants turned to the northern reaches of the Baltic Sea. Riga became the foremost timber port, and its hinterland the chief source of 'great masts' – those over 12 inches in diameter.[41] The timber trade spread northwards from Riga to Parnu and Narva, and in the eighteenth century to the Gulf of Bothnia. Norway was a source for smaller masts, and pitch and tar for caulking were obtained from most parts of the coniferous forest belt. Little timber was shipped from Sweden owing to the competition of the iron industry and the conservationist policies of the Swedish government. Shipments from western Sweden and southern Norway had, however, the advantage of a shorter voyage to western Europe and of freedom from the obligation to pass through the Sound.

The growing size both of navies and of individual ships, coupled with the demand for construction timber and wainscoting, placed a great pressure on the supply of Baltic timber. It became the practice for landowners to concede cutting rights to individuals who employed local labour to fell the trees and to drag them to the nearest navigable river.

There they were floated to the sawmills on the coast, where the logs were cut up and prepared for shipment. Cutting and transport were largely carried on in winter, when prolonged deep snow provided the most suitable conditions.[42] In large areas of the Baltic hinterland forest occupations provided a valuable, even an essential, supplement to the income of the peasantry.

A third group of exports from the Baltic region was made up of flax and hemp. These formed the chief cash crop of the east Baltic peasant. Flax, already retted and scutched, was brought down the Baltic rivers in small boats, and, with hemp, dominated the export trade of some ports. Together they made up about 60 per cent by value of the exports of Riga in the seventeenth century, and were shipped mostly to London or Amsterdam.[43]

Russia was the objective of many of the early Baltic merchants, who wanted not only the pelts of its fur-bearing animals, but also the trade which crossed Russia from 'Inner' Asia. The Baltic traders had, however, to compete with those who dealt with Russia by the sea route to Archangel, but in the course of the seventeenth century the former gained the upper hand.[44] The Russian trade was at first carried on mainly by way of Narva and Novgorod. In 1582 Narva was taken by the Swedes, and the trade continued through Tartu and Pskov. Riga was the chief rival of Tartu for this commerce, and after the destruction of Tartu in the war of 1654–60 Riga was left as the undisputed gateway to Russia.[45] In 1710 Riga was absorbed into the Russian empire, but not even the foundation of St Petersburg (Leningrad) in 1706 affected its fortunes adversely.

Russia's exports came mainly from her Baltic provinces until the rise of the Russian iron industry (see p. 277). The latter in the second half of the eighteenth century dominated the international market for bar-iron, and was able to undersell Swedish iron in the British market. The reason lay not, as might have been expected, in the superiority of Russian resources in ore and timber, but in lower costs of transport. For the iron trade was intimately linked with the export of flax and hemp. The latter were bulky but very light, and ships which loaded flax at Riga needed also to take on ballast; iron served as ballast and, furthermore, paid a small freight. In 1755, Hildebrand has recorded, a large amount of iron remained in Russia, unexported because there was no flax for it to accompany.[46] The Russian iron export lasted only into the early nineteenth century, when the spread of the puddling process (see p. 252) restored self-sufficiency to western Europe.

The Revolutionary and Napoleonic Wars virtually extinguished Dutch trade with the Baltic, but added immeasurably to the needs and opportunities of their rival. British trade, especially in timber and naval stores, continued to increase, and only tapered off in the nineteenth century with the extinction of the iron trade and the replacement of Baltic timber with supplies from North America.

The Atlantic

In contrast with the long stagnation of Mediterranean trade and the rise and subsequent decline of that of the Baltic, the Atlantic trade of western Europe showed an almost continuous expansion. An increasing proportion of Europe's trade was conducted through its western ports. This trend had been apparent even before the opening up of the oceanic routes, in the salt trade, the wine trade, and the periodic sailing of the Italian galleys for the Low Countries. It received an immense impetus from the development of Portuguese trade with Africa and Asia and from Spain's commerce with the New World.

The trade of Spain and Portugal. The twin foci of this new trade were Lisbon and Seville. The former had been the port of departure for the Portuguese voyagers, and it was in Lisbon that the earliest cargoes of spices brought to Europe by the sea route were unloaded. Lisbon continued to be the home port of the Portuguese merchant fleet. But Portuguese trade remained relatively small. Its chief problem was that Portugal produced nothing of importance with which to requite its imports from Africa and Asia. It was, in fact, obliged to export bullion, and for this was dependent on its neighbour, Spain.

The Spanish voyages to the New World had all set out from ports in south-western Spain, much frequented by Genoese and other Italians.[47] The ships in which the Spaniards sailed were mostly made along the creeks of Galicia and the Basque territory, but the focus of their seafaring activities lay in the small ports near the mouth of the Guadalquivir: Palos, Huelva, Cadiz, San Lucar de Barrameda. Inland, dominating them and controlling their commercial activities, was Seville, where the Casa de Contratación had its headquarters. Through this cluster of ports flowed almost all the commerce between Europe and the New World. 'Compared with other trade of the period', wrote Chaunu, 'the Spanish–American was enormous.'[48] The transatlantic trade of Seville and its dependencies grew from some 3–4000 tonneaux[49] at the beginning of the sixteenth century to about 30,000 by 1580. There was a decline in the volume of trade during the closing years of the century owing to the Spanish losses in the defeat of the Armada. The early seventeenth century, however, marked the culmination of Spanish Atlantic trade, which in 1608 reached 45,078 tonneaux.[50] Thereafter there was a gradual decline in Spanish trade, until in the eighteenth century Spain was left struggling to protect what remained of it from British and Dutch predators.

The Spanish ships returned to Spain with cargoes made up in part of the precious metals. The Spanish import of gold and silver began soon after 1500 and grew at an accelerating rate until the 1590s. Thereafter it declined equally rapidly, and was of little significance by the second half of the seventeenth century. But returning ships did not carry bullion only. They lacked the spices which the Spaniards had hoped to find, but they brought subtropical plants, including maize, which they had within a generation established in Europe (see p. 184). Cargoes outwards from Seville consisted overwhelmingly of corn, wine and olive oil, that Mediterranean trilogy on which the Spanish settlers long subsisted in the New World. Spain continued for almost a century with what Chaunu has called this 'folie économique' – shipping goods of low value at a very high cost. The settlers then began to produce their own food supply, and imports to the New World came to consist mainly of manufactured goods, especially cloth, which Spain did not produce. One must, however, beware of exaggerating the scale of Spanish Atlantic trade. No more than seventy ships as a general rule sailed from Spain in a year, and the total tonnage of the Spanish fleet in the later sixteenth century was appreciably less than that of the revolting Netherlands at the same time. It has even been suggested that the shipping which frequented Seville and its outports was less in total tonnage than that which plied with cargoes of wool and iron along the coast of northern Spain.[51]

Antwerp and Amsterdam. Seville and Lisbon, near the meeting place of Mediterranean and Atlantic trade, were complemented by the ports of the Low Countries, in which Atlantic merchants met those of northern Europe. During the later Middle Ages the latter had consisted primarily of the havens of the river Zwin, known collectively as the port of Bruges. In the fifteenth century these were gradually replaced by Antwerp, which became for more than half a century the focus of trade in north-western Europe.[52] Its rise was as meteoric as that of Seville had been, and its eclipse a great deal more sudden (see p. 129). To the advantages of accessibility from the sea and relatively easy communications with the Rhineland and Germany Antwerp added those of a liberal city administration and an industrially developed hinterland. The Italians began to use Antwerp as their commercial base in north-western Europe; the English used it as the staple from which their cloth was distributed in northern Europe, and when in 1499 the Portuguese also chose the city as the staple for their spice trade, the seal was put upon Antwerp's greatness. The Portuguese needed cloth and metal goods with which to purchase oriental spices; these they could obtain in Antwerp, thus providing a return freight to Lisbon. Antwerp had already become a centre for trade in the metal goods of Liège and the Eifel; it also attracted metal goods from central Europe, and when the Fuggers developed the copper industry of the Carpathian region, it was only natural that they should send their metal by river and sea to the port of Antwerp.[53]

The prosperity of Antwerp was at its height in the 1540s and 50s. Here were to be found colonies of merchants from every trading country of Europe. Agents bought cloth and metal goods on behalf of their Italian principals, and their correspondence reveals an intimate picture of the variety and volume of the goods which passed through the port of Antwerp.[54] In 1553–4 there are said to have been no less than 283 Spanish and Portuguese merchants and factors in Antwerp, together with 17 from Italy and a large number from Germany.[55] Amongst the foreign residents of Antwerp was Ludovico Guicciardini, who described the commerce of the city at the height of its prosperity.[56] Every variety of Italian and English cloth; dyestuffs and leather; alum from Tolfa and salt from the Bay of Bourgneuf; wool from Spain and Germany; French and Rhenish wines; metal goods and copper 'en quantité incroiable';[57] Baltic wheat and rye; flax, honey, skins and furs, and even amber from the forests of Poland.[58] He estimated the value of goods entering Antwerp at 16 million crowns yearly, of which English cloth amounted to 5 and Italian to nearly 3. Corn and Rhenish and French wines were each worth from 1 to 2 million crowns. All in all the commerce of the Scheldt was incomparably greater than that passing through Seville and its outports or, indeed, any other European trading centre at this time.

Antwerp was primarily an entrepôt, in which goods from distant sources were traded or exchanged, but it was also, with its Flemish and Brabantine hinterland, a manufacturing region. Part of the trade of the Scheldt consisted of wool for the local cloth industries, and amongst the exports were the serges, linens and other fabrics made in this region. Part of the metal imported was also fabricated here, and exports included metal goods from local workshops.[59]

The glory of Antwerp was short-lived. A recession in the 1560s was followed by the Dutch revolt, and this in turn by the 'eighty years' war' which destroyed the basis of the city's prosperity. In 1576 mutinous Spanish soldiery did irreparable damage to the city. Many of Antwerp's merchants migrated northwards and helped to build the prosperity of Amsterdam. Lastly, the truce of 1609 drew a boundary across the Scheldt a few kilometres below the city, thus cutting it off from the sea. Much has been made of this so-called 'closure of the Scheldt', and it has commonly been taken to mark the end of Antwerp as a port until the river was reopened by the French in 1792. The Scheldt and its estuary, the Honte, had never been easy to navigate, and many 'great' ships had normally been offloaded on to lighters which then carried their cargoes up to the city.[60] Indeed, it is improbable that Antwerp could ever have accommodated all the ships that regularly came to the Scheldt. The effect of the closure was to prevent any ship from sailing directly from the sea to the city. All had henceforward to unload at Middelburg into river craft. This somewhat limited traffic was never interfered with except in time of war. The chief obstacle to the use of the Scheldt became, in fact, the high tolls imposed by the Dutch on this transit trade.

The 'closure' of the Scheldt proved not to be a complete disaster; it was, as Van Houtte remarked, 'loin d'être hermétique'.[61] The population of Antwerp, which had fallen by half by 1595, began to increase again during the following century. Merchants continued to use Antwerp as a business centre, if no longer as a commercial base. They devised ways of circumventing the Scheldt, including the use of the Flemish port of Dunkirk and even of Calais, and they were able to maintain their overland trade with the Rhineland and Germany.[62]

In most respects, however, the mantle of Antwerp was assumed by Amsterdam, but it underwent a number of alterations in the process. In the first place, Antwerp had never developed a merchant fleet, owned and based in the city. At most, an Antwerp 'registration' extended only to a number of small coasting vessels.[63] Amsterdam, on the other hand, built up a large fleet of vessels whose home ports lay around the Zuider Zee. The Dutch fleet, most of it based on Amsterdam, was without question the largest in Europe – or indeed in the world – in the later sixteenth century. The commerce of Amsterdam and of its neighbouring ports of the Zuider Zee had developed in the later Middle Ages primarily as a northern trade. The expanding traffic in corn and timber offered the opportunity and Dutch energy and initiative provided the means for the rapid growth of this northern trade in the later sixteenth century; 'they shame us with their industry', wrote Owen Feltham in 1660; ' 'tis their Diligence makes them rich'.[64]   At the same time the Dutch developed financial organisations and institutions in advance of those known in Antwerp and more suited to their new commercial role. A new bourse was begun in 1608; an exchange bank was opened during the next year, followed by a bank for loan transactions, and, in 1616, by a special bourse for the Baltic grain trade.[65]

The trading activities of Amsterdam soon extended far beyond the scope of the northern trade. The influx of refugees from Antwerp brought with it an interest in the Atlantic, the Mediterranean and the oriental trades. 'Of the 320 greatest depositors in the exchange bank', wrote Barbour, 'more than a half had come from the southern provinces', and by 1631 'about one-third of the richest Amsterdammers were of southern origin'.[66] It was the merchants of Amsterdam who established a connection between the northern and the Mediterranean trades, exchanging the grain and timber of the one for the wine, oil, cotton and silk of the other. The opening up of Dutch trade with the Orient created a third dimension to their commerce. The Portuguese had pioneered the route to the east, but no longer had the strength to defend it. The first Dutch voyage to Asia, in 1595, promised well, and during the following half century they created an empire in south-eastern Asia, from which they virtually expelled the Portuguese and excluded the British. For the first half century spices and pepper made up more than two-thirds of Dutch imports from Asia; during the second, textiles and textile materials increased almost to a half of a greatly increased total. During the eighteenth century, when the value of Dutch Asiatic trade grew only to a small extent, that of spices and pepper declined, while the value of tea and coffee increased to a quarter of the total.[67]

To these maritime commercial activities the Dutch added the most highly developed fishery known to this date. In the 1660s they are said to have had a thousand specially built craft of 50 to 60 tonneaux.[68] Most important was the 'great fishery', the herring fishery carried on off the east coast of Great Britain between June and January. During the rest of the year the 'small fishery' was conducted in the area of the Dogger Bank. These were supplemented by the less important North Atlantic and Newfoundland fisheries. These fisheries supplied an important item in the Dutch diet as well as an export commodity, particularly to the Mediterranean. '. . . it is difficult', wrote Wilson, 'to overestimate the value of the fisheries in the Dutch economy. They were basic to it, as agriculture was basic to most other contemporary economies.'[69]

The Atlantic coast of Europe. Between Seville and the Sound lay countless small ports, carrying on an active trade with one another, receiving goods from the major ports and feeding cargoes into the systems of long-distance commerce. Many lay at or near the mouths of rivers which provided a link with their hinterlands. Some – those for example on the rock-bound coasts of Brittany and Galicia – supplied ships and sailors rather than commodities, serving as carriers for western Europe. The Breton was 'le transporteur universel'.[70] There was an intense maritime activity. Around the coast of north-western France alone, from Mont-Saint-Michel to the Bay of Bourgneuf – some 600 kilometres – there lay the astonishing total of 123 small ports.[71] At Saint-Malo, probably the largest port on this coast, there were about two thousand arrivals a year in the 1680s.[72] Only about 5 per cent of these ships belonged to *le grand commerce* and were over 100 tonneaux burden. Nearly 60 per cent were each of less than 20 tonneaux, and carried on only a short-distance trade with neighbouring ports.[73] Le Havre, Dieppe, La Rochelle and Nantes were comparable with Saint-Malo. All others had a very much smaller trade and were visited by very few 'great ships'. Most harbours were in fact too small to receive them.

Every port, however small, handled an immense variety of merchandise. The ports of Normandy exported grain and cloth, and imported wine, salt, timber, iron and a vast range of exotic goods relayed from Britain or the Netherlands.[74] Saint-Malo gathered by means of *le petit cabotage* coarse linen cloth for export to Spain or America; grain from Normandy; wood and fuel; slates and lime; wine and salt, and fish from both inshore and deep-sea fisheries.[75] Brest also exported coarse Breton cloth.[76] La Rochelle shipped wines from Saintonge and salt from the local salines, and distributed Spanish wool to the clothiers of Poitou.[77] The traffic of Nantes was augmented by the wheat and wine brought down the Loire. In return salt, metals from Spain and England, salt fish from Brittany and the Netherlands, and Breton *toiles* brought in coasting vessels, were sent upstream.[78] In the later seventeenth century the trade of Nantes was expanding despite the depressed economic climate of the times;[79] it seems probable that the French were beginning to take over some of the traffic previously handled by the Dutch.

The most rapid expansion in these years was, however, in the trade of Bordeaux and of the ports of the Seine estuary. Bordeaux had long been the chief port of Aquitaine and handled most of its large wine export. In the late seventeenth century it began also to trade with the French overseas dependencies, and in the eighteenth century became the foremost French port in the New World trade. On average 150 ships a year cleared the Gironde for the West Indies, laden with cloth, wine, grain, salted meat, fish and butter. Their return cargoes were made up chiefly of sugar – mostly in the form of molasses – coffee and indigo which were distributed by coastal shipping to the ports of north-western and northern Europe.[80] Much of the sugar went to Amsterdam, Hamburg and Stettin. Bordeaux was slowly taking over much of the colonial trade in which a century earlier the merchants of Amsterdam had been supreme.

The ports of Rouen and Le Havre, despite the difficult channel leading to the former and the lack of protection of the latter, also developed during the eighteenth century. They commanded the largest and the richest hinterland of any European port at this time. They imported, not only wine, grain, fish and other foodstuffs, but also industrial raw materials – cotton and Spanish wool – for the cloth industries of their hinterland. Rouen and Le Havre also developed a Baltic trade, and in the eighteenth century were second only to Bordeaux in that with the West Indies.[81]

The growth of the major French ports during the eighteenth century was paralleled by that of the German North Sea ports. Both groups were in part heirs to the commercial predominance of the Dutch. In the early seventeenth century Emden enjoyed a short-lived prosperity largely because it provided, as it were, a flag of convenience for Dutch merchants, allowing them to continue to trade with Spain, with which their country was at war. Hamburg and Bremen remained ports of little more than regional importance until the early eighteenth century, when they began to take on the role, formerly played by the Dutch, of exporters of German – particularly Silesian – cloth and of forwarders of French sugar and wines to the Baltic.[82] By the later eighteenth century the Bordeaux–Hamburg trade had gone far towards supplanting the older Amsterdam–Danzig relationship.

Hamburg had considerable advantages: its freedom from serious disturbance during the wars of the sixteenth and seventeenth centuries when its rivals were destroyed; its links by river and canal with eastern and south-eastern Germany, and its social structure, which resembled more closely that of Amsterdam or London than that of the gild-ridden towns of Germany. The completion of the system of canals in Brandenburg, linking the Elbe with the Oder, extended the port's hinterland, while the orderliness of Prussian rule greatly facilitated trade. The large export of Silesian linen, according to Mirabeau, went exclusively by way of Hamburg, and the latter became the chief centre for the distribution of colonial wares in central Europe.[83] On the eve of the French Revolution, it has been said,[84] Hamburg absorbed 'fully one-third of all French exports', which it transhipped to central Europe. Bremen came a distant second in the foreign trade of Germany at this time, largely because it lacked easy communications with an extensive hinterland such as Hamburg enjoyed. Its forwarding trade tended, in consequence, to make greater use of the Danish Sound and the Baltic ports.

Internal trade

Only part, and probably a very small part, of Europe's trade passed through its ports; most crossed its internal boundaries, despite the obstacles which these presented to the movement of goods. Tolls and tariffs were charged at most boundary crossings and also at many points within each country. This led in a few instances to the keeping of records of the flow of merchandise; more often it led to smuggling, for which there is no statistical record. There was during the eighteenth century a gradual relaxation of internal obstacles to trade. In Germany many such restraints disappeared during the Thirty Years' War; within the Habsburg lands internal tariffs were abolished in 1775, and this free-trade area was extended in 1796 to include the Austrian share in the Partitions of Poland. In France internal barriers to trade were more restrictive than elsewhere. Every historic province had at one time imposed its system of duties. In 1664 Colbert succeeded in forming a customs union for northern France, known as 'les Cinq Grosses Fermes', but his attempts to extend it to the rest of France were wrecked on the parochialism and vested interests of the remaining provinces. Not until 1790 were all obstacles to internal trade abolished; 'instead of more than a thousand bureaux scattered over the country, slowing up traffic by their inspections and bureaucratic controls, there were now some 750 concentrated on the frontiers alone'.[85] At the same time the *gabelle* and the *tabac*, highly variable local taxes on salt and tobacco, were also abolished. A unified customs system was a necessary condition of its use as an instrument of national policy. In Germany, where the multiplicity of staple rights (see p. 357) and tariff barriers reached their extreme, the situation was not resolved until the nineteenth century.

Markets and fairs

The mechanics of trade changed little during the period. It continued, as during the later Middle Ages, to be built on the broad foundation of market and fair, and, if the role of fairs had begun to decline in western Europe, they remained very active into the nineteenth century in central and eastern. Europe was strewn with markets, each serving its market area of a hundred square kilometres or more. The market was held once or twice weekly. Here the peasant disposed of his surplus produce and bought those necessities which he could not grow or make himself. Here came the petty merchants and dealers, offering a few exotic goods for sale and buying up corn, skins, leather and live animals for the supply of larger and more distant places. The small town or village was the first stage in provisioning the large city and in the export of coarse cloth for the colonial trade. The market was also a social occasion, the 'principal distraction' of the peasant, who would often go to market even if he had nothing to sell or buy.[86]

The fair served a somewhat different purpose, complementing the activities of the market. It met less frequently, often only once a year and rarely more than three or four times. It usually lasted for several days, and its business often included some specialised activity. It attracted traders from a much wider area than the market, and it was an occasion when the peasant or the inhabitant of the small town could make an exceptional or unusual purchase. Fairs tended to disappear from the larger towns, from Paris and Antwerp, for example, and the attempt to establish a fair at Nuremberg failed.[87] This was because the occasional gathering of traders at a fair could offer nothing that was not normally available in a rich and prosperous city. Fairs belonged to regions of Europe where towns were few and small.

There was nonetheless no lack of fairs in France; no less than about 130 were active in the *généralité* of Paris, but their most important activity was the seasonal trade in horses, other animals or wine. Fairs in the thinly populated province of Quercy, where there were no towns of significance, had a very much wider range of function.[88] The Guibray fair in western Normandy and that of Beaucaire in Languedoc were amongst the most active in France, but the Parisian fairs of Lendit, Saint-Germain and Saint-Laurent were becoming the occasion more for jollification than for commerce,[89] and the Lyons fairs, founded in the fifteenth century to detract from the importance of those of Geneva, were of steadily diminishing importance in the seventeenth and eighteenth centuries.[90]

The most important fairs in the Low Countries were those of Antwerp and of Bergen op Zoom. They had been very important in the fifteenth century for trade in cloth and general merchandise, but in the sixteenth they were becoming increasingly superfluous, and they did not outlast the century.[91] In the northern Netherlands the chief medieval fair, that of Deventer, declined with the growth of Amsterdam.[92]

If the role of fairs was declining in western Europe in the face of the growing commercial importance of the larger towns, this was far from being so in central and eastern Europe. In Germany there were an immense number of fairs, many of them merely *Krammärkte*, at which only goods of trifling value were sold; some concerned mainly with the sale of horses and cattle. In the Prussian Rhineland province there were no less than six hundred in the early nineteenth century,[93] though most were of negligible importance. At least until the end of the eighteenth century a dozen or more leading German fairs continued to play an important, even a decisive, role in German trade. Foremost amongst them were the Rhineland fairs at Frankfurt, Strasbourg and Zurzach, the last held at a village of that name on the Swiss bank of the upper Rhine.[94] It was pre-eminently the fair of south-western Germany and the Swiss plateau. It had lost something of its earlier significance with the decline of the south German cloth industry, but was still a fair of regional importance.[95] Frankfurt, however, never lost its importance as a general fair. A French report of 1810 showed the immense range of goods bought and sold and the very great area from which its clientele was drawn.[96] Every variety of cloth and leather and of metalwork and jewellery could be bought there, and it was still, even at this late date, frequented by traders from as far away as Poland and the Danube basin. The smaller size and lower frequency of towns in east-central Europe led to the growth of many other important fairs: Nördlingen in south Germany; Brunswick, Naumburg, Erfurt and above all, Leipzig in central Europe, and Breslau (Wrocław), Frankfurt-on-Oder, Poznań and Danzig on the borders of Poland. In the Balkan peninsula the relative importance of fairs was even greater than central and eastern Europe. Here the fairs served as fixed points in the otherwise unstructured movements of traders. The medieval fairs, most numerous and important in the mining districts of Bosnia and Serbia, were destroyed by the Turkish invasions. In the fifteenth and sixteenth centuries another group of fairs developed, mainly along the traditional highways: in Transylvania, near the Danube, and in the Marica valley of Thrace.[97] Thessaloníki had never lost its medieval importance as a fair town, and there were other fairs in Macedonia and Greece. As late as the mid-nineteenth century the fair of Uzundžovo, held on the old imperial road from Istanbul to Sofia, still had three thousand stalls, and the fairs of the Balkans decayed only with the coming of the railway and the creation of the modern boundaries, which obstructed the freedom of movement on which the fairs had depended.

Transport and travel

Most of the internal movement of goods before the railway age was by road, despite the problems presented by poor surfaces, steep inclines, and the slowness and clumsiness of the vehicles in general use. The greater convenience of water transport was recognised, but few rivers were without obstacles to navigation and they rarely flowed in directions in which merchants most often needed to go. Nevertheless, attempts were made at intervals from the later Middle Ages to the present to make rivers more navigable and to link river basins together by canals.

Roads. The network of roads described in the first chapter underwent no significant change before the nineteenth century. Some roads passed into disuse; traffic was intensified on others. But no new roads were created and few improvements were made. Travellers would still use hilly roads rather than those across the level plain, because the former were likely to be dry, though rough, and the latter, muddy and impassable. The route taken between Paris and the Rhône valley, which today follows river valleys for most of its course, more often crossed to the Loire and threaded the mountains of the Lyonnais. Occasionally a river was used to supplement the roads, and travellers, their baggage and even their horses were taken on to flat-bottomed boats. The transcontinental routes which linked Italy with Germany incorporated sections of river, and many were the travellers who rested as they glided down the Rhine or the Po after the rigours of the Alpine crossing.

There was a gradual shift in emphasis between these great routes which linked the north with the south of Europe. Medieval merchants and travellers had tended to use the more westerly passes, especially the Mont Cenis and the two St Bernard passes. The ascendancy of Antwerp led to a greater use of the Rhineland route which led to the central passes, of which the St Gotthard was the easiest and most favoured.[98] More easterly routes, notably that from Hamburg by way of Nuremberg and Augsburg, tended to use the passes of the Engadine, particularly the Splügen and Septimer, now largely abandoned in favour of the Maloja and Julier. Much of the traffic to and from Venice crossed the Alps by the Brenner Pass, but there was also a considerable movement of goods over the low Tarvis and Semmering passes to Vienna and Bohemia.

Within the Alps traffic was concentrated on a half-dozen routes. The passes were in consequence heavily used. Bishop Burnet, who crossed the Splügen Pass in the mid-seventeenth century, described Splügen itself as 'a large village of above two hundred Houses, that are well built, and the Inhabitants seem to live at their Ease, tho' they have no sort of Soil but a little Meadow-Ground about them . . . Those of this Village are the Carriers between Italy and Germany, so they drive a great Trade; for there is here a perpetual Carriage going and coming; and we were told, that there pass generally a hundred Horses thro' this Town, one day with another; and there are above five hundred carriage-Horses that belong to the Town.'[99] Thousands must have been employed in carting merchandise and assisting travellers across the mountains. Bertrand de la Broquière in the fifteenth century described how guides were used on the Mont Cenis whenever the path was hidden by snow.[100]

The volume of traffic on the roads of Europe was increasing in the sixteenth century. In France Louis XI had in the previous century established a system of couriers; this had the effect of emphasising certain roads and of attracting more travellers to them. In 1599, Henry IV's minister Sully appointed an official with responsibility for maintaining and improving the roads. Some work was done on bridges in the first two decades of the seventeenth century, but then the project languished[101] until it was revived by Colbert in the 1660s. He directed that roads linking the more important towns, including the ports, should be kept in good order. But he was obstructed, like Sully before him, both by those provinces – the *pays d'élection* – over which he had little authority, and by certain vested interests which had no reason to welcome competition from outside their local areas.[102] The intendants were given responsibility for roads, and in some instances made attempts to improve their appalling condition. In Burgundy, the provincial estates in 1682 took up the problem, though without any significant results.[103] The turning point came, however, towards the middle of the eighteenth century. In 1738 a new form of *corvée, la corvée royale*, was imposed on the peasantry, an obligation to contribute labour towards the improvement of the roads. Even more significant for the future was the creation in 1747 of the Ecole des Ponts et Chaussées, and, three years later, a corps of engineers was established. Henceforward there was, in Trénard's expression, 'une véritable politique routière',[104] and France began to develop a network of trunk roads radiating from the capital and spanning most of the country.

Thus the task of creating a road system, which in England was entrusted to the unco-ordinated activities of turnpike trusts, was assumed by the state. Nowhere else in Europe, not even in Prussia, was anything significant done to make land travel less difficult before the nineteenth century.

Rivers and canals. These provided the only alternative to the roads. Water transport was generally cheaper and often safer, but it was usually very slow. Tavernier travelled from Vienna to Budapest early in the seventeenth century by boat, for, he wrote, 'the Road by Land is seldom travell'd, in regard that the Fontiers of both Empires [i.e. Habsburg and Ottoman] are full of Thieves and Boothaylers [i.e. those who carry off booty]. In fair weather you may go from Buda to Belgrade in less than eight days, but we were forc'd to stay longer upon the water, in regard of the Cold weather.'[105] The distance by road would not have been more than 350 kilometres, which could certainly have been covered in less than half the time. Few travellers made use of rivers, except for short distances. There was no navigable river which was not, at some time during the year, rendered impassable for boats by low water, floods or ice. In the Mediterranean region this closure lasted for much of the summer. The design of boats had to be adjusted to the conditions of the stream, just as navigation was to the seasons. The capacity of river boats was in most instances small, never more than 10 tonneaux (about 15 cubic metres), except on a few large rivers, and generally less than 5.[106] Boats normally tied up at the river's bank for loading and unloading; only in a few cities were there masonry-built quays. The boats were usually owned by the boatmen who sailed them, and river navigation was for many of them only a secondary occupation. Not surprisingly, inland navigation was 'saisonnière, sporadique, inter-mittente'.[107]

In Italy there was a regular traffic on the Po, and the Tiber was used to transport supplies, chiefly corn and timber, to Rome. In Spain only the Guadalquivir was much used, but there was some navigation on the lowermost stretches of the Tagus, Duero and Ebro. Some Spaniards nevertheless formed the extraordinary opinion that internal navigation had a future in their country, and proposed the construction of canals to join up the river basin.

France was well endowed with navigable rivers. Their radial pattern and their relatively even flow encouraged not only their use for local traffic but also fostered the opinion that they could be linked into a national system. Sully included the improvement of rivers and the construction of canals in his plan to revolutionise internal transport. Late in the seventeenth century Vauban saw in the improvement of navigation the chief means of increasing trade, and listed the rivers which he thought most suited for navigation and capable of improvement.[108] The intendants showed a praiseworthy, but not always effective, zeal in improving rivers, and one of their most frequent recommendations during the crisis years of the 1690s was for navigable waterways, which alone, it seemed, could bring relief to their afflicted provinces.

Most French rivers were in fact used only irregularly. The Rhône was easily navigated in its deltaic course, but above Arles there was little or no upstream traffic, and not a great deal came down the river. The Loire, despite its shallow and shifting bed, was used more than most rivers, since, alone amongst French rivers, it flowed westwards, thus allowing a sail-driven boat to move upstream with the wind for much of the time. It carried a good deal of salt from the Bay of Bourgneuf, and, after the completion of the Canal de Briare in 1642, timber, corn and coal for the Paris market were brought down its upper course. Only the Seine appears to have been used more regularly than the Loire, and this because of the immense demands made by Paris.[109] Food, wine, metals and salt were brought upstream from Rouen and Le Havre, as well as the farm products of Normandy. Downstream traffic included timber for construction and rough wood for fuel. In fact almost all Paris's supply arrived by water.[110] In 1725 this amounted to 420,000 *voies*. Much came from the Morvan by way of the Yonne; most was floated to Paris in winter when the level of the river was at its highest. Other downstream cargoes included corn from Champagne and Brie and wine from Burgundy. Paris was the focus of one of the largest – perhaps the largest – system of waterborne commerce in Europe, but its volume must not be exaggerated. If all the boats which passed upstream from Normandy had been fully loaded – which they were not – they could not in the eighteenth century have carried more than 75,000 tonnes of cargo. In fact, they probably carried no more than about 45,000.[111]

On most other French rivers the traffic was small and irregular. The tributaries of the Garonne had long been used to convey wine to Bordeaux, more because the smooth movement of the boat was less damaging to the wine than the road journey than for any reasons of

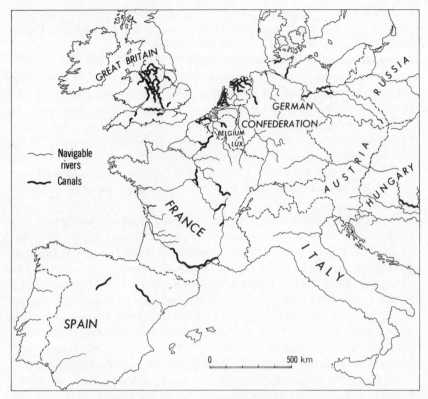

Fig. 6.2 European canals and navigable rivers, early nineteenth century

economy. On the Dordogne, for example, traffic was significant only in winter and spring, and consisted, in addition to wine, of chestnuts, cheese and building materials from the Central Massif.[112] Most rivers were, however, used, if only intermittently: the Somme to above Amiens, the Aa to Saint-Omer, and the lowermost courses of other rivers despite the continued silting which impeded navigation.[113]

Rivers were very much more important in the network of transport and communication in the Low Countries than elsewhere in Europe. Road construction in the alluvial region of north-western Europe was difficult. Bromley, at the end of the seventeenth century, found the road from Emden to Groningen 'only passable in Summer, for most of the Winter it is under Water'.[114] Within the Netherlands, however, he travelled 'in large cover'd Boats drawn by Horses, which is not only easy but expeditious; the Hour of the Boats coming in, and going out, is so punctually observed, that upon the Ringing of a bell it goes off, without staying for any Person whatsoever'.[115] This highly organised system of canal travel was made possible by the close control which the Dutch were obliged to maintain over the level of the water in their rivers and drainage canals. There was no significant current; the banks were maintained; there was no danger of low water and little of flood, and only ice in winter held up navigation. Sir William Temple noted 'the great Rivers, and the strange number of Canals . . . [which] do not only lead to every great town, but almost to every Village, and every Farm-House in the country; and the infinity of Sails that are seen every where coursing up and down upon them'.[116] It is likely that the Netherlands, and here only the more westerly provinces, formed one part of Europe where transport by water was more important than by land.

The Rhine is today the most-used internal waterway in Europe, yet the primitive river was not an easily navigable stream. Its upper course could generally be used only for downstream travel, and from Basel to Strasbourg very little traffic moved against the current. Not until Mainz was approached did one find a really active river traffic. This continued to Cologne, where *Stapel-* and *Umschlagsrechte* effectively ended through navigation, and there was little traffic on the lower Rhine. The seventeenth century saw a decline in long-distance traffic; the local *Marktschiffe* were as active as ever, but the larger boats had disappeared from the river. Some of the princes of Baden and the Palatinate tried to open up a through trade, but tolls, the vested interests of some of the riverine cities, and the physical conditions of the river always defeated them. Gothein described the 'öde Stille' of the river, disturbed only for a short period each year by the traffic of the Frankfurt fair.[117] In fact, the rafting of timber remained the most important activity on the river above Mainz.

Two changes were necessary before the Rhine could become a major commercial highway. The first, legal and political, would sweep away the toll-stations and abolish the rights of certain cities to hinder and obstruct the movement of boats. The second was technological, the straightening and deepening of the bed of the stream in certain critical sections of its course. The former was accomplished between 1803, when France advanced her boundary to the Rhine, and 1831, when the Convention of Mainz abolished the last of the medieval restrictions on the freedom of the river.[118] In 1816 the first steamboat appeared on the Rhine, and in the following year the first steps were taken to straighten the very difficult section of the river above Speyer. The work was entrusted to the Baden engineer Tulla. His method was to cut a new bed for the river through its convoluted meanders. The effect was to steepen the stream-bed and thus to increase the speed of flow.[119] This in turn scoured the bed and kept it free of sediment. Unfortunately it also made upstream travel more difficult, so that the success of Tulla's work was in fact contingent upon the use of steam-powered ships. Work continued on the river during most of the century, and by about 1850 the effective limit for barges pulled by a steam tug was Mannheim. By this date, however, the railway had been built along the Rhine valley and was drawing traffic away from the river. The importance of the latter was restored only by the development of the bulk transport of goods of relatively low value – coal, iron-ore, crude oil – late in the century.

The tributaries of the Rhine had little importance as navigable waterways before the present age. The poet Goethe, in his hasty retreat from the battle of Valmy (1792), took a boat down the Moselle, but the river was in fact very little used. The lower Main was used for local traffic, but goods coming upstream from the Rhine had to be tran-shipped at Mainz into smaller craft. The little river Lahn was used primarily to transport iron-ore and charcoal from the hills of Nassau,[120] and there was some movement on the lower course of the Neckar. Coal was shipped down the river Ruhr to Duisburg for the supply of Rhineland towns, but of long-distance trade there was little evidence. On no European river did the volume of trade before the industrial age fall so far short of its potential as on the Rhine.

The north German rivers, the Weser,[121] Elbe and Oder, were used in the sixteenth century mainly for local traffic. The Weser in particular was used for shipping timber and grain to Bremen as well as salt from the numerous salt-springs of the vicinity. The importance of the Elbe lay in the linkages which it provided with the Baltic region, allowing merchants to circumvent the Danish Sound. The Stecknitz Canal joined Lübeck with the Elbe at Lauenburg. Plans were made in the sixteenth century to join the Elbe with the Oder, though the first such connection was not completed until 1620.

The Vistula was much used, even though its physical conditions were far from favourable. Its bed was shallow and changing, and the river was obstructed by ice in winter and liable to severe floods. On the other hand there were few fiscal or political obstacles, and boats had a relatively unimpeded voyage from the limit of navigation to Danzig at the river's mouth. There was, however, little navigation above Kazimierz Dolny, where the road from Ruthenia reached the river. Here a number of granaries, many of which still survive, were built in the sixteenth century, to hold the corn until shipment in 'great Flatt-bottomed lighters called Canes, off which some tymes 1500 or 2000 att once ly Neare the Citty [of Danzig] and May have, one with the other, aboutt 15 men each. By report above 160,000 tonnes of Corne is shipped from hence every Summer.'[122] Peter Mundy left a sketch of the *canes* passing under the great wooden bridge at Toruń, the lowest on the river, 'comming downe laden with Corne rowed with paddles ... Another setting uppe against the stream and with poles and staves, laden with Herrings, wyne, etts. Commodities from Dantzigk.'[123]

The boats were adapted to navigating the shallow river. In the sixteenth century they had a capacity of about 12 lasts, or over 10 tons. This was increased in the seventeenth century to about 38 lasts.[124] The river was generally open for navigation from March to November, when the grain from the *previous* year's harvest was sent down to the Baltic. Figures survive for a few years in the mid-sixteenth century of the amount of grain passing the toll station at Wrocławek, between Toruń and Płock; it amounted at most to about 20,000 lasts,[125] only a fraction of the volume suggested by Mundy. The river trade is said to have employed up to 28,000 boatmen. Cargoes were made up overwhelmingly of rye, though the quantity of wheat increased during the eighteenth and early nineteenth centuries with changes in demand in western Europe.[126] The amount of river traffic fluctuated with political conditions. It declined during the period of the Partitions, but remained important until the coming of the railway swept the last grain ships from the river.

Canals were constructed to supplement the rivers, to extend their range and to link two or more river systems together. Most canals crossed a watershed, necessitating not only the construction of sluices or locks, but also the provision of water at the highest point of their course. The first European canal to breach a watershed was the Stecknitz Canal (see p. 297 above). In the 1540s plans were prepared for linking respectively the Havel and the Spree with the Oder, using a marshy *Urstromtal* or glacial river valley for the purpose and thus minimising the need for locks. The canal from the Spree to the Oder was in fact completed by the Great Elector and was opened in 1669. The link between the Havel and the Oder, later known as the Finow Canal, was begun in 1605 and completed in 1620. But its life was short. It had been poorly constructed; it fell to ruin during the Thirty Years' War, and had to be rebuilt under Frederick the Great. The annexation of West Prussia by Frederick in 1772 gave him the opportunity to construct a link between the Oder and the Vistula. The Noteć, which joined the Wartha, a tributary of the Oder, approached to within 30 kilometres of the Vistula in the vicinity of Bydgoszcz, and the two rivers were separated only by a marshy valley. In 1773–4 a canal was cut through this depression, an army of 8000 peasants being drafted for the purpose. During the following years the canal was much used by boats sailing from as far away as Poznań to the port of Danzig.[127] Nowhere else in Germany was a comparable work undertaken before the late nineteenth century.

At the end of the eighteenth century the Upper Silesian coalfield promised to become a major source of fuel for Prussia, and in 1788 it was proposed to construct a canal along the valley of the little river Kłodnica from the Oder to the coal basin. Work was begun in 1792, and by 1806 a section of the canal from Gliwice to the mines at Zabrze was open for traffic. The main section of the canal, from Gliwice to Koźle on the Oder, was not completed until 1812. It was used almost exclusively to transport coal, which then passed down the Oder and through the canals of Brandenburg to Berlin. The waterway was not particularly successful. A normal coal barge proved to be too large for the shallow, twisting Oder, and no more than 60,000 tonnes ever passed downstream in a single year before the coming of the railway made the canal superfluous.[128]

The magnates of Poland were much impressed by the potentialities of water transport; many of them owed their fortunes to the shipment of corn by way of the Vistula. In the later eighteenth century plans were laid for the eastward extension of the catchment area of Baltic trade. First in the field was Michał Ogiński, who in 1765 began the construction of a canal to join the Niemen with the Prypeć and thus with the Dnepr (fig. 6.3). The Ogiński Canal was opened in 1784. At the same time work was completed on the so-called Royal Canal, which linked the Bug, a tributary of the Vistula, with the Prypeć. A third canal, the Augustów Canal, was cut to join the Vistula system with the Niemen. This activity was then brought to an end by the final Partition and the Napoleonic Wars, and there was to be no further development before the twentieth century.

Early in the sixteenth century Gustavus Vasa had envisaged a canal across southern Sweden both to serve the needs of Swedish internal commerce and to circumvent the Danish Sound. Nothing came of this idea, but canals were cut to join lakes Mälar and Hjalmar, and in the seventeenth century surveys were made near lakes Vättern and Vänern with a view to extending this canal westwards to the newly founded port of Göteborg. It was not, however, until the end of the eighteenth century that this difficult project was undertaken. The resulting canal was not opened until 1832, and was replaced by the Göta Canal later in the century.[129]

The most ambitious canal-building projects in Europe before the industrial age were in France, where they were encouraged by the gentle relief, by the interpenetrating river basins and, above all, by political unity. The plan to connect the great river basins of France, and thus to link the Atlantic coasts with the Mediterranean, was initiated by Francis I, who discussed it with Leonardo da Vinci and had a survey made of possible routes. The project lapsed during the religious wars of the

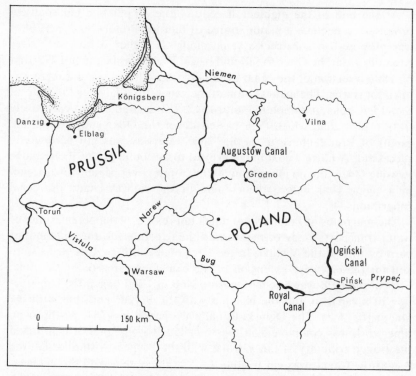

Fig. 6.3 Canals and navigable rivers in eastern Europe

second half of the sixteenth century, but was revived by Henry IV and Sully. Only one of the projected canals was completed at this time, that linking the Loire at Briare with the Loing, a tributary of the Seine, at Montargis. It was begun in 1608, interrupted after the assassination of Henry IV and not completed until 1642. Paris had come to depend on the Central Massif and the Loire valley especially for wine, timber and coal. These goods now used the canal, together with the salt which was brought up the Loire from the sea. The canal was a financial success, and it has been claimed that during the seventeenth century 200,000 tonnes of merchandise a year were carried along it.[130] This encouraged the construction of a further canal from the Loire near Orléans to Montargis. The river Loing was itself replaced for navigational purposes by a lateral canal during the following century.

The Languedoc Canal, or Canal des Deux Mers, was a much more ambitious project, and work was not begun on it until nearly a century and a half after Francis I had first proposed it. It was designed to join the

Garonne at Toulouse with the Mediterranean at Sète, a distance of 240 kilometres, and it called for a rise of 190 metres and the construction of seventy-four locks. The project received strong support from Colbert, and was completed in the years 1665–81. It was, in Skempton's words, 'the greatest feat of civil engineering in Europe between Roman times and the nineteenth century'.[131] It aroused the admiration of contemporaries. John Locke described it before its completion, with its '17 locks between Castelnaudary and Toulouse, and at each the goods are to be carried from one boat to another, for at each lock the boat is changed'.[132] There was even a daily packet-boat from Castelnaudary to Toulouse a year or two before the canal was completed. To Arthur Young the Languedoc Canal was 'a noble and stupendous work . . . alive with commerce'. At Béziers was a 'port . . . broad enough for four large vessels to lie abreast; the greatest of them carries from 90 to 100 tons', and, he concluded, 'This is the best sight I have seen in France.'[133]

There is no question but that both the Orléans–Briare and the Languedoc canals were technically and economically successful. They were, however, followed by a multiplicity of projects, most of them unsuccessful or left incomplete. Plans to link the Moselle with both the Meuse and the Saar were never put into effect;[134] the Picardy Canal from the Oise to the Somme was left unfinished owing to lack of money,[135] as was also the Burgundy Canal from the Seine system to Dijon and the Saône. The only other canal to be completed in the eighteenth century was the Canal du Centre, cut from the Loire at Digoin to the Saône at Chalons. The French did not lack vision or technical skill; they were defeated primarily by the cost of canal-construction. The Canal de Briare, it should be noted, was completed only because Sully drafted 6000 soldiers to assist in the laborious work of digging and carting earth. Under Napoleon the Saint-Quentin Canal was finished to allow coal from the département of Nord to reach Paris, and the short Ourcq Canal was cut *around* Paris from the Marne to the Seine. After the Napoleonic Wars a veritable canal mania seized the French. In 1820, the engineer in charge of transport, Louis Becquey, secured approval for an ambitious plan which would, in effect, complete the canals left unfinished before the Revolution and add a number of others which were thought to have a political or economic significance. Between 1820 and the mid-century no less than 2500 kilometres of canal were constructed. Apart from the canal from the Loire to Brest, built for strategic purposes, the new canals either focussed on the developing industrial region of Le Centre (see p. 340) or linked the Paris basin with the coalfield of the north and the increasingly important industrial regions of the north-east and east (see fig. 6.2). By 1850 France had an integrated system of internal navigation. Its many segments had, however, been constructed at differing times and to varying specifications. It remained only to standardise their sizes and to build canal barges to suit them. This was done by the Freycinet reform, beginning in 1879.

In the Low Countries it was sometimes difficult to distinguish between rivers and canals, for most rivers were in some degree canalised. Nor were the canals constructed primarily for navigation. Most served in the first instance to evacuate the water pumped from the fields. The first modern canal cut exclusively for navigation was the Brussels Canal, which in 1550–60 was dug from the city to the river Rupel. Its purpose was to improve connections with the port of Antwerp, though these expectations were ended by the Spanish war and the closure of the Scheldt. The latter did, however, contribute to a flurry of canal-building in Flanders. The Scheldt was linked with Bruges and the coastal ports from Ostend to Dunkirk, which served as one of Antwerp's outlets to the sea.

The reopening of the Scheldt in 1792 and the formation of the United Netherlands led to a further programme of canal-building. A canal link between Antwerp and the Meuse was begun under Napoleon, and after 1815 the Ghent–Terneuzen Canal was enlarged to take sea-going ships. A canal was also cut from Brussels to the coal basin at Charleroi.

In the northern Low Countries transport and communication were already in the sixteenth century heavily dependent on waterways, natural and artificial, and subsequent works were in the main designed to improve them. In particular, the Voorne Canal was constructed in 1827–9 to improve access to the port of Rotterdam, and the North Holland Canal (1820–5) linked Amsterdam with the sea at Den Helder. Attempts to improve Amsterdam's connections with the Rhine were less successful. Canals cut through Gouda and Utrecht silted up, and the problem was not solved until late in the century.

Spain's halting economic progress in the later eighteenth century encouraged plans to develop a canal network. Attempts had been made as early as the sixteenth to canalise the Ebro. In 1768 the project was revived. It was to consist of a canal, the Aragon Canal, along the Ebro valley and through the mountains to the north of Burgos to the coast. This was then to link with the Castile Canal, to be cut through Old Castile to Valladolid, Zamora and Segovia. Lastly, the navigable Guadalquivir was to be extended northwards, across the Sierra Morena, to La Mancha and thus to Madrid.[136] Improved communications with the coast, it was expected, would revive the moribund economy of the interior. This project was pursued only intermittently, and was probably beyond the financial and technical resources of Spain. In all some 300 kilometres of canal were built, but 'none of the critical junctions was ever

made, with the result that for economic purposes the canals began nowhere
and ended nowhere'.[137] By 1840 only two sections of canal were in use:
from Valladolid to Palencia, and along the Ebro valley from Zaragoza to
Tudela.

European trade at the end of the eighteenth century

The Revolutionary and Napoleonic Wars came at the end of a period of
steadily increasing external trade. There are, however, no statistical
series which measure its rate of growth other than those of the trade of
Great Britain with continental Europe. The aggregate trade of England
and Wales rose from £20,471 thousand in 1750 to £39,173 in 1791.
Growth was even more rapid during the next decade. The total trade of
Great Britain increased from £42,402 thousand in 1791 to £73,723 in
1800. A significant fraction of this was with continental Europe (table
6.1).[138] These figures, when allowances are made for inflation, show a
stagnating trade with the Mediterranean and a rapidly expanding trade
with northern Europe. Since Great Britain had become the dominant
commercial power in the latter region, one must assume that the volume
of trade of northern Europe was growing steadily through the second
half of the eighteenth century.

Table 6.1a

	Northern Europe	Southern Europe	Total	Percentage of British trade
1750	6511	5791	12,302	60.1
1791	9914	7339	17,253	44.1
1800	21,351	5807	27,158	38.8

a In thousands of pounds sterling. Figures for 1791 and 1800 relate to Great
Britain; those for 1750, to England and Wales.

Nevertheless, European trade constituted a steadily diminishing
fraction of Great Britain's external trade during these years. This was in
part due to the reduced export of Swedish iron to Great Britain; in part
to wartime interference with trade, but, above all, to the increase in the
colonial and New World trade. Amongst imports the biggest increases
were in raw cotton, sugar, tea and, towards the end of the period, coffee.
Exports which showed the sharpest increases were cotton yarn and
cloth, but there were also noteworthy increases in shipments of coal,
woollen cloth and, in the last decade of the century, iron.
  One cannot of course use British statistics to throw light on the trade

of continental Europe, except insofar as their trade was mutual, but the qualitative evidence suggests that the more important ports of western Europe also experienced a considerable increase in their colonial trade, greatest probably in the case of France;[139] least in that of Spain and Portugal. There is no evidence for a comparable expansion in internal trade, except insofar as this was linked with external. The increased export of Silesian linen, for example, mainly through the ports of Stettin and Hamburg, is well documented, and must have been accompanied by a movement of bread grains and other consumer goods into the weaving towns and villages along the foot of the Sudeten mountains. But over continental Europe as a whole there was no mass demand for consumer goods until well into the nineteenth century.

The northern trade

Aside from the colonial and New World trade, that of northern Europe was the most active at the end of the eighteenth century. This was due in large measure to the fact that Scandinavia and the Baltic region constituted the most important source by far of ships' timbers and naval supplies, the demand for which was increasing at the end of the century. Great Britain, in particular, considered the Baltic trade to be of critical importance, and in 1801 fought a naval battle in the Danish Sound in order to keep it open for British trade. Four years later Jepson Oddy published his treatise on European trade, which, despite its title, was restricted to the commerce of Russia, Germany and the Baltic.[140] It was the most detailed and comprehensive study of the trade of this region to have been published up to this time.

Oddy's study showed the exports of northern Europe to be dominated by timber, flax and hemp from the more northerly ports, and by grain from the more southerly. Russia was the source of most of the timber, half of it coming from St Petersburg. '. . . by far the best fir wood in Europe, and the finest masts came by way of Riga', but an immense amount also came from Russia through Memel and Danzig. The Ogiński and Royal canals greatly extended the hinterlands of Russia's Baltic ports, and the trade of Memel, previously very small, was increased by the timber 'from the forests of Prince Radziwiłł, whose father would not suffer the forests to be cut in his time'. Hardwood timber from the Carpathians was rafted down the Dunajec and other tributaries of the Vistula, but it is evident that forest products had been reduced to minor importance in Poland.

Hemp, flax and the oil expressed from them were particularly important exports of the east Baltic region, making up no less than a third by value of all Russia's exports. There was also an export of coarse linen. Tallow, grain and iron made up most of the remaining cargo shipped from Russia's Baltic ports. The hinterland of the latter was delimited by the catchment area of the Russian rivers. Transport was almost entirely by water. The Dvina a few miles above Riga became navigable only 'when the water is high in spring, by the melting of the snow, and in autumn by the fall of rains, when the barks and floats of masts descend and bring down grain, hemp and produce, impelled by the current'. In this way timber sometimes took two years to reach Riga. Much was expected from the recently constructed canals. It was, for example, confidently hoped that a great deal of Britain's trade with the Ottoman empire would go by these river routes across Russia, especially as ships were sailing to Riga in ballast and freight rates were low. These expectations, however, never materialised; a trans-Russian trade proved to be impracticable.

Grain, predominantly rye, but with an increasing percentage of wheat, remained the chief export of Danzig. It continued to be brought down the Vistula, some in properly constructed ships of 40 or 50 lasts, but much of it still on rafts: 'floats clumsily put together of different dimensions and descriptions according to the rivers or places they are first sent from'. The grain had little protection on its journey and had often to be dried out on arrival at Danzig. This trade, Oddy noted, 'is chiefly in the hands of the Jews, whose interest, one would suppose, would instruct them better'. Shipments varied greatly from year to year, depending not so much on the size of the crop 'as the plenty of water in the rivers for easy navigation in summer, and the high prices in Dantzic, as an inducement to bring it down'. The sphere of the Baltic grain trade was being extended at this time. Not only the San but also the Bug was being used to bring grain from Galicia and the Ukraine. Wheat from Lithuania and the Ukraine had once been reckoned inferior to that of southern Poland, but its quality had in recent years been improved, and the best was now said to come from Russia by way of the Bug. High grain prices in the west, coupled with improvements to agriculture in Brandenburg and Mecklenburg, also led to a grain export, from, in particular, Hamburg, Stettin and the minor ports of the south Baltic coast. Lübeck continued to serve as an emporium for the southern Baltic, and sent much of its commerce by way of the Stecknitz Canal to the Elbe. A hundred boats were said to be constantly employed on this waterway.

Sweden, wrote Oddy, 'has never been a country very famous for its commerce'. Iron was the most important export, but amounted to little more than 50,000 tonnes a year at this time. Denmark's trade was very small, though the Holstein Canal carried an increasing transit trade between the Baltic and the North seas. Hamburg, despite its lack of docks, was becoming more important as an intermediary in the trade between central Europe and the Atlantic, exporting mainly corn and linen and importing sugar, coffee and colonial products. Ships usually anchored at Cuxhaven or in the Elbe and were off-loaded on to lighters. Bremen was the port of the Weser basin, and Emden by means of a network of canals served Groningen, Friesland and the northern Netherlands.

Norway exported timber, especially masts, and fish. Salted fish were its chief product, and were prepared and shipped from dozens of small ports in the southern half of the country. Imports, as Oddy summarised them, 'consist of such necessaries, and the few luxuries that a poor people require, and such a northerly latitude does not produce'.

The southern trade

Little remains to be said of the commerce of southern Europe at this time. North Africa and the Levant were a potential market of great size for the products of European industry, but they supplied few commodities needed by the developing regions of Europe, and oriental goods, once handled in the markets of Alexandria and Antioch, were now brought to Europe in the holds of British, French and Dutch ships. The Middle East continued to provide a market for light cloth, especially for that woven in Languedoc, and raw cotton, dried fruit and even wine provided return cargoes. Mediterranean trade was unquestionably more important for France,[141] Spain and Italy than it was for Great Britain, but for none was it of profound significance, and in volume it paled before the large cargoes handled in the Baltic ports.

7
Europe on the eve of the Industrial Revolution

In 1815 the old order in Europe was restored insofar as the politicians gathered in Vienna could bring back the institutions and attitudes of a vanished age. The map of Europe was, it is true, modified and simplified. The Austrian Low Countries were merged into a kingdom of the United Netherlands; the number of German states was reduced, and the area of Prussia greatly increased and its power augmented; in Italy, Lombardy and Venezia were incorporated into the empire of the Habsburgs. Poland had disappeared, and Napoleon's Grand Duchy of Warsaw, which had temporarily taken its place, was ruled by the Russian Tsar. In many respects, however, it was a very different Europe from that which had been so rudely shaken by the revolutionary ideas of the French and fought over by the armies of Napoleon. The spirit of nationalism had been intensified, and there was a widespread feeling that government should not only be responsive to public feeling, but should reflect national aspirations.

The previous quarter of a century had been marked by war and civil disturbance in most parts of Europe. A hundred years earlier warfare in Europe had been accompanied by famine crises and epidemics, and the resulting mortality had been heavy. The Revolutionary and Napoleonic Wars had also been accompanied by shortages but there was no famine crisis and no major epidemic. The years immediately following the peace of 1815 were marked by poor harvests and resulting scarcity and high price of food, but there was no abnormal rise in mortality as there had been a century earlier.[1]

The nineteenth century was indeed a different world from the eighteenth, one in which the quality of housing was better, and standards of cleanliness were higher; when more people wore underclothing and changed it more frequently, with a consequent decline in the lice population and thus in susceptibility to typhus. The plague had vanished from Europe and smallpox was under control. The human diet was marginally better, and shortages were more easily remedied. The result of small changes and marginal improvements in so many directions was a spectacular increase in population, almost certainly the most rapid that Europe had ever experienced.

The practice of agriculture improved only slowly during the early decades of the nineteenth century (pp. 209–12), but barriers to change, both institutional and psychological, were being broken down. There was a greater willingness in many parts of Europe to adopt new crops and cropping systems, to employ better tools and to invest more heavily in draining and fertilising the soil. It was evident to travellers in continental Europe that a wave of progress was spreading through agriculture. If its results were not spectacular they were at least irreversible. There could be no return to the agricultural practice of the *ancien régime*. Europe geared itself to an expanding agricultural production.

A change in attitudes was no less marked in the field of industrial enterprise. Before the Revolutionary Wars continental entrepreneurs had done little more than toy with the technical innovations which had come from Great Britain. The failure of continental ironworkers to master the use of coal in smelting and refining (p. 263) was typical of the aristocratic and amateur attitudes which prevailed. By 1815 this had changed. The floodgates were opened and Europe was inundated by British technology, as innovations were diffused across the continent at a speed, in many instances, far greater than that at which they had spread through Great Britain itself during the previous century. Education, especially technical education, made important advances during these years, and the development of a technological literature, especially a periodical literature, disseminated the knowledge of advances in manufacturing.

Attitudes to investment and risk-taking, to the size of the firm and to participation in industry all underwent a change between the eighteenth century and the nineteenth. The amount of capital available in the eighteenth century was admittedly not large, but little was in fact invested productively in either agriculture or industry. Those with capital saw little profit in such developments and, indeed, little reason for them. After 1815, investment became a normal preoccupation of those with the means to engage in it. The squandering of wealth, all too prevalent under the *ancien régime*, did not by any means cease, but conspicuous consumption began to take second place at least in western and central Europe to the demands for investment capital. This was an essential feature of what Rostow has called 'the take-off into sustained growth ... the interval', as he defined it, 'when the old blocks and resistances to steady growth are finally overcome. The forces making for economic progress, which yielded limited bursts and enclaves of modern activity, expand and come to dominate the society. Growth becomes its normal condition. Compound interest becomes built, as it were, into its habits and institutional structure.'[2]

Great Britain, it is generally recognised, had reached this phase of sustained growth well before the end of the eighteenth century. The corresponding phase of development was deferred in continental Europe until after the Revolutionary and Napoleonic Wars. Rostow places its beginnings in France and Belgium in the 1830s, though it may have come a little earlier in the latter. In Germany it did not begin until the mid-century. Such precision is not possible in other parts of Europe, but the beginnings of sustained growth can probably be placed early in the second half of the century in the Netherlands, Switzerland and the Czech lands. It was to follow within a decade or two in Sweden and in parts of Spain and Italy.

Economic growth is most conveniently measured by the increase in gross national product per head. The compilation of such data is, however, complicated by the absence of an adequate statistical base for much of Europe before the late nineteenth century. All figures for the first half of the century are tentative. Estimates compiled by Bairoch[3] show no sharp increase for the continent as a whole before the mid-nineteenth century. Growth was, however, significant in western Europe a decade or more earlier.

Population

The sharp increase in population which characterised the first half of the nineteenth century was achieved in spite of an average age at marriage which was tending in many parts of Europe to increase and a diminishing birth-rate. The latter had been declining very slightly in the later eighteenth century and more sharply in the nineteenth, though there were not only short-term fluctuations with changing economic circumstances but also distinct regional variations.[4] In Norway, for example, the age at marriage was strongly influenced by the quality of the harvest and the price of food.[5] The decline in fertility, irregular and local though it may have been, can nevertheless be recognised as 'the beginning of the secular movement to restrict births voluntarily'.[6]

This fall in the rate of reproduction was accompanied by an even more marked change in death-rates which was marginally steeper than that of birth-rates.[7] The expectation of life increased almost everywhere. In Sweden it rose thus:[8]

	Males	Females
1755–75	33.88 years	36.6 years
1841–55	41.28 years	45.6 years

The most significant aspect of the diminished mortality rate was the survival into adulthood of a larger proportion of children.[9] At the same

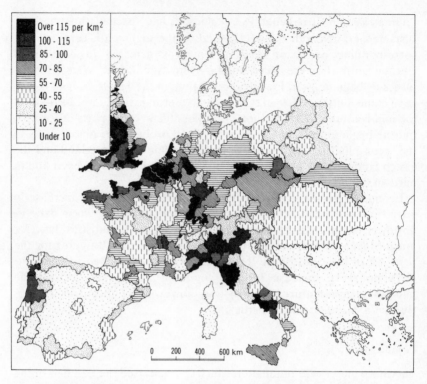

Fig. 7.1 Distribution of population in Europe, about 1840

time more women were living through the child-bearing period; more families were completed, and a very much higher proportion of those born grew up to have families of their own. This is why, despite an overall decline in the birth-rate, the population of Europe was able to increase during the period from 1815 to 1850 at an annual rate of from 1 to 2 per cent.

There nevertheless continued to be local and regional crises. Outbreaks of cholera and typhus were locally severe, but famine crises were becoming rarer.

The rate of population growth was in many areas directly related to the economy. Duprez for example distinguished between the respective birth-rates on three different soil types in Flanders. It was lowest on the good agricultural soils and highest on the poor.[10] The reason lay in the fact that domestic crafts had been developed to supplement agriculture in the poorest areas, and that the peasant who relied primarily on his wife's facility with the distaff and his own with the loom did not need to wait before marrying until he could inherit a tenement. Early marriage might in fact be advantageous as an additional pair of hands helped to supply him with thread and children still offered an economic advantage.[11] It has been demonstrated from under-developed societies today that if the average age at marriage of women falls below 20, the net reproduction rate may rise almost to three and the fertility rate to seven.[12] Marriage at 27 is likely to reduce fertility by at least two births per family.

In all parts of Europe where the tradition of domestic crafts was strong, birth-rates tended to be higher than elsewhere. This was as true of the sandy heathland regions of the Netherlands[13] as of the mountain regions of Bohemia[14] and Saxony.[15] In each instance it was the availability of employment which encouraged early marriage. A map of France showing the baptismal- and hence approximately the birth-rate in the late eighteenth century shows a relatively low rate in a broad belt extending from Artois and the Channel coast south and south-west to Aquitaine. At the same time baptismal-rates were very high (over 46 per thousand) in much of the east and south-east.[16] Birth-rates are seen to have been consistently lower in areas of the highest agricultural productivity, such as the Beauce and eastern Normandy, where peasants commonly waited before marriage to inherit a commonly impartible inheritance. 'It is', wrote Eversley, 'the industrial element in the agrarian sector which causes population increases.'[17]

France

The population of France at the end of the Napoleonic Wars has been put, following estimates by the *préfets*, at about 30 million. Losses during the wars which had just ended had been heavy – perhaps as many as 860,000, almost all of them men[18] – and this restricted the rate of growth during the following years. By 1831 the population within the boundaries established by the Treaty of Vienna reached 32,569,000, and 34,230,000 by 1841. The densest population continued to be in a broad belt along the Channel coast from Brittany to Nord, and the only other areas with densities considerably above the average were Alsace and the Lyonnais, which included the coal-mining region of Saint-Etienne. Over most of the empty heart of France population was failing to increase. In the Alpine départements, including Savoy which was not ceded to France until 1860, there was a very slow increase until about 1830, followed by a decline, so that some areas were less populous at the mid-century than they had been at its beginning.[19] Here, as also in the Jura, Central Massif and Pyrenees, there was an outward migration during the middle decades of the nineteenth century.

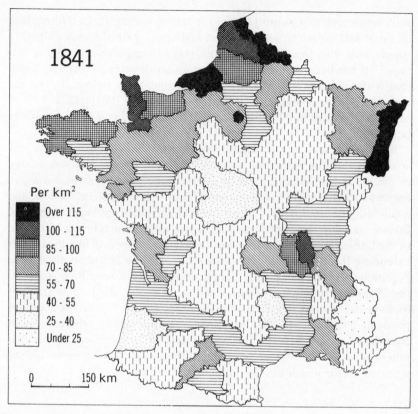

Fig. 7.2 Distribution of population in France, 1841

The Low Countries

In the Low Countries arable farming was relatively unimportant, and large numbers were employed in the textile industries, in peat-digging and in navigation on the system of inland waterways. There were few constraints on population growth, and increase was rapid in those areas, in Flanders in particular, where domestic weaving was important. The population of the *châtellenie* of Audenarde grew by over 60 per cent in a little over half a century,[20] and there was a similarly rapid growth in other areas where manufacturing was well established. The population of the northern provinces of Belgium increased by 40 per cent between 1801 and 1829,[21] and that of the country as a whole from about 3,000,000 in 1800 to about 3,760,000 in 1830.[22]

Rate of growth in the Netherlands was similar to that in Belgium. The total population was about 2,150,000 at the beginning of the century, rising to 2,660,000 by 1830.

Germany

The political fragmentation of Germany makes it difficult to measure the course of population change, and only for the larger states are series available. The German Confederation which included Austria and the Czech lands, probably had about 23,500,000 in 1816 and 36,500,000 a half century later.[23] The kingdom of Prussia made up almost 30 per cent of the area of the Confederation, and the Habsburg lands a further 30 per cent. Bavaria composed about 12 per cent, and the rest was divided into no less than thirty-seven separate states, several of them fragmented, some covering only a few square kilometres. Their statistics constitute a demographic nightmare.

The population of Prussia increased from 10.35 million at the end of the Napoleonic Wars to 16.33 million in 1849; that of Bavaria from 3.7 million in 1818 to 4.5 million in 1849, and of Saxony from 1.56 million in 1832 to 1.89 million in 1849. The available statistics, some of which are estimates rather than census figures, suggest a rapid growth during the first ten years of peace, followed by a much reduced rate of increase for a decade, and then by a sharper growth rate which lasted through the mid-century. The increasing population of the earlier period may have been the natural consequence of the termination of the longest and most costly period of warfare since the early seventeenth century; the second increase was the consequence of improvements in agriculture and in public health and of the growing opportunities for employment in manufacturing. Nevertheless the rate of increase varied greatly within Germany. Prussia showed an overall increase of 65 per cent in forty years; Saxony of 71, and Mecklenburg–Schwerin of 75.6. On the other hand, the increase in Baden was only 31.2 per cent; in Bavaria, 24.97, and in Württemberg, 18.6. No great precision can be claimed for these figures, but it is nonetheless clear that the rate of increase in northern Germany was a great deal sharper than in southern. One is tempted to relate this differential to the expansion of manufacturing in northern Germany, especially in Saxony and Rhineland–Westphalia. The industrialising regions of Prussia do not, however, show a more rapid increase than those which remained predominantly agricultural. Indeed, the overall increase between 1816 and the mid-century was much greater in the agricultural eastern provinces than in the more industrialised western. The percentage growth in Pomerania is calculated to have been 88; in West and East Prussia, over 80, and in Posen province, almost 70. Growth in the very much more highly industrialised province of Silesia was 55.6 per cent; in the Rhine province, 57.4, and in Westphalia, only

43.2 – very similar to the growth rates in Belgium and the Netherlands. This very high rate of growth of population in the eastern provinces of Germany, as well as in Congress Poland, may have been the result of the low densities which existed hitherto and of the relative abundance of land available for settlement and cultivation. It was probably also related to the abolition of serfdom within the Prussian state as part of the reforms of von Stein. On the other hand, those regions of Prussia in which manufacturing industries were developing – Silesia and the lower Rhineland, for example – had long been the scene of important craft industries, and it was to some extent a question of diverting labour from the older branch of industry to the newer. The expansion of the latter did not call for the immigration of labour on a large scale until later in the century, and when this did take place, the rural masses of eastern Germany were ready to crowd into the factories of western.

By the 1830s the population map of Germany was coming to be characterised by a belt of high density extending from the Belgian and Dutch borders in the west, across the lower Rhineland and eastwards to Saxony, reaching 200 to the square kilometre on the good soils, but less than 20 on the heathlands. Densities were also low in the hilly regions of Upper Bavaria and central Germany, except where metal industries had given rise to local concentrations.

Population growth was in general slower in the Habsburg lands. It increased from about 3.63 million in Austria itself to 4.6 million, and in the Czech lands from 4.7 to 6 million.[24] Increase was most rapid in Bohemia, which had become the most heavily industrialised region within the Habsburg empire.[25] The population of Switzerland grew from about 1.66 million in 1798 to 2.4 million, a rate of growth similar to that experienced in western Germany and the Low Countries.[26]

Scandinavia

Population had long been pressing against resources, and in this region of harsh climate and, except in Denmark, poor soil, famine crises occurred more frequently and more severely than in most other parts of Europe. Small climatic fluctuations such as might elsewhere have had little measurable effect could, as Utterström has emphasised,[27] have disastrous consequences so close to the climatic margin of cultivation. Heckscher has emphasised that in pre-industrial Sweden there was a truly Malthusian situation,[28] and Malthus himself found much to support his thesis when travelling in Norway.[29] Drake has suggested that it was the introduction of the heavy-cropping potato which did much in the early nineteenth century to permit population growth.[30] Birth-rates rose sharply in the 1820s, reflecting in all probability the greater availability of food, but then began to fall. Death-rates fluctuated, but their general trend was not downwards until after 1810, a half century later than in western Europe.

Scandinavia remained the least populous region in Europe. The population of Norway was almost wholly coastal, and almost a quarter of it lived close to the shores of Oslo Fjord. In Sweden less than 14 per cent of the population lived in the northern three-quarters of the country, where lumbering and ironworking provided almost the only means of livelihood. The demographic history of Denmark followed a similar course: slow increase in the eighteenth century followed by more rapid growth in the nineteenth.[31] Density was, however, much greater but varied roughly with soil quality, being highest in the islands of Sjaelland and Fyn and in Holstein, then part of Denmark, and lowest in the morainic region of Jutland, where domestic crafts had never been developed to compensate for the poverty of the soil.

Table 7.1   *Population of Scandinavia (in thousands)*

	1800	1830	1850
Denmark	987	1264	1499
Norway	883	1131	1400
Sweden	2347	2888	3483

Southern Europe

Spanish and Portuguese statistics are amongst the least reliable, but they nonetheless demonstrate a rate of growth which was amongst the lowest in Europe. The population of Spain was about 10,500,000 at the end of the eighteenth century. It must have fallen during the Peninsular War, but by 1833 had climbed to about 12,250,000. The Carlist Wars again reduced the total and at the mid-century it may not have been much over 12 million.[32] Portugal may have suffered even more severely. Its population was about 2,900,000 in 1800.[33] Twenty years later it had increased to only 3 million, and by the mid-century had probably not reached more than 3.5 million. The population of the Iberian peninsula was essentially peripheral, with areas of moderately dense population only on the coastal plains of the south and south-east and in the hills which border the Bay of Biscay. But even here population was dense only by contrast with that of the Meseta where prevailing densities were less than 20 to the square kilometre except in Madrid province.

The Italian peninsula was very much more densely populated than the Iberian. Its population, including that of Sicily but not of Sardinia, was about 17,417,500 in 1800.[34] By 1820 this had risen to about 17.9 million, and to 20.5 million by 1840,[35] when the overall density was about three times that of Spain and Portugal. The Lombardy plain, Liguria, Tuscany and Campania had densities amongst the highest in Europe, and even the rugged and mountainous kingdom of Naples and Sicily had average densities far above those of any province of the Iberian peninsula.

Eastern and south-eastern Europe

There are few data for the size of the population in the early nineteenth century, and for some areas there are no statistics before the twentieth. Qualitative evidence suggests that the rate of growth was well above the European average. The population of Congress Poland is said to have increased by 80 per cent – from 2.7 to 4.8 million – between 1816 and 1864, and similar rates of growth are claimed for Prussian-[36] and Austrian-held Poland.[37] Estimates of the population of the Balkan peninsula are little better than guesses, based on the level of the economy and inferred density. Bosnia and Serbia may each have had a million people by 1850 – Serbia certainly had about 1.7 million in 1878.[38] The Romanian provinces of Wallachia and Moldavia may have had about 1.5 million in 1815 and 4.2 million thirty years later. Greece had 6,700,000 at the time of its independence in 1832. The rest of the Balkan peninsula was still under Ottoman rule. There are no firm statistics, and a total of about 9 million at the mid-century can be reached only by projecting back from figures of a much later date.

The population map

Fig. 7.1 is an attempt to show the distribution of population in the mid-nineteenth century. For some areas, notably France, the Low Countries and Switzerland, it is relatively accurate, but for much of Europe only crude estimates for extensive areas are available. The distribution of population anticipated in many ways that of a century later. It was densest in north-western Europe from Finisterre to Friesland, with extensions inland to include the Paris region and the Rhineland. Comparable densities were also to be found in the Lyonnais, northern Italy and 'royal' Saxony. Densities appreciably below the European average (about 30 to the square kilometre) were to be found over Scandinavia, most of Spain, the whole Alpine region and the Balkan peninsula.

One assumes that in this pre-industrial age the density of population would bear a close relationship to the fertility of the soil, though the tendency already discussed for the peasantry in some of the poorer agricultural areas to develop craft industries would have gone some way to level up the densities in some of the less populous regions.

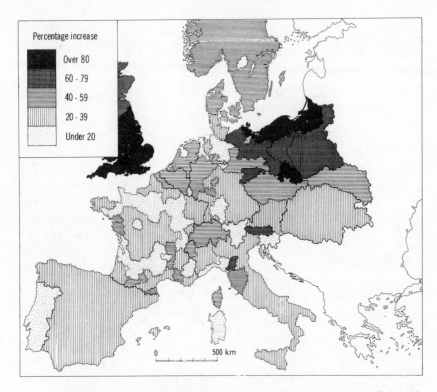

Fig. 7.3 Percentage population growth in Europe during the first half of the nineteenth century

Nevertheless some of the highest densities occurred in rural areas where domestic crafts provided no effective supplement of agriculture. The high density of the Italian peninsula far exceeded the capacity of the land to support it adequately, as countless travellers noted. The low densities of Spain, by contrast, fell considerably short of what could have been fed. It is surely anomalous that the rugged Abruzzi and Molise had densities greater than the province of Valencia with its irrigated *huertas*, and the Beauce, the 'granary of Paris'. In other areas also one finds a density of population greater than the local agriculture could provide for: Sicily, the Dalmatian coast with its Croatian hinterland, Galicia and Lodomeria (Ruthenia and L'vov). There had not by the 1840s, to which most of these data relate, been a sufficient migration within Europe to relieve these local pressures. In the second half of the century these were not only to populate the growing industrial regions but also to provide a stream of migrants to the New World.

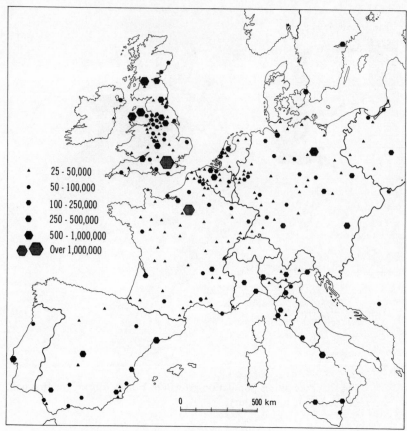

25 - 50,000
50 - 100,000
100 - 250,000
250 - 500,000
500 - 1,000,000
Over 1,000,000

0   500 km

Fig. 7.4 The larger cities of Europe, about 1840

Rates of population growth

These ranged on a national basis from less than 30 per cent in France
between 1800 and 1850 to more than 50 per cent in Denmark.[39] On a
local scale the range was far greater. The highest rates of growth were in
Prussia's eastern provinces, but with only local exceptions they were
high in most of northern Europe. The lowest growth rates were
registered in the interior of France and in Portugal, Spain and peninsular Italy. A Malthusian situation may provide an adequate reason for the
slow growth in much of Italy, but hardly in Spain, where social
conditions and the difficulty of obtaining a tenement offer a more
acceptable explanation. In France, there can be little doubt, the
impartible status of farms was a major factor in reducing the birth-rate.
Fig. 7.3 summarises the available data on the rate of population growth
in the first half of the nineteenth century.

Urban growth

It has sometimes been assumed that the growth of population was in the main an urban phenomenon, and that rural population grew little if at all during the first half of the nineteenth century. The evidence, fragmentary though it is, does little to support this view. The nineteenth century was unquestionably a period of urban growth, but it was, at least during its first fifty years, a highly selective growth. A few cities, amongst them political and regional capitals and the leading ports, increased rapidly in size. Most other towns were growing very much more slowly. Small towns – those of less than 10,000 or 15,000 – were in relation to total population even smaller in 1850 than they had been a half century earlier.[40]

Capital cities, even those of the small German and Italian states, grew rapidly, and became indisputably the 'primate' cities of their respective countries. Paris, which had for centuries stood head and shoulders above other French cities, grew from 547,750 in 1801 to 1,093,250 in 1851, an increase of over 90 per cent. Berlin grew within the same period by about 160 per cent; Brussels by over 250, and Oslo by 180. Growth was slower in The Hague (about 64 per cent), Madrid and Lisbon, but some of the lesser capitals, such as Munich and Turin, more than doubled in size. Regional capitals – the business and cultural centres for their respective provinces – also grew rapidly. Such cities as Toulouse, Trier and Metz; Strasbourg, Cologne and Breslau increased by from 40 to 100 per cent. Growth was no less marked in port cities, notably Le Havre, Antwerp, Rotterdam, Hamburg and Marseilles.

Nevertheless, the ratio of urban to total population did not greatly increase, largely because the population of the small and medium-sized towns, which constituted the great majority, increased as a general rule less rapidly than the population as a whole. Toutain, assuming that all settlements of over 2000 inhabitants were urban, has calculated that the urban population of France increased from 16 per cent in 1806 to 24.4 per cent in 1846.[41] That of Prussia grew from 26 per cent in 1825 only to 28 per cent in 1846.[42] Saxony was in percentage terms less urbanised in 1843 than it had been in 1750. Württemberg was said to have been 24 per cent urban in 1846, and even in Belgium only a quarter of the population lived in towns in that year. Only 12 per cent of the population of Norway and less than 11 per cent of that of Sweden were urban in the mid-nineteenth century.[43] Too much credence must not be given to these figures. The data from which they were derived are not wholly reliable, and there was no accepted definition of urban population. It is nevertheless clear that the rate of growth of the urban sector was but little greater than that of the population as a whole. In no

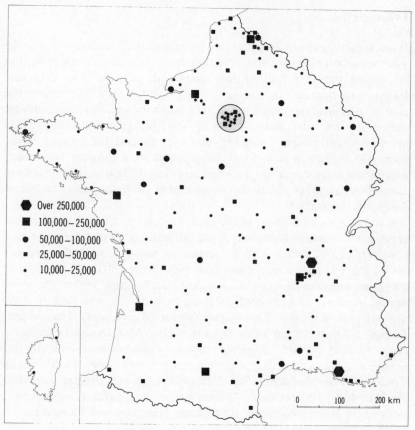

Fig. 7.5 Cities and towns of France in the mid-nineteenth century.
Compare with fig. 3.5

country except Great Britain, where urban population first exceeded
rural in 1851, did the former comprise much more than a quarter. It was
highest – perhaps 40 per cent – in the Netherlands, and was about 35
per cent in Saxony.[44]

It is evident that the 'vital revolution' in continental Europe, and the
rapid growth in population which followed, was not the result of
urbanisation; nor, indeed, did it contribute immediately to a rapid
increase in the urban sector of the total population. In much of Europe
the labour factor in agriculture was not overabundant, and in only a few
areas – notably southern Italy and parts of eastern Europe – was there
severe rural overpopulation. There was in consequence little forced
migration to the towns. Nor was there much opportunity for most towns

to absorb immigrants from the countryside. Their social structure and economic functions changed little, and immigration was in most instances little more than was necessary to compensate for the lower net reproduction rate in towns.

The development of large towns was dependent upon either an increase in the areas which they served or on the creation of new urban functions in manufacturing or business. Both called for improved means of transport and communication, and these did not come until the railway age. The first public railway in continental Europe was not opened until 1835, and by 1840 the total length of all railways was only 1481 kilometres, two-thirds of the length of the contemporary railway system in Great Britain.[45] It was only when towns were linked with markets and with one another that constraints on their growth were at last removed, and this did not happen until the second half of the century.

The industrial town

There were few large industrial towns in the mid-nineteenth century. Manufacturing was still as much a rural as an urban pursuit, though many industrial villages were rapidly assuming the aspect of sprawling, shapeless urban agglomerations. Most older towns continued to be dominated by crafts. Factory industries require power, either water power, which was available only in rural areas, or steam power, which could be used economically only on or near the coalfields. The new industrial towns developed near sources of mechanical power. They were of two kinds: those which had grown from villages, and older incorporated towns which happened to lie conveniently for the supply of power and had not the ability or the will to resist the newer types of industrial organisation. The former included some of the weaving centres of northern France, such as Roubaix and Tourcoing; iron-working centres like Charleroi, and the spreading mining villages of the Belgian coalfield. Similar towns grew up in the lower Rhineland, supported by clothworking and iron-fabricating. On the Ruhr coalfield they developed around the iron works and the mines: Oberhausen, Gelsenkirchen, Mülheim, Borbeck and Ruhrort. Similarly on the coalfield of Upper Silesia villages were growing into towns. The urban settlement which grew up around the largest iron works of the early nineteenth century could find no name more suitable than Königshütte, rendered into Polish as Królewska Huta. Zabrze, Sosnowiec and Katowice all grew from villages or even farmsteads with the opening of mines and construction of smelters.

There were inevitably some older, incorporated towns in these industrialising areas. Most were small; some, Essen for example, tried to resist the new industrial age, but all succumbed and were transformed by it. Modern industry was, as a general rule, established *outside* the walls of the town. Krupp, for example, founded his *Gussstahlwerk* outside Essen, and the earliest works at Dortmund and at Gliwice and Bytom in Upper Silesia lay well beyond the urban limits. Gradually, however, the old town was engulfed within a zone of factories, tenement blocks and terraced workers' housing. The town walls disappeared, and the town began to provide services for its industrial suburbs, and the contrast in townscape and social attitudes between the two were gradually reduced if not obliterated. Such towns usually grew rapidly. The population of the Upper Silesian industrial region increased by over 40 per cent between 1819 and 1849, and Bytom, its most important urban centre, by more than 400 per cent.[46]

Towns whose industries had relied heavily on water power found their growth limited. Some, Elberfeld and Barmen[47] in the Rhineland, for example, and Chemnitz and Zwickau in Saxony, were able to overcome this obstacle because sources of mineral fuel lay nearby, but some of the textile centres which bordered the Ardennes and Eifel had no such advantage, and declined absolutely.[48]

The pre-industrial urban scene

The hand of the past still lay heavily on most European towns. Streets may have been widened but their plan had in most instances not changed significantly since the end of the Middle Ages. Houses had undergone continuous rebuilding and renovation, and brick and stone had in many cases replaced timber, wattle and clay. Disastrous fires were less frequent; domestic waste was less often thrown into the streets, but animals continued to be kept within the walls for milk or meat, and there was everywhere the stench of stables and tanyards. The market-place still came alive on one or two days of the week, as carts brought peasants and their produce to the town. Most gild organisations had disappeared at the Revolution, but small-town society remained no less exclusive than the gild-ridden society of a century earlier.[49] Hufton's description of this society of Bayeux on the eve of the Revolution could have been applied to most small towns a half century later: 'predominantly . . . composed of shopkeepers and petty tradesmen and those involved in the administration of the town and surrounding area. Over half of those rated in the tax lists hovered dangerously on the fringe of destitution . . . the rest lived either by exploiting someone else or were dependent on income from property. The town was in fact parasitic upon the countryside.'[50] Not even the coming of the railway altogether broke down the self-sufficiency and isolation of the European town. The winds of change were already blowing through the larger cities. They had lost their walls; their centres were rebuilt, their streets widened, and that rural presence, so conspicuous in the smaller towns, had disappeared. The modern age had in many instances announced its arrival with a railway station, built usually just beyond the line of the demolished town walls, where land could be had more cheaply and the track more conveniently laid. Around every large city from Madrid to Warsaw workshops and factories were springing up in the social no-man's-land which lay beyond the line of the walls and close to the railways which brought their raw materials and the food supply of their workers.[51]

Agriculture

After the Napoleonic Wars the social and institutional barriers to change in agricultural practice were gradually removed, and by the mid-century Europe was feeding with only a marginal import from overseas a population at least three times that which it had supported three centuries earlier. This was achieved by marginal advances in a dozen directions. Fallow was abandoned in much of Europe, and rotation systems were made more intensive. Animal husbandry was increased and integrated more closely with arable. Animals were bred with greater care; better tools were used, and seed was selected with a view to perpetuating the good strains. Improvements in transport encouraged local specialisation and the adaptation of cropping to local circumstances. At the same time the area in agricultural use was extended by draining wet lands and reclaiming heath and waste. Average yield-ratios increased despite the fact that much marginal land was brought under cultivation.

The expansion of agriculture was a response to the increase in population and the rising demand for foodstuffs, but it was also a factor in population growth. People were on average fed better than ever before. In many parts of Europe the heavy-cropping maize and potato supplemented the cereal crops, and amongst the latter there was a gradual shift away from rye and the coarse grains and towards wheat as the basic human foodstuff. The factors in this general improvement of agriculture varied from one region to another. In Mayenne it was asserted that 'the use of lime had increased the productivity of the land fourfold'.[52] Elsewhere it was ascribed to the abandonment of fallow and its replacement with fodder crops and roots. Almost everywhere there was an increase in yield-ratios. A worker in the Brunswick area noted in 1832 that only the oldest inhabitants could remember 'when the fallow was left undisturbed; there was no clover; only a few parcels of land were planted with potatoes, and crop yields were slim'.[53] It was a case of marginal improvements in almost every branch of farming.

Population was still predominantly rural. Though declining, the proportion which lived by agriculture made up from two-thirds to three-quarters in France in 1801; by 1851 this had declined only to 55 per cent.[54] The agricultural component was higher in Germany. In Switzerland, 65 per cent of the active population was in agriculture in 1798; this fell to 62 per cent in 1820 and to 54.4 per cent in 1850.[55] In the lands of the Austrian crown as late as 1869 more than two-thirds of the active population was still engaged in agriculture, and the proportion was higher in Hungary.[56] Agriculture contributed a large part of the gross national product in every country of continental Europe. In France this is said to have been of the order of 50 per cent about 1850, and in Italy more than 55 per cent. In Germany in the 1860s it was still 32 per cent and in Sweden 39.[57]

Throughout western and central Europe the land was cultivated by peasants who held their tenements either as freeholds or by some form of long-term tenancy or leasehold. In France most had gained complete possession of their lands at the Revolution, but in much of Europe they owed a money rent. Ploughing obligations and other services had almost wholly disappeared except from Europe's eastern borderland, where in Poland it was not finally abolished until 1864. In western and central Europe it had long been the practice to lease the demesne to a yeoman farmer. In much of southern France and Italy peasants more often held their land *en métayage* (p. 171). A traveller in Italy observed that 'scarcely any of the farmers are proprietors; they all occupy on the condition of paying half the produce to the landlord. This tenure is universal.'[58] In Spain, southern Italy and above all in eastern Germany the great estate had survived, owned by a non-resident landlord and managed by his bailiff.

The overriding problem of the peasant was no longer his lack of personal freedom – except in Russian-held Poland – but rather the smallness and fragmented character of his holding and his lack of capital for tools, equipment and land improvement. There is little evidence for the size of peasant holdings in the early nineteenth century. In France the obligation to divide them between heirs was embodied in the Code Napoléon, with dangerous consequences in some areas. 'It is certain', a report on Languedoc of 1869 noted, 'that the land is becoming daily more divided. This is in large measure the inevitable consequence of our civil law which has placed too many constraints on the natural rights of parents to dispose of their belongings, and has given to each co-heir the right to claim a share in landed and personal property.'[59] Farm-holdings, the report continued, were being eroded, and only a restriction on the size of families could preserve them. In Sweden it became necessary to legislate in order to prevent the endless subdivision of holdings,[60] but in Germany only those areas – basically the south-west – where partible inheritance was the rule suffered from this evil.[61] In Italy peasant holdings became excessively subdivided, so that Chateauvieux found none in Tuscany of more than 10 hectares. In a hill village of the Ligurian Apennines, 89 per cent of tenements were of under 3 hectares and only 2 per cent had more than 10.[62] The trend was always towards further subdivision.

In very few regions had farms ever consisted of a single compact area of land. Most were intensely fragmented, and the division of a tenement between heirs consisted all too often of the simple division of each part of it. The consolidation of the resulting strips has had to wait until the twentieth century.[63]

Measures of agricultural progress were not diffused uniformly over Europe. They spread relatively quickly through the agricultural regions of north-western Europe, but they came late, if at all, to many remote and mountainous regions. Here, for example, in the Central Massif, the Alpine region and throughout the Balkans primitive tools and methods survived into the twentieth century. Here the seventeenth-century sequence of famine crises continued, moderated only by improved transport and the greater ease of bringing relief. In the Oisans region of the French Alps, 'poverty led to sickness and sickness to poverty. A low agricultural production was joined with an unbalanced diet and a lack of education.'[64] A means to break out of this cycle had not yet been found in these areas. In the Nivernais and Morvan the diet was said to have consisted essentially of rye and barley bread even in the mid-nineteenth century,[65] and in the Tuscan Apennines chestnuts, cooked into a flat cake, were a staple diet in remote areas.[66] If superior food crops were grown they had as a general rule to be sold in the market or given to the lord as his *mi-produit*.

Much of Europe still practised a three-course system of husbandry, but there were few areas, at least in western and central Europe, where traditional methods had not in some degree been modified. Only in eastern Europe was the traditional rotation with fallow still widely used, and here the chief obstacle to change lay in the rights of *vaine pâture* exercised by the peasants after harvest. Even here the greater economy of growing a fodder crop instead of permitting indiscriminate grazing on fallow and stubble gradually became apparent. In northern France the cultivation of *prairies artificielles* was spreading and by the mid-century naked fallow was still customary only on poorer soils,[67] though in some instances it was made obligatory by the conditions of leases. Elsewhere it was abandoned with some reluctance by the peasants,[68] and in the Rhône valley some peasants resolutely opposed attempts to induce them to take a fodder crop between the sequence of cereals.[69] In Germany fallowing had been abandoned most widely in the Rhineland, but it is noteworthy that traditional methods were abandoned more readily on the poorer soils than on the rich loess, where animals were fewer, the demand for fodder less, and the constraints of the village economy more powerful.[70] At the beginning of the century naked fallow is estimated to have covered almost 29 per cent of the cultivated land;[71] its extent gradually diminished, but was still quite great in 1850. In Poland a three-course system with fallow was general, and in a few areas of the east rye still alternated with fallow.[72] Agriculture was probably more advanced on the Habsburg lands than in eastern Europe,[73] and in Italy, where cereals had customarily alternated with fallow, the latter appears to have been extensively replaced by maize, beans and artificial grasses.[74]

Outside the area of two- and three-field agriculture cropping was more flexible. Fields were usually enclosed and the peasant was free to modify his farming practice in the light of physical and farming conditions. One must not exaggerate the peasant's propensity to experiment. He was in general stubbornly conservative, but at least the opportunity was present for those inclined to innovate. Various forms of 'convertible' husbandry were adopted in 'Atlantic' Europe and in most mountainous and hilly areas, with a few years under crops alternating with a period under grass. Such systems even encroached on traditionally open-field regions as farmers tried to achieve an integration of crop- and animal-farming.

Cereals continued to dominate the cropping systems, but were slowly yielding to other forms of land-use. In East Prussia grain crops occupied about 73 per cent of the cultivated area in 1805, but only 55 per cent in 1883. In West Prussia the decline was from 74 to 62 per cent.[75] In Alpine regions the relative decline of cereals was greater. Only in France did the area under cereals increase, a consequence in all probability of the multiplication of small subsistence farms. There was almost everywhere a change in the cereals grown. Wheat was increasing at the expense of rye, and the breakdown of the three-course system meant that spring-sown grains were no longer produced in approximately the same amounts as autumn-sown. On the other hand there was an increase in coarse grains as more marginal land was brought under cultivation. In France, for example, there was a significant increase in buckwheat (*sarrasin*), which about 1850 made up nearly 5 per cent of all cereals.

Maize also was of growing importance. It was valued chiefly for its high yield-ratio and its ability to produce both human and animal food. In some parts of northern Italy it was commonly grown in each field

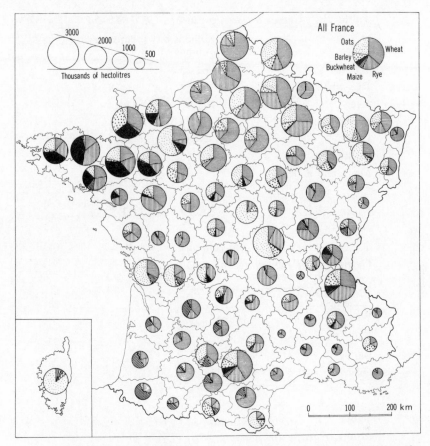

Fig. 7.6 The cultivation of grain crops in France in the early nineteenth century, by départements

every fourth year, and 'constitutes almost the sole article of subsistence with the country people, who eat it under every form of preparation'.[76] It had also spread widely in southern France and was increasingly important in central Europe and the Balkans.

Rye was disappearing from all except the mountainous areas of France, but remained the dominant cereal throughout central and eastern Europe. In France the average cereal production, 1845–54, is shown in table 7.2.[77] But wheat declined in importance in Belgium,[78] and in Germany the balance was tipped yet more strongly in favour of rye, as table 7.3 shows.[79] In Congress Poland the proportions were similar,[80] and the Schwarzenberg lands in Bohemia differed only in their reversal of the roles of barley and oats (table 7.4). In northern Europe winter-sown grain was comparatively rare. Oats and barley were the

Table 7.2   *Cereal production in France, 1845–54*

	Millions of quintals	Percentage
Wheat	62.25	42.5
Rye–wheat mixture	8.54	5.8
Rye	21.00	14.3
Barley	12.37	8.4
Oats	28.81	19.7
Buckwheat	6.80	4.6
Maize and millet	5.83	4.7
	145.60	100.0

Table 7.3   *Cereal cultivation in Germany (in percentage of area cultivated)*

	1800	1861
Wheat	8.1	10.3
Rye	44.1	47.3
Barley	20.4	14.8
Oats	27.4	27.6

Table 7.4   *Cereal production in eastern Europe (in percentage of crop)*

	Poland	Bohemia
Wheat	6.4	6.5
Rye	42.3	49.9
Barley	16.6	35.0
Oats	34.7	8.6

chief cereals in Norway; barley and rye in Sweden. Denmark practised a similar cropping pattern to Germany with, however, even less emphasis on wheat. South of the Alpine system rye and oats almost disappeared. Wheat was the most widely cultivated cereal and in Spain was grown over a vast area of Castile.[81] Barley was of secondary importance, but maize was much grown wherever summer rainfall or irrigation provided sufficient moisture.

Higher yield-ratios played a significant role in securing the greater

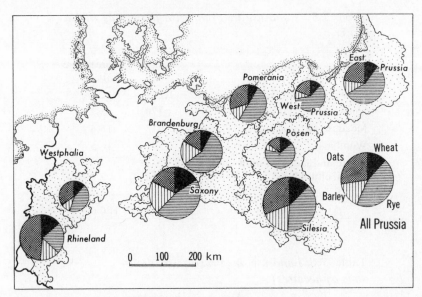

Fig. 7.7 Cereal cultivation in Prussia

cereal production of the nineteenth century. On good soils in western Europe wheat and rye commonly yielded from six- to sevenfold, but on the poorer usually less than fivefold. Ratios were good on the loess lands of western Germany, but declined eastwards and were lowest in Poland where a fourfold return for wheat and rye was reckoned to be good and a fivefold yield exceptional.[82]

Although cereals occupied the greater part of the cropland almost everywhere, secondary crops were gaining in importance. These included legumes, flax and oleaginous plants. On an estate in the Pas de Calais these occupied a quarter of the cropland,[83] and they were important in the Low Countries. In Westphalia and the lower Rhineland 'the cultivation of flax seemed to be universal but in small patches on each farm'.[84] The potato recommended itself to the peasant with only a smallholding, and it was spreading throughout north-western and northern Europe.[85] In Limburg it was grown on almost 8 per cent of the cultivated land,[86] and in Prussia the volume of potatoes grown greatly exceeded that of all the cereals. There was also some increase in such minor and commonly local crops as hops, tobacco and vegetable dyestuffs.

The vine and tree crops such as the apple and olive occupied only a relatively small area. The grapevine was still in retreat in north-western and northern Europe and had almost disappeared from the lower Seine, the lower Rhineland and Saxony. On the other hand vineyards were

Table 7.5   *Land-use in France (in thousands of hectares)*

	Area	Percentage
Arable land	22,818	50.2
Gardens and specialised crops	1,221	2.7
Vines, olives and tree crops	2,379	5.2
Meadow and grazing	7,013	15.5
Woodland	7,501	16.5
Waste and land not used agriculturally	4,513	9.9
	45,445	100.0

Table 7.6 *Land-use in Prussia (in thousands of hectares)*

	Area	Percentage
Arable	29,225	39.7
Gardens	295	
Vineyards	37	
Meadow and pasture	14,672	19.9
Woodland	17,574	23.9
Waste, water, built-up	11,800	16.0
	73,603	99.5

Table 7.7   *Land-use in the Habsburg lands (in percentages)*

	Czech lands	Hungary	Habsburg Empire
Arable	50.4	33.5	37.6
Vineyards	0.2	2.8	1.8
Meadow and garden	10.7	10.0	11.8
Pasture	8.7	15.4	12.6
Forest and waste	30.0	38.3	36.0
Other	–	–	0.2
	100.0	100.0	100.0

increasing in southern France and Italy and also in Hungary where grapes were found to do well on the sandy soils of the Puszta. There were parts of Provence, Languedoc and Aquitaine where wine made up a quarter by value of all agricultural production,[87] and in the Apennine hill village described by Giorgio Doria vineyards covered over half the cultivated land. The market for wine was undoubtedly increasing, but viticulture was also labour-intensive, employing according to a report of 1828 26 per cent more labour than an equivalent area of cropland.[88] At a time of rising population and fragmenting tenements this was an important consideration. The olive was less important than in the eighteenth century,[89] but the mulberry which provided the food of the silkworm was spreading in southern Europe.[90] In north-western Europe apple orchards succeeded to the disappearing vineyards as cider began to replace wine as a popular drink.

There are few data on the overall pattern of land-use. The cultivated area was increasing and it seems likely that in some areas, such as the Spanish Meseta, too much marginal land was brought under cultivation. In north-western Europe the tendency was rather to abandon arable farming on heavy soils and to use the land for grazing. Chaptal's figures for land-use in France, reduced to categories commonly used, are shown in table 7.5.[91] Agricultural land made up a much smaller fraction of the whole of Germany. There are no general statistics but Jacob published the figures in table 7.6 for Prussia.[92] Comparable figures for the Habsburg lands in 1845 are shown in table 7.7.[93] Land-use figures for the continent as a whole are unobtainable. It is unlikely, however, that cropland made up more than 30 per cent of its total area in the mid-eighteenth century, and forest and waste probably covered at least a half. The corresponding percentages in the 1970s are 25 and 30 respectively.

Animal husbandry

Animal-farming was increasing in importance relative to arable during the first half of the nineteenth century, in part because the wisdom became apparent of integrating farm stock with crops, in part because heavy soils tended more and more to be left under grass. In northern France animals contributed about 25 per cent of farm income, but in southern France only 22 per cent.[94] In Germany the pastoral sector accounted for about a quarter,[95] but the fraction tended to become smaller towards the east.[96] The pastoral contribution was very much greater in mountainous and hilly regions and wherever the climate was wet and soils heavy.[97] It was at this time that Normandy and Switzerland established their reputations for butter and cheese.[98] There was in general an inverse relationship between the practice of open-field agriculture and animal husbandry.

In hilly and mountainous areas transhumance continued to be practised in order to make use of marginal land. It was important throughout the Alpine system as well as in Norway, Sweden and the Balkan peninsula. Transhumant pastoralism may even have been increasing in importance in Italy, where Lillen de Chateauvieux described how sheep were kept on Piedmont farms because they could be sent for five months of summer into the Alps; 'on their return, they have the benefit of the after-crop for about six weeks, and are then fed from the rack'.[99] In the plain of Lombardy wealth consisted 'more in cattle than in corn', and many of the small farms combined to operate co-operative dairies for making Parmesan cheese. Transhumant sheep and goats of the Apennines produced wool and 'hard, sour cheeses', important in the local diet.[100] In Spain, however, the transhumant flocks which had at one time traversed the Meseta twice yearly had almost disappeared, victims of the age-old struggle between the steppe and the sown, the pastoralist and the 'dirt-farmer'. Large flocks continued to be kept in Castile, but the traditional migration routes were mostly obstructed by the cultivator.[101]

Agricultural production

Food production increased steadily between the 1820s and the mid-century. This was a condition of the contemporary population growth, and it is likely that in some areas food supply increased faster than population with a consequent improvement in living standards. In France Chaptal gloated over the changes which he had witnessed: 'if one were to compare agriculture now with what it had been in 1789', he wrote, 'one would be astonished at the improvements . . . healthy and abundant food, clean and pleasant houses, simple but becoming clothes – such is the lot of the country-dweller; misery has been banished'.[102] Such praise was exaggerated; there remained areas of extreme poverty and destitution. A report on Brittany praised the progress made in the coastal region but found the interior 'as ill-cultivated and therefore as sterile [i.e. unproductive] as it is possible to conceive . . . In the former, it is intelligent, advanced and productive; in the latter, it is ignorant, prejudiced and unproductive.'[103]

The report went on to describe in terms which Friedrich Engels could not have improved upon, the home of the Breton peasant – 'his crumbling hut, whose roof descends to the ground, its interior blackened by the continual smoke of the heath and rushes, the only fuel of his hearth. It is this miserable hut, into which the light penetrates only thro' the door . . . that he and his family live, half naked, possessing for their entire furniture only a bad table, a bench, an iron pot, and a few wooden and earthen utensils, with no bed but a sort of box, where he sleeps, without bed-clothing, on a mattress stuffed with oaten chaff instead of wool, while in another corner of this melancholy habitation lies, on a little litter, the lean and sorry cow (lucky indeed if he possesses one), which supports his children and himself with its milk.'

This was in a country in which the total production of cereals had increased from about 94.5 million quintals on average in 1803–12 to 146.6 million in the period 1845–54. The proportion of wheat in this total had grown from 41 to 43 per cent, and that of rye had declined.[104] The production of potatoes more than trebled, and if milk consumption declined marginally the consumption of butter, cheese and meat all increased. The value of agricultural production per head of those *vivant de l'agriculture* increased within the half century by 55 per cent.

The nineteenth-century expansion of agriculture is less well documented in other countries. Sweden, which had previously imported up to 15 per cent of its needs, became on balance self-sufficing in bread grains.[105] Baranowski claims that cereal production in Poland increased by almost 50 per cent while that of potatoes more than doubled.[106] Throughout central Europe the trend in agricultural production was sharply upwards.

There is, as Bairoch has demonstrated,[107] a close correlation between industrial development and agricultural progress. In the pre-industrial age at least 80 per cent of the population lived and worked on the land, so that each agricultural unit would on average have had to spare about a quarter of its production to support the non-agricultural classes at the same standard of living. The effect of industrial growth was to increase the demand in the manufacturing sector for foodstuffs and raw materials of vegetable origin. This could be satisfied in the absence of a significant import from outside Europe only by the extension and intensification of agriculture within Europe. Complementary to the satisfaction of urban and industrial demand for foodstuffs was the creation of a rural market for the products of manufacturing. The metal and the textile industries could not have developed as they did through the early nineteenth century without a rural market for their products and a large and growing supply of foodstuffs from the countryside.

Manufacturing industries

By the mid-century Great Britain was in all respects the foremost industrial country in the world. Almost half the population was engaged in manufacturing and mining and over 40 per cent could be classed as urban. There were twenty-eight towns with a population of over 50,000, all of them in large measure industrial, and only 27 per cent of the work force wholly agricultural. No continental country could approach this. Indeed, Great Britain's output of coal was more than twice that of the rest of Europe; she produced more than 50 per cent more pig-iron; consumed two and a half times as much raw cotton, and had more than three times as many spindles. Only in its length of railway track had continental Europe drawn ahead of Great Britain, and this was a significant omen for the future.

In continental Europe manufacturing still provided employment for no more, at a rough estimate, than 5 to 10 per cent of the active population, and despite the existence of a few large mills and industrial plants, much of it was still carried on in domestic workshops. The growth of industrial towns had only just begun, and a high proportion of manufacturing industry – it is impossible to be precise – was still carried on in the countryside, making use, if it used mechanical power at all, only of water power. It would have needed a prophetic vision to recognise the future shape of such industrial regions as central Belgium, the Ruhr and Upper Silesia. Yet the seeds of future industrial growth had been sown, and were germinating under the watchful care of attentive governments and émigré British technicians. All significant coalfields were being explored and exploited, and, if the amount of coal which they yielded at the mid-century was still small, they were nonetheless ready for a great surge forward during the coming years.

Industrial technology

After about 1825 a serious attempt was made to narrow the technical gap between continental Europe and Great Britain. Continental entrepreneurs needed British industrial equipment and trained technicians who came readily enough if the price was right. By 1825 there were in Landes' estimation 2000 or more skilled British workers imparting the secrets of their machines to continental Europeans. Ten years later it was the British who not only built but also drove the first steam-locomotives.

Industrial growth was hesitant for a generation. There was a severe shortage of investment capital; a market for the products of factory industries was slow in developing; the system of transport was inadequate, and, lastly, a class of entrepreneurs to replace the fickle patronage of governments and nobility grew slowly. These factors help to explain why continental Europe still lagged so far behind its British prototype. They also provide a reason for spectacular growth later in the century.

Coalfields

The emerging pattern of industry at this time was being determined by the coalfields. All were being worked to some degree, and the high cost

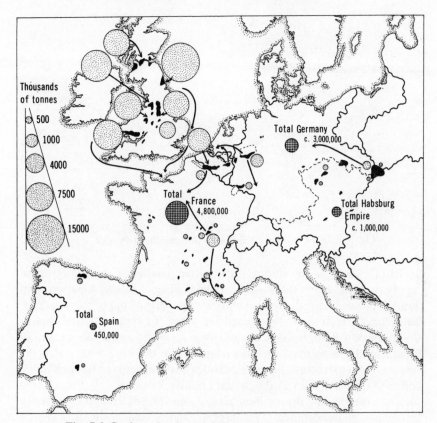

Fig. 7.8 Coal production and the coal trade in the 1840s

of transport gave even the least-economic field some price advantage in its local area. It is difficult to form a precise estimate of the volume of coal production owing to the paucity and unreliability of statistics in much of Europe. Reliable figures exist only for France, Belgium and parts of Germany. It seems however that total output was of the order of 17 million tonnes, with perhaps 2 million tonnes of sub-bituminous coal and lignite. The Belgian coalfield was the most developed. Its Liège sector supported a complex of iron-smelting and fabricating works, but the Hainault sector, lying farther to the west, was less industrialised.[108] By 1846 there were 436 steam-engines at work on the Belgian coalfield, 102 of them used for pumping water from the mines and most of the others for hauling coal to the surface.[109] Belgium was at this time by far the largest coal-producer in continental Europe, but exported perhaps a third of its output, most of it to France and the Netherlands.

France, with a coal production of about 4.8 million tonnes, was a net

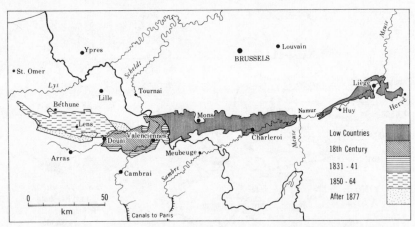

Fig. 7.9 The coalfield of Belgium and northern France

importer. There were about sixty active coalfields, many of them supplying little more than a few scuttles of coal to the local population.[110] The most productive field by far was that of the département of Loire which contained the industrial towns of Saint-Etienne, Saint-Chamond and Rive de Gier. In the 1840s it yielded about 40 per cent of French coal production. Its advantages lay in the ease with which the coal could be extracted from the hillsides and transported by the Rhône and Loire, rather than in the actual abundance of coal.[111] Indeed, the coalfield retained its pre-eminence only into the 1850s, and then began to decline in importance. The largest French coal basin, that of the départements of Nord and Pas-de-Calais, was only partially developed and its extension to the west of Douai almost unexplored.[112] There was a significant production from the Alès field (dép. Gard) and from Blanzy–Le Creusot (dép. Saône-et-Loire), but almost 30 per cent of France's coal still came from the multitude of minute fields most of which yielded annually less than 50,000 tonnes.

Germany was the most richly endowed of all the countries of Europe. The Ruhr and Upper Silesian coalfields alone embraced about 60 per cent of the total reserves of the continent. Yet their intensive exploitation had scarcely begun by 1850. Only a small part of the Ruhr coalfield was accessible, and this yielded little of the better-quality coal. Not until the later nineteenth century did developments take place in the hidden field, where most of the coking coal was found. In 1850 the Ruhr produced about 1.7 million tonnes, but output was increasing rapidly and reached 4.4 million tonnes by 1860. The other important German coalfield lay in Upper Silesia with extensions into Austrian and Russian-held territory. Its resources rivalled those of the Ruhr; it was

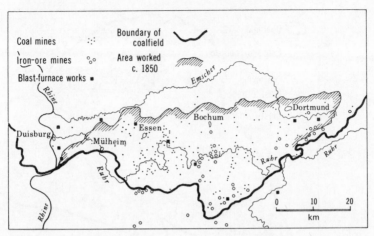

Fig. 7.10 The Ruhr coalfield in the mid-nineteenth century

the most easily worked of Europe's major coalfields, and its pit-head prices were the lowest in the continent, only a quarter of those in the small Saxon fields.[113] But mining was gravely restricted by the lack of market except in the local smelting industries, to supply which many of the mines were in fact opened up. Nearly half the coal was being used in zinc-smelters and much of the remainder in ironworks.[114]

The small coalfields in Germany were disproportionately important. The Saar and Aachen–Düren fields each yielded about half a million tonnes a year. The very small fields at Ibbenbüren, Minden, Lobejun and Wettin were all being exploited, and the Lower Silesian or Waldenburg (Wałbrzych) field was one of the most highly regarded in Europe.[115]

Most of the coal produced within the Habsburg empire came from the mines of Bohemia and northern Moravia, the latter an extension of the Upper Silesian field. Coal-mining was of negligible importance in Austria and Hungary. The Bohemian field consisted of two basins, each of major importance, at Plzeň and Kladno, together with a few small fields which have long since been abandoned. The Ostrava–Karviná field of northern Moravia contained very large reserves, especially of coking coal, which had recently come into use in the iron industry.[116] A feature of coal-mining in the Czech lands was the relatively great importance of the very small and now almost abandoned Rosice–Oslavany field near Brno. Its output was a major factor in the development of manufacturing industry at Brno.

There was a small output of coal in Spain, particularly in Asturias.[117] No production was recorded in Italy, and that of the Danube basin and

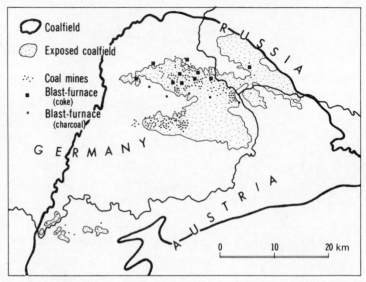

Fig. 7.11 The Silesian coalfield in the mid-nineteenth century

Balkan peninsula was minute. There was in addition a small but growing production of brown coal and lignite. The chief source was – and long remained – the deposits of northern Bohemia, especially those of Teplice–Most–Chomutov. Output in 1848 was about 200,000 tonnes.[118] Brown coal was also dug in Nassau and elsewhere in Germany, but was at this time of only minor and local importance.[119]

The iron industry

No branch of manufacturing showed more clearly the contrast between the old and the new patterns of industry than the smelting and processing of iron. The industry was carried on at three levels. In a few remote areas, such, for example, as the eastern Pyrenees and Corsica, the direct method of producing a soft iron from its ore on a hearth was still practised by a handful of traditional craftsmen. But this had only a local significance and was destined soon to disappear. For the rest, the iron industry was divided between the traditional process of smelting with charcoal and refining on the hearth, and the new method which used coke in the blast-furnace and refined the metal in the puddling furnace. The distinction between the old and the new was not, however, clear-cut. Many furnaces used a mixture of charcoal and coke, and some charcoal-smelted iron was refined in a puddling furnace with coal.

Europe's blast-furnaces were producing a million tonnes of iron a year in the 1840s, of which not more than a third was smelted with mineral fuel.[120] But the situation was changing rapidly. Charcoal was

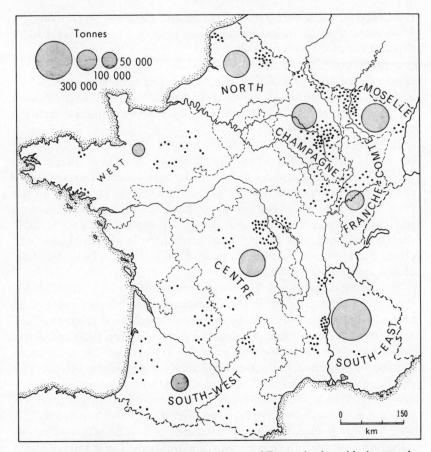

Fig. 7.12 The iron and steel industry of France in the mid-nineteenth century

becoming scarce and expensive, but it was not until the present century that the last of the old-fashioned furnaces was put to rest. Iron-masters continued to be concerned for the quality of the coke available and to have technical difficulties in using it. The coke-fired furnace ran at a higher temperature than one which used charcoal and required a more powerful blast. In effect it had to be rebuilt if it was converted from one fuel to the other. Furnace-masters often lacked the capital for such a change, the success of which they would have considered problematic. Most charcoal furnaces lay far from the coalfields and in many instances the cost of transporting coal would have been prohibitive. Even on the coalfields, coke was adopted only after a long period of trial and experiment.

Belgium was in this, as in other respects, the pioneer. Two groups of coke-fired furnaces were built near Liège and Charleroi respectively. By 1844 there were 51 furnaces which used coke out of a total of 130.[121] Most of the charcoal furnaces lay in the Ardennes. Some attempted to convert to coke, but were defeated by the cost of transport. The last charcoal furnace in Hainault closed in 1851, and most of those in Namur and Liège were blown out within a generation. In 1850 90 per cent of Belgium's output of 145,000 tonnes of pig-iron and castings came from coke-fired furnaces.[122]

In France the charcoal industry resisted the competition of the coke-fired furnace more successfully. It was very widely distributed (see Fig. 7.12), and few furnaces had access to coal. Indeed, the production of charcoal iron continued to increase until 1857. In 1850 only 43 per cent of the total iron production of about 400,000 tonnes had been smelted with coke.[123] Thereafter change was more rapid and by 1870 charcoal iron had sunk to only 8 per cent of the total. The change was effected not so much by the conversion of old furnaces as by the building of new on or close to the coalfields.

The foremost centre of the newer iron industry was unquestionably the Saint-Etienne region.[124] The abundance and cheapness of its coal proved an attraction to the industry, even though local reserves of ore were small. It became the practice to import ore from Elba and North Africa by way of the Rhône, and a number of works was located close to the river at Gisors and Chasse. Le Creusot was similarly placed, with adequate coal, but limited ore resources. The Centre, consisting of Berry and the Nivernais, had a well-established charcoal-iron industry, but this region was distinguished by its large number of small coalfields. This was, in consequence, one of the few areas of Europe where coke was introduced successfully into a traditional industry. The system of rivers and canals was used to convey coal from Commentry, Blanzy and other fields to the furnaces at Montluçon, Fourchambault (near Nevers) and other sites in Berry. Other small coalfields in the Central Massif gave rise to iron-working. The Duc Decazes built furnaces to use the coal of Aubin in Aveyron, thus founding the small industrial town of Decazeville. The Alès coalfield (dép. Gard) also attracted iron works which at first used local and then imported ore. In retrospect it seems strange that contemporaries should have rated so highly the industrial prospects of the Centre. They clearly overestimated the local resources, just as they underrated the potential of the greater coalfields of north-western Europe.

It was, in fact, many years before the industrial development of the Belgian coalfield was emulated on its extension in northern France. Coke-smelting was first practised at Maubeuge in the Sambre valley, but in general it was more profitable to use the coal to refine charcoal iron

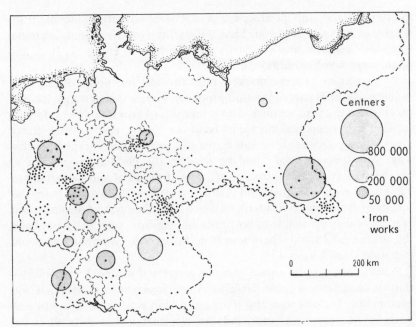

Fig. 7.13 The iron and steel industry of Germany in the mid-nineteenth century

brought into the area. The only coke-fired blast-furnace on the coalfield of northern France about 1850 was the Denain plant near Valenciennes.

East of the Rhine the iron industry was a great deal less advanced, and traditional methods continued to be used close to the coalfields of the Ruhr and Upper Silesia. Although coke had been used successfully in the blast-furnace in Upper Silesia before the end of the eighteenth century, it was not until 1849 that it was introduced in the Ruhr. This followed a long period of experiment during which coke was used in smelting non-ferrous metals, burned on the railways and mixed with charcoal in the blast-furnaces of the Siegerland.[125] The successful use of coke in the Friedrich-Wilhelms Hütte at Mülheim came at a time when demand for iron was increasing sharply and the seams of coking coal (*Fettkohle*) were being discovered in the Ruhr. It was followed by a rapid expansion of coke smelting and a parallel decline in the use of charcoal. Nevertheless, in the eyes of contemporaries the greatest promise for the future within Germany seemed to lie not in the Ruhr but in Upper Silesia, heralded as 'the equal of England and the foremost on the continent of Europe'.[126]

Coke smelting had also been introduced in northern Moravia before the mid-century, but had made no great progress. More than three-quarters of the iron produced was still smelted with charcoal. Elsewhere, in Poland, Bohemia, Styria, Carinthia and Krain only charcoal was used, and the iron industries of Scandinavia, Hungary, Italy and Spain were wholly traditional.

The smelting process marked only the starting point of the iron industry. A small part of the iron produced was used in castings; the rest was refined to make wrought-iron or converted into steel. The puddling furnace had been making rapid headway during the previous thirty years, and by 1850 at least half of the soft iron had been refined in this way. Any form of coal could be used in the puddling furnace, and pig-iron was transported from the forests of the Eifel and Siegerland to be refined with coal from the Aachen and Ruhr fields, and from the forests of Bohemia to Kladno and Plzeň. Puddling was also established at places easily accessible to both coal and pig-iron, such as the banks of the Seine near Rouen where iron from furnaces in Normandy met coal imported from England.[127]

A small amount of refined iron was converted to steel by a combination of cementation (case-hardening) and fusion in a crucible. It was used mainly for weapons and tools but a limit was set to its usefulness both by its very high price and the fact that it was difficult if not impossible to produce large ingots. Krupp astonished the world at the Great Exhibition of 1851 by putting on show a mass of steel weighing almost two tonnes. Attempts were made to produce steel in the puddling furnace, but without success, and the mass production of steel had to await the perfecting of the Bessemer and Siemens–Martin processes. About 1850 steel was being made at only a few works, principally by Krupp at Essen, at the Bochumerverein at Bochum, Schneider Frères at Le Creusot, Terrenoire at Saint-Etienne, and Cockerill at Seraing–Liège.

Puddled iron served many purposes, foremost at this time the rolling of rails. Next in importance was the manufacture of hardware from screws and hinges to ploughs and other agricultural equipment. Improved farming tools, including the plough with a steel coulter and mouldboard, were amongst the many factors which contributed at this time to the increased food production. Cast-iron was used increasingly for pipes for drainage and water supply and for cooking ranges. The wood-burning iron stove had an almost revolutionary effect on life in rural areas.[128] Such *quincaillerie* was beginning to pour from the workshops of eastern France, southern Belgium and the Rhineland.

Non-ferrous metal industries

The most important non-ferrous metals in the mid-nineteenth century were lead, zinc, copper and tin. Other metals, produced in very much smaller quantities, were mercury, manganese, cobalt and nickel, but the precious metals were of negligible importance. The development of the steam-engine had allowed mines to reach new depths, and improvements in smelting techniques had led to great increases in the volume of metals marketed. About 1850 Europe was still largely dependent upon its internal resources, and only the precious metals were obtained in significant amounts from overseas. Metalliferous mining was geographically more concentrated than it had been in the eighteenth century, since many of the small deposits had been exhausted and an increasing proportion of the metal was now coming from a few more highly mineralised regions. Statistics are not available for their direct comparison, but some half dozen regions yielded most of the metal produced in Europe at this time. These included the Ardennes, where Vieille Montagne near Aachen was the leading source of lead and zinc in western Europe and supplied the brass and bronze industries of Stolberg and Eschweiler; the Siegerland and Sauerland, which produced copper and lead in addition to iron; the Harz, which supplied lead and zinc from the Rammelsberg and copper from Mansfeld, and the Ore mountains of Saxony and Bohemia, with their silver–lead as well as a number of metalliferous minerals of lesser importance.

The most vigorous development of these years was, however, taking place in Upper Silesia. By a quirk of geology very large deposits of lead and zinc ores were found as replacement deposits in limestone which directly overlaid the coal measures. The latter were exploited primarily to provide fuel for the pumps and smelters in the metals industry. There had long been a small lead-smelting industry, but zinc became important only with the expansion of its industrial uses in brass-making and galvanising. At the same time the introduction of the muffle furnace (p. 271) allowed this particularly intractable metal to be refined economically, and crude-zinc production had reached more than 20,000 tonnes a year, the largest output in Europe.[129]

Other once-famous mining regions had sunk to relative unimportance. In Sweden the copper ores had been very largely exhausted and in Cornwall the great copper boom was over. In Spain, however, there was a revival of metalliferous mining. Lead was worked at Linares and other sites in south-western Spain. Mercury ore was at this time obtained chiefly from Almaden in southern Spain and from Idrija in Krain.

Textile industries

The textile industries were geographically more widespread and employed a much greater number of people than the metal industries. They too were progressing from a traditional to a modern technology and

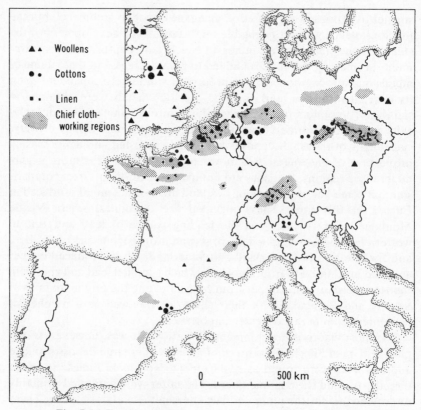

Fig. 7.14 European textile industries in the mid-nineteenth century

distributional pattern, but the contrast between the new and the old was a great deal less clear-cut than with iron manufacture. Progress in the latter consisted in the adoption of new methods and called for new technical skills. In the textile industries, on the other hand, there were no new processes – not, at least until the development of man-made fibres – and progress consisted essentially in speeding up and cheapening the old and familiar methods of production. Innovation in the textile industry was, by and large, a response to the scarcity or inadequacy of labour, and consisted chiefly in better organisation and management and in the application of mechanical power to spinning and weaving. Changes in the textile industries lay at the heart of the British Industrial Revolution, but they were not in themselves revolutionary and in continental Europe they played a much smaller role.

There was no significant alteration in the raw-material base of the textile industries, though there was a change in emphasis as between wool, flax and cotton. There was little inducement to relocate the textile industries. Most of the processes were still carried out manually or by water power and, though steam-powered mills were increasing in number, the textile industries showed little inclination to move to the coalfields. Railways had in fact been developed on a scale sufficient to bring fuel to those textile mills which required it. The trend towards concentration in industrial regions, so marked a feature of the British cotton and woollen industries, was scarcely apparent in France or, indeed, anywhere in continental Europe.[130] The closest parallel to the industrial development of Lancashire or of the West Riding of Yorkshire was to be found in Lille and its satellite towns, but these long antedated the Industrial Revolution and indeed developed, at least in their earlier stages, quite independently of the coal measures, which had not yet been opened up. There was in fact no important centre of the textile industries in 1840 – Łódź in Poland excepted – which was not also significant in 1750, and most had emerged long before this date.

The use of steam power came late to the textile industries. The 'jenny' and the 'mule' had been widely adopted before the end of the eighteenth century, thus increasing the productivity of the individual spinner, but mechanical spinning and the power loom were very slow in gaining acceptance. Lack of capital was in part the reason, but there was furthermore no scarcity of labour and thus no inducement to replace the older labour-intensive methods with newer. The first powered machines were made by the Cockerills, who had settled near Liège in 1794. They built the first steam-powered mill at Verviers in 1816; thirty years later there were 40 in Verviers and no less than 117 in the province of Liège.[131] Hand-spinning had been reduced to minor importance in this area, but mechanical progress was less rapid elsewhere. In northern France, steam power was adopted only very slowly, and at Roubaix, a major weaving centre, the industry remained largely domestic until the second half of the century.[132] The cotton industry was growing rapidly in Alsace, but the number of power looms did not begin to exceed that of hand looms before the mid-century. In Flanders the linen industry is said to have employed in the 1840s almost 300,000 part-time workers, wholly on a domestic basis, and no powered machines were introduced until late in the century. Machine-spinning and the power loom were a great deal more important at Elbeuf and along the lower Seine valley, but the widespread textile industry of western Normandy, Maine and all north-western France, as well as the cloth industry of Languedoc, was still carried on in the home or in small workshops and without mechanical aids.[133]

A broadly similar situation prevailed in the Rhineland. The cotton industry was increasingly mechanised, but much of the woollen and almost all the linen industry continued to use traditional methods, and power was not applied to flax-spinning and linen-weaving until the 1850s.[134] In the eastern Netherlands machine spinning began to be adopted in 1830, but the power loom did not appear for another twenty years.[135] In Switzerland a number of 'factories' was built early in the century, but they used the jenny or mule, and their only advantage lay in closer control over production. Mechanical spinning and weaving were not introduced before the 1820s and 30s.[136] In Bohemia mechanisation was adopted earlier, and by 1830 the textile industry was dominated by a few large mills, which by 1841 were employing twenty-four steam-engines. The woollen industry of Moravia was largely mechanised by 1850, and only the linen industry continued to be carried on largely by traditional methods. In Spain, the expanding textile industry made little use even of water power,[137] and in Italy the powered mill was only in its infancy in the towns of Lombardy.[138]

The very success of the British industry helped to retard development on the continent by inundating it with fabrics, especially cottons, at prices which few manufacturers were able to match. In the second third of the century, however, some countries, including France, began to protect their textile industries by raising tariffs on imported fabrics and yarn. This encouraged the mechanisation of some branches of the industry, and soon after 1850 hand spinning disappeared from the cotton industry and diminished rapidly in other branches.

The chief centres of the textile industry in continental Europe were, unlike those in Great Britain, relatively unspecialised. There was no significant area which concentrated only on one branch, and in every major textile region there was a tendency to change from one branch to another according to market conditions. Specialisation was, however, tending to increase, largely because the growing complexity of the finishing branches, calling for a heavier capital investment, was making such changes too costly.

The cotton industry. Cotton textiles were the most rapidly expanding branch of the textile industry. Their growth, however, is difficult to measure. At Mulhouse in Alsace the number of spindles increased sixfold between 1831 and 1850; according to Adelmann, the number of spindles in the Lower Rhineland grew from 57,642 to 77,801 in the space of only twelve years,[139] and in the town of Rheydt the number of cotton looms was increasing rapidly but largely at the expense of linen-weaving.[140] The cotton industry was expanding no less rapidly in Elberfeld and Barmen, where it was tending to replace silk- and linen-weaving, and at Chemnitz in Saxony,[141] in northern Bohemia,[142] and in Austria. Within the boundary of Congress Poland entrepreneurs from Chemnitz established a textile and in particular a cotton industry at

Łódź in order to avoid the high duties on manufactures imported into the Tsarist empire. By the 1840s the town had become one of the most important centres of the cotton industry in central Europe.[143] At about the same time a cotton industry was established at Turku in Finland, and later shifted to Tampere in the interior of the country.[144] The Spanish cotton industry in Barcelona and its neighbouring towns was growing during the middle years of the century.[145]

The linen industry. Linen-weaving was a traditional peasant industry and from Brittany to Silesia flax was grown, retted and scutched by the peasantry, and its spinning and weaving provided both employment during the winter months and a vitally important source of income. There were five major areas of linen manufacture: Normandy and Brittany; northern France and the southern Low Countries; north-western Germany, including the Münsterland; the mountainous regions of Saxony, Silesia and northern Bohemia, and, lastly, the Swiss plateau and Swabia. All were physically suited to the growing of flax, though local production was increasingly supplemented by imports from the Baltic region. In general the domestic linen industry characterised areas which were poorly endowed agriculturally, and was never firmly established where open-field cultivation prevailed and the peasants had been subjected to the constraints of a manorial economy.

During the first half of the nineteenth century, the market for linen was declining, in part owing to the coarse quality of the peasant product, in part to the competition of the cheaper and more versatile cottons. In the Düsseldorf region spinners and weavers were turning from flax to cotton, but in many rural areas this choice was not available. In Flanders many of the peasantry faced starvation when the market for their linen collapsed in the later 1840s.[146] Linen-weaving was disappearing also from central Europe, and the industry was saved only by the establishment of mechanically operated mills, notably in Bielefeld and the small towns of Silesia, as well as in Ghent and northern France.

The woollen industry. The manufacture of woollen cloth continued to be the most widespread branch of the textile industry, and was carried on in every part of Europe. But already certain areas with slight local advantages had become specialised producers with a wide market for their cloth. Three such regions were in France: the Elbeuf–Darnetal–Louviers district in the lower Seine valley; Sedan and its vicinity in eastern France, and, lastly, the north, where it had declined in its earlier centres such as Amiens, Abbeville and Beauvais, and was concentrating in the area of Lille.[147] At Tourcoing, for example, woollens and woollen–cotton mixtures were increasingly important and their weaving was replacing that of cottons and linen.[148]

The traditional woollen-cloth industry of Languedoc had lost much of its Levant market; the weavers were drawn to viticulture, and the manufacture was reduced to very small proportions.[149] The cloth industry of Flanders and Brabant had similarly been almost extinguished, and its place taken by that of Verviers, which was in the mid-nineteenth century the focus of one of the most concentrated areas of cloth production in Europe. The local wool which had supplied the early industry was now largely replaced by Spanish wool imported through the Belgian and Dutch ports.[150] Aachen and its satellite towns, in effect an eastward extension of the Verviers region to which it owed much of its entrepreneurial skill,[151] had become the most important German centre of the woollens industry. Wool-weaving was a specialised industry in Saxony,[152] but had almost disappeared from Switzerland.[153]

In central Europe the woollen industry was developed in Bohemia, especially at Liberec (Reichenberg), but was overall smaller and less important than linen- and cotton-weaving.[154] Its most important centres were at Brno in Moravia and in Slovakia,[155] where there was still a widespread domestic weaving industry. The market for Czech and Slovak cloth was mainly in Austria, Hungary and the Balkan peninsula.

'In one sphere after another', wrote Stoianovich, 'Balkan industry faltered before the onslaught of European technology.'[156] If manufacturers in western Europe had been for a time inhibited by the competition of the cheaper products of British factories, those of south-eastern Europe were almost extinguished by that of central European manufactures. A handful of undertakings managed to survive in Budapest and in Slovenia and Croatia, most of them controlled by Austrians.[157] In the 1830s, however, Balkan industry had begun to revive in the areas farthest from central European competition. A woollen mill was built in 1836 at Sliven in Bulgaria and equipped with French machinery. It was the first modern factory to be built within the Ottoman empire, and marked the beginning of a significant industrial revival.

Other textile industries. Not all the thread produced by domestic spinsters went into cloth-making. Much was used in lace, muslin and knitwear, especially stockings. In the mid-nineteenth century these crafts were being drawn into the factory, but much – probably the greater part – was still produced in rural cottages. This was especially so of lace, in which traditional patterns were of great importance.

Another industry which had expanded greatly during the nineteenth century was calico-printing. Rolls had replaced wooden blocks for printing patterns on the cloth, and the industry was now to be found mainly in the more important cotton-weaving centres.

Silk-weaving was the most sophisticated branch of the textile industry. It was definitely not a cottage industry and was in the nineteenth century concentrated in a few centres and carried on by skilled craftsmen. Foremost of the centres was Lyons, where the domestic weaver was still a significant figure, but production was increasingly from steam-powered Jacquard looms, established in factories outside the city.[158] Amongst the industries which in this way derived from Lyons was the ribbon manufacture at Saint-Etienne and Saint-Chamond. Other centres of the silk industry in France were Avignon, Ganges (Hérault), Tours and Saint-Didier, but the only real rival to the Lyons region was the lower Rhineland. Here Krefeld was still the undisputed leader,[159] though a greater volume of silks was being manufactured at Elberfeld and along the Wupper valley, where the mills concentrated on making goods at the lower end of the scale such as ribbon, velvet and plush. The Swiss industry had expanded greatly, with mills in Zurich, Solothurn, Appenzell and, above all, Basel, which was outstanding for the man-ufacture of figured silk ribbons and neckties.[160]

At the opposite end of the scale of textiles was hemp, grown over most of Europe except the south and used in making cordage, canvas and even a very coarse fabric. It was exclusively a cottage industry, most practised in the coastal belt of north-western Europe where there was a large demand for ropes and sailcloth. All ports had some form of hemp industry, though the raw hemp had increasingly to be imported from the Baltic region. The traditional role of hemp was, however, being challenged by jute, a product of India. In 1832 it began to be used for making a coarse fabric for packaging. The earliest centre of jute-working was Dundee, in Scotland, but the industry quickly spread to the Netherlands, where hessian proved invaluable for handling coffee and other products of the Dutch empire.

Other manufacturing industries

Most other branches of manufacturing continued to be characterised by a craft organisation. Most processed locally produced materials and sold them into a local market. The manufacture of soap, paint and other household goods; the tanning of leather and making of saddlery and footwear; food-processing, milling and brewing; paper-making and printing were all small-scale industries, and were carried on in all the more densely peopled areas of Europe. Many of them were still predominantly rural because of their reliance on water power or heavy consumption of water. Printing was an urban craft and was particularly important in the political capitals and the leading commercial centres. Tanning was in the main a rural occupation, but the manufacture of footwear, harness and other leather goods was carried on mostly in towns and by traditional methods in small workshops. The mass production of furniture had not begun and indeed could not do so until an efficient means of transporting it had been developed.

The concentration of many of these branches of industry and the emergence of large units of production were hindered both by shortage of capital and by the difficulty of transporting goods which were sometimes heavy and invariably bulky. The introduction of the factory system was in many instances dependent upon the completion of a railway net and the further development of a mass market.

Greater progress had been made in the chemical industry, but in this also the scale remained small, the methods imprecise and the equipment poor. 'Most chemical manufacturers', wrote Landes, 'were kitchen cooks on a large scale.' The chemical industry consisted at this time essentially of the manufacture of the common acids and alkalis, and of soda, bleach and alum. It was heavily dependent on the market provided by the textile industry, and this, coupled with its demand for fuel, tended to dictate its location. The coalfield regions of northern France and Belgium were the most important centres of the manufacture of chemicals, and most of the small central European industry was to be found in the coal basins of Moravia and Bohemia.[161] The manufacture of chemicals was the 'most polygamous of all industries'; there were few branches of manufacture which were not linked with it either as sources of raw materials or as consumers of its products.[162]

Amongst the earliest of such linkages were those with the soap and glass industries. Soap was made by digesting fats and oils with an alkali,[163] and the simplest glass was produced by fusing silica also with an alkali. In the past the most commonly used alkali had been wood-ash, but even before the eighteenth century the growing demand for soap and glass, combined with the growing scarcity of wood, led to the search for an alternative source of alkali. The most successful method of synthesising alkali was that devised by Leblanc late in the eighteenth century, but not used commercially until after the Napoleonic Wars. The improvements in health and the quality of life during the nineteenth century owed not a little to the increased availability of soda.[164] The process was based on common salt and sulphuric acid, the demand for both of which increased sharply. The provision of sulphuric acid was made possible by the contemporary introduction of the lead-chamber process, which used crude sulphur, most of it obtained from Italy, and nitre. The increased supply of sulphuric acid also permitted the development of the mineral-fertiliser industry, in particular the manufacture of superphosphate. At the same time the recently discovered element chlorine was used in the production of bleach, without which, according to Liebig, the growth of the cotton industry would have been severely restricted.

The soap industry was as a general rule established where vegetable or animal fats were readily available. At Marseilles olive oil was used, but in the course of the century this was supplemented and then replaced by vegetable oils of tropical origin, and wood-ash was replaced with soda, much of it imported from Great Britain, which held a secure lead in the manufacture of the basic chemicals. Other important centres of soap manufacture were Rouen and Le Havre, Amsterdam and Rotterdam and Hamburg, all of them port cities.

Glass manufacture also underwent great changes. The traditional industry had been carried on in small workshops located generally where wood-ash and quartz-sand were available. There were glass-furnaces in many of the forested areas of Europe, especially central Germany and northern Bohemia, but quality glass was also made at Venice and near large consuming centres such as Paris. The first half of the nineteenth century was characterised by the mass production of sheet- and plate-glass, suitable for the large windows which were becoming more popular. Conservatories in particular were fashionable and culminated in such glass-and-iron structures as the Crystal Palace (1851). This development called for a larger capital investment than the traditional industry could command. It was carried on in large factories accessible generally speaking to the coalfields. Belgium became a foremost producer of these types of glass.

A feature of the chemical and related industries in the mid-nineteenth century was the wide gap between the experimental chemist and the industrialist, a consequence in part of the lack of scientific training amongst the latter, in part of a failure in communication between them. This accounts at least partially for the appalling wastefulness of manufacturing. By-products of smelting, combustion and other processes were customarily thrown away, and no significant attempt was made until after 1850 to recover and use the waste products of the coking process.[165] Attempts were made to reduce fuel consumption in the iron industry, but in general there was little regard to heat economy, and industry at the mid-century was notoriously extravagant of the fuel and materials which it used.

The pottery and ceramics industry was simpler in its processes and less capital-intensive than glass manufacture. It continued until late in the century to be carried on mainly in small units, sometimes clustered near a good bed of clay as in the English Potteries, at Delft and at Dresden. Difficulties of transport, combined with the fragile nature of china, led to a very wide dispersion of the industry. The emergence of a mass demand for a cheap functional china as well as for a coarser earthenware or *Steingut* led to an expansion of the lower end of the ceramics market. The quality of mass-produced china was improved by the use of better glaze, the application of patterns by means of transfers and generally higher standards of design.

Transport and trade

The growth of manufacturing and its increasing specialisation were made possible by improvements in the means of transport and communication. The canal net was extended; at least the main roads were made suitable for wheeled traffic, and above all the railway net had begun to spread across the continent. Nevertheless much of Europe remained in the 1840s in the road and canal age and much of the bulk transport was by water. New factories, especially those in the iron industry, were located with regard to rivers and canals rather than railways, and in France the Becquey plan (p. 301) to extend existing waterways and to link them into a system was still being pursued at this time. By this date France had an elaborate system of navigable waterways, and it remained only for Freycinet to co-ordinate and standardise them. The French canals were a monument to the skill of French engineers and to the vision of the administration of Ponts et Chaussées. But in some instances the canals linked rivers which were barely navigable. It was possible in some instances to locate manufacturing on the banks of waterways as happened at Nevers and Fourchambault, or to extend canals into industrialised areas, as at Montluçon and Rive de Gier, but many manufacturing centres had no such advantage. Paris enjoyed the benefit of one of the best waterways to Rouen and the sea, but links with the northern coalfield, essential if the capital was to be supplied with fuel, were far from satisfactory. Too little money was available to remedy the defects of the northern canals, and in some cases projects encountered the successful opposition of landed and local interests. French navigable waterways spanned enormous distances. Coal from Saint-Etienne, for example, travelled 600 kilometres to the Paris market, and for much of this distance navigation was difficult and liable to interruption. The barges which carried it were, furthermore, broken up and sold at their destination because it was impossible for them to make the return voyage. The northern canals (see fig. 6.2), despite their obvious problems, were well managed and intensively used, and in the mid-century Nord and Belgium were replacing the coalfields of the Central Massif in the coal market of Paris. The French canal system was clearly not an unqualified success and its shortcomings hastened the building of the railways. Though better built than the English, the French canals 'performed fewer services and carried less goods'.[166]

Internal navigation had been developed more fully and more success-fully in the Low Countries, which had great initial advantages; a flatter terrain and a number of navigable rivers. The opening up of the Scheldt during the Revolutionary Wars and the gradual freeing of the Rhine from legal and fiscal obstacles encouraged the use of waterways. Canal links were constructed between the Scheldt and the Meuse, and a waterway was cut through the Hainault coalfield to join the canal which had been cut from Charleroi through Brussels to the Scheldt. The Meuse was itself in course of improvement below Liège, and a ship canal was cut from Ghent to the Scheldt estuary at Terneuzen. These waterways were well used, especially for the movement of iron ore and for the export of coal. The Vienna Treaty of 1815 had subjected the Meuse and Scheldt, along with the Rhine, to the régime of international rivers, so that there could be no legal impediment to their use, even after the separation of Belgium from the Netherlands in 1831.

In the Netherlands canal construction was primarily to improve access to the country's principal navigable highway, the Rhine. Rotterdam was linked with the sea by the Voorne Canal, thus obviating the circuitous routes in use hitherto, and Amsterdam not only improved its waterway connections with the Lek, the more northerly branch of the Rhine, but also in 1820–5 was linked by the North Holland Canal with the sea at Den Helder. Despite these improvements, however, Amsterdam's connections with its hinterland in western Germany remained difficult, and an increasing proportion of a growing body of trade was now passing through Rotterdam.

The increasing use of the Dutch waterways was bound up with that of the Rhine, the best navigable river in Europe. Almost freed by 1850 of its burdensome tolls and its course straightened and improved by Tulla and other engineers (see p. 296), the Rhine with some of its tributaries had become a very important artery of commerce. The steam-tug was of increasing importance and about the mid-century was pulling most of the upstream traffic on the lower river, and more than half on the upper.[167] Traffic on the Rhine suffered, however, from the shortcom-ings of its tributaries. The Ruhr was used by coal barges and the lower Lahn by small vessels carrying iron ore,[168] but the Moselle, potentially the most valuable of them all, was used only by a passenger service between Trier and Coblenz, and only the lowermost courses of the Main and Neckar could be used. The volume of traffic carried on the Rhine expanded considerably in the middle third of the century. There was a 74-per-cent increase in the amount of goods passing Emmerich on the Dutch–German border, but a growth of only 36 per cent at Mannheim on the upper river.[169] The reason is not far to seek. Shipping on the

Rhine at first carried cargoes of all kinds, but the lighter and more valuable were being attracted to the newly built railways, leaving only bulk cargoes – mainly coal, iron ore and timber – for the river boats. Coal distributed from the newly built port of Ruhrort was by far the most important cargo, and in 1816 the coal-producers of the Ruhr basin began to operate their own fleet of coal-carriers. Large amounts of coal were then sent downriver to the Netherlands, but comparatively little moved farther upstream than Cologne. Lastly, the failure to develop shipping on most of the Rhine's tributaries meant that the river could serve only places on its banks. Although the earliest railways were built as feeders to the river, it was soon found that a break-of-bulk at the river port was not economic.[170] The railway gradually replaced the river for all cargoes which required handling between their terminal points. Mannheim, where a new dock was built in 1840, became the effective limit of navigation.

Other central European rivers were of trifling importance compared with the Rhine. Improvements in the Elbe and Oder were made by the Prussian government, but these rivers served to transport little more than local agricultural produce. A small amount of coal was brought down the Oder from the Upper Silesian coalfield. Although waterways were improved and extended in the Berlin region, there were no significant canal-building projects in central Europe. In fact, the only new canal was the ill-considered project of King Ludwig of Bavaria to link the Rhine system with the Danube. This narrow and shallow waterway, from Bamberg to the Altmühl tributary of the Danube, was completed in 1845, but could not, owing to the inadequacies of the river Main, be integrated into the Rhine system, and remained little used. Little regular use was made of the Danube, and other navigable rivers, such as the Po and Guadalquivir, and the uncompleted canals of Spain, were significant only for local traffic.

Road traffic

By far the largest part of Europe's internal traffic continued to follow the roads, as it had done for centuries. The growth of the economy called for road services of ever growing complexity and scale. There are no data on the increase in the volume of goods or the number of people transported by road vehicles, but there is no doubt that it was considerable. Contemporaries refer to the crowded roads, in contrast with the absence of traffic in the eighteenth century, and firms were being established almost daily to forward goods from one city to another. In France there was a regular service of *postes* between towns, and the volume of mail carried increased at least threefold between 1815 and the mid-century.[171]

At the same time travel was becoming quicker and cheaper. The journey by coach from Paris to Bordeaux in 1816 had taken five days in summer and six in winter. By 1831 this was reduced to three, and before the mid-century the journey was being accomplished in forty hours in summer and only forty-eight even in winter.[172] Merchandise moved at comparable speeds; the silk ribbons of Basel for export to the New World were taken to Le Havre by way of Belfort or Strasbourg 'at a trot in five to six days with relays of horses and Breton drivers'. The return journey was made with dyestuffs, cotton, coffee and sugar.[173] In those regions in which manufacturing industries were of growing importance, such, for example, as the Verviers–Liège district and the Sauerland–Siegerland, there was a regular movement of carters transporting not only raw materials and manufactured goods, but also foodstuffs for the growing industrial proletariat.

In Spain the necessary movement of goods between the Meseta and the coastal regions was accomplished by carters who commonly moved in groups of twenty or thirty. Richard Ford found few travellers on the Spanish roads 'save the migratory caravans which bring corn down from Salamanca and take back salt from Cadiz. Nothing can be more savage or nomadic.'[174] According to Ringrose some 14,000 carts were supplemented by almost 150,000 pack animals in this traffic.[175]

This growing road traffic in most parts of Europe was made possible not only by the greater safety of the roads, but also by their improving quality. In several countries the government took an active part in building and maintaining at least a system of trunk roads. Their quality was improved by the introduction of the methods of Telford and McAdam by which crushed stone of carefully graded size was used to make a firm and waterproof surface. The creation of a harder surface encouraged the use of vehicles with narrower wheels and better springs which could travel at a faster pace than the heavy waggons previously used. Roads were further improved from the 1840s by the use of asphalt to bind the broken stones together into a firm, smooth and impermeable surface.[176] The process was restricted at first to areas where asphalt was naturally available, notably Switzerland, but after 1840 it spread more widely with the use of imported asphalt.

The railway system

It was the railways which ultimately triumphed over the waterways and successfully rivalled the roads. They required more capital than either, but were incomparably more flexible than the one and faster than the other. They crept in slowly, serving at first only to funnel merchandise to the rivers, but there were people like Friedrich List who foresaw a vastly more important role for them. As early as 1833 he had visualised a

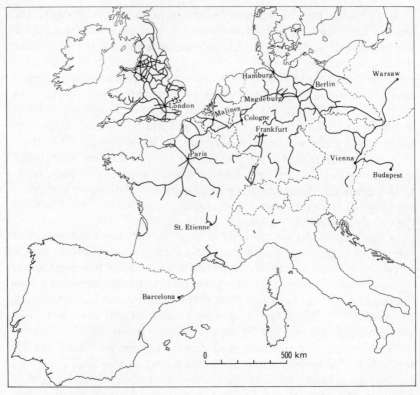

Fig. 7.15 Railway development in Europe before the mid-nineteenth century

central European system linking the major cities and connected with the Atlantic ports. Such a project was unattainable in Germany's current political circumstances, and the German railway system, like the French, began as a series of short and widely separated lengths of track designed to satisfy wholly local needs.

The earliest French railways were built, as in Great Britain, to transport coal. The leading coalfield, that of Saint-Etienne, had poor road connections with the rivers, the Loire and Rhône, which carried much of its coal to the market. The first two railways, completed respectively in 1823 and 1832, were designed to remedy this. But the authorities were still not convinced that the future lay with the railways and held up the extension of the Saint-Etienne–Loire-valley line because they had plans for a canal along this route. Saint-Simon had advocated a railway system for France similar to, though less precisely drawn than, that of List, and it was his disciples who consistently advocated a network of railways focussed on Paris. In the 1840s a radial pattern began to evolve, paralleling the roads and joining Paris with the industrial north, with Le Havre and with the Loire valley and Nantes, and probing towards Bordeaux, Lyons and Strasbourg (fig. 7.15).

Belgium was the first European country to have a public, steam-operated railway. In 1834 the construction was authorised of a system centring in Malines, and during the next year the line from Malines to Brussels was opened, a few months before the Nuremberg–Fürth line in Bavaria. The earliest French railways were built to transport coal and to supplement the canal system, and the construction of a network of lines radiating from Paris had barely begun in the 1830s. In Belgium work started on a national railway system in 1834, but in Germany, despite the vigorous advocacy of Friedrich List, there were only a few short lengths of track. Elsewhere the railway age had not yet dawned.[177]

The pattern of trade

The middle years of the nineteenth century were a period of rapid change in the organisation of trade, in the range of commodities handled, and in its underlying philosophy. In the 1840s Great Britain initiated a movement towards freer trade, and was in time followed by most European countries. It cannot, however, be said that by 1850 this movement had progressed far enough to influence significantly either the volume or the direction of trade. In Germany, on the other hand, the abolition of internal barriers to trade had begun in 1818 with Prussia's law to permit customs unions with neighbouring states. By 1848 the development of the Zollverein was virtually complete, and in 1850 proposals – abortive, as events were to show – were made to form a broader union of Germany and the Habsburg monarchy. A comparable project to form a common market between France and Belgium foundered, but nevertheless resulted in mutual tariff concessions. While France was raising tariffs against imported British goods, especially textiles, Great Britain was negotiating a series of bilateral agreements to reduce obstacles to trade. The movement during these years was hesitatingly towards a freer pattern of commerce than had prevailed at any time in the past.

The mechanism of trade was also undergoing a profound change. The traditional small-town markets continued to be held at their regular times, and in many instances their prosperity was undiminished. But in larger towns they went largely unnoticed, and their functions were assumed by the urban shops. One is struck in the pre-industrial town by the high ratio of small shops to total population.[178] Retailing was small-scale, and customers were accustomed to haggle over prices and to strike a bargain for every item furnished. But the trend was towards larger shops with fixed but reasonable prices and a more rapid turnover. No longer did they deal directly with rural or industrial producers; instead, they usually bought their goods through wholesalers, who understood the market, drew from a wider area and offered a greater range of goods. Manufacturers often advertised their goods in the press or by means of printed catalogues, and some already had travelling salesmen who sold on the basis of samples which they carried with them. This was especially the case with semi-luxury products such as silks, printed calicoes and ribbons. Commodity markets, especially in the so-called colonial goods, emerged and were regularly visited by wholesale merchants and even by retailers. Many were in the great ports, which thus acquired reputations for the particular goods traded. The more modern system of trading was greatly assisted by the development of postal services and of the means for rapid and regular deliveries.[179]

The periodic fairs which had supplemented the weekly markets suffered even more from the development of urban shopping centres in which almost every kind of commodity was available. They had long been declining in importance in north-western Europe and had become a social event rather than an occasion for the exchange of goods. The business transacted at the Beaucaire fairs, for example, declined sharply with the coming of the railway; people just travelled to the nearest town.[180] In eastern and south-eastern Europe on the other hand fairs took on a new lease of life. In areas where the intensification of trade was not matched by the growth of large towns or the creation of commercial institutions fairs had still an important role to play. The Leipzig fair, which served the needs of much of eastern Europe, and the neighbouring fair of Frankfurt-on-Oder continued to develop even into the second half of the century. Fairs had traditionally served not only for the exchange of commodities but also for the settlement of accounts. Here merchants had been accustomed to meet, to set off their obligations to one another and to pay their debts. Banks, the postal system and the use of cheques and drafts not only ended these periodic reunions of merchants but also speeded up the settlement of accounts and removed one of the last justifications for a system of regular fairs.

Internal trade

There are no statistics of the volume of trade within separate countries, but the qualitative evidence suggests that foodstuffs, which had previously constituted the greater part, were now relatively much less important and that fuel, industrial raw materials and consumer goods now accounted for the greater part of it. In volume coal was probably the most important commodity even though its long-distance movement was practicable only by water. In France, for example, large quantities – amounting to millions of tonnes – were sent halfway across the country from the coalfields of the north and Saint-Etienne by a combination of rail and canal transport.[181] Almost a million tonnes a year were shipped from Mülheim and Ruhrort to Rhineland towns, and the Upper Silesian coalfield distributed coal as far as Berlin.

Second in importance to the trade in coal was that in industrial raw materials, especially cotton, wool, iron ore. Most of the cotton entered Europe through its north-western ports and was transported by a variety of means, but chiefly by water, to the consuming centres. Baltic flax and Spanish wool were imported by sea and distributed wherever possible by canal and river barge. Iron ore was being transported over increasing distances to supply the smelting furnaces, and the growing separation of smelting from refining also necessitated the distant transport of pig-iron.

Trade and transport in foodstuffs became more regular and predictable and were handled more professionally and expertly. There was a greater margin of safety in food supply, and famine crises in effect ceased; that of 1846–7 was probably the last. Except for the Low Countries, where there was a significant import of bread grains, most of Europe was still self-sufficing in the basic foodstuffs. Surplus production in Poland and eastern Germany continued to satisfy the small import needs of the rest of Europe and Danzig prices to sway those of most of the continent. Most European countries protected their agriculture by tariffs and discouraged the import of foodstuffs. There was in consequence little international trade in foodstuffs, apart from those of colonial origin. The consumption of meat, butter and cheese was increasing in western and central Europe. Live animals were driven to the market, not irregularly and in vast herds as in the eighteenth century, but as a steady and organised movement from the fattening areas. The consequence of the better-organised and more regular flow of food from farm to market was a general improvement in diet and health. In the utilitarian phraseology of the day, never had so much been enjoyed by so many.

Overseas trade

Europe's seaborne commerce was made up in part of trade with the non-European world, and in part of that part of the internal trade which was carried on between European ports. The latter included the flax, hemp and timber imported by western Europe from the Baltic as well as grain from Stettin, Danzig and Königsberg. It included also the very considerable trade which Great Britain carried on with continental Europe. Great Britain was by far the most important commercial country in the world, and almost half of her total trade by value was with the rest of Europe. Seventeen per cent of Great Britain's exports were to the Baltic region, where there was a large market for her manufactures. This was requited mainly by the export of flax, hemp, timber and corn. Naval stores, it must be remembered, were no less important in the mid-nineteenth century than they had been a century earlier. Great Britain also imported large quantities of French, German and Portuguese wines and of silks and luxury fabrics, while British travellers to the continent contributed then, as today, an important invisible element to Europe's commercial balance. British manufacturers found it difficult to scale the immense tariff wall which the French had erected around themselves, but large quantities were exported to the Low Countries and to Mediterranean Europe.

The volume of trade with the non-European world was increasing steadily. It was made up largely of the import of goods of tropical and sub-tropical origin, paid for by the export of manufactured goods, chiefly cloth and hardware. Spain and Portugal still possessed extensive empires with which, however, they carried on a negligible volume of trade. Great Britain, France and the Netherlands, on the other hand, had a highly important trade with their colonies. Much of this colonial trade was carried on in British or American ships.[182] No less than 70 per cent of Europe's merchant shipping was British-owned, and only a third of all ships calling at French ports were in fact owned in France. A large part of the colonial goods imported into Europe was received in London or Amsterdam where it was transhipped and re-exported to other European ports.

Foremost amongst the commodities imported into Europe in this way were raw cotton, sugar, tea and coffee. In 1832, 38,480 tonnes of raw cotton were re-exported from London to western Europe; fifteen years later this had doubled. Most went to the French port of Le Havre in 1832. Twenty years later 70 per cent of the increased volume still went to France, but Germany now took a fifth of the total. The total west European import of raw cotton in 1832 was less than a third of Great Britain's retained import, and only a slightly larger fraction in 1850. This may in some degree minimise the scale of continental industry, since Great Britain exported considerable quantities of spun thread to mills elsewhere in Europe.

The maritime ports. Europe's growing seaborne trade was concentrated increasingly on a small number of ports. The contrast between large ports and small was becoming greater, and a category of great ports was slowly emerging. Many factors contributed to this development. Small ports were in many instances silting at a time when ships were becoming larger and their draught deeper. Communications were being improved between the larger ports and their hinterlands, thus attracting more traffic to them, and by 1850 a dozen ports in north-west Europe from Nantes to Stettin were linked by rail with developing national railway systems. The growing volume of trade nonetheless created problems even for the best-sited ports. Most had navigational hazards which necessitated the deepening and straightening of their access channels, the cutting of approach canals and the building of dykes to control the flow of tidal waters. In extreme cases the port authorities undertook the building of an outport, situated where a navigable estuary opened into the ocean, in order to avoid the tedious and sometimes dangerous voyage upriver.[183] Seville had done this when Cadiz was developed as the chief port for Spain's transatlantic trade. Bremen similarly founded Bremerhaven at the mouth of the Weser in 1824–30, and a few years later Nantes began to lose trade to Saint-Nazaire on the Loire estuary.

Mediterranean ports. Europe's Mediterranean ports reached their lowest ebb in the early nineteenth century. Their hinterlands remained in large measure unindustrialised, and the commerce of the inland sea was reduced to small proportions. No extensions and few improvements were made in most Spanish and Italian ports. Genoa and Venice handled no more trade than they had done a century earlier, and if the port of Piraeus was more active this was only because Athens had become the capital of an independent state. In only three Mediterranean ports did prospects for growth look good. Barcelona served the commercial needs of the expanding textile region of Catalonia (see p. 239), importing raw cotton and exporting cloth on a small but growing scale. Marseilles had become the chief maritime link with Algeria, which had been conquered in 1830, and the flow of commercial and military goods was bringing about a very considerable growth in the activities of the port. The third centre of growth was Trieste. It was the chief port of the Austro-Hungarian empire, and, though the railway from Vienna, by way of Graz and Ljubljana, was still unfinished in 1850, prospects for the port seemed bright.

Northern ports. The Baltic ports had been amongst the most active in Europe during the eighteenth century. Their commerce, primarily in grain and forest products, continued through the nineteenth, but was of diminishing importance. The Russian absorption of much of Poland, coupled with very high tariffs, effectively reduced the hinterlands of the south-eastern Baltic ports. Königsberg and its satellites, Memel, Pillau and Elbląg, which had formerly been the chief avenues for the export trade of Lithuania and White Russia, were depressed. Only Danzig in virtue of its control of the grain trade of the Vistula basin still retained something of its old prosperity. Most south Baltic ports had only a local trade, but Lübeck and Stettin were linked by rail with Berlin by 1850 and served as commercial outlets for the Prussian state. At Stettin new quays had been built along the Oder and navigation was improved on the difficult lower river. All Baltic trade, however, continued until 1857 to be burdened by the tolls levied by the Danish government on commerce passing through the Sound.

Atlantic ports. By contrast with that of the Mediterranean and Baltic, the trade of Atlantic ports was steadily expanding. Yet it was a highly selective growth. German ports were bedevilled by political rivalries. Hamburg, with the greatest potential of them all, remained a small, self-governing city-state hemmed in by the territory of Denmark, Holstein and Hanover and obstructed in its trade both upstream and down by tolls. Nonetheless, Hamburg merchants began in the 1840s to develop trade with East Africa and with the South Pacific and ultimately monopolised the trade of some parts of Africa. At the same time regular transatlantic sailings were initiated, and in 1847 the Hamburg–America Line was founded. Bremen had fewer natural advantages than Hamburg but at the same time fewer political obstacles. It lay 55 kilometres from the sea and could be reached only after a long voyage up the Weser. Tolls imposed by the Hanoverians on shipping were abolished in 1820, but the difficulties of river navigation nevertheless led the city to acquire a tract of land close to its mouth and to build the port of Bremerhaven (1827–30), the first example of the deliberate *creation* of an outport. Bremen became the foremost transatlantic passenger port in Europe at a time when migration to the New World was increasing to a flood. A new dock was built to the north of the city and, like Hamburg, Bremen began to develop a colonial trade.

The three ports of the Low Countries – Amsterdam, Rotterdam and Antwerp – today form the most important port complex in Europe. In the mid-nineteenth century their primacy had not yet been clearly established, partly because the industrial growth of their hinterland, the Rhine valley, was still in its initial stages, partly because they had not yet solved their individual problems of access to the sea and communication by land. Amsterdam was accessible to sea-going shipping only across the very shallow Zuider Zee, and this severely limited the growth of the port. In 1819–24 a ship canal had been cut through North Holland to the sea at Den Helder, but this was proving inadequate and the problem was ultimately to be solved only by the construction of the North Sea Canal (1875) from Amsterdam to the sea at IJmuiden.

Rotterdam faced a similar problem. The branch of the Rhine on which it lay silted badly between the city and the sea and was at times barely navigable. In 1830 a canal was cut from Rotterdam across the island of Voorne to the navigable Haringvliet. This, however, had only limited success and the problem was not solved until the New Waterway was cut (1866–72) directly to the sea at the Hook of Holland. Nevertheless, Rotterdam held one significant advantage over Amsterdam. Its links with the Rhineland were incomparably better than the tortuous waterways of Holland and Utrecht on which Amsterdam was forced to rely. The longer the completion of the Dutch railway system was postponed the greater became Rotterdam's competitive advantage.

Antwerp was opened up to maritime shipping in 1792, and in 1803 in a perhaps over-sanguine gesture Napoleon ordered the construction of the first two dock basins. Freedom to navigate the Scheldt was confirmed in 1815, but the abolition of tolls was not secured until 1863. Yet the trade of Antwerp grew only slowly, lagging behind that of its Low Country rivals. The reason lay, of course, in the inadequacy of its landward communications. Even the Belgian industrial centres of Liège and Verviers had better links with Rotterdam than with Antwerp. This was remedied only by the completion of the initial railway system and, in 1859, of a canal link between the Meuse and Scheldt. Ghent, like Antwerp, had been cut off from direct access to the sea by the closure of the Scheldt. In 1824–7 a canal was cut from the city to the Wester Scheldt at Terneuzen, and a dock built in the city itself. Ghent at once became an ocean port, a factor of no small importance in the contemporary development of its cotton-textile industry.

Dunkirk was heir to the many small ports of west Flanders, and a net of small canals was cut to link it with the growing industrial region of Belgium and northern France. Its growth was rapid. The port was improved and a commercial dock was built in 1845, and three years later the port was linked with the French railway system. In 1850 no less than 4000 ships are said to have entered and cleared the harbour. The ferry ports on the Channel coast were developing at the same time.

Calais had long been the most important point from which to cross to England. In 1820 a steam ferry was introduced, and in 1845 a dock basin was built. The Boulogne packet service was begun in 1843, and that from Dieppe, hitherto primarily a deep-sea fishing port, was opened in 1856.

The ports of Rouen and Le Havre served the Paris region and the industrial centres of the lower Seine valley. Rouen lay 125 kilometres from the sea. Navigation up to the city had always been hindered by silting and changes in the navigable channel. Shipping was restricted to vessels of little more than 200 tons, and the port was not greatly used before, in the 1840s, extensive work was begun on the river and its channel was deepened and regulated. In the meanwhile, however, Le

Havre was growing rapidly. In 1845 an ambitious programme of dock construction was undertaken to cope with the increasing traffic, which began to include large quantities of British coal.

The ports of north-western France had in the eighteenth century been amongst the largest and most important, and much of France's trade had been carried on through Saint-Malo and Nantes. Most of these ports declined in relative, and some also in absolute, importance in the nineteenth century. Industry was stagnating in their hinterlands, and their links with the growing industrial centres were quite inadequate. Caen tried to revive its lagging fortunes by cutting a canal along the valley of the Orne to the sea. The contemporary growth of Cherbourg was due as much to military considerations as commercial. Saint-Malo grew very little and Brest remained primarily a naval base. Nantes had once been the most active French port, linked with a vast hinterland by the river Loire. Navigational difficulties were increasing on the river and Nantes was saved as a port only by the coming of the railway. In the meanwhile problems of navigation below the city had led to the creation of the outport of Saint-Nazaire, but in 1850 it was still only a very small port and its first dock basin had not yet been dug.

The Biscay coast of France was strewn with decaying ports, cut off from the sea by silting and from their hinterlands by poor communications. Eventually, in the 1860s and 70s, the coming of the railway rescued some of them. Lorient, founded in the seventeenth century in high hopes of an expanding trade with the Orient from which it derived its name, lived on as a modest coal port. La Rochelle, once a major port in France's trade with the New World, was little more than a fishing port, and such commerce as it retained subsequently passed to its outport of La Pallice.

Bordeaux, as the premier port of south-western France and chief commercial outlet for Gascony, might have been expected to survive the decay of other ports on this coast. Yet its growth was slow during the first half of the nineteenth century, and the construction of docks and the regulation of its approach through the Gironde were not undertaken until late in the century, when Bordeaux had already been linked with the French railway system.

In Spain, the commercial revival which followed the Napoleonic Wars was in large measure restricted to the Catalan ports (see p. 276). There was a modest activity at Cadiz, but the development of the Basque and Galician ports did not begin until late in the century.[184] Most of Portugal's small trade was carried on through Oporto or Lisbon. The former with a narrow and difficult waterway was used only by the wine boats; the latter, endowed with the finest natural harbour in western Europe, was scarcely used at all. Portugal's former colonial trade had been dissipated during the Napoleonic Wars, and political disturbances had since prevented its revival.

Conclusion

This chapter has attempted to present a picture of Europe on the eve of its period of rapid industrial growth. It has, however, not been easy to determine when this expansion began. Many of the barriers to change – institutional, social and psychological – were broken down in the course of the Revolutionary and Napoleonic Wars, but change nonetheless came very slowly thereafter and its pace varied greatly from one part of the continent to another. The first public railway in continental Europe was opened only a decade after the first had been built in Britain, but it can hardly be said that the continent was ready for it. It was for many years under-used and the first railways served no essential economic purpose. From the 1820s to the 1840s economic growth was slow. It was as if the new industrial technology was being absorbed and assimilated in preparation for a great forward leap.

Change became more rapid in the 1840s. The revolutions of 1848 swept away such elements as had survived of the *ancien régime*. By 1850, after fifteen years of slow progress, the many short lengths of railway were at last knit together into the semblance of a system. The old technology was yielding more rapidly to the new. It was as if the entrepreneur had gained faith in the future and was prepared to invest in new plant and equipment, in new methods and processes. In this shift of attitude and emphasis the Great Exhibition which was held in London in 1851 played an important role in emphasising the progress which had been made in the more advanced areas of Europe.

The 1850s were a period of advance and expansion in almost every aspect of the European economy. During this decade iron production increased by nearly 90 per cent; the number of cotton spindles by 42 per cent and the consumption of raw cotton by 35 per cent. Coal production was expanded by 116 per cent, and the length of railway by 175 per cent. In France the gross national product increased by a third within a decade and in Germany by nearly two-thirds. Every available measure of production shows a rate of growth during the years following the mid-century immeasurably greater than had ever been experienced previously and probably faster than Europe was again to experience within the century. The volume of international trade, at least in the few instances where it is measurable, increased no less rapidly. In Sweden and France it more than doubled, and in the Austrian empire the increase was by 90 per cent.

Rapid industrial growth with its concomitant intensification of agriculture and creation of the infrastructure of commerce and industry, transformed the geographical pattern of the continent. Urban growth, which had been comparatively slow during the first half of the century, became very much more strongly marked in the latter half. Rural industry largely disappeared from much of the continent as manufacturing expanded in the cities and towns. It was during the decades following the 1840s that the principal industrialised regions, from northern France to Upper Silesia, largely assumed their present shape. Population continued to increase, and every country registered a sharp increase in the third quarter of the century with the exceptions only of France, whose growth was well below the European average, and Ireland, which showed a decline. A geographical study of Europe in the closing years of the century would reveal a scene which differed far more radically from that presented in this chapter than the latter did from the Europe of the early sixteenth century.

Notes

Chapter 1. Europe in the early sixteenth century

1. Ferdinand Lot, *Recherches sur les effectifs des armées françaises* (Paris, 1962), 186.
2. Henry Kamen, *The Iron Century* (London, 1971), 331–85.
3. 'The German Peasants' War: The Memmingen Articles (1525)', in *Renaissance and Reformation, 1300–1648*, ed. G. R. Elton (New York, 1968), 280–2.
4. Montaigne, *Journal de voyage en Italie par la Suisse et l'Allemagne* (Paris, 1946), 156.
5. *Bishop Burnet's Travels through France, Italy, Germany and Switzerland*, 1750 edn (London), 88.
6. J. W. Goethe, *Italienische Reise*, Goldmann edn (Munich, 1957), 16–18.
7. *Phoenix: The Posthumous Papers of D. H. Lawrence* (London, 1936), 49.
8. G. J. Marcus, 'The Greenland Trade-Route', *Ec. Hist. Rev.*, 7 (1954–5), 71–80; *id.*, 'The Norse Traffic with Iceland', *ibid.* 9 (1956–7), 408–19.
9. H. H. Lamb, 'Our Changing Climate Past and Present', in *The Changing Climate* (London, 1966), 1–20.
10. Curt Weikinn, *Quellentexte zur Witterungsgeschichte Europas von der Zeitwende bis zum Jahre 1850*, vols. I (Berlin, 1958), II (1960).
11. *Le journal d'un bourgeois sous le règne de François I*, ed. V.-L. Bourilly (Paris, 1910), 155.
12. Maurice Champion, *Les inondations en France depuis le XVe siècle à nos jours*, 6 vols. (Paris, 1858), II, 17
13. E. Le Roy Ladurie, *Histoire du climat depuis l'an mil* (Paris, 1967), 228; *id.*, 'Le climat des XIe et XVIe siècles: séries comparées', *Ann. ESC*, 20 (1965), 899–922.
14. 'Changes of Climate', in *Arid Zone Research Publications*, Unesco, 20 (1963), 28–46.
15. M. K. E. Gottschalk, 'Some Aspects of the Development of Historical Geography in the Netherlands', *T.K.N.A.G.*, 77 (1960), 319–23; J. P. Bakker, 'The Significance of Physical Geography and Pedology for Historical Geography in the Netherlands', *T. Ec. S.G.*, 49 (1958), 214–26.
16. E. H. L. Krause, 'Florenkarte von Deutschland für das 12. bis 15.

Jahrhundert', *Pet. Mitt.*, 38 (1892), 231–5; Johannes Hoops, *Wald-bäume und Kulturpflanzen im germanischen Altertum* (Strasbourg, 1905), 227–51.

17. F. C. Lane, *Venetian Ships and Shipbuilders of the Renaissance* (Baltimore, Md., 1934), 217–33.

18. Friedrich Mager, *Der Wald in Altpreussen als Wirtschaftsraum*, I (Cologne–Graz, 1960), 29.

19. M. Malowist, 'L'approvisionnement des ports de la Baltique en produits forestières pour les constructions navales aux XVᵉ et XVIᵉ siècles', in *Le navire et l'économie maritime du nord de l'Europe du Moyen Age au XVIIIᵉ siècle*, ed. M. Mollat (Paris, 1960), 25–43.

20. Fernand Braudel, *The Mediterranean and the Mediterranean World in the Age of Philip II*, 2 vols. (London, 1972–3), I, 141–3.

21. Vauban, *Projet d'une dixme royale*, Collection des Principaux Economistes (Paris, 1933), 167.

22. *Journal of a Younger Brother*, trans S. Jennett (London, 1963), 47.

23. Robert Forster, *The House of Saulx-Tavanes* (Baltimore, Md., 1971), 70–2.

24. André Bossual, 'Les usages dans le Donzais: la forêt de Bellefaye et la Côte de Suilly', *Bull. Phil. Hist.*, 1966, 291–9.

25. Michel Duval, 'Economie forestière et féodalité dans l'ouest à la veille de la Révolution', *Ann. Bret.*, 64 (1957), 347–58; Michel Devèze, *La vie de la forêt française au XVIᵉ siècle*, 2 vols. (Paris, 1961).

26. Michel Devèze, 'Superficie et propriété des forêts du nord et de l'est de la France', *Ann. ESC*, 15 (1960), 485–92.

27. *Id.*, *La vie de la forêt*, I, 269.

28. Cited in A. Brette, *Les limites et les divisions territoriales de la France en 1789* (Paris, 1897), 18.

29. *Mémoires de Martin et Guillaume du Bellay*, ed. V. L. Bourilly and F. Vindry, Société de l'Histoire de France, 4 (Paris, 1908), 1325.

30. H. Stein and L. LeGrand, *La frontière de l'Argonne: procès de Claude de la Vallée* (Paris, 1905).

31. M.-A. Arnould, 'La superficie du Tournaisis à l'époque moderne', in *Mélanges offerts à G. Jacquemyns* (Brussels, 1968), 1–19.

32. Edward J. Hertslet, *The Map of Europe by Treaty* (London, 1875–91), II, 718–21.

33. G. N. Clark, *The Seventeenth Century* (Oxford, 1931), 142.

34. Aeneas Sylvius, *Opera* (Basel, 1571), 1034–86.

35. Gilles le Bouvier, *Le livre de la description des pays*, ed. E.-T. Hamy, Recueil des Voyages, 22 (Paris, 1908).

36. *Le débat des hérauts d'armes de France et d'Angleterre*, ed. Léopold Pannier and Paul Meyer, Société des Anciens Textes Français (Paris, 1877).

37. The text has been printed in *Romania*, 21 (1892), 50–2.

38. Dorothy Kirkland, 'The Growth of National Sentiment in France before the Fifteenth Century', *Hist.*, 23 (1938–9), 12–24.

39. *Selections from Conrad Celtis, 1459–1508*, trans. L. Forster (Cam-

bridge, 1948), 43.

40. Cited in Gerald Strauss, *Sixteenth Century Germany: Its Topography and Topographers* (Madison, Wisc., 1959), 40.

41. *Ibid.*

42. *Selections from Conrad Celtis*, 47.

43. A fuller discussion of this question in N. J. G. Pounds, 'The Origin of the Idea of Natural Frontiers in France', *A.A.A.G.*, 41 (1951), 146–57.

44. Felix Gilbert, *Machiavelli and Guicciardini* (Princeton, N.J., 1965); *id.*, 'The Concept of Nationalism in Machiavelli's *Prince*', *Studies in the Renaissance* (Austin, Tex.), 1 (1954), 38–48.

45. *Maxims and Reflections of a Renaissance Statesman*, trans. Mario Domandi (New York, 1965), 144.

46. G. J. Renier, *The Dutch Nation: An Historical Study* (London, 1944), 10.

47. Sir George Clark, *War and Society in the Seventeenth Century* (Cambridge, 1958), 76–7.

48. Jorge Nadal, *La población española (siglos XVI á XX)* (Barcelona, 1966), 76; J. H. Elliott, *The Old World and the New* (Cambridge, 1970), 76.

49. J. C. Russell, 'Late Ancient and Medieval Population', *Tr. Am. Phil. Soc.*, n.s., 48, pt 3 (1958), 148.

50. For sources see N. J. G. Pounds and C. C. Roome, 'Population Density in Fifteenth Century France and the Low Countries', *A.A.A.G.*, 61 (1971), 116–30.

51. J. Cuvelier, *Les dénombrements de foyers en Brabant*, Comm. Roy. Hist. (1912), cccxiv.

52. M.-A. Arnould, *Les dénombrements de foyers dans le comté de Hainaut*, Comm. Roy. Hist. (1956), 298.

53. J. A. Faber *et al.*, 'Population Changes and Economic Developments in the Netherlands: An Historical Survey', *A.A.G. Bij.*, 12 (1965), 47–113.

54. J. C. Russell, 'Late Ancient and Medieval Population', 148; R. Kötzschke, *Deutsche Wirtschaftsgeschichte bis zum 17. Jahrhundert* (Leipzig, 1908), 131.

55. Hildegard Ditt, 'Zur kulturgeographischen Struktur und Stellung des Westmünsterlandes im Mittelalter', in *Landschaft und Geschichte: Festschrift für Franz Petri* (Bonn, 1970), 116–36.

56. F. Stuhr, 'Die Bevölkerung Mecklenburgs am Ausgang des Mittelalters', *Jb. Ver. Meck. Gesch.*, 58 (1893), 232–78.

57. Karlheinz Blaschke, *Zur Bevölkerungsgeschichte Sachsens vor der industriellen Revolution* (Berlin, 1962); *id.*, 'Bevölkerungsgang und Wüstungen in Sachsen während des späten Mittelalters', *Jb. Nat. Stat.*, 174 (1962), 414–29.

58. Ingomar Bog, 'Wachstumsprobleme der oberdeutschen Wirtschaft 1540–1618', in *Wirtschaftliche und soziale Probleme der gewerblichen Entwicklung*, ed. F. Lutge, Forsch. Soz. Wtg., 10 (1968), 44–89.

59. Witold Kula, 'Stan i potrzeby badań nad demografią historyczną

dawniej Polski', *Rocz. Dz. Społ. Gosp.*, 13 (1951), 23–109; Irena Gieysztorowa, 'Badania nad historią zaludnienia Polski', *Kw. Hist. Kult. Mat.*, 11 (1963), 523–62.

60. Edouard Baratier, *La démographie provençale du XIIIᵉ au XVIᵉ siècle* (Paris, 1961), 97–101.

61. Placide Rambaud, *Economie et sociologie de la montagne* (Paris, 1962), 92.

62. W. Schnyder, 'Die Bevölkerung der Stadt und Landschaft Zürich vom 14. bis 17. Jahrhundert', *Schweizer Studien zur Geschichtswissenschaft*, 14, 1 (1925).

63. H. Ammann, 'Die Bevölkerung von Stadt und Landschaft Basel am Ausgang des Mittelalters', *Basl. Zt.*, 49 (1950), 25–52.

64. *La visite des églises du diocèse de Lausanne en 1416–1417*, Soc. Hist. Suisse Rom., Mém. et Doc., 2nd ser., 11 (1921).

65. W. Bickel, *Bevölkerungsgeschichte und Bevölkerungspolitik der Schweiz seit dem Ausgang des Mittelalters* (Zurich, 1947), 39–41; H. Ammann, 'Die Bevölkerung der Westschweiz im ausgehenden Mittelalter', in *Festschrift für Friedrich Emil Welti* (Aarau, 1937), 390–447; J.-F. Bergier, *Problèmes de l'histoire économique de la Suisse* (Bern, 1968), 14–26.

66. Heinrich Rubner, 'En forêt de Bohême: immigration et émigration 1500–1600', *Ann. Dém. Hist.*, 1970, 135–42.

67. Vaclav Husa, 'Notes d'information sur les sources et les recherches de démographie historique en Tchécoslovaquie', *Actes Coll. Int. Dém. Hist.*, 237–47.

68. G. Györffy, 'Einwohnerzahl und Bevölkerungsdichte in Ungarn bis zum Anfang des XIV Jahrhunderts', *Et. Hist.* (B), 1 (1960), 163–92; E. Fugedi, 'Pour une analyse démographique de la Hongrie médiévale', *Ann. ESC*, 24 (1969), 1299–312; Imre Wellmann, 'Esquisse d'une histoire rurale de la Hongrie depuis la première moitié du XVIIIᵉ siècle jusqu'au milieu du XIXᵉ siècle', *Ann. ESC*, 23 (1968), 1181–210; Joseph Kavcsics, 'An Account of Research Work in Historical Demography in Hungary', *Actes Coll. Int. Dém. Hist.*, 249–72.

69. Stafan Pascu, 'Les sources et les recherches démographiques en Roumanie', *Actes Coll. Int. Dém. Hist.*, 283–303.

70. O. L. Barkan, 'Essai sur les données statistiques des Registres de Recensement dans l'Empire Ottoman aux XVᵉ et XVIᵉ siècles', *Jn. Ec. Soc. Hist. Orient*, 1 (1958), 9–36.

71. Julius Beloch, *Bevölkerungsgeschichte Italiens*, 3 vols. (Berlin, 1937–61).

72. Carlo M. Cipolla, 'Four Centuries of Italian Demographic Development', in *Population in History*, ed. D. V. Glass and D. E. C. Eversley (London, 1965), 570–87.

73. H. G. Koenigsberger, 'The Parliament of Piedmont duing the Renaissance, 1460–1560', *Rec. Trav. Hist. Phil.*, 3rd ser., 45 (1952), 67–122.

74. Quoted in R.-H. Bautier, 'La valeur démographique du feu d'après les

recensements de Chieri (Piedmont) 1473–1530', *Bull. Phil. Hist.*, 1965, 235–46.

75. C. M. Cipolla, 'Per la storia della popolazione lombarde nel secolo XVI', in *Studi Gino Luzzatto*, vol. II (Barcelona, 1966), 144–55.

76. Daniele Beltrami, 'Saggio di storia dell'agricoltura nella republica di Venezia durante l'età moderna', *Civ. Venex.*, 1 (1954).

77. 'Gli atti della visita apostolica di S. Carlo Borromeo a Bergamo (1575)', ed. A. G. Roncalli and P. Forno, *Fontes Ambrosiani* (Milan), vols. 15–17 (1939–57).

78. Beloch, *Bevölkerungsgeschichte Italiens*, III, 142.

79. Nadal, *Población española*, 20; José-Gentil da Silva, 'Au Portugal: structure démographique et développement économique', *Studi Fanfani*, II, 491–510; Alvaro Castillo, 'Population et "richesse" en Castille durant la seconde moitié du XVIe siècle', *Ann. ESC*, 20 (1965), 719–33.

80. Ruth Pike, *Aristocrats and Traders: Sevillian Society in the Sixteenth Century* (Ithaca, N.Y., 1972), 100.

81. *Novelas ejemplares*, ed. Marín, II (Madrid, 1957), 235.

82. Pierre Vilar, *La Catalogne dans l'Espagne moderne*, E.P.H.E., 1 (1962), 521–7; *id.*, 'Quelques problèmes de démographie historique en Catalogne et en Espagne', *Ann. Dém. Hist.*, 1965, 11–30.

83. E. Coornaert, *La Flandre françoise de langue flamande* (Paris, 1970), 101; A. M. van der Woude, 'Variations in the Size and Structure of the Household in the United Provinces of the Netherlands in the Seventeenth and Eighteenth Centuries', in *Household and Family in Past Time*, ed. P. Laslett (Cambridge, 1972), 299–318.

84. J. J. Siegrist, *Lenzburg im Mittelalter und im 16. Jahrhundert* (Aarau, 1955).

85. Jean Adhémar, 'Notes sur les plans de villes de France au XVIe siècle', in *Urbanisme et architecture* (Paris, 1954), 17–19.

86. E. Pognon, 'Les plus anciens plans de villes gravés et les évènements militaires', *Imago Mundi*, 22 (1968), 13–19.

87. Gerald Strauss, *Nuremberg in the Sixteenth Century* (New York, 1966), 7.

88. G. Botero, 'A Treatise Concerning the Causes of the Magnificency and Greatness of Cities', trans. R. Petersen, in *The Reason of State*, ed. P. J. and D. P. Waley (New Haven, Conn., 1956), 225–80.

89. Judith Hook, *The Sack of Rome* (London, 1972), 29–35.

90. Joseph Cuvelier, 'La population de Louvain aux XVIe et XVIIe siècles', *Ann. Soc. Arch. Brux.*, 22 (1908), 337–76.

91. Mack Walker, *German Home Towns: Community, State and General Estate 1648–1871* (London, 1971), 32.

92. Michel Rochefort, *L'organisation urbaine de l'Alsace*, Pub. Fac. Strasbourg, 139 (1960), 160.

93. Hans W. Jürgens, 'Sozialanthropologische Probleme der Stadt-Land Bezienhungen', *Stud. Gen.*, 16 (1963), 500–12.

94. Wilhelm Abel, in *Handbuch der deutschen Wirtschafts- und Sozial-*

geschichte, ed. H. Aubin and W. Zorn, I (Stuttgart, 1971), 500.

95. E. Labrousse, P. Léon, P. Goubert, J. Bouvier, C. Carrière and P. Harsin, *Histoire économique et sociale de la France*, II, *1660–1789* (Paris, 1970), 125–9.

96. Michel Mollat and Philippe Wolff, *The Popular Revolutions of the Late Middle Ages* (London, 1973), 271–317.

97. *Maison Rustique or The Country Compiled in the French Tongue by Charles Stevens and John Liebault*, trans. Richard Surfleet (London, 1616), 11.

98. E. Juillard, *La vie rurale dans la plaine de Basse-Alsace*, Pub. Fac. Strasbourg, 123 (1953); J. Jacquart, 'La production agricole dans la France du XVIIᵉ siècle', *XVIIᵉ S.*, nos. 70–1 (1966), 21–46.

99. Olivier de Serres, *Le théâtre d'agriculture et mesnage des champs* (1605 edn), 108.

100. François Granville, 'Histoire d'Ans et Glain des origines à 1789', *Bull. Inst. Arch. Liège*, 74 (1961), 5–252.

101. Andrzej Wychański, 'En Pologne: l'économie du domaine nobiliaire moyen (1500–1580)', *Ann. ESC*, 18 (1963), 81–7.

102. *Ibid.*; yield-ratios from Wychański, 'Le niveau de la récolte des céréales en Pologne du XVIᵉ au XVIIIᵉ siècle', *Int. Conf. Ec. Hist.*, *Stockholm: Communications* (Paris, 1960), 585–90.

103. *The Travel Diaries of Thomas Robert Malthus*, ed. Patricia James (Cambridge, 1966), 156 and *passim*.

104. E. Juillard, 'Villes et campagnes: la région du Rhin moyen avant la révolution industrielle', in *Eventail de l'histoire vivante* (Paris, 1953), 151–3.

105. Fredo Gestrin, 'Economie et société en Slovénie au XVIᵉ siècle', *Ann. ESC*, 17 (1962), 663–90.

106. B. H. Slicher van Bath, 'The Rise of Intensive Husbandry in the Low Countries', in *Britain and the Netherlands*, ed. J. S. Bromley and E. H. Kossmann (London, 1960), 130–53.

107. *Maison Rustique*, 12.

108. Olivier de Serres, *Le théâtre d'agriculture*, 3–4.

109. These ploughs are illustrated in Ernst Klein, *Die historischen Pflüge*, Quell. Forsch. Aggesch., 16 (1967).

110. J. Topolski, *Gospodarstwo wiejskie w dobrach Arcybiskupstwa Gnieźnieńskiego od XVI do XVIII wieku* (Poznań, 1958), 23–5.

111. Abel, in *Handbuch der deutschen Wirtschafts- und Sozialgeschichte*, I, 387.

112. Gabriel Debien, 'En Haut-Poitou: défricheurs au travail XVᵉ–XVIIIᵉ siècles', *Cah. Ann.*, 7 (1952), 40–1; J.-P. Barry and E. Le Roy Ladurie, 'Histoire agricole et phytogéographie', *Ann. ESC*, 17 (1962), 434–47.

113. B. H. Slicher van Bath, 'Yield Ratios', *A.A.G. Bij.*, 10 (1963).

114. Pierre Goubert, 'Les techniques agricoles dans les pays picards aux XVIIᵉ et XVIIIᵉ siècles', *Rev. Hist. Ec. Soc.*, 35 (1957), 24–40.

115. P.-A. Février, 'Quelques aspects de la vie agricole en Basse-Provence à la fin du moyen âge', *Bull. Phil. Hist.*, 1957, 299–317; J. Goasguen,

'Aspects de la vie économique, sociale et municipale à Villeneuve d'Agenais au XVIIᵉ et XVIIIᵉ siècles d'après les archives de la famille de Galaup', *Ann. Midi*, 74 (1962), 361–400.

116. F. Gay, 'Production, prix et rentabilité de la terre en Berry au XVIIᵉ siècle', *Rev. Hist. Ec. Soc.*, 36 (1958), 399–411.

117. Paul Percevaux, 'Structures et rélations économiques en Dombes à la fin du moyen âge', *Cah. Hist.*, 12 (1967), 339–57.

118. W. Szczygielski, 'Le rendement de la production agricole en Pologne du XVIᵉ siècle au XVIIIᵉ siècle sur le fond européen', *Kw. Hist. Kult. Mat.* (*Ergon* suppl., 5), 14 (1966), 795–803.

119. Goubert, 'Les techniques agricoles dans les pays picards'.

120. Lucien Badey, 'Le peuplement du Vivarais à la fin du XVIIIᵉ siècle', *Rev. Hist. Ec. Soc.*, 27 (1948–9), 127–52.

121. *Oesterreichische Urbäre herausgegeben von der Kaiserlichen Akademie der Wissenschaften* (Vienna, 1904–55).

122. Bergier, *Problèmes de l'histoire économique de la Suisse*, 50–2.

123. Wilhelm Abel, 'Zur Entwicklung des Sozialprodukts in Deutschland im 16. Jahrhundert', *Jb. Nat. Stat.*, 173 (1961), 448–89.

124. H. Wiese and J. Bölts, *Rinderhandel und Rinderhaltung im nordwesteuropäischen Küstengebiet vom 15. bis zum 19. Jahrhundert* (Stuttgart, 1966), 23–93; H. Wiese, 'Die Fleischversorgung der nordwesteuropäischen Grossstädte vom XV. bis XIX. Jahrhundert unter besonderer Berücksichtigung des interterritorialen Rinderhandels', *Jb. Nat. Stat.*, 179 (1966), 125–39.

125. Z. P. Pach, 'Die ungarische Agrarentwicklung im 16–17. Jahrhundert', *Stud. Hist* (B), 54 (1964), 20–1.

126. Braudel, *The Mediterranean*, I, 85–102.

127. Elli Müller, 'Die Herdenwanderungen im Mittelmeergebiet', *Pet. Mitt.*, 84 (1938), 364–70.

128. Thérèse Sclafert, *Cultures en Haute-Provence,* E.P.H.E. (1959), 156.

129. Peter Partner, *The Lands of St. Peter* (London, 1972), 423–4.

130. Julius Klein, *The Mesta* (Cambridge, Mass., 1920), 26–9.

131. B. H. Slicher van Bath, 'Agriculture in the Low Countries', in *Relazioni del X Congresso Internationale di Scienze Storiche*, IV (Florence, 1955), 169–203.

132. Jan de Vries, *The Dutch Rural Economy in the Golden Age, 1500–1700* (New Haven, Conn., 1974), 137–44.

133. Guicciardini was clearly wrong in his attribution of extensive vineyards to the Netherlands.

134. Sources given in Strauss, *Sixteenth Century Germany*, 63, 73; Abel, 'Zur Entwicklung des Sozialprodukts in Deutschland im 16. Jahrhundert'.

135. Thérèse Sclafert, 'Sisteron au début du XVIᵉ siècle d'après un cadastre', *Ann. Géog.*, 37 (1928), 167–73.

136. Louis Merle, *La métairie et l'évolution agraire de la gâtine poitevine de la fin du Moyen Age à la Révolution*, E.P.H.E. (1958), 40–73; Gabriel Bernet, 'Un village du Lauragais au XVIIᵉ siècle: le consulat de

Pugnères de 1593 à 1715', *Ann. Midi*, 80 (1968), 27–64.

137. Georges Duby, 'Le grand domaine de la fin du moyen âge en France', *Int. Conf. Ec. Hist., Stockholm: Communications* (Paris, 1960), 333–42.

138. Paul Raveau, *L'agriculture et les classes paysannes* (Paris, 1926), 38.

139. Suzanne Savey, 'Essai de reconstitution de la structure agraire des villages de Sardon et d'Aspères (Gard) sous l'Ancien Régime à l'aide des compoix', *Ann. Midi*, 81 (1969), 41–54.

140. Abel, in *Handbuch der deutschen Wirtschafts- und Sozialgeschichte*, I, 91–7.

141. B. H. Slicher van Bath, 'Vrijheid en lijfeigenschap in agrarisch Europa (16e–18e eeuw)', *A.A.G. Bij.*, 15 (1970), 75–104.

142. Jerome Blum, 'The Rise of Serfdom in Eastern Europe', *Am. Hist. Rev.*, 62 (1956–7), 807–36.

143. I. Simkovics, 'Le servage héréditaire en Hongrie aux 16–17e siècles', in *La Renaissance et la Réformation en Pologne et en Hongrie, Stud. Hist.* (B), 53 (1963), 47–89.

144. Jerzy Ochmanski, 'La grande réforme agraire en Lituanie et en Ruthénie', *Kw. Hist. Kult. Mat. (Ergon* suppl.), 8 (1960), 327–42.

145. P. J. Jones, 'From Manor to Mezzadria: A Tuscan Case-Study in the Medieval Origins of Modern Agrarian Society', in *Florentine Studies*, ed. N. Rubinstein (London, 1968), 193–241.

146. Giorgio Giorgetti, 'Agricoltura e sviluppo capitalistico nella Toscana del '700', *Stud. Stor.*, 9 (1968), 742–83; Gino Luzzatto, *An Economic History of Italy from the Fall of the Roman Empire to the Beginning of the Sixteenth Century* (London, 1961), 100.

147. Giorgio Doria, *Uomini e terre di un borgo collinare* (Milan, 1968), 10.

148. L. S. Stavrianos, *The Balkans since 1453* (New York, 1958), 138–43.

149. N. J. G. Pounds, *An Historial Geography of Europe 450 BC–AD 1330* (Cambridge, 1973), 196–201.

150. R.-H. Bautier, 'Notes sur le commerce du fer en Europe occidentale du XIIIe au XVIe siècle', *Rev. Hist. Sid.*, 1, 4 (1960), 7–35; Vannoccio Biringuccio, *Pirotechnia*, ed. C. S. and M. T. Smith (New York, 1942), 61–7.

151. Illustrated in Georg Agricola, *De re Metallica,* and Biringuccio, *Pirotechnia.*

152. Biringuccio, *Pirotechnia*, 370.

153. R. Sprandel, 'La production du fer au Moyen Age', *Ann. ESC*, 24 (1969), 305–21.

154. F. C. Lane, 'The Mediterranean Spice Trade: Further Evidence of its Revival in the Sixteenth Century', *Am. Hist. Rev.*, 45 (1940), 581–90.

155. F. Edler de Roover, 'The Market for Spices in Antwerp, 1538–1544', *Rev. Belge Phil. Hist.*, 17 (1938), 212–21.

156. Charles Verlinden, 'From the Mediterranean to the Atlantic: Aspects of an Economic Shift (12th–18th Century)', *Jn. Eur. Ec. Hist.*, 1 (1972), 625–46.

157. J. A. van Houtte and E. Stols, 'Les Pays-Bas et la Méditerrané

atlantique au XVIᵉ siècles', *Mélanges F. Braudel*, I, 645–59.

158. Jean Tangay, *Le commerce du port de Nantes au milieu du XVIᵉ siècle*, E.P.H.E. (1956), 16–19; Henri Touchard, *Le commerce maritime breton à la fin du Moyen Age*, Ann. Litt. Nantes, 1 (1967), 314.

159. Etienne Trocme and Marcel Delafosse, *Le commerce rochelais de la fin du XVᵉ siècle au début du XVIIᵉ*, E.P.H.E. (1952), 73; M. Delafosse, 'Trafics rochelais au XVIᵉ siècle', *Ann. ESC*, 12 (1957), 594–601.

160. W. Jappe Alberts, 'Overijssel und die benachbarten Territorien in ihren wirtschaftlichen Verflechtungen im 14. und 15. Jahrhundert', *Rhein. Vbl.*, 23 (1958), 40–57.

161. Philippe Dollinger, *The German Hanse* (London, 1970), 311–20.

162. M. Małowist, 'Poland, Russia and Western Trade in the 15th and 16th Centuries', *P & P*, 13 (1958), 26–41; *id.*, 'Les produits des pays de la Baltique dans le commerce international au XVIᵉ siècle', *Rev. Nord*, 42 (1960), 175–206.

163. J. Zoutis, 'Riga dans le commerce maritime en Baltique au XVIIᵉ siècle', in *Le navire et l'économie maritime du nord de l'Europe du Moyen Age au XVIIIᵉ siècle* (Paris, 1960), 81–92.

164. P. Jeannin, 'Le cuivre, les Fugger et la Hanse', *Ann. ESC*, 10 (1955), 229–36.

165. M.-L. Fanchamps, 'Transport et commerce du bois sur la Meuse au Moyen Age', *Moy. Age*, 21 (1966), 59–81; J. Niquille, 'La navigation sur la Sarine', *Schw. Zt. Gesch.*, 2 (1952), 206–27.

166. Paul Wegner, 'Die mittelalterlichen Flussschiffahrt im Wesergebiet', *Hans. Gbl.*, 19 (1913), 93–161.

167. N. J. G. Pounds, 'Patterns of Trade in the Rhineland', in E. Ashworth Underwood (ed.), *Science, Medicine and History: Essays on the Evolution of Scientific Thought and Medical Practice in Honour of Charles Singer*, 2 vols. (Oxford, 1953), II, 419–34.

168. Gustave Guilmoto, *Etude sur les droits de navigation de la Seine de Paris à la Roche-Guyon du XIᵉ au XVIIIᵉ siècle* (Paris, 1889).

169. K. F. Klöden, *Beiträge zur Geschichte des Oderhandels*, 8 pts (Berlin, 1845–52), 1, 44–5.

170. Marjorie N. Boyer, 'Roads and Rivers: Their Use and Disuse in Late Medieval France', *Med. Hum.*, 13 (1960), 68–80.

171. R.-H. Bautier and M. Mollat, 'Le traffic fluvial sur la Seine au pont de Meulan au milieu du XVᵉ siècle', *Bull. Phil. Hist.*, 1959, 251–96.

172. R. Marquant, *La vie économique à Lille sous Philippe le Bon*, Bibl. Ec. Htes Et., 277 (1940), 94–9.

173. A. W. Skempton, 'Canals and River Navigations before 1750', in Charles Singer, E. J. Holmyard, A. R. Hall and T. I. Williams (eds.), *A History of Technology*, III (Oxford, 1957), 438–70.

174. R.-H. Bautier, 'Recherches sur les routes de l'Europe médiévale', *Bull. Phil. Hist.*, 1960, vol. 1, 99–143.

175. F. Imberdis, 'Les routes médiévales: mythes et réalités historiques', *Ann. Hist. Soc.*, 1 (1939), 411–16.

176. Charles Etienne, *La guide des chemins de France de 1553*, Bibl. Ec.

Htes. Et., 265 and 267 (1936).

177. Hans Wertheim, 'Der erste europäische Strassenatlas', *Imago Mundi*, 50 (1935), 41–4.

178. F. Rauers, 'Zur Geschichte der alten Handelsstrassen in Deutschland', *Pet. Mitt.*, 52 (1906), 49–59.

179. E. Oehlmann, 'Die Alpenpässe im Mittelalter', *Jb. Schw. Gesch.*, 3 (1878), 165–289; 4 (1879), 163–324.

180. Fynes Moryson, *The Itinerary of Fynes Moryson*, 4 vols. (Glasgow, 1908), III, 467.

181. Gabriel Wymans, 'Compte et itinéraire d'un voyage des Pays-Bas à Naples en 1532', *Bull. Inst. Hist. Belge Rome*, 35 (1963), 133–58; *Le voyage d'Outremer de Bertrandon de la Broquière*, ed. C. Schefer (Paris, 1892), 2–3. See also Monique Somme, 'Les déplacements d'Isabelle de Portugal et la circulation dans les Pays-Bas bourgignons au milieu du XVe siècle', *Rev. Nord*, 52 (1970), 183–97.

182. Braudel, *The Mediterranean*, I, 363–9.

183. Richard Gascon, *Grand commerce et vie urbaine au XVIe siècle: Lyon et ses marchands* (Paris, 1971), 169 and fig. 16.

184. Edler de Roover, 'The Market for Spices in Antwerp'.

185. R. Gascon, 'Un siècle du commerce des épices à Lyon: fin X – fin XVIIe siècles', *Ann. ESC*, 15 (1960), 638–66.

186. Kristof Glamann suggests 3–4 million pounds: 'European Trade 1500–1750', in *The Fontana Economic History of Europe*, II (London, 1974), 477.

187. V. Prévot, 'Une grande industrie d'exportation: l'industrie linière dans le nord de la France sous l'Ancien Régime', *Rev. Nord*, 39 (1957), 205–26; E. Coornaert, *La draperie–sayetterie d'Hondschoote (XIVe–XVIIIe siècles)* (Rennes, 1930), 237–51.

188. Aloys Schulte, *Geschichte der grossen Ravensburger Handelsgesellschaft 1380—1530,* 4 vols. (Stuttgart, 1923), I, 10–40.

189. Hermann Mols, 'Der Leinwandhandel in Norddeutschland vom Mittelalter bis zum 17. Jahrhundert', *Hans. Gbl.*, 31 (1926), 116–58.

190. Coornaert, *La draperie–sayetterie*, 251; Prévot, 'Une grande industrie d'exportation'.

191. Josef Janáček, 'L'argent tchèque et la Méditerranée', *Mélanges F. Braudel*, I, 245–61.

192. John Hatcher, *English Tin Production and Trade before 1550* (Oxford, 1973), 118–35.

193. J. Kořan and V. Vaněček, 'Czech Mining and Mining Law', *Cah. Hist. Mond.*, 7 (1962), 27–45; Biringuccio, *Pirotechnia*, ch. 5.

194. Suzanne Deck, *La ville d'Eu: son histoire, ses institutions*, Bibl. Ec. Htes Et., 243 (1924), 191–3; *id.*, 'Les salines de Bouteilles', *Ann. Norm.*, 14 (1964), 445–54.

195. A. R. Bridbury, *England and the Salt Trade in the Later Middle Ages* (Oxford, 1955), 76–93.

196. Walter Fellmann, 'Die Salzproduktion im Hanseraum', in *Hansische Studien Heinrich Sproemberg zum 70. Geburtstag* (Berlin, 1961),

56–71; *Le rôle du sel dans l'histoire*, ed. M. Mollat (Paris, 1968).

197. J. J. Bouquet, 'Le problème du sel au pays de Vaud jusqu'au début du XVIIe siècle', *Schw. Zt. Gesch.*, 7 (1957), 289–344; René Lacour, 'Traffic du sel en Valais et rivalité franco-espagnole', *Cah. Hist.*, 12 (1967), 283–8.

198. N. S. B. Gras, *The Evolution of the English Corn Market*, Harvard Economic Studies, 13 (Cambridge, Mass., 1915), 42.

199. Braudel, *The Mediterranean*, I, 576–9.

200. J. Godard, 'Contributions à l'étude de l'histoire du commerce des grains à Douai du XIVe au XVIIe siècle', *Rev. Nord*, 27 (1944), 171–205; G. Bigwood, 'Gand et la circulation des grains en Flandre du XIVe au XVIIIe siècle', *V.S.W.G.*, 4 (1906), 397–460.

201. Z. W. Sneller, 'Le commerce du blé des Hollandais dans la région de la Somme au XVe siècle', *Bull. Soc. Ant. Pic.*, 42 (1947–8), 140–60.

202. A. P. Usher, *The History of the Grain Trade in France 1400–1710* (Cambridge, Mass., 1913), 48–56.

203. J.-F. Bergier, 'Commerce et politique du blé à Genève aux XVe et XVIe siècles', *Schw. Zt. Gesch.*, 14 (1964), 521–50.

204. Antoni Mączak, 'Export of Grain and the Problem of Distribution of National Income in the Years 1550–1650', *Acta Pol. Hist.*, 18 (1968), 75–98.

205. S. Mielczarski, 'Koszta transportu i ich wpływ na udział kupców w handlu zbożowym w Polsce XVI wieku', *Kw. Hist. Kult. Mat.*, 13 (1965), 269–79.

206. W. Naudé, *Die Getreidehandelspolitik der europäischen Staaten vom 13. bis zum 18. Jahrhundert*, Acta Bor. (1896), 25–31.

207. Maurice Aymard, *Venise, Raguse et le commerce du blé pendant la seconde moitié du XVIe siècle* (Paris, 1966), 15–18.

208. Braudel, *The Mediterranean*, I, 579–83.

209. Octavian Iliescu, 'Notes sur l'apport roumain au ravitaillement de Byzance', *Nouv. Et. Hist.*, 3 (1965), 105–16.

210. Yves Renouard, 'La consommation des grands vins de Bourgogne à la cour pontificale d'Avignon', *Ann. Bourg.*, 24 (1952), 221–44.

211. M. K. James, 'Les activités commerciales des négociants en vins gascons en Angleterre durant la fin du moyen âge', *Ann. Midi*, 65 (1953), 35–48; Y. Renouard, 'Le grand commerce des vins de Gascogne au Moyen Age', *Rev. Hist.*, 221 (1959), 261–304.

212. Roger Dion, *Histoire de la vigne et du vin en France des origines au XIXe siècle* (Paris, 1959), 540–93.

213. Jan Craebeckx, *Un grand commerce d'importation: les vins de France aux anciens Pays-Bas* (Paris, 1958), 11.

214. Douglass C. North and Robert P. Thomas, *The Rise of the Western World* (Cambridge, 1973), esp. 1–18, 91–119.

Chapter 2. The population of Europe

1. Jean Lederer, 'Les mendiants de Bruegel, un document pour l'histoire de Flandres sous l'occupation espagnole', *Scrinium Lovaniense*, 24

(1961), 452–65.

2. Jean Meuvret, 'Crises de subsistances et la démographie de la France d'Ancien Régime', *Pop.*, 1 (1946), 643–50.

3. J.-P. Goubert, 'Le phénomène épidémique en Bretagne à la fin du XVIIIᵉ siècle (1770–1787)', in *Médecins, climat et épidémies à la fin du XVIIIᵉ siècle* (Paris, 1972), 225–52.

4. Catherine Rollet, 'L'effet des crises économiques du début du XIXᵉ siècle sur la population', *Rev. Hist. Mod. Cont.*, 17 (1970), 391–410.

5. John D. Post, 'Famine, Mortality and Epidemic Disease in the Process of Modernization', *Ec. Hist. Rev.*, 29 (1976), 14–37.

6. *Correspondance des Contrôleurs-Généraux des Finances avec les provinces*, ed. A. M. de Boislisle, 4 vols. (Paris, 1874–97). Vol. I contains the correspondence relating to the crisis of 1693–4.

7. Gisèle Van Houtte, *Leuven in 1740, een krisisjaar: ekonomische, sociale en demografische aspekten* (Brussels, 1964).

8. Guy Lemarchand, 'Les troubles de subsistances dans la généralité de Rouen', *Ann. Hist. Rév. Fr.*, 35 (1963), 401–27.

9. Hans Van Werveke, 'La mortalité catastrophique en Flandre au XVIIᵉ siècle', *Actes Coll. Int. Dém. Hist.*, 457–64.

10. J. Charlier, *La peste à Bruxelles de 1667 à 1669 et ses conséquences démographiques*, Pro Civitate Collection, 8 (Brussels, 1969), 192–4; Jacques Revel, 'Autour d'une épidémie ancienne: la peste de 1666–1670', *Rev. Hist. Mod. Cont.*, 17 (1970), 953–83.

11. Pierre Deyon, *Amiens: capitale provinciale* (Paris, 1967), 17–31.

12. Gaston Roupnel, *La ville et la campagne au XVIIᵉ siècle: étude sur les populations du pays dijonnais* (Paris, 1955), 25–7.

13. Gunther Franz, *Der Dreissigjahrige Krieg und das deutsche Volk*, Quell. Forsch. Aggesch., 7 (1961), 5–7; E. Keyser, 'Die Peste in Deutschland und ihre Erforschung', *Actes Coll. Int. Dém. Hist.*, 367–77.

14. J. Nadal and E. Giralt, *La population catalane de 1553 à 1717* (Paris, 1960), 25–45.

15. Bartolomé Bennassar, 'Organisation municipale et communautés d'habitants en temps de peste: l'exemple du nord de l'Espagne et de la Castille à la fin du XVIᵉ siècle', in *Villes de l'Europe méditerranéenne*, 2 vols., Ann. Fac. Nice, 9 and 10 (1969), 139–43.

16. K. F. Helleiner, 'The Vital Revolution Reconsidered', in D. V. Glass and D. E. C. Eversley (eds.), *Population in History* (London, 1965), 79–86.

17. N. J. G. Pounds, 'John Huxham's Medical Diary: 1728–1725', *Loc. Pop. St.*, no. 12 (1974), 34–7.

18. *The Complete Letters of Lady Mary Wortley Montagu*, 3 vols., ed. Robert Halsband (Oxford, 1965), I, 338–9, 392.

19. L. Bradley, *Smallpox Inoculation: An Eighteenth Century Mathematical Controversy* (Nottingham, [c. 1970]; pamphlet), summarises views on the demographic significance of smallpox.

20. Fielding H. Garrison, *An Introduction to the History of Medicine*

(Philadelphia, Pa., 1929), 304–7.

21. Raymond Crawfurd, 'Contributions from the History of Medicine to the Problem of the Transmission of Typhus', *Proc. Roy. Soc. Med., History of Medicine Section*, 6 (1913), 6–17.

22. Lt-Col. MacArthur, 'Old-Time Typhus in Britain', *Trans. Roy. Soc. Tropical Medicine and Hygiene* (London), 20 (1926–7), 487–503.

23. Franz, *Der Dreissigjahrige Krieg*, 5–21.

24. H. J. C. Grimmelshausen, *Der abenteuerliche Simplicissimus* (1669).

25. Sir George Clark, *War and Society in the Seventeenth Century* (Cambridge, 1958), 78.

26. *Ibid.* 87.

27. D. C. Coleman, 'Economic Problems and Policies', *New Camb. Mod. Hist.*, V (1961), 19–46.

28. M. Moheau, *Recherches et considérations sur la population de la France 1778* (Paris, 1778), ed. R. Gonnard in Coll. Ec. Réf. Soc. (1912), 60; probably an underestimate.

29. Marcel Duval in 'A travers la Normandie des XVIIe et XVIIIe siècles', *Cah. Ann. Norm.*, no. 3 (1963), 155–271.

30. Pierre Gouhier, 'Port-en-Bessin 1597–1792', *ibid.*, no. 1 (1962), 38–40.

31. Deyon, *Amiens*, 36.

32. Louis Henry, *Anciennes familles genévoises: étude démographique,* Inst. Nat. Et. Dém., Trav. et Doc., no. 26 (1956), 174.

33. Denise Leymond, 'La communauté de Duravel au XVIIIe siècle', *Ann. Midi*, 79 (1967), 363–85.

34. Jean Delumeau, 'Démographie d'un port français sous l'Ancien Régime: Saint-Malo (1651–1750)', *XVIIe S.*, nos. 86–7 (1970), 3–20.

35. Etienne Gautier and Louis Henry, *La population de Crulai*, Inst. Nat. Et. Dém., 1958; also J.-P. Kintz, 'Etudes alsaciennes', *Ann. Dém. Hist.*, 1969, 261–92.

36. G. Ohlin, 'Mortality, Marriage and Growth in Pre-Industrial Populations', *Pop. Stud.*, 14 (1960–1), 190–7.

37. Quoted in E. Labrousse, P. Léon, P. Goubert, J. Bouvier, C. Carrière and P. Harsin, *Histoire économique et sociale de la France*, vol. II, *1660–1789* (Paris, 1970), 33.

38. Moheau, *Recherches sur la population de la France 1778*, 20–3.

39. P. Deprez, 'The Demographic Development of Flanders in the Eighteenth Century', in Glass and Eversley (eds.), *Population in History*, 608–30.

40. Leymond, 'La communauté de Duravel'.

41. René Baehrel, 'La mortalité sous l'ancien régime', *Ann. ESC*, 12 (1957), 85–96.

42. J.-C. Toutain, *La population de la France de 1700 à 1959, Hist. Quant. Ec. Fr.*, 3 (1963), 34; Raymond Deniel and Louis Henry, 'La population d'un village du nord de la France: Sainghin-en-Melantois, de 1665 à 1851', *Pop.*, 20 (1965), 563–602.

43. J. Godeschot and Suzanne Moncassin, 'Démographie et subsistances

en Languedoc', *Bull. Comm. Hist. Ec. Soc. Rév. Fr.*, 1964, 19–60; P. Goubert, *Beauvais et le Beauvaisis de 1600 à 1730* (Paris, 1960), 61–3.

44. Louis Henry, 'The Population of France in the Eighteenth Century', in Glass and Eversley (eds.), *Population in History*, 434–56; also Serge Dontenwill, 'Les crises démographiques à Charlieu et dans la campagne environnante de 1690 à 1720', *Cah. Hist.*, 14 (1969), 113–40.

45. Moheau, *Recherches sur la population de la France 1778*, 18.

46. F. Tomas, 'Problèmes de démographie historique; le Forez au XVIIIe siècle', *Cah. Hist.*, 13 (1968), 381–99.

47. Etienne Hélin, 'Size of Households before the Industrial Revolution: The Case of Liège in 1801', in *Household and Family in Past Time*, ed. P. Laslett (Cambridge, 1972), 319–34.

48. Philip E. Mosely, 'The Distribution of the Zadruga within Southeastern Europe', in *The Joshua Starr Memorial Volume*, Jewish Social Studies, 5 (New York, 1953), 219–30.

49. Lutz K. Berkner, 'The Peasant Household in Eighteenth Century Austria', unpublished Ph.D. thesis, Harvard University; also *id*., 'The Stem Family and the Developmental Cycle of the Peasant Household: An Eighteenth Century Austrian Example', *Am. Hist. Rev.*, 77 (1972), 398–418, and Peter Laslett, 'The History of the Family', in Laslett (ed.), *Household and Family in Past Time* (Cambridge, 1972), 1–89.

50. J. Ruwet, 'Les inégalités devant la mort: les Pays-Bas et la principauté de Liège du XVIe au XVIIIe siècle', *Actes Coll. Int. Dém. Hist.*, 441–55.

51. Raymond Noël, 'La population de la paroise de Inières, d'après un recensement nominatif du diocèse de Rodez', *Ann. Midi*, 80 (1968), 139–56.

52. Quoted by M.-A. Carron, 'Prélude à l'exode rural en France: les migrations anciennes des travailleurs creusois', *Rev. Hist. Ec. Soc.*, 43 (1965), 289–320.

53. *Correspondence des Contrôleurs-Généraux*, I, no. 312.

54. Quoted in H. Onde, 'L'émigration en Maurienne et Tarentaise', *Bull. Soc. Sci. Dauph.*, 60 (1942), 41–99.

55. Memoir of 1778–9, quoted by Carron, 'Prélude à l'exode rural en France'.

56. Thomas Platter, *Autobiographie*, ed. M. Helmer, *Cah. Ann.*, 22 (1964), 21.

57. Quoted in Domenico Sella, 'Au dossier des migrations montagnardes: l'exemple de la Lombardie au XVIIe siècle', *Mélanges F. Braudel*, I, 547–54.

58. Roger Béteille, 'Les migrations saisonnières en France sous le Premier Empire: essai de synthèse', *Rev. Hist. Mod. Cont.*, 17 (1970), 424–41.

59. Georges Lefebvre, *Etudes orléanais: I. Contributions à l'étude des structures sociales à la fin du XVIIIe siècle*, *Comm. Hist. Ec. Soc. Rév. Fr.*, *Mém. et Doc.*, 15 (1962), 149.

60. P. Clemendot, 'Evolution de la population de Nancy de 1788 à 1815', in *Con. Hist. Dém. Rév. Fr.*, 18 (1965), 181–220.

61. Martine Sevegrand, 'La section de Popincourt', *ibid.*, 25 (1970), 9.
62. F. Rousseau-Vigneron, 'La section de la Place des Fédérés', *ibid.*, 155–84.
63. Henri Lapeyre, *Géographie de l'Espagne morisque* (Paris, 1959), 198–200, 204–5.
64. Warren C. Scoville, *The Persecution of Huguenots and French Economic Development, 1680–1720* (Berkeley, Calif., 1960), 123–7.
65. Albert Hauser, 'Schweizer Bauern als Kolonisten in Preussen und Litauen', *Zt. Aggesch.*, 13 (1965), 212–19.
66. Henry Marczali, *Hungary in the Eighteenth Century* (Cambridge, 1910), 201–46.
67. Jovan Cvijic, *La péninsule balkanique* (Paris, 1918), 112–52 and map of *courants métanastiques*.
68. Vitorino Magalhães-Godinho, 'L'émigration portugaise du XVᵉ siècle à nos jours', *Hommage Labrousse*, 253–68.
69. A. M. Carr-Saunders, *World Population* (Oxford, 1936), 46–50.
70. J. Garnier, *La recherche des feux en Bourgogne aux XIVᵉ et XVᵉ siècles* (Dijon, 1876), 25–62.
71. E. Le Roy Ladurie, 'Les paysans français du XVIᵉ siècle', *Hommage Labrousse*, 333–52.
72. Pierre Goubert, 'Recent Theories and Research in French Population between 1500 and 1700', in Glass and Eversley (eds.), *Population in History*, 457–73.
73. Robert Mandrou, *La France au XVIIᵉ et XVIIIᵉ siècles* (Paris, 1970), 72–3.
74. Deyon, *Amiens*, 36.
75. Marcel Lachiver, *La population de Meulan du XVIIᵉ au XIXᵉ siècle* (Paris, 1969), 50.
76. Goubert, 'Recent Theories and Research in French Population', 469.
77. Jacques Dupâquier, 'Sur la population française au XVIIᵉ et au XVIIIᵉ siècle', *Rev. Hist.*, 239 (1968), 43–79; Bertrand Gille, *Les sources statistiques de l'histoire de France, Htes Et. Méd. Mod.*, 5 (1964).
78. *Mémoires des intendants sur l'état des généralités*, I, *Mémoire de la généralité de Paris*, ed. A. M. de Boislisle (Paris, 1881).
79. Listed in Gille, *Les sources statistiques*, 28–46.
80. Le comte de Boulainvilliers, *Etat de la France*, 6 vols. (London, [*c.* 1730]).
81. Published in *Mémoires des intendants*, I, 738–49.
82. Saugrain, *Dénombrement du royaume de France* (Paris, 1709); *Nouvelle dénombrement* (Paris, 1720).
83. Dupâquier, 'Sur la population française'.
84. Paul E. Vincent, 'French Demography in the Eighteenth Century', *Pop. Stud.*, 1 (1947–8), 44–71.
85. François de Dainville, 'Un dénombrement inédit au XVIIIᵉ siècle', *Pop.*, 7 (1952), 49–68.
86. L'abbé Expilly, *Dictionnaire géographique, historique et politique des Gaules et de la France*, 6 vols. (Paris, 1762–70).

87. E. Esmonin, 'L'abbé Expilly et ses travaux statistiques', *Rev. Hist. Mod. Cont.*, 4 (1957), 241–80.

88. M. Moheau, *Recherches et considérations sur la population de la France 1778* (Paris, 1778), ed. R. Gonnard, Coll. Ec. Réf. Soc. (1912).

89. Jacques Neckar, 'De l'administration des finances de la France', in *Oeuvres complètes*, ed. Baron de Staël, vol. IV (Paris, 1821), 288.

90. Charles Pouthas, *La population française pendant la première moitié du XIXᵉ siècle*, Inst. Nat. Et. Dém., Trav. et Doc., 25 (1956), 22; Toutain, *La population de la France de 1700 à 1959*.

91. P. Goubert, in E. Labrousse *et al.*, *Histoire économique et sociale de la France*, II, 74.

92. Raymond Rousseau, *La population de la Savoie jusqu'en 1861* (Paris, 1960), esp. maps 8, 9.

93. Tomas, 'Problèmes de démographie historique'.

94. Jacques Dupâquier, 'Les mystères de la croissance: soixante-trois paroisses d'Ile de France', *Hommage Labrousse*, 269–86.

95. *Id.*, 'Le peuplement du bassin parisien en 1711', *Ann. ESC*, 24 (1969), 976–98.

96. A. Cosemans, *De bevolking van Brabant in de XVIIᵈᵉ en XVIIIᵈᵉ eeuw*, Comm. Roy. Hist. (1939).

97. R. Boumans, 'L'évolution démographique d'Anvers (XVᵉ–XVIIᵉ siècle), *Bull. Stat.*, 34 (1948), 1683–93.

98. Quoted in Emile Brouette, 'Notes sur l'économie rurale du Namurois au siècle de Malheur (1500–1648)', *Rev. Nord*, 32 (1950), 105–18.

99. Roger Mols, 'Une source d'histoire démographique locale: les anciens registres paroissiaux de Theux', in *Miscellanea Historica in Honorem Alberti de Meyer*, 2 vols. (Louvain, 1946), II, 1048–64.

100. D. Van Assche-Vancauwenbergh, 'Deux villages du Brabant sous l'Ancien Régime: Bièrges et Overyse', in *Cinq études de démographie locale* (Brussels, 1963), 9–66.

101. Cosemans, *De bevolking van Brabant*, 58–9.

102. J. de Brouwere, 'Les dénombrements de la châtellenie d'Audenarde (1469–1801)', *Bull. Comm. Roy. Hist.*, 103 (1938), 513–46.

103. Calculated from tables in J. de Smet, 'Les dénombrements de la population dans la châtellenie d'Ypres (1610 et 1615 à 1620)', *ibid.*, 96 (1932), 255–332.

104. Etienne Hélin, 'Croissance démographique et transformation des campagnes: Chenée, Olne, Gemmerich aux XVIIIᵉ et XIXᵉ siècles', in *Cinq études de démographie locale* (Brussels, 1963), 195–240.

105. Charlier, *La peste à Bruxelles de 1667 à 1669*; Hans Van Werveke, 'La mortalité catastrophique en Flandre au XVIIᵉ siècle', *Actes Coll. Int. Dém. Hist.*, 457–64.

106. Van Houtte, *Leuven in 1740*, 244–8.

107. Joseph Ruwet, *L'agriculture et les classes rurales au pays de Hervé sous l'Ancien Régime*, Bibl. Fac. Liège, 100 (1943), 250–63.

108. Roger Mols, 'Die Bevölkerungsgeschichte Belgiens im Lichte der heutigen Forschung', *V.S.W.G.*, 46 (1959), 491–511.

109. A. Quatelet, 'Sur les anciens recensements de la population belge', *Bull. de la Commission Centrale de Statistiques* (Brussels), 3 (1847), 1–38.

110. A. M. van der Woude, 'Evolution démographique et progrès économique aux Pays-Bas: vue perspective', *Ann. Dém. Hist.*, 1965, 199–226.

111. Sir William Temple, *Observations upon the United Provinces of the Netherlands*, ed. G. N. Clark (Oxford, 1932), 46–7.

112. Violet Barbour, *Capitalism in Amsterdam in the 17th Century* (Baltimore, Md., 1950), 17–18.

113. Jan de Vries, *The Dutch Rural Economy in the Golden Age, 1500–1700* (New Haven, Conn., 1974), 102–4.

114. Mainly after J. A. Faber, 'Economic Development and Population Changes in the Netherlands up to 1800', *Third Int. Conf. Ec. Hist.*, IV, *Demography and Economy* (Paris, 1972), 67–78; Faber *et al.*, 'Population Changes and Economic Development in the Netherlands: A Historical Survey', *A.A.G. Bij.*, 12 (1965), 47–113.

115. J. A. Faber, 'Drie eeuwen Friesland: economische en sociale ontwikkelingen van 1500 tot 1800', *A.A.G. Bij.*, 17 (1972).

116. M. Kuhlmann, 'Bevölkerungsgeographie des Landes Lippe', *Forsch. D. Landesk.*, 76 (1954), 79–110.

117. Karlheinz Blaschke, *Bevölkerungsgeschichte von Sachsen bis zur Industriellen Revolution* (Weimar, 1967), 79.

118. Roger Mols, 'Population in Europe 1500–1700', in *The Fontana Economic History of Europe*, II (London, 1974), 38; the author does not indicate boundaries. K. Kotzschke claimed 20 million in 1600: *Deutsche Wirtschaftsgeschichte bis zum 17. Jahrhundert* (Leipzig, 1908), 131.

119. Gunther Franz, *Der Dreissigjahrige Krieg*, 5–21.

120. Quoted in Henry Kamen, *The Iron Century* (London, 1971), 42.

121. Quoted in W. Abel, *Geschichte der deutschen Landwirtschaft* (Stuttgart, 1962), 251.

122. K. Obermann, 'Quelques données statistiques sur les états de la Confédération Germanique dans la première moitié du XIXe siècle', *Ann. Dém. Hist.*, 1966, 79–98.

123. After Fritz Schulte, 'Die Entwicklung der gewerblichen Wirtschaft in Rheinland–Westfalen', *Schr. Rhein.–Westf. Wtgesch.*, 1 (1959), 47–8; figures marked with an asterisk are taken from Mirabeau, *De l'économie prussienne*, 4 vols. (London, 1788), I, 308, 311.

124. P. Levy, *Histoire linguistique d'Alsace et de la Lorraine*, 2 vols. (Paris, 1929), I, 264–6.

125. J. P. Süssmilch, *Die göttliche Ordnung in den Veränderungen des menschlichen Geschlechts*, 2 vols. (Berlin, 1762).

126. Hans Mauersperg, *Wirtschafts- und Sozialgeschichte zentraleuropäischer Städte in neueren Zeit* (Göttingen, 1960), 23–9.

127. Kurt B. Mayer, *The Population of Switzerland* (New York, 1952), 192–7.

128. W. Bickel, *Bevölkerungsgeschichte und Bevölkerungspolitik der*

Schweiz seit dem Ausgang des Mittelalters (Zurich, 1947), 89.

129. Hektor Ammann, 'Die Bevölkerung der Westschweiz im ausgehenden Mittelalter', *Festschrift Friedrich Emil Welti* (Aarau, 1937), 390–447.

130. Jean-François Bergier, *Problèmes de l'histoire économique de la Suisse* (Bern, 1968), 17–19.

131. Aksel Lassen, 'The Population of Denmark in 1660', *Sc. Ec. Hist. Rev.*, 13 (1965), 1–30; *id.*, 'The Population of Denmark 1660–1960', *ibid.* 134–57.

132. Gustaf Utterström, 'Population and Agriculture in Sweden', *ibid.* 9 (1961), 176–94.

133. N. Friberg, 'Population Growth in a Mining District in Sweden, 1650–1750, and its Economic Background', *Third Int. Conf. Ec. Hist.*, IV, *Demography and Economy* (Paris, 1972), 79–90.

134. Eino Jutikkala, 'The Great Finnish Famine in 1696–97', *Sc. Ec. Hist. Rev.*, 3 (1955), 48–63.

135. E. F. Heckscher, *An Economic History of Sweden* (Cambridge, Mass., 1954), 116–17; Frederick Hendricks, 'On the Vital Statistics of Sweden from 1749 to 1855', *Jn. Roy. Stat. Soc.*, 25 (1862), 111–74.

136. Gustaf Utterström, 'Some Population Problems in Pre-Industrial Sweden', *Sc. Ec. Hist. Rev.*, 2 (1954), 103–65.

137. Michael Drake, *Population and Society in Norway 1735–1865* (Cambridge, 1969), 45–62; *id.*, 'The Growth of Population in Norway 1735–1855', *Sc. Ec. Hist. Rev.*, 13 (1965), 97–127.

138. Irena Gieysztorowa, 'Badania nad historia zaludnienia Polski', *Kw. Hist. Kult. Mat.*, 11 (1963), 523–62.

139. *Id.*, 'Research into the Demographic History of Poland', *Acta Pol. Hist.*, 18 (1968), 5–17.

140. *Historia Polski*, Polish Academy of Science, vol. I, pt 2 (Warsaw, 1958), 618.

141. T. Korzon, *Wewnętrzne dzieje Polski za Stanisława Augusta*, 3 vols. (Warsaw, 1897), I, 78, 160–1.

142. *Historia Polski*, II, pt 1 (1958), 104–6.

143. Frank Lorrimer, *The Population of the Soviet Union*, League of Nations (Geneva, 1946).

144. Statistics mainly from K. Obermann, 'Quelques données statistiques', and *Raum und Bevölkerung in der Weltgeschichte*, ed. E. Kirsten, E. W. Buchholz and W. Kollmann, II (Würzburg, 1956).

145. A. Petranova, 'L'influence du développement des centres industriels sur les structures économiques, démographiques et sociales en Bohême du seizième au dix-huitième siècle', *Third Int. Conf. Ec. Hist.*, IV, *Demography and Economy* (Paris, 1972), 191–8.

146. Heinrich Rubner, 'En forêt de Bohême: immigration et émigration 1500–1960', *Ann. Dém. Hist.*, 1970, 135–42.

147. Pavla Horska, 'L'état actuel des recherches sur l'évolution de la population dans les pays tchèques aux XVIIIe et XIXe siècles', *Ann. Dém. Hist.*, 1967, 173–95; Vaclav Husa, 'Notes d'information sur les

sources et les recherches de démographie historique en Tchécoslovaquie', *Actes Coll. Int. Dém. Hist.*, 237–47.

148. Joseph Kovacsics, 'An Account of Research Work in Historical Demography in Hungary', *ibid.*, 249–72.

149. *The Complete Letters of Lady Mary Wortley Montagu*, I, 338–9.

150. Jozsef Kovacsics, 'Situation démographique de la Hongrie à la fin du XVIIIᵉ siècle (1789–1815)', *Ann. Dém. Hist.*, 1965, 83–104; *id.*, 'The Population of Hungary in the Eighteenth Century', *Third Int. Conf. Ec. Hist.*, vol. IV, *Demography and Economy* (Paris, 1972), 137–145.

151. O. L. Barkan, 'Essai sur les données statistiques des registres de recensement dans l'Empire Ottoman aux XVᵉ et XVIᵉ siècles', *Jn. Ec. Soc. Hist. Orient*, 1 (1958), 9–36.

152. Stefan Pascu, 'Les sources et les recherches démographiques en Roumanie', *Actes Coll. Int. Dém. Hist.*, 283–303; Traian Stoianovich, *A Study in Balkan Civilization* (New York, 1957), 164.

153. David Herlihy, 'The Tuscan Town in the Quattrocento: A Demographic Profile', *Med. Hum.*, n.s., 1 (1970), 81–109; *id.*, 'The Population of Verona in the First Century of Venetian Rule', in *Renaissance Venice*, ed. J. R. Hale (London, 1973), 91–120.

154. Pietro Donnazzolo and Mario Saibante, 'Lo sviluppo demografico di Verona e della sua provincia dalla fine del sec. XV ai giorni nostri', *Metron*, 6, 2–3 (1926), 56–180.

155. Maurice Aymard, 'Une croissance sélective: la population sicilienne au XVIIᵉ siècle', *Casa Veláz.*, 4 (1968), 203–27.

156. Daniele Beltrami, 'Saggio di storia dell'agricoltura nella repubblica di Venezia durante l'eta moderna', *Civ. Venez.*, 1 (1954), 13.

157. Jorge Nadal, *La población española (siglos XVI á XX)* (Barcelona, 1966), 20.

158. Albert Girard, 'La répartition de la population en Espagne dans les temps modernes: XVIᵉ, XVIIᵉ, XVIIIᵉ siècles', *Rev. Hist. Ec. Soc.*, 17 (1929), 347–62.

159. Nadal and Giralt, *La population catalane*, 19.

160. Michael Weisser, 'The Decline of Castile Revisited: The Case of Toledo', *Jn. Eur. Ec. Hist.*, 2 (1973), 614–40.

161. J. H. Elliott, 'The Decline of Spain', *P & P*, 20 (Nov. 1961), 52–75.

162. Bennassar, 'Organisation municipale et communautés d'habitants en temps de peste', 139–43; *id.*, *Recherches sur les grandes épidemies dans le nord de l'Espagne à la fin du XVIᵉ siècle* (Paris, 1969), 40–2.

163. Nadal, *La población española*, 53. The older work of Robert S. Smith, 'Barcelona "Bills of Mortality" and Population, 1457–1590', *Jn. Pol. Ec.*, 44 (1936), 84–93, gives slightly different totals.

164. Elliott, 'The Decline of Spain'.

165. José-Gentil da Silva, *En Espagne: développement économique, subsistance, décline* (Paris, 1965), 106–7; Richard Herr, *The Eighteenth Century Revolution in Spain* (Princeton, N.J., 1958), 86.

Chapter 3. The pattern of cities

1. G. Botero, 'A Treatise Concerning the Causes of the Magnificency and Greatness of Cities', in *The Reason of State*, trans. P. J. and D. P. Waley (New Haven, Conn., 1956), 259.

2. Quoted in G. G. Coulton, *From St. Francis to Dante* (London, 1907), 140.

3. Botero, 'Magnificency and Greatness of Cities', 26.

4. *Paris et ses historiens aux XIVe et XVe siècles*, ed. Le Roux de Lincy and L. M. Tisserand (Paris, 1867), 485–96.

5. Simone Roux, 'L'habitat urbain au Moyen Age: le quartier de l'Université à Paris', *Ann. ESC*, 24 (1969), 1196–219; Madeleine Jurgens and Pierre Couperie, 'Le logement à Paris aux XVIe et XVIIe siècles', *ibid.* 17 (1962), 488–50.

6. Martin Lister, *A Journey to Paris in the Year 1698*, ed. R. P. Stearns (Champagne–Urbana, Ill., 1967), 7.

7. Jean-Louis Bourgeon, 'L'Ile de la Cité pendant la Fronde: structure sociale', *Paris–Ile*, 13 (1962), 23–144.

8. Jean Favier, 'Les contributables parisiennes à la fin de la Guerre de Cent Ans', *Htes Et. Méd. Mod.*, 11 (1970), esp. p. 69.

9. Jean Vidalenc, 'L'approvisionnement de Paris en viande sous l'Ancien Régime', *Rev. Hist. Ec. Soc.*, 30 (1952), 116–32.

10. 'Marchés de Paris', in *Mémoires des intendants sur l'état de généralités*, I, *Mémoire de la généralité de Paris*, ed. A. M. de Boislisle (Paris, 1881), 656–75.

11. Louis Sebastien Mercier, *Tableau de Paris*, 2 vols. (Amsterdam, 1782), I, 220.

12. Lister, *A Journey to Paris*, 181; anon., *Description nouvelle de ce qu'il y a de plus remarquable dans la ville de Paris*, 2 vols. in 1 (Paris, 1717), II, 176.

13. J.-C. Goeury, 'Evolution démographique et sociale du Faubourg Saint-Germain', *Con. Hist. Dém. Rév. Fr.*, 25–60.

14. Quoted by Marcel Reinhard in 'La population des villes: sa mesure sous la Révolution et l'Empire', *Pop.*, 9 (1954), 278–88.

15. Bartolomé Bennassar, *Valladolid au Siècle d'Or; une ville de Castille et sa campagne au XVIe siècle* (Paris, 1967), 166.

16. Charles E. Kany, *Life and Manners in Madrid, 1750–1800* (Berkeley, Calif., 1932), 7–9.

17. R. Davico, 'Démographie et économie: ville et campagne en Piedmont a l'époque française', *Ann. Dém. Hist.*, 1968, 139–64.

18. Yves Renouard, 'Trois villes italiennes au XVe siècle', in *Etudes d'histoire médiévale* (Paris, 1968), 181–90.

19. See Lafréry's map of Rome, 1557.

20. Judith Hook, *The Sack of Rome* (London, 1972), 29.

21. Jean Delumeau, *Vie économique et sociale de Rome sous la seconde moitié du XVIe siècle*, *Bibl. Ec. Fr. Ath. Rome*, 184 (1957), 138–42. For Renaissance accounts of the city see *Codice topografico della città*

di Roma, 3 vols., ed. R. Valentini and G. Zucchetti, Fonti per la Storia d'Italia, 91 (1953), vol. III.

22. Delumeau, *Vie économique et sociale de Rome*, 626–46.
23. A. Cosemans, *De bevolking van Brabant in de XVII^{de} en XVIII^{de} eeuw*, Comm. Roy. Hist. (1939), 58–9, 211.
24. Władysław Tomkiewicz, 'Varsovie au XVIIe siècle', *Acta Pol. Hist.*, 15 (1967), 39–64.
25. *An Account of Sweden*, anon. but probably by John Robinson (London, 1694), 26.
26. A. H. Lybyer, 'Constantinople as Capital of the Ottoman Empire', *Am. Hist. Assn Ann. Rept*, 1 (1916), 373–88.
27. Robert Montran, *Istanbul dans la seconde moitié du XVIIe siècle*, Bibl. Arch. Hist. Inst. Fr. Arch., 12 (1962), 44–7.
28. *Memoirs of the Baron de Tott*, 3 vols. (Dublin, 1785), I, 35–51.
29. Montran, *Istanbul*, 97.
30. *Memoirs of the Baron de Tott*, I, 64–9.
31. Huguette et Pierre Chaunu, *Séville et l'Atlantique (1504–1650)*, 8 vols. in 10 (Paris, 1955–9), I, 12.
32. Ruth Pike, *Enterprise and Adventure: The Genoese in Seville and the Opening of the New World* (Ithaca, N.Y., 1966), 2–3.
33. Ramon Carande, *Carlos V y sus banqueros* (Madrid, 1943), 38.
34. Ruth Pike, *Aristocrats and Traders: Sevillian Society in the Sixteenth Century* (Ithaca, N.Y., 1972), 17. Estimates of population given in F. M. Padron, 'The Commercial World of Seville in Early Modern Times', *Jn. Eur. Ec. Hist.*, 2 (1973), 294–319, appear to be exaggerated.
35. Richard Heer, *The Eighteenth Century Revolution in Spain* (Princeton, N.J., 1958), 87.
36. Pierre Chaunu, 'Séville, pole de croissance?' in *Città mercanti dottrine nell'economia europea*, ed. A. Fanfani (Milan, 1964), 253–76.
37. C. R. Boxer, *The Portuguese Seaborne Empire, 1415–1825* (Harmondsworth, 1973), 4–5.
38. José-Augusto Franca, *La Lisbonne de Pombal* (Paris, 1965), 18–20.
39. Pierre Dardel, *Navires et marchandises dans les ports de Rouen et du Havre au XVIIIe siècle* (Paris, 1963), 238–52; *id.*, 'Les rélations maritimes et commerciales entre la France notamment les ports de Rouen et du Havre, et les ports de la mer baltique', *Ann. Norm.*, 19 (1969), 29–57; Michel Mollat, *Le commerce maritime normand à la fin du Moyen Age* (Paris, 1952), 297.
40. The definitive work on the rise of Antwerp is H. Van der Wee, *The Growth of the Antwerp Market and the European Economy*, 3 vols. (Louvain, 1963), II, *Interpretation*.
41. R. Boumans, 'L'évolution démographique d'Anvers', *Bull. Stat.*, 34 (1948), 1683–93.
42. Ludovico Guicciardini, *Description de to le pais-bas autrement dict la Germanie Inférieure ou Basse-Allemaigne* (Antwerp, 1567), 84–169. Also John J. Murray, *Antwerp in the Age of Plantin and Brueghel*

(Newton Abbot, 1972).

43. W. Brulez, 'Anwers de 1585 à 1650', *V.S.W.G.*, 55 (1967), 75–99; Jean-A. Van Houtte, 'Anvers', in *Città mercanti dottrine nell'economia europea*, ed. A. Fanfani (Milan, 1974), 297–319.

44. Guicciardini, *Description de to le pais-bas*, 252.

45. Kristof Glamann, *Dutch–Asiatic Trade 1620–1740* (Copenhagen, 1958), 13–14.

46. John J. Murray, *Amsterdam in the Age of Rembrandt* (Norman, Okla., 1967), 6.

47. Violet Barbour, *Capitalism in Amsterdam in the 17th Century* (Ann Arbor, Mich., 1963), 28.

48. Sir William Temple, *Observations upon the United Provinces of the Netherlands*, ed. G. N. Clark (Oxford, 1932), 94.

49. Cited in J. Delumeau, 'Démographie d'un port français sous l'Ancien Régime: Saint-Malo (1651–1750)', *XVIIᵉ S.*, nos. 86–7 (1970), 3–20.

50. Helen Liebel, 'Laissez-Faire vs. Mercantilism: The Rise of Hamburg and the Hamburg Bourgeoisie vs. Frederick the Great in the Crisis of 1763', *V.S.W.G.*, 52 (1965), 207–38.

51. *Handbuch der deutschen Wirtschafts- und Sozialgeschichte*, ed. H. Aubin and W. Zorn, I (Stuttgart, 1971), 441.

52. Justus Möser, quoted in *European Society in the Eighteenth Century*, ed. R. & E. Forster (New York, 1969), 185.

53. Hans Mauersperg, *Wirtschafts- und Sozialgeschichte zentraleuropäischer Städte in neuerer Zeit* (Göttingen, 1960), 40–7.

54. Jerzy Stankiewicz and Bohdan Szermer, *Gdańsk* (Warsaw, 1959), 82, 128; Wilhelm Franke, 'Der Volkszahl der deutschen Städte Ende des 18. und Anfang des 19. Jahrhunderts', *Pet. Mitt.*, 69 (1923), 70–4.

55. Figures from Franke, 'Der Volkszahl'.

56. J. Heers, 'Urbanisme et structure sociale à Gênes au moyen âge', *Studi Fanfani*, I, 369–412.

57. *Le journal d'un bourgeois de Mons (1505–1536)*, ed. Armand Louant, Comm. Roy. Hist. (1969), 132.

58. Montran, *Istanbul*, 36.

59. W. F. Robins, *The Story of Water Supply* (Oxford, 1946), 129–40.

60. J. Godechot, 'L'histoire sociale et économique de Toulouse au XVIIIᵉ siècle', *Ann. Midi*, 78 (1966), 363–74.

61. R. Gascon, 'Immigration et croissance au XVIᵉ siècle: l'exemple de Lyon (1529–1563)', *Ann. ESC, 25* (1970), 988–1001.

62. M. Rochefort, *L'organisation urbaine de l'Alsace*, Pub. Fac. Strasbourg, 139 (1960).

63. *Ibid.* 161.

64. Quoted in *A History of Technology*, ed. Charles Singer *et al.*, III (Oxford, 1957), 286.

65. Pierre Levedan, *Histoire de l'urbanisme: Renaissance et temps modernes* (Paris, 1959), 9–70.

66. Frederick R. Hiorns, *Townbuilding in History* (London, 1956), 227.

67. Fernand Braudel and Ruggiero Romano, *Navires et marchandises à*

l'entrée du port de Livourne (1547–1611), (Paris, 1951), 16.

68. M.-A. Lauguier, *Essai sur l'architecture* (1755), as quoted in E. A. Gutkind, *International History of City Development*, V, *Urban Development in Western Europe: France and Belgium* (New York, 1970), 125.

69. Lavedan, *Histoire de l'urbanisme*, 249–55.

70. Eli F. Heckscher, *An Economic History of Sweden* (Cambridge, Mass., 1954), 110.

71. Mack Walker, *German Home Towns: Community, State and General Estate 1648–1871* (London, 1971), 32.

72. Rochefort, *L'organisation urbaine de l'Alsace*, 14, 140–4.

73. Roger Mols, *Introduction à la démographie historique des villes d'Europe du XIVᵉ au XVIIIᵉ siècle*, 3 vols. (Louvain, 1955), II, 40–2.

74. Anton F. Büsching, *A New System of Geography* (London, 1762).

75. William Jacob, *A View of the Agriculture, Manufactures, Statistics and State of Society of Germany* (London, 1820), 234.

76. H. Samsonowicz, 'Das polnische Burgertum in der Renaissancezeit', *Stud. Hist.* (B), 53 (1963), 91–6.

77. Walker, *German Home Towns*, 221.

78. *Ibid.* 76.

79. *Correspondance des Contrôleurs-Généraux des Finances avec les provinces*, ed. A. M. de Boislisle (4 vols., Paris, 1874–97), I, 175–7.

80. Honoré de Balzac, *Béatrix*, edn of 1941, 319–23; author's trans.

81. Samsonowicz, 'Das polnische Burgertum'; A. Klima, 'Industrial Development in Poland, 1648–1781', *P & P*, no. 11 (1957), 87–99.

82. E. Martin, 'La population de la ville de Vannes au début et à la fin du XVIIIᵉ siècle', *Ann. Bret.*, 35 (1921–3), 610–26.

83. G. Roupnel, *La ville et la campagne au XVIIᵉ siècle: étude sur les populations du pays dijonnais* (Paris, 1955), 134.

84. Olwen H. Hufton, *Bayeux in the Late Eighteenth Century* (Oxford, 1967), 5.

85. J. Cuvelier, 'La population de Louvain aux XVIᵉ et XVIIᵉ siècles', *Ann. Soc. Arch. Brux.*, 22 (1908), 337–76.

86. Hufton, *Bayeux*, 41.

87. E. Martin, 'La population de Vannes'.

88. Roupnel, *La ville et la campagne*, 129.

89. *Ibid.* 158.

90. Hufton, *Bayeux*, 57–8.

91. Bennassar, *Valladolid au Siècle d'Or*, 215.

92. E. Martin, 'La population de Vannes'.

93. Hufton, *Bayeux*, 58.

94. *The Diary of Montaigne's Journey to Italy in 1580 and 1581*, trans. E. J. Trenchmann (London, 1929), 149–50.

95. J. Addison, *Remarks on Several Parts of Italy etc. in the Years 1701, 1702, 1703* (London, 1705), 182.

96. *Bishop Burnet's Travels through France, Italy, Germany and Switzerland* (London, 1750), 2.

97. Maurice Aymard, *Venise, Raguse et le commerce de blé pendant la seconde moitié du XVIIᵉ siècle* (Paris, 1966), 156–7.

98. Jean-François Bergier, 'Genève', in *Città mercanti dottrine nell'economia europea*, ed. A. Fanfani (Milan 1964), 151–69.

99. I. Batori, *Die Reichsstadt Augsburg im 18. Jahrhundert, Veröff. Planck*, 22 (1969).

100. J. Godard, 'Contribution à l'étude de l'histoire du commerce des grains à Douai du XIVᵉ au XVIIᵉ siècle', *Rev. Nord*, 27 (1944), 171–205; G. Bigwood, 'Gand et la circulation des grains en Flandre du XIVᵉ au XVIIIᵉ siècle', *V.S.W.G.*, 4 (1906), 397–460.

101. Aymard, *Venise, Raguse et le commerce de blé*, 17.

102. W. Naude, *Die Getreidehandelspolitik der europäischen Staaten vom 13. bis zum 18. Jahrhundert*, Acta Bor., 2 (1896), esp. 313–443.

103. *Paris et ses historiens aux XIVᵉ et XVᵉ siècles*, 485–96; Jean Meuvret, 'Le commerce des grains et des farines à Paris et les marchands parisiens à l'époque de Louis XIV', *Rev. Hist. Mod. Cont.*, 3 (1956), 169–203.

104. *Mémoires des intendants sur l'état des generalités*, I, *Mémoire de la généralité de Paris*, ed. A. M. de Boislisle (Paris, 1881), 1–397.

105. 'Marchés de Paris', in *ibid.* 656–75.

106. A. P. Usher, *The History of the Grain Trade in France 1400–1710* (Cambridge, Mass., 1913), 20–118.

107. Pierre Goubert, *Beauvais et le Beauvaisis de 1600 à 1730* (Paris, 1960), 261.

108. Maria Bogucka, 'Urząd Zapasów a konsumpcja Gdańska w pierwszej połowie XVII w.', *Kw. Hist. Kult. Mat.*, 18 (1970), 255–60.

109. S. P. Pach, 'Die Getreideversorgung der ungarischen Städte vom XV. bis XVII. Jahrhundert', *Jb. Nat. Stat.*, 179 (1966), 140–59.

110. 'Silks of Lyons', *Ciba Rev.*, no. 8 (1938).

111. Leon Halkin, *Une description inédite de la ville de Liège en 1705*, Bibl. Fac. Liège, 113 (1948), 23.

112. Jean Yernaux, *Contrats de travail liégeois du XVIIᵐᵉ siècle*, Comm. Roy. Hist (1941), 19–20.

113. E. Coornaert, 'Une capitale de la laine: Leyde', *Ann. ESC*, 1 (1946), 169–77.

114. Frédéric Mauro, *Le XVIᵉ siècle européen: aspects économiques* (Paris, 1966), 120–3.

115. E. Maugis, 'La saietterie à Amiens, 1480–1587', *V.S.W.G.*, 5 (1970), 1–114.

116. Pierre Deyon, *Amiens: capitale provinciale* (Paris, 1967), 179–83.

117. *Mémoires des intendants sur l'état des généralités*, I, 620; Goubert, *Beauvais et le Beauvaisis*, 258, 282–3; Georges Clause, 'L'industrie lainière rémoise à l'époque napoléonienne', *Rev. Hist. Mod. Cont.*, 17 (1970), 574–95.

118. Bennassar, *Valladolid au Siècle d'Or*, 101–3.

119. *Id.*, 'Medina del Campo: un exemple des structures urbaines de l'Espagne au XVIᵉ siècle', *Rev. Hist. Ec. Soc.*, 39 (1961), 474–95.

120. Domenico Sella, 'Les mouvements longs de l'industrie lainière à Venise aux XVIe et XVIIe siècles', *Ann. ESC*, 12 (1957), 29–45.

121. Heinrich Sieveking, 'Die genueser Seidenindustrie im 15. und 16. Jahrhundert', *Schm. Jb.*, 21 (1897), 101–33; Jacques Heers, *Gênes au XVe sièclé* (Paris, 1961), 230–51.

122. R. Romano, 'A Florence au XVIIe siècle: industries textiles et conjoncture', *Ann. ESC*, 7 (1952), 508–12.

123. E. Coornaert, *La draperie–sayetterie d'Hondschoote (XIVe–XVIIIe siècles)* (Rennes, 1930), 22–43.

124. P. Deyon and Alain Lottin, 'Evolution de la production textile à Lille aux XVIe et XVIIe siècles', *Rev. Nord*, 49 (1967), 23–33.

125. 'Description de Lille en 1698', in *Textes historiques sur Lille et le Nord de la France avant 1789*, Bibl. Soc. Hist. Dr. Flam., 5 (1931), 142–4.

126. Jean Lejeune, *La formation du capitalisme moderne dans la principauté de Liège au XVIe siècle*, Bibl. Fac. Liège, 87 (1939), 223.

127. Max Barkhausen, 'Verviers: Die Enstehung einer neuzeitlichen Industriedstadt im 17. und 18. Jahrhundert', *V.S.W.G.*, 47 (1960), 363–75; Georges Lefebvre, 'A Verviers: capitalisme et draperie', *Ann. ESC*, 5 (1950), 49–55.

128. Jeffry Kaplow, *Elbeuf during the Revolutionary Period: History and Social Structure* (Baltimore, Md., 1964), 22–3.

129. Jean Vidalenc, 'Les sociétés urbaines et les villes dans les arrondissements littoraux de la Seine-Inférieure sous le Premier Empire', in *Villes de l'Europe médiévale et de l'Europe occidentale du Moyen Age au XIXe siècle*, Ann. Fac. Nice, 9–10 (1969), 291–314.

Chapter 4. Agriculture

1. William Jacob, *A View of the Agriculture, Manufactures, Statistics and State of Society of Germany* (London, 1920), 102–3.

2. A list of exceptional years in the south of France is given in René Baehrel, *Une croissance: la Basse-Provence rurale (fin XVIe siècle–1789)* (Paris, 1961), 94–9.

3. Published in Duhamel de Monceau, *Practical Treatise of Husbandry* (London, 1759), 473–90.

4. Pierre Vilar, 'Réflexions sur la "crise de l'ancien type": "inégalités des récoltes" et "sous-développement" ', *Hommage Labrousse*, 38–58.

5. Catherine Rollet, 'L'effet des crises économiques au début du XIXe siècle sur la population', *Rev. Hist. Mod. Cont.*, 17 (1970), 391–410.

6. J. D. Post, 'A Study in Meteorological and Trade Cycle History: The Economic Crisis Following the Napoleonic Wars', *Jn. Ec. Hist.*, 34 (1974), 315–49.

7. André Thuillier, *Economie et société nivernais au début du XIXe siècle* (Paris, 1966), 97–131.

8. Eberhard Weis, 'Ergebnisse eines Vergleichs der grundherrschaftlichen Strukturen Deutschlands und Frankreichs vom 13. bis zum Ausgang de 18. Jahrhunderts', *V.S.W.G.*, 57 (1970), 1–14.

9. Pierre Goubert, *Beauvais et le Beauvaisis de 1600 à 1730* (Paris, 1960), 156.

10. Henri Sée, *Esquisse d'une histoire du régime agraire* (Paris, 1921), 16.

11. Robert Forster, *The Nobility of Toulouse in the Eighteenth Century: A Social and Economic Study* (Baltimore, Md., 1960), 22.

12. Ivan Delatte, *Les classes rurales dans la principalité de Liège*, Bibl. Fac. Liège, 105 (1945), 48.

13. Jaime Vicens Vives, *An Economic History of Spain* (Princeton, N.J., 1969), 165.

14. See for example P. J. Jones, 'From Manor to Mezzadria: A Tuscan Case-Study in the Medieval Origins of Modern Agrarian Society', in *Florentine Studies*, ed. N. Rubinstein (London, 1968), 193–241.

15. E. Le Roy Ladurie, 'Sur Montpellier et sa campagne au XVIe et XVIIIe siècles', *Ann. ESC*, 12 (1957), 223–30.

16. G. Roupnel, *La ville et la campagne au XVIIe siècle: étude sur les populations du pays dijonnais* (Paris, 1955), 205–49.

17. Weis, 'Ergebnisse eines Vergleichs der grundherrschaftlichen Strukturen Deutschlands und Frankreichs'.

18. Jean Georgelin, 'Une grande propriété en Vénétie au XVIIIe siècle: Anguillara', *Ann. ESC*, 23 (1968), 483–519.

19. Jerome Blum, 'The Rise of Serfdom in Eastern Europe', *Am. Hist. Rev.*, 62 (1956–7), 807–36.

20. I. Simkovics, 'Le servage héréditaire en Hongrie aux 16–17e siècles', in *La Renaissance et la Réformation en Pologne et en Hongrie*, *Stud. Hist.* (B), 53 (1963), 47–89.

21. Leonid Żytkowicz, 'The Peasant's Farm and the Landlord's Farm in Poland from the 16th to the Middle of the 18th Century', *Jn. Eur. Ec. Hist.*, 1 (1972), 135–54.

22. James C. Miller, 'The Nobility in Polish Renaissance Society', unpublished Ph.D. thesis, Indiana University (1976), puts the typical szlachcic's demesne even smaller: 3 *lany* (*c*. 50 hectares) in the early sixteenth century and 3.5–4 near its end.

23. Leonid Żytkowica, 'Następstwa ekonomiczne i społeczne niskich plonów zbóz w Polsce od połowy XVI do połowy XVIII wieku', *Rocz. Dz. społ. Gosp.*, 34 (1973), 1–30.

24. Andrzej Wyczański, 'Proba oszacowania obrotu żytem w Polsce XVI w.', *Kw. Hist. Kult. Mat.*, 9 (1961), 23–33; Leonid Zytkowicz, 'An Investigation into Agricultural Production in Masowia in the First Half of the 17th Century', *Acta Pol. Hist.*, 18 (1968), 99–118.

25. W. Abel, 'Die landwirtschaftlichen Grossbetriebe Deutschlands', *Int. Conf. Ec. Hist., Stockholm: Communications* (Paris, 1960), 311–19; also *id.*, 'Landwirtschaft 1500–1648', in *Handbuch der deutschen Wirtschafts- und Sozialgeschichte*, ed. H. Aubin and W. Zorn, I (Stuttgart, 1971), 394–5.

26. Rudolf Berthold, 'Einige Bemerkungen über den Entwicklungsstand des bauerlichen Ackerbaus vor den Agrarreformen des 19. Jahrhunderts', in his *Beiträge zur deutschen Wirtschafts- und Sozialgeschichte*

des 18. und 19. Jahrhunderts (Berlin, 1962), 81–131.

27. W. Abel, *Geschichte der deutschen Landwirtschaft* (Stuttgart, 1962), 188.

28. Werner Conze, 'L'émancipation des paysans d'après de récents travaux allemands', *Cah. Hist. Mond.*, 1 (1953), 179–94; Béla K. Kiraly, 'The Emancipation of the Serfs of East Central Europe', *Antem.*, 15 (1971), 63–85; Sée, *Esquisse d'une histoire du régime agraire*, 13–15, 27–8.

29. *Introduction to European Society in the Eighteenth Century*, ed. R. and E. Forster (New York, 1969), 100.

30. Pierre Goubert, 'The French Peasantry of the Seventeenth Century', *P & P*, 10 (1956), 55–77; Alun Davies, 'The Origins of the French Peasant Revolution', *Hist.*, 49 (1964), 24–41.

31. Olwen H. Hufton, *The Poor of Eighteenth Century France* (Oxford, 1974), 69–106, esp. 73.

32. *The Characters of Jean de la Bruyère*, trans. Henri van Laun, XI (London, 1929), 128.

33. Robert Darlington, *The View of France, 1604*, Shakespeare Association Facsimiles, 13 (Oxford, 1936).

34. Paul Raveau, *L'agriculture et les classes paysannes* (Paris, 1926), 39; *id.*, 'L'agriculture et les classes paysannes dans le Haut-Poitou au XVIe siècle', *Rev. Hist. Ec. Soc.*, 12 (1924), 1–52.

35. Félix Ferrand, 'La propriété rurale au milieu du XVIIe siècle dans la commune de Pontcharra (Haut-Grésivaudan)', *Bull. Phil. Hist.*, 1957, 267–97.

36. Denise Leymond, 'La communauté de Duravel au XVIIIe siècle', *Ann. Midi*, 79 (1967), 363–85.

37. Delatte, *Les classes rurales dans la principalité de Liège*, 110.

38. Joseph Ruwet, *L'agriculture et les classes rurales au pays de Hervé sous l'Ancien Régime*, Bibl. Fac. Liège, 100 (1943), 235.

39. Berthold, 'Einige Bemerkungen über den Entwicklungsstand des bauerlichen Ackerbaus vor den Agrarreformen'.

40. Giorgio Doria, *Uomini e terri di un borgo collinare* (Milan, 1968), 10.

41. Cited in Abel, *Geschichte der deutschen Landwirtschaft*, 194.

42. Raveau, 'L'agriculture et les classes paysannes dans le Haut-Poitou'.

43. R. Forster, *The Nobility of Toulouse*, 55–7; *id.*, 'Obstacles to Agricultural Growth in Eighteenth Century France', *Am. Hist. Rev.*, 75 (1970), 1600–15.

44. P. de Saint-Jacob, *Les paysans de la Bourgogne du nord au dernier siècle de l'Ancien Régime*, Pub. Univ. Dijon, 21 (1960), 152–3.

45. Forster, 'Obstacles to Agricultural Growth'.

46. *Ibid.*

47. Vauban, 'Description de l'élection de Vézelay', in *Projet d'une dixme royale*, ed. E. Coornaert (Paris, 1933), 279.

48. R.-J. Bernard, 'L'alimentation paysanne en Gévaudan au XVIIIe siècle', *Ann. ESC*, 24 (1969), 1449–63.

49. *Locke's Travels in France 1675–1679*, ed. John Lough (Cambridge, 1953), 237.

50. *The Travel Diaries of Thomas Robert Malthus*, ed. Patricia James (Cambridge, 1966), 60.

51. Quoted in Anne-Marie Piuz, 'Alimentation populaire et sous-alimentation au XVIIᵉ siècle: le cas de Genève', *Schw. Zt. Gesch.*, 18 (1968), 23–46.

52. J.-J. Hémardinquer, 'Note sur l'alimentation à la fin du XVIIIᵉ siècle', *Ann. ESC*, 23, 2 (1968), 819–22.

53. A. Wyczański, 'Uwagi o konsumpcji żywności w Polsce XVI w.', *Kw. Hist. Kult. Mat.*, 8 (1960), 15–40.

54. Etienne Juillard, *La vie rurale dans la plaine de Basse-Alsace*, Pub. Fac. Strasbourg, 123 (1953), 39; *id.*, 'Villes et campagnes: la région du Rhin moyen avant la révolution industrielle', in *Eventail de l'histoire vivante*, 2 vols. (Paris, 1953), I, 151–3.

55. B. H. Slicher van Bath, *The Agrarian History of Western Europe, A.D. 500–1850* (London, 1963), 264–5.

56. Henri Fréville, *L'intendance de Bretagne (1689–1790)*, 2 vols. (Rennes, 1953), I, 27.

57. Olivier de Serres, *Le théâtre d'agriculture et mesnage des champs* (Paris, 1605 edn), 108; Ruwet, *L'agriculture et les classes rurales au pays de Hervé*, 159.

58. Robert Gradmann, *Der Getreidebau im deutschen und römischen Altertum* (Jena, 1909), 48–57, 80–99.

59. Berthold, 'Einige Bemerkungen über den Entwicklungsstand des bauerlichen Ackerbaus vor den Agrarreformen'.

60. Quoted in Abel, *Geschichte der deutschen Landwirtschaft*, 300.

61. A lease of 1596 cited in Raveau, 'L'agriculture et les classes paysannes dans le Haut-Poitou'.

62. Georges Lefebvre, *Etudes orléanaises, I. Contributions à l'étude des structures sociales à la fin du XVIIIᵉ siècle*, Comm. Hist. Ec. Soc. Rév. Fr., Mém. et Doc., 15 (1962), 40–3; Jean Jacquart, 'La productivité agricole dans la France du Nord aux XVIᵉ et XVIIᵉ siècles', *Third Int. Conf. Ec. Hist.*, II, *Production et productivité agricole* (Paris, 1968), 65–74.

63. Michel Fontenay, 'Paysans et marchands ruraux de la vallée de l'Essonnes dans la seconde moitié du XVIIᵉ siècle', *Paris–Ile*, 9 (1957–8), 157–282.

64. Abel Poitrineau, *La vie rurale en Basse-Auvergne au XVIIIᵉ siècle (1726–1789)*, Pub. Fac. Lett. Clermont-Ferrand, 2nd ser., 23 (1965), 266–9.

65. Bernard, 'L'alimentation paysanne en Gévaudan'.

66. Eugène Sol, 'Les céréales inférieures en Quercy: les prix de 1751 à 1789', *Rev. Hist. Ec. Soc.*, 24 (1938), 335–55.

67. Quoted in Thomas F. Sheppard, *Lourmarin in the Eighteenth Century* (Baltimore, Md., 1971), 11.

68. Lefebvre, *Etudes orléanaises*, I, 42.

69. Jean Delvert, 'L'évolution économique de la plaine d'Alençon', *Ann. Norm.*, 2 (1952), 263–79.

70. Lefebvre, *Etudes orléanaises*, I, 42.
71. Juillard, *La vie rurale en Basse-Auvergne*, 36–9.
72. *The Travel Dairies of Malthus*, 41.
73. Diedrich Saalfeld, 'Die Produktion und Intensität der Landwirtschaft in Deutschland und angrenzenden Gebieten um 1800', *Zt. Aggesch.*, 15 (1967), 137–75.
74. Berthold, 'Einige Bermerkungen über den Entwicklungsstand des bauerlichen Ackerbaus vor den Agrarreformen'.
75. Christof Römer, 'Das Kloster Berge bei Magdeburg und seine Dörfer 968–1565', *Veröff. Planck*, 30 (1970), 124–5.
76. A. Wyczański, 'Tentative Estimate of Polish Rye Trade in the Sixteenth Century', *Acta Pol. Hist.*, 4 (1961), 119–31.
77. Jerzy Topolski, *Gospodarstwo wiejski w dobrach Arcybiskupstwa Gnieźnieńskiego od XVI do XVIII wieku* (Poznań, 1958), 409.
78. Berthold, 'Einige Bemerkungen', 99.
79. François Matejek, 'La production agricole dans les pays tchécoslovaques à partir du XVIe siècle jusqu'à la première guerre mondiale', *Third Int. Conf. Ec. Hist.*, II, *Production et productivité agricole* (Paris, 1968), 205–19.
80. Zs. Kirilly and István N. Kiss, 'Productivité de céréales et exploitations paysannes en Hongrie aux XVIe et XVIIe siècles', *Ann. ESC,* 23 (1968), 1211–36.
81. František Sedlák, 'Obilná produkcia a výnos pôdy na panstvách šmtava', *Historické Štúdie* (Bratislava), 13 (1968), 29–50.
82. N. J. G. Pounds, 'Barton Farming in Eighteenth Century Cornwall', *Jn. Roy. Institution of Cornwall* (Truro), 7, 1 (1973), 55–75.
83. François Gay, 'Production, prix et rentabilité de la terre en Berry au XVIIIe siècle', *Rev. Hist. Ec. Soc.*, 36 (1958), 399–411.
84. B. H. Slicher van Bath, 'Yield Ratios', *A.A.G. Bij.*, 10 (1963).
85. A. Wyczański, 'Le niveau de la récolte des céréales en Pologne du XVIe au XVIIIe siècle', *Int. Conf. Ec. Hist., Stockholm: Communications* (Paris, 1960), 585–90.
86. Wojciech Szczygielski, 'Le rendement de la production agricole en Pologne du XVIe au XVIIIe siècle sur le fond européen', *Kw. Hist. Kult. Mat.*, 14 (*Ergon* suppl.) (1966), 795–803.
87. Georgelin, 'Une grande propriété en Vénétie: Anguillara'.
88. Pierre Goubert, 'Les techniques agricoles dans les pays picards aux XVIIe et XVIIIe siècles', *Rev. Hist. Ec. Soc.*, 35 (1957), 24–40.
89. Quoted in Hufton, *The Poor of Eighteenth Century France*, 276.
90. Cited by Lefebvre in *Etudes orléanaises*, I, 192.
91. *The Whole Art and Trade of Husbandry, Contained in Foure Bookes* (London, 1614).
92. *Documents de l'histoire de la Normandie*, ed. Michel de Boüard (Paris, 1972), 224–5.
93. Georges Lefebvre, *Les paysans du nord pendant la Révolution Française* (Lille, 1924), 195–6.
94. R. J. Forbes, 'The Rise of Food Technology (1500–1900)', *Janus*

(Amsterdam), 47 (1958), 101–27, 139–55.
95. J.-J. Hémardinquer, 'Les débuts du maïs en Méditerranée', *Mélanges F. Braudel*, I, 227–33.
96. Virginia Rau, 'Large-Scale Agricultural Enterprise in Post-Medieval Portugal', *First Int. Conf. Ec. Hist., Stockholm: Communications* (Paris, 1960), 425–32; Fernand Braudel, *Capitalism and Material Life 1400–1800* (London, 1973), 112–13.
97. Gabriel Bernet, 'L'économie d'un village du Lauragais au XVIIᵉ siècle: le consulat de Pugnères de 1593 à 1715', *Ann. Midi*, 78 (1966), 481–512; Georges Frêche, 'Une enquête sur les prix des produits agricoles dans la région toulousain: XVᵉ–XIXᵉ siècle', *Ann. Midi*, 81 (1969), 17–39.
98. H. L. Duhamel de Monceau, *Practical Treatise of Husbandry* (London, 1759), 283–6.
99. L. Ligeron, 'Notes sur la culture du maïs dans la vallée moyenne de la Saône', *Ann. Bourg.*, 40 (1968), 197–204.
100. Troian Stoianovich and George C. Haupt, 'Le maïs arrive dans les Balkans', *Ann. ESC*, 17 (1962), 84–93.
101. *Locke's Travels in France*, 236.
102. Imre Wellmann, 'Systemy uprawy roli na Węgrzech w XVIII w.', *Kw. Hist. Kult. Mat.*, 8 (1960), 479–98.
103. Forbes, 'The Rise of Food Technology'; also R. N. Salaman, *The History and Social Influence of the Potato* (Cambridge, 1949).
104. Slicher van Bath, *The Agrarian History of Western Europe*, 266–8.
105. Wilhelm Abel in Hermann Aubin and Wolfgang Zorn (eds.), *Handbuch der deutschen Wirtschafts- und Sozialgeschichte*, I (Stuttgart, 1971), 520.
106. Octave Festy, *L'agriculture pendant la Révolution Française: l'utilisation des jachères 1789–1795* (Paris, 1950), 89–144.
107. G. Désert, 'La couture de la pomme de terre dans le Calvados au XIXᵉ siècle', *Ann. Norm.*, 5 (1955), 261–70; Jean Vidalenc, 'L'agriculture dans les départements normands à la fin du Premier Empire', *ibid.* 7 (1957), 179–201.
108. Le comte de Chaptal, *De l'industrie française* (Paris, 1819), 147.
109. E. F. Heckscher, *An Economic History of Sweden* (Cambridge, Mass., 1954), 150–1.
110. This account relies heavily on Noel Deerr, *The History of Sugar*, 2 vols. (London, 1950), II, 471–500.
111. Roland Villeneuve, 'Le financement de l'industrie sucrière en France entre 1815 et 1850', *Rev. Hist. Ec. Soc.*, 38 (1960), 285–319; Fernand Lentacker, 'Sucre et betterave dans le département du Nord à la fin du Premier Empire', *Rev. Nord*, 36 (1954), 325–7.
112. Chaptal, *De l'industrie française*, 159.
113. Joseph Halkin, 'Etude historique sur la culture de la vigne en Belgique', *Bull. Soc. d'Art et d'Histoire du Diocèse de Liège*, 9 (1895), 1–146; W. Abel, 'Zur Entwicklung des Sozialprodukts in Deutschland im 16. Jahrhundert', *Jb. Nat. Stat.*, 173 (1961), 448–89.

114. Ludovico Guicciardini, *Description de to le pais-bas autrement dict la Germanie Inférieure ou Basse-Allemaigne* (Antwerp, 1567), 9.
115. Kirilly and Kiss, 'Productivité de céréales en Hongrie'.
116. *Mémoires historiques du comte Betlem-Niklos* (Amsterdam, 1736), I, 268.
117. A. Huetz de Lemps, 'Le vignoble de la "Tierra de Medina" aux XVIIᵉ et XVIIIᵉ siècles', *Ann. ESC*, 12 (1957), 403–17.
118. *Id.*, 'Les terroirs en Vieille Castille et Léon', *Ann. ESC*, 17 (1962), 239–51.
119. Robert Boutruche, *La crise d'une société: seigneurs et paysans du Bordelais pendant la Guerre de Cent Ans* (Paris, 1947).
120. *Documents de l'histoire de Normandie*, 232; Vidalenc, 'L'agriculture dans les départements normands'.
121. Roger Dion, *Histoire de la vigne et du vin en France des origines au XIXᵉ siècle* (Paris, 1959).
122. Forbes, 'The Rise of Food Technology'.
123. Baehrel, *Une croissance: la Basse-Provence rurale*, 123.
124. Suzanne Savey, 'Essai de reconstitution de la structure agraire des villages de Sardan et d'Aspères (Gard) sous l'ancien régime à l'aide des compoix', *Ann. Midi*, 81 (1969), 41–54.
125. Delvert, 'L'évolution économique de la plaine d'Alençon'.
126. Jean Vidalenc, 'La vie économique des départements méditerranéens pendant l'Empire', *Rev. Hist. Mod. Cont.*, 1 (1954), 165–96.
127. Olivier de Serres, *Le théatre d'agriculture*, 486.
128. Lucien Badey, 'Le peuplement du Vivarais à la fin du XVIIIᵉ siècle', *Rev. Hist. Ec. Soc.*, 27 (1948–9), 127–52.
129. Arthur Young, *Travels in France during the Years 1787, 1788, 1789* (London, 1915), 107; Lefebvre, *Les paysans du nord*, 194–5.
130. Braudel, *Capitalism and Material Life*, 168–9.
131. R. J. Forbes, 'Food and Drink', in *A History of Technology*, ed. Charles Singer, E. J. Holmyard, A. R. Hall and T. E. Williams, III (Oxford, 1957), 11.
132. Lefebvre, *Les paysans du nord*, 195; Abel, *Geschichte der deutschen Landwirtschaft*, 209.
133. *Documents de l'histoire de Normandie*, 231.
134. *Maison Rustique* (Paris, 1616 edn), 411.
135. Braudel, *Capitalism and Material Life*, 169–70.
136. Poitrineau, *La vie rurale en Basse-Auvergne au XVIIIᵉ siècle*, 265.
137. Topolski, *Gospodarstwo wiejski w dobrach Arcybisckupstwa Gnieźnieńskiego*, 23–5.
138. Zofia Podwińska, 'Origines et propagation de la charrue sur les territoires polonais', *Kw. Hist. Kult. Mat.*, 8 (*Ergon* suppl.) (1960), 300–10.
139. F. Braudel, *The Mediterranean and the Mediterranean World in the Age of Philip II*, 2 vols. (London, 1972–3), I, 426.
140. Olivier de Serres, *Le théatre d'agriculture*, 74.
141. *Ibid.* 102–3.

142. Forster, *The Nobility of Toulouse in the Eighteenth Century*, 44.
143. See esp. Václav Husa, *Traditional Crafts and Skills* (Prague, 1967), pls. 115–21.
144. B. H. Slicher van Bath, 'Les problèmes fondamentaux de la société pré-industrielle en Europe occidentale', *A.A.G. Bij.*, 12 (1965), 3–46.
145. Abel, 'Zur Entwicklung des Sozialprodukts in Deutschland im 16. Jahrhundert'; J.-P. Barry and E. Le Roy Ladurie, 'Histoire agricole et phytogéographie', *Ann. ESC*, 17 (1962), 434–47; Jean-Jacques Letrait, 'Les actes d'habitation en Provence 1460–1560', *Bull. Phil. Hist.*, 1965, 183–226.
146. Slicher van Bath, *The Agrarian History of Western Europe*, 214–15.
147. Paul Wagret, *Polderlands* (London, 1968), 11.
148. Rex Wailes, 'A Note on Windmills', in *A History of Technology*, ed. C. Singer *et al.*, II (Oxford, 1956), 623–8.
149. W. Abel, 'Landwirtschaft 1500–1648', 387.
150. R. Blanchard, *La Flandre* (Paris, 1906), 171.
151. Abel Briquet, *Le littoral du nord de la France et son évolution morphologique* (Paris, 1930), 378–9.
152. J. Duhergne, *Le Bas-Poitou à la veille de la Révolution, Comm. Hist. Ec. Soc. Rév. Fr., Mém. et Doc.*, 16 (1963), 33–6.
153. Carlo Poni, 'Hydraulic Systems in the Venetian States in the Second Half of the XVIth Century', *Third Int. Conf. Ec. Hist.*, II, *Production et productivité agricole* (Paris, 1968), 61–3; Angelo Ventura, 'Considerazioni sull'agricoltura veneta e sulla accumulazione originaria del capitale nei secoli XVI e XVII', *Stud. Stor.*, 9 (1968), 674–722; S. J. Woolf, 'Venice and the Terrafirma: Problems of Change from Commercial to Landed Activities', in B. Pullan (ed.), *Crisis and Change in the Venetian Economy* (London, 1968), 175–203.
154. F. Overbeck, K. O. Münnich, L. Aletsee and F. R. Averdiek, 'Das Alter des 'Grenzhorizonts' nord-deutscher Hochmoore nach Radiocarbon Datierung', *Flora* (Stuttgart), 145 (1957), 37–71.
155. Lefebvre, *Les paysans du nord*, 217–18; Ernest Labrousse, Pierre Léon, Pierre Goubert, Jean Bouvier, Charles Carrière and Paul Harsin, *Histoire économique et sociale de la France*, II, *1660–1789* (Paris, 1970), 427–8.
156. Saint-Jacob, *Les paysans de la Bourgogne du nord*.
157. Labrousse *et al.*, *Histoire économique et sociale*, II, 429.
158. Zenon Guldon, 'Zmiany areału uprawnego i zaludnienia w badaniach nad osadnictwem nowożytnym', *Kw. Hist. Kult. Mat.*, 10 (1962), 653–61.
159. Vauban, in *Projet d'une dixme royale*, 165.
160. Savey, 'Essai de reconstitution de la structure agraire des villages de Sardan et d'Aspères (Gard)'.
161. Saalfeld, 'Die Produktion und Intensität der Landwirtschaft in Deutschland und angrenzenden Gebieten'.
162. Tadeusz Sobczak, 'O pierwszej statystyce użytków rolnych w Królestwie Polskim', *Kw. Hist. Kult. Mat.*, 12 (1963), 429–49.

163. *The Travel Diaries of Malthus*, 109.
164. M. de Réaumur, 'Réflexions sur l'état des bois du royaume', *Mém. Acad. Roy. Sci.*, 1721, 284–301.
165. M. de Buffon, 'Mémoire sur la conservation et le rétablissement des forêts', *ibid.* 1739, 140–56.
166. 'Notice sur l'état des bois et des forêts en France, et particulièrement dans le midi de la république', *Jn. Mines*, 4, 21 (1972), 49–64.
167. Henri Sée, 'Les forêts et la question du déboisement en Bretagne à la fin de l'Ancien Régime', *Ann. Bret.*, 36 (1924), 1–30, 355–79.
168. Arvo M. Soininen, 'Burn-Beating as the Technical Basis of Colonisation in Finland in the 16th and 17th Centuries', *Sc. Ec. Hist. Rev.*, 7 (1959), 150–66; F. Skubbeltrang, 'The History of the Finnish Peasant', *ibid.* 12 (1964), 165–80; W. R. Mead, *Farming in Finland* (London, 1953), 44–9.
169. F. Monkhouse, *The Belgian Kempenland* (Liverpool, 1949), 37–9.
170. *Documents de l'histoire de Normandie*, 230.
171. Abel, *Geschichte der deutschen Landwirtschaft*, 228–30.
172. Goubert, *Beauvais et le Beauvaisis*, 93–4, 110.
173. *Documents de l'histoire de Normandie*, 230.
174. F. H. Gilbert, *Traité des prairies artificielles* (1789), quoted in Festy, *L'agriculture pendant la Révolution Française*, 145–6.
175. Vidalenc, 'L'agriculture dans les départements normands'; Jean-Michel Lévy, 'Situation économique et esprit public en Basse-Normandie lors de l'aventure fédéraliste (été 1793)', *Ann. Hist. Rév. Fr.*, 35 (1963), 215–28.
176. *Documents de l'histoire de Normandie*, 229.
177. Fréville, *L'intendance de Bretagne*, I, 27.
178. Léon Dubreuil, 'Le paysan breton au XVIIIᵉ siècle', *Rev. Hist. Ec. Soc.*, 12 (1924), 478–92.
179. Jean Vidalenc, 'L'approvisionnement de Paris en viande sous l'ancien régime', *Rev. Hist. Ec. Soc.*, 30 (1952), 116–32.
180. James L. Goldsmith, 'Agricultural Specialization and Stagnation in Early Modern Auvergne', *Agr. Hist.*, 47 (1973), 216–34; Poitrineau, *La vie rurale en Basse-Auvergne au XVIIIᵉ siècle*, 291.
181. Guicciardini, *Description de to le pais-bas*, 240.
182. Sir William Temple, *Observations upon the United Provinces of the Netherlands*, ed. G. N. Clark (Oxford, 1972), 79.
183. Lefebvre, *Les paysans du nord*, 215.
184. Ruwet, *L'agriculture et les classes rurales au pays de Hervé*, 62–6.
185. J.-F. Bergier, *Problèmes de l'histoire économique de la Suisse* (Bern, 1968), 50.
186. Ferdinand Tremel, 'Zur Geschichte des Viehhandels aus Steiermark nach Tirol', *Festschrift zum 70. Geburtstag von Fritz Popelka*, Veröffentlichungen des Steiermärkischen Landesarchives, 2 (Graz, 1960), 98.
187. Lioba Beyer, *Der Siedlungenbereich von Jerzens im Pitztal*, *Westf. Geogr. Stud.*, 21 (1969), 26.

188. Römer, 'Das Kloster Berge bei Magdeburg', 124–5.
189. Quoted in *Handbuch der deutschen Wirtschafts- und Sozialgeschichte*, ed. H. Aubin and W. Zorn, I (Stuttgart, 1971), 492.
190. Topolski, *Gospodarstwo wiejski w dobrach Arcybiskupstwa Gnieźnieńskiego*, 410.
191. H. Wiese and J. Bölts, *Rinderhandel und Rinderhaltung im nordwesteuropäischen Küstengebiet vom 15. bis zum 19. Jahrhundert* (Stuttgart, 1966), 93.
192. H. Wiese, 'Die Fleischversorgung der nordwesteuropäischen Grossstädte vom XV. bis XIX. Jahrhundert unter besonderer Berücksichtigung des interterritorialen Rinderhandels', *Jb. Nat. Stat.*, 179 (1966), 125–39.
193. Henry Marczali, *Hungary in the Eighteenth Century* (Cambridge, 1910), 47–61.
194. Wiese, 'Die Fleischversorgung der nordwesteuropäischen Grossstädte'.
195. Gertrud Schröder-Lembke, 'Englische Einflüsse auf die deutsche Gutswirtschaft im 18. Jahrhundert', *Zt. Aggesch.*, 12 (1964), 29–48.
196. D. Faucher, 'L'avortement de la renaissance agricole à la fin du XVIe siècle', *Congrès de Rodez, 1958*, Sociéte des Lettres et Arts de l'Aveyron (Rodez, 1958); Lefebvre, *Les paysans du nord*, 206–10.
197. B. H. Slicher van Bath, 'Agriculture in the Low Countries (*ca.* 1600–1800)', *Relazioni del X. Congresso Internationale di Scienze Storiche*, IV (Florence, 1955), 169–203.
198. Michel Morineau, 'Y a-t-il eu une révolution agricole en France au XVIIIe siècle?' *Rev. Hist.*, 239 (1968), 299–326.
199. Heckscher, *An Economic History of Sweden*, 156–7; Sven Dahl, 'Strip Fields and Enclosures in Sweden', *Sc. Ec. Hist. Rev.*, 9 (1961), 56–67.
200. H. L. Duhamel de Monceau, *Traité de la culture des terres*, 6 vols. (Paris, 1753–61).
201. *Id., Practical Treatise of Husbandry*.
202. André J. Bourde, *The Influence of England on the French Agronomes* (Cambridge, 1953), 68.
203. Schröder-Lembke, 'Englische Einflusse auf die deutsche Gutswirtschaft'.
204. Jacob, *A View of the Agriculture . . . of Germany*, 88, 101, 301.
205. Heckscher, *An Economic History of Sweden*, 152–3.
206. Arvo M. Soininen, 'Burn-Beating'; Mead, *Farming in Finland*, 43–50.
207. Young, *Travels in France*, 7.

Chapter 5. Manufacturing and mining

1. W. W. Rostow, *The Stages of Economic Growth* (Cambridge, 1960), 36–40.
2. N. S. B. Gras, *The Evolution of the English Corn Market from the Twelfth to the Eighteenth Century* (Cambridge, Mass., 1915), 64.
3. David S. Landes, 'Technological Change and Industrial Development in Western Europe, 1750–1914', in *Camb. Ec. Hist.*, VI (1965), 356.
4. *Ibid.*
5. Arthur Young, *Travels in France during the Years 1787, 1788, 1789*

(London, 1915), 27.

6. John U. Nef, 'Industrial Europe at the Time of the Reformation', *Jn. Pol. Ec.*, 49 (1941), 183–224, 221.

7. *Id., Industry and Government in France and England 1540–1640* (Ithaca, N.Y., 1957), 88.

8. Carlo M. Cipolla, 'The Decline of Italy: The Case of a Fully Matured Economy', *Ec. Hist. Rev.*, 5 (1952–3), 178–87.

9. J. Hartung, 'Die direkten Steuern und die Vermögensentwicklung in Augsburg von der Mitte des 16. bis zum 18. Jahrhundert', *Schm. Jb.*, 22 (1898), 167–209; Friedrich Lutge, 'Die wirtschaftliche Lage Deutschlands vor Ausbruch des Dreissigjahrigen Krieges', *Jb. Nat. Stat.*, 170 (1958), 43–99.

10. Ingomar Bog, 'Wachstumsprobleme der oberdeutschen Wirtschaft 1540–1618', *Jb. Nat. Stat.*, 179 (1966), 493–537.

11. Stefan Inglot, 'Economic Relations of Silesia with Poland from the XVI Century to the Beginning of the XVIII Century', *Ann. Siles.*, 1, 2 (1960), 153–70.

12. Sven-Erik Astrom, 'The Swedish Economy and Sweden's Role as a Great Power, 1632–1697', in *Sweden's Age of Greatness*, ed. Michael Roberts (London, 1973), 58–101.

13. René Baehrel, *Une croissance: la Basse-Provence rurale* (Paris, 1961).

14. Robert Mandrou, *La France aux XVIIe et XVIIIe siècles* (Paris, 1970), 116–23; but compare E. Labrousse, P. Léon, P. Goubert, J. Bouvier, C. Carrière and P. Harsin, *Histoire économique et sociale de la France*, II, *1660–1789* (Paris, 1970), 367–416.

15. *Ibid.* 133–5.

16. Quoted in *Ciba Rev.* (1968), no. 1, 4.

17. *Royal Commission on the Distribution of the Industrial Population*, H.M.S.O. (London, 1940), 32.

18. E. J. Hobsbawm, *Industry and Empire* (Harmondsworth, 1969), 54.

19. E. H. Robinson, 'The Early Diffusion of Steam Power', *Jn. Ec. Hist.*, 34 (1974), 91–107; J. Tann and M. J. Breckin, 'The International Diffusion of the Watt Engine, 1775–1825', *Ec. Hist. Rev.*, 31 (1978), 541–64.

20. Hermann Kellenbenz, 'Industries rurales en Occident de la fin du Moyen Age au XVIIIe siècle', *Ann. ESC*, 18 (1963), 823–82.

21. Pierre Goubert, *Beauvais et le Beauvaisis* (Paris, 1960), 123–5.

22. Pierre Deyon, *Amiens: capitale provinciale* (Paris, 1967), 199–208; *id.*, 'La production manufacturière en France au XVIIe siècle', *XVIIe S.*, nos. 70–1 (1966), 47–63.

23. The text is published in *European Society in the Eighteenth Century*, ed. R. and E. Forster (New York, 1969), 226–32.

24. In *ibid.* 211.

25. Le comte de Mirabeau, *De la monarchie prussienne*, 4 vols. (London, 1788), II, 157.

26. E. Coornaert, *La Flandre française de langue flamande* (Paris, 1970), 105.

27. *Id.*, 'L'organisation administrative et économique du travail dans une draperie rurale en Flandre du XVᵉ au XVIIIᵉ siècle: la draperie–sayetterie d'Hondschoote', *Rev. Hist. Ec. Soc.*, 15 (1927), 351–8.

28. Hermann Kellenbenz, 'Landliches gewerbe und bauerliches Unternehmertum in Westeuropa vom Spätmittelalter bis ins 18. Jahrhundert', *Second Int. Conf. Ec. Hist.* (Paris, 1965), 377–427.

29. N. W. Postumus, *De geschiedenis van de leidsche lakenindustrie*, 3 vols. (The Hague, 1908–39), III, 882; E. Coornaert, 'Une capitale de la laine: Leyde', *Ann. ESC*, 1 (1946), 169–77.

30. Charles Wilson, 'Cloth Production and International Competition in the Seventeenth Century', *Ec. Hist. Rev.*, 13 (1960–1), 209–21.

31. Z. W. Sneller, 'La naissance de l'industrie rurale dans les Pays-Bas aux XVIIᵉ et XVIIIᵉ siècles', *Ann. Hist. Ec. Soc.*, 1 (1929), 193–202.

32. H. K. Roessingh, 'Village and Hamlet in a Sandy Region of the Netherlands in the Middle of the 18th Century', *Acta Hist. Neer.*, 4 (1970), 105–29.

33. Max Barkhausen, 'Verviers: die Entstehung einer neuzeitlichen Industriestadt im 17. und 18. Jahrhundert', *V.S.W.G.*, 47 (1960), 363–75.

34. Pierre Lebrun, *L'industrie de la laine à Verviers pendant le XVIIIᵉ siècle*, Bibl. Fac. Liège, 114 (1948), 130–2; *id.*, 'Croissance et industrialisation: l'expérience de l'industrie drapière verviétoise 1750–1850', *Int. Conf. Econ. Hist., Stockholm: Communications* (Paris, 1960), 531–68.

35. Georges Lefebvre, 'A Verviers: capitalisme et draperie', *Ann. ESC*, 5 (1950), 49–55.

36. V. Prévot, 'Une grande industrie d'exportation: l'industrie linière dans le nord de la France sous l'Ancien Régime', *Rev. Nord*, 39 (1957), 205–26.

37. Paul Leuilliot, 'Houille et coton en Belgique', *Ann. ESC*, 7 (1952), 199–209.

38. 'Art de la draperie, principalement pour ce qui regarde les draps fins', *Description des arts et des métiers*, ed. H. L. Duhamel de Monceau (27 vols., Paris, 1761–88), XXV.

39. Pierre Deyon and A. Lottin, 'Evolution de la production textile à Lille aux XVIᵉ et XVIIᵉ siècles', *Rev. Nord*, 49 (1967), 23–33.

40. E. Maugis, 'La saietterie à Amiens 1480–1587', *V.S.W.G.*, 5 (1907), 1–114; Deyon, *Amiens*, 179–83.

41. Labrousse *et al.*, *Histoire économique et sociale de la France*, II, 222–3.

42. Louis Fontvieille, 'Documents statistiques: les premiers enquêtes industrielles de la France: 1692 et 1703', *Hist. Quant. Ec. Fr.*, 3, 6 (1969), 1085–280.

43. Calculated from tables in T. J. Markovitch, 'L'industrie française au XVIIIᵉ siècle', *ibid.* 2, 8 (1968), 1517–697.

44. Deyon, *Amiens*, 173–83.

45. *Correspondance des Contrôleurs-Généraux des Finances avec les intendants des provinces*, ed. A. M. de Boislisle, 4 vols. (Paris, 1874–91), II, *1699–1708*, no. 27, p. 8.

46. 'Mémoire fourni par Henri Noette, 1708', in *Mémoires des intendants sur l'état des généralités*, I, *Mémoire de la généralité de Paris*, ed. A. M. de Boislisle (Paris, 1881), 624–34.

47. Michel Mollat, *Le commerce maritime normand à la fin du Moyen Age* (Paris, 1952), 273–7.

48. *Correspondance des Contrôleurs-Généraux*, II, no. 1338, p. 443.

49. *Documents de l'histoire de la Normandie*, ed. Michel de Boüard (Paris, 1972), 235.

50. 'Rapport du Sieur Barolet', in *Mémoire de la généralité de Paris*, 634–8.

51. Quoted in T. J. Markovitch, 'L'industrie française au XVIIIe siècle', *Hist. Quant. Ec. Fr.*, 2 (1968), 1517–697; also Charles Carrière, 'La draperie languedocienne dans la second moitié du XVIIe siècle: contribution a l'étude de la conjoncture levantine', *Hommage Labrousse*, 157–72; also T. J. Markovitch, 'L'industrie lainière française au début du XVIIIe siècle', *Rev. Hist. Ec. Soc.*, 46 (1968), 550–79.

52. *Correspondence des Contrôleurs-Généraux*, no. 1237, p. 403.

53. *Ibid.* I, *1683–99*, no. 1143, p. 303.

54. *Ibid.* III, *1708–15*, no. 74, p. 27.

55. *Ibid.* II, no. 596, p. 178.

56. Georges Lefebvre, *Etudes orléanaises*, I. *Contributions à l'étude des structures sociales à la fin du XVIIIe siècle, Comm. Hist. Ec. Soc. Rév. Fr., Mém. et Doc.*, 15 (1962), 101–3; J. Dehergne, *Le Bas-Poitou à la veille de la Révolution, ibid.* 16 (1963), 68–70; Paul Raveau, 'Essai sur la situation économique et l'état social en Poitou au XVIe siècle', *Rev. Hist. Ec. Soc.*, 18 (1930), 15–51.

57. Germain Martin, *La grande industrie en France sous le règne de Louis XV* (Paris, 1900), 101–22; Pierre Deyon, 'Le mouvement de la production textile à Amiens au XVIIIe siècle', *Rev. Nord*, 44 (1962), 201–11.

58. *Documents de l'histoire d'Alsace*, ed. Philippe Dollinger (Toulouse, 1972), 360.

59. Markovitch, 'L'industrie française au XVIIIe siècle', 1519.

60. Prévot, 'Une grande industrie d'exportation: l'industrie linière dans le nord de la France sous l'Ancien Régime'.

61. Georges Lefebvre, *Les paysans du Nord pendant la Révolution Française* (Lille, 1924), 285.

62. F. Dornic, 'L'évolution de l'industrie textile aux XVIIIe et XIXe siècles: l'activité de la famille Cohen', *Rev. Hist. Mod. Cont.*, 3 (1956), 38–66.

63. Jean Vidalenc, 'L'industrie dans les départements normands à la fin du Premier Empire', *Ann. Norm.*, 7 (1957), 281–307.

64. Dehergne, *Le Bas-Poitou à la veille de la Révolution*, 72.

65. *Documents de l'histoire de la Bretagne*, ed. Jean Delumeau (Toulouse, 1971), 255–6.

66. 'Rouen – French Textile Centre', *Ciba Rev.*, no. 135 (Dec. 1959).

67. *La grande industrie en France sous le règne de Louis XV*, 129;

Documents de l'histoire de Normandie, 236.

68. Fr. de Beaurepaire, 'Le commerce du coton à Yvetôt vers 1787', *Ann. Norm.*, 11 (1961), 325–7.

69. Henri Causse, 'Un industriel toulousain au temps de la Révolution et de l'Empire: François-Bernard Boyer-Fonfrède', *Ann. Midi*, 69 (1957), 121–33; Pierre Vayssière, 'Un pionnier de la révolution industrielle en Languedoc au XVIIIᵉ siècle: John Holker', *Ann. Midi*, 79 (1967), 269–86.

70. Fontvieille, 'Documents statistiques: 1692 et 1703'.

71. Hermann Aubin, 'Formen und Verbreitung des Verlagswesens in der Altnürnberger Wirtschaft', *Beitr. Wtgesch. Nürn.*, 2 (1967), 620–68.

72. Herbert Kisch, 'Das Erbe des Mittelalters, ein Hemmnis wirtschaftlicher Entwicklung: Aachens Tuchgewerbe vor 1790', *Rhein. Vbl.*, 30 (1965), 253–308; Clemens Bruckner, 'Zur Wirtschaftsgeschichte des Regierungsbezirks Aachen', *Schr. Rhein.–Westf. Wtgesch.*, 16 (1967), 320, 362–71.

73. Mirabeau, *De la monarchie prussienne*, II, 34–5.

74. Gustav Otruba, 'Die alteste Manufaktur- und Gewerbestatistik Bohmens', *Boh.*, 5 (1964), 161–241.

75. Heinrich Benedikt, 'Die Anfange der Industrie in Mahren', *Der Donau*, 2 (1957), 38–51.

76. Hermann Kellenbenz, 'Die wirstschaftlichen Beziehungen zwischen Westdeutschland und Bohmen–Mahren im Zeitalter der Industrialisierung', *Boh.*, 3 (1962), 239–59.

77. Arnost Klima, 'Die Textilmanufaktur in Bohmen des 18. Jahrhunderts', *Hist.* (P), 15 (1967), 123–81.

78. Gustav Otruba, 'Anfange und Verbreitung der bohmischen Manufakturen bis zum Beginn des 19. Jahrhunderts', *Boh.*, 6 (1965), 230–331.

79. Hermann Freundenberg, 'The Woolen Goods Industry of the Habsburg Monarchy in the Eighteenth Century', *Jn. Ec. Hist.*, 20 (1960), 383–406.

80. Wolfgang Zorn, 'Schwerpunkte der deutschen Ausfuhrindustrie im 18. Jahrhundert', *Jb. Nat. Stat.*, 173 (1961), 422–47; Arnost Klima, 'Industrial Development in Bohemia 1648–1781', *P & P*, 11 (Apr. 1957), 87–99.

81. Wolfgang Zorn, 'Handels- und Industriegeschichte Bayerisch–Schwabens 1648–1870', *Veröffentlichungen der Schwäbischen Forschungsgemeinschaft* (Augsburg), 1961, 71–98.

82. Mirabeau, *De la monarchie prussienne*, II, 149.

83. William Jacob, *A View of the Agriculture, Manufactures, Statistics and State of Society of Germany* (London, 1820), 78, 91.

84. Edith Schmidt, 'Leinengewerbe and Leinenhandel in Nordwestdeutschland (1650–1850)', *Schr. Rhein.–Westf. Wtgesch.*, 15 (1967), 25–45, 76–82.

85. Walter Bodmer, *Die Entwicklung der schweizerischen Textilwirtschaft im Rahmen der übrigen Industrien und übrigen Wirtschaftszweige* (Zurich, 1960), 172–6.

86. Arnost Klima, 'English Merchant Capital in Bohemia in the Eighteenth Century', *Ec. Hist. Rev.*, 12 (1959–60), 34–48.
87. *Id.*, 'The Domestic Industry and the Putting-Out System in the Period of Transition from Feudalism to Capitalism', *Second Int. Conf. Ec. Hist.* (Paris, 1965), 477–81.
88. R. Forberger, *Die Manufaktur in Sachsen vom Ende des 16. bis zum Anfang des 19. Jahrhunderts* (Berlin, 1958), 170.
89. Wolfram Fischer, 'Ansätze zur Industrialisierung in Baden 1770–1870', *V.S.W.G.*, 47 (1960), 186–231.
90. Alfred Engels, 'Die Zollgrenze in der Eifel', *Schr. Rhein.–Westf. Wtgesch.*, 2 (1959), 32.
91. James Clayburn La Force, *The Development of the Spanish Textile Industry, 1750–1800* (Berkeley, Calif., 1965), 19–22; 'The Catalan Textile Industry', *Ciba Rev.*, 1963, no. 3.
92. James Clayburn La Force, 'Royal Textile Factories in Spain, 1700–1800', *Jn. Ec. Hist.*, 24 (1964), 337–63; Richard Heer, *The Eighteenth Century Revolution in Spain* (Princeton, N.J., 1958), 122–32.
93. La Force, *The Development of the Spanish Textile Industry*, 13–14.
94. Jaime Vicens Vives, *An Economic History of Spain* (Princeton, N.J., 1969), 668–70.
95. Robert Davidsohn, 'Blüte und Niedergang der Florentiner Tuchindustrie', *Zt. Ges. Staatsw.*, 85 (1928), 225–55.
96. Aldo de Maddalena, 'L'industria tesssile a Mantova nell'500 e all'inizio del 600', *Studi Fanfani*, IV, 607–53.
97. Domenico Sella, 'Les mouvements longs de l'industrie lainière à Venise aux XVIᵉ et XVIIᵉ siècles', *Ann. ESC*, 12 (1957), 29–45.
98. *Id.*, 'Industrial Production in Seventeenth Century Italy: A Reappraisal', *Expl. Entr. Hist.*, 2nd ser., 6 (1969), 235–53.
99. I. Ghica, quoted in D. Warriner, *Contrasts in Emerging Societies* (Bloomington, Ind., 1965), 165.
100. Heinrich Sieveking, 'Die genueser Seidenindustrie im 15. und 16. Jahrhundert., *Schm. Jb.*, 21 (1897), 101–33.
101. Ilja Mieck, 'Preussischer Seidenbau im 18. Jahrhundert', *V.S.W.G.*, 56 (1969), 478–98.
102. D. Sella, 'Les mouvements longs de l'industrie lainière à Venise'; 'Venetian Silks', *Ciba Rev.*, no. 19 (Jan. 1940).
103. 'Zurich Silks', *Ciba Rev.*, no. 119 (Mar. 1957).
104. Quoted in 'Silk Industries of Crefeld', *Ciba Rev.*, no. 83 (Dec. 1950), 3013.
105. 'Damask', *Ciba Rev.*, no. 110 (June 1955).
106. H. Pirenne, 'Note sur la fabrication des tapisseries en Flandre au XVIᵉ siècle', *V.S.W.G.*, 4 (1906), 325–39; Valentin Vasquez de Prada, 'Tapisseries et tableaux flamands en Espagne au XVIᵉ siècle', *Ann. ESC*, 10 (1955), 37–45.
107. *Description des arts et des métiers*, ed. H. L. Duhamel de Monceau, 27 vols. (Paris, 1761–88).

108. Henri Sée, 'L'industrie et le commerce de la Bretagne dans la première moitié du XVIIIe siècle', *Ann. Bret.*, 35 (1921–3), 187–208, 433–55.

109. 'Etat des manufactures et des produits des terres dans la généralité de Paris, 1740 et 1750', in *Mémoire de la généralité de Paris*, 650–5.

110. *Description des arts et des métiers*, XXV.

111. Herbert Milz, *Das Kölner Grossgewerbe von 1750 bis 1835*, *Schr. Rhein.–Westf. Wtgesch.*, 7 (1962), 57.

112. *Correspondance des Contrôleurs-Généraux*, II, no. 1237, p. 403.

113. *Ibid.* I, no. 427, p. 109.

114. Martin, *La grande industrie en France sous le règne de Louis XV*, 144–5.

115. Fernand Braudel, *Capitalism and Material Life 1400–1800* (London 1973), 295–300; Colin Clair, *A History of European Printing* (London, 1976).

116. N. J. G. Pounds, 'The Discovery of China Clay', *Ec. Hist. Rev.*, 1 (1948), 20–33.

117. W. B. Honey, *European Ceramic Art to 1815*, 2 vols. (London, 1949–52); vol. II contains a list of potteries.

118. Jean Yernaux, *Contrats de travail liégeois du XVIIe siècle*, Comm. Roy. Hist. (1941), 270.

119. P.-M. Bondois, 'Le développement de l'industrie verrière dans la région parisienne de 1515 à 1665', *Rev. Hist. Ec. Soc.*, 23 (1936–7), 49–72; *id.*, 'Le développement de la verrerie française au XVIIIe siècle', *ibid.* 23 (1936–7), 238–61, 333–61.

120. R. Ludloff, 'Industrial Development in 16th–17th Century Germany', *P & P*, 12 (1957), 58–75.

121. E. Poche, 'Le verre de Bohême', *Cah. Hist. Mond.*, 5 (1959), 434–62.

122. Eberhard Gothein, *Wirtschaftsgeschichte des Schwarzewaldes* (Strasbourg, 1892), 831–44.

123. Bodmer, *Die Entwicklung der Schweizerischen Textilwirtschaft*, 239.

124. *The Itinerary of Fynes Moryson* (London, 1903), 372.

125. C. M. Cipolla, 'Clocks and Culture', in his *European Culture and Overseas Expansion* (Harmondsworth, 1970), 128–9.

126. 'Industrial Europe at the Time of the Reformation'.

127. *Descriptions des arts et métiers*, XIX, pls. 5, 7.

128. *Correspondance des Contrôleurs-Généraux*, II, no. 355, p. 100.

129. Sven Tunberg, 'Die Entstehung und erste Entwicklung des schwedischen Bergbaues', *Hans. Gbl.*, 63 (1938), 11–26.

130. E. F. Heckscher, *An Economic History of Sweden* (Cambridge, Mass., 1954), 93.

131. *Id.*, 'Un grand chapitre de l'histoire du fer: le monopole suédois', *Ann. Hist. Ec. Soc.*, 4 (1932), 127–39, 225–41.

132. Ludwig Beck, *Geschichte des Eisens*, II, *1893–5* (Brunswick, 1886); this total may have been too high.

133. Gabriel Jars, *Voyages métallurgiques*, 3 vols. (Paris, 1774), I, 134, 144, 157–9.

134. Thérèse Sclafert, 'L'industrie du fer dans la région d'Allevard au moyen

âge', *Rev. Géog. Alp*., 14 (1926), 239–355; Pierre Léon, 'Deux siècles d'activité minière et métallurgique en Dauphiné: l'usine d'Allevard (1675–1870)', *ibid*. 36 (1948), 215–58.

135. Armando Frumento, *Imprese lombarde nella storia della siderurgia italiana*, 2 vols. (Milan, 1952), 92, 186.
136. Gianfranco Faina, 'Note sur les bas foyers ligures aux XVIIe et XVIIIe siècles', *Rev. Hist. Sid*., 9 (1968), 123–43.
137. Kurt Kaser, *Eisenverarbeitung und Eisenhandel*, Beitr. Öst. Eis., sect. 2, pt 1 (1932), 113–92.
138. Beck, *Geschichte des Eisens*, II, *1893–5*, 796.
139. Max Roesler, *The Iron-Ore Resources of Europe*, U.S. Geological Survey, Bulletin 706 (Washington, D.C., 1921).
140. Leon Puzenat, *La sidérurgie armoricaine*, Mémoires de la Société Géologique et Minéralogique de Bretagne, 4 (Rennes, 1939), 53–104.
141. Philippe Moureaux, 'Las sidérurgie belge et luxembourgeoise d'ancien régime', *Rev. Hist. Sid*., 5 (1964), 139–52; Jean Lejeune, *La formation du capitalisme moderne dans la principauté de Liège au XVIe siècle*, Pub. Fac. Liège (1939), 145–57.
142. Roesler, *The Iron-Ore Resources of Europe*, 77.
143. F. A. A. Eversmann, *Die Eisen und Stahl Erzeugung auf Wasserwerken zwischen Lahn und Lippe* (Dortmund, 1804).
144. A. M. Heron de Villefosse, *De la richesse minérale*, I (Paris, 1819).
145. Hermann Wedding, 'Beiträge zur Geschichte des Eisenhüttenwesens im Harz', *Zt. Harz Gesch*., 14 (1881), 1–32.
146. Gustav Otruba, 'Anfange und Verbreitung der Böhmischen Manufakturen bis zum Beginn des 19. Jahrhunderts', *Boh*., 6 (1965), 230–331.
147. N. J. G. Pounds, *The Upper Silesian Industrial Region*, Slavic and East European Series, Indiana University, 11 (Bloomington, Ind., 1958).
148. J. Pazdur, 'Materiały do dziejow hutnictwa żelaza w Polsce w XVIII wieku', *Stud. Dz. Gór. Hutn*., 1 (1957), 319–59.
149. Baron de Verneilh, 'Les anciennes forges du Périgord et du Limousin', *Revue des Sociétés Savantes des Départements* (Paris), 6th ser., 4 (1876), 537–60.
150. C. N. Allou, 'Observations sur les mines et usines du département de la Dordogne', *Jn. Mines*, 37 (1815), 41–65, 81–100.
151. M. Lieffroy, 'L'industrie métallurgique en Franche-Comté', *Acad. Besanç*., 1892, 220–33; Louis Mazoyer, 'Exploitation forestière et conflits sociaux en Franche-Comté à la fin de l'Ancien Régime', *Ann. Hist. Ec. Soc*., 4 (1932), 339–58.
152. Marcel Bulard, 'L'industrie du fer dans la Haute-Marne', *Ann. Géog*., 13 (1904), 223–42, 310–21.
153. 'Mémoire sur la statistique minérologique du département de la Haute-Marne', *Jn. Mines*, 17 (Year 13 [1804–5]), no. 102, 405–36; F. Rigaud, 'Notice sur les minières de la Haute-Marne', *Ann. Mines*, 7th ser., 14 (1878), 9–62.
154. A. Weyhmann, 'Geschichte der älteren Lothringischen Eisenindustrie', *Jb. Ges. Loth. Gesch*., 17 (1905), 1–210; George Hot-

tenger, *L'ancienne industrie du fer en Lorraine* (Nancy, n.d.), 23–36.

155. Citoyen Colchen, *Mémoire statistique du département de la Moselle* (Paris, Year 11 [1802–3]), 162.

156. Arthur Kipgen, 'L'industrie sidérurgique luxembourgeoise', *Revue Technique Luxembourgeois* (Luxembourg), 26 (1934), 103–10.

157. Jars, *Voyages métallurgiques*, I; see also N. J. G. Pounds and W. N. Parker, *Coal and Steel in Western Europe* (London, 1957), 71.

158. Cécile Douxchamps-Lefèvre, 'Les premiers essais de fabrication du coke dans les charbonnages du nord de la France et la région de Charleroi à la fin du XVIIIᵉ siècle', *Rev. Nord*, 50 (1968), 25–24.

159. Jean Chevalier, *Le Creusot* (Paris, 1935), 62–140; C. Ballot, 'La rývolution technique et ses débuts dans la métallurgie française: l'introduction de la fonte au coke en France et la fondation du Creusot', *Revue d'Histoire des Doctrines Economiques* (Paris), 5 (1912), 29–62.

160. C. Northcote Parkinson (ed.), *The Trade Winds* (London, 1948), 92–3.

161. R. G. Albion, *Forests and Sea Power* (Cambridge, Mass., 1926), 139–99.

162. Stanislaw Gierszewski, *Elblqski przemysł okrętowy w latach 1570–1815* (Danzig, 1961).

163. Louis Trenard, 'Le charbon avant l'ère industrielle', in *Charbon et sciences humaines* (Paris, 1966), 53–101.

164. John Evelyn, *Fumifugium* (London, 1661); John U. Nef, *Rise of the British Coal Industry*, I (London, 1932), 156–64.

165. *Descriptions des arts et des métiers*, II, xv.

166. Le comte de Buffon, *Histoire Naturelle, générale et particulière*, 44 vols. (Paris, 1753–67), I, 525.

167. Gonzalès Descamps, *Mèmoire historique sur l'origine et les développements de l'industrie houillère dans le bassin du Couchant de Mons*, Mémoires et Publications de la Société des Sciences, des Arts et des Lettres du Hainaut, 4th ser., 5 (1880) and 5th ser., 1 (1889).

168. Marcel Gillet, 'Charbonnages belges et charbonnages du nord de la France aux XVIIIᵉ et XIXᵉ siècles', in *Mélanges offerts à G. Jacquemyns* (Brussels, 1968), 361–84; *id.*, *Les charbonnages du nord de la France* (Paris, 1973), 25–30.

169. Léon Jacques, 'Etude sur la houille du bassin de Liège', *Rev. Universelle des Mines* (Liège), 22 (1867), 149–342.

170. Based on Héron de Villefosse, *De la richesse minérale*, I; *Jn. Mines*, 9 (Year 10 [1801–2]), 257–66; 36 (1814), 321–94; *Ann. Mines*, 2 (1832), 203–32, 431–92; *Zt. Berg. Hüt. Sal.*, 8 (1849), 332–3; 55 (1907), 547–74.

171. H. Reader Lack, 'The Mining Resources of France, 1841 to 1852', *Jn. Roy. Stat. Soc.*, 18 (1855), 345–55.

172. *Die Graftschaft Mark: Festschrift zum Gedächtnis der 300 jährigen Vereinigung mit Brandenburg–Preussen*, 2 vols. (Dortmund, 1909), I, 541.

173. J. F. Daubuisson, 'Notice sur l'exploitation des houillères de Waldenburg en Silesie', *Jn. Mines*, 15 (Year 12 [1803–4]), 88–103; Héron de

Villefosse, *De la richesse minérale*, II (Paris, 1819), 514–27.

174. Gustav Otruba and Rudolf Kropf, 'Bergbau und Industrie in der Epoche der Frühindustrialisierung', *Boh.*, 12 (1972), 53–233; Otruba, 'Anfange und Verbreitung der Bohmischen Manufakturen bis zum Beginn des 19. Jahrhunderts'.

175. B. R. Mitchell, 'Statistical Appendix 1700–1914', in *The Fontana Economic History of Europe*, IV (London, 1973), 738–820.

176. John U. Nef, 'Silver Production in Central Europe, 1450–1618', *Jn. Pol. Ec.*, 49 (1941), 575–91; Richard Dietrich, 'Untersuchungen zum Frühkapitalismus im mitteldeutschen Erzbergbau und Metallhandel', *Jb. Gesch. Mitt. Ostd.*, 7 (1958), 141–206, 8 (1959), 51–119, 9 (1960), 127–94; Josef Janacek, 'Die Fugger und Joachimstal', *Hist.* (P), 6 (1963), 109–44; Jan Kořan and Vaclav Vaneček, 'Czech Mining and Mining Law', *Cah. Hist. Mond.*, 7 (1962), 27–45.

177. Götz von Pölnitz, *Jakob Fugger: Kaiser, Kirche und Kapital in der oberdeutschen Renaissance* (Tübingen, 1949); Pierre Jeannin, 'Le cuivre, les Fugger et la Hanse', *Ann. ESC*, 10 (1955), 229–36.

178. Pierre Jeannin, 'Conjoncture et production du cuivre dans les Vosges méridionales à la fin du XVIᵉ et au début du XVIIᵉ siècle', *Hommage Labrousse*, 121–38.

179. Jozef Vlachovic, 'Slovak Copper Boom in World Markets of the Sixteenth and in the First Quarter of the 17th Centuries', *Studia Historica Slovaca* (Bratislava), 1 (1963), 63–95.

180. Jars, *Voyages métallurgiques*, III, 1ff.

181. J. Vlachovic, 'Slovak Copper Boom'.

182. Sven Tunberg, 'Die Entstehung und erste Entwicklung des schwedischen Bergbaues'.

183. Michael Roberts, *Gustavus Adolphus and the Rise of Sweden* (London, 1973), 121.

184. Jars, *Voyages métallurgiques*, II, 358–495.

185. See Héron de Villefosse, *De la richesse minérale*, I, though his statistics do not appear to be particularly reliable.

186. T. C. Banfield, 'The Progress of the Prussian Nation, 1805, 1831, 1842', *Jn. Roy. Stat. Soc.*, 11 (1848), 25–37.

Chapter 6. The pattern of trade

1. Thomas Mun, *England's Treasure by fforaign Trade* (1664) (Oxford, 1928), 4.

2. B. R. Mitchell and Phyllis Deane, *Abstract of British Historical Statistics* (Cambridge, 1962), 279–81.

3. E. Labrousse, P. Léon, P. Goubert, J. Bouvier, C. Carrière and P. Harsin, *Histoire économique et sociale de la France*, II, *1660–1789* (Paris, 1970), 503.

4. Charles Wilson, *Profit and Power: A Study of England and the Dutch Wars* (London, 1957), 40–1.

5. Kristof Glamann, *Dutch–Asiatic Trade 1620–1740* (Copenhagen,

1958), 14.

6. *Correspondance des Contrôleurs-Généraux des Finances avec les intendants des provinces*, ed. A. M. de Boislisle, 4 vols. (Paris, 1874–97), I, *1683–99*, no. 18.

7. *Ibid*. III, *1708–15*, no. 1772.

8. *Ibid*. II, *1699–1708*, no. 820.

9. *Ibid*. II, no. 733.

10. J. Heers, *Gênes au XVᵉ siècle* (Paris, 1961), 416–500.

11. Brian Pullan, Introduction to Pullen (ed.), *Crisis and Change in the Venetian Economy* (London, 1968), 5.

12. Fernand Braudel and R. Romano, *Navires et marchandises à l'entrée du port de Livourne (1547–1611)* (Paris, 1951), 31–61.

13. Peter Earle, 'The Commercial Development of Ancona, 1479–1551', *Ec. Hist. Rev.*, 22 (1969), 28–44.

14. Torjo Tadic, 'Le port de Raguse et sa flotte au XVIᵉ siècle', in *Le navire et l'économie maritime au Moyen Age au XVIIIᵉ siècle, principalement en Méditerranée*, ed. M. Mollat (Paris, 1960), 9–26.

15. Earle, 'The Commercial Development of Ancona', 35.

16. Alberto Tenenti, *Piracy and the Decline of Venice 1580–1615* (London, 1967), 19.

17. Henry Simonsfeld, *Der Fondaco dei Tedeschi in Venedig und die deutsch–venetianischen Handelsbeziehungen*, 2 vols. (Stuttgart, 1887), II, 13.

18. Domenico Sella, 'Crisis and Transformation in Venetian Trade', in Brian Pullan (ed.), *Crisis and Change in the Venetian Economy* (London, 1968), 88–105.

19. Ralph Davis, 'England and the Mediterranean, 1570–1670', in *Essays in the Economic and Social History of Tudor and Stuart England*, ed. F. J. Fisher (Cambridge, 1961), 117–37.

20. E. Lipson, *The Economic History of England*, II (London, 1948), 335–52.

21. H. Koenigsberger, 'English Merchants in Naples and Sicily in the Seventeenth Century', *Eng. Hist. Rev.*, 62 (1947), 304–26.

22. W. Brulez, 'La navigation flamande vers la Méditerranée à la fin du XVIᵉ siècle', *Rev. Belge Phil. Hist.*, 36 (1958), 1210–42.

23. *Id.*, *De firma della Faille en de internationale handel van vlaamse firma's in de 16e eeuw* (Brussels, 1959); *id.*, 'L'exportation des Pays-Bas vers l'Italie par voie de terre au milieu du XVIᵉ siècle', *Ann. ESC*, 14 (1959), 461–91.

24. F. Braudel, *The Mediterranean and the Mediterranean World in the Age of Philip II*, 2 vols. (London, 1972–3), I, 599–602.

25. Pierre Jeannin, 'Entreprises hanséatiques et commerce méditerranéen à la fin du XVIᵉ siècle', *Mélanges F. Braudel*, I, 263–76.

26. Henryk Samsonowicz, 'Relations commerciales entre la Baltique et la Méditerranée', *ibid*. I, 537–45.

27. Pierre Jeannin, 'Le commerce de Lübeck aux environs de 1580', *Ann. ESC*, 16 (1961), 36–65.

28. Henryk Zins, *England and the Baltic in the Elizabethan Era* (Manchester, 1972), 45–9.

29. Lipson, *Economic History of England*, II, 315–34.

30. Astrid Friis, *Alderman Cockayne's Project and the Cloth Trade* (Copenhagen, 1927), 224–38.

31. R. W. K. Hinton, *The Eastland Trade and the Common Weal in the Seventeenth Century* (Cambridge, 1959), 34–42.

32. Sven-Erik Astrom, *From Cloth to Iron: The Anglo-Baltic Trade in the Late Seventeenth Century*, Societas Scientiarum Fennica, 33 (Helsinki, 1963), 29–52.

33. Pierre Jeannin, 'Les relations économiques des villes de la Baltique avec Anvers', *V.S.W.G.*, 43 (1956), 193–217, 323–55.

34. Aksel E. Christensen, *Dutch Trade to the Baltic about 1600* (Copenhagen, 1941), 17.

35. Wilson, *Profit and Power*, 41.

36. Christensen, *Dutch Trade to the Baltic*, 465.

37. Published by Nina Ellinger Bang, *Tabeller over skibsfart og varetransport gennen Öresund 1497–1660*, 2 vols. (Copenhagen, 1906–22); *ibid. 1661–1783*, 2 vols. (Copenhagen, 1930–53).

38. Pierre Jeannin, 'Les comptes du Sund comme source pour la construction d'indices généraux de l'activité économique en Europe (XVIe–XVIIIe siècle)', *Rev. Hist.*, 231 (1964), 55–102, 307–40; *id.*, 'Anvers et la Baltique au XVIe siècle', *Rev. Nord*, 37 (1955), 93–114.

39. J. A. Faber, 'Het probleem van de dalende graanaanvoer uit de Oostzeelanden in de tweede helft van zeventiene eeuw', *A.A.G. Bij.*, 9 (1963), 3–28.

40. M. Malowist, 'L'approvisionnement des ports de la Baltique en produits forestiers pour les constructions navales', in Mollat (ed.), *Le navire et l'économie maritime*, 25–43.

41. Arnold Soom, 'Der Ostbaltische Holzhandel und die Holzindustrie im 17. Jahrhundert', *Hans. Gbl.*, 79 (1961), 80–100.

42. R. G. Albion, *Forests and Sea Power* (Cambridge, Mass., 1926), 139–99; H. S. K. Kent, *War and Trade in the Northern Seas* (Cambridge, 1973), 39–54.

43. J. Zoutis, 'Riga dans le commerce maritime en Baltique au XVIIe siècle', in Mollat (ed.), *Le navire et l'économie maritime*, 81–92.

44. Hermann Kellenbenz, 'The Economic Significance of the Archangel Route', *Jn. Eur. Ec. Hist.*, 2 (1973), 541–81.

45. Georgij Jens, 'Rivalry between Riga and Tartu for the Trade with Pskov in the XVI and XVII Centuries', *Balt. Scand.*, 4 (1938), 145–54.

46. M. K. G. Hildebrand, 'Exportation du fer et navigation en Baltique', in Mollat (ed.), *Le navire et l'économie maritime*, 111–20.

47. Charles Verlinden, 'From the Mediterranean to the Atlantic: Aspects of an Economic Shift', *Jn. Eur. Ec. Hist.*, 1 (1972), 625–46.

48. H. and P. Chaunu, *Séville et l'Atlantique (1504–1650)*, I (Paris, 1955), 12.

49. A measure of volume; the tonneau or tun was about 1.5 cubic metres.

50. H. and P. Chaunu, 'Economie atlantique: économie mondiale (1504–1650)', *Cah. Hist. Mond.*, 1 (1953), 91–104.

51. A. P. Usher, 'Spanish Ships and Shipping in the Sixteenth and Seventeenth Centuries', in *Facts and Factors in Economic History* (E. F. Gay Festschrift), ed. A. H. Cole, A. L. Duncan and N. S. B. Gras (Cambridge, Mass., 1932), 189–213.

52. J. A. Van Houtte, 'La genèse du grand marché international d'Anvers à la fin du Moyen Age', *Rev. Belge Phil. Hist.*, 19 (1940), 87–126; H. Van der Wee, *The Growth of the Antwerp Market and the European Economy*, 2 vols. (Louvain, 1963), esp. I, 130–207.

53. E. Coornaert, 'Note sur le commerce d'Anvers au XVIᵉ siècle', *Rev. Nord*, 13 (1927), 123–7.

54. W. Brulez, 'Lettres commerciales de Daniel et Antoine Bombergen à Antonio Grimani (1532–1543)', *Bull. Inst. Hist. Belge Rome*, 31 (1958), 169–205; F. Edler, 'The Van der Molen, Commission Merchants of Antwerp: Trade with Italy, 1538–44', in *Medieval and Historiographical Essays*, ed. J. L. Cate and E. N. Anderson (Chicago, 1938), 78–145; Brulez, *De firma della Faille*.

55. Léon van der Essen, 'Contribution à l'histoire du port d'Anvers et du commerce d'exportation des Pays-Bas vers l'Espagne et le Portugal à l'époque de Charles Quint', *Acad. Roy. Arch. Belge*, 1920, fasc. 3, 39–64.

56. Ludovico Guicciardini, *Description de to le pais-bas autrement dict la Germanie Inferieure ou Basse-Allemaigne* (Antwerp, 1567).

57. *Ibid.* 158–66.

58. W. Brulez, 'Le commerce international des Pays-Bas au XVIᵉ siècle: essai d'appréciation quantitative', *Rev. Belge Phil. Hist.*, 46 (1968), 1205–21.

59. E. Coornaert, 'Le rayonnement d'Anvers dans le nord de la France au XVIᵉ siècle', *Rev. Nord*, 41 (1959), 251–63; W. Brulez, 'The Balance of Trade of the Netherlands in the Middle of the 16th Century', *Acta Hist. Neer.*, 4 (1970), 20–48.

60. S. T. Bindoff, 'The Greatness of Antwerp', in *New Camb. Mod. Hist.*, II (1958), 50–69; *id.*, *The Scheldt Question* (London, 1945), 108–37.

61. J. A. Van Houtte, 'Déclin et survivance d'Anvers (1550–1700)', *Studi Fanfani*, V, 703–26.

62. Frank J. Smolar, 'Resiliency of Enterprise: Economic Crises and Recovery in the Spanish Netherlands in the Early Seventeenth Century', in *From the Renaissance to the Counter-Reformation*, ed. C. H. Carter (London, 1966), 247–68; W. Brulez, 'Anvers de 1585 à 1650', *V.S.W.G.*, 54 (1967), 75–99.

63. E. Coornaert, 'Anvers a-t-elle eu une flotte marchande au XVIᵉ siècle?' in Mollat (ed.), *Le navire et l'économie maritime*, 71–80.

64. Owen Feltham, *A Brief Character of the Low Countries under the States* (London, 1660), 72.

65. André-E. Sayous, 'Le rôle d'Amsterdam dans l'histoire du capitalisme

commercial et financier', *Rev. Hist.*, 183 (1938), 242–80; Violet Barbour, *Capitalism in Amsterdam in the 17th Century* (Ann Arbor, Mich., 1963), 17, 43–53.

66. Barbour, *Capitalism in Amsterdam*, 24.
67. Glamann, *Dutch–Asiatic Trade 1620–1740*, 11–14.
68. Henri Sée, 'L'activité commerciale de la Hollande à la fin du XVIIᵉ siècle', *Rev. Hist. Ec. Soc.*, 14 (1926), 200–53.
69. Wilson, *Profit and Power: A Study of England and the Dutch Wars,* 34.
70. Etienne Trocme and Marcel Delafosse, *Le commerce rochelais de la fin du XVᵉ siècle au début du XVIIᵉ* (Paris, 1952), 73.
71. Jean Tanguy, *Le commerce du port de Nantes au milieu du XVIᵉ siècle* (Paris, 1956), 63.
72. Jean Delumeau, 'Le commerce malouin à la fin du XVIIᵉ siècle', *Ann. Bret.*, 66 (1959), 263–86; Robert Faveau, 'Les ports de la côte poitevine du XVIᵉ siècle', *Bull. Phil. Hist.*, 1962, 13–61.
73. Jean Delumeau, 'Le commerce malouin sous l'ancien régime d'après les registres de l'Amirauté', in *Les sources de l'histoire maritime*, ed. M. Mollat (Paris, 1962), 299–310.
74. M. Mollat, *Le commerce maritime normand à la fin du Moyen Age* (Paris, 1952), 200–69.
75. J. Delumeau, 'Le commerce malouin à la fin du XVIIᵉ siècle'.
76. Henri Touchard, *Le commerce maritime breton à la fin du Moyen Age,* Ann. Litt. Nantes, 1 (1967), 334–5; André Plaisse, 'Le commerce du port de Brest à la fin du XVIᵉ siècle', *Rev. Hist. Ec. Soc.*, 42 (1964), 499–545.
77. Trocme and Delafosse, *Le commerce rochelais*, 75–88; M. Delafosse, 'Trafic rochelais aux XVᵉ–XVIᵉ siècles: marchands poitevins et laines d'Espagne', *Ann. ESC*, 7 (1952), 61–4.
78. Tanguy, *Le commerce du port de Nantes*, 22–57.
79. *Documents de l'histoire de la Bretagne*, ed. J. Delumeau (Toulouse, 1971), 266.
80. P. Butel, 'Le trafic colonial de Bordeaux de la guerre d'Amérique à la Révolution', *Ann. Midi*, 78 (1966), 37–82; (1967), 287–306; J. Fayard, 'Notes sur le trafic maritime entre Bordeaux et Hambourg à la fin du XVIIᵉ siècle', *ibid.* 79 (1967), 219–28.
81. Pierre Dardel, *Navires et marchandises dans les ports de Rouen et du Havre* (Paris, 1963), 163–231.
82. Helen Liebel, 'Laissez-Faire vs. Mercantilism: The Rise of Hamburg and the Hamburg Bourgeoisie vs. Frederick the Great in the Crisis of 1763'. *V.S.W.G.*, 52 (1965), 207–38.
83. Le comte de Mirabeau, *De la monarchie prussienne,* 4 vols. (London, 1788), II, 246–7.
84. Liebel, 'Laissez-Faire vs. Mercantilism', 215–16; also Hermann Kellenbenz, 'Der deutschen Aussenhandel gegen Ausgang des 18. Jahrhunderts', in *Die wirtschaftliche Situation in Deutschland und Österreich um die Wende vom 18. zum 19. Jahrhundert*, ed. F. Lütge

(Stuttgart, 1964), 4–60.

85. J. F. Bosher, 'French Administration and Public Finance in their European Setting', in *New Camb. Mod. Hist.*, VIII (1965), 565–91.
86. Georges Lefebvre, *Etudes orléanaises: I. Contributions à l'étude des strucures sociales à la fin du XVIIIᵉ siècle, Comm. Hist. Ec. Soc. Rév. Fr., Mém. et Doc.*, 15 (1962), 231–3.
87. F. Lütge, 'Der Untergang der nürnberger Heiltumsmesse', *Jb. Nat. Stat*, 178 (1965), 133–57.
88. J.-F. Henry de Richeprey, *Journal de voyage*, quoted in *Histoire de l'Aquitaine: documents*, ed. Charles Higounet (Toulouse, 1973), 266.
89. Labrousse *et al.*, *Histoire économique et sociale de la France*, II, 184–6.
90. Domenico Cioffre, *Gênes et les foires de change de Lyon à Besançon* (Paris, 1960), 25–7, 72.
91. Van der Wee, *The Growth of the Antwerp Market*; E. Coornaert, *Les français et le commerce international à Antwerp*, 2 vols. (Paris, 1961), II, 138–45; C. F. J. Slootmans, 'Les marchands brabançons et plus specialement les marchands bruxellois aux foires de Bergen-op-Zoom', *Cah. Brux.*, 8 (1963), 13–64.
92. Z. W. Sneller, *Deventer die Stadt der Jahrmärkte*, Hansische Pfingst-blätter, 25 (Lübeck, 1936).
93. Helmuth Toepfer, 'Die Jahrmärkte in der preussischen Rheinprovinz um 1845', *Rhein. Vbl.*, 35 (1971), 288–300.
94. H. Aubin and W. Zorn, *Handbuch der deutschen Wirtschafts- und Sozialgeschichte*, I (Stuttgart, 1971), 437.
95. H. Ammann, 'Die Zurzacher Messen im Mittelalter', *Taschb. Aargau*, 1923, 1–154.
96. Gottfried Glocke, 'Ein französcher Bericht über die Messen in Frank-furt und Leipzig im Jahre 1810', *Arch. Frank. Gesch. Kunst*, 49 (1965), 99–121.
97. Arno Mehlan, 'Die grossen Balkanmessen in der Turkenzeit', *V.S.W.G.*, 31 (1938), 10–49.
98. Fritz Glauser, 'Der internationale Gotthardtransit im Lichte des Luzerner Zentnerzolls von 1493 bis 1505', *Schw. Zt. Gesch.*, 18 (1968), 177–245.
99. Bishop Burnet, *Travels through France, Italy, Germany and Switzer-land* (London, 1750 edn), 88.
100. *Le voyage d'Outremer de Bertrandon de la Broquière*, ed. C. Schefer (Paris, 1892), 2–3.
101. D. J. Buisseret, 'The Communications of France during the Recon-struction of Henri IV', *Ec. Hist. Rev.*, 18 (1965), 267–77.
102. Georges Livet, 'La route royale et la civilisation française de la fin du XVᵉ au milieu du XVIII siècle', in *Les routes de France* (Paris, 1959), 57–100.
103. P. de Saint-Jacob, 'Le réseau routier bourguignan au XVIIIᵉ siècle', *Ann. Bourg.*, 28 (1956), 253–63.
104. Louis Trénard, 'De la route royale à l'âge d'or des diligences', in *Les routes de France* (Paris, 1959), 101–32.

105. *The Six Voyages of John Baptista Tavernier through Turky, into Persia and the East Indies* (London, 1677).

106. Jacques Heers, 'Rivalité ou collaboration de la terre et de l'eau?' in *Les grandes voies maritimes dans le monde* (Paris, 1965), 13–63.

107. J.-Y. Tirat, 'Circulation et commerce intérieur dans la France du XVIIᵉ siècle', *XVIIᵉ S.*, nos. 70–1 (1966), 65–79.

108. 'Mémoire sur la navigation des rivières', in *Mémoires des intendants sur l'état des généralités*, I, *Mémoire de la généralité de Paris*, ed. A. M. de Boislisle (Paris, 1881), 399–414.

109. Gustave Guilmoto, *Etude sur les droits de navigation de la Seine de Paris à la Roche-Guyon du XIᵉ au XVIIIᵉ siècle* (Paris, 1889).

110. Marie-Hélène Bourquin, 'L'approvisionnement de Paris en bois de la Régence à la Révolution', in *Etudes d'histoire du droit parisien* (Paris, 1970), 158–228.

111. Léon Cohen, 'Ce qu'on enseigne un péage du XVIIIᵉ siècle: la Seine entre Rouen et Paris et les caractères de l'économie parisienne', *Ann. Hist. Ec. Soc.*, 3 (1931), 487–518.

112. Anne-Marie Cocula, 'L'activité d'un maître de bâteau sur la Dordogne au milieu du XVIIᵉ siècle', *Ann. Midi*, 82 (1970), 21–43.

113. J. de Pas, 'Débouchés fluviaux et maritimes du Bas-Artois au moyen-âge et jusqu'au dix-huitième siècle', *Rev. Nord*, 15 (1929), 5–46.

114. William Bromley, *Several Years Travels, Performed by a Gentleman* (London, 1702), 271.

115. *Ibid.* 280; also *The Journal of James Yonge (1647–1721)*, ed. F. N. L. Poynter (London, 1963), 106.

116. Sir William Temple, *Observations upon the United Provinces of the Netherlands*, ed. G. N. Clark (Oxford, 1932), 93.

117. Eberhard Gothein, *Geschichtliche Entwicklung der Rheinschiffahrt im XIX. Jahrhundert* (Leipzig, 1903), 12.

118. Sir Osborne Mance, *International River and Canal Transport* (Oxford, 1944), 27–34. The Convention of Mainz was modified and extended by that of Mannheim, 1868.

119. For Tulla's engineering see *Der Rhein: Ausbau–Verkehr–Verwaltung* (Duisburg, 1951), 100–37.

120. Konrad Fuchs, 'Die Lahn als Schiffahrtsweg im 19. Jahrhundert', *Nass. Ann.*, 75 (1964), 160–201.

121. Paul Segner, 'Die mittelalterliche Flussschiffahrt im Wesergebiet', *Hans. Gbl.*, 19 (1913), 93–161.

122. *The Travels of Peter Mundy, Vol. 4*, Hakluyt Society, 2nd ser., 55 (London, 1924), 182.

123. *Ibid.* 197.

124. H. Obuchowska-Pysiowa, 'Warunki naturalne, technika i organizacja spławu wiślanego w XVII wieku', *Kw. Hist. Kult. Mat.*, 13 (1965), 281–97.

125. *Regestra thelonei aquatici Wladislawiensis saeculi XVI*, ed. S. Kutrzeba and F. Duda (Kraków, 1915).

126. Stanislaw Hoszowski, 'Z dziejow handlu zbożowego w Toruniu

1760–1860', *Rocz. Dz. Społ. Gosp.*, 11 (1949), 51–118.

127. Jan Rutkowski, *Historia gospodarcza Polski (do 1864 r.)* (Warsaw, 1953), 373.

128. N. J. G. Pounds, *The Upper Silesian Industrial Region* (Bloomington, Ind., 1958), 37.

129. T. Telford, 'Inland Navigation', *The Edinburgh Encyclopaedia*, XV (Edinburgh, 1830), 209–315.

130. A. W. Skempton, 'Canals and River Navigation before 1750', in *A History of Technology*, ed. C. Singer, E. J. Holmyard, A. R. Hall and T. I. Williams, III (Oxford, 1957), 438–70; this estimate appears to be too high.

131. *Ibid.* 459.

132. *Locke's Travels in France 1675–1679*, ed. John Lough (Cambridge, 1953), 134–38.

133. Arthur Young, *Travels in France during the Years 1787, 1788, 1789* (London, 1915), 32, 46.

134. Marlies Kutz, 'Beiträge zur Geschichte der Moselkanalisierung', *Schr. Rhein.–Westf. Gesch.*, 14 (1967), 25–44.

135. Young, *Travels in France*, 106.

136. David R. Ringrose, *Transportation and Economic Stagnation in Spain 1750–1850* (Durham, N.C., 1970), 16–17.

137. *Ibid.* 17.

138. Mitchell and Dean, *Abstract of British Historical Statistics*, 279–81, 309–11, 288–95.

139. Pierre Léon, 'Structure du commerce extérieur et évolution industrielle de la France à la fin du XVIII siècle', *Hommage Labrousse*, 407–32.

140. J. Jepson Oddy, *European Commerce* (London, 1805). The quotations that follow are on pp. 75, 139, 248, 250 and 297.

141. Le comte d'Arnould, *De la balance du commerce*, 2 vols. (Paris, 1788), I, 140–59.

Chapter 7. Europe on the eve of the Industrial Revolution

1. John D. Post, 'Famine, Mortality, and Epidemic Disease in the Process of Modernization', *Ec. Hist. Rev.*, 29 (1976), 14–37.

2. Walt W. Rostow, *The Stages of Economic Growth* (Cambridge, 1960), 7.

3. Paul Bairoch, 'Europe's Gross National Product 1800–1975', *Jn. Eur. Ec. Hist.*, 5 (1976), 273–340.

4. Marcel Lachiver, *La population de Meulan du XVIIe au XIXe siècle* (Paris, 1969), 139; B. H. Slicher van Bath, 'Report on the Study of Historical Demography in the Netherlands', *Actes Coll. Int. Dém. Hist.*, 185–98.

5. Michael Drake, *Population and Society in Norway 1735–1865* (Cambridge, 1969), 67.

6. Jacques Houdaille, 'La population de Boulay (Moselle) avant 1850',

Pop., 22 (1967), 1055–84; Colin Clark, *Population Growth and Land Use* (London, 1967), 7–9.

7. J. Bourgeois-Pichat, 'Evolution générale de la population française depuis le XVIIIe siècle', *Pop.*, 6 (1951), 635–62; P. Deprez, 'The Demographic Development of Flanders in the Eighteenth Century', in *Population in History*, ed. D. V. Glass and D. E. C. Eversley (London, 1965), 608–30.

8. Frederick Hendricks, 'On the Vital Statistics of Sweden from 1749 to 1855', *Jn. Roy. Stat. Soc.*, 25 (1862), 111–74.

9. Gerard Engelmann, 'Etude démographique d'un village de la commune de Toulouse: Pouvourville (1756–1798)', *Ann. Midi*, 77 (1965), 427–42; S. Poitrineau, *La vie rurale en Basse-Auvergne au XVIIIe siècle*, Pub. Fac. Lett. Clermont-Ferrand, 2nd ser., 23 (1965), 61.

10. P. Duprez, 'Evolution démographique et évolution économique en Flandre au dix-huitième siècle', *Third Int. Conf. Ec. Hist.*, IV, *Demography and Economy* (Paris, 1972), 49–53.

11. Clark, *Population Growth and Land Use*, 178–92.

12. J. William Leasure, 'Malthus, Marriage and Multiplication', *Milbank Memorial Fund Quarterly* (New York), 41, 4 (1963), 19–35.

13. Slicher van Bath, 'Historical Demography in the Netherlands'.

14. Pavla Horska, 'L'état actuel des recherches sur l'évolution de la population dans les pays tchèques aux XVIIIe et XIXe siècles', *Ann. Dém. Hist.*, 1967, 173–95.

15. Karl Blaschke, 'The Development of Population in an Area of Early Industrialisation: Saxony from the Sixteenth to the Nineteenth Century', *Third Int. Conf. Ec. Hist.*, IV, *Demography and Economy* (Paris, 1972), 45–7.

16. Marcel Reinhard, 'La population de la France et sa mesure, de l'Ancien Régime au Consulat', *Con. Hist. Dém. Rév. Fr.*, 257–74.

17. D. E. C. Eversley, 'Demography and Economics', *Third Int. Conf. Ec. Hist.*, IV, *Demography and Economy* (Paris, 1972), 15–35.

18. J.-C. Toutain, *La population de la France de 1700 à 1959*, Hist. Quant. Ec. Fr., no. 3 (1963), 17.

19. Raymond Rousseau, *La population de la Savoie jusqu'en 1861* (Paris, 1960), 180–221 and map 8.

20. J. De Brouwere, 'Les dénombrements de la Châtellenie d'Audenarde', *Bull. Comm. Roy. Hist.*, 103 (1938), 513–46.

21. A. Quatelet, 'Sur les anciens recensements de la population belge', *Bulletin de la Commission Centrale de Statistiques* (Brussels), 3 (1847), 1–38.

22. Based in part on *Raum und Bevölkerung in der Weltgeschichte*, ed. E. Kirsten, E. W. Buchholz and W. Kollmann, II (Würzburg, 1956); *Almanach de Gotha* summarises national statistics for the late 1840s.

23. K. Obermann, 'Quelques données statistiques sur les états de la confédération germanique dans la première moitié du XIXe siècle', *Ann. Dém. Hist.*, 1966, 79–98.

24. Horska, 'L'état actuel des recherches sur l'évolution de la population

dans les pays tchèques'.
25. Obermann, 'Quelques données statistiques sur les états de la confédération germanique'.
26. Kurt B. Mayer, *The Population of Switzerland* (New York, 1952), 28, 30.
27. Gustaf Utterström, 'Population and Agriculture, c. 1700–1830', *Sc. Ec. Hist. Rev.*, 9 (1960), 176–94.
28. E. F. Heckscher, *An Economic History of Sweden* (Cambridge, Mass., 1954), 137.
29. *The Travel Diaries of Thomas Robert Malthus*, ed. Patricia James (Cambridge, 1966), 68, 153.
30. Drake, *Population and Society in Norway*, 45–53; *id*., 'The Growth of Population in Norway', *Sc. Ec. Hist. Rev.*, 13 (1965), 97–127.
31. Axel Nielsen, *Dänische Wirtschaftsgeschichte* (Jena, 1933), 341; Aksel Lassen, 'The Population of Denmark, 1660–1960', *Sc. Ec. Hist. Rev.*, 14 (1966), 134–57.
32. Frederick Hendricks, 'A Review of the Statistics of Spain down to the Years 1857 and 1858', *Jn. Roy. Stat. Soc.*, 23 (1860), 147–200.
33. Albert Silbert, *Le Portugal méditerranéen à la fin de l'Ancien Régime*, 2 vols. (Paris, 1966), I, 114–19.
34. K. J. Beloch, *Bevölkerungsgeschichte Italiens*, III (Berlin, 1961), 353.
35. C. M. Cipolla, 'Four Centuries of Italian Demographic Development', in *Population in History*, ed. Glass and Eversley, 570–87.
36. I. Kostrowicka, Z. Landau and J. Tomaszewski, *Historia gospodarcza Polski XIX i XX wieku* (Warsaw, 1966), 139.
37. J. Kovascsics, 'Situation démographique de la Hongrie à la fin du XVIII siècle', *Ann. Dém. Hist.*, 1965, 83–104; the totals given in *Raum und Bevölkerung* seem to be much too high.
38. L. S. Stavrianos, *The Balkans since 1453* (New York, 1958), 420.
39. Tabulated in Mayer, *The Population of Switzerland*, 26.
40. K. T. Eheberg, 'Strassburgs Bevölkerungszahl seit Ende des 15. Jahrhunderts bis zur Gegenwart', *Jb. Nat. Stat.*, 42 (1884), 413–30; J.-C. Perrot, 'Documents sur la population du Calvados pendant la Révolution et l'Empire', *Ann. Norm.*, 15 (1965), 77–128.
41. Toutain, *La population de la France de 1700 à 1959*, 47–50.
42. H. W. Graf Finck von Finckenstein, *Die Entwicklung der Landwirtschaft in Preussen und Deutschland, 1800–1930*, Göttinger Arbeitskreis (Würzburg, 1960), 168.
43. F. Hendricks, 'On the Vital Statistics of Sweden from 1749 to 1855', *Jn. Roy. Stat. Soc.*, 25 (1862), 111–74.
44. Blaschke, 'The Development of Population in an Area of Early Industrialisation: Saxony', 45–7.
45. From B. R. Mitchell, 'Statistical Appendix 1700–1914', in *Fontana Economic History of Europe*, IX, pt 2 (London, 1973), 738–820.
46. Pawel Rybicki, 'Rozwój ludności Górnego Śląska od początku XIX wieku', in *Górny Slask* (Kraków, 1955).
47. W. Koellmann, 'The Population of Barmen before and during the

Period of Industrialization', in *Population in History*, ed. Glass and Eversley, 588–607.

48. Pierre Lebrun, *L'industrie de la laine à Verviers pendant le XVIIIᵉ et le début du XIXᵉ siècle*, Bibl. Fac. Liège, 114 (1948), 105–6.

49. Mack Walker, 'Weissenburg 1780–1825', in his *German Home Towns: Community, State and General Estate 1648–1871* (Ithaca, N.Y., 1971), 217–47.

50. O. H. Hufton, *Bayeux in the Late Eighteenth Century: A Social Study* (Oxford, 1967), 58, 78.

51. See in particular R. E. Dickinson, *The West European City* (London, 1951).

52. J. Suret-Canale, 'L'état économique et sociale de la Mayenne au milieu du XIXᵉ siècle', *Rev. Hist. Ec. Soc.*, 36 (1958), 294–331.

53. Quoted in E. W. Buchholz, 'Landliche Bevölkerung an der Schwelle des Industriezeitalters', *Quell. Forsch. Aggesch.*, 11 (1966), 5.

54. Toutain, *La population de la France de 1700 à 1959*, 54–5.

55. J.-F. Bergier, *Problèmes de l'histoire économique de la Suisse* (Bern, 1968), 58.

56. Jerome Blum, *Noble Landowners and Agriculture in Austria 1815–1848* (Baltimore, Md., 1948), 43.

57. Simon Kuznets, *Modern Economic Growth* (New Haven, Conn., 1966), 88–93.

58. Frederick Lillin de Chateauvieux, 'Travels in Italy Descriptive of the Rural Manners and Economy of that Country', in his *New Voyages and Travels* (London, n.d.), 4.

59. Quoted in *Documents de l'histoire de Languedoc*, ed. P. Wolff (Toulouse, 1969), 329; also Octave Festy, 'Les progrès de l'agriculture française durant le Premier Empire', *Rev. Hist. Ec. Soc.*, 35 (1957), 266–92.

60. G. A. Montgomery, *The Rise of Modern Industry in Sweden*, Stockholm Economic Series, 8 (London, 1939), 5.

61. A. Mayhew, *Rural Settlement and Farming in Germany* (London, 1973), 132.

62. G. Doria, *Uomini e terri di un borgo collinare* (Milan, 1968), 10.

63. Lioba Beyer, 'Der Siedlungsbereich von Jerzens in Pitztal', *Westf. Geog. Stud.*, 21 (1969), 24–6.

64. J. Paquet, 'La misère dans un village de l'Oisans en 1809', *Cah. Hist.*, 11 (1966), 247–56.

65. Guy Thuillier, 'L'alimentation en Nivernais au XIXᵉ siècle', in *Pour une histoire de l'alimentation, Cah. Ann.*, 28 (1970), 154–73.

66. Lillin de Chateauvieux, 'Travels in Italy', 20.

67. R. H. Hubscher, 'Le livre de compte de la famille Flahaut (1811–1877)', *Rev. Hist. Ec. Soc.*, 47 (1969), 361–403.

68. J. Vidalenc, 'L'agriculture dans le départements normands à la fin du Premier Empire', *Ann. Norm.*, 7 (1957), 179–201; H. Sée, 'L'économie rurale de l'Anjou dans la première moitié du XIXᵉ siècle', *Rev. Hist. Ec. Soc.*, 15 (1927), 104–22.

69. Georges Castellan, 'Les céréales dans l'économie rurale de la Restauration', *Rev. Hist. Ec. Soc.*, 40 (1962), 175–99.
70. Georg Droege, 'Zur Lage der rheinischen Landwirtschaft in der ersten Hälfte des 19. Jahrhunderts', in *Landschaft und Geschichte: Festschrift für Franz Petri* (Bonn, 1970), 143–56.
71. D. Saalfeld, 'Die Produktion und Intensität der Landwirtschaft in Deutschland und angrenzenden Gebieten um 1800', *Zt. Aggesch.*, 15 (1967), 137–75.
72. Maria Różycka-Glassowa, 'Productivité du travail dans l'agriculture des grands domaines fonciers du Royaume de Pologne (1800–1864)', *Kw. Hist. Kult. Mat.*, 21 (1973), 69–84.
73. Blum, *Noble Landowners and Agriculture in Austria*, 155–8.
74. Lillin de Chateauvieux, 'Travels in Italy', 10–12.
75. Graf Finck von Finckenstein, *Die Entwicklung der Landwirtschaft in Preussen und Deutschland*, 34.
76. Lillin de Chateauvieux, 'Travels in Italy', 11.
77. J.-C. Toutain, *Le produit de l'agriculture française de 1700 à 1958*, *Hist. Quant. Ec. Fr.*, 2 (1961), 16.
78. J. F. R. Philips, 'Die Agrarstruktur Sudlimburgs in der ersten Hälfte des 19. Jahrhunderts', *Acta Hist. Neer.*, 4 (1970), 84–104.
79. Rudolf Berthold, *Einige Bemerkungen über den Entwicklungsstand des bäuerlichen Ackerbaus vor den Agrarreformen des 19. Jahrhunderts*, Deutsch. Akad. Wiss., 10 (1962); Graf Finck von Finckenstein, *Die Entwicklung der Landwirtschaft in Preussen und Deutschland*, 100.
80. Bohdan Baranowski, 'Proba obliczenia rozmiarów produkcji rolniczej i jej konsumpcji w czascach Księstwa Warszawskiego', *Kw. Hist. Kult. Mat.*, 8 (1960), 209–28; the figures relate to 1827.
81. J. Vicens Vives, *An Economic History of Spain* (Princeton, N.J., 1969), 645.
82. Różycka-Glassowa, 'Productivité du travail dans l'agriculture des grands domains fonciers du Royaume de Pologne'.
83. Hubscher, 'Le livre de compte de la famille Flahaut'.
84. William Jacob, *A View of the Agriculture, Manufactures, Statistics and State of Society of Germany* (London, 1920), 78.
85. G. Desert, 'La culture de la pomme de terre dans le Calvados au XIXe siècle', *Ann. Norm.*, 5 (1955), 261–70.
86. Philips, 'Die agrarstruktur Sudlimburgs'.
87. Vidalenc, 'L'agriculture dans les départements normands'.
88. T. A. Welton, 'Observations on French Population Statistics', *Jn. Roy. Stat. Soc.*, 29 (1866), 254–81.
89. Quoted in *Histoire de l'Aquitaine: documents*, ed. C. Higounet (Toulouse, 1973), 348–51.
90. J. Vidalenc, 'La vie économique des départements méditerranéens pendant l'Empire', *Rev. Hist. Mod. Cont.*, 1 (1954), 165–98.
91. Le comte de Chaptal, *De l'industrie française*, 2 vols. (Paris, 1819), I, 189.
92. Jacob, *A View of the Agriculture . . . Germany*, 237.

93. After Blum, *Noble Landowners and Agriculture in Austria*, 149, and I. Wellmann, 'Esquisse d'une histoire rurale de la Hongrie depuis la première moitié du XVIIIᵉ siècle jusqu'au milieu du XIXᵉ siècle', *Ann. ESC*, 23 (1968), 1181–210.

94. Welton, 'Observations on French Population Statistics'.

95. W. Abel, 'Die Lage der deutschen Land- und Ernährungswirtschaft um 1800', *Jb. Nat. Stat.*, 175 (1963), 319–34.

96. Saalfeld, 'Die Produktion und Intensität der Landwirtschaft in Deutschland und angrenzenden Gebieten'.

97. Guy Thuillier, 'Les transformations agricoles en Nivernais de 1815 à 1840', *Rev. Hist. Ec. Soc.*, 34 (1956), 426–56.

98. Fritz Glauser, 'Handel mit Entlebucher Käse und Butter vom 16. bis 19. Jahrhundert', *Schw. Zt. Gesch.*, 21 (1971), 1–63.

99. Lillin de Chateauvieux, 'Travels in Italy', 11.

100. *Ibid.* 14–15.

101. Julius Klein, *The Mesta* (Cambridge, Mass., 1920), 331–49.

102. Chaptal, *De l'industrie française*, vol. I.

103. 'Abstract of the Report of a Tour in the Five Departments of Brittany, during the Years 1840 and 1841', *Jn. Roy. Stat. Soc.*, 13 (1850), 134–51.

104. Calculated from figures in Toutain, *Le produit de l'agriculture*.

105. Montgomery, *The Rise of Modern Industry in Sweden*, 3, 50–7.

106. Baranowski, 'Próba obliczenia rozmiarów produkcji rolniczej i jej konsumpcji w czasach Księstwa Warszawskiego'.

107. Paul Bairoch, 'Agriculture and the Industrial Revolution', in *The Fontana Economic History of Europe*, III (London, 1973), 425–506.

108. E. A. Wrigley, *Industrial Growth and Population Change* (Cambridge, 1961), 12–25.

109. J. A. Van Houtte, *Esquisse d'une histoire économique de la Belgique* (Louvain, 1943), 154.

110. H. Reader, 'The Mining Resources of France, 1841 to 1852', *Jn. Roy. Stat. Soc.*, 18 (1855), 345–55.

111. Maxime Perrin, *Saint-Etienne et sa région économique* (Tours, 1937), 89–92.

112. Marcel Gillet, 'L'âge du charbon et l'essor du bassin houiller du Nord et du Pas-de-Calais', *Charbon et sciences humaines: Actes du colloque organisé par la Faculté des Lettres de l'Université de Lille en mai 1963* (Paris, 1966), 25–52.

113. See *Zt. Berg. Hüt. Sal.*, 10 (1862), 18. Wage-rates in Upper Silesia were also the lowest.

114. 'Die Lage des Bergbaues in Preussen und die Verwerthung seiner Erzeugnisse', *Bg. Hüt. Zt.*, 9 (1850), 245.

115. S. Michalkiewicz, 'Les conditions de travail dans l'industries minière de la Basse-Silésie dans la première moitié du XIXᵉ siècle', *Rev. Nord*, 48 (1966), 51–66.

116. Ludmila Kárníková, *Vývoj uhelného průmyslu v českych zemích do r. 1880* (Prague, 1960), 334–5.

117. Vicens Vives, *An Economic History of Spain*, 660. Asturian production was about 278,400 tonnes in 1860; that of the whole of Spain, about 450,000 in 1865.

118. Kárníková, *Vývoj uhelného průmyslu v českých zemích do r. 1880*, 356.

119. Konrad Fuchs, 'Die Bergwerks- und Hüttenproduktion im Herzogtum Nassau', *Nass. Ann.*, 79 (1968), 368–77.

120. *Bg. Hüt. Zt.*, 8 (1849), 331–2.

121. Eck, 'Ueber den Betrieb der Koakshochöfen in Belgien', *Bg. Hüt. Zt.*, 9 (1850).

122. P. L. Michotte, 'Localisation de la grosse sidérurgie belgo-luxembourgeoise, avant et après 1830', *Bull. Soc. Belge Géog.*, 2 (1932), 43–73.

123. Charles Fohlen, 'Charbon et révolution industrielle en France (1815–1850)', in *Charbon et sciences humaines* (Paris, 1966), 141–51; Jean Vial, *L'industrialisation de la sidérurgie française 1814–1864* (Paris, 1967), 125.

124. Harry Scrivenor, *A Comprehensive History of the Iron Trade* (London, 1841), 187.

125. Hans Spethmann, *Die Anfänge der ruhrländischen Koksindustrie*, Beiträge zur Geschichte von Stadt und Stift Essen, 62 (Essen, 1947); F. A. von Waldthausen, *Geschichte des Steinkohlenbergwerks Vereinigte Sälzer und Neuack* (Essen, 1902), 86–7.

126. *Bg. Hüt. Zt.*, 1 (1842), 58.

127. G. Richard, 'La révolution industrielle et ses aspects techniques dans la métallurgie du fer en Haute-Normandie', *Ann. Norm.*, 14 (1964), 339–63.

128. Jan Slomka, *From Serfdom to Self-Government* (London, 1941).

129. N. J. G. Pounds, *The Upper Silesian Industrial Region*, Slavic and East European Series, 11 (Bloomington, Ind., 1958), 81–93.

130. Claude Fohlen, 'La concentration dans l'industrie textile française au milieu du XIXᵉ siècle', *Rev. Hist. Mod. Cont.*, 2 (1955), 46–58.

131. Lebrun, *L'industrie de la laine à Verviers*, 235–82; *id.*, 'Croissance et industrialisation: l'expérience de l'industrie drapière verviétoise 1750–1850', *Int. Conf. Ec. Hist.*, *Stockholm: Communications* (Paris, 1960), 531–68.

132. Claude Fohlen, 'Esquisse d'une évolution industrielle: Roubaix au XIXᵉ siècle', *Rev. Nord*, 33 (1951), 92–102.

133. David Landes, *The Unbound Prometheus* (Cambridge, 1969), 159–62.

134. Gerhard Adelmann, 'Strukturwandlungen der rheinischen Leinen- und Baumwollgewerbe zu Beginn der Industrialisierung', *V.S.W.G.*, 53 (1966), 162–84; Edith Schmitz, *Leinengewerbe und Leinenhandel in Nordwestdeutschland (1650–1850)*, *Schr. Rhein.–Westf. Wtgesch.*, 15 (1967), 57.

135. I. J. Brugmans, 'Die industrielle Révolution in den Niederlanden', *Rhein. Vbl.*, 29 (1964), 124–37.

136. Walter Bodmer, *Die Entwicklung der schweizerischen Textilwirtschaft*

im Rahmen der übrigen Industrien und Wirtschaftszweige (Zurich, 1960), 277–96.

137. Vicens Vives, *An Economic History of Spain,* 668–70; the statistical data appear to be quite unreliable.

138. Domenico Demarco, 'L'économie italienne du nord et du sud avant l'unité', *Rev. Hist. Ec. Soc.,* 34 (1956), 369–91.

139. Adelmann, 'Strukturwandlungen der rheinischen Leinen- and Baumwollgewerbe'.

140. Willy Franken, *Die Entwicklung des Gewerbes in den Städten Mönchen-Gladbach und Rheydt im 19. Jahrhundert, Schr. Rhein.–Westf. Wtgesch.,* 19 (1969), 25.

141. W. Zorn, 'Neues von der historischen Wirtschaftskarte der Rheinlande', *Rhein. Vbl.,* 30 (1965), 334–45.

142. J. Purs, 'The Industrial Revolution and Czech Lands', *Hist.* (P), 2 (1960), 183–272; *id.,* 'Die Aufhebung der Hörigkeit und die Grundentlastung in der böhmischen Ländern', *Second Int. Conf. Ec. Hist.* (Paris, 1965), p. 257 (map).

143. Adam Ginsbert, *Łodź* (Łodź, 1962).

144. Penttu Virrankoski, 'Replacement of Flax by Cotton in the Domestic Textile Industry of South-West Finland', *Sc. Ec. Hist. Rev.,* 11 (1963), 27–42.

145. Vicens Vives, *An Economic History of Spain,* 669–70.

146. Jean de Béthune, 'La crise linière et le pauperisme dans le Courtraisis entre 1825 et 1850', *35ᵉ Cong., Fédération Historique et Archéologique de Belgique,* 1953, vol. II, 71–133.

147. Chaptal, *De l'industrie française,* I, 120–2.

148. Jacques Toulemonde, 'Notes sur l'industrie roubaisienne et tourquennoise dans la première moitié du XIXᵉ siècle', *Rev. Nord,* 48 (1966), 321–36.

149. Etienne Baux, 'Les draperies audoises sous le Premier Empire', *Rev. Hist. Ec. Soc.,* 38 (1960), 418–32. A map of the industry is given in *Documents de l'histoire de Languedoc,* 248. See also Claude Fohlen, 'En Languedoc: vigne contre draperie', *Ann. ESC,* 4 (1949), 290–7.

150. Lebrun, *L'industrie de la laine à Verviers,* 130–2, 143.

151. Clemens Bruckner, *Zur Wirtschaftsgeschichte des Regierungsbezirk Aachen, Schr. Rhein.–Westf. Wtgesch.,* 16 (1967), 195–9.

152. Rudolf Forberger, *Die Manufaktur in Sachsen vom Ende des 16. bis zum Anfang des 19. Jahrhunderts,* Deutsch. Akad. Wiss., 13 (1958), 155–61.

153. Bodmer, *Die Entwicklung der schweizerischen Textilwirtschaft,* 315.

154. G. Otruba, 'Anfänge und Verbreitung der böhmischen Manufackturen bis zum Beginn des 19. Jahrhunderts', *Boh.,* 6 (1965), 230–331; Purs, 'The Industrial Revolution in Czech Lands'.

155. György Tolnai, 'Textilná manufaktúra a rolnícka tkáčska a pradiarska výroba na Slovensku (1850–1867)', *Historické Stúdie* (Bratislava), 14 (1969), 17–46.

156. Traian Stoianovich, *A Study in Balkan Civilisation* (New York, 1967), 87.
157. W. Zorn, 'Umrisse der frühen Industrialisierung Südosteuropas im 19. Jahrhundert', *V.S.W.G.*, 57 (1970), 500–33.
158. 'Silks of Lyon', *Ciba Rev.*, no. 6 (Feb. 1938).
159. 'The Silk and Velvet Industries of Krefeld', *Ciba Rev.*, no. 83 (Dec. 1950).
160. 'The Basel Ribbon Industry', *Ciba Rev.*, no. 24 (Aug. 1939).
161. G. Otruba and R. Kropf, 'Bergbau und Industrie Böhmens in der Epoche der Frühindustrialisierung (1820–1848)', *Boh.*, 12 (1971), 53–232.
162. A. and N. L. Clow, 'The Chemical Industry: Interaction with the Industrial Revolution', in *A History of Technology*, ed. C. Singer, E. J. Holmyard, A. R. Hall and T. I. Williams, IV (Oxford, 1958), 230–57, 230.
163. Either sodium carbonate (Na_2CO_3) or caustic soda ($NaOH$).
164. Quoted in A. and N. L. Clow, 'The Chemical Industry', 248.
165. *The History of Coke Making and of the Coke Oven Managers' Association* (Cambridge, 1936), 64–83.
166. A. L. Dunham, *La Révolution Industrielle en France (1815–1848)* (Paris, 1953), 37.
167. N. J. G. Pounds, 'Patterns of Trade in the Rhineland', in *Science, Medicine and History*, ed. E. Ashworth Underwood, 2 vols. (Oxford, 1953), II, 419–34.
168. Konrad Fuchs, 'Die Lahn als Schiffahrtsweg im 19. Jahrhundert', *Nass. Ann.*, 75 (1964), 160–201.
169. A. Sartorius von Sartorius von Waltershausen, *Deutsche Wirtschaftsgeschichte 1815–1914* (Jena, 1923), 108–9.
170. E. Gothein, *Geschichtliche Entwicklung der Rheinschiffahrt im XIX. Jahrhundert* (Leipzig, 1903), 270–7.
171. Henri Cavaillés, *La route française: son histoire, sa fonction* (Paris, 1946), 264–5.
172. Quoted in *ibid.* 266.
173. 'The Basel Ribbon Industry', *Ciba Rev.*, no. 24 (Aug. 1939).
174. Richard Ford, *A Hand-Book for Travellers in Spain, and Readers at Home* (repr. London, 1966).
175. David R. Ringrose, *Transportation and Economic Stagnation in Spain 1750–1850* (Durham, N.C., 1970), 120.
176. R. J. Forbes, 'Roads to c. 1900', in *A History of Technology*, IV (Oxford, 1958), 520–47.
177. Dionysius Lardner, *Railway Economy* (London, 1850; repr. 1968).
178. Gideon Sjoberg, *The Preindustrial City* (New York, 1960), 199–203.
179. See, for example, W. Zorn, 'Zur Nürnberger Handels- und Unternehmergeschichte des 19. Jahrhunderts', *Beitr. Wtesch. Nürn.*, 2 (1967), 851–64.
180. Report of 1857, quoted in *Documents de l'histoire de Languedoc*, 271.
181. H. Reader Lack, 'The Mining Resources of France, 1841 to 1852', *Jn.*

Roy. Stat. Soc., 18 (1855), 345–55; E. Gruner and G. Bousquet, *Atlas général des houillères*, pt 2 (Paris, 1911), 37.

182. J. H. Clapham, *The Economic Development of France and Germany, 1815–1914* (Cambridge, 1945), 112.

183. N. J. G. Pounds, 'Port and Outport in North-West Europe', *Geographical Journal* (London), 109 (1947), 216–28.

184. Vicens Vives, *An Economic History of Spain*, 688–91.

Index

DATE DUE
